公能教育文库

张元龙/总主编　张鉴鼺/总策划

全球人权治理的中国智慧

张彭春在联合国人权委员会及联大第三委员会等的发言

孙平华　编著

天津社会科学院出版社

图书在版编目（CIP）数据

全球人权治理的中国智慧：张彭春在联合国人权委
员会及联大第三委员会等的发言：汉、英 / 孙平华编著
. -- 天津：天津社会科学院出版社，2024.1
（公能教育文库 / 张元龙总主编）
ISBN 978-7-5563-0885-9

Ⅰ. ①全… Ⅱ. ①孙… Ⅲ. ①人权－研究－中国－汉
、英 Ⅳ. ①D621.5

中国国家版本馆 CIP 数据核字(2023)第 088233 号

全球人权治理的中国智慧：
张彭春在联合国人权委员会及联大第三委员会等的发言
QUANQIU RENQUAN ZHILI DE ZHONGGUO ZHIHUI: ZHANG PENGCHUN ZAI LIANHEGUO RENQUAN
WEIYUANHUI JI LIANDA DISAN WEIYUANHUI DENG DE FAYAN

选题策划：韩　鹏
责任编辑：吴　琼
责任校对：付聿炜
装帧设计：高馨月
出版发行：天津社会科学院出版社
地　　址：天津市南开区迎水道 7 号
邮　　编：300191
电　　话：(022) 23360165
印　　刷：北京盛通印刷股份有限公司
开　　本：710×1000　　1/16
印　　张：51
字　　数：600 千字
版　　次：2024 年 1 月第 1 版　　2024 年 1 月第 1 次印刷
定　　价：130.00 元

该书系 2020 年度"教育部哲学社会科学研究后期资助项目"(重大项目)——"国际人权话语中的中国声音研究"(批准号:20JHQ010)的阶段性成果,得到"中央高校基本科研业务费专项资金"资助(Supported by "the Fundamental Research Funds for the Central Universities")及张伯苓研究会的资助

前　　言①

一、概述

2022年2月25日下午,习近平总书记在中共中央政治局第三十七次集体学习时,不仅从六个方面高屋建瓴地总结了我国人权发展的道路,还明确指出"要弘扬正确人权观,广泛开展人权宣传和知识普及,营造尊重和保障人权的良好氛围。……着力培养一批理论扎实、学术精湛、熟悉国

---

① 　作者系中国政法大学教授、人权法学博士(系我国第一位人权法学博士);英国埃克塞特大学法学院访问学者;美国、加拿大、新加坡及国内多家中英文学术期刊特约审稿人;兼任国家社科基金通讯评审专家、国家留学基金评审专家、教育部学位与研究生教育中心评估专家等;兼任中国政法大学全面依法治国研究院研究员、中南大学人权研究中心(国家人权教育与培训基地)研究员、山东大学习近平法治思想研究中心特聘研究员、西北政法大学刑事法律科学研究中心客座研究员等。主持完成三项国家社科基金项目,在《外语界》《外语与外语教学》《课程·教材·教法》《法学家》《安徽大学学报》《浙江工商大学学报》等及 Human Rights Quarterly, Journal of East Asia and International Law, China Legal Science 等发表中英文学术论文及译文110余篇,其中8篇被中国人民大学书报资料《国际法学》《宪法学 行政法学》《中国政治》等全文转载。代表性成果有《〈世界人权宣言〉研究》(系国家社科基金后期资助项目成果,2014年荣获"北京市第十三届哲学社会科学优秀成果奖"二等奖)、《张彭春:世界人权体系的重要设计师》(入选2016年度"国家哲学社会科学成果文库")、《国际人权话语中的中国声音研究》(系2020年度教育部哲学社会科学研究后期资助重大项目成果)和两部国家社科基金中华学术外译项目成果及一部得到国家社科基金重大课题资助的英文成果:Human Rights Protection System in China (Springer 2014); Historic Achievement of a Common Standard: Pengchun Chang and the Universal Declaration of Human Rights (Springer 2018); Chinese Contributions to International Discourse of Human Rights (Springer 2022)。另外,编著出版的《世界合作共赢的中国贡献》《全球人权治理的中国智慧》系"2020年度教育部哲学社会科学研究后期资助"(重大项目)阶段性成果,得到"中央高校基本科研业务费专项资金"资助及张伯苓研究会资助等;2021年、2022年分别荣获"张伯苓研究贡献奖""钱端升法学研究成果奖三等奖"等。主要研究领域:人权法学、全球治理、应用语言学、英语语言教学等。

际规则、会讲中国人权故事的高端人权专家队伍。"①习近平强调："要积极推动全球人权治理，弘扬全人类共同价值观、坚持平等互信、包容互鉴、合作共赢、共同发展的理念，推动全球人权治理朝着更加公平公正合理包容的方向发展。"②习近平旗帜鲜明地反对空谈人权、反对在人权方面搞双重标准、反对把人权当作干涉别国内政的政治工具，并明确指出："要把握战略主动，着力讲好中国人权故事，运用形象化、具体化的表达方式，增强当代中国人权观的吸引力、感染力、影响力。"③中共中央政治局围绕人权话题开展集体学习，这无疑是继 1991 年的《中国人权状况白皮书》的发布、2004 年"国家尊重和保障人权"载入宪法、2009 年《国家人权行动计划（2009—2010）》的发布实施之后第四个里程碑的大事件。而习近平总书记的有关人权的重要讲话，更是为我国参与全球人权治理指明了方向。

习近平总书记在其重要讲话中先后两次强调讲述中国人权故事的重要性，第一要求"会讲"，第二要求"讲好"中国人权故事，而且要下大功夫，充分利用"形象化、具体化"的形式来加以讲述，这就要求我们在讲述中国人权故事时，必须以生动的形式来讲述具体的内容。为了积极响应习总书记的号召，也借此机会简要介绍一下笔者学习人权、探讨人权、参与国际人权交流、讲述中国人权故事的情况。

2022 年 4 月 7 日，笔者撰写的第三部英文专著 *Chinese Contributions to International Discourse of Human Rights*（《国际人权话语中的中国贡献》）由施普林格出版社出版。该书中有插图 137 幅，其中 80 幅彩色插图标题为

---

① 《习近平在中共中央政治局第三十七次集体学习时强调 坚定不移走中国人权发展道路 更好推动我国人权事业发展》，见人民网：http://cpc. people. com. cn/n1/2022/0226/c64094-32360358. html(访问时间 2022 年 4 月 12 日)

② 《习近平在中共中央政治局第三十七次集体学习时强调 坚定不移走中国人权发展道路 更好推动我国人权事业发展》，见人民网：http://cpc. people. com. cn/n1/2022/0226/c64094-32360358. html(访问时间 2022 年 4 月 12 日)

③ 《习近平在中共中央政治局第三十七次集体学习时强调 坚定不移走中国人权发展道路 更好推动我国人权事业发展》，见人民网：http://cpc. people. com. cn/n1/2022/0226/c64094-32360358. html(访问时间 2022 年 4 月 12 日)

"*Telling a Chinese human rights story*（2010–2020）"①（可以大致翻译为"十年讲述中国人权故事"），而这80幅彩色插图包含了239张照片或截图，是笔者近10年来从事人权学术研究和学术交流的缩影。笔者曾在"欧美及国内数十所著名高校开展学术交流活动，成为中国人权故事和中国人权话语的研究者、讲述者和贡献者"。② 回想起2012年莫言在获得诺贝尔文学奖并发表感言时称，他其实就是讲述一个故事，那么笔者在这里也不妨采取叙事体倒叙方式③来讨论一个严肃的学术问题，积极响应习近平总书记的号召，以期能够"着力讲好中国人权故事"。

2022年5月12日，笔者应邀为中国政法大学全面依法治国研究院举办了讲座，题目为"中国在全球人权治理中的重要贡献——以张彭春和钱端升的人权思想为例"，该讲座中笔者认为："钱端升先生参与起草新中国第一部宪法，为新中国法治建设做出了卓越贡献，这是全球人权治理的重要组成部分；张彭春先生将其多元主义人权观引入《世界人权宣言》的订立过程，并在长达两年之久的起草过程中，其系统的人权哲学思想得以阐发，为国际人权共同标准的达成做出了不朽的贡献。"④该讲座还播放了有关张彭春生平的视频短片，而该短片是专门为2022年4月22日上午在天津市干部俱乐部院内天谊英伦会议楼举行的"纪念张彭春先生诞辰130周年研讨会"准备的，该研讨会由南开大学、哥伦比亚大学和张伯苓研究会共同举办。作为《世界合作共赢的中国贡献》一书的作者，笔者应邀在研讨会上发言。发言内容除了简要回顾了该书的选题依据、研究历程、主要发现和现存问题外，也重点总结了张彭春在联合国经济及社会理事会（简称"经社理事会"）代表中国所做出的杰出贡献。

---

① Sun, Pinghua. 2022. *Chinese Contributions to International Discourse of Human Rights*. Singapore：Springer. pp. 311–351.

② 孙平华编著，《世界合作共赢的中国贡献：张彭春在联合国经济及社会理事会上的发言》，天津：天津社会科学院出版社，2023年1月版。（见封面勒口作者简介）

③ 倒叙，即把故事的结局或某个最重要、最突出的片段提到文章前边，然后从事件开头按事情发展顺序进行叙述。

④ https：//mp.weixin.qq.com/s/WHdqR0_OwEz5mT6cLZENBw

插图1:纪念张彭春先生诞辰130周年研讨会于2022年4月22日
在天津召开,与会人员合影

　　由于经社理事会在联合国的地位十分重要,它在推动国际合作共赢方面发挥了至关重要的作用。它"在处理人口、世界贸易、经济、社会福利、文化、自然资源、工业化、人权、教育科技、妇女地位、卫生及其他有关事项中发挥了重要作用"①。如果说,当今世界人类所面临的三大主题是安全、发展和人权的话,那么,经社理事会当时则担负起其中两大主题任务,一是解决世界经济和社会发展问题,二是搭建国际人权保障制度。这是因为该理事会不仅负责经济及社会领域的国际合作,还作为领导机关负责成立了联合国人权委员会,这为国际人权机制的构建发挥了重要的作用。正是因为理事会工作的重要性,当时各国代表中就不止一人认为一旦理事会的工作做好了,消除了贫困让全人类都享有各种人权保障,那么,必然将有利于国际安全与和平,那么联合国安全理事会的工作就没得做了。这种观点虽然说可能有点夸大了经社理事会的作用,但却从一个侧面反映了经社理事

---

　　① 孙平华编著,《世界合作共赢的中国贡献:张彭春在联合国经济及社会理事会的发言》,天津:天津社会科学院出版社2023年1月版,前言第3页。

会所发挥的作用是极为重要的。

张彭春作为中国常驻联合国经社理事会首席代表,出席了理事会十一届会议,为理事会历史使命的担当、工作机制的建构、国际组织的创建、各项工作的开展,付出了艰辛的努力,并做出了突出的贡献。即使是在不完全统计的情况下,张彭春先生至少在理事会所召开的165次会议上发言,代表中国就世界合作、经济发展、社会进步等阐述了一系列的观点和主张,并提出了一系列合理化建议案,被国际社会所接受和采纳。联合国档案的初步研究,使得我们对张彭春先生的在理事会的工作成就有了崭新的认识。就像笔者在《世界合作共赢的中国贡献》一书前言中所述的那样,他在经社理事会的主要贡献包括以下五个方面[①]:

首先、张彭春先生作为中国驻联合国经济及社会理事会首席代表,所做的第一件大事就是倡议召开国际卫生大会,促使由中国和巴西代表团在旧金山会议期间所提出建立世界卫生组织的议案,能够具体落实下来,为世界卫生组织的创建立下了汗马功劳。

其次、在联合国经济及社会理事会的指导下,建立了联合国人权委员会,张彭春在人权委员会第一届会议上当选为副主席,参与起草《世界人权宣言》和国际人权两公约,为国际人权保障机制的构建倾注了大量心血,成为构建国际人权体系的重要设计师,他当年的努力和付出为全球人权治理打下了坚实的基础。

第三、张彭春善于运用儒家经典名言的风格,彰显了中国传统文化思想的光芒,为国际社会全球治理做出了卓越贡献。

第四、张彭春担任亚洲和远东工作组主席,在积极促成和建立亚洲和远东经济委员会(即亚洲及太平洋经济委员会的前身)方面,起到了重要的主导作用,并做出了杰出贡献。

第五、张彭春不仅为审议新闻自由小组委员会的报告、审议麻醉药品委员会的报告、审议理事会关于世界卫生组织的决议草案、审议和讨论国

---

① 孙平华编著,《世界合作共赢的中国贡献:张彭春在联合国经济及社会理事会的发言》,天津:天津社会科学院出版社2023年1月版,前言第9-13页。

际难民组织决议草案及修正案、审议建立人口委员会议案、审议国际难民组织特别委员会财政报告、审议人权委员会的报告、审议经济委员会报告、审议理事会非政府组织报告、审议专门机构的报告、审议欧洲经济委员会的报告、审议国际劳工组织的报告、审议拉丁美洲经济委员会的报告等做出诸多重要贡献，还详细阐述了对世界经济形势的看法和主张，提出了许多建设性意见，为完善联合国工作机制和促进理事会各项工作的顺利开展做出了卓越的贡献。

二、参与学术交流，讲述中国人权故事

与上述张彭春在联合国经济及社会理事会的贡献相比，他由于参与起草了具有人类历史里程碑意义的《世界人权宣言》，张彭春先生对国际人权事业的贡献彪炳史册，成为国际人权事业的一位卓越领导者。他的思想、主张和众多合理化建议和提案受到各国与会代表的大力支持，并在国际社会赢得了崇高威望，得到了欧美许多著名学者的称颂和赞赏。这些学者包括联合国人权理事会特别程序委员会主席迈克尔·阿多（Michael K. Addo）教授、美国哈佛大学玛丽·格伦登（Mary A. Glendon）教授、哥伦比亚大学刘禾（Lydia H. Liu）教授、弗洛里达州立大学萨姆纳·特威斯（Sumner Twiss）教授、普度大学杨凤岗教授、密西根大学苏珊·华尔兹（Suzan Waltz）教授、杨百翰大学布雷特·沙夫斯（Brett Scharffs）教授、澳大利亚迪肯大学何包钢教授、法国法兰西学院著名汉学家魏丕信（Pierre-Étienne Will）教授、德国著名汉学家海德堡大学鲁道夫·瓦格纳（Ruldolf Wagner）教授、瑞典斯德哥尔摩大学汉斯·罗特（Hans I. Roth）教授、德国国家智库年轻学者弗雷德里克·克伦宾（Frédéric Krumbein）博士①等。下面笔者将讲述一下近10多年来所从事人权研究、开展人权学术交流的真实故事，以期能够解释笔者与人权结下的这段不解情缘。

---

① Krumbein, F. 2015. P. C. Chang—The Chinese father of human rights. *Journal of Human Rights*, 14(3)：333–352.

故事场景一:"半路出家",开启人权研究之旅。笔者本来无缘从事人权研究,从山东省单县师范学校毕业成为一名中学物理教师,后通过自学改教中学英语,从而执教了多年中学英语,从农村到县城、从县城到城市、从城市到北京。为了一个"不安于现状"求学的梦想,从小中专到大专、从大专到本科,从学士到硕士、从硕士到博士,从国内到国外、从国外又回到国内。20世纪末与21世纪初,笔者有幸在外语教学与研究出版社担任过几年英语编辑,期间在北京师范大学攻读了英语语言文学硕士学位,也赴英国华威大学(the University of Warwick)攻读了英语语言教学硕士学位,毕业后以人才引进首都北京。2005年初经教育部留学服务中心派遣到中国政法大学外国语学院任教,2007年考入中国政法大学法学院,秋季学期开始攻读人权法学博士学位,2009年12月份通过了博士论文(《〈世界人权宣言〉研究》)答辩,提前半年毕业,并于2010年1月8日获得人权法学博士学位。这样"半路出家",一边从事外语教学,一边"业余"从事人权研究。所撰写的博士论文2010年通过申报获批了国家社科基金后期资助项目,在博士论文的修改和出版过程中,开始关注张彭春对《世界人权宣言》的贡献。

故事场景二:访学英伦,助力学术科研。2011年2月至2012年1月,笔者有幸在英国埃克塞特大学(the University of Exeter)法学院访学一年,与当时任职于该法学院的迈克尔·阿多(Michael K. Addo)先生有过较多的交流,并由于笔者为该院硕士研究生开设"中国人权"课程,而开始系统研究中国代表张彭春在起草《世界人权宣言》所做的贡献,且借助英国研究生课堂讲述了中国对世界人权事业的贡献,取得了意想不到的效果,不仅顺利完成了博士论文的修改工作,2012年经修改后的博士论文由北京大学出版社出版①,而且,由于访学期间的研究和积累,笔者2012年还成功获批了国家社科基金中华学术外译项目——"中国特色社会主义人权保障制度研究",这是我国人权研究领域获批的第一个中华学术外译项目,

---

① 孙平华著,《〈世界人权宣言〉研究》,北京:北京大学出版社2012年版。

其最终成果《中国人权保障制度》①（英文版）由国际著名出版机构施普林格出版社出版。2014年习近平总书记访问欧洲，并在素有欧洲政治家摇篮之称的比利时欧洲学院发表演讲，而这本英文版著作被中宣部和国务院新闻办选作赠书，在欧洲学院中国馆展出，在重大国际外交场合发挥了作用。同时，该书也是首批纳入联合国电子图书馆检索的570种图书之一。该书不仅已经被数十位不同国家学者在不同语言论著中引用，还被联合国教科文组织有关人员译为波斯语版，即将由伊朗一家出版社出版。上述两项国家社科基金项目成果的出版，无疑得益于笔者英国访学期间的不懈努力。

故事场景三：博士论文成功出版，得到专家和学界和认可。中国政法大学博士生导师杨宇冠教授不仅对笔者的博士论文——《〈世界人权宣言〉研究》给予了精心指导，还应邀为该书撰写了序言，认为："这是我国第一部系统研究这一具有划时代意义的人权文献的专著，填补了我国学术研究领域的一项空白，具有极其重要的理论价值和实践意义。"②获悉该书获批国家社科基金后期资助项目并将由北京大学出版社出版，他评价道："这一成就的取得令人羡慕，他那孜孜以求的探索精神值得称道，为其他人权法学博士项目的研究树立了楷模。"③另外，联合国人权理事会特别程序委员会主席迈克尔·阿多教授也对该成果给予了高度评价，他认为该成果将东、西方世界的学者和决策者之间的辩论巧妙地结合起来，将激发中、外参与者就人权这一与中国有关的主题展开一个公开的和引人入胜的对话。中国政法大学校长黄进教授应邀为该书撰写了题为"一部填补我国学术界研究空白的扛鼎之作——评孙平华老师所著的《〈世界人权宣言〉研究》"，这篇书评刊发在《中国法律》2012年第5期，他认为："孙平华老

---

① Sun, Pinghua. 2014. *Human Rights Protection System in China*. Heidelberg/New York/Dordrecht/London：Springer.

② 杨宇冠，序言二，载于孙平华著：《〈世界人权宣言〉研究》，北京：北京大学出版社2012年版，序言二第3页。

③ 杨宇冠，序言二，载于孙平华著：《〈世界人权宣言〉研究》，北京：北京大学出版社2012年版，序言二第3页。

师的《〈世界人权宣言〉研究》一书对构建我国人权理论体系做出了积极的探索,该书不仅对这一具有划时代意义的世界文献进行了深入剖析,而且在很多章节都提出了新观点和新主张,这对一项原创性研究来说,是至关重要的,也是难能可贵的,而作者新观点和新主张是在分析、比较和综合的基础上提出来的,如对国际人权机制和国内人权保护成就的研究等。"①中国政法大学研究生院院长助理肖宝兴博士也以"世界人权宣言研究的崭新成果"为题为该成果撰写书评并刊发在《人权》2013 年第 1 期,他认为:"这本新著中令人印象深刻的地方有四点。第一,系统探讨了人权的思想基础和制度路径;第二,深入挖掘了《世界人权宣言》制定过程的珍贵史料;第三,进行了《世界人权宣言》的多语种、多文本比较研究;第四,构建了研究国际经典人权文献的新范式。概言之,该书是一本研究《世界人权宣言》集大成的专著,是我国研究《世界人权宣言》的最新成果。相信该书的面世,对人权知识的普及,人权意识的培育,人权理念的提升,人权精神的推广,人权研究水平的提高,人权制度的建设和人权事业的发展,都将起到积极的促进作用。"②另外,《中国法律》和《人权》还刊发了上述两篇书评的英文版。2014 年笔者的《〈世界人权宣言〉研究》一书申报获批了"北京市第十三届哲学社会科学优秀成果二等奖"。上述杨宇冠教授、迈克尔·阿多教授、黄进教授和肖宝兴博士等的评价及优秀成果奖的取得对刚踏入人权研究大门不久的笔者无疑是巨大的激励和鞭策。

故事场景四:欧美学术交流,扩大人权共识。2011 年 11 月,笔者在英访学期间,应邀赴瑞士日内瓦办事处参加了联合国经济、社会和文化权利委员会第 47 届会议,并借机系统查阅了联合国万国宫图书馆相关的历史

---

① 黄进,"一部填补我国学术界研究空白的扛鼎之作——评孙平华老师所著的《〈世界人权宣言〉研究》",《中国法律》2012 年第 5 期,第 38-40 页。//Huang, Jin. (2012). An epic work filling blanks in human rights research in China's academia—Review of *the Study of the Universal Declaration of Human Rights* by Associate Professor Sun Pinghua. *China Law*, 5, pp. 97-99.

② 肖宝兴,2013,世界人权宣言研究的崭新成果,《人权》第 1 期,第 52-53 页。//Xiao, Baoxing 2013. Latest results on studying the Universal Declaration of Human Rights. *Human Rights* 2:31-32.

档案资料,使得对张彭春的研究从一开始就具有了实证研究的性质。2012年5月,笔者应邀赴意大利博洛尼亚大学参加"中欧人权论坛",并在论坛上发表了"中国实现国际人权标准的基本原则"①的演讲,演讲内容2013年收入意大利科学出版社出版的《中欧基本权利:区域认同和普遍主义》一书。2013年2月,应邀赴美国纽约州首府奥尔伯尼法学院参加2013年国际人权论坛,并应邀主持两个分论坛,根据在两个论坛上的发言内容撰写的学术论文"现代世界的人口买卖与性奴隶制"②,刊发在《奥尔巴尼政府法律评论》2014年第7卷第1期;会议期间应邀为该校师生举办了题为"中国人权事业的发展"的学术报告,介绍了中国人权事业的发展与进步。2014年10月初,笔者应邀为美国普度大学举办了题为"儒家学者张彭春与《世界人权宣言》"的报告。接着,采访了密西根大学苏珊·华尔兹教授、哈佛大学法学院玛丽·格伦登教授、纽约大学杰罗姆·科恩(Jerome Cohen)教授等,并先后两次赴联合国纽约总部查阅有关资料和文献。虽然这次调研和学术交流收获满满,但却也是一次充满艰辛的冒险之旅。因为这次旅行,在短短的10天内,笔者乘坐了9个航班,而且,由于天气原因,遇到多次航班延误,不是在等航班就是在去机场、去宾馆、去采访的路上,为了赶航班,常常顾不上吃饭,返回北京时掉了8斤肉。几天时间穿越了大半个美国,还有一次因乘坐小飞机在空中遭遇强气流撞击,被撞击的声音至今回想起来都心有余悸。然而,这些欧美学术交流活动,促进了在人权议题上达成诸多国际共识。

故事场景五:推出中华学术外译成果,在重大国际外交场合发挥作用,为东西方学界的学术交流打开了一扇窗口。2011年2月至2012年1月,笔者有幸获得国家留学基金委的资助,应邀到英国埃克塞特大学法学院访学一年。埃克斯特大学法学院非常重视笔者的研究,并为笔者在英国访学

---

① Sun, Pinghua. 2013. Fundamental principles for achieving international human-rights standards in China. In Lucia Serena Rossi & Giacomo Di Federico (eds.), *Fundamental Rights in Europe and China: Regional identities and universalism.* Napoli: Editoriale Scientifica.

② Sun, Pinghua and Xie, Yan. 2014. Human trafficking and sex slavery in the modern world. *Albany Government Law Review*, 7(1): 91-110.

期间提供了奖学金。访学期间,笔者为该法学院开设了"中国人权"硕士研究生课程,并利用便利的条件,借助备课的实际,撰写了 *Human Rights Protection System in China* 一书,该书稿在 2012 年回国后,成功获批了我国人权研究领域的第一个中华学术外译项目("中国特色社会主义人权保障制度研究",批准号:12WFX001)。2013 年,该项目的最终学术外译成果 *Human Rights Protection System in China*[①] 由施普林格(Springer)在美国、德国、荷兰和英国同时出版,销往全球一百二十多个国家和地区,这是我国人权研究领域中第一部"获得中华社会科学基金资助"的项目成果。该成果引起国内外顶级人权专家的关注,联合国跨国公司和其他工商企业人权事务工作组专家迈克尔·阿多(Michael Addo)教授、时任山东大学校长徐显明教授、中国政法大学校长黄进教授和美国哥伦比亚大学法学院中国法律研究中心主任李本(Benjamin Liebman)教授等均给予积极的肯定和评价。2014 年 1 月 7 日,《中国日报》英文版(*China Daily*)刊文简要介绍了该书;2014 年 5 月,该书封面及内容介绍被全国哲学社会科学规划办公室收入《国家社科基金项目年度报告(2013)》;全国哲学社会科学规划办公室官方网站上 2014 年 9 月推出"国家社科基金中华学术外译项目成果选介",该成果成功入选。如故事场景二所述,2014 年 3-4 月,为了配合国家主席习近平的欧洲访问,该书作为赠书在素有"欧盟重要智囊和欧洲未来政治家摇篮之称"的比利时欧洲学院"中国馆"展出,并永久收藏,在国际重大外交场合发挥了作用。2017 年 7 月 17 日,《光明日报》第一版头条刊登了一篇综合报道,题目是"中国声音 世界回响",该文系统回顾了国家社科基金中华学术外译项目设立五年来的发展状况,其中两次提及该项目成果。另外,该书还被纳入联合国电子图书馆检索,是全球首批纳入检索的 570 本图书之一。该书已被数十个不同语言国家的专家学者在其论著中所引用,为东西方学术交流打开了一扇窗口。

故事场景六:借助学术研究,应邀开展校际学术交流,取得了较好的学

---

① Sun, Pinghua. 2014. *Human Rights Protection System in China*. Heidelberg/New York/Dordrecht/London:Springer.

术交流效果。2013 年 11 月至 2014 年 11 月间,笔者应北京师范大学武尊民教授、河北大学政法学院院长孟庆瑜教授、西北政法大学科研处处长冯卫国教授和南开大学人权研究中心主任常健教授的邀请,为上述几所高校师生举办了五场学术讲座,他们的邀请为笔者提供了与这些学校师生交流的机会。(1)2013 年 11 月 28 日,北京师范大学著名的武尊民教授邀请笔者为母校北京师范大学外国语言文学学院举办了题为"跨越外语学科局限,构建中国人权话语体系"的讲座;(2)2014 年 3 月 12 日,院长孟庆瑜教授邀请笔者为河北大学政法学院师生做了题为"国际关系中的中国人权话语体系"的学术报告;(3)2014 年 5 月 15 日至 16 日,西北政法大学科研处处长冯卫国教授邀请笔者为该校本科生和硕士研究生举办了两场学术报告,为本科生举办的学术报告题目是"构建国际人权体系过程中的中华智慧",为硕士研究生举办的学术报告题目是"论中国人权话语体系的构建";(4)2014 年 11 月 19 日,南开大学人权研究中心主任常健教授邀请笔者为该校法学院学生做了题为"历史性共同标准的达成——张彭春与世界人权宣言"的学术讲座。上述学术讲座和报告的举办使笔者有机会与我国多所高校师生开展了较为广泛的学术交流,促进了笔者在人权领域的研究。同时,在上述高校的几次学术报告也取得了较好的学术交流效果,并在我国学术研究领域产生了一定的影响。

故事场景七:"一面之交",达成合作伙伴。作为世界王牌的高等学府著名教授,玛丽·格伦登在学术界和国际交往中都颇具影响力,是名副其实的世界顶级学者和活动家,她是哈佛大学勒尼德·汉德(Learned Hand)法学讲席教授,系美国人文与科学院(American Academy of Arts and Sciences)院士、曾担任联合国教科文组织资助的学术团体"法律科学国际联合会"(International Association of Legal Science)主席、曾任美国驻梵蒂冈大使、2005 年作为美国代表团团长参加在北京举办的第四届"世界妇女大会"等。她的经典著作《一个新世界的诞生:埃莉诺·罗斯福与世界人权宣言》享誉全球,现已被翻译为中文版出版。① 就是这样一位享誉全球的顶级学者,笔者仅通过邮件联系,她就欣然答应并如约接受了采访(2014年10月1日),还为笔者的两部中、英文著作撰写了长篇序言,对张彭春在人权领域的贡献给予了高度评价,这同时也是对笔者著作的认可和肯定。采访过程中,笔者曾带着一份英文著作草稿,她翻阅草稿后表示希望能够留存在哈佛大学图书馆供学者们参考,但当时鉴于草稿还需要进一步修改完善,以免见笑于国际学界,笔者只好婉言谢绝,并答应待书出版后,赠送她一本。不过她接着表示,如果下次笔者再访哈佛,她将预先召集她的同事一起座谈。2018年3月,笔者的英文著作《历史性共同标准的达成:张彭春与世界人权宣言》(系笔者所主持完成的第二项国家社科基金中华学术外译项目成果)②由施普林格出版社出版,笔者收到样书后写邮件要将新书邮寄给她一本,她回复说哈佛大学图书馆已经购买了该书,她已经看到了这部著作,并明确表示不要邮寄给她样书了。回顾那次采访,格伦登教授对张彭春的评价是极高的,她认为张彭春是"一位智力和学识非凡的人"③、"人权委员会中最有学问、最有文化的人"④、有着伟大的"外交天赋"⑤、称张彭春对《宣言》的普遍性贡献巨大,"多亏了张(彭春),它才不是一份从美国权利传统的角度来看通俗易懂的个人主义的宣言。"⑥

故事场景八:"三次谋面",畅谈学术友谊。笔者与哥伦比亚大学刘禾教授的"三次谋面"。哥伦比亚大学刘禾教授曾在2014年发表过一篇题

① 玛丽·安·葛兰顿著,刘轶圣译,《美丽新世界:〈世界人权宣言〉诞生记》,北京:中国政法大学出版社2016年版。

② Sun, Pinghua. 2018. *Historic Achievement of a Common Standard: Pengchun Chang and the Universal Declaration of Human Rights*. Singapore: Springer.

③ 孙平华著,《张彭春:世界人权体系的重要设计师》,北京:社会科学文献出版社2017年版,第124页。

④ 孙平华著,《张彭春:世界人权体系的重要设计师》,北京:社会科学文献出版社2017年版,第124页。

⑤ 孙平华著,《张彭春:世界人权体系的重要设计师》,北京:社会科学文献出版社2017年版,第127页。

⑥ 孙平华著,《张彭春:世界人权体系的重要设计师》,北京:社会科学文献出版社2017年版,第125页。

为"普遍主义的影子：1948 年前后未讲述的人权故事"①，对张彭春在国际人权史上的历史地位给予了高度评价，称张彭春为"人权先驱"。同年 7 月 7 日，她还在哥伦比亚大学举办了一个讲座，题目是"刘禾教授论人权先驱和哥伦比亚大学校友张彭春"。后来 2015 年仲夏的一个下午，笔者与刘禾教授相约在北京紫竹院公园北码头茶叙，在愉快的交流过程中，刘禾教授根据自己的研究经验，提供了新的研究线索，这对笔者启发颇多。2016 年 6 月下旬，刘禾教授主编的《世界秩序与文明等级：全球史研究的新路径》新书发布座谈会在清华大学举行，笔者应邀在这次座谈会发言②，不仅对新书给予了积极评价，也对张彭春在人权领域的贡献进行了概括介绍。本年度，笔者的《张彭春：世界人权体系的重要设计师》入选《国家哲学社会科学成果文库》，并于 2017 年春季由社会科学文献出版社出版，而刘禾教授恰好夏季来清华任教，因此，笔者将新出版的这部文库成果送到刘禾教授在北京紫竹院旁边的家中，看到笔者的新书，刘禾教授非常高兴地表示随时欢迎笔者到哥伦比亚大学访学，并承诺为笔者提供大力帮助。以上就是笔者与哥伦比亚大学刘禾教授的"三次谋面"。这里笔者也借此机会介绍一下刘禾教授对张彭春先生的概括评价，她认为在哥大的校友中，有许多著名校友的历史影响被提及，如号称民国第一外交家的顾维钧、在五四新文化运动中发挥重要作用的胡适、在中国创建了哲学学科的冯友兰。刘禾教授认为："从长远来看，在这些来自哥伦比亚大学的著名知识分子中，张彭春比其他任何人都更值得纪念，因为他参与起草了对世界具有深远影响的《世界人权宣言》。"③她认为张彭春的影响力高于其他任何人，因为他的学识、政治远见，并且他决心创建他那个时代的人们难以想象的东

---

① Liu, H. L. Shadow of Universalism: The untold story of human rights around 1948. *Critical Enquiry*（40）2014：385-417.

② 三联书店《世界秩序与文明等级》新书研讨会在清华大学举行：重塑中国文明话语，见网址：https://www.guancha.cn/culture/2016_07_01_366094.shtml（2022 年 4 月 12 日访问）

③ 孙平华著，《张彭春：世界人权体系的重要设计师》，北京：社会科学文献出版社 2017 年版，第 140 页。

西:那就是一个真正普遍享有人权的世界"。①

故事场景九:京津沪讲学,引起媒体关注。如上述故事场景六所述,2014 年 11 月 19 日,笔者应首批国家人权教育与培训基地南开大学人权研究中心主任常健教授的邀请,举办了题为"历史性共同标准的达成:张彭春与《世界人权宣言》"的讲座,人权研究中心副主任唐颖侠博士主持了这次讲座,南开大学崔国良先生亲临讲座现场,并应邀发表了精彩点评。这次讲座的题目也正是笔者本年度所获批立项的第二个国家社科基金中华学术外译项目的题目,而该项目的最终成果 *Historic Achievement of a Common Standard：Pengchun Chang and the Universal Declaration of Human Rights* 于 2018 年 3 月 22 日出版发行,这是国内外学术界第一部以张彭春为主题的英文论著。② 而这一天正好笔者应邀在复旦大学举办了题为"《世界人权宣言》中的中国理念"的讲座。复旦大学国家人权教育与培训基地执行主任、法学院陆志安博士还专门别出心裁地为这部英文专著举行了新书发布会。在该书出版之前,由于笔者所撰写的《张彭春:世界人权体系的重要设计师》入选 2016 年《国家哲学社会科学成果文库》,并于 2017 年由社会科学文献出版社出版,这是一部较为全面研究张彭春对国际人权贡献的专著。2017 年 12 月 10 日,是《世界人权宣言》发布 69 周年纪念日,笔者应中国人民大学法学院院长、国家人权教育与培训基地主任韩大元教授的邀请,举办了"张彭春与国际人权共同标准的确立:聚焦历史贡献、人权思

---

① Liu, H. L. Professor Lydia H. Liu on Human Rights Pioneer and Columbia Alum P. C. Chnag. http://weaicolumbia. wordpress. com/2014/07/07professor-lydia-h-liu-on-human-rights-pioneer-and-columbia-alum-p-c-chang/Human right pioneer and Columbia alum P. C. Chang.

② 瑞典斯德哥尔摩大学汉斯·罗特(Hans I. Roth)教授的 *P. C. Chang and the Universal Declaration of Human Rights* 在 2018 年冬季在美国由宾夕法尼亚大学出版社出版发行。2018 年暑假期间在牛津大学基督堂学院举行的国际学术研讨会上,笔者与这位早年毕业于牛津大学的瑞典学者罗特教授进行了很多交流,并将一本 *Historic Achievement of a Common Standard：Pengchun Chang and the Universal Declaration of Human Rights* 复印本赠送给他,而他让我翻阅了他那本瑞典语版书,并且讲述了他与张彭春儿子张远峰的交往,而我说我曾与张彭春的女儿张新月多次通过电话,我们在牛津大学基督堂学院交流很是开心,期间他提到他的那本瑞典语版的书,其英文版即将在美国出版。

想和当代价值"的学术讲座,讲座中所提到的"张彭春多元主义人权哲学观"对全面认识张彭春对世界人权事业的贡献有着重要的参考价值。该讲座内容被光明网、中国网络日报、人民日报海外网、CCTV,凤凰网、百度、腾讯、新浪、搜狐、人权网、头条等20多家新闻媒体所报道。[①] 上述京、津、沪三所国内著名大学的讲座,都是围绕着《世界人权宣言》和张彭春的贡献进行的,也意味着张彭春对国际人权事业的贡献被越来越多的人所熟悉和认识。

故事场景十:积极参与校内外学术交流,并发表学术见解。2014年11月14日,应中国人民大学人权研究中心副主任朱力宇教授的邀请,参加了在中国人民大学苏州校区举办的"中国法治与人权"研讨会,并提交了学术论文"国际关系中的中国人权话语体系"。2014年12月20日,应中央党校政法教研部副主任、中央党校人权研究中心主任张晓玲教授的邀请,参加了在中央党校举办的"纪念'五四宪法颁布六十周年与人权入宪十周年'——暨学习十八届四中全会精神研讨会",并在该研讨会上发表"人权入宪——开启我国人权保护的新时代的讲话"。2015年4月23日,应邀在学院路校区科研楼B209会议室为中国政法大学外国语学院师生举办学术讲座,题目是"藉出国访学,寻自我超越——论学术视野拓展之路"。2015年7月22日至23日,笔者应邀参加了由中国人权研究会和东北财经大学联合举办的"中国经济发展新常态:发展权的可持续保护"理论研讨会,并在会议上做了题为"经济新常态下发展权对促进人权的作用"的大会发言。2016年6月24日,应清华大学人文学院的邀请,在清华大学甲所,参加"告别金字塔——《世界秩序与文明等级》新书座谈会",并应邀在座谈会上发言。2016年12月6日,应邀参加在由中国人权研究会、南开大学人权研究中心和南开大学法学院联合举办的"第五届跨文化人权国际研讨会",并在大会上做"论张彭春多元主义人权观的文化渊源"的发言,

---

① Sun, Pinghua. 2022. *Chinese Contributions to International Discourse of Human Rights*. Singapore：Springer. pp. xxii–xxiii.

其发言内容①收入本届国际研讨会论文集。通过积极参与校内外学术交流，发表了学术见解，取得了良好的交流效果。

故事场景十一：入选成果文库，荣获钱端升法学研究成果奖。2015年，笔者申报获批的中国政法大学校级人文社会科学规划项目——"张彭春：世界人权体系的主要设计师"，名列立项名单榜首（课题编号：15ZFG82001）。通过进一步研究，《张彭春：世界人权体系的重要设计师》入选 2016 年《国家哲学社会科学成果文库》（批准号：16KFX015），并得到五位匿名评审专家的一致好评。这是中国政法大学继 2014 年蔡拓教授所撰写的《全球学导论》和李雪梅教授所撰写的《法制"镂之金石"传统与明清碑禁体系》两项成果之后入选的第三部成果，该成果 2022 年荣获"钱端升法学研究成果奖"三等奖。美国哈佛大学玛丽·格伦登教授应邀为本成果撰写的序言，对该成果给予了高度评价；中国政法大学杨宇冠教授也应邀为本成果撰写了序言，其序言（节选）部分刊发在《中国政法大学校报》（第 500 期）2016 年 11 月 22 日，第三版。序言中对该成果的学术价值评价如下："第一，具有原创性和学术引领作用。第二，具有独特的研究方法、重大的研究价值。第三，该书主题鲜明、结构严谨，首次系统地展示了中国在国际人权体系构建中的作用。第四，该书探讨了相关研究缺失的原因，展现了具有历史跨度的广泛视野。"该成果 2017 年 3 月由社会科学文献出版社出版，中国社会科学院荣誉学部委员刘海年教授为本成果撰写书评，并给予高度评价，认为该成果："不仅在国内而且在国际人权领域，都是一部开拓性的重要研究成果。它的出版，对弘扬中华文化，增进我国人权建设制度自信、理论自信，以及国际人权交流与合作，都将产生深刻影响。"②该成果出版后，被包括中国社会科学院法学所和国际法研究所、中国人民大学法学院、复旦大学国际问题研究院、中南大学法学院、南开大学

---

① 孙平华，论张彭春多元主义人权观的文化渊源，载于常健，汤姆·茨瓦特主编：《传统精神和文化价值观念与人权本土源头》，北京：五洲传播出版社 2018 年 9 月版，第 95-103 页。

② http://www. humanrights. cn/html/2017/4_1122/33075. html

周恩来政府管理学院和历史学院、上海交通大学法学院、南京师范大学法学院等十多位博士生导师(如柳华文、赵建文、孙世彦、朱力宇、任晓、周刚志、常健、侯杰、范进学、毛俊响、严海良等)引证,现已被 SSCI、CSSCI、ESCI 及《中国法学》(英文版) 等引证 80 余次,产生了跨学科影响力和国际影响力。

故事场景十二:再次出版学术外译成果,填补国际学界重要空白。2018 年 3 月 22 日,笔者的英文学术专著,即国家社科基金中华学术外译项目成果——*Historic Achievement of a Common Standard: Pengchun Chang and the Universal Declaration of Human Rights* 由施普林格出版社出版,这是国际学界第一部有关张彭春对《世界人权宣言》所做贡献的英文专著,填补了国际学界一项重要空白,在人权研究领域具有重要的学术价值。这是因为当年参与起草《世界人权宣言》的三位主要人物,包括美国代表罗斯福夫人、中国代表张彭春先生和黎巴嫩代表马利克先生,其中哈佛大学法学院玛丽·格伦登教授撰写了一部以罗斯福夫人为主题的英文专著,马利克的儿子编撰了一部有关马利克当年发言的著作,之前国际学界尚未出版过有关张彭春的英文专著。联合国人权理事会专家、联合国人权理事会特别程序协调委员会主席迈克尔·阿多教授,中国社会科学院荣誉学部委员、中国社会科学院人权研究中心原主任刘海年教授,中共中央党校政法部副主任、中共中央党校人权研究中心主任张晓玲教授,中国政法大学博士生导师杨宇冠教授,美国哈佛大学法学院世界著名专家玛丽·格伦登教授,国际宪法学会终身名誉主席、中国社会科学院大学法学院院长莫纪宏教授等,分别对该英文著作给予高度评价。另外,台湾师范大学刘蔚之教授还专门为该书撰写了英文书评①,刊发在韩国英文期刊 *China and WTO Review*(《中国和世贸组织评论》)2020 年第 1 期上。该书出版后,不仅为国内学术交流提供了便利,也对国际学术交流产生了很大影响。刘蔚之教授认为:"在有关张彭春的著作中,这本书包含了最完整、最全面的信息资

---

① Liou, Wer-Chih, (2020). Book Review. *China and WTO Review*, 2: 433-436.

料,要研究张彭春和《世界人权宣言》,该书就是一本必读书。"①笔者也因该书的出版建立了国际学术声誉,不仅先后多次应邀参加国际学术会议并做大会主旨发言,还引起联合国有关机构的关注并得到其认可(参见下述故事场景十六)。

故事场景十三:广州高校讲座,扩大学术交流范围。2018 年 4 月 17 日至 19 日,笔者应邀在广州四所著名大学开展学术交流。4 月 17 日下午 2 时至 4 时,应暨南大学法学院/知识产权学院邀请,在暨南大学番禺校区教学楼 420 课室,举办了题为"《世界人权宣言》的中国贡献"的讲座,沈太霞副教授主持了讲座,并发表了精彩点评。4 月 17 日晚上 7 时至 9 时,应广州大学法学院的邀请,在广州大学行政东楼前座 201 法学院会议室,举办题为"《世界人权宣言》中的中国方案"的讲座,法学院副院长蒋银华教授主持了讲座,并对讲座内容给予了精彩点评。4 月 18 日上午 10 时至 12 时,应广州大学国家人权教育与培训基地、广州大学人权研究院的邀请,在行政东楼前座 209 人权研究院会议室,举办了题为"课题研究和学术外译主题座谈会",座谈会由广州大学人权研究院常务副院长杨松才教授主持,我国著名法学家、广州大学国家人权教育与培训基地主任、法学元老之一的李步云教授亲临座谈会现场,并发表了精彩点评,基地副主任陈佑武教授以及人权研究院部分教师参加了座谈会,这次座谈会也是"步云人权论坛"开坛活动,具有重要的纪念意义。4 月 19 日下午 3 时至 5 时,应华南理工大学外国语学院的邀请,在华南理工大学外国语学院 4502 报告厅,举办了题为"学术外译中的中华元素"的讲座,外国语学院部分师生听取了讲座,外国语学院李昀教授主持了讲座,并对讲座内容进行了精彩点评。

---

① Liou Wei-Chih. (2020). Book review (*Historic Achievement of a Common Standard: Pengchun Chang and the Universal Declaration of Human Rights*). *China and WTO Review*, 2: 433-436. (Among books about P. C. Chang, this book contains the most complete and thorough information, which makes it a necessity when studying P. C. Chang and the UDHR. This book also clarifies historical facts and restores the status that P. C. Chang deserves. Furthermore, the author provides concrete explanations about the unique contributions of Confucianism to the UDHR.)

4月19日晚上7时20分至9时50分,应中山大学法学院的邀请,在东校园法学院模拟仲裁庭,举办了题为"《世界人权宣言》的中华文化元素"的讲座,讲座由中山大学人权研究中心主任谢进杰教授主持,黄建武教授、刘诚副教授对讲座内容发表了精彩点评。三天时间内,笔者有幸与广州四所著名大学和一个首批国家人权教育与培训基地的师生开展了学术交流,进一步扩大了交流范围,收获颇丰。同时,也从不同的角度将中国对世界人权事业的贡献进行了深入剖析,包括张彭春参与起草《世界人权宣言》的贡献等,取得了较好的交流效果。

故事场景十四:中美学术交流,参与国际合作。2018年暑假,由于中美高校之间的交流与合作,美国杨百翰大学著名学者布雷特·沙夫斯(Brett Scharffs)教授,曾应邀来访中国政法大学并为法学院暑期班授课,在法学院宴请布雷特教授的一次晚餐会上布雷特教授提到了有一位中国人对世界人权事业做出了重要贡献时,法学院院长焦洪昌教授提到了笔者对张彭春的研究,引起了这位美国学者的极大兴趣。焦院长当即打来电话,让笔者与这位美国学者交流起来,通话中布雷特教授便约定一个时间请笔者在他下榻的北京香格里拉酒店见面,并共进晚餐,通过这次交流增进了彼此之间的了解。笔者将复印的一本新出版的 *Historic Achievement of a Common Standard:Pengchun Chang and the Universal Declaration of Human Rights* 赠送给他,而他邀请笔者为在牛津大学基督堂学院举行的国际会议上做题为"张彭春人权思想中的人的尊严"的大会主题报告(2018年8月3日),系该次牛津大学国际会议的三大主题报告之一,与来自欧美国家的20多位专家学者共同出席了大会,大会期间参与《人的尊严宣言》初稿的讨论和起草,该宣言全称为《全世界人人享有尊严的埃斯特角宣言》(简称:《埃斯特角宣言》),2018年12月10日是《世界人权宣言》发布70周年纪念日,也是《埃斯特角宣言》发布日。笔者有幸成为该宣言的中国唯一原始签署人①,并将该宣言译成中文版。② 2019 年春,布雷特教授应邀参加中国社会科学院的学术会议,他再次邀请笔者到香格里拉酒店共进晚餐叙谈。同年 7 月初,布雷特教授再次受邀为中国政法大学法学院暑期班授课,在课程设计中他邀请笔者一起参与暑期班授课,讲述中国对世界人权事业的贡献。2019 年 7 月 25 日,笔者再次应邀参加在牛津大学举办的牛津出版工作坊,并在工作坊发表了题为"《全世界人人享有尊严的埃斯特角宣言》的中国应对策略"主题讲话。暨南大学法学院/知识产权学院的沈太霞博士也应邀参加了本次牛津出版工作坊活动,并在工作坊发表了主题讲话,赢得国际学界的关注。

故事场景十五:英文论文发表,扩大国际学术影响。2018 年参加牛津大学国际会议的还有瑞典斯德哥尔摩大学汉斯·罗特(Hans I. Roth)教授,他是《张彭春与世界人权宣言》一书的作者,他的这本最初为瑞典语版的著作,其英文版于 2018 年年底前由美国宾夕法尼亚大学出版社出版。美国著名的《人权季刊》主编伯特·洛克伍德(Bert B. Lockwood)教授在 2019 年中国政法大学暑期班授课时,赠送笔者一本该书,并应邀在该书扉页题写了如下赠言:*To Pinghua Sun: I hope that you find this study as developing some of this important insights that you have made in your work on P. C. Chang. Your colleague with deep respect, Bert Lockwood.*(译文:致孙平华:我希望你会发现,这项研究拓展了你在研究张彭春时所获得的一些重要见解。你的同事伯特·洛克伍德。)因为笔者 2019 年在《人权季刊》发表了一篇题为"全球治理中张彭春对国际人权的贡献"③一文,这是自该刊创刊

① https://www.dignityforeveryone.org/signatories-to-the-punta-del-este-declaration-of-human-rights/

② https://www.dignityforeveryone.org/wp-content/uploads/2019/02/《埃斯特角宣言》(中文).pdf

③ Sun, Pinghua. 2019. Pengchun Chang's contributions to international human rights in global governance. *Human Rights Quarterly* 41(4): 982-1002.

41 年来,内地学者在该刊所刊发的第三篇学术论文①。联合国人权理事会特别程序委员会主席迈克尔·阿多(Michael K. Addo)教授在邮件中写道:"我很高兴通读了您在《人权季刊》上发表的文章,获悉您业已成为关于张彭春工作的主要权威,这给了我极大的快乐。这是对文献的一项重要贡献。太棒了。"("I have enjoyed reading through your HRQ article and it gives me immense pleasure to know that you have become the leading authority on P. C. Chang's work. This is an important contribution to the literature. Bravo!"—Michael Addo, Jan. 4, 2021.)这一点也从一个侧面说明了,张彭春的人权思想已经在国际学界深入人心。

故事场景十六:英文著作出版,得到联合国有关部门认可。2018 年 11 月 23 日,笔者因本年度英文著作的出版意外地收到联合国人权高专出版部主任 Ahmad Azadi 的邮件,邀请笔者根据对联合国档案资料的掌握,提供一份张彭春的经典言论和主张,以便能够概括张彭春的人权观,以纪念《世界人权宣言》发布 70 周年。通过整理与研究,笔者提供了 11 段相关内容,这里列举三条,供大家参考:1. A human being has to be constantly conscious of other men, in whose society he lives. (译文:一个人必须时刻意识到他所生活的社会中的其他人。) 2. Rights must be protected by law, but laws are necessary also to promote the best in men. (译文:权利必须受到法律的保护,但法律也有必要促进人的优秀品质。) 3. A standard should be established with a view to elevating the concept of man's dignity and emphasizing the respect of man: that principle should be embodied in a preamble to the International Bill of Rights. (译文:应该制定一项标准,以提升人的尊严的概念,强调对人的尊重:这项原则应该体现在《国际权利法案》的序言中。) 联合国人权高专出版部主任主动写邮件向笔者征集有关张彭春在联合国发言的经典言论和主张,这件事本身不仅反映了笔者的有关研究引起了联合

---

① 另外两篇学术论文其中一篇是由曾任中国社会科学院美国研究所所长的周琪教授于 2005 年在美国宾夕法尼亚大学攻读博士学位时刊发的,而另一篇是现任浙江大学光华法学院副院长赵骏教授(系哈佛大学硕士、康奈尔大学博士)于 2015 年刊发的。

国人权高专有关部门领导的关注,也反映了当下联合国工作人员对张彭春当年所做贡献的重视和认可。

故事场景十七:上海高校讲座,促进京沪人文交流。2019 年 12 月 13 日至 15 日,笔者应邀赴上海参加由复旦大学法学院主办的"百年变局下的国际法与人权"研讨会,会议期间应邀为上海三所全国著名高校举办了学术讲座,与相关师生进行了交流。其中,2019 年 12 月 13 日上午,为上海外国语大学举办了题为"论全球治理中的中国人权话语体系"的学术讲座,上海外国语大学教务处副处长王雪梅教授主持了讲座,该校部分教师及博士生、硕士生和本科生参加了这次讲座;13 日下午为华东政法大学外国语学院举办了题为"中华学术外译项目研究"的学术讲座,华东政法大学外国语学院翻译系主任曹嬿老师主持了讲座,外国语学院部分教师参加了讲座;2019 年 12 月 15 日,为复旦大学举办了题为"论《世界人权宣言》的中国元素"的学术报告,复旦大学法学院马忠法教授主持了讲座,中国社会科学院朱伟东教授对讲座给予了精彩点评。上海三所著名高校的讲座以及在复旦大学研讨会上的发言,笔者运用中国人权话语,来讲述中国人权故事,起到了良好的学术交流效果。

故事场景十八:应邀参加庆祝大会,发表获奖感言。2021 年 10 月 14 日,笔者应邀参加"张伯苓研究会成立十五周年庆祝大会",并发表视频获奖感言。会议期间笔者荣获"伯苓研究贡献奖"奖牌,获奖证书载明:"孙平华教授:鉴于您对张彭春及其在世界人权体系构建中的贡献有着深入研究,并出版多部论著,为张伯苓和南开的研究事业做出重要贡献,特授予您'伯苓研究贡献奖'。特发此证,以资鼓励。"由于上课时间冲突,笔者无法亲自前往天津领取奖牌,特录制了时长 3 分钟的获奖感言小视频,对张伯苓研究会成立十五周年表示祝贺,并感谢研究会对笔者研究的认可和奖励。这里简要回顾一下笔者所撰写的"多部论著":(1)2010 年笔者的《〈世界人权宣言〉研究》一书获批国家社科基金后期资助项目,该书的最终成果 2012 年 8 月由北京大学出版社出版,该书 2014 年荣获"北京市第十三届哲学社会科学优秀成果奖(二等奖)"。该项成果既是中国政法大学外国语学院所获批的第一项国家社科基金项目成果,也是该院第一部荣获省部级科研奖励的学术成果。(2)笔者所撰写的《张彭春:世界人权体系的重要设计师》成功入选 2016 年度《国家哲学社会科学成果文库》,成为中国政法大学入选的第三部文库成果,入选《成果文库》被学界认为是荣获我国哲学社会科学领域最高级别的奖励。(3)笔者分别于 2014 年、2018 年和 2022 年出版了三部英文著作,即:*Human Rights Protection System in China*(Springer 2014),*Historic Achievement of a Common Standard:Pengchun Chang and the Universal Declaration of Human Rights*(Springer 2018),*Chinese Contributions to International Discourse of Human Rights*(Springer 2022)。其中,第一部英文成果是我国人权领域荣获中华社科基金资助的第一部外译项目成果;第二部英文成果系国际学界第一部有关张彭春所做贡献的英文专著,也是笔者所主持的第二项国家社科基金中华学术外译项目成果;第三部英文成果系得到国家社科基金重大项目重点资助的学术成果。(4)笔者依托所主持的 2020 年度教育部哲学社会科学研究后期资助重大项目,撰写了两部阶段性成果,包括《世界合作共赢的中国贡献》和《全球人权治理的中国智慧》,均由天津社会科学院出版社出版。而该项目的最终成果——《国际人权话语中的中国声音研究》一书,通过结项评审后,目前已经提交天津社会科学院出版社,进入审核和出版流程。上述成果即为获奖证书中所提到的笔者的"多部论著"。

故事场景十九:郑大线上授课,讲好中国人权故事。由于近三年来新冠疫情的暴发和传播,给人们的生活方式带来了诸多不便,也严重影响了国内外学术交流,国际的面对面交流基本上按下了暂停键,即使国内学术交流也只好改为网上进行。2021 年 7 月,笔者应郑州大学外国语与国际关系学院与中国外交话语研究院的邀请,为该校师生举办了一个题为"论西方人权话语霸权"的学术讲座(2021-7-14),郑州大学中国外交话语研究院院长杨明星教授主持了讲座,牛桂玲教授对讲座内容发表了精彩点评①,大约四百名师生在线听取了讲座。随后,笔者应邀为该校国际学校暑期班,执教了四个专题系列人权课程,包括:第一讲:中国对世界人权的贡献:以张彭春对《世界人权宣言》的贡献为例(2021-7-19);第二讲:论全球治理中的中国人权话语体系(2021-7-20);第三讲:实现国际人权标准的原则与措施(2021-7-26);第四讲:借助学术交流讲好中国人权故事(2021-7-27)。郑州大学硕士研究生张瑞宇同学②和山东政法学院学生孙璐同学③在听了上述课程后,分别撰写了听讲感言,对讲座内容给予了高度评价。借助上述五个专题,并通过自己的探索和总结,力图着力讲好中国人权故事。④ 这些探索完全符合习近平总书记的最新指示精神,能够"讲好中国人权故事"也是笔者孜孜以求的努力方向。

故事场景二十:推出新的学术论著,强化校内外学术交流与合作。笔者 2022 年 4 月 7 日由施普林格出版社出版的 *Chinese Contributions to International Discourse of Human Rights* 一书⑤,汇集了笔者近十年来在人权研究领域的代表性英语学术成果,正是对外讲好中国人权故事的一次有益的尝试。而由笔者历经数月艰辛所倾情编著的《世界合作共赢的中国贡献:张彭春在联合国经济及社会理事会的发言》一书,2022 年 4 月 20 日由天津

① Niu, Guiling. 2022. A brief review of Professor Sun Pinghua's lecture on Western hegemony in human rights discourse. In Sun, Pinghua. *Chinese Contributions to International Discourse of Human Rights*. Singapore: Springer. pp. 285-288,

② Zhang, Ruiyu. 2022. My thoughts about Professor Sun Pinghua's four lectures for the 2021 International Summer School at Zhengzhou University. In Sun, Pinghua. *Chinese Contributions to International Discourse of Human Rights*. Singapore: Springer. pp. 288-293.

③ Sun, Lu. 2022. My thoughts about Professor Sun Pinghua's lectures. In Sun, Pinghua. *Chinese Contributions to International Discourse of Human Rights*. Singapore: Springer. pp. 293-296.

④ Sun, Pinghua. 2022. Chinese Contributions to International Discourse of Human Rights. Singapore: Springer. pp. 285-296.

⑤ 该书是笔者继所主持完成的两项国家社科基金中华学术外译项目成果之后,由施普林格出版社出版的第三部英文著作,得到国家社科基金重大项目的重点支持。

社会科学院出版社出版了部分样书①,也作为 4 月 22 日在天津举办的"中国价值 世界贡献"纪念张彭春先生诞辰 130 周年研讨会的一份献礼。在这次研讨会上,笔者应邀以"论张彭春对世界经济及社会合作的贡献"为题进行了发言,该发言内容的修改稿,收入研讨会论文集《中国价值 世界贡献——张彭春诞辰 130 周年纪念文辑》②。如前所述,2022 年 5 月 12 日,笔者应邀为中国政法大学全面依法治国研究院举办了"中国在全球人权治理中的重要贡献——以张彭春和钱端升的人权思想为例"的学术讲座;6 月 9 日和 10 日,应邀分别为天津大学法学院和南京师范大学法学院举办了题为"全球人权治理的中国智慧——张彭春对国际人权事业的贡献"的学术讲座;6 月 12 日,笔者还应邀作为与谈人参加了由天津大学法学院举办的"工商业与人权"前沿法律问题研讨会。另外,2022 年 5 月,笔者的成果文库作品《张彭春:世界人权体系的重要设计师》荣获"钱端升法学研究成果奖"三等奖。

故事场景二十一:参加亚洲人权论坛,破解西方话语霸权。2022 年 11 月 26 日,笔者应邀参加中国人民大学主办的"亚洲人权论坛——环境、气候变化与人权"国际学术研讨会,并在第一单元"亚洲视野下的人权观"做了题为"张彭春对国际人权理念的贡献"的主题发言(《中国人权网》进行了专门报道),而《中国新闻网》对其发言内容进行了相关的报道,题目是"亚洲学者呼以'亚洲人权共识'回应话语霸权"。该报道引用了笔者的发言内容:"西方人权观受到'弱肉强食、适者生存'的社会达尔文主义影响,

---

① 该书的正式出版时间是 2023 年 1 月,而 2022 年 4 月 22 日研讨会上为参会人员分发的样书(大概 30 本左右)标注的出版时间是 2022 年 5 月第 1 版,南开大学侯杰教授和曲敏君在其论文"张彭春:中国在联合国和世界上的一座丰碑"一文中所引证 28 次的便是 2022 年 5 月版样书,见南开大学校史办公室等编:《中国价值 世界贡献——张彭春诞辰 130 周年纪念文辑》,天津:天津社会科学院出版社 2022 年 12 月版,第 61-76 页。

② 孙平华,论张彭春对世界经济及社会合作的贡献,载于南开大学校史办公室等编:《中国价值 世界贡献——张彭春诞辰 130 周年纪念文辑》,天津:天津社会科学院出版社 2022 年 12 月版,第 31-46 页。

已经形成了思维定式,比如一些国家动辄使用武力制裁。"①报道中接着这样写道:"这位长期研究人权的学者分析,从实践来看,美西方国家并不是真正关心亚洲或其他国家的人权成就,而是试图站在道义制高点,将人权作为打压他国的工具。面对这种话语霸权,亚洲国家必须寻求更多共识,破解看待人权的单一视角。"②这篇报道的最后一段:"孙平华举例说,中国代表张彭春当年参与起草《世界人权宣言》时秉持儒家哲学思想,尊重文化多元主义,换言之,现有的国际人权话语体系中蕴含着丰富的中国人权理念和主张。'人权并不是西方国家的专利。'他说,为建设一个更加合理公平的国际人权治理新秩序,中国各界还将继续作出贡献。"③从话语分析的角度来看,这段报道题目中"话语霸权"来自笔者对问题的回应及大家对国际人权话语格局的共识;三个小标题(破解人权单一视角、形成共识已有基础、中国发挥积极作用)中有两个涉及到笔者的观点,也许因受到笔者的发言浅见的启发;报道的 12 段文字中有三段提到笔者的见解,足见报道者对当下国际人权问题的深刻思索;报道以笔者的见解作结尾,既表明了笔者发言契合了大家的期待,凸显了中国的历史性贡献和中国当下对国际人权事业的作用,也发出了积极的倡议。《中国网》《中国人权网》《腾讯网》《新浪网》《搜狐网》《齐鲁网》《荆楚网》《扬子晚报》等对其报道进行了转载,产生了一定的社会影响。

故事场景二十二:参加国际会议,发出中国学术声音。2023 年 4 月 18 日,笔者应国际学术界邀请,在线参加美国夏威夷"亚洲人的尊严观"国际学术会议,并在会议上以"Chinese Perspectives on Human Dignity"(人的尊

① 亚洲学者吁以"亚洲人权共识"回应话语霸权,《中国新闻网》2022 年 11 月 27 日。见网址:https://www.chinanews.com.cn/gn/2022/11-27/9903498.shtml(访问时间 2023 年 5 月 10 日)。

② 亚洲学者吁以"亚洲人权共识"回应话语霸权,《中国新闻网》2022 年 11 月 27 日。见网址:https://www.chinanews.com.cn/gn/2022/11-27/9903498.shtml(访问时间 2023 年 5 月 10 日)。

③ 亚洲学者吁以"亚洲人权共识"回应话语霸权,《中国新闻网》2022 年 11 月 27 日。见网址:https://www.chinanews.com.cn/gn/2022/11-27/9903498.shtml(访问时间 2023 年 5 月 10 日)。

严的中国观)为题进行大会发言。一位在杨百翰大学夏威夷分校读研的台湾学生江濡秀同学,听后发来邮件表示:"我只想对您关于中国人对人类尊严的看法的发言表示感谢。看到中国人是如何看待这一思想的,这是一次令人惊奇的经历和令人大开眼界的发言,特别是对我这个来自台湾的学生来说。感谢您的讲述。("I just want to express my appreciation for your presentations on Chinese perspectives on Human Dignity. It is an amazing experience and eye-opening presentation to see how Chinese view on this thought, especially for me as a student from Taiwan. I appreciate your input.")预计笔者这篇发言稿也将与其他发言稿一起由 Routledge 出版。

故事场景二十三:借助国际学校课堂教学,为建构国家对外话语体系添砖加瓦。2023 年 7 月 5 日至 6 日,笔者再次应邀为郑州大学国际暑期学校授课时,就自己的研究成果与师生们进行了系统交流,交流的题目共有四个,包括"论西方人权话语霸权的成因、破解案例及对策""全球治理的中国贡献:基于联合国档案研究""论全球治理中的中国人权话语体系"和"世界卫生组织的中国渊源研究",每个题目讲授两个小时,两天时间上午和下午各讲授一个题目。其中,在讲述论西方人权话语霸权时,从全球史的角度分析了西方人权话语霸权的成因、并借助联合国档案的研究提供了西方人权话语霸权的破解案例,从而提出应对西方人权话语霸权的策略。在讲述全球治理的中国贡献时,笔者从对联合国档案的整理和研究,不仅系统总结了中国对人权事业的贡献,展现了丰富的中国人权话语,还从全球治理的角度分析了中国对世界经济及社会发展所做出的杰出历史贡献,这是目前国际学术研究的一个重要空白。另外,在讲述世界卫生组织的中国渊源时,系统地阐述了中国对世界卫生组织创建所做出的卓越贡献,这些贡献是其他任何国家都难以比拟的,中国堪称是世界卫生组织的倡议者和缔造者。通过上述这些课堂交流,为建构我国的人权话语体系、法学话语体系和国家对外话语体系添砖加瓦。

故事场景二十四:编撰出版《全球人权治理的中国智慧》,并被京、鲁、湘三所著名高校研究机构聘请为研究员。2023 年 1 月,笔者继所编著的

《世界合作共赢的中国贡献：张彭春在联合国经济及社会理事会的发言》一书之后，为了全面探究全球治理的中国贡献，笔者又编撰了《全球人权治理的中国智慧：张彭春在联合国人权委员会及联大第三委员会等的发言》，该书即将由天津社会科学院出版社出版，系 2020 年教育部哲学社会科学后期资助重大项目——"国际人权话语中的中国声音研究"的阶段性研究成果（批准号：20JHQ010），得到"中央高校基本科研业务费专项资金"资助（Supported by "the Fundamental Research Funds for the Central Universities"）及张伯苓研究会的资助。2023 年 7 月 17 日，笔者应邀参加了由山东大学习近平法治思想研究中心和山东大学法学院联合主办的"习近平法治思想与法学三大体系建设学术研讨会"，被聘为"山东大学习近平法治思想研究中心特聘研究员"、主持了第二单元的发言和讨论，并在第三单元做了题为"促进法学话语体系建设的几点想法"的大会发言。而恰在同日，"光石法学苑"发布了"群雄逐鹿，2023 年度法学高贡献学者都来自哪些高校？"一文[1]，笔者有幸被列入"校友会 2023 中国大学法学高贡献学者名单"[2]。另外，本年度还被中国政法大学全面依法治国研究院、中南大学人权研究中心（国家人权教育与培训基地）分别聘为研究员等。被上述三所高校科研机构聘为研究员这对笔者来说是一份荣耀，也是对笔者研究工作的激励和鞭策。

　　故事场景二十五：美国学者再次来访法大，笔者赠送一部新作——《世界合作共赢的中国贡献》。2023 年 9 月 18 日，美国杨百翰大学布雷特·沙夫斯（Brett Scharffs）教授再次来访北京，笔者与他在喜来登酒店相聚交流共进晚餐、具体了解了他近年来所开展的国际学术交流活动。9 月 19 日下午，笔者参加了布雷特·沙夫斯教授在中国政法大学举办的学术讲座，讲座的题目为"文明视域下的人类尊严——《世界人权宣言》75 周年之际"（Civilizational Perspective on Human Dignity—on the 75th Anniversary of the Universal Declaration of Human Rights），并应邀在讲座最后对讲座演

---

① https://mp. weixin. qq. com/s/ZMUbeTvZs0xlnirD3g2ZDw（2023 年 8 月 31 日访问）
② https://mp. weixin. qq. com/s/ZMUbeTvZs0xlnirD3g2ZDw（2023 年 8 月 31 日访问）

讲者及演讲内容作了简要点评,对学者的信仰与使命、采取的措施和开展的学术活动,以及取得的成就和做出的贡献等进行了简短评价,并对讲座的成功举办表示感谢,赢得在座同学们的热烈掌声。有趣的是在该讲座开始前,笔者将一部《世界合作共赢的中国贡献:张彭春在联合国经济及社会理事会的发言》①赠送给布雷特·沙夫斯教授,并展示了另一部待版的《全球人权治理的中国智慧:张彭春在联合国人权委员会及联大第三委员会等的发言》(双语版)样书,看到每部 800 页的两部样书,这位学者惊叹道:"编写这些内容需要做大量的工作!"另外,令人意外的是,这位美国学者在讲座的课件中还专门展示了笔者的英文专著 *Historic Achievement of a Common Standard*:*Pengchun Chang and the Universal Declaration of Human Rights* 的封面,并对作者给予了高度评价,将笔者誉为研究《世界人权宣言》的"国际知名权威专家"(well-known international leading authority)。记得笔者曾经在 2018 年在香格里拉酒店与其共进晚餐时,赠送了这部英文著作的复印本,从本次讲座课件来看,这位美国学者对笔者这部英文专著极为重视和认可。

故事场景二十六:完成重大课题成果,并刊发"论应对西方人权话语霸权"。2023 年恰逢《世界人权宣言》发布 75 周年,笔者在已有编著的《世界合作共赢的中国贡献:张彭春在联合国经济及社会理事会的发言》(天津社会科学院出版社 2023 年版)和《全球人权治理的中国智慧:张彭春在联合国人权委员会和联大第三委员会等的发言》(天津社会科学院出版社 2024 年版)两项阶段性成果的基础上,也完成了 2020 年度教育部哲学社会科学研究后期资助重大项目(批准号:20JHQ010)——"国际人权话语中的中国声音研究"的最终研究成果,并通过了结项专家评审,结合评审意见经笔者进一步修改之后,结题成果《国际人权话语中的中国声音研究》(英文书名:*The Study of China's Voice in the International Discourse of Human Rights*)书稿进入审核和出版阶段。另外,笔者的"论应对西方人权话

---

① 孙平华编著:《世界合作共赢的中国贡献:张彭春在联合国经济及社会理事会的发言》,天津:天津社会科学院出版社 2023 年 1 月版。

语霸权"一文刊发在《中共青岛市委党校 青岛行政学院学报》2023年第5期。该文从全球史的角度,聚焦西方人权话语霸权成因的剖析,并借助联合国档案资料提供了破解案例,从而进一步提出应对策略,这不仅旗帜鲜明地反对西方人权话语霸权,宣传中国对《世界人权宣言》卓越贡献,还对拓展学术视野、培养具备国际视野的外语和法治人才有着重要的现实指导意义。综上所述,笔者通过教育部重大课题研究、完成成果结项、刊发相关学术论文,为全面探究全球治理的中国贡献,为深入参与全球治理提供了智力支撑。

故事场景二十七:张元龙先生的大力支持,为笔者的人权研究助力。(1)2013年7月5日,张元龙先生首次接受了笔者的采访,在随后的研究过程中他为笔者提供了很大帮助,并提供了他在2003年对张彭春女儿——张新月的采访录像,这给笔者开展对张彭春的系统研究增加了新的视角。张元龙先生历任天津人大常委会副主任、全国工商联副主席、天津工商联主席,他是张彭春胞兄张伯苓的嫡孙。(2)笔者于2014年9月30日至10月11日在美国开展了初步采访和调查研究,这为进一步开展对张彭春的研究提供了助力,这次调研活动得到了张元龙先生的大力支持,并得到天津复方光电技术有限公司的赞助。(3)如前所述,2014年11月19日,笔者应邀为南开大学法学院举办题为"历史性共同标准的达成——张彭春与世界人权宣言"的学术讲座,张元龙先生获悉后,专门派摄影师到课堂拍摄,为笔者的南开大学学术讲座留下了宝贵的音像资料。(4)2017年6月8日,在南开大学新校区周恩来政府管理学院为张彭春先生雕像举办了揭幕仪式,张伯苓、张彭春先生后人张元龙,校长龚克出席揭幕仪式,仪式由副校长朱光磊主持。张彭春雕像由南开大学社会学系1992级校友张洪涛捐资设立,南开大学文学院教授李军设计。张元龙先生在致辞时说,张彭春不但在《世界人权宣言》的起草中发挥了重要组织作用,还把中国传统文化中的哲学思想、人权思想融入《世界人权宣言》,是世界人权体系的重要设计者。其实,就在揭幕仪式举行前的3月份,笔者的"国家哲学社会科学成果文库"成果——《张彭春：世界人权体系的重要设计师》①一书由社会科学文献出版社出版，张元龙先生出资购买一百册，这也是对笔者研究成果的肯定和支持。(5)2019年4月5日，为纪念爱国教育家、南开系列学校创办人张伯苓先生诞辰143周年，《别有中华》中文版首发式暨"南开·中国·世界"学术研讨会在南开大学举行，笔者应邀参加了该学术研讨会，并在会议上以"《别有中华》来自跨学科的世界赞誉"为主题发言，而该部《别有中华》中文版收入了笔者撰写的"张彭春：《别有中华》的幕后主持人和实际编辑者"②一文。(6)2022年4月22日，"纪念张彭春诞辰130周年研讨会"在天津举行，笔者应邀参加了会议并在会议上做了题为"张彭春对世界经济及社会合作的贡献"的主题发言，该发言内容经过修改和扩充，收入天津社会科学院出版社2022年12月出版的《中国价值 世界贡献——张彭春诞辰130周年纪念文辑》③。在这次研讨会上，还分发了笔者编著的《世界合作共赢的中国贡献：张彭春在联合国经济及社会理事会的发言》④一书的部分样书，得到了与会人员的好评，而该书得到了张伯苓研究会的资助。(7)另外，得到张元龙先生大力支持的还有笔者所编著的《全球人权治理的中国智慧：张彭春在联合国人权委员会和联大第三委员会等的发言》⑤一书，该书作为2020年度教育部哲学社会科学研究后期资助重大项目的阶段性成果(批准号：20JHQ010)，还得到了"中央高校基本科研业务费专项资金"资助(Supported by "the Fundamental Research Funds for the Central Universities")，该书即将由天津社科院出版社

① 孙平华：《张彭春：世界人权体系的重要设计师》，北京：社会科学文献出版社2017年3月版。

② 孙平华：张彭春：《别有中华》的幕后主持人和实际编辑者，载于[美]司徒雷登，胡适等著，张昊苏，陈熹等译：《别有中华》，天津：南开大学出版社2019年版，第271-275页。

③ 孙平华：张彭春对世界经济及社会合作的贡献，载于南开大学校史研究室编，《中国价值 世界贡献——张彭春诞辰130周年纪念文辑》，天津：天津社会科学院出版社2022年12月版，第31-46页。

④ 孙平华编著：《世界合作共赢的中国贡献：张彭春在联合国经济及社会理事会的发言》，天津：天津社会科学院出版社2023年1月版。

⑤ 孙平华编著：《全球人权治理的中国智慧：张彭春在联合国人权委员会和联大第三委员会等的发言》，天津：天津社会科学院出版社2023年11月版。

出版发行。

　　故事场景二十八:刘海年教授撰写书评,鞭策笔者坚持人权研究。承蒙中国社会科学院荣誉学部委员刘海年教授的大力支持,他为笔者的两部中英文论著撰写的书评刊发在"中国人权网"和《中国政法大学校报》,其英文版收入笔者英文学术专著。(1)2013年11月5—6日,笔者应邀参加了在武汉大学举办的"第五届全国人权研究机构工作经验交流会",并在会议上对自己的人权研究工作进行了介绍,得到了中国社会科学院荣誉学部委员刘海年教授的肯定、认可和鼓励,会议期间也结识了人权研究领域许多知名的学者,如李步云教授、陈世球大使、张晓玲教授、柳华文教授等。(2)2014年11月14日,笔者应邀在中国人民大学苏州校区举办的"法治中国与人权"理论研讨会,为本次学术研讨会提交了一篇题为"国际关系中的中国人权话语体系"的学术论文,并在大会上做了介绍与交流,再次得到了我国著名法学专家、中国社会科学院荣誉学部委员刘海年教授的高度评价。(3)2017年9月26日,《中国政法大学校报》第三版,刊发了刘海年教授为笔者的英文著作(*Historic Achievement of a Common Standard: Pengchun Chang and the Universal Declaration of Human Rights*)撰写的书评,题目为"论述中国专家张彭春为打造国际人权宪章所做贡献的力作——孙平华著《历史性共同标准的达成》(英文版)"。[①] (4)2017年11月22日,"中国人权网"刊发了刘海年教授的书评,题目是"论述中国专家张彭春为打造国际人权宪章所做贡献的力作——评孙平华教授著《张彭春:世界人权体系的重要设计师》"[②]。刘海年教授认为:笔者的著作"不仅在国内而且在国际人权领域,都是一部开拓性的重要研究成果。它的出版,对弘扬中华文化,增进我国人权建设制度自信、理论自信,以及国际人权交流

---

　　① 刘海年:论述中国专家张彭春为打造国际人权宪章所做贡献的力作——孙平华著《历史性共同标准的达成》(英文版),《中国政法大学校报》2017年9月26日第527期(总第933期)第三版。

　　② http://www.humanrights.cn/html/2017/4_1122/33075.html

与合作,都将产生深刻影响。"①另外,刘海年教授还将他的几部论著和刚发表不久的论文期刊赠送给笔者,并留言鼓励和鞭策笔者继续从事人权研究。

故事场景二十九:莫纪宏教授等撰写序言及书评,笔者最新研究成果得到权威认可。承蒙中国社会科学院大学法学院院长莫纪宏教授的大力支持,他对笔者的最新研究成果给予了高度评价。莫纪宏教授系我国法学界和人权研究领域的国家队领军人物,系国际宪法学协会终身名誉主席、中国社会科学院大学法学院院长、中国社会科学院法学研究所所长、中国社会科学院人权研究中心主任、中国社会科学院大学教授、博士生导师。(1)2009年12月12日上午,"中国政法大学法学院博士毕业论文答辩会"在学院路校区举行,笔者于2007年考入法学院攻读人权法学博士学位,学院提前半年为笔者召开了毕业论文答辩会,这次答辩会莫纪宏教授担任答辩委员会主席,主持了笔者的博士论文答辩。这是笔者首次长时间的与莫教授等五位校内外专家面对面,通过这次毕业论文答辩活动,莫老师渊博学识和法语运用能力给笔者留下了深刻印象,尤其是莫教授所提出的问题给笔者进一步思索和研究指明了方向。(2)莫纪宏教授应邀为笔者的两部中英文论著(《国际人权话语中的中国声音研究》和 Chinese Contributions to International Discourse of Human Rights②)撰写了序言,并全面地介绍了笔者的科研经历及学术交流与研究情况,对笔者的四部主要论著给予了高度评价,这是对笔者人权研究的支持、鼓励和鞭策。(3)莫纪宏教授在《中国政法大学校报》2023年4月25日第三版刊发了以"我国人权研究领域的一部重要力作——评孙平华教授《国际人权话语中的中国声音研究》"为题的书评,对笔者所主持完成的2020年度教育部哲学社会科学研究后期资助(重大)项目成果给予了充分的肯定,他认为:"该书内容对构建适合

---

① 刘海年:论述中国专家张彭春为打造国际人权宪章所做贡献的力作——孙平华著《历史性共同标准的达成》(英文版),《中国政法大学校报》2017年9月26日第527期(总第933期)第三版。/又见:http://www. humanrights. cn/html/2017/4_1122/33075. html

② Mo Jihong: Foreword by Mo Jihong. In Sun, Pinghua. 2022. *Chinese Contributions to International Discourse of Human Rights*. Singapore: Springer.

我国大国地位的人权话语体系,掌握国际交往中的人权话语权和主导权,具有重要的现实意义。其学术创新和学术价值体现在以下几个方面:一、该成果对国际人权议题的原创性研究,展现和丰富了国际人权话语中的中国贡献,在人权话语研究中具有重要学术引领作用。二、该成果研究方法科学、学术视野宽泛,理论价值重大。三、该成果首次较为系统地展示了中国对国际人权事业的贡献,成为国际人权话语中的中国声音,对开展国际人权交流与合作具有重要现实意义。总之,该书选题具有重要价值,其研究方法科学、学术观点鲜明、结构设计合理、论证逻辑严谨、语言使用规范、结论令人信服,是一部不可多得的原创佳作。"[①](4)莫纪宏教授和赵江寒同学共同撰写的书评,题目是"历史担当与未来使命——评孙平华教授《历史性共同标准的达成:张彭春与〈世界人权宣言〉》",该书评从四个方面对笔者的第二部英文专著给予了较高的评价:"该书通过发掘翔实的文献史料,系统研究了中国外交家张彭春在《世界人权宣言》起草过程中所发挥的关键作用,向世界展示了张彭春基于其多元主义人权观对联合国达成人权共同标准所做出的历史性贡献,诠释了中华文化对国际人权事业的历史担当与未来使命。在中华文化复兴的新时代,从历史展望未来,该书的价值已超越了其初衷及内容。一、浓缩起草历程,彰显《宣言》价值;二、填补学界空白,突出中国贡献;三、寻求理论建树,体现学术创新;四、立足中华文明,推进人类人权事业。"[②]该书评最后指出:"孙平华教授通过研究与实践所形成的人文主义和集体主义人权思想与张彭春先生一脉相承,根植于厚重的以儒家文化为核心的中华文明,是现代世界人权理论的重要根基和组成部分。他们就是中华文化中求索于理想与现实之间的"士",怀有神圣的使命感,献身于现代人类人权事业,助力全球人权治理朝着更加

[①] 莫纪宏:我国人权研究领域的一部重要力作——评孙平华教授《国际人权话语中的中国声音研究》,《中国政法大学校报》2023 年 4 月 25 日第 721 期(总第 1127 期)第三版。

[②] 莫纪宏,赵江寒:历史担当与未来使命——评孙平华教授《历史性共同标准的达成:张彭春与〈世界人权宣言〉》,《语言与法律研究》2024 年第 1 期。

公平公正的方向发展。"①莫纪宏教授提携、支持和鼓励后进的师德风范及博闻广识、乐于助人的学术关怀永远成为笔者前进的不懈动力。

故事场景三十:利用受众较多的几次学术演讲与讲座,不断讲述中国人权故事。回顾笔者近十多年来所从事的学术交流活动,听众一般为高校师生或者相关研究领域的专家学者,但从听众人数来说,规模较大的有如下几次:(1)2013年11月5-6日,笔者应邀参加在武汉大学举办的"第五次全国人权研究机构工作经验交流会",并在大会上发言,向来自于全国人权研究领域的一百多位专家学者介绍了笔者的人权研究和所取得的研究成果等,受到了与会专家的好评。通过参与本次会议,笔者也结识了我国众多的人权专家,包括全国十届政协副主席罗豪才教授、中国社会科学院荣誉学部委员、人权研究中心主任刘海年教授、我国著名的三大法学元老之一的李步云教授、陈世球大使等,并在与他们的交流中受益匪浅。(2)2014年5月15-16日,笔者应邀为西北政法大学举办了两场学术讲座。其中,5月15日为该校本科生举办的题为"国际人权保护体系构建中的中华智慧",科研处处长冯卫国教授主持了报告会,参与听讲的学生一百五十多人,取得了良好的交流效果(见上述故事场景六)。(3)2014年11月19日,笔者应邀在南开大学法学院举办了"历史性共同标准的达成:张彭春与世界人权宣言"的学术讲座,参与该次讲座的同学有一百三十多人,南开大学人权研究中心副主任唐颖侠副教授主持了这次讲座活动,崔国良先生应邀对讲座内容发表了精彩点评,张伯苓研究会还专门派摄影师对讲座进行了全程录像和拍照(见上述故事场景六)。(4)2018年4月21日,应北京大学外国语学院的邀请,在北京大学英杰交流中心阳光厅参加了"中国翻译职业交流大会",并做主题发言,题目为"《世界人权宣言》中的中国故事",与会代表与北京大学师生约三百人参加交流活动。(5)2018年5月16-17日,笔者应邀为河北大学政法学院(2019年9月改名"法学院")和外国语学院举办了两场学术讲座,其中,5月16日为政法学

---

① 莫纪宏,赵江寒:历史担当与未来使命——评孙平华教授《历史性共同标准的达成:张彭春与〈世界人权宣言〉》,《语言与法律研究》2023年第2期。

院在该院模拟法庭举办的题为"《世界人权宣言》的中国渊源"的学术讲座，政法学院院长孟庆瑜教授主持了讲座，刘晓蜜副教授对讲座进行了点评，孟庆瑜院长发表了感言，近三百名师生参加了这次学术交流活动。（6）2021年7月14日，笔者应邀为郑州大学外国语与国际关系学院举办了题为"论西方人权话语霸权"的学术讲座，郑州大学中国外交话语研究院院长杨明星教授主持了讲座，牛桂玲教授对讲座内容发表了精彩评论，约四百名师生在线听取了讲座，这也是在疫情期间笔者所做的重要学术报告之一。总之，笔者通过上述几次学术活动，不断讲述中国人权故事，使得中国对世界人权事业的贡献为越来越多的高校师生所知悉和了解。

故事场景三十一：探究全球治理的中国贡献，借机为宣传《宣言》鼓与呼。今年是《世界人权宣言》发布75周年，是《维也纳宣言和行动纲领》发布30周年，也是《埃斯特角宣言》发布5周年，笔者结合已经完成的教育部重大项目的相关成果，应邀为国内著名高校举办了多个相关的学术讲座，涉的具体高校、讲座时间及主题内容分别如下：（1）作为山东大学习近平法治思想研究中心特聘研究员，2023年10月25日应邀为山东大学法学院和人权研究中心举办了"全球人权治理中的中国贡献"的学术讲座，从全球治理的角度和视野，侧重全球人权治理中的中国贡献，尤其是中国对起草《世界人权宣言》的所发挥的重要作用等，为全面了解中国对全球人权治理的作用和贡献提供了详实依据。（2）作为中国政法大学法学院校友，笔者于2023年10月27日应邀为中国政法大学"萌才讲坛"举办了"全球人权治理中的中国贡献"的学术报告。来自法学院本科生一百多位同学参加了该讲座，讲座内容不仅对全球人权治理中的中国贡献做了分析和讲述，还对培养学生的爱国主义情怀，树立和增强四个自信都有着十分重要的现实意义。（3）2023年11月8日，笔者应邀为西南政法大学外国语学院举办了"全球治理中的西方人权话语霸权"的学术讲座，从全球史的角度，剖析了西方人权话语霸权的成因、并借助联合国档案资料提供了破解案例进一步提出应对策略，不仅旗帜鲜明地反对西方人权话语霸权，宣传中国对《世界人权宣言》卓越贡献，还对拓展学术视野、培养具备国际视野的外语和法治人才有着重要的指导意义。这也是继在西北政法大学、华东政法大学和中国政法大学之后,笔者开展学术交流的第四所我国著名政法类院校。(4)2023 年 11 月 23 日应邀为广州大学人权研究院举办了"西方人权话语霸权的成因分析及应对策略"的学术讲座,人权研究院副院长周露露博士主持了讲座,这是继 2018 年之后,笔者再次应邀在广州大学举办学术讲座。广州大学人权研究院是三大首批国家人权教育与培训基地之一(另外两个基地设在南开大学和中国政法大学),是中国人权研究的重镇,造就了一流的人权专家队伍、成就了一批国家社科基金项目成果,并为国家人权事业培养了合格人才。(5)2023 年 11 月 24 日应邀为广州暨南大学法学院与知识产权学院举办了"全球人权治理的中国贡献"的学术讲座,这是继 2018 年在该校举办讲座后,笔者再次受邀举办学术讲座。总之,笔者借机 2023 年重要时间节点,为宣传《宣言》和中国对全球治理的贡献,与上述几所高校师生就三大主题内容开展了学术交流活动,取得了良好的交流效果。

故事待续:弘扬人类命运共同体理念,为参与全球治理提供智力支撑。笔者的论文"人类命运共同体理念下的全球人权治理"一文,拟刊发在《法学论坛》(CSSCI)2024 年第 3 期,该文弘扬人类命运共同体理念,为参与全球治理提供了智力支撑。笔者的另一篇"论人的尊严的中国观:以中国学者的研究为视角"(英文稿)也将由 Routledge 出版社收入论文集在美国出版。同时,笔者将于 2024 年春季学期应邀为国内几所高校举办学术讲座,为弘扬人类命运共同体理念提供助力,为我国参与全球人权治理摇旗呐喊,为培养涉外法律人才做出应有的贡献。另外,笔者也将积极参与国际学术交流,在国际学界发出中国声音。

生命不息,探索不止、讲述不尽,为构建我国的人权学科体系、学术体系和话语体系,为我国积极参与全球人权治理,笔者将竭尽所能,奉献自己一份微薄的力量,与各位学界同仁一道,形成合力,为建设和完善我国的人权话语体系而不懈努力。

三、张彭春在全球治理中对国际人权事业的贡献

张彭春对国际人权事业的贡献可以从多个角度来研究,可以从对相关文献的研究开始,通过对联合国档案会议记录的全面研究,较为全面把握其巨大贡献。再一个常用的方法就是通过对张彭春同事的评价来概括和总结张彭春对世界人权事业的贡献。

(一) 张彭春同事的评价

张彭春先生在国际人权体系的建构过程的作用以及他个人的人格魅力,给他的联合国同事留下了深刻印象。其中联合国人权委员会主席、美国代表罗斯福夫人认为张彭春先生"给我们大家都带来了极大的快乐,因为他具有幽默感,且从哲学的角度考虑问题,几乎在任何场合他都能够引述机智的中国谚语来应场。"①就在《世界人权宣言》发布的前夕,曾任联大第 13 届主席、联合国第三委员会主席、联合国经济及社会理事会主席、联合国人权委员会报告员的黎巴嫩代表马利克先生在联大全会的发言中,对张彭春先生给予了高度评价:"我们必须提及张彭春博士,他是人权委员会和起草委员会一位杰出的副主席。他经常引用东方智慧和东方哲学,每次都成功地开阔了我们的视野,而且他借助其特殊的起草天才,能够愉快地调整我们的许多条款。"②

---

① Roosevelt E. 1958. *On My Own*. London:Hutchinson & Co. Ltd. p. 95. / 又见:孙平华著,《张彭春:世界人权体系的重要设计师》,北京:社会科学文献出版社 2017 年版,第 142-143 页。

② Charles Malik, December 9, 1948, speech to the General Assembly, in H. C. Malik (ed.)(2000). *The Challenge of Human Rights*:*Charles Malik and the Universal Declaration*. Oxford:Charles Malik Foundation in association with the Centre for Lebanese Studies. p. 121. (I must refer to Dr. P. C. Chang, the distinguished vice-chairman of the Commission and drafting committee. He never failed to broaden our perspective by his frequent references to the wisdom and philosophy of the Orient and, by a special drafting gift, was able happily to rectify many of our terms.)

　　联合国秘书处首任人权司司长加拿大人汉弗莱先生更是给予张彭春先生以高度评价:"他是一位调和的艺术大师,心中有一整套儒家的经典名言,他经常能够提出规则以使人权委员会能够摆脱僵局。"①汉弗莱回顾说:"张彭春设想可以设置三个文件:一份以简单语句起草的宣言,一份对每一条款的注释和一份执行建议。后来他提出包含三部分规则的法案——宣言、公约和执行措施——这一建议最后被采纳。"②汉弗莱在 1948年 12 月 4 日的日记中这样评价了张彭春先生:"在才智声望上,他远远高于委员会中任何其他一位成员。"③在获悉张彭春去世的消息后,汉弗莱在日记中写道:"在理事会所有代表中,我感觉到他是我在精神上和学识上交流最多的一位,也是我最喜欢的一位……他是一位学者,并且在某种程度上,他又是一位艺术大师。尽管他有这些出众的天赋,他的外交职责也行使的很好。与那些随波逐流者相比,他堪称一位巨人。"④据中国社会科学院荣誉学部委员刘海年教授回忆说,他在 20 世纪 80 年代初的一次学术交流中幸好与汉弗莱相见,而汉弗莱先生听说是来自中国的学者,原先的交流主题还没说上几句,就将话题转移到对张彭春先生介绍上,并且兴奋地侃侃而谈,从而也可以看出张彭春给汉弗莱所留下的历久弥新的印象。

　　然而,无论是当年张彭春的联合国同事,还是当今中外学界,都还没一个人对张彭春所涉及的所有联合国档案内容进行过系统的研究,这也是我

---

　　①　Humphrey, J. P. 1983. The Memoirs of John P. Humphrey, the First Director of the United Nations Division of Human Rights. *Human Rights Quarterly* 5(4): 387–439.

　　②　Humphrey, J. P. 1983. The Memoirs of John P. Humphrey, the First Director of the United Nations Division of Human Rights. *Human Rights Quarterly* 5(4): 387–439.

　　③　Hobbins, A. J. (ed.), 1994. *On the Edge of Greatness: The Diaries of John Humphrey, First Director of the United Nations Division of Human Rights*, Volume 1, 1948–1949. Montreal: McGill University Libraries.

　　④　Glendon, M. A. 2001. *A World Made New: Eleanor Roosevelt and the Universal Declaration of Human Rights*. New York: Random House. pp. 211–212. (Of all the delegates who came into the Council, he was the one with whom I felt most in spiritual and intellectual communion. And the one I liked the best. . . He was a scholar, in a way, an artist although he performed his diplomatic functions well in spite of these superior gifts. What a giant he seems in contrast with the time-servers.)

们今天通过整理联合国档案资料,来研究张彭春在国际人权领域所做贡献的重要依据。正是基于这些认识,借助多年研究的积累,再加上近年来的不懈努力,终于将这部《全球人权治理的中国智慧:张彭春在联合国人权委员会及联大第三委员会等的发言》(简称:《全球人权治理的中国智慧》)呈现给世人。

插图 2:他们消除了自然来自不同委员会成员群体的分歧

(二)基本结构和具体内容

该书的基本结构分为两大部分,其中,第一部分是张彭春在联合国人权委员会及起草委员会的发言,共涉及人权委员会第一届会议、起草委员会第一届会议、人权委员会第三届会议、人权委员会第四届会议、人权委员会第五届会议和人权委员会第六届会议。在大致 4 年的时间内,这几届会议,共举办了 197 次会议,其中张彭春参加了 178 次会议,并在其中的 139 次会议上发言(见表 1)。本书第二部分是张彭春在联大第三委员会第一届会议、第二届会议、第三届会议(第一部分)、第三届会议(第二部分)、第四届会议、第五届会议和联大全会上的发言,在联合国创建之初的大约五六年的时间内,张彭春参加了联大第三委员会的绝大多数会议及联大全会的部分会议,并在其中的 82 次会议上发言(见表 2)。因此,本书两大部分中,张彭春涉及人权的发言为 221 次会议,这还不包括在联合国经社理事会的相关发言,而如果将本书与笔者所编著的《世界合作共赢的中国贡献》结合起来比较研究,相信必将会有更多的研究发现。

表 1:张彭春在联合国人权委员会及起草委员会会议的发言情况(1947-1950)

届会名称	会议时间	会议地点	会议总次数(会次)	张彭春参会次数	张彭春发言会议次数
人权委员会第一届	1947-1-27—1947-2-10	纽约成功湖	22(第 1-22 次会议)	22	16
起草委员会第一届	1947-6-9—1947-6-25	纽约成功湖	19(第 1-19 次会议)	19	19
人权委员会第三届	1948-5-24—1948-6-18	纽约成功湖	36(第 46-81 次会议)	33	30
人权委员会第四届	1949-4-1	纽约成功湖	1(第 82 次会议、特别会议)	1	0
人权委员会第五届	1949-5-9—1949-6-20	纽约成功湖	53(第 83-135 次会议)	46	30
人权委员会第六届	1950-3-27—1950-5-19	纽约成功湖	66(第 136-201 次会议)	57	44
合计	大约 4 年时间	纽约成功湖	197 次会议	178	139

表 2:张彭春在联大第三委员会及联大全会的发言情况

届会名称	会议时间	会议地点	会议总次数(会次)	档案资料情况	张彭春会议发言情况
联大第三委员会第一届	1946-1-11—1946-2-10;1946-10-24—1946-12-12	伦敦圣公会总部大楼;纽约成功湖	11(1—11)37(12—48)	会议纪要	在 3 次会议发言
联大第三委员会第二届	1947-4-28;1947-9-16—1947-11-11	纽约法拉盛草地公园;纽约成功湖	44(49—82)	会议纪要	在 6 次会议上发言

届会名称	会议时间	会议地点	会议总次数（会次）	档案资料情况	张彭春会议发言情况
联大第三委员会第三届（第一部分）	1948-4-16—1948-12-8	纽约法拉盛草地公园+纽约成功湖+巴黎夏洛宫	98(83—180)	会议纪要	在45次会议上发言
联大第三委员会第三届（第二部分）	1949-4-6—1949-5-12	纽约成功湖	49(181—229)	会议纪要	在11次会议上发言
联大第三委员会第四届	1949-9-20—1949-11-28	纽约成功湖	40(230—269)	会议纪要	在1次会议上发言
联大第三委员会第五届	1950-9-20—1950-12-11	纽约成功湖	53(270—345)	会议纪要	在15次会议上发言
联大全体会议	1948-12-9—1948-12-10	巴黎夏洛宫	4(180—183)	会议纪要	在1次会议上发言
合计	大约6年	伦敦、纽约、巴黎等地	349	会议纪要	在82次会议上发言

(三) 以张彭春为代表的中国智慧对全球人权治理的
意义与价值

这里仅简要地提出如下五点，以便能够抛砖引玉。

第一，全面掌握张彭春在联合国人权委员会及联大第三委员会等的发言内容，不仅对全面研究国际人权领域的中国贡献有着极为重要的意义和价值，也能够进一步拓展我国人权研究的新领域。大家知道，张彭春作为彪炳国际人权发展史册的中国杰出代表，为起草《世界人权宣言》做出了卓越贡献，但他代表中国参与起草国际人权两公约的贡献则很少有人提及，这部新书收入了张彭春在联合国人权委员会第五届和第六届会议的大量发言内容，这两届涉及他74次会议上的发言，张彭春在联大第三委员会第四届和第五届会议也涉及到他 16 次会议上的发言,而上述共计 90 次会议上的发言都是在《世界人权宣言》发布之后做出的,所针对的主要议题是国际人权公约和实施措施部分,尤其是国际人权核心两公约,即《公民权利和政治权利国际公约》和《经济、社会和文化权利国际公约》。尽管这两个公约是在 1966 年才通过生效的,但其起草基本上是与《世界人权宣言》同步进行的,只是早期侧重于宣言的起草进程,但在 1948 年 12 月 10 日《世界人权宣言》发布之后,人权委员会第五届和第六届会议和联大第三委员会第五届会议上其实主要是对两个核心公约的内容进行了大量的起草和审议工作。这部分发言内容,将无疑极大地丰富人们对我国为国际人权事业做出的贡献的认识,加深对作为"世界人权体系的重要设计师"[①]的张彭春的认识更是有着十分重要的意义,从而也将进一步拓展潜在的人权学术研究领域。

第二,现有的国际人权话语体系中蕴含着丰富的中国人权思想和主张,人权并不是西方国家的专利,中国的价值观与哲学理念对世界人权的历史贡献是巨大的。作为 2020 年教育部哲学社会科学研究后期资助重大项目——"国际人权话语的中国声音研究"(批准号:20JHQ010)的又一阶段性研究成果,张彭春在联合国人权委员会和起草委员会、联大第三委员会及联大全会上的发言,成为建构国际人权话语体系的重要组成部分,"在世界人权保障机制的构建过程中,他以其博大精深的中国智慧,积极建言献策、赢得各国同事的赞赏,为联合国人权机制建设贡献了中国人的聪明才智,也为全球人权治理打下了坚实的基础。"[②]这也是张彭春代表中国对国际社会和全人类所做出的重大贡献,正是因为这些发言内容使得张彭春先生的英名永载联合国发展史册,他也因此将引起国际学术界越来越多的关注,而中国对世界人权事业的历史贡献也将被国际社会所永远

① 孙平华著,《张彭春:世界人权体系的重要设计师》,北京:社会科学文献出版社 2017 年版。

② 孙平华编著:《世界合作共赢的中国贡献:张彭春在联合国经济及社会理事会的发言》,天津:天津社会科学院出版社 2023 年 1 月版,前言第 9 页。

铭记。

第三,张彭春坚持以人为本、关注人类命运,为我国在全球治理中大力倡导"人类命运共同体"理念,提供了历史依据。他既强调立法措施,也强调实施方案;既讲究求同存异化解矛盾,也坚持文化的包容等思想。张彭春在谈到联合国经社理事会的使命时强调:"全世界人民都渴望生活水平的提高,对其中一些人来说,生活水平的提高目前意味着他们摆脱饥饿。除非为实现这一目标而采取行动,否则世界的良心就无法得以安宁。"[①]在起草委员会第一届第 11 次会议上,张彭春引用了孟子的两句话:"徒善不足以为政,徒法不能以自行。"[②]"他坚持认为,目的和目标应该是培养更好的人,而不仅仅是惩罚那些侵犯人权的人。权利必须受到法律的保护,但法律也有必要促进人的优秀品质。它们应强调通过教育和道德手段促进人权的扩展和完善。实施不仅意味着惩罚,而且意味着促进人的全面发展的措施。"[③]在联大第三委员会第三届第 96 次会议上,张彭春明确指出:"宣言无疑将为(联合国)多数成员国接受时,在人权领域人口的多数性不应该被忘记。中国代表认为他的国家的人口占(世界)总人口的很大部分。这部分人口有着不同于基督教西方的理想和传统。那些思想中包括得体的举止、礼貌、礼仪和为他人着想。然而,尽管中国文化作为伦理道德的一个组成部分,对人们的行为方式有着极其重要的影响,但是,中国代表并没有提议在宣言中应该提及这些。他希望他的同事们表现出平等的态度,撤回在第 1 条修正案中提出的某些形而上学的东西。同样,对西方文明来说,宗教不容忍时代结束了。"[④]

第四,当下全球人权治理可以从中国对国际人权事业的历史贡献中借鉴经验,进一步调动和发挥中华民族的聪明才智,进一步提升中国在全球人权治理中的主人翁意识,建设一个更加合理公正的国际人权治理新秩

---

① UN Document:E/PV.7, pp. 25–36.

② 《孟子·离娄章句上》

③ UN Document: E/CN.4/AC.1/SR.11, pp. 10–11.

④ UN Document: A/C.3/SR/96, pp. 98–99.

插图3：张彭春(左)、罗斯福夫人(中)和查尔斯·马利克(右)
共同主导着《世界人权宣言》的起草工作

序。本书中所收入的张彭春在联合国人权委员会及联大第三委员会等的发言，是张彭春先生代表中华民族在联合国层面所贡献的聪明才智，他所提出的一系列建议和措施，为世界各国代表不同意见的达成妥协并形成共识发挥了不可替代的作用。张彭春也因此成为中国驻联合国机构的杰出代言人。正如联合国人权司首任司长汉弗莱所评价的那样："在才智的声望上，他远远高于委员会中任何其他一位成员。"①汉弗莱所说的委员会即联大第三委员会，包括当时五十多个国家的代表，张彭春作为在该委员会的中国代表，其才智的卓尔不群是中华民族智慧的象征，具体体现了中华民族智慧和传统文化思想。他的发言，被联合国会议纪要或全文记录所永远铭记，成为我们深入研究和系统挖掘的宝藏，当下的全球人权治理可以

---

① Hobbins, A. J. (ed.), *On the Edge of Greatness: The Diaries of John Humphrey, First Director of the United Nations Division of Human Rights.* Volume 1. 1948–1949 (Montreal: McGill University Libraries, 1994), p. 88.

从当年中国代表所发表的主张以及所提出的解决方案中得到启迪,为未来国际人权治理新秩序的构建提供智力支撑。笔者坚信,勤劳智慧的中华民族必将在百年未有之大变局中掌握更多的人权话语权和主动权,为全球人权治理做出新的更大的贡献。

第五,笔者曾在之前出版的两部中英文著作中所概括的"张彭春的多元主义人权思想"(见《张彭春:世界人权体系的重要设计师》与 *Historic Achievement of a Common Standard: Pengchun Chang and the Universal Declaration of Human rights*),是基于对联合国档案资料的全面研究而总结的,对丰富全球人权治理背景下的中国人权话语体系,有着极其重要的现实意义和理论意义。该书(《全球人权治理的中国智慧》)与之前出版的《世界合作共赢的中国贡献》所包含的内容,是张彭春先生代表中国在联合国层面发出的中国声音、阐述的中国主张、提出的中国方案,为全球治理尤其是全球人权治理谱写的精彩篇章,也是为全人类所做出的卓越贡献。

四、结 论

笔者作为中国人权话语和中国人权故事的研究者、讲述者,在过去的十多年间,通过对《世界人权宣言》和国际人权公约起草历史的回顾,发现中国代表张彭春不仅对《世界人权宣言》的起草发挥了重要作用,也对整个国际人权机制的构建做出了卓越的贡献。这一发现,对目前我国积极参与全球人权治理、推进全球人权治理朝着更加公正合理的方向发展,提供了范例。这也是中华民族智慧在全球人权治理中所做出的突出贡献。

但愿本项研究能够为构筑中国话语体系尤其是中国人权话语体系尽一份绵薄之力,做出自己应有的贡献,为弘扬全球人权治理中的中国智慧、为探讨国际人权体系构建的中国贡献、为习近平新时代"人类命运共同体"理念的国际传播、为深入学习和落实习近平总书记在中共中央政治局第三十七次集体学习时所阐述的人权主张、为积极参与全球人权治理推进构建"人类命运共同体"再续写新的篇章。

由于笔者水平有限,加之时间仓促,书中定有不当之处,敬请学界同仁批评指正!

孙平华

中国政法大学教授

中国第一位人权法学博士

英国埃克塞特大学法学院访问学者

《埃斯特角宣言》中国唯一原始签署人

加拿大《政治与法律杂志》特约审稿人

新加坡《国际中国研究杂志》特约审稿人

美国《政治科学与公共事务杂志》特约审稿人

于北京市海淀区昆玉河畔

目 录

联合国人权委员会和起草委员会

第一章　联合国人权委员会第一届会议 ……………………………… 3

1. 张彭春在人权委员会第一届第 1 次会议当选为副主席 ………… 4

2. 张彭春在人权委员会第一届第 3 次会议的发言 ……………… 5

3. 张彭春在人权委员会第一届第 4 次会议的发言 ……………… 7

4. 张彭春在人权委员会第一届第 5 次会议的发言 ……………… 8

5. 张彭春在人权委员会第一届第 6 次会议的发言 …………… 12

6. 张彭春在人权委员会第一届第 7 次会议的发言 …………… 16

7. 张彭春在人权委员会第一届第 11 次会议的发言 …………… 19

8. 张彭春在人权委员会第一届第 12 次会议的发言 …………… 21

9. 张彭春在人权委员会第一届第 13 次会议的发言 …………… 23

10. 张彭春在人权委员会第一届第 14 次会议的发言 …………… 25

11. 张彭春在人权委员会第一届第 16 次会议的发言 …………… 27

12. 张彭春在人权委员会第一届第 18 次会议的发言 …………… 30

13. 张彭春在人权委员会第一届第 19 次会议的发言 …………… 31

14. 张彭春在人权委员会第一届第 20 次会议的发言 …………… 32

15. 张彭春在人权委员会第一届第 21 次会议的发言 …………… 33

16. 张彭春在人权委员会第一届第 22 次会议的发言 …………… 38

第二章　起草委员会第一届会议 ·· 42

　　1. 张彭春在起草委员会第一届第 1 次会议上的发言 ·············· 43

　　2. 张彭春在起草委员会第一届第 2 次会议上的发言 ·············· 47

　　3. 张彭春在起草委员会第一届第 3 次会议上的发言 ·············· 48

　　4. 张彭春在起草委员会第一届第 4 次会议上的发言 ·············· 54

　　5. 张彭春在起草委员会第一届第 5 次会议上的发言 ·············· 58

　　6. 张彭春在起草委员会第一届第 6 次会议上的发言 ·············· 60

　　7. 张彭春在起草委员会第一届第 7 次会议上的发言 ·············· 64

　　8. 张彭春在起草委员会第一届第 8 次会议上的发言 ·············· 67

　　9. 张彭春在起草委员会第一届第 9 次会议上的发言 ·············· 76

　　10. 张彭春在起草委员会第一届第 10 次会议上的发言 ·············· 81

　　11. 张彭春在起草委员会第一届第 11 次会议上的发言 ·············· 84

　　12. 张彭春在起草委员会第一届第 12 次会议上的发言 ·············· 87

　　13. 张彭春在起草委员会第一届第 13 次会议上的发言 ·············· 92

　　14. 张彭春在起草委员会第一届第 14 次会议上的发言 ·············· 99

　　15. 张彭春在起草委员会第一届第 15 次会议上的发言 ············ 101

　　16. 张彭春在起草委员会第一届第 16 次会议上的发言 ············ 105

　　17. 张彭春在起草委员会第一届第 17 次会议上的发言 ············ 108

　　18. 张彭春在起草委员会第一届第 18 次会议上的发言 ············ 112

　　19. 张彭春在起草委员会第一届第 19 次会议上的发言 ············ 116

第三章　联合国人权委员会第三届会议 ····························· 118

　　1. 张彭春在联合国人权委员会第三届第 48 次会议上的发言 ······ 119

　　2. 张彭春在联合国人权委员会第三届第 50 次会议上的发言 ······ 120

　　3. 张彭春在联合国人权委员会第三届第 51 次会议上的发言 ······ 125

　　4. 张彭春在联合国人权委员会第三届第 52 次会议上的发言 ······ 127

　　5. 张彭春在联合国人权委员会第三届第 53 次会议上的发言 ······ 132

　　6. 张彭春在联合国人权委员会第三届第 54 次会议上的发言 ······ 136

7. 张彭春在联合国人权委员会第三届第 55 次会议上的发言 …… 142

8. 张彭春在联合国人权委员会第三届第 56 次会议上的发言 …… 145

9. 张彭春在联合国人权委员会第三届第 57 次会议上的发言 …… 147

10. 张彭春在联合国人权委员会第三届第 58 次会议上的发言 … 152

11. 张彭春在联合国人权委员会第三届第 59 次会议上的发言 … 153

12. 张彭春在联合国人权委员会第三届第 60 次会议上的发言 … 154

13. 张彭春在联合国人权委员会第三届第 61 次会议上的发言 … 156

14. 张彭春在联合国人权委员会第三届第 62 次会议上的发言 … 160

15. 张彭春在联合国人权委员会第三届第 63 次会议上的发言 … 162

16. 张彭春在联合国人权委员会第三届第 64 次会议上的发言 … 165

17. 张彭春在联合国人权委员会第三届第 65 次会议上的发言 … 168

18. 张彭春在联合国人权委员会第三届第 67 次会议上的发言 … 172

19. 张彭春在联合国人权委员会第三届第 68 次会议上的发言 … 178

20. 张彭春在联合国人权委员会第三届第 69 次会议上的发言 … 180

21. 张彭春在联合国人权委员会第三届第 70 次会议上的发言 … 184

22. 张彭春在联合国人权委员会第三届第 71 次会议上的发言 … 186

23. 张彭春在联合国人权委员会第三届第 72 次会议上的发言 … 190

24. 张彭春在联合国人权委员会第三届第 74 次会议上的发言 … 193

25. 张彭春在联合国人权委员会第三届第 75 次会议上的发言 … 198

26. 张彭春在联合国人权委员会第三届第 76 次会议上的发言 … 205

27. 张彭春在联合国人权委员会第三届第 77 次会议上的发言 … 209

28. 张彭春在联合国人权委员会第三届第 78 次会议上的发言 … 216

29. 张彭春在联合国人权委员会第三届第 80 次会议上的发言 … 222

30. 张彭春在联合国人权委员会第三届第 81 次会议上的发言 … 226

第四章　联合国人权委员会第五届会议 …………………… 235

1. 张彭春在人权委员会第五届第 84 次会议上的发言 ………… 236

2. 张彭春在人权委员会第五届第 85 次会议上的发言 ………… 239

3. 张彭春在人权委员会第五届第 87 次会议上的发言 ………… 242

4. 张彭春在人权委员会第五届第 88 次会议发言纪要 ………… 245

5. 张彭春在人权委员会第五届第 90 次会议发言纪要 ………… 248

6. 张彭春在人权委员会第五届第 91 次会议发言纪要 ………… 252

7. 张彭春在人权委员会第五届第 93 次会议发言纪要 ………… 254

8. 张彭春在人权委员会第五届第 95 次会议发言纪要 ………… 256

9. 张彭春在人权委员会第五届第 96 次会议发言纪要 ………… 259

10. 张彭春在人权委员会第五届第 98 次会议发言纪要　………… 260

11. 张彭春在人权委员会第五届第 99 次会议发言纪要　………… 262

12. 张彭春在人权委员会第五届第 100 次会议发言纪要 ………… 265

13. 张彭春在人权委员会第五届第 102 次会议发言纪要 ………… 267

14. 张彭春在人权委员会第五届第 103 次会议发言纪要 ………… 269

15. 张彭春在人权委员会第五届第 104 次会议发言纪要 ………… 273

16. 张彭春在人权委员会第五届第 115 次会议发言纪要 ………… 276

17. 张彭春在人权委员会第五届第 117 次会议发言纪要 ………… 279

18. 张彭春在人权委员会第五届第 118 次会议发言纪要 ………… 281

19. 张彭春在人权委员会第五届第 119 次会议发言纪要 ………… 285

20. 张彭春在人权委员会第五届第 120 次会议发言纪要 ………… 288

21. 张彭春在人权委员会第五届第 121 次会议发言纪要 ………… 291

22. 张彭春在人权委员会第五届第 122 次会议发言纪要 ………… 293

23. 张彭春在人权委员会第五届第 123 次会议发言纪要 ………… 296

24. 张彭春在人权委员会第五届第 124 次会议发言纪要 ………… 300

25. 张彭春在人权委员会第五届第 126 次会议发言纪要 ………… 302

26. 张彭春在人权委员会第五届第 127 次会议发言纪要 ………… 306

27. 张彭春在人权委员会第五届第 129 次会议发言纪要 ………… 309

28. 张彭春在人权委员会第五届第 131 次会议发言纪要 ………… 313

29. 张彭春在人权委员会第五届第 133 次会议发言纪要 ………… 315

30. 张彭春在人权委员会第五届第 134 次会议发言纪要 ………… 316

第五章　联合国人权委员会第六届会议 ┈┈┈┈┈┈┈┈┈┈┈ 319

  1. 张彭春在人权委员会第六届第 136 次会议发言纪要 ┈┈┈ 320

  2. 张彭春在人权委员会第六届第 137 次会议发言纪要 ┈┈┈ 323

  3. 张彭春在人权委员会第六届第 138 次会议发言纪要 ┈┈┈ 329

  4. 张彭春在人权委员会第六届第 139 次会议发言纪要 ┈┈┈ 333

  5. 张彭春在人权委员会第六届第 140 次会议发言纪要 ┈┈┈ 336

  6. 张彭春在人权委员会第六届第 142 次会议发言纪要 ┈┈┈ 338

  7. 张彭春在人权委员会第六届第 143 次会议发言纪要 ┈┈┈ 339

  8. 张彭春在人权委员会第六届第 145 次会议发言纪要 ┈┈┈ 341

  9. 张彭春在人权委员会第六届第 146 次会议发言纪要 ┈┈┈ 343

  10. 张彭春在人权委员会第六届第 147 次会议发言纪要 ┈┈┈ 345

  11. 张彭春在人权委员会第六届第 148 次会议发言纪要 ┈┈┈ 348

  12. 张彭春在人权委员会第六届第 149 次会议发言纪要 ┈┈┈ 350

  13. 张彭春在人权委员会第六届第 150 次会议发言纪要 ┈┈┈ 353

  14. 张彭春在人权委员会第六届第 151 次会议发言纪要 ┈┈┈ 355

  15. 张彭春在人权委员会第六届第 152 次会议发言纪要 ┈┈┈ 357

  16. 张彭春在人权委员会第六届第 153 次会议发言纪要 ┈┈┈ 359

  17. 张彭春在人权委员会第六届第 155 次会议发言纪要 ┈┈┈ 361

  18. 张彭春在人权委员会第六届第 156 次会议发言纪要 ┈┈┈ 362

  19. 张彭春在人权委员会第六届第 157 次会议发言纪要 ┈┈┈ 363

  20. 张彭春在人权委员会第六届第 158 次会议发言纪要 ┈┈┈ 364

  21. 张彭春在人权委员会第六届第 159 次会议发言纪要 ┈┈┈ 366

  22. 张彭春在人权委员会第六届第 161 次会议发言纪要 ┈┈┈ 367

  23. 张彭春在人权委员会第六届第 163 次会议发言纪要 ┈┈┈ 368

  24. 张彭春在人权委员会第六届第 164 次会议发言纪要 ┈┈┈ 372

  25. 张彭春在人权委员会第六届第 165 次会议发言纪要 ┈┈┈ 377

  26. 张彭春在人权委员会第六届第 166 次会议发言纪要 ┈┈┈ 380

  27. 张彭春在人权委员会第六届第 167 次会议发言纪要 ┈┈┈ 383

目 录

28. 张彭春在人权委员会第六届第 170 次会议发言纪要 ………… 389

29. 张彭春在人权委员会第六届第 171 次会议发言纪要 ………… 392

30. 张彭春在人权委员会第六届第 173 次会议发言纪要 ………… 395

31. 张彭春在人权委员会第六届第 174 次会议发言纪要 ………… 398

32. 张彭春在人权委员会第六届第 175 次会议发言纪要 ………… 401

33. 张彭春在人权委员会第六届第 182 次会议发言纪要 ………… 406

34. 张彭春在人权委员会第六届第 183 次会议发言纪要 ………… 408

35. 张彭春在人权委员会第六届第 184 次会议发言纪要 ………… 412

36. 张彭春在人权委员会第六届第 186 次会议发言纪要 ………… 413

37. 张彭春在人权委员会第六届第 189 次会议发言纪要 ………… 417

38. 张彭春在人权委员会第六届第 192 次会议发言纪要 ………… 418

39. 张彭春在人权委员会第六届第 193 次会议发言纪要 ………… 420

40. 张彭春在人权委员会第六届第 195 次会议发言纪要 ………… 421

41. 张彭春在人权委员会第六届第 197 次会议发言纪要 ………… 422

42. 张彭春在人权委员会第六届第 198 次会议发言纪要 ………… 423

43. 张彭春在人权委员会第六届第 199 次会议发言纪要 ………… 427

44. 张彭春在人权委员会第六届第 201 次会议发言纪要 ………… 429

联大第三委员会及联大全会

第一章 联大第三委员会第一届会议 ………………………… 433

　　1. 张彭春在联大第三委员会第一届第 10 次会议上的发言 ……… 434

　　2. 张彭春在联大第三委员会第一届第 14 次会议上的发言 ……… 436

　　3. 张彭春在联大第三委员会第一届第 15 次会议上的发言 ……… 437

第二章 联大第三委员会第二届会议 ………………………… 439

　　1. 张彭春在联大第三委员会第二届第 55 次会议上的发言 ……… 439

　　2. 张彭春在联大第三委员会第二届第 57 次会议上的发言 ……… 441

3. 张彭春在联大第三委员会第二届第 58 次会议上的发言 ········· 444

4. 张彭春在联大第三委员会第二届第 59 次会议上的发言 ········· 447

5. 张彭春在联大第三委员会第二届第 60 次会议上的发言 ········· 448

6. 张彭春在联大第三委员会第二届第 67 次会议上的发言 ········· 451

第三章　联大第三委员会第三届会议（第一部分） ·················· 453

1. 张彭春在联大第三委员会第三届第 88 次会议上的发言 ········· 454

2. 张彭春在联大第三委员会第三届第 91 次会议上的发言 ········· 458

3. 张彭春在联大第三委员会第三届第 95 次会议上的发言 ········· 461

4. 张彭春在联大第三委员会第三届第 96 次会议上的发言 ········· 464

5. 张彭春在联大第三委员会第三届第 97 次会议上的发言 ········· 468

6. 张彭春在联大第三委员会第三届第 98 次会议上的发言 ········· 470

7. 张彭春在联大第三委员会第三届第 99 次会议上的发言 ········· 474

8. 张彭春在联大第三委员会第三届第 100 次会议上的发言 ······ 475

9. 张彭春在联大第三委员会第三届第 101 次会议上的发言 ······ 478

10. 张彭春在联大第三委员会第三届第 103 次会议上的发言 ······ 480

11. 张彭春在联大第三委员会第三届第 105 次会议上的发言 ······ 484

12. 张彭春在联大第三委员会第三届第 107 次会议上的发言 ······ 487

13. 张彭春在联大第三委员会第三届第 108 次会议上的发言 ······ 490

14. 张彭春在联大第三委员会第三届第 109 次会议上的发言 ······ 493

15. 张彭春在联大第三委员会第三届第 110 次会议上的发言 ······ 495

16. 张彭春在联大第三委员会第三届第 113 次会议上的发言 ······ 498

17. 张彭春在联大第三委员会第三届第 114 次会议上的发言 ······ 500

18. 张彭春在联大第三委员会第三届第 119 次会议上的发言 ······ 501

19. 张彭春在联大第三委员会第三届第 125 次会议上的发言 ······ 504

20. 张彭春在联大第三委员会第三届第 126 次会议上的发言 ······ 505

21. 张彭春在联大第三委员会第三届第 127 次会议上的发言 ······ 507

22. 张彭春在联大第三委员会第三届第 131 次会议上的发言 ······ 510

目

录

23. 张彭春在联大第三委员会第三届第 133 次会议上的发言 …… 512

24. 张彭春在联大第三委员会第三届第 134 次会议上的发言 …… 515

25. 张彭春在联大第三委员会第三届第 141 次会议上的发言 …… 517

26. 张彭春在联大第三委员会第三届第 142 次会议上的发言 …… 519

27. 张彭春在联大第三委员会第三届第 143 次会议上的发言 …… 521

28. 张彭春在联大第三委员会第三届第 144 次会议上的发言 …… 524

29. 张彭春在联大第三委员会第三届第 145 次会议上的发言 …… 527

30. 张彭春在联大第三委员会第三届第 146 次会议上的发言 …… 530

31. 张彭春在联大第三委员会第三届第 149 次会议上的发言 …… 532

32. 张彭春在联大第三委员会第三届第 150 次会议上的发言 …… 533

33. 张彭春在联大第三委员会第三届第 151 次会议上的发言 …… 535

34. 张彭春在联大第三委员会第三届第 152 次会议上的发言 …… 538

35. 张彭春在联大第三委员会第三届第 153 次会议上的发言 …… 540

36. 张彭春在联大第三委员会第三届第 154 次会议上的发言 …… 542

37. 张彭春在联大第三委员会第三届第 156 次会议上的发言 …… 544

38. 张彭春在联大第三委员会第三届第 157 次会议上的发言 …… 546

39. 张彭春在联大第三委员会第三届第 158 次会议上的发言 …… 548

40. 张彭春在联大第三委员会第三届第 166 次会议上的发言 …… 549

41. 张彭春在联大第三委员会第三届第 167 次会议上的发言 …… 552

42. 张彭春在联大第三委员会第三届第 175 次会议上的发言 …… 555

43. 张彭春在联大第三委员会第三届第 176 次会议上的发言 …… 557

44. 张彭春在联大第三委员会第三届第 177 次会议上的发言 …… 559

45. 张彭春在联大第三委员会第三届第 178 次会议上的发言 …… 562

第四章 联大第三委员会第三届会议（第二部分） ……………… 567

1. 张彭春在联大第三委员会第三届第 182 次会议上的发言 …… 568

2. 张彭春在联大第三委员会第三届第 183 次会议上的发言 …… 573

3. 张彭春在联大第三委员会第三届第 184 次会议上的发言 …… 579

4. 张彭春在联大第三委员会第三届第185次会议上的发言 ······ 584

5. 张彭春在联大第三委员会第三届第188次会议上的发言 ······ 588

6. 张彭春在联大第三委员会第三届第189次会议上的发言 ······ 591

7. 张彭春在联大第三委员会第三届第190次会议上的发言 ······ 593

8. 张彭春在联大第三委员会第三届第193次会议上的发言 ······ 597

9. 张彭春在联大第三委员会第三届第194次会议上的发言 ······ 600

10. 张彭春在联大第三委员会第三届第218次会议上的发言 ······ 602

11. 张彭春在联大第三委员会第三届第219次会议上的发言 ······ 606

第五章　联大第三委员会第四届会议 ······ 608

1. 张彭春在联大第三委员会第四届第255次会议上的发言 ······ 609

第六章　联大第三委员会第五届会议 ······ 613

1. 张彭春在联大第三委员会第五届第291次会议上的发言 ······ 615

2. 张彭春在联大第三委员会第五届第292次会议上的发言 ······ 619

3. 张彭春在联大第三委员会第五届第295次会议上的发言 ······ 621

4. 张彭春在联大第三委员会第五届第299次会议上的发言 ······ 626

5. 张彭春在联大第三委员会第五届第301次会议上的发言 ······ 631

6. 张彭春在联大第三委员会第五届第302次会议上的发言 ······ 635

7. 张彭春在联大第三委员会第五届第304次会议上的发言 ······ 636

8. 张彭春在联大第三委员会第五届第308次会议上的发言 ······ 637

9. 张彭春在联大第三委员会第五届第309次会议上的发言 ······ 640

10. 张彭春在联大第三委员会第五届第312次会议上的发言 ······ 642

11. 张彭春在联大第三委员会第五届第313次会议上的发言 ······ 645

12. 张彭春在联大第三委员会第五届第315次会议上的发言 ······ 646

13. 张彭春在联大第三委员会第五届第316次会议上的发言 ······ 648

14. 张彭春在联大第三委员会第五届第318次会议上的发言 ······ 649

15. 张彭春在联大第三委员会第五届第322次会议上的发言 ······ 650

目

录

第七章　联合国大会全体会议 ·········· 655

　　1. 张彭春在联大第 182 次全会上的发言 ·········· 655

附　录

《世界合作共赢的中国贡献：张彭春在联合国经济及社会理事会的发言》
内容补正说明 ·········· 663

第三章　联合国经社理事会第三届会议 ·········· 665

　　1. 张彭春在经社理事会第三届第 1 次会议上的发言 ·········· 667

　　2. 张彭春在经社理事会第三届第 2 次会议上的发言 ·········· 672

　　3. 张彭春在经社理事会第三届第 3 次会议上的发言 ·········· 680

　　4. 张彭春在经社理事会第三届第 5 次会议上的发言 ·········· 695

　　5. 张彭春在经社理事会第三届第 6 次会议上的发言 ·········· 696

　　6. 张彭春在经社理事会第三届第 7 次会议上的发言 ·········· 704

　　7. 张彭春在经社理事会第三届第 12 次会议上的发言 ·········· 706

　　8. 张彭春在经社理事会第三届第 14 次会议上的发言 ·········· 711

　　9. 张彭春在经社理事会第三届第 15 次会议上的发言 ·········· 714

　　10. 张彭春在经社理事会第三届第 16 次会议上的发言 ·········· 716

　　11. 张彭春在经社理事会第三届第 17 次会议上的发言 ·········· 717

　　12. 张彭春在经社理事会第三届第 18 次会议上的发言 ·········· 724

　　13. 张彭春在经社理事会第三届第 19 次会议上的发言 ·········· 727

　　14. 张彭春在经社理事会第三届第 20 次会议上的发言 ·········· 731

　　15. 张彭春在经社理事会第三届第 21 次会议上的发言 ·········· 738

　　16. 张彭春在经社理事会第三届特别会议上的发言 ·········· 749

联合国人权委员会和起草委员会

表 1:张彭春在联合国人权委员会及起草委员会会议的发言情况

(1947-1950)

届会名称	会议时间	会议地点	会议总次数（会次）	张彭春参会次数	张彭春发言会议次数
人权委员会第一届	1947-1-27—1947-2-10	纽约成功湖	22（第 1-22 次会议）	22	16
起草委员会第一届	1947-6-9—1947-6-25	纽约成功湖	19（第 1-19 次会议）	19	19
人权委员会第三届	1948-5-24—1948-6-18	纽约成功湖	36（第 46-81 次会议）	33	30
人权委员会第四届	1949-4-1	纽约成功湖	1（第 82 次会议、特别会议）	1	0
人权委员会第五届	1949-5-9—1949-6-20	纽约成功湖	53（第 83-135 次会议）	46	30
人权委员会第六届	1950-3-27—1950-5-19	纽约成功湖	66（第 136-201 次会议）	57	44
合计	大约 4 年时间	纽约成功湖	196 次会议	178	139

第一章　联合国人权委员会
第一届会议

1947 年 1 月 27 日至 2 月 10 日,联合国人权委员会第一届会议,在美国纽约成功湖召开。在其第 1 次会议上一致选举埃莉诺·罗斯福(美国代表)为主席,张彭春(中国代表)为副主席,查尔斯·马利克(黎巴嫩代表)为报告员(E/CN.4/SR.1)。

人权司司长兼委员会秘书约翰·汉弗莱出席了委员会的会议,并参与了起草过程。委员会成员之间存在不同意见:是起草一份具有强有力的执行部分的法律文书更重要,还是起草一份作为人权标准制定文件的国际权利法案更重要。这个问题在整个起草过程中一直存在,委员会努力同时实现这两个目标。

在本届会议上,联合国人权委员会做出决定:

(1)主席、副主席和报告员在秘书处的协助下,根据委员会第一届会议的指示和决定,承担起草国际人权法案初稿的任务,提交委员会第二届会议彻底审查;

(2)主席在进行这项工作的过程中,可以争取委员会任何成员的合作,并应该得到他们口头或书面的任何意见和建议;

(3)主席可征求经联合国会员国政府同意挑选的专家的意见;

(4)主席、副主席和报告员在起草国际人权法案初稿时,可向他们认为与其工作相关的任何人或文件征求意见。

中国代表张彭春参加了本届全部会议,即联合国人权委员会第一届第 1 次至第 22 次会议,并在其中的 16 次会议上发言,包括第 1 次会议当选为副主席、第 3 次会议、第 4 次会议、第 5 次会议、第 6 次会议、第 7 次会议、第 11 次会议、第 12 次会议、第 13 次会议、第 14 次会议、第 16 次会议、第

18 次会议、第 19 次会议、第 20 次会议、第 21 次会议和第 22 次会议。张彭春先生在本届会议上的发言为国际人权法案的起草发挥了重要的作用,其具体发言内容以"会议纪要""纪要影像"和"纪要译文"形式加以整理,并依次标明发言内容所在的页码,以便学者参考引用。

1. 张彭春在人权委员会
第一届第 1 次会议当选为副主席

1947 年 1 月 27 日上午 11 时,联合国人权委员会第一届第 1 次会议,在纽约成功湖开幕,本次会议的主要议题是致开幕词、选举委员会主席、副主席和报告员、通过临时议程、通过议事规则、审查职权范围。中国代表张彭春参加了本次会议,并在会议上当选为副主席,其具体内容①会议纪要、纪要影像和纪要译文如下:

【会议纪要】

3. Election of the Vice chairman

Mr. DUKES (UNITED KINGDOM) proposed Dr. P. C. Chang, mentioning the quality of his work in the field of Human Rights. Dr. Chang was unanimously elected.

---

① UN Document:E/CN. 4/SR. 1, p. 4. 本次会议虽然张彭春并未直接发言,但他当选为人权委员会副主席这件事的本身就说明,他在委员会的威望是很高的并得到英美国家的高度赞赏,这也将预示着他将代表中国甚至代表联合国人权委员会发出强有力的声音,在构筑世界人权保障制度体系的过程中发挥重要的作用,为全球人权治理奠定良好的基础。真可谓此处无声胜有声,故此,也把本次列出发言范畴。

3. **Election of Vice-Chairman**
Mr. DUKES (UNITED KINGDOM) proposed Dr. P. C. Chang, mentioning the quality of his work in the field of Human Rights. Dr. Chang was unanimously elected.

图片 1.1.1:张彭春在联合国人权委员会第一届第 1 次会议当选为副主席会议纪要

【纪要译文】

3. 选举副主席

杜克斯(Dukes)先生(英国)提名张彭春博士,提到他在人权领域的工作质量。张博士被一致推选。

2. 张彭春在人权委员会
第一届第 3 次会议的发言

1947 年 1 月 28 日上午 11 时,联合国人权委员会第一届第 3 次会议,在纽约成功湖召开,本次会议的主要议题是通过议事规则、审议收到的来文。中国代表张彭春参加了本次会议,并在会议上发言,其具体发言内容①会议纪要、纪要影像和纪要译文如下:

【会议纪要】

Dr. CHANG (CHINA) felt that of the three solutions suggested in Paragraph 4 of the document submitted by the Secretariat, (E/CN. 4/W. 7), the second, namely to adopt the proposed Rules of Procedure for the first session

---

① UN Document: E/CN. 4/SR. 3, p. 3, p. 5.

only and to postpone examination and amendment to the second session, was certainly the most reasonable.

Dr. CHANG (CHINA), seconded by General ROMULO (PHILIPPINE REPUBLIC), proposed setting up a committee of three persons to study such amendments as might be made to the rules of procedure.

DECISION: *This proposal was adopted. The CHAIRMAN appointed the representatives of Australia, China and the Union of Soviet Socialist Republics to serve on this committee.*

【纪要影像】

Dr. CHANG (CHINA) felt that of the three solutions suggested in paragraph 4 of the document submitted by the Secretariat, (E/CN.4/W.7), the second, namely to adopt the proposed Rules of Procedure for the first session only and to postpone examination and amendment to the second session, was certainly the most reasonable.

Dr. CHANG (CHINA), seconded by General ROMULO (PHILIPPINE REPUBLIC), proposed setting up a committee of three persons to study such amendments as might be made to the rules of procedure.

DECISION: This proposal was adopted. The CHAIRMAN appointed the representatives of Australia, China and the Union of Soviet Socialist Republics to serve on this committee.

图片 1.1.2:张彭春在联合国人权委员会第一届第 3 次会议发言纪要

【纪要译文】

张博士(中国)认为,由秘书处提交的文件(E/CN.4/W.7)第 4 段提出的三种解决办法中,第二种办法,即仅通过第一届会议拟定的议事规则,并将审查和修正推迟到第二届会议,肯定是最合理的。

张博士(中国)在罗慕洛(Romulo)将军(菲律宾共和国)的附议下,提议设立一个三人委员会,研究对议事规则可能作出的修正。

决定:这项提议获得通过。主席任命澳大利亚、中国和苏联代表在该委员会任职。

3. 张彭春在人权委员会
第一届第4次会议的发言

1947年1月28日下午2时30分,联合国人权委员会第一届第4次会议,在纽约成功湖召开,本次会议的主要议题是继续审议收到的来文。中国代表张彭春参加了本次会议,并在会议上发言,其具体发言内容①会议纪要、纪要影像和纪要译文如下:

【会议纪要】

Mr. CHANG（CHINA）suggested that the Commission should postpone consideration of the proposal dealing with item 8 on its provisional agenda （Consideration of ways and means for the effective implementation of human rights and fundamental freedoms—document E/CN. 4/3）.

【纪要影像】

Mr. CHANG (CHINA) suggested that the Commission should postpone consideration of the proposal dealing with item 8 on its provisional agenda (Consideration of ways and means for the effective implementation of human rights and fundamental freedoms - document E/CN.4/3).

图片1.1.3:张彭春在联合国人权委员会第一届第4次会议发言纪要

【纪要译文】

张先生(中国)建议委员会推迟审议关于临时议程项目8(审议有效落实人权和基本自由的方式和方法——E/CN.4/3号文件)的提案。

---

① UN Document：E/CN. 4/SR. 4, p. 7.

4. 张彭春在人权委员会
第一届第 5 次会议的发言

1947 年 1 月 29 日上午 11 时,联合国人权委员会第一届第 5 次会议,在纽约成功湖召开,本次会议的主要议题是讨论议程项目 2,即新闻和出版自由分设委员会的设立和职权范围。中国代表张彭春参加了本次会议,并在会议上发言,其具体发言内容①会议纪要、纪要影像和纪要译文如下:

【会议纪要】

General ROMULO (PHILIPPINE REPUBLIC) said he wished to place on record paragraph 15 of document E/CN. 4/W. 11. He moved "that the Commission of Human Rights establish a Sub-Commission on Freedom of Information and of the Press in accordance with our terms of reference."

Mr. CHANG (CHINA) suggested that the motion would be more clear if the last phrase were dropped.

General ROMULO (PHILIPPINE REPUBLIC) agreed with Mr. Chang, and accordingly moved "that the Commission on Human Rights establish a Sub-Commission on Freedom of Information and of the Press."

This was seconded by Mr. Dukes and carried by 10 votes to nil.

The CHAIRMAN said that before proceeding to discussion of the composition of the Sub-Commission and Terms of Reference, a document incorporating suggestions made by the United States would be circulated (documents E/CN. 4/7 and E/CN. 4/8).

Mr. CHANG (CHINA) supported the proposal of the Lebanese Repre-

---

① UN Document: E/CN. 4/SR. 5, p. 4, p. 5, p. 6, p. 7.

sentative to appoint a sub-committee of three to go over the various points, formulate Teams of Reference, and report back to the Commission. He emphasized the importance of responsibility of the press as well as freedom of the press.

Mr. CHANG (CHINA) said that perhaps the Sub-Commission's Terms of Reference should be a little more definitive, suggestive, and inclusive than the words of the resolution of the Economic and Social Council, even though the general principles were acceptable.

Mr. CHANG (CHINA) suggested that the sub-committee also be given the task of determining the composition of the Sub-Commission.

Mr. TEPLIAKOV (USSR) recalled his previous motion on the issue of composition, and suggested that it now be considered.

Mr. CHANG (CHINA) pointed out that there were several problems such as relationship with Specialized Agencies to be discussed in relation to the composition of the Sub-Commission. The Representative of the USSR, who was also on the recently appointed sub-committee, could place his suggestions before it.

Mr. MORA (URUGUAY) called the Commission's attention to paragraphs 9 and 10 of the working paper (document E/CN. 4/W. 11).

Mrs. MEHTA (INDIA) agreed with Mr. Chang that it was wise to let the sub-committee discuss the composition as well as the Terms of Reference of the Sub-Commission, and seconded his motion.

Mr. TEPLIAKOV (USSR) said he was willing to withdraw his motion provided the question of composition was considered later along with the composition of the other Sub-Commission or Sub-Commissions.

Mr. CHAHG's proposal was carried by 9 votes to 2.

【纪要影像】

General ROMULO (PHILIPPINE REPUBLIC) said he wished to place on record paragraph 15 of document E/CN.4/W.11. He moved "that the Commission of Human Rights establish a Sub-Commission on Freedom of Information and of the Press in accordance with our terms of reference."

Mr. CHANG (CHINA) suggested that the motion would be more clear if the last phrase were dropped.

General ROMULO (PHILIPPINE REPUBLIC) agreed with Mr. Chang, and accordingly moved "that the Commission on Human Rights establish a Sub-Commission on Freedom of Information and of the Press."

This was seconded by Mr. Dukes and carried by 10 votes to nil.

The CHAIRMAN said that before proceeding to discussion of the composition of the Sub-Commission and Terms of Reference, a document incorporating suggestions made by the United States would be circulated (documents E/CN.4/7 and E/CN.4/8).

图片 1.1.4：张彭春在联合国人权委员会第一届第 5 会议发言纪要(1)

Mr. CHANG (CHINA) supported the proposal of the Lebanese Representative to appoint a sub-committee of three to go over the various points, formulate Terms of Reference, and report back to the Commission. He emphasized the importance of responsibility of the press as well as freedom of the press.

Mr. CHANG (CHINA) said that perhaps the Sub-Commission's Terms of Reference should be a little more definitive, suggestive, and inclusive than the words of the resolution of the Economic and Social Council, even though the general principles were acceptable.

Mr. CHANG (CHINA) suggested that the sub-committee also be given the task of determining the composition of the Sub-Commission.

Mr. TEPLIAKOV (USSR) recalled his previous motion on the issue of composition, and suggested that it now be considered.

Mr. CHANG (CHINA) pointed out that there were several problems such as relationship with Specialized Agencies to be discussed in relation to the composition of the Sub-Commission. The Representative of the USSR, who was also on the recently appointed sub-committee, could place his suggestions before it.

图片 1.1.5：张彭春在联合国人权委员会第一届第 5 会议发言纪要(2)

Mr. MORA (URUGUAY) called the Commission's attention to paragraphs 9 and 10 of the working paper (document E/CN.4/W.11).

Mrs. MEHTA (INDIA) agreed with Mr. Chang that it was wise to let the sub-committee discuss the composition as well as the Terms of Reference of the Sub-Commission, and seconded his motion.

Mr. TEPLIAKOV (USSR) said he was willing to withdraw his motion provided the question of composition was considered later along with the composition of the other Sub-Commission or Sub-Commissions.

Mr. CHANG's proposal was carried by 9 votes to 2.

图片 1.1.6:张彭春在联合国人权委员会第一届第 5 会议发言纪要(3)

【纪要译文】

罗慕洛将军(菲律宾共和国)说,他希望将 E/CN.4/W.11 号文件第 15 段记录在案。他提议"人权委员会根据我们的职权范围设立一个新闻和出版自由分设委员会"①。

张先生(中国)建议,如果删除最后一个短语②,该动议将更加明确。

罗慕洛将军(菲律宾共和国)同意张先生的意见,并据此提议"人权委员会设立一个新闻和出版自由分设委员会"。

这项提议得到了杜克斯先生的附议,并以 10 票对 0 票获得通过。

主席说,在开始讨论分设委员会的组成和职权范围之前,将分发一份载有美国建议的文件(E/CN.4/7 和 E/CN.4/8 号文件)。

张先生(中国)支持黎巴嫩代表的建议,即任命一个三人小组委员会审查各个要点,拟订职权范围,并向委员会报告。他强调了新闻责任和新闻自由的重要性。

张先生(中国)说,也许分设委员会的职权范围应该比经济及社会理事会决议的措辞更明确、更具建议性和更具包容性,尽管决议的一般原则

---

① 编著者注:为了区分将英文 sub-commission 译为"分设委员会",而将英文 sub-committee 译为"小组委员会"

② 编著者注:由于中英文句子语序不同,"最后一个短语"这里指的是:"根据我们的职权范围"。

是可以接受的。

张先生(中国)建议也赋予小组委员会决定分设委员会组成的任务。

特普利亚科夫(Tepliakov)先生(苏联)回顾了他以前关于组成问题的动议,并建议现在审议该动议。

张先生(中国)指出,在分设委员会的组成方面,有几个问题需要讨论,如与专门机构的关系。苏联代表也是最近任命的小组委员会的成员,他可以向分设委员会提出建议。

莫拉(Mora)先生(乌拉圭)提请委员会注意工作文件(E/CN.4/W.11号文件)第9段和第10段。

梅赫塔(Mehta)女士(印度)同意张先生的意见,让小组委员会讨论分设委员会的组成和职权范围是明智的,并支持他的动议。

特普利亚科夫先生(苏联)说,如果以后连同其他分设委员会的组成一起审议组成问题,他愿意撤回他的动议。

张先生的提议以9票对2票获得通过。

5. 张彭春在人权委员会
第一届第6次会议的发言

1947年1月29日下午2时30分,联合国人权委员会第一届第6次会议,在纽约成功湖召开,本次会议的主要议题是讨论保护少数者小组委员会的设立和职权范围(议程项目11;E/CN.4/1/Rev.1)、讨论防止歧视及保护少数者分设委员会的职权范围。中国代表张彭春参加了本次会议,并在会议上发言,其具体发言内容①会议纪要、纪要影像和纪要译文如下:

---

① UN Document:E/CN.4/SR.6, p.2, p.3, p.4, p.7.

Dr. CHANG (CHINA) considered that the prevention of discrimination was more inclusive than the protection of minorities, and suggested that the Australian proposal should therefore be amended to refer to the contemplated sub-commission as the sub-commission on the prevention of discrimination and protection of minorities.

Dr. CHANG (CHINA) explaining that this suggestion was no doubt intended to improve the general definition of discrimination, assured the USSR representative that the matter would be taken up during the discussion of the terms of reference of the sub-commission.

Dr. CHANG (CHINA) said that numerous points of the United States document required detailed discussion; the suggestion of the USSR representative should be given consideration; the composition of the sub-commission in question should be studied in connection with that of other sub-commissions. Inasmuch as the Commission had appointed a drafting sub-committee to consider the terms of reference of another sub-commission, Dr. CHANG moved that the terms of reference and the composition of the Sub-Commission on the Prevention of Discrimination and the Protection of Minorities should also be referred to that sub-committee. He further moved that, in view of the added work which the sub-committee would be called upon to perform, two new members should be added to it.

Dr. CHANG (CHINA) proposed that his two motions should be put to the vote separately.

The CHAIRMAN put to the vote the Chinese motion to refer the terms of reference and composition of the Sub-Commission on the Prevention of Discrimination and the Protection of Minorities to the drafting sub-committee.

DECISION: The motion was adopted by ten votes to none.

联合国人权委员会和起草委员会

The CHAIRMAN put to the vote the Chinese motion to add two members to the drafting sub-committee.

DECISION: The motion was adopted by ten votes to none.

The suggestion of Dr. CHANG (CHINA) that the Commission should adjourn to study the documents with respect to the International Bill of Rights was accepted. It was decided that the drafting sub-committee would sit immediately following the Commission's adjournment.

【纪要影像】

Dr. CHANG (CHINA) considered that the prevention of discrimination was more inclusive than the protection of minorities, and suggested that the Australian proposal should therefore be amended to refer to the contemplated sub-commission as the sub-commission on the prevention of discrimination and protection of minorities.

Dr. CHANG (CHINA) explaining that this suggestion was no doubt intended to improve the general definition of discrimination, assured the USSR representative that the matter would be taken up during the discussion of the terms of reference of the sub-commission.

图片 1.1.7:张彭春在联合国人权委员会第一届第 6 次会议发言纪要(1)

Dr. CHANG (CHINA) said that numerous points of the United States document required detailed discussion; the suggestion of the USSR representative should be given consideration; the composition of the sub-commission in question should be studied in connection with that of other sub-commissions. Inasmuch as the Commission had appointed a drafting sub-committee to consider the terms of reference of another sub-commission, Dr. CHANG moved that the terms of reference and the composition of the Sub-Commission on the Prevention of Discrimination and the Protection of Minorities should also be referred to that sub-committee. He further moved that, in view of the added work which the sub-committee would be called upon to perform, two new members should be added to it.

图片1.1.8:张彭春在联合国人权委员会第一届第6次会议发言纪要(2)

Dr. CHANG (CHINA) proposed that his two motions should be put to the vote separately.

The CHAIRMAN put to the vote the Chinese motion to refer the terms of reference and composition of the Sub-Commission on the Prevention of Discrimination and the Protection of Minorities to the drafting sub-committee.

DECISION: The motion was adopted by ten votes to none.

The CHAIRMAN put to the vote the Chinese motion to add two members to the drafting sub-committee.

DECISION: The motion was adopted by ten votes to none.

The suggestion of Dr. CHANG (CHINA) that the Commission should adjourn to study documents with respect to the International Bill of Rights was accepted. It was decided that the drafting sub-committee would sit immediately following the Commission's adjournment.

图片1.1.9:张彭春在联合国人权委员会第一届第6次会议发言纪要(3)

【纪要译文】

张博士(中国)认为,防止歧视比保护少数者更具包容性,因此建议修改澳大利亚的提案,将设想的分设委员会称为防止歧视及保护少数者分设委员会。

张博士(中国)解释说,这一建议无疑是为了改进歧视的一般定义,他向苏联代表保证,在讨论分设委员会的职权范围时将会讨论这个问题。

张博士(中国)说,美国文件中有许多要点需要详细讨论;应当考虑苏联代表的建议;正在讨论的分设委员会的组成应与其他分设委员会的组成一起研究。由于人权委员会已委任一个草拟小组委员会考虑另一个分设委员会的职权范围,张博士动议防止歧视及保护少数者分设委员会的职权范围及成员组成亦应提交该小组委员会。他进一步提议,鉴于小组委员会需要完成的工作量增加,应增加两名新成员。

张博士(中国)建议对他的两项动议分别进行表决。

主席将中国关于将防止歧视及保护少数者分设委员会的职权范围和组成提交起草小组委员会的动议付诸表决。

决定:该动议以 10 票对 0 票获得通过。

主席将中国提出的在起草小组委员会中增加两名成员的动议付诸表决。

决定:该动议以 10 票对 0 票获得通过。

张博士(中国)建议委员会休会,研究有关国际人权法案的文件,这项建议获得接受。会议决定,起草小组委员会将在委员会休会后立即开会。

6. 张彭春在人权委员会
第一届第 7 次会议的发言

1947 年 1 月 31 日上午 11 时,联合国人权委员会第一届第 7 次会议,在纽约成功湖召开,本次会议的主要议题是讨论议程项目 2:国际权利法案(E/CN.4/4,E/CN.4/W.4)。中国代表张彭春参加了本次会议,并在会议上发言,其具体发言内容①会议纪要、纪要影像和纪要译文如下:

---

① UN Document:E/CN.4/SR.7, p. 3, pp. 3-4.

Mr. CHANG (China) considered that the Commission should take no vote at the present stage of discussion; he suggested, however, that it should proceed on the assumption that the bill would be drafted as a General Assembly resolution, and discuss the substance of the bill on that basis.

The Commission agreed to follow the procedure proposed by the representative of China.

Mr. CHANG (China) pointed out that the preamble suggested in the document prepared by the Secretariat appeared to have been omitted from the United States proposals. He emphasized that the bill should include a preamble propounding the philosophy on which the bill was based.

At the present time it was necessary to affirm and enlarge the difference existing between man and animal. A standard should be established with a view to elevating the concept of man's dignity and emphasizing the respect of man: that principle should be embodied in a preamble to the International Bill of Rights.

In reply to a question from the representative of Australia regarding the nature of the standard envisaged for the application of human rights, Mr. Chang went on to explain that the principle of human rights should be given universal application regardless of human level. He had referred to a minimum standard as a means of increasing the stature of man as opposed to animal.

In conclusion, the representative of China urged the Commission to bear in mind the historical background of human rights, particularly the emphasis placed on human values by the 16th century thinkers, in elaborating a preamble propounding the philosophy on which the future International Bill of Rights would be based.

【纪要影像】

Mr. CHANG (China) considered that the Commission should take no vote at the present stage of discussion; he suggested, however, that it should proceed on the assumption that the bill would be drafted as a General Assembly resolution, and discuss the substance of the bill on that basis.

The Commission agreed to follow the procedure proposed by the representative of China.

Mr. CHANG (China) pointed out that the preamble suggested in the document prepared by the Secretariat appeared to have been omitted from the United States proposals. He emphasized that the bill should include a preamble propounding the philosophy on which the bill was based.

At the present time it was necessary to affirm and enlarge the difference existing between man and animal. A standard should be established with a view to elevating the concept of man's dignity and emphasizing the respect of man: that principle should be embodied in a preamble to the International Bill of Rights.

图片 1.1.10:张彭春在联合国人权委员会第一届第 7 次会议发言纪要(1)

In reply to a question from the representative of Australia regarding the nature of the standard envisaged for the application of human rights, Mr. Chang went on to explain that the principle of human rights should be given universal application regardless of human level. He had referred to a minimum standard as a means of increasing the stature of man as opposed to animal.

In conclusion, the representative of China urged the Commission to bear in mind the historical background of human rights, particularly the emphasis placed on human values by the 16th century thinkers, in elaborating a preamble propounding the philosophy on which the future International Bill of Rights would be based.

图片 1.1.11:张彭春在联合国人权委员会第一届第 7 次会议发言纪要(2)

【纪要译文】

张先生(中国)认为,委员会在目前讨论阶段不应进行表决;然而,他建议,应当假定该法案将作为大会决议起草,并在此基础上讨论该法案的实质内容。

委员会同意遵循中国代表提议的程序。

张先生(中国)指出,美国的提案似乎遗漏了秘书处准备的文件中建议的序言。他强调,该法案应包括一个序言,提出该法案所依据的理念。

目前有必要肯定和扩大人和动物之间存在的差异。应该制定一项标准,以提升人的尊严的概念,强调对人的尊重:这项原则应该体现在《国际权利法案》①的序言中。

在回答澳大利亚代表关于适用人权所设想的标准的性质的问题时,张先生继续解释说,人权原则应当普遍适用,不论人的地位如何。他提到最低标准是提高人的地位而不是动物的地位的一种手段。

最后,中国代表敦促委员会铭记人权的历史背景,特别是 16 世纪思想家对人的价值的重视,拟定序言,提出未来《国际权利法案》将依据的哲学。

7. 张彭春在人权委员会
第一届第 11 次会议的发言

1947 年 2 月 3 日上午 11 时,联合国人权委员会第一届第 11 次会议,在纽约成功湖召开,本次会议的主要议题是讨论起草《国际权利法案》应遵循

---

① 《国际权利法案》(International Bill of Rights)与后文中出现的《国际人权法案》(International Bill of Human Rights)为同一文件,因会议纪要原文中存在不同提法,故在翻译上有所区别。

的程序(E/CN. 4/12 和 13 号文件)。中国代表张彭春参加了本次会议,并在会议上发言,其具体发言内容①会议纪要、纪要影像和纪要译文如下:

【会议纪要】

Mr. CHANG(China)thought that the difficulty might be solved by the Commission sitting as a whole as a Committee, to draft the International Bill of Human Rights, The Chairman could call a meeting every two weeks, at which those members or their deputies who were in New York could be present. No formal voting would be done, but the Committee would give its views on the drafts prepared by the Secretariat with the assistance of experts.

He considered it was more desirable to arrive at a practical compromise such as that than to take a vote which would give the impression of a difference of opinion on a matter of such vital importance.

【纪要影像】

Mr. CHANG (China) thought that the difficulty might be solved by the Commission sitting as a whole as a Committee, to draft the International Bill of Human Rights. The Chairman could call a meeting every two weeks, at which those members or their deputies who were in New York could be present. No formal voting would be done, but the Committee would give its views on the drafts prepared by the Secretariat with the assistance of experts.

He considered it was more desirable to arrive at a practical compromise such as that than to take a vote which would give the impression of a difference of opinion on a matter of such vital importance.

图片 1.1.12:张彭春在联合国人权委员会第一届第 11 次会议发言纪要

① UN Document:E/CN. 4/SR. 11, p. 4, p. 5.

张先生(中国)认为,委员会作为一个整体开会可能会解决这个问题,为了起草《国际人权法案》,主席可以每两周召开一次会议,让在纽约的成员或其代表出席。不会进行正式表决,但委员会将对秘书处在专家协助下准备的草案发表意见。

他认为,达成这样一种切实可行的妥协比进行表决更为可取,因为表决会给人一种在如此重要的问题上存在意见分歧的印象。

8. 张彭春在人权委员会
第一届第 12 次会议的发言

1947 年 2 月 3 日下午 2 时 30 分,联合国人权委员会第一届第 12 次会议,在纽约成功湖召开,本次会议的主要议题是讨论并表决人权委员会的决议,即制定《国际人权法案》初稿的议题。中国代表张彭春参加了本次会议,并在会议上发言,其具体发言内容①会议纪要、纪要影像和纪要译文如下:

【会议纪要】

Dr. CHANG (China) and Professor CASSIN (France) requested that the phrase "in co-operation with the Secretariat" be changed to "with the co-operation of the Secretariat".

At the request of Dr. CHANG (China), the Commission decided to take a vote by paragraphs.

DECISION: The United Kingdom representative's amendment, which was

---

① UN Document: E/CN. 4/SR. 12, p. 2.

put to the vote first, was rejected.

DECISION: The Lebanese representative's amendment was adopted.

Mr. TEPLIAKOV (Union of Soviet Socialist Republics) stated that the question of co-operation with those organizations was on the Commission's agenda and would come up for discussion, in due course.

Supported by Dr. CHANG (China), he stated that the members of the Commission should have the right to express their opinion at any stage in the drafting of the declaration.

【纪要影像】

Dr. CHANG (China) and Professor CASSIN (France) requested that the phrase "in co-operation with the Secretariat" be changed to "with the co-operation of the Secretariat".

At the request of Dr. CHANG (China), the Commission decided to take a vote by paragraphs.

DECISION: The United Kingdom representative's amendment, which was put to the vote first, was rejected.

DECISION: The Lebanese representative's amendment was adopted.

Mr. TEPLIAKOV (Union of Soviet Socialist Republics) stated that the question of co-operation with those organizations was on the Commission's agenda and would come up for discussion in due course.

Supported by Dr. CHANG (China), he stated that the members of the Commission should have the right to express their opinion at any stage in the drafting of the declaration.

1.1.13:张彭春在联合国人权委员会第一届第12次会议发言纪要

【纪要译文】

张博士(中国)和卡森教授(法国)要求将"与秘书处合作"(in co-operation with the Secretariat)改为"和秘书处合作"(with the co-operation of the Secretariat)。

应张博士(中国)的要求,委员会决定分段进行表决。

决定:先付诸表决的英国代表的修正案被否决。

决定:黎巴嫩代表的修正案获得通过。

特普利亚科夫先生(苏联)表示,与这些组织的合作问题已列入委员会的议程,并将在适当时候提出讨论。

在张博士(中国)的支持下,他说,委员会成员应有权在起草宣言的任何阶段发表意见。

9. 张彭春在人权委员会 第一届第 13 次会议的发言

1947 年 2 月 4 日上午 11 时,联合国人权委员会第一届第 13 次会议,在纽约成功湖召开,本次会议的主要议题是 E/CN/18 号文件的审议。中国代表张彭春参加了本次会议,并在会议上发言,其具体发言内容①会议纪要、纪要影像和纪要译文如下:

【会议纪要】

Dr. CHANG (China) considered that the principle of equality should be examined, bearing in mind the concept of human dignity.

Dr. CHANG (China) considered that, in order to comply with the wishes of the Representatives of France and the Philippine Republic, a sentence might be included in the summary record to the effect that the Commission considered it necessary to emphasize this idea of the solidarity or unity of the human race. It would thereby be ensured that the Declaration of Human Rights would always be correctly understood, and that it would be possible at all times to see what had been formulated on the morrow of a war waged by the enemy in the name of

---

① UN Document: E/CN. 4/SR. 13, pp. 3-4, p. 5, pp. 5-6, p. 7.

racial inequality.

Dr. CHANG（China）emphasized that his country's Constitution already contained the majority of the rights enumerated in paragraph 2, and he added that he would have copies of the Chinese Constitution distributed among the members of the Commission.

Dr. CHANG（China）drew the Commission's attention to Article 18 of the Chinese Constitution which prescribed the system of public examinations for the admission to public office. He considered that that right should exist in all countries, and suggested that it be mentioned in the Bill of Human Rights.

【纪要影像】

Dr. CHANG (China) considered that the principle of equality should be examined, bearing in mind the concept of human dignity.

Dr. CHANG (China) considered that, in order to comply with the wishes of the Representatives of France and the Philippine Republic, a sentence might be included in the summary record to the effect that the Commission considered it necessary to emphasize this idea of the solidarity or unity of the human race. It would thereby be ensured that the Declaration of Human Rights would always be correctly understood, and that it would be possible at all times to see what had been formulated on the morrow of a war waged by the enemy in the name of racial inequality.

图片 1.1.14:张彭春在联合国人权委员会第一届第 13 次会议发言纪要(1)

Dr. CHANG (China) emphasized that his country's Constitution already contained the majority of the rights enumerated in paragraph 2, and he added that he would have copies of the Chinese Constitution distributed among the members of the Commission.

Dr. CHANG (China) drew the Commission's attention to Article 18 of the Chinese Constitution which prescribed the system of public examinations for the admission to public office. He considered that that right should exist in all countries, and suggested that it be mentioned in the Bill of Human Rights.

图片 1.1.15:张彭春在联合国人权委员会第一届第 13 次会议发言纪要(2)

张博士（中国）认为，应审查平等原则，同时铭记人类尊严的概念。

张博士（中国）认为，为了顺应法国和菲律宾代表的愿望，可在摘要记录中列入一句话，大意是委员会认为有必要强调人类团结或联合的思想。这样就可以确保《人权宣言》永远得到正确的理解，而且在任何时候都有可能明白敌人以种族不平等的名义发动战争随后所制定的内容。

张博士（中国）强调说，中国的《宪法》已经包含了第 2 款列举的大多数权利，他还说，他将把中国《宪法》的副本分发给委员会成员。

张博士（中国）提请委员会注意中国《宪法》第 18 条，该条规定了录用公职人员的公共考试制度。他认为这项权利应该存在于所有国家，并建议在《人权法案》中提及。

10. 张彭春在人权委员会第一届第 14 次会议的发言

1947 年 2 月 4 日下午 2 时，联合国人权委员会第一届第 14 次会议，在纽约成功湖召开，本次会议的主要议题是继续就《国际人权法案》草案的内容进行辩论。中国代表张彭春参加了本次会议，并在会议上发言，其具体发言内容①会议纪要、纪要影像和纪要译文如下：

【会议纪要】

Mr. CHANG（CHINA）warned against the danger of producing a document which would ill accord with the times owing to its being out of time with the spirit and atomosphere of the past war era；he would like to see the expres-

---

① UN Document：E/CN.4/SR.14, p. 6, p. 7.

sion "freedom from want" appear somewhere, either in the preamble or in the text itself.

Mr. CHANG (China), supported by Mr. TEPLIAKOV (Union of Soviet Socialist Republics), thought the Commission ought, first of all, with the assistance of the Drafting Committee, to draw up a Bill of Rights incorporated in a draft resolution.

【纪要影像】

Mr. CHANG (China) warned against the danger of producing a document which would ill accord with the times owing to its being out of time with the spirit and atmosphere of the post war era; he would like to see the expression "freedom from want" appear somewhere, either in the preamble or in the text itself.

Mr. CHANG (China), supported by Mr. TEPLIAKOV (Union of Soviet Socialist Republics), thought the Commission ought, first of all, with the assistance of the Drafting Committee, to draw up a Bill of Rights incorporated in a .. draft resolution.

图片 1.1.16:张彭春在联合国人权委员会第一届第 14 次会议发言纪要

【纪要译文】

张先生(中国)警告说,编写一份不符合时代精神的文件是有危险的,因为它与过去战争时代的精神和气氛不符;他希望"免于匮乏的自由"这一表述出现在序言或案文本身的某处。

张先生(中国)在特普利亚科夫先生(苏联)的支持下认为,委员会首先应在起草委员会的协助下,起草一份纳入决议草案的《人权法案》。

11. 张彭春在人权委员会第一届第16次会议的发言

1947年2月5日下午2时45分,联合国人权委员会第一届第16次会议,在纽约成功湖召开,本次会议的主要议题是讨论澳大利亚代表提交的关于《国际人权法案》的决议草案(E/CN. 4/15号文件)、讨论小组委员会关于处理来文的报告(E/CN. 4/14/Rev. 1号文件)。中国代表张彭春参加了本次会议,并在会议上发言,其具体发言内容①会议纪要、纪要影像和纪要译文如下:

【会议纪要】

Mr. CHANG (China) agreed that the drafting group had been entrusted with the task of drafting a bill of rights. If suggestions concerning implementation were also to be referred to that group, that fact should be clearly stated. In order to meet the different points of view expressed, the Chinese representative suggested that the Lebanese amendment should also state that the drafting group should be allowed to explore all aspects of the problem, including implementation.

Mr. CHANG (China) said that the chief function of the Commission was to draft the International Bill of Human Rights. Therefore all communications on that subject should be brought to the Commission's notice immediately. As regards all other communications, the Commission should therefore refrain from raising false hopes.

Mr. Chang accordingly suggested that paragraph 5 of the report might be

① UN Document: E/CN. 4/SR. 16, p. 5, pp. 7-8, p. 9, p. 10.

adopted at once, and that the question of the proposed sub-committee might be deferred to the next session of the Commission.

Mr. CHANG (China) said that the functions of the Commission might be misconstrued by the general public unless the position were clarified.

He proposed that paragraph 5 should be adopted at once, section (d) being amended in the manner suggested by the Belgian representative and the words "before each meeting of the Sub-Committee" in section (a) being deleted. The rest of the report should be referred back to the Sub-Committee in accordance with the suggestion of the United Kingdom representative.

Mr. CHANG (China) remarked that communications dealing with human rights would continue to arrive whether or not there was a special sub-committee to receive them. Many of those communications might contain the accounts of serious wrongs.

【纪要影像】

Mr. CHANG (China) agreed that the drafting group had been entrusted with the task of drafting a bill of rights. If suggestions concerning implementation were also to be referred to that group, that fact should be clearly stated. In order to meet the different points of view expressed, the Chinese representative suggested that the Lebanese amendment should also state that the drafting group should be allowed to explore all aspects of the problem, including implementation.

Mr. CHANG (China) said that the chief function of the Commission was to draft the International Bill of Human Rights. Therefore all communications on that subject should be brought to the Commission's notice immediately. As regards all other communications, the Commission should therefore refrain from raising false hopes.

Mr. Chang accordingly suggested that paragraph 5 of the report might be adopted at once, and that the question of the proposed sub-committee might be deferred to the next session of the Commission.

图片 1.1.17：张彭春在联合国人权委员会第一届第 16 次会议发言纪要(1)

Mr. CHANG (China) said that the functions of the Commission might be misconstrued by the general public unless the position were clarified.

He proposed that paragraph 5 should be adopted at once, section (d) being amended in the manner suggested by the Belgian representative and the words "before each meeting of the Sub-Committee" in section (a) being deleted. The rest of the report should be referred back to the Sub-Committee in accordance with the suggestion of the United Kingdom representative.

Mr. CHANG (China) remarked that communications dealing with human rights would continue to arrive whether or not there was a special sub-committee to receive them. Many of those communications might contain the accounts of serious wrongs.

图片 1.1.18：张彭春在联合国人权委员会第一届第 16 次会议发言纪要(2)

【纪要译文】

张先生(中国)同意委托起草小组起草《人权法案》的任务。如果关于实施的建议也提交给该小组，则应明确说明这一事实。为了满足所表达的不同观点，中国代表建议，黎巴嫩的修正案还应说明，应允许起草小组探讨问题的所有方面，包括实施问题。

张先生(中国)说，委员会的首要职能是起草《国际人权法案》。因此，关于这一主题的所有来文都应立即提请委员会注意。因此，关于所有其他来文，委员会应避免产生不切实际的希望。

因此，张先生建议，报告第 5 段可以立即通过，拟议的小组委员会问题可以推迟到委员会下届会议。

张先生(中国)说，除非澄清立场，否则公众可能会误解委员会的职能。

他建议立即通过第 5 段，按照比利时代表建议的方式修改(d)节，删除(a)节中的"在小组委员会每次会议之前"字样。根据英国代表的建议，报告的其余部分应发回小组委员会。

张先生(中国)说，无论是否有一个特别小组委员会来接收有关人权的来文，这些来文都将会继续收到。其中许多来文可能包含对严重冤案的描述。

12. 张彭春在人权委员会
第一届第 18 次会议的发言

1947 年 2 月 6 日下午 12 时 45 分,联合国人权委员会第一届第 18 次会议,在纽约成功湖召开,本次会议的主要议题是议程项目 7:与其他委员会的协调等。中国代表张彭春参加了本次会议,并在会议上发言,其具体发言内容①会议纪要、纪要影像和纪要译文如下:

【会议纪要】

Dr. CHANG (China), Vice-Chairman, thought that this question should be left aside until the next session, and that for the moment the system should be kept as simple and practical as possible.

【纪要影像】

Dr. CHANG (China), Vice-Chairman, thought that this question should be left aside until the next session, and that for the moment the system should be kept as simple and practical as possible.

图片 1.1.19:张彭春在联合国人权委员会第一届第 18 次会议发言纪要

【纪要译文】

副主席张博士(中国)认为,这个问题应留到下届会议讨论,目前该制度应尽可能保持简单实用。

---

① UN Document:E/CN. 4/SR. 18, p. 6.

13. 张彭春在人权委员会
第一届第 19 次会议的发言

1947 年 2 月 7 日上午 11 时,联合国人权委员会第一届第 19 次会议,在纽约成功湖召开,本次会议的主要议题是讨论议事规则委员会的报告等。中国代表张彭春参加了本次会议,并在会议上发言,其具体发言内容①会议纪要、纪要影像和纪要译文如下:

【会议纪要】

Mr. CHANG（China）remarked that the question of location required greater attention than the date, in view of its political significance. Any decision in that respect should be in the hands of the Commission. At the same time, he emphasized the basic principle that the Commission should meet at Headquarters.

【纪要影像】

> Mr. CHANG (China) remarked that the question of location required greater attention than the date, in view of its political significance. Any decision in that respect should be in the hands of the Commission. At the same time, he emphasized the basic principle that the Commission should meet at Headquarters.

图片 1.1.20:张彭春在联合国人权委员会第一届第 19 次会议发言纪要

---

① UN Document: E/CN. 4/SR. 19, p. 7.

【纪要译文】

张先生(中国)说,鉴于地点问题的政治意义,它比日期问题更值得注意。这方面的任何决定都应由委员会做出。同时,他强调了委员会应在总部开会的基本原则。

14. 张彭春在人权委员会
第一届第 20 次会议的发言

1947 年 2 月 7 日下午 3 时,联合国人权委员会第一届第 20 次会议,在纽约成功湖召开,本次会议的主要议题是讨论并表决处理来文小组委员会的报告、讨论人权委员会提交经济及社会理事会的报告草稿。中国代表张彭春参加了本次会议,并在会议上发言,其具体发言内容①会议纪要、纪要影像和纪要译文如下:

【会议纪要】

Mr. CHANG (China) was ready to vote for paragraph 5 but was against paragraph 4 because it raised a question of principle. He thought it premature to say that the Commission was qualified to receive communications officially.

The CHAIRMAN invited the members of the Commission to submit proposals for amendments as the Rapporteur, Mr. Malik (Lebanon), read through the text of the document.

In Chapter I, paragraph 2, the Commission decided, on the proposal of Mr. Chang (China), to delete the word "substitutes" in line 2 and to insert "represented" instead of "replaced" in the last line.

---

① UN Document：E/CN. 4/SR. 20, p. 3, p. 6.

【纪要影像】

Mr. CHANG (China) was ready to vote for paragraph 5 but was against paragraph 4 because it raised a question of principle. He thought it premature to say that the Commission was qualified to receive communications officially.

The CHAIRMAN invited the members of the Commission to submit proposals for amendments as the Rapporteur, Mr. Malik (Lebanon), read through the text of the document.

In Chapter I, paragraph 2, the Commission decided, on the proposal of Mr. Chang (China), to delete the word "substitutes" in line 2 and to insert "represented" instead of "replaced" in the last line.

图片 1.1.21：张彭春在联合国人权委员会第一届第 20 次会议发言纪要

【纪要译文】

张先生(中国)准备对第 5 段投赞成票,但反对第 4 段,因为它提出了一个原则问题。他认为说委员会有资格正式接收来文还为时过早。

主席请委员会成员在报告员马利克先生(黎巴嫩)宣读文件案文时提交修正提案。

在第一章第 2 段中,根据张先生(中国)的建议,委员会决定删除第 2 行中的"替代"一词,并在最后一行中插入"代表"而不是"被取代"。

15. 张彭春在人权委员会
第一届第 21 次会议的发言

1947 年 2 月 10 日上午 10 时,联合国人权委员会第一届第 21 次会议,在纽约成功湖召开,本次会议的主要议题是讨论提交经济及社会理事会的报告草稿(E/CN.4/19 号文件)、讨论美国关于新闻和出版自由小组委员会(E/CN.4/7号文件)和保护少数者和防止歧视小组委员会的建议(E/CN.4/6号文件)。中国代表张彭春参加了本次会议,并在会议上发言,其具体发言内容①会议纪要、纪要影像和纪要译文如下:

【会议纪要】

Mr. CHANG (China) agreed with the representative of Australia and suggested that the Commission should postpone the setting up of Sub-Commissions until its next session, but if the Sub-Commission on Freedom of Information and of the Press was considered more urgent, then the report of the Rapporteur should be approved and that Sub-Commission set up immediately.

Mr. CHANG (China) said there might not be time to receive nominations from certain distant areas, and the Council would be faced with the responsibility of choosing from perhaps some hundred names, while several important geographical sections might not figure among the nominations.

Col. HODGSON (Australia) asked the representative of China, since he was also a representative of the Economic and Social Council whether it was a fact that it was not because of difficulties of communications or through inadvertence that many important governments had refused to submit nominations, but as a matter of principle, and whether consequently, if the method under discussion were to be adopted, it would be impossible for the Economic and Social Council to carry out the intentions of the Commission.

Mr. CHANG (China) said the reasons for nominations not coming in had never been clearly stated.

Mr. CHANG (China) made a formal amendment to change the term of office from two years to one year, especially in view of the preparation for the Conference. The matter could be reconsidered at the end of one year.

Mr. CHANG (China) pointed out that the terms of reference of the Sub-

---

① UN Document: E/CN.4/SR.21, p. 7, p. 9, p. 10, p. 11, pp. 12–13, p. 13.

Commission were to examine what rights, obligations and practices should be included in the concept "Freedom of Information". It should be possible to make some headway on that subject in one or two sessions, and the Commission might wish to change the terms of reference after one year.

Furthermore, he did not consider it practical to set up permanent Sub-Commissions, as the budget might make that impossible.

DECISION: *The Chinese amendment, for the term of office of members of the Sub-Commission to be one year only, was adopted by seven votes to three.*

In answer to a question from Mr. CHANG (China) as to whether those sub-commissions had been chosen already and what decision had been reached by the Economic and Employment Commission, Mr. HUMPHREY said that according to the draft report before him the members had not yet been appointed.

Mr. CHANG (China) suggested that in view of the difficulty of referring the matter to the Council, it might be advisable to have a meeting of the sub-committee of seven, to talk the matter over before the afternoon meeting.

【纪要影像】

Mr. CHANG (China) agreed with the representative of Australia and suggested that the Commission should postpone the setting up of Sub-Commissions until its next session, but if the Sub-Commission on Freedom of Information and of the Press was considered more urgent, then the report of the Rapporteur should be approved and that Sub-Commission set up immediately.

Mr. CHANG (China) said there might not be time to receive nominations from certain distant areas, and the Council would be faced with the responsibility of choosing from perhaps some hundred names, while several important geographical sections might not figure among the nominations.

图片 1.1.22:张彭春在联合国人权委员会第一届第 21 次会议发言纪要(1)

Col. HODGSON (Australia) asked the representative of China, since he was also a representative of the Economic and Social Council whether it was a fact that it was not because of difficulties of communications or through inadvertence that many important governments had refused to submit nominations, but as a matter of principle, and whether consequently, if the method under discussion were to be adopted, it would be impossible for the Economic and Social Council to carry out the intentions of the Commission.

Mr. CHANG (China) said the reasons for nominations not coming in had never been clearly stated.

Mr. CHANG (China) made a formal amendment to change the term of office from two years to one year, especially in view of the preparation for the Conference. The matter could be reconsidered at the end of one year.

图片 1.1.23：张彭春在联合国人权委员会第一届第 21 次会议发言纪要（2）

Mr. CHANG (China) pointed out that the terms of reference of the Sub-Commission were to examine what rights, obligations and practices should be included in the concept "Freedom of Information". It should be possible to make some headway on that subject in one or two sessions, and the Commission might wish to change the terms of reference after one year.

Furthermore, he did not consider it practical to set up permanent Sub-Commissions, as the budget might make that impossible.

DECISION: The Chinese amendment, for the term of office of members of the Sub-Commission to be one year only, was adopted by seven votes to three.

In answer to a question from Mr. CHANG (China) as to whether those sub-commissions had been chosen already and what decision had been reached by the Economic and Employment Commission, Mr. HUMPHREY said that according to the draft report before him the members had not yet been appointed.

Mr. CHANG (China) suggested that in view of the difficulty of referring the matter to the Council, it might be advisable to have a meeting of the sub-committee of seven, to talk the matter over before the afternoon meeting.

图片 1.1.24：张彭春在联合国人权委员会第一届第 21 次会议发言纪要（3）

【纪要译文】

张先生（中国）同意澳大利亚代表的意见，并建议委员会将设立分设委员会的工作推迟到下届会议，但如果认为新闻和出版自由分设委员会更为紧迫，则应批准报告员的报告，并立即设立该分设委员会。

张先生（中国）说，可能没有时间接受某些偏远地区的提名，理事会将面临从数百个名字中进行选择的责任，而几个重要的地理区域可能不在提名之列。

霍奇森（Hodgson）上校（澳大利亚）询问中国代表，因为他也是经济及社会理事会的代表，许多重要国家政府拒绝提名不是因为沟通困难或疏忽，而是出于原则，因此，如果采用正在讨论的方法，经济及社会理事会是否无法实现委员会的意图。

张先生（中国）说，没有收到提名的原因从未得到明确说明。

张先生（中国）提出了一项正式修正案，将任期从两年改为一年，特别是考虑到会议的筹备工作。这件事可以在一年后重新考虑。

张先生（中国）指出，小组委员会的职权范围是审查"新闻自由"概念中应包括哪些权利、义务和做法。在一届或两届会议上应该有可能在这个问题上取得一些进展，委员会可能希望在一年后改变职权范围。

此外，他认为设立常任分设委员会是不切实际的，因为可能预算不允许。

决定：关于分设委员会成员任期仅为一年的中国修正案以 7 票对 3 票获得通过。

在回答张先生（中国）关于这些分设委员会成员是否已经选定以及经济和就业委员会作出了什么决定的问题时，汉弗莱（Humphrey）先生说，根据他面前的报告草稿，成员尚未任命。

张先生（中国）建议，鉴于很难将此事提交理事会，不妨召开一次七人小组委员会会议，在下午会议之前讨论此事。

16. 张彭春在人权委员会
第一届第 22 次会议的发言

1947 年 2 月 10 日下午 2 时 30 分,联合国人权委员会第一届第 22 次会议,在纽约成功湖召开,本次会议的主要议题是讨论并通过人权委员会提交经济及社会理事会的报告草稿(E/CN. 4/19 号文件)、讨论并决定人权委员会下届会议的结束日期、人权委员会第一届会议辩论总结等。中国代表张彭春参加了本次会议,并在会议上发言,其具体发言内容①会议纪要、纪要影像和纪要译文如下:

【会议纪要】

Mr. CHANG (China) proposed that the suggestions of the specialized agencies and the non-governmental organizations should be transmitted orally to the Economic and Social Council by the Rapporteur.

DECISION: The proposal of the representative of China was adopted by nine votes to none.

Mr. CHANG (China) proposed that the session should take place at the seat of the United Nations, and that the Economic and Social Council should fix the date. The rules of procedure of the Council provided for three annual sessions and the Council had decided to hold three or four sessions in 1947. In order to economize in budget funds, he asked that the session should take place at the seat of the United Nations.

In reply to a question from Dr. CHANG (China), Mr. STANCZYK (Secretariat) said that the Commission's vote was only a guide to the Secretariat.

---

① UN Document: E/CN. 4/SR. 22, p. 7, p. 8, p. 9, p. 10.

Dr. CHANG (China) asked that the following statement be included in the summary record for transmission to all concerned:

"The Commission on Human Rights expresses to the Secretary-General its appreciation of the extremely able manner in which the work of his staff was performed, both in preparation for and during the first session of this Commission.

"The opening address of Monsieur Laugier, delivered at real sacrifice to his personal convenience and his health, will not soon be forgotten. The Commission further feels that the Secretary-General is to be congratulated on having on his staff Dr. Humphrey, who acted as Secretary during this session. The success of the Commission's work has been due in no small measure to the careful planning and the high degree of intelligence and tireless devotion which Dr. Humphrey has given to this work.

"The Commission wishes also to express its appreciation and gratitude for the devoted and inspiring leadership of its Chairman, whose charming and irresistible spirit of patience and humor elicits our sincerest admiration."

Colonal HODGSON (Australia), Professor CASSIN (France), Mr. MALIK (Lebanon), Mr. DUKES (United Kingdom), Mr. RIBNIKAR (Yugoslavia), Mr. EBEID (Egypt), associated themselves with the sentiments expressed by the representative of China.

The meeting rose at 6.30 p. m.

【纪要影像】

Mr. CHANG (China) proposed that the suggestions of the specialized
agencies and the non-governmental organizations should be transmitted orally
to the Economic and Social Council by the Rapporteur.
  DECISION: The proposal of the representative of China was adopted by
          nine votes to none.

Mr. CHANG (China) proposed that the session should take place at the seat of the United Nations, and that the Economic and Social Council should fix the date. The rules of procedure of the Council provided for three annual sessions and the Council had decided to hold three or four sessions in 1947. In order to economize in budget funds, he asked that the session should take place at the seat of the United Nations.

In reply to a question from Dr. CHANG (China), Mr. STANCZYK (Secretariat) said that the Commission's vote was only a guide to the Secretariat.

图片 1.1.25：张彭春在联合国人权委员会第一届第 22 次会议发言纪要(1)

Dr. CHANG (China) asked that the following statement be included in the summary record for transmission to all concerned:

"The Commission on Human Rights expresses to the Secretary-General its appreciation of the extremely able manner in which the work of his staff was performed, both in preparation for and during the first session of this Commission.

"The opening address of Monsieur Laugier, delivered at real sacrifice to his personal convenience and his health, will not soon be forgotten. The Commission further feels that the Secretary-General is to be congratulated on having on his staff Dr. Humphrey, who acted as Secretary during this session. The success of the Commission's work has been due in no small measure to the careful planning and the high degree of intelligence and tireless devotion which Dr. Humphrey has given to this work.

图片 1.1.26：张彭春在联合国人权委员会第一届第 22 次会议发言纪要(2)

"The Commission wishes also to express its appreciation and gratitude for the devoted and inspiring leadership of its Chairman, whose charming and irresistible spirit of patience and humor elicits our sincerest admiration."

Colonel HODGSON (Australia), Professor CASSIN (France), Mr. MALIK (Lebanon), Mr. DUKES (United Kingdom), Mr. RIBNIKAR (Yugoslavia), Mr. EBEID (Egypt), associated themselves with the sentiments expressed by the representative of China.

The meeting rose at 6:30 p.m.

图片 1.1.27：张彭春在联合国人权委员会第一届第 22 次会议发言纪要(3)

【纪要译文】

张先生(中国)提议由报告员向经济及社会理事会口头转达各专门机构和非政府组织的建议。

决定:中国代表的提案以9票对0票获得通过。(E/CN. 4/SR. 22第7页)

张先生(中国)提议,该届会议应在联合国所在地举行,并由经济及社会理事会确定日期。理事会的议事规则规定每年举行三届会议,理事会决定在1947年举行三届或四届会议。为了节省预算资金,他要求该届会议在联合国所在地举行。(E/CN. 4/SR. 22第8页)

在回答张博士(中国)的问题时,斯坦奇克(Stanczyk)先生(秘书处)说,委员会的表决只是秘书处的一个指南。

张博士(中国)要求将以下发言列入摘要记录,以便分发给所有有关方面:

"人权委员会向秘书长表示感谢,感谢他的工作人员在筹备委员会第一届会议以及期间极其干练地开展了工作。

"劳吉尔(Laugier)先生发表的开幕词,为此他牺牲了个人的方便和健康,不会立即被忘记。委员会还认为,应该祝贺秘书长拥有汉弗莱博士这样的工作人员,后者在本届会议期间担任秘书。委员会工作的成功在很大程度上归功于汉弗莱博士对这项工作的精心规划、高度智慧和不懈奉献。

"委员会还希望对其主席专心致志和鼓舞人心的领导表示赞赏和感谢,他迷人和不可抗拒的耐心和幽默精神赢得了我们最真诚的钦佩。"

霍奇森上校(澳大利亚)、卡森教授(法国)、马利克先生(黎巴嫩)、杜克斯先生(英国)、里布尼卡尔(Ribnikar)先生(南斯拉夫)、埃贝德(Ebeid)先生(埃及)赞同中国代表表达的意见。(E/CN. 4/SR. 22第10页)

下午6时30分散会。

第二章　起草委员会第一届会议

　　1947 年 6 月 9 日至 25 日，联合国人权委员的专门起草委员会第一届会议，在美国纽约成功湖举行，本届会议共召开了 19 次会议。

　　回顾起草的最初经历，1947 年 2 月，根据人权委员会第一届会议作出的决定（E/259），在委员会会议结束后，由主席埃莉诺·罗斯福、副主席张彭春和报告员查尔斯·马利克组成的一个小型起草小组在联合国秘书处的协助下，开始起草《国际人权法案》。拟订《国际人权法案》初稿的任务交给了秘书处人权司司长约翰·汉弗莱。

　　在人权委员会主席于 1947 年 3 月 27 日致函经济及社会理事会主席（E/383）之后，该起草委员会得到扩大，除了中国、法国、黎巴嫩和美国的代表之外，还包括了澳大利亚、智利、法国、苏联和英国的代表。

　　秘书处编写的初稿作为 E/CN. 4/AC. 1/3 号文件国际权利法案纲要草案提交给了委员会。该文件包含 48 条概述人权的条款。秘书处提交起草委员会审议的其他文件载于 E/CN. 4/AC. 1/3 的增编文件。其中，E/CN. 4/AC. 1/3/Add. 1 列出了个人权利，随后是人权委员会成员的意见。该文件阐述了与提交委员会的其他国际宣言和建议草案的关系，并概述了个人人权与成员国宪法之间的关系。最后，它将每项人权与非政府组织提交的建议联系起来。而 E/CN. 4/AC. 1/3/Add. 2 列出了 48 条拟议条款，分为四章：自由、社会权利、平等和一般处置。

　　英国提出了一项法律文书形式的《国际人权法案》草案，E/CN. 4/AC. 1/4。这一提案也提交给了起草委员会，并在讨论中得到了审议。

　　在本届会议上，起草委员会设立了一个临时工作组，由法国代表（勒内·卡森）、黎巴嫩代表（查尔斯·马利克）和英国代表（杰弗莱·威尔逊）以及主席（埃莉诺·罗斯福）组成。临时工作组的任务是建议对秘书处提供的大纲草案的条款进行合理的重新安排;根据起草委员会的讨论,建议重新起草各条款;并建议起草委员会将条款的实质内容分为"宣言"和"公约"。在临时工作组内,根据秘书处的纲要草案重新起草一份宣言的任务交给了勒内·卡森(法国)。①

　　起草委员会提交人权委员会的报告(E/CN.4/21),包括国际人权宣言草案(附件F)和考虑列入公约的条款草案(附件G),以及人权司应起草委员会的要求编写的执行备忘录。

　　作为起草委员会副主席,中国代表张彭春参加了本届全部共计19次会议,并在每次会议上发言,其具体发言内容以"会议纪要""纪要影像"和"纪要译文"形式加以整理,并依次标明发言内容所在的页码,以便学者参考引用。

1. 张彭春在起草委员会
第一届第1次会议上的发言

　　《国际人权法案》起草委员会(简称"起草委员会")第一届第1次会议,于1947年6月9日上午11时,在纽约成功湖开幕。本次会议的主要议题是开幕式、选举起草委员会官员、通过临时议程、根据秘书处提供的文件编写《国际人权法案》初稿等。中国代表张彭春参加了本次会议,并在会议上发言,其具体发言内容②会议纪要、纪要影像和纪要译文如下:

---

①　UN Document:E/CN.4/AC.1/SR.6.

②　UN Document:E/CN.4/AC.1/SR.1, p.2, p.3, p.7.

【会议纪要】

2. *Election of Officers*

Col. HODGSON (Australia) referred to the decision of the Commission on Human Rights, that its officers, Mrs. Roosevelt (Chairman), Dr. Chang (Vice chairman), and Dr. Malik (Rapporteur) should undertake, with the assistance of the Secretariat, the task of formulating a preliminary draft of an International Bill of Human Rights. He suggested that the officers of the Drafting Committee be the same as those of the Commission on Human Rights.

3. *Adoption of Provisional Agenda (Document E/CN. 4/AC. 1/1)*

Dr. CHANG (China) moved the adoption of the provisional agenda as the agenda of the Drafting Committee. Prof. CASSIN (France) supported the motion. Col. Hodgson (Australia) pointed out that the question of implementation was not on the provisional agenda. He said that he felt that the Drafting Committee was obliged and the resolution relating to implementation adopted by the Commission on Human Rights to study this question.

DECISION: Without objection the provisional agenda was adopted unanimously as the agenda of the Drafting Committee.

6. *Preparation of a Preliminary Draft of an International Bill of Human Rights on the Basis of Documentation Supplied by the Secretariat*

The CHAIRMAN agreed that the preamble should be decided upon after the remainder of the draft bill had been agreed upon, but she pointed out that all Prof. Cassin had suggested was that a Committee be appointed on Wednesday. That Committee would consider the preamble and would be prepared to bring in a draft at the appropriate time. Prof. CASSIN agreed with this interpretation. Dr. CHANG (China) agreed to postpone the second meeting of the Committee until Wednesday. Dr. MALIK (Lebanon) also stated that in his opinion Wednesday was the right day. However, he did not believe that a final programme of work for Wednesday could be decided at that time. He stated that in his opinion any decision as to such a programme of work ought to be tentative and open to reconsideration.

【纪要影像】

2. Election of Officers

   Col. HODGSON (Australia) referred to the decision of the Commission on Human Rights, that its officers, Mrs. Roosevelt (Chairman), Dr. Chang (Vice-Chairman), and Dr. Malik (Rapporteur) should undertake, with the

3. Adoption of Provisional Agenda (Document E/CN.4/AC.1/1)

   Dr. CHANG (China) moved the adoption of the provisional agenda as the agenda of the Drafting Committee. Prof. CASSIN (France) supported the motion. Col. HODGSON (Australia) pointed out that the question of implementation was not on the provisional agenda. He said that he felt that the Drafting Committee was obliged, under the resolution relating to implementation adopted by the Commission on Human Rights, to study this question.

   DECISION: Without objection the provisional agenda was adopted unanimously as the agenda of the Drafting Committee.

图片 1.2.1:张彭春在起草委员会第一届第 1 次会议发言纪要(1)

6. <u>Preparation of a Preliminary Draft of an International Bill of Human Rights on the Basis of Documentation Supplied by the Secretariat</u>

The CHAIRMAN agreed that the preamble should be decided upon after the remainder of the draft bill had been agreed upon, but she pointed out that all Prof. Cassin had suggested was that a Committee be appointed on Wednesday. That Committee would consider the preamble and would be prepared to bring in a draft at the appropriate time. Prof. CASSIN agreed with this interpretation. Dr. CHANG (China) agreed to postpone the second meeting of the Committee until Wednesday. Dr. MALIK (Lebanon) also stated that in his opinion Wednesday was the right day. However, he did not believe that a final programme of work for Wednesday could be decided at that time. He stated that in his opinion any decision as to such a programme of work ought to be tentative and open to reconsideration.

图片 1.2.2：张彭春在起草委员会第一届第 1 次会议发言纪要(2)

【纪要译文】

2. 选举主席团成员

霍奇森上校(澳大利亚)提到人权委员会的决定,即其主席团成员罗斯福夫人(主席)、张博士(副主席)和马利克博士(报告员)应在秘书处的协助下,承担起编写国际人权法案初稿的任务。他建议起草委员会的主席团成员与人权委员会的主席团成员相同。

3. 通过临时议程(E/CN.4/AC.1/1 号文件)

张博士(中国)提议通过临时议程,作为起草委员会的议程。卡森教授(法国)支持该动议。霍奇森上校(澳大利亚)指出,执行问题不在临时议程上。他说,他认为起草委员会和人权委员会通过的关于执行的决议有义务研究这个问题。

决定:无异议一致通过临时议程,作为起草委员会的议程。

6. 根据秘书处提供的文件编写国际人权法案初稿

主席同意在就法案草案的其余部分达成一致意见后再决定序言,但她指出,卡森教授所建议的只是在星期三任命一个委员会。该委员会将审议序言,并准备在适当的时候提出草案。卡森教授同意这种解释。张博士(中国)同意将委员会第二次会议推迟到星期三举行。马利克博士(黎巴嫩)也说,他认为星期三是合适的日子。然而,他不认为星期三的最后工作方案能够在那个时候决定。他说,他认为关于这一工作计划的任何决定都应该是临时性的,可以重新考虑。

2. 张彭春在起草委员会
第一届第 2 次会议上的发言

1947 年 6 月 11 日上午 11 时,起草委员会第一届第 2 次会议,在纽约成功湖召开,本次会议的主要议题是讨论起草程序及秘书处大纲等。中国代表张彭春参加了本次会议,并在会议上发言,其具体发言内容①会议纪要、纪要影像和纪要译文如下:

【会议纪要】

Dr. CHANG (China) maintained that the discussion should proceed from the concrete to the abstract, that it should start with articles in the Secretariat draft on which all members of the Committee could agree and then go on to consider other articles appearing either in the United Kingdom draft or in a proposal by one of the other members. He urged that the Committee attain as wide a perspective as possible and that it be always conscious of the historical context of the formulation of this International Bill of Rights. He particularly urged that it not be allowed to become a stale duplication of previous Bills of Rights.

① UN Document: E/CN. 4/AC. 1/SR. 2, p. 4.

【纪要影像】

Dr. CHANG (China) maintained that the discussion should proceed from the concrete to the abstract, that it should start with articles in the Secretariat draft on which all members of the Committee could agree and then go on to consider other articles appearing either in the United Kingdom draft or in a proposal by one of the other members. He urged that the Committee attain as wide a perspective as possible and that it be always conscious of the historical context of the formulation of this International Bill of Rights. He particularly urged that it not be allowed to become a stale duplication of previous Bills of Rights.

图片 1.2.3：张彭春在起草委员会第一届第 2 次会议发言纪要

【纪要译文】

张博士(中国)坚持认为,讨论应当从具体到抽象,应该从委员会所有成员都能同意的秘书处草案中的条款开始,然后再审议英国草案或其他成员提案中的其他条款。他敦促委员会尽可能扩大视野,并始终意识到制定这一《国际人权法案》的历史背景。他特别敦促不要让它成为以前的《人权法案》的过时翻版。

3. 张彭春在起草委员会第一届第 3 次会议上的发言

1947 年 6 月 11 日下午 2 时 30 分,起草委员会第一届第 3 次会议,在纽约成功湖召开,本次会议的主要议题是审议英国代表团提交的草案及秘书处草案大纲等。中国代表张彭春参加了本次会议,并在会议上发言,其具体发言内容①会议纪要、纪要影像和纪要译文如下：

【会议纪要】

Article 14 of the Secretariat Draft Outline and Part II Article 13 of the United Kingdom Draft

Dr. CHANG (China) remarked that in his opinion China was perhaps the least bothersome nation insofar as religious discrimination was concerned. This fact, he added, had attracted the attention of the English philosophers in the eighteenth century. He added that the relative brevity or detail to be contained in each article of the draft would have to be discussed article by article.

Article 17 of the Secretariat Draft Outline and Part II Article 14 of the United Kingdom draft

Dr. CHANG (China) remarked that the United Kingdom draft put the affirmative ideas first and that this appeared to be a better arrangement.

2. Consideration of the Draft Outline of the International Bill of Rights prepared by the Division of Human Rights (E/CN. 4/AC. 1/3)

Mr. SANTA CRUZ (Chile) stated that he had no comments to make at the moment on either Article 1 or Article 8. Mr. HARRY (Australia) felt that attention should be drawn to the general duty of the individual comparing to each general right. He said that he would make a statement on this subject later. Dr. CHANG (China) remarked that the Committee should not tend to set up the possibility of the State and the individual being so sharply contrasted.

Article 2 of the Secretariat Draft Outline

Dr. CHANG (China) pointed out that the modification proposed by the United States was clearly worded. In his opinion it contained two different ideas which might be separated. The middle sentence might logically be permitted to

---

① UN Document：E/CN. 4/AC. 1/SR. 3, p. 4, p. 5, p. 9, p. 11, pp. 11-12, p. 13, p. 14.

stand by itself. He formally suggested using the United States modification by separating it into two articles, one a statement of the relation of individuals to the State and the other a statement of the relation of one individual to another.

Article 3 of the Secretariat Draft Outline and the United States Alternate Text

Dr. CHANG (China) observed that it was obvious that all members of the Committee would agree that the right to life should be included in a Bill of Rights. He suggested, however, that more thought should be put into a definition of the word "life"—was it intended to mean mere physical existence or did it imply something more than that?

Article 4 of the Secretariat Draft Outline

Dr. CHANG (China) felt that the article was tied up with the previous article and that both should be included in the Committee's draft. He felt that the draft somehow should stress the goodness of life itself.

Article 5 of the Secretariat Draft Outline

Dr. CHANG (China) called the attention of the members of the Committee to document E/CN. 4/AC. 1/3/Add. 2 and pointed out that there were seven articles numbered 5 to 11, all dealing with liberty of the person. He suggested that in the Committee's draft all of the articles on this subject should be grouped together. Dr. MALIK (Lebanon) supported his suggestion and Mr. WILSON (United Kingdom) said that he also was in favour of this arrangement.

Article 14 of the Secretariat Draft Outline and Part II Article 13 of the United Kingdom Draft

Dr. CHANG (China) remarked that in his opinion China was perhaps the least bothersome nation insofar as religious discrimination was concerned. This fact, he added, had attracted the attention of the English philosophers in the eighteenth century. He added that the relative brevity or detail to be contained in each article of the draft would have to be discussed article by article.

Article 17 of the Secretariat Draft Outline and Part II Article 14 of the United Kingdom Draft

Dr. CHANG (China) remarked that the United Kingdom draft put the affirmative ideas first and that this appeared to be a better arrangement.

2.   Consideration of the Draft Outline of the International Bill of Rights prepared by the Division of Human Rights (E/CN.4/AC.1/3)

Mr. SANTA CRUZ (Chile) stated that he had no comments to make at the moment on either Article 1 or Article 8. Mr. HARRY (Australia) felt that attention should be drawn to the general duty of the individual comparing to each general right. He said that he would make a statement on this subject later. Dr. CHANG (China) remarked that the Committee should not tend to set up the possibility of the State and the individual being so sharply contrasted.

图片 1.2.4：张彭春在起草委员会第一届第 3 次会议发言纪要(1)

Article 2 of the Secretariat Draft Outline

Dr. CHANG (China) pointed out that the modification proposed by the United States was clearly worded. In his opinion it contained two different ideas which might be separated. The middle sentence might logically be permitted to stand by itself. He formally suggested using the United States modification by separating it into two articles, one a statement of the relation of individuals to the State and the other a statement of the relation of one individual to another.

Dr. CHANG (China) pointed out that the modification proposed by the United States was clearly worded. In his opinion it contained two different ideas which might be separated. The middle sentence might logically be permitted to stand by itself. He formally suggested using the United States modification by separating it into two articles, one a statement of the relation of individuals to the State and the other a statement of the relation of one individual to another.

Article 3 of the Secretariat Draft Outline and the United States Alternate Text

Dr. CHANG (China) observed that it was obvious that all members of the Committee would agree that the right to life should be included in a Bill of Rights. He suggested, however, that more thought should be put into a definition of the word "life" - was it intended to mean mere physical existence or did it imply something more than that?

图片 1.2.5：张彭春在起草委员会第一届第 3 次会议发言纪要(2)

Article 4 of the Secretariat Draft Outline

Dr. CHANG (China) felt that the article was tied up with the previous article and that both should be included in the Committee's draft. He felt that the draft somehow should stress the goodness of life itself.

Article 5 of the Secretariat Draft Outline

Dr. CHANG (China) called the attention or the members of the Committee to document E/CN.4/AC.1/3/Add.2 and pointed out that there were seven articles numbered 5 to 11, all dealing with liberty of the person. He suggested that in the Committee's draft all of the articles on this subject should be grouped together. Dr. MALIK (Lebanon) supported his suggestion and Mr. WILSON (United Kingdom) said that he also was in favour of this arrangement.

图片 1.2.6:张彭春在起草委员会第一届第 3 次会议发言纪要(3)

【纪要译文】

秘书处草案大纲第 14 条和英国草案第二部分第 13 条

张博士(中国)说,他认为就宗教歧视而言,中国也许是麻烦最少的国家。他补充说,这个事实已经引起了 18 世纪英国哲学家的注意。他补充说,草案中每一项条款所包含的相对简洁或细节必须逐条讨论。

秘书处草案大纲第 17 条和英国草案第二部分第 14 条

张博士(中国)说,英国的草案把肯定的想法放在第一位,这似乎是一个更好的安排。

2. 审议人权司编写的国际权利法案草案大纲(E/CN.4/AC.1/3)

桑塔·克鲁兹(Santa Cruz)先生(智利)说,目前他对第 1 条和第 8 条都没有意见。哈里(Harry)先生(澳大利亚)认为,与每项一般权利相比,应提请注意个人的一般义务。他说他将在晚些时候就这个问题发表声明。张博士(中国)说,委员会不应倾向于设定国家和个人形成如此鲜明对比的可能性。

秘书处草案大纲第 2 条

张博士(中国)指出,美国提出的修改措辞明确。在他看来,它包含可以分开的两种不同的想法。中间那句话在逻辑上可以单独成立。他正式建议采用美国的修改,将其分为两条,一条是关于个人与国家关系的声明,另一条是关于个人与他人关系的声明。

秘书处草案大纲第 3 条和美国备选案文

张博士(中国)说,很明显,委员会所有成员都同意生命权应列入《人权法案》。然而,他建议应该对"生命"一词的定义进行更多的思考——它是指单纯的物质存在,还是意味着更多的东西?

秘书处草案大纲第 4 条

张博士(中国)认为该条与前一条联系在一起,两者都应列入委员会的草案。他觉得草案应该强调生命本身的美好。

秘书处草案大纲第 5 条

张博士(中国)提请委员会成员注意 E/CN. 4/AC. 1/3/Add. 2 号文件,并指出其中有 7 条,编号为 5 至 11,都涉及人身自由。他建议,在委员会的草案中,关于这一主题的所有条款应归在一起。马利克博士(黎巴嫩)支持他的建议,威尔逊(Wilson)先生(英国)说,他也赞成这种安排。

4. 张彭春在起草委员会
第一届第 4 次会议上的发言

1947 年 6 月 12 日上午 10 时 30 分,起草委员会第一届第 4 次会议,在纽约成功湖召开,本次会议的主要议题是逐条审议秘书处《国际人权法案》草案大纲。中国代表张彭春参加了本次会议,并在会议上发言,其具体发言内容①会议纪要、纪要影像和纪要译文如下:

---

① UN Document:E/CN. 4/AC. 1/SR. 4, p. 2, p. 3, p. 5, p. 7, p. 8, p. 9, p. 10, p. 11.

Article 6

Dr. CHANG (China) pointed out that it would be necessary to clarify the term "national emergency" used in the Secretariat draft.

Article 8

Dr. CHANG (China) also preferred the United States draft. He considered the phrase "prohibited by this Bill of Rights" unsuitable, and felt that reference to livelihood and work should be made at another point. "Contractual obligations," in his opinion, would have to be qualified inasmuch as laws relating to contracts differed throughout the world.

Article 10

Dr. CHANG (China) said he believed liberty of movement to be fundamental. A statement of principle might be drawn up, he felt, but its implementation would have to be the concern of the individual countries.

Article 21

The inclusion of the substance of Article 21 was sponsored by Dr. CHANG (China).

Article 28

The inclusion of the substance of Article 28 was sponsored by Dr. CHANG (China). He pointed out, however, that what the United Nations could do about grievances would have to be made clear.

Article 31

The inclusion of the substance of Article 31 was sponsored by Dr. CHANG (China). He felt, however, that a change of wording might be necessary.

Article 34

The inclusion of the substance of Article 34 was sponsored by Dr. MALIK (Lebanon) and Dr. CHANG (China).

联合国人权委员会和起草委员会

Article 47

Dr. CHANG (China) pointed out that Article 47 dealt with a method of implementing the Bill of Rights. For this reason he felt that it should not be discussed immediately.

Article 48

Dr. CHANG (China) envisaged three distinct documents: one a Declaration, drafted in simple phrases; the second a commentary on each Article of the Declaration; the third a series of proposals for implementation.

【纪要影像】

Article 6

Dr. CHANG (China) pointed out that it would be necessary to clarify the term "national emergency" used in the Secretariat draft.

Article 8

Dr. CHANG (China) also preferred the United States draft. He considered the phrase "prohibited by this Bill of Rights" unsuitable, and felt that reference to livelihood and work should be made at another point. "Contractual obligations," in his opinion, would have to be qualified inasmuch as laws relating to contracts differed throughout the world.

Article 10

Dr. CHANG (China) said he believed liberty of movement to be fundamental. A statement of principle might be drawn up, he felt, but its implementation would have to be the concern of the individual countries.

Article 21

The inclusion of the substance of Article 21 was sponsored by Dr. CHANG (China).

图片 1.2.7:张彭春在起草委员会第一届第 4 次会议发言纪要(1)

Article 28

The inclusion of the substance of Article 28 was sponsored by Dr. CHANG (China). He pointed out, however, that what the United Nations could do about grievances would have to be made clear.

Article 31

The inclusion of the substance of Article 31 was sponsored by Dr. CHANG (China). He felt, however, that a change of wording might be necessary.

Article 34

The inclusion of the substance of Article 34 was sponsored by Dr. MALIK (Lebanon) and Dr. CHANG (China).

Article 47

Dr. CHANG (China) pointed out that Article 47 dealt with a method of implementing the Bill of Rights. For this reason he felt that it should not be discussed immediately.

Article 48

Dr. CHANG (China) envisaged three distinct documents: one a Declaration, drafted in simple phrases; the second a commentary on each Article of the Declaration; the third a series of proposals for implementation.

图片 1.2.8:张彭春在起草委员会第一届第 4 次会议发言纪要(2

【纪要译文】

第 6 条

张博士(中国)指出,有必要澄清秘书处草案中使用的"国家紧急状态"一词。

第 8 条

张博士(中国)也倾向于美国的草案。他认为"本《人权法案》所禁止的"一语不合适,并认为应在另一处提及生计和工作。他认为,"合同义务"必须加以限定,因为世界各地有关合同的法律各不相同。

第 10 条

张博士(中国)说,他认为迁徙自由是根本。他认为,可以起草一份原则声明,但其实施必须是各个国家的事。

第 21 条

张博士(中国)提议列入第 21 条的内容。

第 28 条

张博士(中国)提议列入第 28 条的内容。然而,他指出,必须明确联合国可以对冤情做些什么。

第 31 条

张博士(中国)提议列入第 31 条的内容。然而,他认为可能有必要改变措辞。

第 34 条

马利克博士(黎巴嫩)和张博士(中国)提议列入第 34 条的内容。

第 47 条

张博士(中国)指出,第 47 条涉及实施《人权法案》的方法。因此,他认为不应该立即讨论这个问题。

第 48 条

张博士(中国)设想了三份不同的文件:一份是《宣言》,用简单的短句起草;第二份是对《宣言》每一条款的评论;第三是一系列实施建议。

5. 张彭春在起草委员会第一届第 5 次会议上的发言

1947 年 6 月 12 日下午 2 时 30 分,起草委员会第一届第 5 次会议,在纽约成功湖召开,本次会议的主要议题是根据秘书处提供的文件编写《国际人权法案》初稿。中国代表张彭春参加了本次会议,并在会议上发言,其具体发言内容①会议纪要、纪要影像和纪要译文如下：

【会议纪要】

Dr. CHANG (China) stated that at this stage the Committee could only hope to draw up a list of general principles and rights, putting them into the form of a draft Declaration for consideration by the General Assembly. A commentary might be attached to that list of principles and rights, defining the terms in simple formulations. Later the Committee could consider practical methods of implementation. He emphasized that the number of articles should not be limited at this stage, and that the Committee might, at the first stage, allow itself to err on the side of too many articles rather than too few.

【纪要影像】

Dr. CHANG (China) stated that at this stage the Committee could only hope to draw up a list of general principles and rights, putting them into the form of a draft Declaration for consideration by the General Assembly. A commentary might be attached to that list of principles and rights, defining the terms in simple formulations. Later the Committee could consider practical methods of implementation. He emphasized that the number of articles should not be limited at this stage, and that the Committee might, at the first stage, allow itself to err on the side of too many articles rather than too few.

图片 1.2.9：张彭春在起草委员会第一届第 5 次会议发言纪要

【纪要译文】

张博士(中国)说,在现阶段,委员会只能希望草拟一份一般原则和权利清单,以宣言草案的形式提交大会审议。该原则和权利清单可附有一条评注,用简单的措辞对术语进行定义。以后,委员会可以考虑实际的实施

---

① UN Document：E/CN.4/AC.1/SR.5, pp.3-4.

方法。他强调说,在现阶段不应限制条款的数量,委员会在第一阶段可能会犯条款过多而不是过少的错误。

6. 张彭春在起草委员会第一届第 6 次会议上的发言

1947 年 6 月 13 日上午 10 时 30 分,起草委员会第一届第 6 次会议,在纽约成功湖召开,本次会议的主要议题是根据秘书处提供的文件编写《国际人权法案》初稿。中国代表张彭春参加了本次会议,并在会议上发言,其具体发言内容①会议纪要、纪要影像和纪要译文如下:

【会议纪要】

Prof. CASSIN (France) observed that either one group could undertake the writing of the the Manifesto and one group the writing of the Convention, or alternatively each group could take responsibility for certain parts of each document. He thought the suggestion of the United Kingdom was a practical one. Dr. CHANG (China) remarked that the United Kingdom proposal involved every member of the Committee. He thought the suggestion was not impractical, but that it should be made clear that these were not drafting committees but small working groups, each undertaking a part of the preliminary work of the Drafting Committee. He also thought that the division of groups should not be such that the Drafting Committee would be divided permanently.

Dr. CHANG (China) suggested that the Committee instruct the working group to go over the material which had been discussed up to that point and to report back to the Committee as a whole. He thought that the group need do no

---

① UN Document: E/CN. 4/AC. 1/SR. 6, p. 7, p. 8.

more than summarize the discussions and perhaps produce some concrete suggestions. Mr. Wilson (United Kingdom) said it was not very difficult to understand exactly what the working group was to do. The Committee had (1) discussed the Secretariat draft; (2) agreed in substance regarding matters which should find a place in the document; and (3) expressed the opinion that two documents should be prepared. He thought the members of the Committee should now set about drafting the documents themselves, and added that confusion might result if there was a horizontal division of work between the two documents. Dr. CHANG (China) said he would like to have the small group undertake (1) a logical rearrangement of the Secretariat draft, (2) a rough redrafting of the various articles on the basis of discussions which had taken place in the Committee, and (3) a division of the work indicating which articles would require international conventions and which would not.

DECISION: The Committee decided to appoint a Temporary Working Group consisting of the representatives of France, the Lebanon and the United Kingdom, the functions of the Group to be

1. To suggest a logical rearrangement of the articles of the Draft Outline supplied by the Secretariat;

2. To suggest a redraft of the various articles in the light of the discussions of the Drafting Committee;

3. To recommend to the Drafting Committee the division of the substance of the articles between a Manifesto and a Convention.

【纪要影像】

Prof. CASSIN (France) observed that either one group could undertake the writing of the Manifesto and one group the writing of the Convention, or alternatively each group could take responsibility for certain parts of each document. He thought the suggestion of the United Kingdom was a practical one. Dr. CHANG (China) remarked that the United Kingdom proposal involved every member of the Committee. He thought the suggestion was not impractical, but that it should be made clear that these were not drafting committees but small working groups, each undertaking a part of the preliminary work of the Drafting Committee. He also thought that the division of groups should not be such that the Drafting Committee would be divided permanently.

图片 1.2.10：张彭春在起草委员会第一届第 6 次会议发言纪要(1)

Dr. CHANG (China) suggested that the Committee instruct the working group to go over the material which had been discussed up to that point and to report back to the Committee as a whole. He thought that the group need do no more than summarize the discussions and perhaps produce some concrete suggestions. Mr. WILSON (United Kingdom) said it was not very difficult to understand exactly what the working group was to do. The Committee had (1) discussed the Secretariat draft; (2) agreed in substance regarding matters which should find a place in the document; and (3) expressed the opinion that two documents should be prepared. He thought the members of the Committee should now set about drafting the documents themselves, and added that confusion might result if there was a horizontal division of work between the two documents. Dr. CHANG (China) said he would like to have the small group undertake (1) a logical rearrangement of the Secretariat draft, (2) a rough redrafting of the various articles on the basis of discussions which had taken place in the Committee, and (3) a division of the work indicating which articles would require international conventions and which would not.

图片图片 1.2.11：张彭春在起草委员会第一届第 6 次会议发言纪要(2)

```
DECISION: The Committee decided to appoint a Temporary Working Group
         consisting of the representatives of France, the Lebanon
         and the United Kingdom, the functions of the Group to be

         1.  To suggest a logical rearrangement of the articles of
         the Draft Outline supplied by the Secretariat;

         2.  To suggest a redraft of the various articles in the
         light of the discussions of the Drafting Committee;

         3.  To recommend to the Drafting Committee the division
         of the substance of the articles between a Manifesto and
         a Convention.
```

图片 1.2.12:张彭春在起草委员会第一届第 6 次会议发言纪要(3)

【纪要译文】

卡森教授(法国)指出,要么一个小组负责起草宣言,一个小组负责起草公约,要么每个小组负责每个文件的某些部分。他认为英国的建议是切合实际的。张博士(中国)说,英国的提议涉及委员会的每一个成员。他认为这一建议并非不切实际,但应该明确指出,这些不是起草委员会,而是小型工作组,每个工作组承担起草委员会的一部分初步工作。他还认为,分组不应导致起草委员会永久分裂。

张博士(中国)建议委员会指示工作组审查到目前为止已经讨论过的材料,并向整个委员会报告。他认为,工作组只需要总结讨论情况,或许提出一些具体建议。威尔逊(Wilson)先生(英国)说,确切理解工作组要做什么并不十分困难。委员会(1)讨论了秘书处的草案;(2)就应在文件中占有一席之地的事项达成实质一致;(3)表示认为应准备两份文件。他认为委员会成员现在应该自己着手起草文件,并补充说,如果两份文件之间有横向分工,可能会造成混乱。张博士(中国)说,他希望小组能够(1)对秘书处的草案进行合乎逻辑的重新安排,(2)根据委员会进行的讨论对各条款进行粗略的重新起草,以及(3)进行分工,指出国际公约需要哪些条款,不需要哪些条款。

决定:委员会决定任命一个由法国、黎巴嫩和英国代表组成的临时工作组,该工作组的职能是

1.建议对秘书处提供的草案大纲的条款进行合理的重新安排;

2.根据起草委员会的讨论,建议重新起草各条款;

3.向起草委员会建议将条款的实质内容分为宣言和公约。

7.张彭春在起草委员会
第一届第7次会议上的发言

1947年6月17日上午11时,起草委员会第一届第7次会议,在纽约成功湖召开,本次会议的主要议题是根据秘书处提供的文件编写《国际人权法案》初稿。中国代表张彭春参加了本次会议,并在会议上发言,其具体发言内容①会议纪要、纪要影像和纪要译文如下:

【会议纪要】

Dr. CHANG (China) said the Working Group had made a significant step towards orderliness. He felt, however, that the entire Committee should go over each of the proposed articles first.

The CHAIRMAN stated that Dr. Chang apparently agreed with the position of the United States, that there should be a Declaration, followed by one or more Conventions.

Dr. MALIK (Lebanon) pointed out that the Drafting Committee already had agreed that two documents should be prepared, one a general Declaration and the other a Convention, to be submitted simultaneously to the Commission on Human Rights.

Regarding the Declaration, he felt that it should be very brief but should include all the basic principles of a Bill of Human Rights. It should be a fundamental matrix of doctrine from which positive law might be elaborated, a battle

---

① UN Document: E/CN. 4/AC. 1/SR. 7, pp. 3-4.

cry for freedom, for liberty; a Credo embodying the basic philosophy of the U-
nited Nations regarding human rights. From this declaration, there might flow
one or more conventions. The world was awaiting more than mere resolutions. It
wanted maximum assurance against the infringement of human rights and actual
conventions. He pointed out there was already agreement on certain things that
should be made the subject of Conventions at once. The field of personal liberties—protection of the bodily integrity of man—was one such subject. He a-
greed with Dr. Chang (China) that the Committee might work as a whole for
sometime. He felt it should attempt to draft two documents:

1. a Declaration, brief and all-inclusive, and

2. a summary of the maximum agreement as to what ought to go into one or
more Conventions.

【纪要影像】

Dr. CHANG (China) said the Working Group had made a significant
step towards orderliness. He felt, however, that the entire Committee
should go over each of the proposed articles first.

The CHAIRMAN stated that Dr. Chang apparently agreed with the
position of the United States, that there should be a Declaration,
followed by one or more Conventions.

图片 1.2.13:张彭春在起草委员会第一届第 7 次会议发言纪要(1)

Dr. MALIK (Lebanon) pointed out that the Drafting Committee already had agreed that two documents should be prepared, one a general Declaration and the other a Convention, to be submitted simultaneously to the Commission on Human Rights.

Regarding the Declaration, he felt that it should be very brief but should include all the basic principles of a Bill of Human Rights. It should be a fundamental matrix of doctrine from which positive law might be elaborated, a battle cry for freedom, for liberty; a Credo embodying the basic philosophy of the United Nations regarding human rights. From this declaration, there might flow one or more conventions. The world was awaiting more than mere resolutions. It wanted maximum assurance against the infringement of human rights and actual conventions. He pointed out there was already agreement on certain things that should be made the subject of Conventions at once. The field of personal liberties - protection of the bodily integrity of man - was one such subject. He agreed with Dr. Chang (China) that the Committee might work as a whole for sometime. He felt it should attempt to draft two documents:

1. a Declaration, brief and all-inclusive, and

2. a summary of the maximum agreement as to what ought to go into one or more Conventions.

图片 1.2.14：张彭春在起草委员会第一届第 7 次会议发言纪要(2)

【纪要译文】

张博士(中国)说,工作组朝着井然有序的方向迈出了重要一步。然而,他认为,整个委员会应该首先审查每一项拟议的条款。

主席说,张博士显然同意美国的立场,即应该有一项宣言,随之是一项或多项公约。

马利克博士(黎巴嫩)指出,起草委员会已经同意编写两份文件,一份是一般性宣言,另一份是公约,同时提交人权委员会。

关于宣言,他认为宣言应该非常简短,但应该包括《人权法案》的所有基本原则。它应该是一个理论的基本发源地,实在法可以从这个发源地中得到阐述,是一个为自由而战的口号;这一信条体现了联合国关于人权的基本哲学。从这个声明中,可能会产生一个或多个公约。世界期待的不仅仅是决议。它希望最大限度地保证不侵犯人权和不违背实际公约。他指出,已经就应该立即成为公约主题的某些事项达成了一致意见。个人自由领域——保护人的身体完整——就是这样一个主题。他同意张博士(中国)的意见,委员会可以作为一个整体来工作一段时间。他觉得应该尝试起草两个文件:

1.一个简洁和全面的宣言,和

2.关于应该在一个或多个公约中包含哪些内容的最大一致意见的概述。

8. 张彭春在起草委员会
第一届第 8 次会议上的发言

1947 年 6 月 17 日下午 2 时 30 分,起草委员会第一届第 8 次会议,在纽约成功湖召开,本次会议的主要议题是审议工作组提交的《国际人权法案》草案序言及第 1-6 条和第 7-44 条。中国代表张彭春参加了本次会议,并在会议上发言,其具体发言内容①会议纪要、纪要影像和纪要译文如下:

【会议纪要】

Article 1

The CHAIRMAN read Article 1. She stated that the Unitcd States government was not satisfied with the present wording, and invited the members to suggest possible revisions. Dr. CHANG (China) thought that there should be

① UN Document:E/CN. 4/AC. 1/SR. 8, p. 2, p. 5, p. 6, p. 7, p. 9, p. 13.

added to the idea of "reason," the idea which in a literal translation from the Chinese would be "two-man-mindedness". The English equivalent might be "sympathy" or "consciousness of his fellow men." This new idea, he felt, might well be included as an essential human attribute. The CHAIRMAN agreed that Article 1 might be changed to read in substance: "All men, as members of one family, must be free and equal in dignity and rights. Being endowed with reason, they must have the additional sense of understanding of their fellow men about them." She felt that the wording of this would need revision.

Article 6

The CHAIRMAN read Article 6. Dr. CHANG suggested that the word "dignity" be used instead of "life" so that the first sentence would read: "There shall be respect for human dignity." He also felt that the sentence in Article 5 which the United States considered unnecessary might be eliminated.

Article 8

The CHAIRMAN read Article 8. She suggested that it might be improved if changed to read "There shall be inviolability of privacy, home, correspondence and reputation, protected by law."

Dr. CHANG (China), while agreeing with Mr. WILSON's suggestion, felt that certain phrases or sentences appearing in Articles 6 to 13 might be extracted for use in the Declaration. Inclusion of the whole of these articles in the Declaration would make it too complex, he said.

Article 12

Mr. CHANG (China) recalled his previous proposal that in addition to a Declaration and one or more conventions there might be a third category—a commentary. He felt that there should be not more than twenty articles in the Declaration. The commentary would follow those articles which needed to be explained, but which could not be dealt with immediately in a convention. The CHAIRMAN agreed that his suggestion was a good one.

Article 13

Dr. CHANG (China) expressed the hope that by the following day a more concise Declaration could be prepared under the supervision of Professor CASSIN, and a proposed list of topics to be included on conventions by the Secretariat. Professor CASSIN, while agreeing, declared that in his opinion it was incorrect to start with the idea that the Declaration should contain a certain number of Articles it should contain a certain number of ideas and these ideas should determine the number of Articles.

Mr. HARRY (Australia) felt that Dr. Chang's proposal was a practical one. The CHAIRMAN expressed the view that the full Committee should first go through the rest of the Articles presented by Professor CASSIN. There was no objection to this procedure.

Article 14

The CHAIRMAN read Article 14. Dr. CHANG felt that the phrase "legal personality" was a little too technical. Professor CASSIN attempted to explain the philosophical basis of the articles appearing in Chapter IV, headed "Legal Status." The recognition of the juridical personality of all human beings is a second means of abolishing slavery, he pointed out. Slaves were once considered as instruments, as chattels, not as beings who could have rights. Also, just before the war there were instances when the right to marry was refused to refugees under the pretext that they did not have all the necessary papers and documents, that they did not have an authorization of residence, an official permit, and so forth, although they might have been living in a particular country for several years. Through such small detailed regulations the most fundamental human rights were denied. Chapter IV attempts to counteract that situation, he concluded, and in his opinion Article 14 should state that every human being has certain juridical and human rights regardless of whether or not he is a citizen, including the right to marry and the right to conclude contracts. The texts might be difficult to understand, he realized, but they touched upon the rights of millions of human beings in a most concrete and practical manner.

Article 18

The CHAIRMAN read Article 18, and suggested that the fourth paragraph, which seemed to her to be included in the first, did not appear to be necessary. Dr. CHANG (China) felt that the first two paragraphs might be taken to include the last two. He suggested that the first two might serve as a declaration of principle, the latter two as "commentary". Mr. WILSON (United Kingdom) agreed with Dr. CHANG, but felt that the Article might be limited still further, to the first paragraph, "Everyone has a right to own personal property". Regarding the second paragraph, he asked what would happen if a person were fined, by a court, an amount of money which involved selling his automobile. He would be deprived of his property, but whether or not this could be considered for the public welfare was a difficult question. He felt that it was impossible to go beyond saying, as a statement of principle, that a person should have the things he needs in order to carry on and to enjoy his everyday life.

Article 20

Mr. HARRY (Australia) hoped that the bracket of freedoms outlined in Chapter V could be expanded and given precise definition in a Convention, and condensed and crystallized for inclusion in the Declaration. Dr. CHANG (China) suggested as a drafting change that the word "morals" be eliminated, since it already was implied in the phrase "rights and freedoms of others"; and that the sentence might then read, in part, "... to protect public order and the rights and freedoms of others".

Article 24

Professor CASSIN (France) felt that the right of petition might be included among the political rights of man. He suggested that Articles 20, 21, 22, and 23 might be grouped together in the Declaration. Dr. CHANG (China) agreed, and added that Articles 24 and 25 also might be grouped, as political rights. Mr. WILSON (United Kingdom) felt that the substance of Articles 20, 21, 22, and 23 should be included in a convention.

【纪要影像】

Article 1

    The CHAIRMAN read Article 1. She stated that the United States government was not satisfied with the present wording, and invited the members to suggest possible revisions. Dr. CHANG (China) thought that there should be added to the idea of "reason," the idea which in a literal translation from the Chinese would be "two-man-mindedness." The English equivalent might be "sympathy" or "consciousness of his fellow men." This new idea, he felt, might well be included as an essential human attribute. The CHAIRMAN agreed that Article 1 might be changed to read in substance: "All men, as members of one family, must be free and equal in dignity and rights. Being endowed with reason, they must have the additional sense of understanding of their fellow men about them." She felt that the wording of this would need revision.

Article 6

    The CHAIRMAN read Article 6. Dr. CHANG suggested that the word "dignity" be used instead of "life" so that the first sentence would read: "There shall be respect for human dignity." He also felt that the sentence in Article 5 which the United States considered unnecessary might be eliminated.

图片 1.2.15：张彭春在起草委员会第一届第 8 次会议发言纪要(1)

Article 8

    The CHAIRMAN read Article 8. She suggested that it might be improved if changed to read "There shall be inviolability of privacy, home, correspondence and reputation, protected by law."

    Dr. CHANG (China), while agreeing with Mr. WILSON's suggestion, felt that certain phrases or sentences appearing in Articles 6 to 13 might be extracted for use in the Declaration. Inclusion of the whole of these articles in the Declaration would make it too complex, he said.

联合国人权委员会和起草委员会

Article 12

Dr. CHANG (China) recalled his previous proposal that in addition to a Declaration and one or more conventions there might be a third category - a commentary. He felt that there should be not more than twenty articles in the Declaration. The commentary would follow those articles which needed to be explained, but which could not be dealt with immediately in a convention. The CHAIRMAN agreed that his suggestion was a good one.

图片 1.2.16:张彭春在起草委员会第一届第 8 次会议发言纪要(2)

Article 13

Dr. CHANG (China) expressed the hope that by the following day a more concise Declaration could be prepared under the supervision of Professor CASSIN, and a proposed list of topics to be included on conventions by the Secretariat. Professor CASSIN, while agreeing, declared that in his opinion it was incorrect to start with the idea that the Declaration should contain a certain number of Articles it should contain a certain number of ideas and these ideas should determine the number of Articles.

Mr. HARRY (Australia) felt that Dr. Chang's proposal was a practical one. The CHAIRMAN expressed the view that the full Committee should first go through the rest of the Articles presented by Professor CASSIN. There was no objection to this procedure.

图片 1.2.17:张彭春在起草委员会第一届第 8 次会议发言纪要(3)

Article 14

The CHAIRMAN read Article 14. Dr. CHANG felt that the phrase "legal personality" was a little too technical. Professor CASSIN attempted to explain the philosophical basis of the articles appearing in Chapter IV, headed "Legal Status." The recognition of the juridical personality of all human beings is a second means of abolishing slavery, he pointed out. Slaves were once considered as instruments, as chattels, not as beings who could have rights. Also, just before the war there were instances when the right to marry was refused to refugees under the pretext that they did not have all the necessary papers and documents, that they did not have an authorization of residence, an official permit, and so forth, although they might have been living in a particular country for several years. Through such small detailed regulations the most fundamental human rights were denied. Chapter IV attempts to counteract that situation, he concluded, and in his opinion Article 14 should state that every human being has certain juridical and human rights regardless of whether or not he is a citizen, including the right to marry and the right to conclude contracts. The texts might be difficult to understand, he realized, but they touched upon the rights of millions of human beings in a most concrete and practical manner.

图片 1.2.18:张彭春在起草委员会第一届第 8 次会议发言纪要(4)

Article 18

The CHAIRMAN read Article 18, and suggested that the fourth paragraph, which seemed to her to be included in the first, did not appear to be necessary. Dr. CHANG (China) felt that the first two paragraphs might be taken to include the last two. He suggested that the first two might serve as a declaration of principle, the latter two as "commentary". Mr. WILSON (United Kingdom) agreed with Dr. CHANG, but felt that the Article might be limited still further, to the first paragraph, "Everyone has a right to own personal property". Regarding the second paragraph, he asked what would happen if a person were fined, by a court, an amount of money which involved selling his automobile. He would be deprived of his property, but whether or not this could be considered for the public welfare was a difficult question. He felt that it was impossible to go beyond saying, as a statement of principle, that a person should have the things he needs in order to carry on and to enjoy his everyday life.

Article 20

Mr. HARRY (Australia) hoped that the bracket of freedoms outlined in Chapter V could be expanded and given precise definition in a Convention, and condensed and crystallized for inclusion in the Declaration. Dr. CHANG (China) suggested as a drafting change that the word "morals" be eliminated, since it already was implied in the phrase "rights and freedoms of others"; and that the sentence might then read, in part, "...to protect public order and the rights and freedoms of others".

Article 24

Professor CASSIN (France) felt that the right of petition might be included among the political rights of man. He suggested that Articles 20, 21, 22, and 23 might be grouped together in the Declaration. Dr. CHANG (China) agreed, and added that Articles 24 and 25 also might be grouped, as political rights. Mr. WILSON (United Kingdom) felt that the substance of Articles 20, 21, 22, and 23 should be included in a convention.

图片1.2.19:张彭春在起草委员会第一届第8次会议发言纪要(5)

【纪要译文】

第1条

主席宣读了第1条。她说,美国政府对目前的措辞不满意,并请成员们提出可能的修改意见。张博士(中国)认为应在"理性"观念中加上中文里"仁"的思想。英语中的对应词可能是"同情"或"对他人的意识"。他认为,这一新观点很可能被列为人类的一种基本属性。主席同意,第1条的实质内容可以改为:"所有人作为一个家庭的成员,必须自由,在尊严和权利上一律平等。被赋予理性,他们还必须能够理解他们的同胞对他们的感觉。"她认为这一措辞需要修改。

第6条

主席宣读了第6条。张博士建议用"尊严"一词代替"生命",这样第一句就可以读作:"应当尊重人的尊严"。他还认为第5条中美国认为不必要的句子可以删除。

第8条

主席宣读了第8条。她建议,如果改为"隐私、住宅、通信和名誉不受侵犯,受法律保护",可能会有所改进。

张博士(中国)虽然同意威尔逊先生的建议,但认为第6至第13条中的某些短语或句子可以摘录出来用于宣言。他说,将所有这些条款纳入宣言会使其过于复杂。

第 12 条

张先生(中国)回顾了他以前的提议,即除了一项宣言和一项或多项公约之外,还可以有第三个类别,即评注。他认为宣言中的条款不应超过二十条。评注将跟随那些需要解释但不能立即在公约中处理的条款。主席同意他的建议是好的。

第 13 条

张博士(中国)表示,希望到第二天,在卡森教授的指导下,能够拟出一份更为简洁的宣言,并由秘书处拟出一份列入公约的专题清单。卡森教授表示同意,但他认为,一开始就认为宣言应该包含一定数量的条款是不正确的,应该包含一定数量的想法,而这些想法应该决定条款的数量。

哈里(Harry)先生(澳大利亚)认为,张博士的建议是切合实际的。主席认为,全体委员会应首先阅读卡森教授提交的其余条款。没有人反对这一程序。

第 14 条

主席宣读了第 14 条。张博士认为"法律人格"一词有点太专业了。卡森教授试图解释出现在题为"法律地位"的第四章中的条款的哲学基础。他指出,承认所有人类的法律人格是废除奴隶制的第二个手段。奴隶曾经被认为是工具,是动产,而不是可以拥有权利的存在。此外,就在战争之前,有很多难民被拒绝结婚的例子,借口是他们没有所有必要的文件和证件,他们没有居住授权或官方许可等,尽管他们可能已经在某个国家生活了多年。通过如此细微而详细的规定,最基本的人权被剥夺了。他总结说,第四章试图改变这种情况,他认为第 14 条应该规定,每个人都有某些法律权利和人权,不论他是否是公民,包括结婚的权利和签订合同的权利。他意识到,这些文本可能难以理解,但它们以最具体和实用的方式触及了数百万人的权利。

第 18 条

主席阅读了第 18 条,并认为第四段似乎已包括在第一段中,似乎没有必要。张博士(中国)觉得前两段可以理解为包括最后两段。他建议,前两段可以作为原则声明,后两段可以作为"评注"。威尔逊先生(英国)同意张博士的意见,但认为该条可进一步限于第一段,"人人有权拥有个人财产"。关于第二段,他问,如果一个人被法院罚款一笔涉及出售其汽车的款项,会发生什么情况。他将被剥夺他的财产,但这是否能被视为公共福利是一个困难的问题。他认为,作为一种原则声明,一个人应该拥有他继续生活和享受日常生活所需要的东西,这是不可能超越的。

第 20 条

哈里先生(澳大利亚)希望第五章中概述的自由范围可以扩大,并在一份声明中给予精确的定义,并加以浓缩和具体化,以便列入宣言。张博士(中国)建议,作为一项措辞上的修改,删除"道德"一词,因为它已经包含在"他人的权利和自由"一语中;这句话可能会部分读作:"……保护公共秩序和他人的权利和自由。"

第 24 条

卡森教授(法国)认为请愿权可以包括在人的政治权利中。他建议将第 20、21、22 和 23 条放在宣言中。张博士(中国)表示同意,并补充说,第24 条和第 25 条也可以合并为政治权利。威尔逊先生(英国)认为,第 20、21、22 和 23 条的实质内容应列入一项公约。

9. 张彭春在起草委员会第一届第 9 次会议上的发言

1947 年 6 月 18 日上午 10 时 30 分,起草委员会第一届第 9 次会议,在纽约成功湖召开,本次会议的主要议题是审议法国代表关于国际人权宣言条款的议案。中国代表张彭春参加了本次会议,并在会议上就第 29 条、第 30 条和第 32 条发言,其具体发言内容①会议纪要、纪要影像和纪要译文如下:

---

① UN Document:E/CN. 4/AC. 1/SR. 9, p. 4, p. 5, p. 6, p. 8.

Article 29

The CHAIRMAN read Article 29. She pointed out that the English translation did not exactly correspond to the French text. She reminded the Committee that the words "public functions" were to be understood as "public employment". Speaking as a Member, Mrs. ROOSEVELT (United States of America) said that she would prefer to delete the second sentence of Article 29. Dr. CHANG (China) stated that he would prefer to replace the last sentence of Article 29 by the second part of Article 31 of the Secretariat draft Outline (document E/CN. 4/AC. 1/3); reading: "Appointments to the Civil Service shall be by competitive examination". He stressed the fact that as public functions grew more and more numerous and important, all men should have the right to participate in the public life by holding public office. He reviewed the experience of China in this matter and pointed out that competitive examination for public jobs had existed in his country for centuries. In his opinion "free competitive examinations" should be considered as one of the ways to a truly free democracy.

Prof. KORETSKY (Union of Soviet Socialist Republics) asked Dr. CHANG whether or not the complexity and the number of competitive examinations in China had not in part eliminated from public office the common man, who was not able to get the education necessary to be able to pass such examinations. Dr. CHANG (China) explained that this, in his opinion, was not a correct interpretation of Chinese history. He thought that a competitive examination was one way, in settled community life, to give an equal chance of access to public office. Mr. HARRY (Australia) thought that a real equality of opportunity should be given to people to enable them to gain access to public service. He did not feel, however, that a Declaration should specify exactly how appointments should be made. He felt that it could be enough to state the general principle of equal opportunity of access to public office in Article 29, eliminating the last part of the Article.

Article 30

Dr. CHANG (China) called the attention of the Committee to Article 27. In this Article "elections" were mentioned as a method of achieving human rights. He felt that competitive examinations were also a method of achieving human rights, and should therefore be mentioned.

Article 32

Mr. HARRY (Australia) felt that the Article should be formulated from the point of view of human rights rather than the rights of the State. He favoured the Article in the Cuban proposal. Mr. SANTA CRUZ (Chile) pointed out that the principle of asylum had always guided his country, and that he was in favour of including it in the Declaration. Prof. CASSIN (France) proposed the following text: "Every one has the right to flee from persecution and to try to find asylum on the soil of such a country as is willing to grant it to him". Dr. CHANG (China) stated that he would like to see the individual's right to asylum and the State's right to grant asylum stated in the Declaration.

Article 29

The CHAIRMAN read Article 29. She pointed out that the English translation did not exactly correspond to the French text. She reminded the Committee that the words "public functions" were to be understood as "public employment". Speaking as a Member, Mrs. ROOSEVELT (United States of America) said that she would prefer to delete the second sentence of Article 29. Dr. CHANG (China) stated that he would prefer to replace the last sentence of Article 29 by the second part of Article 31 of the Secretariat draft Outline (document E/CN.4/AC.1/3), reading: "Appointments to the Civil Service shall be by competitive examination". He stressed the fact that as public functions grew more and more numerous and important, all men should have the right to participate in the public life by holding public office. He reviewed the experience of China in this matter and pointed out that competitive examination for public jobs had existed in his country for centuries. In his opinion "free competitive examinations" should be considered as one of the ways to a truly free democracy.

图片 1.2.20:张彭春在起草委员会第一届第 9 次会议发言纪要(1)

Prof. KORETSKY (Union of Soviet Socialist Republics) asked Dr. CHANG whether or not the complexity and the number of competitive examinations in China had not in part eliminated from public office the common man, who was not able to get the education necessary to be able to pass such examinations. Dr. CHANG (China) explained that this, in his opinion, was not a correct interpretation of Chinese history. He thought that a competitive examination was one way, in settled community life, to give an equal chance of access to public office. Mr. HARRY (Australia) thought that a real equality of opportunity should be given to people to enable them to gain access to public service. He did not feel, however, that a Declaration should specify exactly how appointments should be made. He felt that it would be enough to state the general principle of equal opportunity of access to public office in Article 29, eliminating the last part of the Article.

图片 1.2.21:张彭春在起草委员会第一届第 9 次会议发言纪要(2)

Article 30

Dr. CHANG (China) called the attention of the Committee to Article 27. In this Article "elections" were mentioned as a method of achieving human rights. He felt that competitive examinations were also a method of achieving human rights, and should therefore be mentioned.

Article 32

Mr. HARRY (Australia) felt that the Article should be formulated from the point of view of human rights rather than the rights of the State. He favoured the Article in the Cuban proposal. Mr. SANTA CRUZ (Chile) pointed out that the principle of asylum had always guided his country, and that he was in favour of including it in the Declaration. Prof. CASSIN (France) proposed the following text: "Every one has the right to flee from persecution and to try to find asylum on the soil of such a country as is willing to grant it to him". Dr. CHANG (China) stated that he would like to see the individual's right to asylum and the State's right to grant asylum stated in the Declaration.

图片 1.2.22：张彭春在起草委员会第一届第 9 次会议发言纪要(3)

【纪要译文】

第 29 条

主席宣读了第 29 条。她指出,英文译文与法文文本不完全相符。她提醒委员会,"公共职能"一词应理解为"担任公职"。罗斯福夫人(美国)作为成员发言时说,她倾向于删除第 29 条第二句。张博士(中国)说,他倾向于用秘书处草案大纲(E/CN. 4/AC. 1/3 号文件)第 31 条第二部分取代第 29 条最后一句:"公务员的任命应通过竞争性考试。"他强调,随着公共职能变得越来越多和越来越重要,所有人都应该有权通过担任公职来参与公共生活。他回顾了中国在这一问题上的经验,并指出,公职竞争性考试在中国已经存在了几个世纪。在他看来,"自由竞争考试"应该被视为通向真正自由民主的途径之一。

科列茨基(Koretsky)教授(苏联)问张博士,中国竞争性考试的复杂性和数量是否在一定程度上把普通人排除在公职之外,这些人无法获得通过这种考试所必需的教育。张博士(中国)解释说,他认为这不是对中国历史的正确解释。他认为在固定的社区生活中,竞争性考试是一种给予平等机会获得公职的方式。哈里先生(澳大利亚)认为,应当给予人们真正的平等机会,使他们能够获得公共服务。然而,他不认为一项声明应具体说明如何作出任命。他认为,在第 29 条中陈述获得公职的平等机会的一般原则就足够了,删除该条的最后一部分。

第 30 条

张博士(中国)提请委员会注意第 27 条。该条提到"选举"是实现人权的一种方法。他认为竞争性考试也是实现人权的一种方法,因此应该提及。

第 32 条

哈里先生(澳大利亚)认为,应该从人权而不是国家权利的角度来拟订该条。他赞成古巴提案中的条款。桑塔·克鲁兹先生(智利)指出,庇护原则一直指导着他的国家,他赞成将其列入宣言。卡森教授(法国)提出以下案文:"人人有权逃避迫害,并在愿意给予他庇护的国家的土地上寻求庇护。"张博士(中国)说,他希望宣言中提到个人的庇护权和国家给予庇护的权利。

10. 张彭春在起草委员会第一届第 10 次会议上的发言

1947 年 6 月 18 日下午 3 时 30 分,起草委员会第一届第 10 次会议,在纽约成功湖召开,本次会议的主要议题是审议《国际人权法案》附件 1。中国代表张彭春参加了本次会议,并在会议上就第 8 条、第 10 条、第 15 条和第 16 条发言,其具体发言内容[①]会议纪要、纪要影像和纪要译文如下:

---

① UN Document:E/CN.4/AC.1/SR.10, p. 2, pp. 8–9, p. 11, p. 12, p. 13.

【会议纪要】

Article 8

Dr. CHANG (China) asked whether that implied that all Articles included were to be enforcible in terms of obligations in a treaty. He thought that Article 8 would be difficult of enforcement.

Article 10

Dr. CHANG (China) thought it was not far from wrong to say that a Declaration had been envisaged first of all, and therefore the Secretariat document had taken that general form. The question was how the Drafting Committee should proceed. All questions of form and substance would have to be decided by the Commission, but the Members of the Commission might wish to bring legal experts with them, who could meet simultaneously with the Commission as an *ad hoc* legal working group.

Article 15

Dr. CHANG (China) said that in his case silence often indicated the need for mature consideration and expert advice.

Dr. CHANG (China) said that he hoped the Members of the Commission might receive (1) all summary records of the meetings of the Drafting Committee, (2) all drafts that had been submitted, (3) a composite draft of the Articles which might be included in a Declaration, and (4) a composite draft of the Articles that might be included in a Convention.

Article 16

Dr. CHANG (China) said that as a non-technician, he was impressed by the importance of the structure of the United Kingdom draft. He felt that Members should not lose sight of its Preamble and of Part III.

Dr. CHANG (China) emphasized again the importance of Parts I and III of the United Kingdom draft.

Article 8

Dr. CHANG (China) asked whether that implied that all Articles included were to be enforcible in terms of obligations in a treaty. He thought that Article 8 would be difficult of enforcement.

Article 10

Dr. CHANG (China) thought it was not far from wrong to say that a Declaration had been envisaged first of all, and therefore the Secretariat document had taken that general form. The question was how the Drafting Committee should proceed. All questions of form and substance would have to be decided by the Commission, but the Members of the Commission might wish to bring legal experts with them, who could meet simultaneously with the Commission as an ad hoc legal working group.

图片 1.2.23:张彭春在起草委员会第一届第 10 次会议发言纪要(1)

Article 15

Dr. CHANG (China) said that in his case silence often indicated the need for mature consideration and expert advice.

Dr. CHANG (China) said that he hoped the Members of the Commission might receive (1) all summary records of the meetings of the Drafting Committee, (2) all drafts that had been submitted, (3) a composite draft of the Articles which might be included in a Declaration, and (4) a composite draft of the Articles that might be included in a Convention.

Article 16

Dr. CHANG (China) said that as a non-technician, he was impressed by the importance of the structure of the United Kingdom draft. He felt that Members should not lose sight of its Preamble and of Part III.

Dr. CHANG (China) emphasized again the importance of Parts I and III of the United Kingdom draft.

图片 1.2.24:张彭春在起草委员会第一届第 10 次会议发言纪要(2)

【纪要译文】

第 8 条

张博士(中国)问,这是否意味着列入条约的所有条款在义务方面都是可执行的。他认为第 8 条难以执行。

第 10 条

张博士(中国)认为,如果说首先设想的是一项宣言,因此秘书处的文件采取了这种笼统的形式,那就差不多了。问题是起草委员会应该如何进行。所有形式和实质问题都必须由委员会决定,但委员会成员不妨带上法律专家,他们可以作为临时法律工作组与委员会同时开会。

第 15 条

张博士(中国)说,在他的情况下,沉默往往表明需要成熟的考虑和专家意见。

张博士(中国)说,他希望委员会成员能收到:(1)起草委员会会议的所有简要记录;(2)提交的所有草案;(3)可能列入宣言的条款综合草案;(4)可能列入公约的条款综合草案。

第 16 条

张博士(中国)说,作为一名非技术人员,他对英国草案结构的重要性印象深刻。他认为,成员们不应忽视其序言和第三部分。

张博士(中国)再次强调英国草案第一和第三部分的重要性。

11. 张彭春在起草委员会
第一届第 11 次会议上的发言

1947 年 6 月 19 日下午 2 时 30 分,起草委员会第一届第 11 次会议,在纽约成功湖召开,本次会议的主要议题是讨论附件 1——英国草案和起草委员会提交人权委员会的报告的形式。中国代表张彭春参加了本次会议，并在会议上发言，其具体发言内容①会议纪要、纪要影像和纪要译文如下：

【会议纪要】

In considering the method of procedure, the CHAIRMAN explained, in answer to a question from Dr. CHANG (China), that the Preamble in the United States paper (E/CN. 4/AC. 1/13), was intended as the Preamble to a Declaration rather than a Convention.

Dr. CHANG (China) complimented the United Kingdom and Australian members on their proposals for implementation but added that he felt the work of the Commission on Human Rights should go a step further than making provision for the punishment of violations of the Bill of Rights. Concerning the suggestion for revising the terms of reference of the Commission, he felt that it would be a mistake to make the Commission merely a court of appeal for petitions for presentation to the Economic and Social Council or the General Assembly, as that would narrow the scope of the Commission to only legal questions.

In illustration of his point of view, Dr. CHANG quoted two Chinese proverbs which he translated as follows: "Good intentions alone are not sufficient for political order," and "Laws alone are not sufficient to bring about results by themselves." The intention and goal should be to build up better human beings, and not merely to punish those who violate human rights, he maintained. Rights must be protected by law, but laws are necessary also to promote the best in men. They should emphasize the promotion of the extension and refinement of human rights through education and moral means. Implementation does not only mean punishment, but also measures for the full development of man.

Dr. CHANG (China) approved of the suggestion for a separate section to cover the discussion on implementation.

----

① UN Document: E/CN. 4/AC. 1/SR. 11, p. 2, pp. 10–11, p. 15.

【纪要影像】

> In considering the method of procedure, the CHAIRMAN explained, in answer to a question from Dr. CHANG (China), that the Preamble in the United States paper (E/CN.4/AC.1/13), was intended as the Preamble to a Declaration rather than a Convention.
>
> Dr. CHANG (China) complimented the United Kingdom and Australian members on their proposals for implementation but added that he felt the work of the Commission on Human Rights should go a step further than making provision for the punishment of violations of the Bill of Rights. Concerning the suggestion for revising the terms of reference of the Commission, he felt that it would be a mistake to make the Commission merely a court of appeal for petitions for presentation to the Economic and Social Council or the General Assembly, as that would narrow the scope of the Commission to only legal questions.
>
> In illustration of his point of view, Dr. CHANG quoted two Chinese proverbs which he translated as follows: "Good intentions alone are not sufficient for political order," and "Laws alone are not sufficient to bring about results by themselves." The intention and goal should be to build up better human beings, and not merely to punish those who violate human rights, he maintained. Rights must be protected by law, but laws are necessary also to promote the best in men. They should emphasize the promotion of the extension and refinement of human rights through education and moral means. Implementation does not only mean punishment, but also measures for the full development of man.
>
> Dr. CHANG (China) approved of the suggestion for a separate section to cover the discussion on implementation.

图片 1.2.25：张彭春在起草委员会第一届第 11 次会议发言纪要

【纪要译文】

在审议程序方法时，主席在回答张博士（中国）的问题时解释说，美国文件（E/CN.4/AC.1/13）中的序言意在作为一项宣言的序言而不是一项公约的序言。

张博士（中国）称赞英国和澳大利亚成员提出的实施建议，但他补充说,他认为人权委员会的工作应更进一步,不仅仅是规定对违反人权法案的行为进行惩罚。关于修改委员会职权范围的建议,他认为,使委员会仅仅成为向经济及社会理事会或大会提交请愿书的上诉法院是错误的,因为这将把委员会的职权范围缩小到仅限于法律问题。

为了说明他的观点,张博士引用了两句中国孟子语录,他翻译如下:"徒善不足以为政"以及"徒法不能以自行"。他坚持认为,目的和目标应该是培养更好的人,而不仅仅是惩罚那些侵犯人权的人。权利必须受到法律的保护,但法律也有必要促进人的优秀品质。它们应强调通过教育和道德手段促进人权的扩展和完善。实施不仅意味着惩罚,而且意味着促进人的全面发展的措施。

张博士(中国)同意关于用单独一节来讨论实施问题的建议。

12. 张彭春在起草委员会
第一届第 12 次会议上的发言

1947 年 6 月 20 日上午 11 时,起草委员会第一届第 12 次会议,在纽约成功湖召开,本次会议的主要议题是审议法国代表为《国际人权宣言》条款所提交的修改后的建议案①。中国代表张彭春参加了本次会议,并在会议上针对建议案中不同的条款进行了发言,其具体发言内容②会议纪要、纪要影像和纪要译文如下:

【会议纪要】

Articles 1 to 4

Dr. CHANG (China) pointed out that the time at the disposal of the Com-

①　UN Document：E/CN. 4/AC. l/W. 2/Rev. 2.

②　UN Document：E/CN. 4/AC. 1/SR. 12, p. 4, p. 5, pp. 7-8, pp. 8-9, p. 9.

mittee was limited and that if redrafts were made of each Article, the work of the Committee would not progress.

Prof. CASSIN (France) stated that he himself reserved the right to make changes in the Articles he had suggested, as he recognized their imperfection.

Dr. CHANG (China) agreed with the suggestion of the United States, that the first four Articles might be merged in some way. He wished, however, to retain the first four words of Article 1, "All men are brothers."

Article 5

The CHAIRMAN read Article 5. She said that the United States would prefer deleting the last sentence and would suggest that the Article be altered to read:

"All are equal before the law and entitled to equal protection of the law. The law applies to public authorities and judges as well as to individuals."

Dr. CHANG (China) and Prof. CASSIN (France) were in favour of the United States revision. Mr. WILSON (United Kingdom) supported the United States suggestion but preferred that the second sentence read "Public authorities and judges, as well as individuals, are subject to the rule of law."

Article 6

The CHAIRMAN read Article 6. She stated that the United States suggested that "hereunder declared" be replaced by "set forth in this Declaration." Dr. CHANG (China) was in favour of this change. He thought the general principle might be included in the Preamble rather than drafted as a separate Article. Dr. MALIK (Lebanon) shared the viewpoint of Dr. CHANG. The CHAIRMAN suggested a foot-note to the effect that if this thought was embodied in the Preamble, it might be deleted in the Declaration.

Articles 7 and 8

Dr. CHANG (China) thought it important to take note of the cultural development of man, to include "the better development of life itself," inasmuch as mere physical existence was not sufficient.

Article 9

Dr. CHANG (China) pointed out that Article 7 was a statement of general principle while Article 8 dealt with a process of law. He thought that the "due process of law" could not be spelled out. He believed that Article 8 should remain but that Articles 9 and 10 might be relegated to a foot-note or commentary.

Mr. WILSON (United Kingdom) thought that his suggested wording of a foot-note would cover Dr. Chang's point inasmuch as "considered" was a broader term than "shortened".

Dr. CHANG (China) suggested that the first sentences of Articles 8, 9 and 10 might form a new Article 8, as they enunciated ideas of a general character. The remaining sentences of the Articles were qualifications and might be added as foot-notes or commentaries.

The CHAIRMAN requested Dr. CHANG to redraft the Articles and foot-note for consideration at the afternoon meeting.

【纪要影像】

Articles 1 to 4

Dr. CHANG (China) pointed out that the time at the disposal of the Committee was limited and that if redrafts were made of each Article, the work of the Committee would not progress.

Prof. CASSIN (France) stated that he himself reserved the right to make changes in the Articles he had suggested, as he recognized their imperfection.

Dr. CHANG (China) agreed with the suggestion of the United States, that the first four Articles might be merged in some way. He wished, however, to retain the first four words of Article 1, "All men are brothers."

Article 5

The CHAIRMAN read Article 5. She said that the United States would prefer deleting the last sentence and would suggest that the Article be altered to read:

"All are equal before the law and entitled to equal protection of the law. The law applies to public authorities and judges as well as to individuals."

Dr. CHANG (China) and Prof. CASSIN (France) were in favour of the United States revision. Mr. WILSON (United Kingdom) supported the United States suggestion but preferred that the second sentence read "Public authorities and judges, as well as individuals, are subject to the rule of law."

图片1.2.26:张彭春在起草委员会第一届第12次会议发言纪要(1)

Article 6

The CHAIRMAN read Article 6. She stated that the United States suggested that "hereunder declared" be replaced by "set forth in this Declaration." Dr. CHANG (China) was in favour of this change. He thought the general principle might be included in the Preamble rather than drafted as a separate Article. Dr. MALIK (Lebanon) shared the viewpoint of Dr. CHANG. The CHAIRMAN suggested a foot-note to the effect that if this thought was embodied in the Preamble, it might be deleted in the Declaration.

Articles 7 and 8

Dr. CHANG (China) thought it important to take note of the cultural development of man, to include "the better development of life itself," inasmuch as mere physical existence was not sufficient.

图片1.2.27:张彭春在起草委员会第一届第12次会议发言纪要(2)

Article 9

Dr. CHANG (China) pointed out that Article 7 was a statement of general principle while Article 8 dealt with a process of law. He thought that the "due process of law" could not be spelled out. He believed that Article 8 should remain but that Articles 9 and 10 might be relegated to a foot-note or commentary.

Mr. WILSON (United Kingdom) thought that his suggested wording of a foot-note would cover Dr. Chang's point inasmuch as "considered" was a broader term than "shortened".

Dr. CHANG (China) suggested that the first sentences of Articles 8, 9 and 10 might form a new Article 8, as they enunciated ideas of a general character. The remaining sentences of the Articles were qualifications and might be added as foot-notes or commentaries.

The CHAIRMAN requested Dr. CHANG to redraft the Articles and foot-note for consideration at the afternoon meeting.

图片 1.2.28：张彭春在起草委员会第一届第 12 次会议发言纪要(3)

【纪要译文】

第 1-4 条

张博士(中国)指出，委员会可支配的时间有限，如果每一条都重新起草，委员会的工作就不会有进展。

卡森教授(法国)说，他本人保留对他建议的条款进行修改的权利，因为他认识到这些条款不完善。

张博士(中国)同意美国的建议，前四条可以以某种方式合并。然而，他希望保留第 1 条的前五个字(英文为四个词)，"人人皆兄弟"。

第 5 条

主席宣读了第 5 条。她说，美国倾向于删除最后一句，并建议将该条改为：

"法律面前人人平等，并有权获得法律的平等保护。法律适用于公共当局和法官以及个人。"

张博士(中国)和卡森教授(法国)赞成美国的修订。威尔逊先生(英国)支持美国的建议，但倾向于将第二句改为"公共当局和法官以及个人都受法治约束"。

第 6 条

主席宣读了第 6 条。她说,美国建议将"在此宣布"改为"在本宣言中规定"。张博士(中国)赞成这一修改。他认为一般原则可以包括在序言中,而不是作为一个单独的条款起草。马利克博士(黎巴嫩)同意张博士的观点。主席提出了一个脚注,大意是,如果这一思想体现在序言中,则可以在宣言中删除。

第 7 条和第 8 条

张博士(中国)认为必须注意到人类的文化发展,包括"生活本身的更好发展",因为仅仅物质是不够的。

第 9 条

张博士(中国)指出,第 7 条是对一般原则的陈述,而第 8 条涉及法律程序。他认为"法律的正当程序"无法详细说明。他认为第 8 条应当保留,但第 9 条和第 10 条可以放在脚注或评注中。

威尔逊先生(英国)认为,他建议的脚注措辞可以涵盖张博士(中国)的观点,因为"考虑过"这个词比"缩短"更宽泛。

张博士(中国)建议,第 8 条、第 9 条和第 10 条的前几句可以组成新的第 8 条,因为它们阐述了一般性的思想。条款的其余句子是限定语,可以作为脚注或评注添加。

主席请张博士重新起草条款和脚注,以便在下午的会议上审议。

13. 张彭春在起草委员会
第一届第 13 次会议上的发言

1947 年 6 月 20 日下午 2 时 30 分,起草委员会第一届第 13 次会议,在纽约成功湖召开,本次会议的主要议题是继续审议法国代表为《国际人权宣言》条款所提交的修改后的建议案。中国代表张彭春参加了本次会议,

并在会议上先后多次发言,其具体发言内容①会议纪要、纪要影像和纪要译文如下:

【会议纪要】

<u>Article 11</u>

The CHAIRMAN read Article 11, and added that the United States suggested that the second sentence should be deleted.

Mr. WILSON (United Kingdom) supported this proposal, adding that the abolition of slavery was the main purpose of the Article: the subject of compulsory labour would be included in the Convention, and would then have to be very carefully examined. Dr. CHANG (China) agreed with this.

Dr. CHANG (China) said he wondered whether Members should not clarify their thinking as to what was meant by a Convention. In this case it might not be possible to have it clarified in a Convention, but it might be possible to clarify it in a comment. Certain things could be clarified in a comment and others enforced in a Convention.

The CHAIRMAN said that in his use of the word "enforced", Dr. CHANG implied that was intended as something to be included in a Convention.

<u>Articles 1, 2, 3, and 4</u>

Dr. CHANG (China) said he was in agreement with the Representative of the Lebanon that short, pithy sentences were needed for the first few articles, but he felt the Australian suggestions were interesting and significant. He agreed with the Representative of the United Kingdom that the word "conscience" should be added, but there should also be some word indicating, aside from "reason", something of a moral significance. He suggested that Article 1 should read as it stands: "All men are brothers. Being endowed with rea-

---

① UN Document: E/CN. 4/AC. 1/SR. 13, p. 2, pp. 5–6, p. 8, p. 10, p. 13, p. 15, p. 16, p. 20.

son and conscience, members of one family, they are free and possess equal dignity and rights. " Articles 2, 3, and 4 should be combined and become Article 2 (taken from the Australian proposal) as follows: "These rights are limited only by the equal rights of others. Man also owes duties to society, through which he is enabled to develop his spirit, mind and body in wider freedom. "

Article 13

Dr. CHANG (China) said he reserved his position, since he, too, realized the difficulties in qualification. He suggested as a drafting change that instead of the words "Subject to", the sentence should begin "There shall be liberty... ".

Dr. CHANG (China) said that it would not be wise at the present stage to go any further. He added that his attention had been drawn to a possible form of presenting a Declaration which included a comment for each Article. In this case, there was no necessity to include a comment to every Article, but he thought that the Articles themselves should be short, and if they were not clear, should then be followed by a comment. For this particular Article, he felt an explanatory comment would be useful.

Article 15

Dr. CHANG (China) said he thought that the first sentence of the third paragraph of Article 15 might be combined with some of the concepts implied in Articles 8, 9 and 10, which were being redrafted. He felt that paragraph 1 required classification.

Dr. CHANG (China) said that the third paragraph was still a little too technical for the common man, who wanted equality, consideration, and wished to know his relationship with the courts. He had already suggested that inasmuch as the first Article might appear too technical, and if a clarification of the relation of the individual to the tribunals was concerned, it might be considered as a part of the consideration of the tribunal relationship with the individual.

Dr. CHANG (China) said that the last sentence might still be a comment rather than a part of the Article. He would like to reserve his position with regard to retaining this Article.

Article 20

Dr. CHANG (China) agreed that it would be useful to include the two forms, but thought that the phrase offered by the Representative of France was not clear.

Dr. CHANG (China) suggested adding the original wording of the Representative of France as a third alternative.

【纪要影像】

Article 11

The CHAIRMAN read Article 11, and added that the United States suggested that the second sentence should be deleted.

Mr. WILSON (United Kingdom) supported this proposal, adding that the abolition of slavery was the main purpose of the Article: the subject of compulsory labour would be included in the Convention, and would then have to be very carefully examined. Dr. CHANG (China) agreed with this.

Dr. CHANG (China) said he wondered whether Members should not clarify their thinking as to what was meant by a Convention. In this case it might not be possible to have it clarified in a Convention, but it might be possible to clarify it in a comment. Certain things could be clarified in a comment and others enforced in a Convention.

The CHAIRMAN said that in his use of the word "enforced", Dr. CHANG implied what was intended as something to be included in a Convention.

图片 1.2.29：张彭春在起草委员会第一届第 13 次会议发言纪要(1)

Articles 1, 2, 3, and 4

Dr. CHANG (China) said he was in agreement with the Representative of the Lebanon that short, pithy sentences were needed for the first few articles, but he felt the Australian suggestions were interesting and significant. He agreed with the Representative of the United Kingdom that the word "conscience" should be added, but there should also be some word indicating, aside from "reason", something of a moral significance. He suggested that Article 1 should read as it stands: "All men are brothers. Being endowed with reason and conscience, members of one family, they are free and possess equal dignity and rights." Articles 2, 3, and 4 should be combined and become Article 2 (taken from the Australian proposal) as follows: "These rights are limited only by the equal rights of others. Man also owes duties to society, through which he is enabled to develop his spirit, mind and body in wider freedom."

图片 1.2.30：张彭春在起草委员会第一届第 13 次会议发言纪要(2)

Article 13

Dr. CHANG (China) said he reserved his position, since he, too, realized the difficulties in qualification. He suggested as a drafting change that instead of the words "Subject to", the sentence should begin "There shall be liberty.....".

Dr. CHANG (China) said that it would not be wise at the present stage to go any further. He added that his attention had been drawn to a possible form of presenting a Declaration which included a comment for each Article. In this case, there was no necessity to include a comment to every Article, but he thought that the Articles themselves should be short, and if they were not clear, should then be followed by a comment. For this particular Article, he felt an explanatory comment would be useful.

图片 1.2.31：张彭春在起草委员会第一届第 13 次会议发言纪要(3)

Article 15

Dr. CHANG (China) said he thought that the first sentence of the third paragraph of Article 15 might be combined with some of the concepts implied in Articles 8, 9, and 10, which were being redrafted. He felt that paragraph 1 required classification.

Dr. CHANG (China) said that the third paragraph was still a little too technical for the common man, who wanted equality, consideration, and wished to know his relationship with the courts. He had already suggested that inasmuch as the first Article might appear too technical, and if a clarification of the relation of the individual to the tribunals was concerned, it might be considered as a part of the consideration of the tribunal relationship with the individual.

Dr. CHANG (China) said that the last sentence might still be a comment rather than a part of the Article. He would like to reserve his position with regard to retaining this Article.

Article 20

Dr. CHANG (China) agreed that it would be useful to include the two forms, but thought that the phrase offered by the Representative of France was not clear.

Dr. CHANG (China) suggested adding the original wording of the Representative of France as a third alternative.

图片 1.2.32:张彭春在起草委员会第一届第 13 次会议发言纪要(4)

【纪要译文】

第 11 条

主席阅读了第 11 条,并补充说,美国建议删除第二句。

威尔逊先生(英国)支持这一提议,并补充说,废除奴隶制是该条的主要目的:强制劳动的问题将列入公约,然后必须非常仔细地加以审查。张博士(中国)对此表示同意。

张博士(中国)说,他不知道各成员是否应该澄清他们对公约的含义的想法。在这种情况下,可能无法在一项公约中予以澄清,但可能在一项评论中予以澄清。某些事情可以在评论中澄清,其他事情可以在公约中强制执行。

主席说,张博士在使用"强制执行"一词时,暗示这是打算列入公约的内容。

第 1、2、3 和 4 条

张博士(中国)说,他同意黎巴嫩代表的意见,前几项条款需要简短扼要,但他认为澳大利亚的建议很有意思,意义重大。他同意英国代表的意见,即应该加上"良心"一词,但除了"理性"之外,还应该有一个表示某种道德意义的词。他建议第 1 条应照原样读作:"人人皆为兄弟。作为一个大家庭的成员,他们赋予理性和良心,人人自由并享有平等的尊严和权利。"第 2 条、第 3 条和第 4 条应合并成为第 2 条(取自澳大利亚的提案),内容如下:"这些权利只受他人平等享有这些权利的限制。人人也对社会负有责任,以此他能够在更广泛的自由中发展他的精神、思想和身体。"

第 13 条

张博士(中国)说,他保留自己的立场,因为他也认识到资格方面的困难。他建议,作为一项措辞上的修改,该句应以"将有······自由"代替"隶属于······"。

张博士(中国)说,在现阶段继续下去是不明智的。他补充说,有人提请他注意提交宣言的一种可能形式,其中包括对每一条款的评论。在这种情况下,没有必要对每一条都作出评论,但他认为条款本身应该简短,如果不清楚,应该在后面加上评论。对于这一特定条款,他认为解释性评论将是有用的。

第 15 条

张博士(中国)说,他认为第 15 条第三段第一句可与正在重新起草的第 8、第 9 和第 10 条中隐含的一些概念合并。他认为第一段需要分类。

张博士(中国)说,第三段对普通人来说还是太专业了一点,普通人想要平等、体贴,并希望知道自己与法院的关系。他已经建议,由于第一条可能显得过于技术性,如果涉及澄清个人与法庭的关系,可以将其视为考虑法庭与个人关系的一部分。

张博士(中国)说,最后一句可能仍然是一个评论,而不是条款的一部分。对于保留该条他持保留意见。

第 20 条

张博士(中国)同意列入这两种形式是有益的,但认为法国代表提出的措辞不清楚。

张博士(中国)建议增加法国代表原来的措辞作为第三个备选案文。

14. 张彭春在起草委员会第一届第 14 次会议上的发言

　　1947 年 6 月 23 日上午 10 时 30 分,起草委员会第一届第 14 次会议,在纽约成功湖召开,本次会议的主要议题是继续审议法国代表为《国际人权宣言》条款所提交的修改后的建议案。中国代表张彭春参加了本次会议,并在会议上发言,其具体发言内容①会议纪要、纪要影像和纪要译文如下:

【会议纪要】

Article 26

Dr. CHANG (China) was in favour of the United States form, adding that Government included all forms of government, and not only State or territorial government as in the other text.

Article 28

Dr. CHANG (China) proposed the addition of the sentence "There shall be free access to public examinations for public employment". He was in favour of the rest of the Article but suggested that the word "offices" might give rise to misunderstanding as some offices are elective.

Mr. SANTA CRUZ (Chile) said that to include this sentence would indi-

---

① UN Document: E/CN.4/AC.1/SR.1, p. 3, p. 4, p. 5.

cate that the Committee was of the opinion that public offices should be filled by competitive examination. He pointed out that in Chile public offices are attained by examination up to a certain point only; the highest appointments are made through the will of the Executive or after consultation with the Legislative power. He felt that this meant too detailed specifications. Dr. CHANG (China) felt there would be no objection to his wording if "offices" were omitted. Mr. WILSON (United Kingdom) had no objection to Dr. Chang's proposal but he pointed out that, as the Article aimed at the prevention of discrimination in public office, it should be referred to the Sub-Commission on the Prevention of Discrimination and the Protection of Minorities.

【纪要影像】

Article 26
    Dr. CHANG (China) was in favour of the United States form, adding that Government included all forms of government, and not only State or territorial government as in the other text.
Article 28
    Dr. CHANG (China) proposed the addition of the sentence "There shall be free access to public examinations for public employment". He was in favour of the rest of the Article but suggested that the word "offices" might give rise to misunderstanding as some offices are elective.
    Mr. SANTA CRUZ (Chile) said that to include this sentence would indicate that the Committee was of the opinion that public offices should be filled by competitive examination. He pointed out that in Chile public offices are attained by examination up to a certain point only; the highest appointments are made through the will of the Executive or after consultation with the Legislative power. He felt that this meant too detailed specifications. Dr. CHANG (China) felt there would be no objection to his wording if "offices" were omitted. Mr. WILSON (United Kingdom) had no objection to Dr. Chang's proposal but he pointed out that, as the Article aimed at the prevention of discrimination in public office, it should be referred to the Sub-Commission on the Prevention of Discrimination and the Protection of Minorities.

图片 1.2.33：张彭春在起草委员会第一届第 14 次会议发言纪要

【纪要译文】

第 26 条

张博士(中国)赞成美国的形式,并补充说,政府应该包括各种形式的政府,而不仅仅是州政府或是另一案文中的地区政府。

第 28 条

张博士(中国)建议添加"公职人员应免费参加公共考试"一句。他赞成该条的其余部分,但认为"职位"一词可能会引起误解,因为有些职位是选举产生的。

桑塔·克鲁兹先生(智利)说,列入这句话将表明委员会认为公职人员应通过竞争性考试来填补。他指出,在智利,公职只有在一定程度上通过考试才能获得;最高职位的任命是根据行政部门的意愿或在与立法部门协商后做出的。他觉得这意味着过于详细的说明。张博士(中国)认为,如果省略"职位"一词,对他的措辞没有异议。威尔逊先生(英国)不反对张博士的提议,但他指出,由于该条旨在防止公职中的歧视,因此应提交防止歧视及保护少数者分设委员会。

15. 张彭春在起草委员会第一届第 15 次会议上的发言

1947 年 6 月 23 日下午 2 时 30 分,起草委员会第一届第 15 次会议,在纽约成功湖召开,本次会议的主要议题是继续审议法国代表为国际人权宣言条款所提交的修改后的建议案。中国代表张彭春参加了本次会议,并在会议上发言,其具体发言内容①会议纪要、纪要影像和纪要译文如下:

① UN Document:E/CN. 4/AC. 1/SR. 15, p. 2, p. 3, p. 4, p. 5.

【会议纪要】

Articles 36 and 37

Dr. CHANG (China) thought that the right to a fair share of rest and leisure might be separated from the right to the knowledge of the outside world which could be included in the subject of education.

The CHAIRMAN stated that Article 36 would now read: "Every one has the right to a fair share of rest and leisure". It was the general consensus of opinion that Article 37 be retained as it stood, with a footnote saying that the substance of the Article might be included in the Preamble instead of being spelt out in the Declaration. Dr. CHANG (China) asked for an explanation of the phrase "share in the benefits of science" in Article 37. Mr. SANTA CRUZ (Chile) said that in the Chilean Draft, it was stated that scientific inventions should belong to society and be enjoyed by all.

Article 35

Returning to Article 35, the CHAIRMAN, speaking as the Representative of the United States, proposed the addition of the following sentence: "This will not exclude private educational facilities and institutions".

Dr. CHANG (China) proposed that the Article should read:

"Every one has the right to education. Primary education shall be obligatory and shall be provided by the State or community in which he lives. There shall be equal access to technical, cultural and higher education as can be provided by the State or community on the basis of merit and without distinction as to race, sex, language or religion."

The CHAIRMAN proposed the deletion of the words "in which he lives" and Dr. CHANG accepted this amendment.

Dr. CHANG（China）stated that he had no objection to the inclusion of reference to social standing or political belief.

【纪要影像】

Articles 36 and 37

Dr. CHANG (China) thought that the right to a fair share of rest and leisure might be separated from the right to the knowledge of the outside world which could be included in the subject of education.

The CHAIRMAN stated that Article 36 would now read: "Every one has the right to a fair share of rest and leisure". It was the general consensus of opinion that Article 37 be retained as it stood, with a footnote saying that the substance of the Article might be included in the Preamble instead of being spelt out in the Declaration. Dr. CHANG (China) asked for an explanation of the phrase "share in the benefits of science" in Article 37. Mr. SANTA CRUZ (Chile) said that in the Chilean Draft, it was stated that scientific inventions should belong to society and be enjoyed by all.

图片 1.2.34：张彭春在起草委员会第一届第 15 次会议发言纪要(1)

Article 35

Returning to Article 35, the CHAIRMAN, speaking as the Representative of the United States, proposed the addition of the following sentence: "This will not exclude private educational facilities and institutions".

Dr. CHANG (China) proposed that the Article should read: "Every one has the right to education. Primary education shall be obligatory and shall be provided by the State or community in which he lives. There shall be equal access to technical, cultural and higher education as can be provided by the State or community on the basis of merit and without distinction as to race,.sex, language or religion."

The CHAIRMAN proposed the deletion of the words "in which he lives" and Dr. CHANG accepted this amendment.

Dr. CHANG (China) stated that he had no objection to the inclusion of reference to social standing or political belief.

图片 1.2.35：张彭春在起草委员会第一届第 15 次会议发言纪要(2)

【纪要译文】

第 36 条和第 37 条

张博士(中国)认为,公平分享休息和闲暇的权利可以与了解外部世界的权利分开,后者可以包括在教育科目中。

主席说,第 36 条现在的内容是:"人人有权享有公平的休息和闲暇。"普遍一致的意见是,第 37 条应保持原样,并加一个脚注,说明该条的实质内容可列入序言,而不是在宣言中阐述。张博士(中国)要求解释第 37 条中的"分享科学的利益"一语。桑塔·克鲁兹先生(智利)说,智利的草案指出,科学发明应属于社会,由所有人享有。

第 35 条

回到第 35 条,主席以美国代表的身份发言,提议添加以下一句:"这不排除私人教育设施和机构。"

张博士(中国)提议将该条改为:

"每个人都有受教育的权利。初等教育应为义务教育,由他所居住的国家或社区提供。应平等获得国家或社区根据成绩提供的技术、文化和高等教育,不分种族、性别、语言或宗教。"

主席提议删除"他所居住的"等字,张博士接受了这一修正。

张博士(中国)说,他不反对提及社会地位或政治信仰。

16. 张彭春在起草委员会
第一届第 16 次会议上的发言

1947 年 6 月 24 日上午 10 时 45 分,起草委员会第一届第 16 次会议,在纽约成功湖召开,本次会议的主要议题是审议起草委员会提交给人权委员会的报告草案。中国代表张彭春参加了本次会议,并在会议上发言,其具体发言内容①会议纪要、纪要影像和纪要译文如下:

【会议纪要】

Paragraph 10

The CHAIRMAN explained that the Committee was submitting the views expressed during the course of its session in a working paper which was not binding upon any individual or Government. Dr. CHANG (China) suggested that the words " it was agreed " be deleted. He felt that it might even be possible to omit the entire paragraph.

The CHAIRMAN agreed that the paragraph might be omitted. Prof. KORETSKY (Union of Soviet Socialist Republics) thought the suggestion of Dr. Chang was a logical one and favoured complete elimination of the paragraph. He said that perhaps some mention might be made of this point in Chapter II. Mr. HARRY (Australia) agreed to elimination of the paragraph. Dr. MALIK (Lebanon) explained that the original terms of reference had requested the Drafting Committee to prepare a preliminary draft of an International Bill of Human Rights. Inasmuch as the Drafting Committee had not actually prepared such a Preliminary Draft, he felt that an explanatory reference to the discrepen-

---

① UN Document: E/CN. 4/AC. 1/SR. 16, p. 4, p. 8, p. 10.

cy was necessary. He would, however, agree, should the Drafting Committee so wish, to the deletion of the paragraph.

Paragraph 14

Dr. CHANG (China) said that inasmuch as the Summary Record had not been passed by the Committee, there might be opportunity to change the phrasing. He proposed that the terminology used at the intermediate stage of discussions might be appropriate; "to undertake a division of the work indicating which Articles would require International Conventions and which would not. "

Paragraph 17

At this point in the meeting, Dr. CHANG (China) Vice-Chairman, took the chair and Mr. HENDRICK replaced Mrs. ROOSEVELT as Representative of the United States.

【纪要影像】

Paragraph 10

The CHAIRMAN explained that the Committee was submitting the views expressed during the course of its session in a working paper which was not binding upon any individual or Government. Dr. CHANG (China) suggested that the words "it was agreed" be deleted. He felt that it might even be possible to omit the entire paragraph.

The CHAIRMAN agreed that the paragraph might be omitted. Prof. KORETSKY (Union of Soviet Socialist Republics) thought the suggestion of Dr. Chang was a logical one and favoured complete elimination of the paragraph. He said that perhaps some mention might be made of this point in Chapter II. Mr. HARRY (Australia) agreed to elimination of the paragraph. Dr. MALIK (Lebanon) explained that the original terms of reference had requested the Drafting Committee to prepare a preliminary draft of an International Bill of Human Rights. Inasmuch as the Drafting Committee had not actually prepared such a Preliminary Draft, he felt that an explanatory reference to the discrepency was necessary. He would, however, agree, should the Drafting Committee so wish, to the deletion of the paragraph.

图片 1.2.36：张彭春在起草委员会第一届第 16 次会议发言纪要(1)

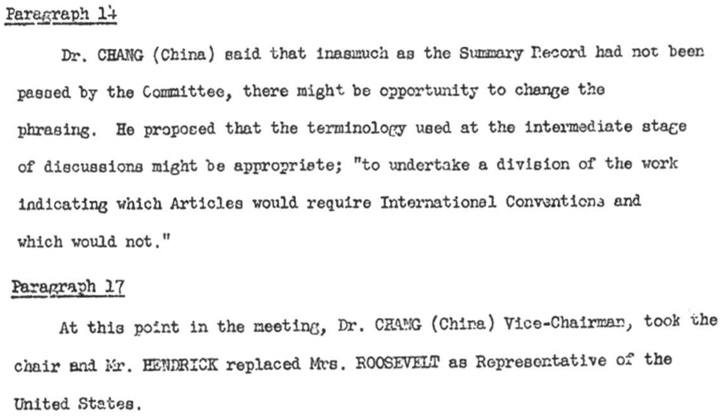

Dr. CHANG (China) said that inasmuch as the Summary Record had not been passed by the Committee, there might be opportunity to change the phrasing. He proposed that the terminology used at the intermediate stage of discussions might be appropriate; "to undertake a division of the work indicating which Articles would require International Conventions and which would not."

Paragraph 17

At this point in the meeting, Dr. CHANG (China) Vice-Chairman, took the chair and Mr. HENDRICK replaced Mrs. ROOSEVELT as Representative of the United States.

图片 1.2.37:张彭春在起草委员会第一届第 16 次会议发言纪要(2)

【纪要译文】

第 10 段

主席解释说,委员会正在提交会议期间在一份工作文件中表达的意见,该文件对任何个人或政府都没有约束力。张博士(中国)建议删除"一致同意"这几个字。他认为甚至可以省略整个段落。

主席同意该段可以省略。考瑞茨基(Koretsky)教授(苏联)认为,张博士的建议是合理的,他赞成完全删除该段。他说,也许可以在第二章中提到这一点。哈里先生(澳大利亚)同意删除该段。马利克博士(黎巴嫩)解释说,最初的职权范围要求起草委员会编写一份《国际人权法案》初稿。由于起草委员会实际上没有编写这样一份初步草案,他认为有必要对这一差异作出解释性说明。然而,如果是起草委员会的意愿,他同意删除该段。

第 14 段

张博士(中国)说,由于摘要记录没有获得委员会通过,可能有机会改变措辞。他提议在讨论的中间阶段使用的术语可能是合适的:"进行工作分工,指出哪些条款需要国际公约,而哪些不需要。"

第 17 段

会议至此,副主席张博士(中国)主持会议,亨德里克先生代替罗斯福夫人担任美国代表。

17. 张彭春在起草委员会
第一届第 17 次会议上的发言

　　1947 年 6 月 24 日下午 2 时 30 分,起草委员会第一届第 17 次会议,在纽约成功湖召开,本次会议的主要议题是继续讨论起草委员会提交人权委员会的报告草稿及附件。① 中国代表张彭春参加了本次会议,在前半场会议在罗斯福夫人缺席的情况下,以主席身份主持了前半场会议并在后半场会议上发言,其具体发言内容②会议纪要、纪要影像和纪要译文如下:

【会议纪要】

In the absence of the CHAIRMAN, Dr. CHANG, the Vice-Chairman, temporarily presided.

Paragraph 19

The CHAIRMAN was also of the opinion that it should be made clear that the decision to draft a Convention rested with the Commission on Human Rights.

The CHAIRMAN felt that the shortness of time and the need to consult legal experts should be included in this paragraph. He was supported by Mr. WILSON (United Kingdom).

The CHAIRMAN pointed out that the shortness of time was already implied in the text before the Committee.

CHAPTER III, Paragraph 20

The CHAIRMAN proposed the deletion of the word "again" on Page 6,

---

　　① UN Document E/CN. 4/AC. 1/14.

　　② UN Document:E/CN. 4/AC. 1/SR. 17, p. 1, p. 4, p. 5, p. 10, p. 12, p. 13, p. 14.

paragraph (f), line 3, which was accepted.

(At this point Mrs. Roosevelt arrived and presided over the remainder of the meeting.)

Paragraph 19

Dr. CHANG (China) supported Mr. HARRY's text, and felt the substance should be retained, but was in favour of a shorter form. He proposed that the RAPPORTEUR and Mr. HARRY should redraft this section.

Dr. CHANG (China) accepted the United Kingdom amendment, but wished to retain the phrase "which the Commission may wish to consider and elaborate" at the end, Mr. WILSON agreed.

There was a general consensus of opinion that the modified text of the United Kingdom Draft should be issued in a separate Annex.

Article 8

The RAPPORTEUR read the text of the Article and the footnotes. Dr. CHANG (China) requested the withdrawal of the footnote containing a Chinese amendment as he intended to present his amendment later to the Commission on Human Rights.

Article 11

The RAPPORTEUR read the text of the Article and footnotes.

The CHAIRMAN said that Mr. CASSIN (France) had accepted that "slavery in all its forms" should be stated. It was her opinion also that the second sentence should be included in a footnote with a note stating that the Committee had considered that its substance might be included in a Convention. Dr. CHANG (China) and Mr. WILSON (United Kingdom) agreed with the CHAIRMAN and the suggestion was adopted.

Article 11 then read: "Slavery, which is inconsistent with the dignity of man, is prohibited in all its forms".

【纪要影像】

In the absence of the CHAIRMAN, Dr. CHANG, the Vice-Chairman, temporarily presided.

Paragraph 19

The CHAIRMAN was also of the opinion that it should be made clear that the decision to draft a Convention rested with the Commission on Human Rights.

The CHAIRMAN felt that the shortness of time and the need to consult legal experts should be included in this paragraph. He was supported by Mr. WILSON (United Kingdom).

The CHAIRMAN pointed out that the shortness of time was already implied in the text before the Committee.

CHAPTER III, Paragraph 20

The CHAIRMAN proposed the deletion of the word "again" on Page 6, paragraph (f), line 3, which was accepted.

(At this point Mrs. Roosevelt arrived and presided over the remainder of the meeting.)

图片 1.2.38:张彭春在起草委员会第一届第 17 次会议发言纪要(1)

Paragraph 19

Dr. CHANG (China) supported Mr. HARRY's text, and felt the substance should be retained, but was in favour of a shorter form. He proposed that the RAPPORTEUR and Mr. HARRY should redraft this section.

Dr. CHANG (China) accepted the United Kingdom amendment, but wished to retain the phrase "which the Commission may wish to consider and elaborate" at the end. Mr. WILSON agreed.

There was a general consensus of opinion that the modified text of the United Kingdom Draft should be issued in a separate Annex.

图片 1.2.39:张彭春在起草委员会第一届第 17 次会议发言纪要(2)

Article 8

  The RAPPORTEUR read the text of the Article and the footnotes.

Dr. CHANG (China) requested the withdrawal of the footnote containing a Chinese amendment as he intended to present his amendment later to the Commission on Human Rights.

Article 11

  The RAPPORTEUR read the text of the Article and footnotes.

  The CHAIRMAN said that M. CASSIN (France) had accepted that "slavery in all its forms" should be stated. It was her opinion also that the second sentence should be included in a footnote with a note stating that the Committee had considered that its substance might be included in a Convention. Dr. CHANG (China) and Mr. WILSON (United Kingdom) agreed with the CHAIRMAN and the suggestion was adopted.

  Article 11 then read: "Slavery, which is inconsistent with the dignity of man, is prohibited in all its forms".

图片 1.2.40:张彭春在起草委员会第一届第 17 次会议发言纪要(3)

【纪要译文】

主席缺席,副主席张博士临时主持会议。

第 19 段

主席还认为,应该明确指出,起草公约的决定属于人权委员会。

主席认为,时间紧迫和咨询法律专家的必要性应包括在这一段中。他得到了威尔逊先生(英国)的支持。

主席指出,委员会面前的案文已经暗示时间紧迫。

第三章,第 20 段

主席提议删除第 6 页(f)段第 3 行中的"再次"一词,该提议被接受。

(这时,罗斯福夫人抵达会场,并主持了余下的会议。)

第 19 段

张博士(中国)支持哈里先生的案文,认为应保留其实质内容,但赞成采用较短的形式。他建议报告员和哈里先生重新起草这一部分。

张博士(中国)接受英国的修正,但希望保留结尾的"委员会有意审议和阐述"一语,威尔逊先生对此表示同意。

普遍一致的意见是,英国草案的修改案文应作为单独的附件印发。

第 8 条

报告员宣读了该条案文和脚注。张博士(中国)要求撤回载有中国修正案的脚注,因为他打算稍后向人权委员会提出他的修正案。

第 11 条

报告员宣读了该条案文和脚注。

主席说,卡森先生(法国)同意应陈述"一切形式的奴隶制"。她还认为,第二句应包括在一个脚注中,并附有说明,指出委员会认为其实质内容可纳入一项公约。张博士(中国)和威尔逊先生(英国)同意主席的意见,该建议获得通过。

那么,第 11 条写道:"所有形式的奴隶制,皆有悖于人的尊严,应予以禁止。"

18. 张彭春在起草委员会第一届第 18 次会议上的发言

1947 年 6 月 25 日上午 10 时 30 分,起草委员会第一届第 18 次会议,在纽约成功湖召开,本次会议的主要议题是讨论起草委员会提交人权委员会的报告草稿第三章(《国际人权法案》的实施问题)及附件 F。中国代表张彭春参加了本次会议,并在会议上发言,其具体发言内容①会议纪要、纪要影像和纪要译文如下:

【会议纪要】

Mr. HARRY(Australia)proposed the following wording:"It was sugges-

---

① UN Document:E/CN. 4/AC. 1/SR. 18, p. 4, p. 6, p. 9.

ted by individual Members of the Committee that such education should be carried out through the existing organs of the United Nations or a possible international organ. "

Dr. CHANG (China) pointed out that the idea of using existing organs had not been clarified during the previous meetings and that therefore he felt it might not be included here.

The CHAIRMAN thought that it might be well to keep the original text of Section 21 with the insertion of "by individual Members" after "It was suggested". Mrs. ROOSEVELT (United States of America) then suggested substituting "there should be some form of implementation with respect to human rights" for "the international community must ensure the observance of . . . " in the second part of Paragraph 20.

Dr. CHANG (China) referring to the same paragraph, pointed out that there was no expression of the consensus of opinion of the Committee regarding these principles. Therefore he suggested the deletion of the first sentence. With regard to the word "session" in the first paragraph of Paragraph 20, he thought that the word "meeting" should be substituted.

Article 15

Mrs. ROOSEVELT stated that the United States suggested that the phrase "he shall have the right to consult with and to be represented by counsel" should not be a footnote but should be included in the Article.

The RAPPORTEUR explained that because of the lack of clear agreement between the Chairman and Professor CASSIN on this point this phrase had been put into a footnote. Dr. CHANG (China) suggested putting it at the end of the Article. The RAPPORTEUR accepted the change.

Article 28

The CHAIRMAN suggested inserting the words "to hold public office" after "public employment". Dr. CHANG (China) suggested adding the following sentence to Article 28: "Access to examinations for public employment shall not be a matter of privilege or favour".

The RAPPORTEUR said the acceptance of this suggestion called for the deletion of the first footnote.

Article 31

Dr. CHANG (China) thought the word "and" in Article 31 might better be changed to "or". The RAPPORTEUR accepted this suggestion and suggested the substitution of "shall" for "should" in this Article.

【纪要影像】

Mr. HARRY (Australia) proposed the following wording: "It was suggested by individual Members of the Committee that such education should be carried out through the existing organs of the United Nations or a possible international organ."

Dr. CHANG (China) pointed out that the idea of using existing organs had not been clarified during the previous meetings and that therefore he felt it might not be included here.

The CHAIRMAN thought that it might be well to keep the original text of Section 21 with the insertion of "by individual Members" after "It was suggested". Mrs. ROOSEVELT (United States of America) then suggested substituting "there should be some form of implementation with respect to human rights" for "the international community must ensure the observance of ..." in the second part of Paragraph 20.

Dr. CHANG (China) referring to the same paragraph, pointed out that there was no expression of the consensus of opinion of the Committee regarding these principles. Therefore he suggested the deletion of the first sentence. With regard to the word "session" in the first paragraph of Paragraph 20, he thought that the word "meeting" should be substituted.

图片 1.2.41:张彭春在起草委员会第一届第 18 次会议发言纪要(1)

Article 15

Mrs. ROOSEVELT stated that the United States suggested that the phrase "he shall have the right to consult with and to be represented by counsel" should not be a footnote but should be included in the Article.

The RAPPORTEUR explained that because of the lack of clear agreement between the Chairman and Professor CASSIN on this point this phrase had been put into a footnote. Dr. CHANG (China) suggested putting it at the end of the Article. The RAPPORTEUR accepted the change.

Article 28

The CHAIRMAN suggested inserting the words "to hold public office" after "public employment". Dr. CHANG (China) suggested adding the following sentence to Article 28: "Access to examinations for public employment shall not be a matter of privilege or favour".

The RAPPORTEUR said the acceptance of this suggestion called for the deletion of the first footnote.

Article 31

Dr. CHANG (China) thought the word "and" in Article 31 might better be changed to "or". The RAPPORTEUR accepted this suggestion and suggested the substitution of "shall" for "should" in this Article.

图片 1.2.42:张彭春在起草委员会第一届第 18 次会议发言纪要(2)

【纪要译文】

哈里先生(澳大利亚)提议采用以下措辞:"委员会个别成员建议,应通过联合国现有机构或可能的国际机构开展这种教育。"

张博士(中国)指出,使用现有机构的主张在之前的会议上没有得以明确,因此他认为可能不列入此处。

主席认为,最好保留第 21 部分的原始案文,并在"建议"之后插入"个别成员"。罗斯福夫人(美国)然后建议将第 20 段的第二部分中的"在人权方面应该有一些实施形式"替换为"国际社会必须确保其遵行"。

张博士(中国)在提到同一段时指出,委员会没有对这些原则达成共识。因此,他建议删除第一句。关于第 20 段第一部分中的"届会"一词,他认为应该用"会议"一词代替。

第 15 条

罗斯福夫人说,美国建议,"他应有权咨询律师,并由律师代理"这一短语不应成为脚注,而应列入该条。

报告员解释说,由于主席和卡森教授在这一点上缺乏明确的一致意见,这一短语被放在脚注中。张博士(中国)建议将其放在该条的末尾。报告员接受了这一修改。

第 28 条

主席建议在"从事公务职业"之后插入"担任公职"的词语。张博士(中国)建议在第 28 条中增加以下一句:"参与公务人员考试将不是特权或恩惠的事情"。

报告员说,接受这一建议需要删除第一个脚注。

第 31 条

张博士(中国)认为,第 31 条中的"和"一词最好改为"或"。报告员接受了这一建议,并建议在该条中用"将"(shall)取代"应"(should)。

19. 张彭春在起草委员会第一届第 19 次会议上的发言

1947 年 6 月 25 日下午 2 时 30 分,起草委员会第一届第 19 次会议,在纽约成功湖召开,本次会议的主要议题是审议包含在公约中的人权和基本自由的界定问题(起草委员会提交人权委员会的报告草稿附件 C)。中国代表张彭春参加了本次会议,并在会议上发言,其具体发言内容①会议纪要、纪要影像和纪要译文如下:

---

① UN Document:E/CN.4/AC.1/SR.19, pp. 2-3.

Dr. CHANG (China) said that he and the Representative of the United Kingdom felt that this document should be headed: "Draft Articles on Human Rights and Fundamental Freedoms to be Considered for Inclusion in a Convention."

The CHAIRMAN said that since there were no comments, this suggestion was accepted. She pointed out that all of the items in Annex G had been taken from other documents which had already been discussed, therefore they might require no further discussion.

【纪要影像】

Dr. CHANG (China) said that he and the Representative of the United Kingdom felt that this document should be headed: "Draft Articles on Human Rights and Fundamental Freedoms to be Considered for Inclusion in a Convention."

The CHAIRMAN said that since there were no comments, this suggestion was accepted. She pointed out that all of the items in Annex G had been taken from other documents which had already been discussed, therefore they might require no further discussion.

图片 1.2.43:张彭春在起草委员会第一届第 19 次会议发言纪要

【纪要译文】

张博士(中国)说,他和英国代表认为,这份文件的标题应为:"考虑列入一项公约的人权和基本自由条款草案。"

主席说,由于没有意见,这一建议被接受。她指出,附件 G 中的所有项目都取自已经讨论过的其他文件,因此可能不需要进 步讨论。

第三章　联合国人权委员会第三届会议

　　联合国人权委员会第三届会议(从第 46 次会议至第 81 次会议),于 1948 年 5 月 24 日至 6 月 18 日,在美国纽约成功湖召开,本届会议共召开了 36 次会议。在这届会议上,委员会的工作以起草委员会第二届会议的报告 E/CN.4/95 为基础。审查了宣言的个别条款,委员会以 12 票赞成、4 票弃权通过了重新起草的宣言。① 最后,人权委员会第三届会议的报告提交给经济及社会理事会第七届会议审议。

　　中国代表张彭春参加了本届会议中的 33 次会议,并在其中的 30 次会议上进行了大会发言,包括第 48 次会议、第 50 次会议、第 51 次会议、第 52 次会议、第 53 次会议、第 54 次会议、第 55 次会议、第 56 次会议、第 57 次会议、第 58 次会议、第 59 次会议、第 60 次会议、第 61 次会议、第 62 次会议、第 63 次会议、第 64 次会议、第 65 次会议、第 67 次会议、第 68 次会议、第 69 次会议、第 70 次会议、第 71 次会议、第 72 次会议、第 74 次会议、第 75 次会议、第 76 次会议、第 77 次会议、第 78 次会议、第 80 次会议和第 81 次会议。另外,参加起草委员会第二届会议的中国代表吴德耀先生也单独参加了本届 3 次会议和与张彭春先生共同参加了 1 次会议。张彭春先生在本届会议上的发言对《世界人权宣言》的起草工作做出了卓越的贡献,其具体发言内容如下:

---

　　①　UN Document: E/CN.4/SR.81.

1. 张彭春在联合国人权委员会第三届第48次会议上的发言

1948 年 5 月 26 日下午 2 时 45 分,联合国人权委员会第三届第 48 次会议,在纽约成功湖召开。中国代表张彭春参加了本次会议,并在会议上发言,具体发言内容①会议纪要、纪要影像和纪要译文如下:

【会议纪要】

Mr. CHANG（China）said that his delegation also reserved the right to ask for a Chinese translation of any resolution, recommendation or official decision if it considered that it needed that translation for the discussion.

He then asked whether "implementation" in the French proposal applied to the Covenant as well as to the Declaration.

【纪要影像】

图片 1.3.1:张彭春在联合国人权委员会第三届第 48 次会议发言纪要

【纪要译文】

张先生(中国)说,如果中国代表团认为讨论需要任何决议、建议或正

---

① UN Document: E/CN. 4/SR. 48, p. 14.

式决定的中文译本,它也保留要求获得该译本的权利。

然后,他问法国提案中的"实施"是否适用于《公约》以及《宣言》。

2. 张彭春在联合国人权委员会第三届第 50 次会议上的发言

1948 年 5 月 27 日下午 2 时 30 分,联合国人权委员会第三届第 50 次会议,在纽约成功湖召开,该次会议的主要议题是审议起草委员会提交的《国际人权宣言》草案。中国代表张彭春参加了本次会议,并在会议上发言,具体发言内容①会议纪要、纪要影像和纪要译文如下:

【会议纪要】

Mr. CHANG (China) drew attention to the shorter draft Declaration submitted by his delegation, and contained in Annex A of the report of the Drafting Committee. The Commission was dealing with one of the most serious questions before the United Nations and the whole world. The principal aim of the Declaration was to call the attention of the world to certain fundamental human rights, with a view to educational advancement. The term "education" was here used in the broad sense of how to improve the quality of life. The Declaration should be as simple as possible and in the form which was easy to grasp. He urged those members of the Commission who had not served on the Drafting Committee to examine carefully the Chinese Draft.

Article 1

Mr. CHANG (China) amended the text submitted by the representatives of the United Kingdom and India by deleting the full stop after the first sentence

---

① UN Document: E/CN. 4/SR. 50, pp. 7-8, p. 11, p. 14, p. 15, p. 17.

and the words "They are endowed by nature with reason and conscience".

The import of that sentence was controversial and its deletion would clarify and shorten the text.

Mrs. MEHTA (India) and Mr. WILSON (United Kingdom) agreed to the deletion proposed by the Chinese representative.

After a brief procedural discussion, it was decided to put the Chinese representative's amendment of the text submitted by the delegations of India and the United Kingdom to the vote in separate parts.

The first sentence was adopted by eleven votes to none, with four abstentions.

The deletion of the first full stop and of the subsequent words up to and including the word "conscience" was rejected by six votes to five, with six abstentions.

The last sentence was adopted by thirteen votes to none, with three abstentions.

The article as a whole was adopted by eleven votes to none, with six abstentions.

Article 2

Mr. CHANG (China) drew the Commission's attention to the Chinese draft of Article 2, which condensed Articles 2 and 3 of the Drafting Committee's text in one paragraph. If the Commission desired to arrive at a brief text for the Declaration, he would suggest using the second sentence of that paragraph for Article 2. However, in his opinion, it would be preferable to place the Article on the restrictions of the rights of the individual at the very end of the Declaration, for it was not logical to proclaim the restrictions before the rights themselves had not been stated.

Mr. WILSON (United Kingdom) agreed with the representative of Chile and with the Chinese representative's plea for brevity. However, the Chinese draft had the disadvantage of being insufficiently specific and he would prefer the phrase "restrictions ... necessary to secure due regard, etc. " to "recognition of the rights of others".

Mr. CHANG (China) once more stressed the fact that the Declaration which the Commission was drafting was intended to be read and understood by large masses of people, and should therefore be as brief and intelligible as possible. He urged the members of the Commission to give consideration to the draft submitted by his delegation, appearing on pages 14 and 15 of document E/CN. 4/95.

【纪要影像】

Mr. CHANG (China) drew attention to the shorter draft Declaration submitted by his delegation, and contained in Annex A of the report of the Drafting Committee. The Commission was dealing with one of the most serious questions before the United Nations and the whole world. The principal aim of the Declaration was to call the attention of the world to certain fundamental human rights, with a view to educational advancement. The term "education" was here used in the broad sense of how to improve the quality of life. The Declaration should be as simple as possible and in a form which was easy to grasp. He urged those members of the Commission who had not served on the Drafting Committee to examine carefully the Chinese Draft.

图片 1.3.2:张彭春在联合国人权委员会第三届第 50 次会议发言纪要(1)

Article 1

Mr. CHANG (China) amended the text submitted by the representatives of the United Kingdom and India by deleting the full stop after the first sentence and the words "They are endowed by nature with reason and conscience".

The import of that sentence was controversial and its deletion would clarify and shorten the text.

Mrs. MEHTA (India) and Mr. WILSON (United Kingdom) agreed to the deletion proposed by the Chinese representative.

After a brief procedural discussion, it was decided to put the Chinese representative's amendment of the text submitted by the delegations of India and the United Kingdom to the vote in separate parts.

The first sentence was adopted by eleven votes to none, with four abstentions.

The deletion of the first full stop and of the subsequent words up to and including the word "conscience" was rejected by six votes to five, with six abstentions.

The last sentence was adopted by thirteen votes to none, with three abstentions.

The article as a whole was adopted by eleven votes to none, with six abstentions.

图片1.3.3:张彭春在联合国人权委员会第三届第50次会议发言纪要(2)

Article 2

Mr. CHANG (China) drew the Commission's attention to the Chinese draft of Article 2, which condensed Articles 2 and 3 of the Drafting Committee's text in one paragraph. If the Commission desired to arrive at a brief text for the Declaration, he would suggest using the second sentence of that paragraph for Article 2. However, in his opinion, it would be preferable to place the Article on the restrictions of the rights of the individual at the very end of the Declaration, for it was not logical to proclaim the restrictions before the rights themselves had not been stated.

Mr. WILSON (United Kingdom) agreed with the representative of Chile and with the Chinese representative's plea for brevity. However, the Chinese draft had the disadvantage of being insufficiently specific and he would prefer the phrase "restrictions...necessary to secure due regard, etc." to "recognition of the rights of others".

Mr. CHANG (China) once more stressed the fact that the Declaration which the Commission was drafting was intended to be read and understood by large masses of people, and should therefore be as brief and intelligible as possible. He urged the members of the Commission to give consideration to the draft submitted by his delegation, appearing on pages 14 and 15 of document E/CN.4/95.

图片1.3.4:张彭春在联合国人权委员会第三届第50次会议发言纪要(3)

【纪要译文】

张先生(中国)提请注意中国代表团提交的较短的《宣言》草案,该草案载于起草委员会报告附件A。委员会正在处理联合国和全世界面临的最严重的问题之一。《宣言》的主要目的是呼吁世界关注某些基本人权,以促进教育发展。这里的"教育"一词是从如何提高生活质量的广泛意义上来使用的。宣言应尽可能简单,并采用易于理解的形式。他敦促没有在起草委员会任职的委员会成员仔细审议中国的草案。

第1条

张先生(中国)对英国和印度代表提交的案文进行了修订,删除了第一句后的句号和"他们天生具有理性和良知"等字样。

这句话的含义是有争议的,删除这句话将会澄清和缩短案文。

梅赫塔夫人(印度)和威尔逊先生(英国)同意中国代表的删除提议。

经过简短的程序性讨论后,决定将中国代表对印度和英国代表团提交的案文的修正案分成不同部分进行表决。

第一句以11票对0票,4票弃权获得通过。

删除第一个句号和随后的直至并包括"良知"一词以6票对5票,6票弃权被否决。

最后一句以13票对0票,3票弃权获得通过。

整个条款以11票对0票,6票弃权获得通过。

第2条

张先生(中国)提请委员会注意第2条的中文草案,该草案将起草委员会案文的第2条和第3条压缩在一段中。如果委员会希望就宣言达成一个简短的案文，他建议将该段第二句用于第2条。但是，他认为，最好把限制个人权利的本条内容放在宣言的末尾，因为权利本身还没有阐明就宣布其限制是不合逻辑的。

威尔逊先生(英国)同意智利代表和中国代表关于简洁的请求。然而，中国的草案有不够具体的缺点，他更喜欢"为确保适当考虑所必要的限制等"胜过"承认他人的权利"。

张先生(中国)再次强调，委员会正在起草的宣言是为了让广大人民阅读和理解，因此应尽可能简明易懂。他敦促委员会成员审议载于 E/CN.4/95 号文件第 14 和 15 页的该国代表团提交的草案。

3. 张彭春在联合国人权委员会第三届第 51 次会议上的发言

1948 年 5 月 28 日上午 10 时 45 分，联合国人权委员会第三届第 51 次会议，在纽约成功湖召开，该次会议的主要议题是审议宣言草案的第 2 条。中国代表张彭春参加了本次会议，并在会议上发言，具体发言内容①会议纪要、纪要影像和纪要译文如下：

【会议纪要】

Mr. CHANG (China) suggested that his amendment should be changed to read as follows："The exercise of these rights requires recognition of the rights of others and the welfare of all. " Welfare included the idea of security; and recognition of the rights of all included the idea of democracy. He stressed the value of the voluntary element in the word "recognition". Emphasis should be

---

① UN Document：E/CN.4/SR.51, pp. 5-6.

placed not on restraining people, but on educating them. The purpose of all social and political education was the voluntary recognition of the rights of others. The Commission's ideal should not be the imposition of restrictions but rather the voluntary recognition by all of the rights of others. That was the ideal which the Declaration should express.

【纪要影像】

Mr. CHANG (China) suggested that his amendment should be changed to read as follows: "The exercise of these rights requires recognition of the rights of others and the welfare of all." Welfare included the idea of security; and recognition of the rights of all included the idea of democracy. He stressed the value of the voluntary element in the word "recognition". Emphasis should be placed not on restraining people, but on educating them. The purpose of all social and political education was the voluntary recognition of the rights of others. The Commission's ideal should not be the imposition of restrictions but rather the voluntary recognition by all of the rights of others. That was the ideal which the Declaration should express.

图片 1.3.5：张彭春在联合国人权委员会第三届第 51 次会议发言纪要

【纪要译文】

张先生(中国)建议将他的修正案改为如下："行使这些权利需要承认他人的权利和所有人的福利。"福利包括安全的概念；承认所有人的权利包括民主的思想。他强调了"承认"一词中自愿成分的价值。重点不应该放在约束人上，而应该放在教育人上。所有社会和政治教育的目的都是自愿承认他人的权利。委员会的理想不应是强加限制，而是所有人自愿承认他人的权利。这是宣言应该表达的理想。

4. 张彭春在联合国人权委员会第三届第 52 次会议上的发言

1948 年 5 月 28 日下午 2 时 30 分,联合国人权委员会第三届第 52 次会议,在纽约成功湖召开,本次会议主要议题是审议《国际人权宣言》的第 3 条等。中国代表张彭春参加了本次会议,并在会议上先后多次发言,具体发言内容①会议纪要、纪要影像和纪要译文如下:

【会议纪要】

Article 3, paragraph 1

Mr. CHANG (China) stated that, in view of the fact that the Commission apparently preferred to draft the Declaration in a more detailed form than the Chinese delegation had envisaged, he withdrew his amendment to the paragraph in question. (Cf. document E/CN. 4/102)

Mr. Klekovkin (Ukrainian Soviet Socialist Republics) accepted the suggestion of Mr. CHANG (China) to insert the words "or other" between the words "property" and "status", which would meet the point he wished to make.

The Ukrainian amendment was adopted by thirteen votes to none, with one abstention.

Mr. CHANG (China) considered the addition of the word "office" unnecessary; the concept was covered by the words "property or other status".

---

① UN Document: E/CN. 4/SR. 52, p. 3, p. 5, p. 6, p. 7, p. 9, p. 11, p. 12, p. 13, p. 15, p. 17.

Article 3, paragraph 2

Mr. CHANG (China) pointed out that those who wished to avoid use of that phrase could vote for the French amendment which did not contain it.

Mr. CHANG (China) supported the observations of the Philippine representative. In the interest of unanimity he was also ready to accept the deletion of the word "arbitrary".

Mr. CHANG (China) proposed to incorporate the Philippine suggestion in the Article so that the phrase would read "without and against any discrimination". The word "discrimination" did not apply to useful distinction.

Mr. CHANG (China) agreed with the United Kingdom representative that the suggested addition might have the effect of limiting the idea of equal protection of the law and advised further consideration of the article. To say "against any discrimination in violation of this Declaration" was perhaps acceptable but was certainly less strong than the phrase "without or against any discrimination".

The meaning of "discrimination" did not present a problem, for the word was unquestionably used in a derogatory sense.

Mr. CHANG (China) did not agree that the phrase was repetitious since in prargraph 2 of the article it was used to describe equal protection of the law.

Mr. CHANG (China) agreed with the United Kingdom representative that the French suggestion was unwise. He proposed that the sentence should end after the word "discrimination" in the second line.

Mr. CHANG (China) thought the meaning of the phrase was clear if it were read with the proper emphasis. Since it had already been accepted by a vote of the Commission it was no longer open to question.

Referring to the last part of his proposal, namely, the deletion of the words "in violation of this Declaration", Mr. CHANG (China) pointed out that the comma should be omitted as it affected the meaning of the text. Without the comma the phrase would apply only to the last part of the sentence and would be acceptable.

Mr. CHANG (China) thought the French amendment would unduly weaken the words "without and against any discrimination". The phrase at the end was sufficient.

The CHAIRMAN appointed a small drafting committee made up of the representatives of China, France and the United Kingdom to draw up a text, or alternative texts, on the basis of the discussion that had taken place.

【纪要影像】

Article 3, paragraph 1
        Mr. CHANG (China) stated that, in view of the fact that the
Commission apparently preferred to draft the Declaration in a more detailed
form than the Chinese delegation had envisaged, he withdrew his amendment to
the paragraph in question. (Cf. document E/CN.4/102)
        Mr. KLEKOVKIN (Ukrainian Soviet Socialist Republics) accepted
the suggestion of Mr. CHANG (China) to insert the words "or other" between
the words "property" and "status", which would meet the point he wished
to make.
        The Ukrainian amendment was adopted by thirteen votes to none, with
one abstention.
        Mr. CHANG (China) considered the addition of the word "office"
unnecessary; the concept was covered by the words "property or other status'

图片 1.3.6:张彭春在联合国人权委员会第三届第 52 次会议发言纪要(1)

Article 3, paragraph 2
        Mr. CHANG (China) pointed out that those who wished to avoid use
of that phrase could vote for the French amendment which did not contain it.
        Mr. CHANG (China) supported the observations of the Philippine
representative. In the interest of unanimity he was also ready to accept
the deletion of the word "arbitrary".
        Mr. CHANG (China) proposed to incorporate the Philippine suggestion
in the Article so that the phrase would read "without and against any discrimination". The word "discrimination" did not apply to useful distinction

Mr. CHANG (China) agreed with the United Kingdom representative that the suggested addition might have the effect of limiting the idea of equal protection of the law and advised further consideration of the article To say "against any discrimination in violation of this Declaration" was perhaps acceptable but was certainly less strong than the phrase "without or against any discrimination".

The meaning of "discrimination" did not present a problem, for the word was unquestionably used in a derogatory sense.

图片 1.3.7：张彭春在联合国人权委员会第三届第 52 次会议发言纪要(2)

Mr. CHANG (China) did not agree that the phrase was repetitious since in paragraph 2 of the article it was used to describe equal protection of the law.

Mr. CHANG (China) agreed with the United Kingdom representative that the French suggestion was unwise. He proposed that the sentence should end after the word "discrimination" in the second line.

Mr. CHANG (China) thought the meaning of the phrase was clear if it were read with the proper emphasis. Since it had already been accepted by a vote of the Commission it was no longer open to question.

Referring to the last part of his proposal, namely, the deletion of the words "in violation of this Declaration", Mr. CHANG (China) pointed out that the comma should be omitted as it affected the meaning of the text. Without the comma the phrase would apply only to the last part of the sentence and would be acceptable.

Mr. CHANG (China) thought the French amendment would unduly weaken the words "without and against any discrimination". The phrase at the end was sufficient.

The CHAIRMAN appointed a small drafting committee made up of the representatives of China, France and the United Kingdom to draw up a text, or alternative texts, on the basis of the discussion that had taken place.

图片 1.3.8：张彭春在联合国人权委员会第三届第 52 次会议发言纪要(3)

【纪要译文】

第 3 条第 1 款

张先生(中国)说,鉴于委员会显然倾向于以比中国代表团所设想的

更详细的形式起草宣言,他撤回对该段的修正。(参见 E/CN. 4/102 号文件)

克列科夫金(Klekovkin)先生(乌克兰苏维埃社会主义共和国)接受张先生(中国)的建议,在"财产"和"身份"之间插入"或其他"几个字,这样就符合他想表达的观点。

乌克兰的修正案以 13 票对 0 票,1 票弃权获得通过。

张先生(中国)认为没有必要增加"办公室"一词;"财产或其他身份"一语涵盖了这一概念。

第 3 条第 2 款

张先生(中国)指出,那些希望避免使用该短语的人可以投票赞成法国的修正案,因为它没有包含该短语。

张先生(中国)支持菲律宾代表的意见。为了全体一致,他也愿意接受删除"任意"一词。

张先生(中国)提议将菲律宾的建议纳入该条,这样该短语将读作"不受和反对任何歧视"。"歧视"一词不适用于有益的区分。

张先生(中国)同意英国代表的意见,即建议增加的词语可能会限制法律平等保护的概念,并建议进一步审议该条。说"反对违反本宣言的任何歧视"也许是可以接受的,但肯定不如"不受或反对任何歧视"这样强烈。

"歧视"的含义并不构成问题,因为这个词无疑是在贬义上使用的。

张先生(中国)不同意这一说法是重复的,因为在该条第 2 款中,它用来描述法律的平等保护的。

张先生(中国)同意英国代表的意见,认为法国的建议是不明智的。他建议该句应在第二行"歧视"一词之后结束。

张先生(中国)认为,如果用适当的重音来读,这个短语的意思就很清楚了。既然它已经被委员会的表决所接受,就不再有问题了。

关于他的建议的最后一部分,即删除"违反本宣言"等字,张先生(中国)指出,逗号应删除,因为它影响了案文的含义。如果没有逗号,该短语将仅适用于句子的最后一部分,是可以接受的。

张先生(中国)认为法国的修正案不适当地削弱了"不受和反对任何歧视"这几个字。结尾的短语就足够了。

主席任命了一个由中国、法国和英国代表组成的小型起草委员会,根据已经进行的讨论起草一份案文或备选案文。

5. 张彭春在联合国人权委员会第三届第 53 次会议上的发言

1948 年 6 月 1 日上午 10 时 45 分,联合国人权委员会第三届第 53 次会议,在纽约成功湖召开,本次会议的主要议题继续审议《人权宣言》草案条款。中国代表张彭春参加了本次会议,并在会议上发言,具体发言内容①会议纪要、纪要影像和纪要译文如下:

【会议纪要】

Article 5

Mr. CHANG (China) drew attention to the Chinese draft for article 5, the first part of which was the same as that used in the United Kingdom and Indian draft. For the present, he thought discussion ought to be limited to article 5, leaving the question of merging articles 5 and 8 to a later stage.

Article 3, paragraph 2

The CHAIRMAN drew the attention of the Commission to the following new draft of article 3, paragraph 2, which had been prepared by the small drafting group set up for that purpose at the previous meeting:

"All are equal before the law and are entitled to equal protection of the

---

① UN Document:E/CN. 4/SR. 53, p. 3, p. 5, p. 6, pp. 7-8, p. 9.

law without any discrimination, and against any discrimination in violation of this Declaration or incitement to such discrimination. "

Mr. CHANG (China) explained that the small drafting group had not been particularly satisfied with the final wording; the text had, however, the advantage of being in conformity with the decisions taken by the Commission at the previous meeting, and could therefore be adopted without the Commission reconsidering the votes already taken.

Mr. CHANG (China) recalled that by the two votes taken at the previous meeting, the Commission had decided that the phrase "without and against any discrimination" was to be included, and that mention was to be made of incitement to discrimination. The only question not decided had been the position of the phrase concerning the principles of the Declaration, the inclusion of which had been suggested by the representative of France. The drafting group had decided, with the agreement of the French representative, that the phrase "in violation of this Declaration" should qualify the phrase "against any discrimination" and not the phrase "without any discrimination".

Mr. Chang contended that in making that decision, the drafting group had in no way overstepped its terms of reference. If, however, any members felt that an unwarranted liberty had been taken with the wording, the Commission could revert to the original text, in which case the Chinese delegation would abandon the compromise text and urge, as before, a shorter paragraph, ending with the words "and against any discrimination".

With regard to the Australian amendment, its acceptance would necessitate a reconsideration of the votes taken at the previous meeting.

Mr. CASSIN (France) confirmed the statement of the Chinese representative. The drafting group had carried out its mandate in strict observance of the instructions of the Commission, and had unanimously decided that the qualifications "in violation of this Declaration" could only be placed after the phrase "against any discrimination".

The drafting group had carried out its mandate in strict observance of the instructions of the Commission, and had unanimously decided that the qualifications" in violation of this Declaration" could only be placed after the phrase "against any discrimination".

The CHAIRMAN proposed that since it was obvious that there would be no agreement at the present stage, the only procedure was for the drafting group, together with the representatives of Australia and the Byelorussian Soviet Socialist Republic, to discuss the text again, and present alternative formulas for the Commission to vote upon.

Mr. CHANG (China) supported that proposal.

【纪要影像】

Article 5

  Mr. CHANG (China) drew attention to the Chinese draft for article 5, the first part of which was the same as that used in the United Kingdom and Indian draft. For the present, he thought discussion ought to be limited to article 5, leaving the question of merging articles 5 and 8 to a later stage.

Article 3, paragraph 2

  Mr. CHANG (China) explained that the small drafting group had not been particularly satisfied with the final wording; the text had, however, the advantage of being in conformity with the decisions taken by the Commission at the previous meeting, and could therefore be adopted without the Commission reconsidering the votes already taken.

  Mr. CHANG (China) recalled that by the two votes taken at the previous meeting, the Commission had decided that the phrase "without and against any discrimination" was to be included, and that mention was to be made of incitement to discrimination. The only question not decided had been the position of the phrase concerning the principles of the Declaration, the inclusion of which had been suggested by the representative of France. The drafting group had decided, with the agreement of the French representative, that the phrase "in violation of this Declaration" should qualify the phrase "against any discrimination" and not the phrase "without any discrimination".

图片 1.3.9:张彭春在联合国人权委员会第三届第 53 次会议发言纪要(1)

Mr. Chang contended that in making that decision, the drafting group had in no way overstepped its terms of reference. If, however, any members felt that an unwarranted liberty had been taken with the wording, the Commission could revert to the original text, in which case the Chinese delegation would abandon the compromise text and urge, as before, a shorter paragraph, ending with the words "and against any discrimination".

With regard to the Australian amendment, its acceptance would necessitate a reconsideration of the votes taken at the previous meeting.

Mr. CASSIN (France) confirmed the statement of the Chinese representative. The drafting group had carried out its mandate in strict observance of the instructions of the Commission, and had unanimously decided that the qualifications "in violation of this Declaration" could only be placed after the phrase "against any discrimination".

The CHAIRMAN proposed that since it was obvious that there would be no agreement at the present stage, the only procedure was for the drafting group, together with the representatives of Australia and the Byelorussian Soviet Socialist Republic, to discuss the text again, and present alternative formulas for the Commission to vote upon.

Mr. CHANG (China) supported that proposal.

图片 1.3.10：张彭春在联合国人权委员会第三届第 53 次会议发言纪要(2)

【纪要译文】

第 5 条

张先生(中国)提请注意中国的第 5 条草案,该条的第一部分与英国和印度草案中使用的相同。目前,他认为讨论应限于第 5 条,将第 5 条和第 8 条合并的问题留待以后解决。

第 3 条第 2 款

主席提请委员会注意第 3 条第 2 款的以下新草案,该草案是在上次会议上为此目的设立的小型起草小组编写的:

"法律面前人人平等,并一律受到法律的平等保护,不受歧视,反对任何违反本宣言的歧视或煽动这种歧视。"

张先生(中国)解释说,小型起草小组对最后的措辞不是特别满意;然而,该案文的优点是符合委员会在上次会议上作出的决定,因此可以在委员会不重新审议已经进行的表决的情况下获得通过。

张先生(中国)回顾说,在上次会议上进行的两次表决中,委员会决定列入"不受和反对任何歧视"一语,并提及煽动歧视。唯一没有决定的问题是关于《宣言》原则的短语的位置,这是法国代表建议列入的。起草小组在法国代表的同意下决定,"违反本《宣言》"一语应修饰"反对任何歧视"一语,而不是"不受任何歧视"一语。

张先生认为,起草小组在作出这一决定时,绝对没有超越其职权范围。但是,如果任何成员认为这一措辞不合理,委员会可以回到原来的案文,在这种情况下,中国代表团将放弃折中案文,并像以前一样敦促缩短一段,以"并反对任何歧视"结尾。

关于澳大利亚的修正案,接受该修正案将需要重新审议上次会议所进行的表决。

卡森先生(法国)证实了中国代表的发言。起草小组严格按照委员会的指示执行了任务,并一致决定,"违反本《宣言》"这一限定语只能放在"反对任何歧视"这一短语之后。

主席提议,由于在现阶段显然不会达成一致意见,唯一的程序是由起草小组与澳大利亚和白俄罗斯苏维埃社会主义共和国的代表一起再次讨论该案文,并提出备选方案供委员会表决。

张先生(中国)支持这一提议。

6. 张彭春在联合国人权委员会第三届第54次会议上的发言

1948年6月1日下午2时30分,联合国人权委员会第三届第54次会议,在纽约成功湖召开,本次会议继续审议《国际人权宣言》草案。中国代表张彭春参加了本次会议,并在会议上先后多次发言,具体发言内容①会议纪要、纪要影像和纪要译文如下:

【会议纪要】

Article 3

Mr. CHANG (China) reported that the drafting sub-committee appointed at the fifty-third meeting had agreed on the text of paragraph 2, Article 3 as originally amended. The Philippine representative had accepted the view of the French representative that the words "in violation" should be retained. The English and the Russian texts would contain the word "discrimination", while the French text would use "distinction", since the words in question were so used in the United Nations Charter.

Article 6

The CHAIRMAN said she would put the text to the vote in the following order: first the China-India-United Kingdom substitute as furthest removed from the original, and then the first sentence of the text adopted at the second session of the Commission.

The China-India-United Kingdom text was adopted by ten votes to four with two abstentions.

Article 7

Mr. CHANG (China) accepted the India-United Kingdom text (E/CN. 4/99) but suggested that it should be changed as follows: "Every one in the determination of any criminal charge against him and of his rights and obligations is entitled . . . " He explained that he suggested the change because the text adopted at the second session of the Commission followed that order.

Mr. WILSON (United Kingdom) was ready to accept the Chinese repre-

---

① UN Document: E/CN. 4/SR. 54, p. 2, p. 6, pp. 7–8, p. 10, p. 11, p. 14.

sentative's suggestion concerning the transposition of the clauses.

Mr. CHANG (China) also felt that the principles of equality before the law and before the tribunal were the same.

Mr. CASSIN (France) appealing for the greatest possible measure of a-greement on the text, urged the Commission to accept the following amend-ment:

"Everyone is entitled in *full equality* to a fair hearing by an *independent* and *impartial* tribunal in the determination of his rights..."

Mr. WILSON (United Kingdom) was not opposed to the addition of the words "independent and", but felt that the expression: "in full equality" was repetitious, and therefore inadvisable.

Mr. CHANG (China) shared the United Kingdom representative's opin-ion.

The Chiese-Indian-United Kingdom draft, as amended, was adopted by thirteen votes to none, with four abstentions.

<u>Article 8</u>

Mr. CHANG (China) noted general agreement on the clear and simple drafting of paragraph 3. As regards the other paragraphs, disagreement might a-rise, not on the principles involved, but with regard to their appropriateness in the present context. He favoured retention of the first sentence of paragraph 1, deletion of the second sentence, and would abstain from voting on the third and fourth sentences. Paragraph 2 could be deleted, and paragraph 3 maintained.

The Chairman then appointed a sub-committee, consisting of the repre-sentatives of the United Kingdom, India, France, China, and Yugoslavia, to compose a new draft of Article 8, paragraphs 1 and 2.

【纪要影像】

Article 3

    Mr. CHANG (China) reported that the drafting sub-committee appointed at the fifty-third meeting had agreed on the text of paragraph 2, Article 3 as originally amended. The Philippine representative had accepted the view of the French representative that the words "in violation" should be retained. The English and the Russian texts would contain the word "discrimination", while the French text would use "distinction", since the words in question were so used in the United Nations Charter.

Article 6.

    The CHAIRMAN said she would put the text to the vote in the following order: first the China-India-United Kingdom substitute as furthest removed from the original, and then the first sentence of the text adopted at the second session of the Commission.

    The China-India-United Kingdom text was adopted by ten votes to four with two abstentions.

图片 1.3.11：张彭春在联合国人权委员会第三届第 54 次会议发言纪要(1)

Article 7

    Mr. CHANG (China) accepted the India-United Kingdom text (E/CN.4/99) but suggested that it should be changed as follows: "Every one in the determination of any criminal charge against him and of his rights and obligations is entitled..." He explained that he suggested the change because the text adopted at the second session of the Commission followed that order.

    Mr. WILSON (United Kingdom) was ready to accept the Chinese representative's suggestion concerning the transposition of the clauses.

    Mr. CHANG (China) also felt that the principles of equality before the law and before the tribunal were the same.

图片 1.3.12：张彭春在联合国人权委员会第三届第 54 次会议发言纪要(2)

联合国人权委员会和起草委员会

Mr. CASSIN (France) appealing for the greatest possible measure of agreement on the text, urged the Commission to accept the following amendment:

"Everyone is entitled in <u>full equality</u> to a fair hearing by an <u>independent</u> and <u>impartial</u> tribunal in the determination of his rights..."

Mr. WILSON (United Kingdom) was not opposed to the addition of the words "independent and", but felt that the expression: "in full equality" was repetitious, and therefore inadvisable.

Mr. CHANG (China) shared the United Kingdom representative's opinion.

<u>The Chinese-Indian-United Kingdom draft, as amended, was adopted by thirteen votes to none, with four abstentions.</u>

图片 1.3.13:张彭春在联合国人权委员会第三届第 54 次会议发言纪要(3)

Article 8

Mr. CHANG (China) noted general agreement on the clear and simple drafting of paragraph 3. As regards the other paragraphs, disagreement might arise, not on the principles involved, but with regard to their appropriateness in the present context. He favoured retention of the first sentence of paragraph 1, deletion of the second sentence, and would abstain from voting on the third and fourth sentences. Paragraph 2 could be deleted, and paragraph 3 maintained.

The Chairman then appointed a sub-committee, consisting of the representatives of the United Kingdom, India, France, China, and Yugoslavia, to compose a new draft of Article 8, paragraphs 1 and 2.

图片 1.3.14:张彭春在联合国人权委员会第三届第 54 次会议发言纪要(4)

【纪要译文】

第 3 条

张先生(中国)报告说,在第 53 次会议上任命的起草小组委员会已同意最初修正的第 3 条第 2 款的案文。菲律宾代表接受了法国代表的观点,即应当保留"违反"一词。英文和俄文文本将包含"歧视"一词,而法文文本将使用"区别",因为《联合国宪章》中就使用了这一词。

第 6 条

主席说,她将按照以下顺序将案文付诸表决:首先是距离原始案文最远的中国-印度-英国联合替代案文,然后是委员会第二届会议通过的案文的第一句。

中国-印度-英国联合案文以 10 票对 4 票,2 票弃权获得通过。

第 7 条

张先生(中国)接受印度-英国的案文(E/CN.4/99),但建议将其修改如下:"在确定对他提出的任何刑事指控时,任何人都有其权利和义务"。他解释说,他提出这一修改是因为委员会第二届会议通过的案文遵循了这一顺序。

威尔逊先生(英国)准备接受中国代表关于调换条款的建议。

张先生(中国)也认为,法律面前和法庭面前平等的原则是相同的。

卡森先生(法国)呼吁就案文达成最大程度的一致,并敦促委员会接受以下修正:

"人人完全平等地有权由一个独立而无偏倚的法庭进行公正的审讯以确定他的权利……"

威尔逊先生(英国)不反对添加"独立而"字样,但认为"完全平等"的表述是重复的,因此不可取。

张先生(中国)同意英国代表的意见。

经修正的中国-印度-英国联合草案以 13 票对 0 票,4 票弃权获得通过。

第 8 条

张先生(中国)注意到大家普遍同意第 3 款的行文简洁明了。至于其他段落,可能会出现分歧,不是在所涉及的原则上,而是在它们在目前情况下是否合适的问题上。他赞成保留第 1 款第一句,删除第二句,并将对第三和第四句投弃权票。可以删除第 2 款,保留第 3 款。

主席随后任命了一个小组委员会,由英国、印度、法国、中国和南斯拉夫的代表组成,负责编写第 8 条第 1 款和第 2 款的新草案。

7. 张彭春在联合国人权委员会
第三届第 55 次会议上的发言

1948 年 6 月 2 日上午 11 时,联合国人权委员会第三届第 55 次会议,在纽约成功湖召开,本次会议的主要议题是审议起草委员会提交给人权委员会的报告、审议宣言条款及各国代表提交的修正案。中国代表张彭春参加了本次会议,并在会议上发言,具体发言内容①会议纪要、纪要影像和纪要译文如下:

【会议纪要】

Article 9

Mr. CHANG (China) drew attention to the negative form in which article 9 was worded in the text proposed by his delegation. The wording "No one shall be subjected to unreasonable interference . . . " affirmed implicitly everyone's right to protection under the law and avoided the ambiguity which might arise as a result of the deletion of the words "under the law" from the Drafting Committee's text.

He thought, moreover, that the order of presentation of the provisions was more logical in his delegation's text beginning as it did with interference with the individual and from there going on to cover interference with his family, home, correspondence and reputation.

The CHAIRMAN put to the vote the Chinese draft of article 9 of the Draft Declaration.

Draft article 9 proposed by China was adopted by 9 votes to 3, with 4 ab-

---

① UN Document: E/CN. 4/SR. 55, pp. 2-3, p. 13.

stentions.

Article 8

Mr. CHANG (China) explained on behalf of the Sub-Committee that the phrase "in a public trial at which he has had all guarantees necessary for his defence" had been placed in brackets to indicate that there had been a difference of opinion on the subject in the Sub-Committee. The Sub-Committee reached a unanimous decision with regard to the first part of paragraph 1 only. He therefore suggested that first the clause in brackets be put to the vote.

The Chairman put to the vote the retention or deletion of the part of the sentence in parentheses.

It was decided by eight votes to six, with two abstentions, to delete the part of the sentence in parentheses from the first paragraph of article 8.

【纪要影像】

Article 9

　　　　Mr. CHANG (China) drew attention to the negative form in which article 9 was worded in the text proposed by his delegation. The wording "No one shall be subjected to unreasonable interference..." affirmed implicitly everyone's right to protection under the law and avoided the ambiguity which might arise as a result of the deletion of the words "under the law" from the Drafting Committee's text.

　　　　He thought, moreover, that the order of presentation of the provisions was more logical in his delegation's text beginning as it did with interference with the individual and from there going on to cover interference with his family, home, correspondence and reputation.

　　　　The CHAIRMAN put to the vote the Chinese draft of article 9 of the Draft Declaration.

　　　　Draft article 9 proposed by China was adopted by 9 votes to 3, with 4 abstentions.

图片 1.3.15：张彭春在联合国人权委员会第三届第 55 次会议发言纪要(1)

Article 8

Mr. CHANG (China) explained on behalf of the Sub-Committee that the phrase "in a public trial at which he has had all guarantees necessary for his defence" had been placed in brackets to indicate that there had been a difference of opinion on the subject in the Sub-Committee. The Sub-Committee reached a unanimous decision with regard to the first part of paragraph 1 only. He therefore suggested that first the clause in brackets be put to the vote.

The CHAIRMAN put to the vote the retention or deletion of the part of the sentence in parentheses.

It was decided by eight votes to six, with two abstentions, to delete the part of the sentence in parentheses from the first paragraph of article 8.

图片 1.3.16：张彭春在联合国人权委员会第三届第 55 次会议发言纪要(2)

【纪要译文】

第 9 条

张先生(中国)提请注意中国代表团提出的案文中第 9 条的否定形式。"任何人不得受到不合理的干涉……"含蓄地肯定了每个人受法律保护的权利,避免了由于删除起草委员会的案文中"根据法律"一词而可能产生的含糊不清。

此外,他认为,在他的代表团的案文中,条款的陈述顺序更符合逻辑,从对个人的干涉开始,然后包括对其家庭、住宅、通信和名誉的干涉。

主席将宣言草案第 9 条的中文草案付诸表决。

中国提议的草案第 9 条以 9 票对 3 票,4 票弃权获得通过。

第 8 条

张先生(中国)代表小组委员会解释说,"在公开审判中,他得到了为其辩护所必需的一切保证"一语被放在方括号内,是为了表明小组委员会对这一问题有不同意见。小组委员会仅就第 1 款的第一部分达成了一致决定。因此,他建议首先将括号中的条款付诸表决。

主席将保留还是删除括号中的句子部分付诸表决。

以 8 票对 6 票,2 票弃权决定删除第 8 条第 1 款括号中的部分句子。

8. 张彭春在联合国人权委员会第三届第 56 次会议上的发言

1948 年 6 月 2 日下午 2 时 30 分,联合国人权委员会第三届第 56 次会议,在纽约成功湖召开,本次会议的主要议题是继续讨论《人权宣言》草案。中国代表张彭春参加了本次会议,并在会议上发言,具体发言内容[①]会议纪要、纪要影像和纪要译文如下:

【会议纪要】

Article 8, paragraph 1

Mr. CHANG (China) proposed to replace the sub-committee's text by the following:

"Everyone charged with a penal offence is presumed to be innocent until proved guilty according to law."

The phrase "according to law" had been inadvertently omitted in the English translation.

Article 8, paragraph 2

In reply to the Chairman, Dr. CHANG (China) agreed to amend his proposal to read as follows: "Everyone has a right to seek and shall be granted temporary asylum from persecution in other countries."

---

① UN Document: E/CN. 4/SR. 56, p. 2, p. 8, p. 11.

Dr. CHANG (China) said that the question of Japanese war criminals in China did not arise, because article 11 dealt with refugees from persecution. The Commission was attempting to draft a declaration of aspirations and therefore no qualifications should be introduced into the text.

【纪要影像】

Article 8, paragraph 1
　　Mr. CHANG (China) proposed to replace the sub-committee's text by the following:
　　"Everyone charged with a penal offence is presumed to be innocent until proved guilty according to law."
　　The phrase "according to law" had been inadvertently omitted in the English translation.

Article 8, paragraph 2
　　In reply to the Chairman, Dr. CHANG (China agreed to amend his proposal to read as follows: "Everyone has a right to seek and shall be granted temporary asylum from persecution in other countries."
　　Dr. CHANG (China) said that the question of Japanese war criminals in China did not arise, because article 11 dealt with refugees from persecution. The Commission was attempting to draft a declaration of aspirations and therefore no qualifications should be introduced into the text.

图片 1.3.17:张彭春在联合国人权委员会第三届第 56 次会议发言纪要

【纪要译文】

第 8 条第 1 款

张先生(中国)建议将小组委员会的案文改为:

"每个被指控犯有刑事罪的人,在依法证明有罪之前,都被假定为无罪。"

英文译文中无意中漏掉了"依法"一词。

第 8 条第 2 款

在答复主席时,张博士(中国)同意将他的建议修改如下:"人人有权寻求并应获得临时庇护,以免在其他国家受到迫害。"

张博士(中国)说,在中国的日本战犯的问题不在其中,因为第11条处理的是逃避迫害的难民。委员会正试图起草一份表达愿望的宣言,因此不应在案文中引入任何限定条件。

9. 张彭春在联合国人权委员会 第三届第 57 次会议上的发言

1948 年 6 月 3 日上午 10 时 45 分,联合国人权委员会第三届第 57 次会议,在纽约成功湖召开,本次会议继续讨论《人权宣言》草案。中国代表张彭春参加了本次会议,并在会议上发言,具体发言内容[①]会议纪要、纪要影像和纪要译文如下:

【会议纪要】

Article 11   Continuation of consideration

Mr. CHANG (China), agreeing with the Belgian representative's interpretation of the two versions, noted the importance of a clear and unambiguous text on the matter. It was true that the first version gave the country of immigration certain control over the granting of asylum. The original Chinese amendment had included that right of states to control immigration. He supported the French proposal which had been rejected in view of the fact that a similar question was under consideration by the Council. Should it be impossible to revert to that proposal, the Commission might go on record as considering that a United Nations organ should deal with that problem. He agreed with the representative of Lebanon regarding the vagueness of the qualification clause which could

---

① UN Document: E/CN. 4/SR. 57, pp. 4-5, p. 10, p. 11.

not be a compromise between the rights of states granting, and persons seeking, asylum. The Commission should state clearly and frankly whether or not countries had control over the granting of asylum. If no qualification clause was included, the question might arise whether countries were obliged to grant asylum whenever asked for it. There were two possibilities, the Commission could either accept the first version without the qualification clause, and in that case it would be well to revert to the French proposal or at least go on record that the French proposal constituted the most desirable solution to the problem; or the Commission should clearly leave it to countries to decide whether they would grant asylum. The first alternative should be put to the vote first as being farthest removed from the Drafting Committee's text.

The CHAIRMAN, referring to the Chinese representative's remarks, explained that the Commission's action with regard to the French proposal had been based on the fact that the Council had called for a separate study of the question of nationality which would probably include the problem of asylum. She also pointed out that the qualification clause had been introduced by the drafting sub-committee partly because the Chinese representative had indicated the danger of an unqualified right of persons to seek and be granted asylum. Such a provision might keep many countries unable to make such a commitment from ratifying the Convention.

After an exchange of views between Mr. WILSON (United Kingdom), and Mr. CHANG (China) on the order in which the vote should proceed, Mr. PAVLOV (Union of Soviet Socialist Republics) expressed the opinion that both alternative texts of the amendment were equally removed from the original. He stated that the text he had previously suggested was furthest removed. The final version of the USSR amendment was as follows: "Everyone has the right to seek and be granted in other countries asylum from persecution as required by humanity, defence of democratic interests, activity in the field of science, and participation in the struggle for national liberty". He requested that his amendment should be voted first.

After a short discussion in which Mr. CASSIN (France), Mr. CHANG (China), Mr. Hood (Australia) and Mr. WILSON (United Kingdom) took part, the CHAIRMAN put the amended version of paragraph 1, article 11 to the vote.

The Commission adopted by twelve votes to one with four abstentions, the following version of paragraph 1: Everyone has the right to seek and be granted in other countries asylum from persecution".

【纪要影像】

Article 11 -- Continuation of consideration.

Mr. CHANG (China), agreeing with the Belgian representative's interpretation of the two versions, noted the importance of a clear and unambiguous text on the matter. It was true that the first version gave the country of immigration certain control over the granting of asylum. The original Chinese amendment had included that right of states to control immigration. He supported the French proposal which had been rejected in view of the fact that a similar question was under consideration by the Council. Should it be impossible to revert to that proposal, the Commission might go on record as considering that a United Nations organ should deal with that problem. He agreed with the representative of Lebanon regarding the vagueness of the qualification clause which could not be a compromise between the rights of states granting, and persons seeking, asylum. The Commission should state clearly and frankly whether or not countries had control over the granting of asylum. If no qualification clause was included, the question might arise whether countries were obliged to grant asylum whenever asked for it. There were two possibilities, the Commission could either accept the first version without the qualification clause, and in that case it would be well to revert to the French proposal or at least go on record that the French proposal constituted the most desirable solution to the problem; or the Commission should clearly leave it to countries to decide whether they would grant asylum. The first alternative should be put to the vote first as being farthest removed from the Drafting Committee's text.

图片 1.3.18:张彭春在联合国人权委员会第三届第 57 次会议发言纪要(1)

The CHAIRMAN, referring to the Chinese representative's remarks, explained that the Commission's action with regard to the French proposal had been based on the fact that the Council had called for a separate study of the question of nationality which would probably include the problem of asylum. She also pointed out that the qualification clause had been introduced by the drafting sub-committee partly because the Chinese representative had indicated the danger of an unqualified right of persons to seek and be granted asylum. Such a provision might keep many countries unable to make such a commitment from ratifying the Convention.

After an exchange of views between Mr. WILSON (United Kingdom), and Mr. CHANG (China) on the order in which the vote should proceed, Mr. PAVLOV (Union of Soviet Socialist Republics) expressed the opinion that both alternative texts of the amendment were equally removed from the original. He stated that the text he had previously suggested was furthest removed. The final version of the USSR amendment was as follows: "Everyone has the right to seek and be granted in other countries asylum from persecution as required by humanity, defence of democratic interests, activity in the field of science, and participation in the struggle for national liberty". He requested that his amendment should be voted first.

After a short discussion in which Mr. CASSIN (France), Mr. CHANG (China), Mr. HOOD (Australia) and Mr. WILSON (United Kingdom) took part, the CHAIRMAN put the amended version of paragraph 1, article 11 to the vote.

The Commission adopted by twelve votes to one with four abstentions, the following version of paragraph 1: "Everyone has the right to seek and be granted in other countries asylum from persecution".

图片 1.3.19:张彭春在联合国人权委员会第三届第 57 次会议发言纪要(2)

【纪要译文】

第 11 条(继续审议)

张先生(中国)同意比利时代表对两个文本的解释,并指出在这个问题上有一个清楚明确的文本是很重要的。的确,第一个版本给予移民国家对提供庇护的某种控制。中国最初修正案包括国家控制移民的权利。他支持法国的提议,该提议遭到拒绝,因为理事会正在审议一个类似的问题。如果不可能回到这一提议,委员会可以记录在案,认为应由一个联合国机构来处理这一问题。他同意黎巴嫩代表关于限定条款含糊不清的意见,该条款不能成为提供庇护的国家和寻求庇护的人的权利之间的妥协。委员会应明确和坦率地说明国家是否对提供庇护拥有控制权。如果不包括资格条款,可能会出现国家是否有义务在请求庇护时提供庇护的问题。有两种可能性,委员会可以接受没有限定条款的第一个版本,在这种情况下,最好回到法国的提案,或者至少记录在案,法国的提案是解决这个问题的最可取的办法;或者委员会应该明确让各国决定是否提供庇护。第一个备选案文应首先付诸表决,因为它离起草委员会的案文最远。

主席在提到中国代表的发言时解释说,委员会对法国提议采取的行动是基于这样一个事实,即理事会要求对国籍问题进行单独研究,这可能包括庇护问题。她还指出,起草小组委员会之所以提出限定条款,部分原因是中国代表指出了人们寻求和获得庇护的权利不受限制的危险。这种规定可能会使许多无法作出这种承诺的国家无法批准公约。

在威尔逊先生(英国)和张先生(中国)就表决的顺序交换意见后,帕夫洛夫(PAVLOV)先生(苏联)表示,修正案的两个备选案文都从原文中删除了。他说,他先前建议的案文距离最远。苏联修正案的最终版本如下:"人人有权根据人道、捍卫民主利益、科学领域的活动和参加争取民族自由的斗争的需要,在其他国家寻求和获得庇护。"他要求先表决他的修正案。

在卡森先生(法国)、张先生(中国)、胡德(Hood)先生(澳大利亚)和威尔逊先生(英国)参加的简短讨论之后,主席将第 11 条第 1 款的修订案文付诸表决。

委员会以 12 票对 1 票,4 票弃权通过了第 1 款的如下案文:"人人有权在其他国家寻求并获得庇护以避免迫害。"

10. 张彭春在联合国人权委员会
第三届第 58 次会议上的发言

1948 年 6 月 3 日下午 2 时 30 分,联合国人权委员会第三届第 58 次会议,在纽约成功湖召开,本次会议继续讨论起草委员会提交给人权委员会的报告。中国代表张彭春参加了本次会议,并在会议上发言,具体发言内容①会议纪要、纪要影像和纪要译文如下:

【会议纪要】

Article 12

Mr. CHANG(China) stated that the law of his country, too, did not clearly define the concept.

Article 13

Mr. CHANG(China) stated his delegation would vote in favour of the most concise text, namely, that proposed by the delegation of India and the United Kingdom.

Mr. CHANG(China) formally proposed the adjournment of the discussion.

【纪要影像】

```
Article 12
        Mr. CHANG (China) stated that the law of his country, too,
did not clearly define the concept.
Article 13
```

---

① UN Document: E/CN. 4/SR. 58, p. 7, p. 17, p. 18.

```
'Mr. CHANG (China) stated his delegation would vote in
favour of the most concise text, namely, that proposed by the
delegations of : India and the United Kingdom.
        Mr. CHANG (China) formally proposed the adjournment of the
discussion.
```

图片1.3.20:张彭春在联合国人权委员会第三届第58次会议发言纪要

【纪要译文】

第 12 条

张先生(中国)说,他的国家的法律也没有明确界定这一概念。

第 13 条

张先生(中国)说,中国代表团将投票赞成最简洁的案文,即印度和英国代表团提出的案文。

张先生(中国)正式提议暂停讨论。

11. 张彭春在联合国人权委员会第三届第59次会议上的发言

1948 年 6 月 4 日上午 10 时 45 分,联合国人权委员会第三届第 59 次会议,在纽约成功湖召开,本次会议的主要议题是继续讨论《人权宣言》草案。中国代表张彭春参加了本次会议,并在会议上发言,具体发言内容①会议纪要、纪要影像和纪要译文如下:

【会议纪要】

<u>Article 15</u>

Mr. CHANG (China) supported the United Kingdom text of article 15 (document E/CN. 4/99).

---

① UN Document:E/CN. 4/SR. 59, p. 6.

【纪要影像】

> Mr. CHANG (China) supported the United Kingdom text of article 15 (document E/CN.4/99).

图片 1.3.21:张彭春在联合国人权委员会第三届第 59 次会议发言纪要

【纪要译文】

第 15 条

张先生(中国)支持英国的第 15 条案文(E/CN.4/99 号文件)。

12. 张彭春在联合国人权委员会第三届第 60 次会议上的发言

1948 年 6 月 4 日下午 3 时,联合国人权委员会第三届第 60 次会议,在纽约成功湖召开,本次会议继续讨论《人权宣言》草案第 15 条。中国代表张彭春参加了本次会议,并在会议上先后多次发言,具体发言内容①会议纪要、纪要影像和纪要译文如下:

【会议纪要】

Article 15 (continued)

Mr. CHANG (China) did not oppose the French representative's request for a vote, but feared that the inclusion of the words he proposed would amount to a repetition.

Mr. CHANG (China) pointed out that the Chinese amendment applied simultaneously to articles 16, 17, 18 and 19, and suggested that it should not

---

① UN Document: E/CN.4/SR.60, p. 4, p. 6, p. 11, p. 13.

be considered at present.

Mr. CHANG (China) preferred the latter amendment. Article 16 should treat only of the protection of freedom of religion and belief; the protection of freedom of thought was dealt with in Articles 17 and 18.

He suggested replacing "either alone or in community with other persons of like mind" by "with others".

He would vote for the Indian and United Kingdom amendment.

Mr. CHANG (China) agreed that according to European ideas freedom of thought was the basis of freedom of belief. Although belief implied thought, freedom of thought had in the course of history actually preceded freedom of belief. But the right to those freedoms implied the right to change them. He therefore suggested simply saying: "the right to freedom of thought, religion and belief."

【纪要影像】

Article 15 (continued)

Mr. CHANG (China) did not oppose the French representative's request for a vote, but feared that the inclusion of the words he proposed would amount to a repetition.

Mr. CHANG (China) pointed out that the Chinese amendment applied simultaneously to articles 16, 17, 18 and 19, and suggested that it should not be considered at present.

Mr. CHANG (China) preferred the latter amendment. Article 16 should treat only of the protection of freedom of religion and belief; the protection of freedom of thought was dealt with in Articles 17 and 18.

He suggested replacing "either alone or in community with other persons of like mind" by "with others".

He would vote for the Indian and United Kingdom amendment.

Mr. CHANG (China) agreed that according to European ideas freedom of thought was the basis of freedom of belief. Although belief implied thought, freedom of thought had in the course of history actually preceded freedom of belief. But the right to those freedoms implied the right to change them. He therefore suggested simply saying: "the right to freedom of thought, religion and belief."

图片 1.3.22:张彭春在联合国人权委员会第三届第 60 次会议发言纪要

【纪要译文】

第 15 条(续)

张先生(中国)不反对法国代表要求进行表决,但担心列入他提议的措辞将等同于重复。

张先生(中国)指出,中国的修正案同时适用于第 16、17、18 和 19 条,并建议目前不应审议该修正案。

张先生(中国)倾向于后一种修正案。第 16 条应仅涉及保护宗教和信仰自由;第 17 条和第 18 条涉及保护思想自由。

他建议将"单独或与志同道合的人一起"改为"与他人一起"。

他将投票赞成印度和英国的修正案。

张先生(中国)同意,根据欧洲的观点,思想自由是信仰自由的基础。虽然信仰意味着思想,但在历史上,思想自由实际上先于信仰自由。但是,享有这些自由的权利意味着有权改变它们。因此,他建议简单地说:"思想、宗教和信仰自由的权利。"

13. 张彭春在联合国人权委员会第三届第 61 次会议上的发言

1948 年 6 月 7 日上午 11 时,联合国人权委员会第三届第 61 次会议,在纽约成功湖召开,本次会议继续审议起草委员会的报告。中国代表张彭春参加了本次会议,并在会议上发言,具体发言内容①会议纪要、纪要影像和纪要译文如下:

【会议纪要】

Article 19

Mr. CHANG (China) said that after studying the different proposals submitted, he wished to stress that his delegation's draft had the advantage of being both complete and concise.

The joint text proposed by the delegations of India and the United Kingdom added to the Chinese proposal a condition taken from the Drafting Committee's text: "for the promotion, defence and protection etc. ..." That rather long reservation did not seem necessary, for the general interest of the democratic societies was the constant aim of the proposed Declaration.

The Drafting Committee's text enumerated moreover the kinds of associations to which a person had a right to belong. But any enumeration was dangerous. It might be argued that religious associations, for example, had the same right to be included in article 19 as trade union organizations. He did not see why the latter should be mentioned any more than the former. The purpose of article 19 should be to grant to every one freedom to organize or join any association provided only that that was done within the framework of democratic interests. The simplified draft advocated by the Chinese delegation best fulfilled that purpose.

The CHAIRMAN then put to the vote the variant proposed by China (document E/CN. 4/102).

The Chinese draft for article 19 *was adopted by seven votes to four with three abstentions.*

---

① UN Document: E/CN. 4/SR. 61, pp. 8-9, p. 12, p. 18.

<u>Articles 21 and 22</u>

Mr. CHANG (China) withdrew his amendment and said the Chinese delegation preferred and accepted the wording proposed by the Indian and United Kingdom delegation.

Mr. CHANG (China) proposed, as regards the English text, to revert to the Drafting Committee's wording and say "access to public employment".

The CHAIRMAN asked the representatives of China, India and of the United Kingdom to work out a formula on which the Commission would vote at its next meeting.

【纪要影像】

Article 19

    Mr. CHANG (China) said that after studying the different proposals submitted, he wished to stress that his delegation's draft had the advantage of being both complete and concise.

    The joint text proposed by the delegations of India and the United Kingdom added to the Chinese proposal a condition taken from the Drafting Committee's text: "for the promotion, defence and protection etc..." That rather long reservation did not seem necessary, for the general interest of the democratic societies was the constant aim of the proposed Declaration.

    The Drafting Committee's text enumerated moreover the kinds of associations to which a person had a right to belong. But any enumeration was dangerous. It might be argued that religious associations, for example, had the same right to be included in article 19 as trade union organizations. He did not see why the latter should be mentioned any more than the former. The purpose of article 19 should be to grant to every one freedom to organize or join any association provided only that that was done within the framework of democratic interests. The simplified draft advocated by the Chinese delegation best fulfilled that purpose.

    The CHAIRMAN then put to the vote the variant proposed by China (document E/CN.4/102).

    <u>The Chinese draft for article 19 was adopted by seven votes to four with three abstentions.</u>

图片 1.3.23:张彭春在联合国人权委员会第三届第 61 次会议发言纪要(1)

Mr. CHANG (China) withdrew his amendment and said the Chinese delegation preferred and accepted the wording proposed by the Indian and United Kingdom delegations.

Mr. CHANG (China) proposed, as regards the English text, to revert to the Drafting Committee's wording and say "access to public employment."

The CHAIRMAN asked the representatives of China, India and of the United Kingdom to work out a formula on which the Commission would vote at its next meeting.

图片 1.3.24:张彭春在联合国人权委员会第三届第 61 次会议发言纪要(2)

【纪要译文】

第 19 条

张先生(中国)说,在研究了提交的不同提案之后,他希望强调,中国代表团的草案具有既完整又简明的优点。

印度和英国代表团提出的联合案文在中国的提案中增加了取自起草委员会案文的一个条件:"促进、防卫和保护等……"这一相当长的保留似乎没有必要,因为民主社会的普遍利益是拟议宣言的一贯目标。

起草委员会的案文还列举了一个人有权加入的各种协会。但是任何列举都是危险的。例如,有人可能会争辩说,宗教协会与工会组织一样,有同样的权利被列入第 19 条。他不明白为什么后者比前者更值得一提。第 19 条的目的应该是给予每个人组织或加入任何社团的自由,只要这是在民主利益的框架内进行的。中国代表团主张的简化草案最符合这一目的。

主席随后将中国提议的备选案文(E/CN.4/102 号文件)付诸表决。

第 19 条的中国草案以 7 票对 4 票,3 票弃权获得通过。

第 21 和 22 条

张先生(中国)撤回其修正案,并说中国代表团倾向于并接受印度和英国代表团提议的措辞。

张先生(中国)建议,关于英文文本,回到起草委员会的措辞,改为"获得公职"。

主席请中国、印度和英国代表制定一个方案,供委员会在下次会议上表决。

14. 张彭春在联合国人权委员会
第三届第 62 次会议上的发言

1948 年 6 月 7 日下午 2 时 30 分,联合国人权委员会第三届第 62 次会议,在纽约成功湖召开,本次会议主要议题是审议起草委员会提交的《国际人权宣言》草案。中国代表张彭春参加了本次会议,并在会议上发言,具体发言内容①会议纪要、纪要影像和纪要译文如下:

【会议纪要】

Articles 21 and 22

Mr. CHANG (China) wondered whether a simplified form would be acceptable, taking into consideration the general structure of the Declaration. He proposed some such simple formula as "The Government shall conform to the will of the people".

Mr. HOOD (Australia) supported the representative of China. It was possible that the Commission had proceeded too rapidly in its consideration of Article 21, and that some mention of the will of the people should be included somewhere in the Declaration. He would go even further than the Chinese representative, and would suggest that the Commission might go back to Article 21 with a view to including that phrase at the end of the first sentence, along the following lines: " ... freely chosen representatives, to the end that the Gov-

---

① UN Document: E/CN. 4/SR. 62, p. 5, p. 6.

ernment shall conform to the will of the people. ”

Mr. FONTAINA (Uruguay) suggested that, before a vote was taken upon the actual text, the Commission should vote whether it was to be included in the Preamble or as a separate article.

After a short discussion, in which Mr. CHANG (China) pointed out that if the text was rejected as an article, members would still have the right to reintroduce it when the Preamble was discussed, Mr. FONTAINA (Uruguay) withdrew his suggestion.

【纪要影像】

Articles 21 and 22

Mr. CHANG (China) wondered whether a simplified form would be acceptable, taking into consideration the general structure of the Declaration. He proposed some such simple formula as "The Government shall conform to the will of the people".

Mr. HOOD (Australia) supported the representative of China. It was possible that the Commission had proceeded too rapidly in its consideration of Article 21, and that some mention of the will of the people should be included somewhere in the Declaration. He would go even further than the Chinese representative, and would suggest that the Commission might go back to Article 21 with a view to including that phrase at the end of the first sentence, along the following lines: "...freely chosen representatives, to the end that the Government shall conform to the will of the people."

Mr. FONTAINA (Uruguay) suggested that, before a vote was taken upon the actual text, the Commission should vote whether it was to be included in the Preamble or as a separate article.

After a short discussion, in which Mr. CHANG (China) pointed out that if the text was rejected as an article, members would still have the right to reintroduce it when the Preamble was discussed, Mr. FONTAINA (Uruguay) withdrew his suggestion.

图片 1.3.25:张彭春在联合国人权委员会第三届第 62 次会议发言纪要

【纪要译文】

第 21 和 22 条

张先生(中国)考虑到声明的一般结构,不知道简化形式是否可以接受。他提出了一些简单的公式,如"政府应符合人民的意愿"。

胡德先生(澳大利亚)支持中国代表。委员会在审议第 21 条时可能进行得太快,宣言的某处应该提到人民的意愿。他将比中国代表更进一步,并建议委员会可以回到第 21 条,以便在第一句的末尾加上这句话,大意如下:"……自由选择的代表,政府应遵从人民的意愿。"

丰泰纳(Fontaina)先生(乌拉圭)建议,在对实际案文进行表决之前,委员会应就是将其纳入序言还是作为独立条文进行表决。

经过简短的讨论,张先生(中国)指出,如果案文作为一条被否决,成员们仍有权在讨论序言时重新提出,丰泰纳先生(乌拉圭)撤回了他的建议。

15. 张彭春在联合国人权委员会第三届第 63 次会议上的发言

1948 年 6 月 8 日上午 10 时 45 分,联合国人权委员会第三届第 63 次会议,在纽约成功湖召开,本次会议的主要议题是审议起草委员会提交的《国际人权宣言》草案。中国代表张彭春参加了本次会议,并在会议上发言,具体发言内容①会议纪要、纪要影像和纪要译文如下:

【会议纪要】

Articles 17 and 18

---

① UN Document:E/CN.4/SR.63, p. 5, p. 12, p. 14.

Mr. CHANG (China) also supported the text submitted by the United Nations Conference on Freedom of Information, but proposed, in view of the previously agreed substitution of the word "opinion" for the word "thought" in the first line of the Geneva text, the following re-arrangement of the article: "Everyone shall have the right to freedom of opinion and expression; this right shall include freedom to seek, receive and impart information and ideas without inference and regardless of frontiers. " The word "by any means" in the third line of the Geneva text seemed superfluous. He would not oppose, however, the inclusion of such an idea, but suggested that the words should be changed to: "through all media of expression".

Mr. CHANG (China) did not think that the suggestions of the Conference on the Freedom of Information were necessarily binding on the Commission but he agreed that the important ideas in the Conference text should be retained. It seemed redundant, however, to keep the phrase "to hold opinions" in the second line, if freedom of opinion had already been mentioned in the first line.

Mr. CHANG (China) suggested that the representatives of Lebanon, Philippines, the United Kingdom and China should try to prepare for the afternoon meeting a text that would be acceptable to the Commission.

The CHAIRMAN stated that the Chinese suggestion would be followed.

【纪要影像】

Articles 17 and 18

       Mr. CHANG (China) also supported the text submitted by the United Nations Conference on Freedom of Information, but proposed, in view of the previously agreed substitution of the word "opinion" for the word "thought" in the first line of the Geneva text, the following re-arrangement of the article: "Everyone shall have the right to freedom of opinion and expression; this right shall include freedom to seek, receive and import information and ideas without inference and regardless of frontiers." The word "by any means" in the third line of the Geneva text seemed superfluous. He would not oppose, however, the inclusion of such an idea, but suggested that the words should be changed to: "through all media of expression".

图片 1.3.26：张彭春在联合国人权委员会第三届第 63 次会议发言纪要(1)

       Mr. CHANG (China) did not think that the suggestions of the Conference on the Freedom of Information were necessarily binding on the Commission but he agreed that the important ideas in the Conference text should be retained. It seemed redundant, however, to keep the phrase "to hold opinions" in the second line, if freedom of opinion had already been mentioned in the first line.

       Mr. CHANG (China) suggested that the representatives of Lebanon, Philippines, the United Kingdom and China should try to prepare for the afternoon meeting a text that would be acceptable to the Commission.

       The CHAIRMAN stated that the Chinese suggestion would be followed.

图片 1.3.27：张彭春在联合国人权委员会第三届第 63 次会议发言纪要(2)

第 17 条和第 18 条

张先生(中国)也支持联合国新闻自由会议提交的案文,但鉴于此前在日内瓦文本第一行中已商定将"思想"一词改为"见解",以下是对条文的重新安排:"人人有权享有见解和言论自由;这项权利包括不受干扰和不分国界地寻求、接受和传递消息和思想的自由。"日内瓦文本第三行中的"以任何方式"一词似乎是多余的。然而,他不反对纳入这一想法,但建议将措辞改为:"通过所有表达媒介。"

张先生(中国)并不认为关于新闻自由会议的建议对委员会一定具有约束力,但他同意会议案文中的重要思想应予保留。然而,如果在第一行已经提到了意见自由,那么在第二行保留"持有意见"似乎是多余的。

张先生(中国)建议黎巴嫩、菲律宾、英国和中国的代表努力为下午的会议准备一份委员会可以接受的案文。

主席表示将遵循中国的建议。

16. 张彭春在联合国人权委员会第三届第 64 次会议上的发言

1948 年 6 月 8 日下午 2 时 30 分,联合国人权委员会第三届第 64 次会议,在纽约成功湖召开,本次会议的主要议题是审议《国际人权宣言》草案。中国代表张彭春参加了本次会议,并在会议上发言,具体发言内容① 会议纪要、纪要影像和纪要译文如下:

---

① UN Document:E/CN.4/SR.64,p. 2,p. 4,p. 6.

【会议纪要】

Articles 17 and 18（Continuation）

The CHAIRMAN requested the representative of China to present the conclusions of the Drafting Sub-Committee on articles 17 and 18.

Mr. CHANG（China）said that the Drafting Sub-Committee had not intended to change the substance of the articles and had limited itself to proposing slight drafting modifications: replacing "freedom of opinion", in the second line, by "freedom of thought", and in the English text, replacing "any means" by "any media".

Mr. CHANG（China）recalled that his delegation had suggested placing article 2 at the end of the Declaration. In addition, since it was apparent that the majority of members favoured a reconsideration of that article, he did not think it appropriate to vote for its reconsideration before it was known in what way it would be modified. He therefore proposed that the Commission should merely mention those two suggestions in its minutes.

Articles 23 and 24

Mr. CHANG（China）thought that the Chinese text would have to be considered subsequently, for it embodied a different conception of how the Declaration should be set out.

Articles 17 and 18 (Continuation)

The CHAIRMAN requested the representative of China to present the conclusions of the Drafting Sub-Committee on articles 17 and 18.

Mr. CHANG (China) said that the Drafting Sub-Committee had not intended to change the substance of the articles and had limited itself to proposing slight drafting modifications: replacing "freedom of opinion", in the second line, by "freedom of thought", and in the English text, replacing "any means" by "any media".

Mr. CHANG (China) recalled that his delegation had suggested placing article 2 at the end of the Declaration. In addition, since it was apparent that the majority of members favoured a reconsideration of that article, he did not think it appropriate to vote for its reconsideration befo it was known in what way it would be modified. He therefore proposed that the Commission should merely mention those two suggestions in its minutes.

Articles 23 and 24

Mr. CHANG (China) thought that the Chinese text would have to be considered subsequently, for it embodied a different conception of how the Declaration should be set out.

图片 1.3.28:张彭春在联合国人权委员会第三届第 64 次会议发言纪要

【纪要译文】

第 17 和 18 条(续)

主席请中国代表介绍起草小组委员会关于第 17 条和第 18 条的结论。

张先生(中国)说,起草小组委员会并不打算改变条款的实质内容,而仅限于提出一些细微的文字修改:将第二行中的"意见自由"改为"思想自由",并将英文文本中的"任何手段"改为"任何媒介"。

张先生(中国)回顾说,中国代表团曾建议将第 2 条放在宣言的末尾。此外,由于大多数成员显然赞成重新审议该条,他认为在知道将以何种方式修改该条之前投票赞成重新审议是不合适的。因此,他建议委员会在其会议记录中仅提及这两项建议。

第 23 条和第 24 条

张先生(中国)认为,中文文本必须在以后审议,因为它体现了关于声明应如何表述的不同概念。

17. 张彭春在联合国人权委员会第三届第 65 次会议上的发言

1948 年 5 月 24 日上午 11 时,联合国人权委员会第三届第 65 次会议,在纽约成功湖召开,本次会议的主要议题是审议《国际人权宣言》草案。中国代表张彭春参加了本次会议,并在会议上发言,具体发言内容①会议纪要、纪要影像和纪要译文如下:

【会议纪要】

Article 23

Mr. CHANG (China) thought that it was difficult to decide whether or not the provision should be included in article 23, since no text was available on which all members agreed. He agreed with the Lebanese representative that reference to unemployment should be made in article 23 and that a general article should be placed at the end of the section devoted to economic and social rights.

He proposed the following text combining the provisions of paragraphs 1 and 2 of article 23;

"Everyone has the right to work and to just and favourable conditions of work and pay; that right includes the adoption of such measures as would create the widest possible opportunities for useful work and prevent unemployment."

---

① UN Document: E/CN.4/SR.65, p.7, p.8, p.9.

He asked that his proposal be put to the vote.

Mr. VILFAN (Yugoslavia) proposed an amendment to the text submitted by the representative of China; involving the addition of the words: "taken by the State or society" after the word: "measures".

Mr. CASSIN (France) also proposed an amendment; he suggested the addition of the words: "taken by the various States, and with international co-operation" after the word: "measures".

Mr. CHANG (China) could accept neither of the two amendments.

The CHAIRMAN read out paragraph 1 as amended by the representative of China. She said that she would vote against that amendment.

Mr. MALIK (Lebanon) felt that his own draft was better; the word "protection", contrary to the views of the United Kingdom representative, was completely unambiguous and included all measures to be taken against unemployment.

Mr. Malik asked for a vote on his amendment. If that amendment were rejected, he would propose, as an amendment to the Chinese text, replacing the words: "the widest possible" by the word: "adequate". He pointed out that, while the French representative's intentions were excellent, his amendment might raise difficulties in introducing a new element which would require further study.

Mr. CHANG (China) accepted the Lebanese representative's amendment to his text.

Mr. Pavlov also proposed that the Chinese draft should be amended by replacing the word: "includes" by the word: "provides".

Mr. CHANG (China) considered that his was a compromise formula; he pointed out that it was impossible to deal with the question of unemployment without mentioning measures to be taken against it.

【纪要影像】

Article 23

Mr. CHANG (China) thought that it was difficult to decide whether or not the provision should be included in article 23, since no text was available on which all members agreed. He agreed with the Lebanese representative that reference to unemployment should be made in article 23 and that a general article should be placed at the end of the section devoted to economic and social rights.

He proposed the following text combining the provisions of paragraphs 1 and 2 of article 23:

"Everyone has the right to work and to just and favourable conditions of work and pay; that right includes the adoption of such measures as would create the widest possible opportunities for useful work and prevent unemployment."

He asked that his proposal be put to the vote.

Mr. VILFAN (Yugoslavia) proposed an amendment to the text submitted by the representative of China; involving the addition of the words: "taken by the State or society" after the word: "measures".

Mr. CASSIN (France) also proposed an amendment; he suggested the addition of the words: "taken by the various States, and with international co-operation" after the word: "measures".

Mr. CHANG (China) could accept neither of the two amendments.

图片 1.3.29：张彭春在联合国人权委员会第三届第 65 次会议发言纪要(1)

The CHAIRMAN read out paragraph 1 as amended by the representative of China. She said that she would vote against that amendment.

Mr. MALIK (Lebanon) felt that his own draft was better; the word "protection", contrary to the views of the United Kingdom representative, was completely unambiguous and included all measures to be taken against unemployment.

Mr. Malik asked for a vote on his amendment. If that amendment were rejected, he would propose, as an amendment to the Chinese text, replacing the words: "the widest possible" by the word: "adequate". He pointed out that, while the French representative's intentions were excellent, his amendment might raise difficulties in introducing a new element which would require further study.

Mr. CHANG (China) accepted the Lebanese representative's amendment to his text.

Mr. Pavlov also proposed that the Chinese draft should be amended by replacing the word: "includes" by the word: "provides".

Mr. CHANG (China) considered that his was a compromise formula; he pointed out that it was impossible to deal with the question of unemployment without mentioning measures to be taken against it.

图片 1.3.30:张彭春在联合国人权委员会第三届第 65 次会议发言纪要(2)

【纪要译文】

第 23 条

张先生(中国)认为,很难决定该条款是否应列入第 23 条,因为没有所有成员都同意的案文。他同意黎巴嫩代表的意见,即应在第 23 条中提及失业问题,并应在专门讨论经济和社会权利的一节末尾增加一个一般性条款。

他提议将第 23 条第 1 款和第 2 款的规定合并成以下案文:

"人人有权工作,并享有公正和良好的工作条件和报酬;这项权利包括采取各种措施,为有益的工作创造尽可能广泛的机会,并防止失业。"

他要求将他的提议付诸表决。

维尔凡(Vilfan)先生(南斯拉夫)提议对中国代表提交的案文进行修正,在"措施"一词之后加上"国家或社会所采取的"。

卡森先生(法国)也提出了一项修正案;他建议在"措施"一词之后加上"各国和在国际合作下所采取的"一语。

张先生(中国)不能接受两个修正案中的任何一个。

主席宣读了经中国代表修正的第 1 款。她说她将投票反对该修正案。

马利克先生(黎巴嫩)认为他自己的草案更好;与英国代表的观点相反,"保护"一词是完全明确的,包括了针对失业采取的所有措施。

马利克先生要求对他的修正案进行表决。如果该修正案被否决,作为对中文文本的一项修正案,他建议将"尽可能广泛"一词改为"充分"。他指出,虽然法国代表的意图很好,但他的修正案可能会在引入一个需要进一步研究的新要素方面造成困难。

张先生(中国)接受黎巴嫩代表对其案文的修正。

帕夫洛夫(Pavlov)先生还提议修改中文草案,将"包括"一词改为"提供"。

张先生(中国)认为他的方案是一种折衷方案;他指出,在处理失业问题时,不可能不提到解决失业问题的措施。

18. 张彭春在联合国人权委员会 第三届第 67 次会议上的发言

1948 年 8 月 10 日上午 11 时,联合国人权委员会第三届第 67 次会议,在纽约成功湖召开,本次会议的主要议题是继续讨论起草委员会提交给人权委员会的报告。中国代表张彭春参加了本次会议,并在会议上先后多次发言,具体发言内容①会议纪要、纪要影像和纪要译文如下:

【会议纪要】

New article

Mr. CHANG (China) suggested that the place to be given to the new articles should not be decided upon immediately. It was sufficient to agree that the articles would be added towards the end of the Declaration.

While supporting the idea that an article of general principle establishing everyone's right to a good social and international order should be included in the Declaration, he thought that the Commission should go further, and should affirm that it was the duty of all to contribute towards the establishment and maintenance of that order.

While stressing the importance of the question, he thought that there was

---

① UN Document: E/CN. 4/SR. 67, pp. 3-4, p. 4, p. 8, pp. 16-17.

no need for an immediate vote on the text proposed by the Sub-Committee. The Commission should reflect on what improvements might be made in it. He, therefore, suggested that the consideration of the question should be postponed till a later date.

If, however, the Commission decided on an immediate discussion of the two new articles, he would propose the inclusion in the first text of a phrase expressing the idea he had just set forth, namely, the need to affirm, side by side with the duties of the State, the individual's duty to contribute to the good social order he demanded. He therefore suggested the words "everyone has the right" either "and the duty to assist in the realization of" or "and the duty to bring about".

Mr. MALIK (Lebanon) entirely agreed with the idea Mr. Chang wished to have included in the Declaration, and realized its importance. That idea should, however, be stated in the Preamble which would mention the rights of States as well as the duties of the individual. To introduce the idea of the individual's duties into an article would be a departure from the form given to the other articles of the Declaration. The Commission should decide whether it considered such a departure justified by the importance of the article in question.

Mr. CHANG (China) said in answer to a question by the CHAIRMAN that article 2 did not fully meet the idea he wished to express by the new article. The duties of the individual mentioned in article 2 were those which he owed to the State of which he was a national, or to other nationals of that State. The article, the addition of which had been recommended by the Sub-Committee introduced a new idea, namely the individual's right to a good social order. As, however, the social order which the individual was entitled to demand, under the terms of that article, depended in the first instance on the individual's contribution to its establishment and maintenance, that right was dependent on the fulfillment of a duty which should be clearly stated.

Mr. CHANG (China) asked for some enlightenment on the functions of the Style Committee. He thought that that Committee would deal mainly with questions of style and with the uniformity of translations, and he was surprised that it should be entrusted with important decisions such as the placing of articles.

Articles 27 and 28

Mr. CHANG (China) proposed the adoption of the following text:

"1. Everyone has the right to education, including free fundamental education and equal access on the basis of merit to higher education.

"2. Education shall be directed to the full development of the human personality and to the strengthening of respect for human rights and fundamental freedoms."

Mr. CHANG pointed out that the first paragraph of that single article retained the two ideas contained in the joint United Kingdom—India text, while the second paragraph set forth, in condensed form, the substance of article 28, the importance of which the Chinese delegation had stressed time and again.

The Chairman then announced that a drafting Sub-Committee would be asked to submit suggestions for redrafting articles 27 and 28. It would be composed of the representatives of China, France, Lebanon, Panama, the United Kingdom, the Union of Soviet Socialist Republics and the United States.

【纪要影像】

New article

Mr. CHANG (China) suggested that the place to be given to the new articles should not be decided upon immediately. It was sufficient to agree that the articles would be added towards the end of the Declaration.

While supporting the idea that an article of general principle establishing everyone's right to a good social and international order should be included in the Declaration, he thought that the Commission should go further, and should affirm that it was the duty of all to contribute towards the establishment and maintenance of that order.

While stressing the importance of the question, he thought that there was no need for an immediate vote on the text proposed by the Sub-Committee. The Commission should reflect on what improvements might be made in it. He, therefore, suggested that the consideration of the question should be postponed till a later date.

If, however, the Commission decided on an immediate discussion of the two new articles, he would propose the inclusion in the first text of a phrase expressing the idea he had just set forth, namely, the need to affirm, side by side with the duties of the State, the individual's duty to contribute to the good social order he demanded. He therefore suggested adding after the words "everyone has the right" either "and the duty to assist in the realization of" or "and the duty to bring about".

图片 1.3.31：张彭春在联合国人权委员会第三届第 67 次会议发言纪要(1)

Mr. MALIK (Lebanon) entirely agreed with the idea Mr. Chang wished to have included in the Declaration, and realized its importance. That idea should, however, be stated in the Preamble which would mention the rights of States as well as the duties of the individual. To introduce the idea of the individual's duties into an article would be a departure from the form given to the other articles of the Declaration. The Commission should decide whether it considered such a departure justified by the importance of the article in question.

联合国人权委员会和起草委员会

Mr. CHANG (China) said in answer to a question by the CHAIRMAN that article 2 did not fully meet the idea he wished to express by the new article. The duties of the individual mentioned in article 2 were those which he owed to the State of which he was a national, or to other nationals of that State. The article, the addition of which had been recommended by the Sub-Committee introduced a new idea, namely the individual's right to a good social order. As, however, the social order which the individual was entitled to demand, under the terms of that article, depended in the first instance on the individual's contribution to its establishment and maintenance, that right was dependent on the fulfillment of a duty which should be clearly stated.

Mr. CHANG (China) asked for some enlightenment on the functions of the Style Committee. He thought that that Committee would deal mainly with questions of style and with the uniformity of translations, and he was surprised that it should be entrusted with important decisions such as the placing of articles.

图片 1.3.32：张彭春在联合国人权委员会第三届第 67 次会议发言纪要(2)

Articles 27 and 28

Mr. CHANG (China) proposed the adoption of the following text:

"1. Everyone has the right to education, including free fundamental education and equal access on the basis of merit to higher education.

"2. Education shall be directed to the full development of the human personality and to the strengthening of respect for human rights and fundamental freedoms."

Mr. Chang pointed out that the first paragraph of that single article retained the two ideas contained in the joint United Kingdom—India text, while the second paragraph set forth, in condensed form, the substance of article 28, the importance of which the Chinese delegation had stressed time and again.

The Chairman then announced that a drafting sub-committee would be asked to submit suggestions for redrafting articles 27 and 28. It would be composed of the representatives of China, France, Lebanon, Panama, the United Kingdom, the Union of Soviet Socialist Republics and the United States.

图片 1.3.33：张彭春在联合国人权委员会第三届第 67 次会议发言纪要(3)

新条款

张先生(中国)建议不要立即决定新条款的位置。同意在宣言末尾增加条款就足够了。

他支持在宣言中列入一项确立人人有权享有良好的社会和国际秩序的一般原则条款的想法,但认为委员会应更进一步,并应申明所有人都有义务为建立和维护这一秩序做出贡献。

他强调这个问题的重要性,但认为没有必要立即对小组委员会提出的案文进行表决。委员会应思考可以对其进行哪些改进。因此,他建议推迟审议这个问题。

但是,如果委员会决定立即讨论这两个新条款,他将提议在第一个案文中列入一个短语,表达他刚才提出的想法,即除了国家的责任之外,还需要申明个人有责任为他所要求的良好社会秩序作出贡献。因此,他建议使用"人人有权"或"有义务协助实现"或"有义务实现"的措辞。

马利克先生(黎巴嫩)完全同意张先生希望列入宣言的想法,并认识到其重要性。然而,这一想法应在序言中说明,序言将提到国家的权利以及个人的义务。将个人义务的概念引入一项条款将偏离《宣言》其他条款的形式。委员会应决定它是否认为这种偏离因有关条款的重要性而具合理性。

张先生(中国)在回答主席的一个问题时说,第2条没有完全满足他希望新条款表达的思想。第2条中提到的个人的责任是他对其为国民的国家或对该国其他国民的责任。这一条是小组委员会建议增加的,它提出了一个新的概念,即个人享有良好社会秩序的权利。然而,根据该条的规定,个人有权要求的社会秩序首先取决于个人对建立和维持社会秩序的贡献,因此,这一权利取决于履行一项应明确规定的义务。

张先生(中国)要求就文体委员会的职能给予一些启发。他认为该委员会将主要处理风格问题和翻译的统一问题,他感到惊讶的是,该委员会竟然被委托作出诸如条款安排等重要决定。

　　<u>第 27 和 28 条</u>

　　张先生(中国)提议通过以下案文:

　　"1. 每个人都有受教育的权利,包括免费基础教育和根据成绩平等接受高等教育。

　　"2. 教育的目的在于充分发展人的个性,加强对人权和基本自由的尊重。"

　　张先生指出,这一条的第一款保留了英国—印度联合案文中的两个观点,而第二款则简要阐述了第 28 条的实质内容,中国代表团曾多次强调其重要性。

　　主席随后宣布,将请一个起草小组委员会提交重新起草第 27 条和第 28 条的建议。它将由中国、法国、黎巴嫩、巴拿马、英国、苏联和美国的代表组成。

19. 张彭春在联合国人权委员会第三届第 68 次会议上的发言

　　1948 年 6 月 10 日下午 3 时 30 分,联合国人权委员会第三届第 68 次会议,在纽约成功湖召开,本次会议的主要议题是继续讨论《人权宣言》草案。中国代表张彭春参加了本次会议,并在会议上发言,具体发言内容①会议纪要、纪要影像和纪要译文如下:

---

　　①　UN Document:E/CN. 4/SR. 68, pp. 4-5, p. 7, p. 11.

Articles 27-28

Mr. CHANG (China) pleaded for support of the concept of "fundamental" education as elucidated by the representative of UNESCO. That new and modern concept was particularly well adapted to countries where adult education became imperative for those persons who had not enjoyed the opportunities of grade-school instruction. Mr. Chang agreed with the representative of the United Kingdom that the word "compulsory" should be deleted.

Mr. CHANG (China) felt that it would be tragic to omit the word "fundamental" from that phrase. He urged the Commission to insert the words "and fundamental" after "elementary", thus making a reference to education for adults.

The Chinese representative's amendment was approved by ten votes to none, with five abstentions.

Mr. CHANG (China) pointed out that in the first paragraph the word "compulsory" referred only to elementary and fundamental education. He did not think it should be used in a paragraph which applied also to higher education.

【纪要影像】

Articles 27-28

Mr. CHANG (China) pleaded for support of the concept of "fundamental" education as elucidated by the representative of UNESCO. That now and modern concept was particularly well adapted to countries where adult education became

imperative for those persons who had not enjoyed the opportunities of grade-school instruction. Mr. Chang agreed with the representative of the United Kingdom that the word "compulsory" should be deleted.

联合国人权委员会和起草委员会

Mr. CEANG (China) felt that it would be tragic to omit the word "fundamental" from that phrase. He urged the Commission to insert the words "and fundamental" after "elementary", thus making a reference to education for adults.

The Chinese representative's amendment was approved by ten votes to none, with five abstentions.

Mr. CHANG (China) pointed out that in the first paragraph the word "compulsory" referred only to elementary and fundamental education. He did not think it should be used in a paragraph which applied also to higher education.

图片 1.3.34：张彭春在联合国人权委员会第三届第 68 次会议发言纪要

【纪要译文】

第 27 至 28 条

张先生(中国)呼吁支持教科文组织代表阐述的"基础"教育概念。这一新的现代概念特别适合那些没有享受过小学教育机会的人必须接受成人教育的国家。张先生同意英国代表的意见,应删除"强制性"一词。

张先生(中国)认为,从该短语中删去"基础"一词将是悲剧性的。他敦促委员会在"初等"一词后插入"和基础"一词,从而提及成人教育。

中国代表的修正案以 10 票对 0 票,5 票弃权获得通过。

张先生(中国)指出,在第一段中,"义务"一词仅指初等和基础教育。他认为不应该在一个也适用于高等教育的段落中使用它。

20. 张彭春在联合国人权委员会第三届第 69 次会议上的发言

1948 年 6 月 11 日上午 11 时,联合国人权委员会第三届第 69 次会议,在纽约成功湖召开,本次会议的主要议题是继续审议《人权宣言》草案第 27 条和第 28 条。中国代表张彭春参加了本次会议,并在会议上先后多次

发言,具体发言内容①会议纪要、纪要影像和纪要译文如下:

【会议纪要】

Mr. CHANG (China) recalled that the Commission had discussed the question of education at length at its last meeting, and that it was essential that the declaration should not be silent on that point. Paragraph 2, as re-drafted by the Drafting Sub-Committee, appeared to him to express adequately the aim which positive education should pursue.

Mr. CHANG (China) suggested that the United Kingdom representative should modify his proposal by applying it not only to article 28, but to the whole of paragraph 2 of article 27, since that paragraph embodied the ideas contained in article 28.

Mr. CHANG (China) proposed the deletion of the words: "and foster international understanding", in order to avoid the two repetition of the same idea in a single paragraph.

Mr. CHANG (China) proposed the following text:

"Education shall be directed to the full development of the human personality, to the strengthening of respect for human rights and fundamental freedoms and to the promotion of international goodwill."

Mr. VILFAN (Yugoslavia) suggested that the following phrase should be added to the text proposed by the Chinese representative:

"and to the combating of the spirit of intolerance and hatred against the nations or racial or religious groups."

The amendment proposed by the representative of Yugoslavia was adopted by 6 votes to 4, with 5 abstentions.

The text submitted by the representative of China was adopted in its amended form by 7 votes to 5, with 2 abstentions.

---

① UN Document: E/CN. 4/SR. 69, p. 5, p. 6, p. 8, p. 9.

Article 27 as a whole was adopted by 7 votes to 4, with 3 abstentions.

【纪要影像】

Mr. CHANG (China) recalled that the Commission had discussed the question of education at length at its last meeting, and that it was essential that the declaration should not be silent on that point. Paragraph 2, as re-drafted by the Drafting Sub-Committee, appeared to him to express adequately the aim which positive education should pursue.

Mr. CHANG (China) suggested that the United Kingdom representative should modify his proposal by applying it not only to article 28, but to the whole of paragraph 2 of article 27, since that paragraph embodied the ideas contained in article 28.

Mr. CHANG (China) proposed the deletion of the words: "and foster international understanding", in order to avoid two repetitions of the same idea in a single paragraph.

图片 1.3.35: 张彭春在联合国人权委员会第三届第 69 次会议发言纪要(1)

Mr. CHANG (China) proposed the following text:

"Education shall be directed to the full development of the human personality, to the strengthening of respect for human rights and fundamental freedoms and to the promotion of international goodwill."

Mr. VILFAN (Yugoslavia) suggested that the following phrase should be added to the text proposed by the Chinese representative:

"and to the combatting of the spirit of intolerance and hatred against the nations or racial or religious groups."

The amendment proposed by the representative of Yugoslavia was adopted by 6 votes to 4, with 5 abstentions.

The text submitted by the representative of China was adopted in its amended form by 7 votes to 5, with 2 abstentions.

Article 27 as a whole was adopted by 7 votes to 4, with 3 abstentions.

图片 1.3.36：张彭春在联合国人权委员会第三届第 69 次会议发言纪要(1)

【纪要译文】

张先生(中国)回顾说，委员会在上次会议上详细讨论了教育问题，宣言不应在这一点上保持沉默。他认为，起草小组委员会重新起草的第 2 款充分表达了积极教育应该追求的目标。

张先生(中国)建议英国代表修改其提议，不仅将其适用于第 28 条，而且适用于第 27 条第 2 款全文，因为该款体现了第 28 条所载的思想。

张先生(中国)提议删除"并促进国际了解"等字，以避免同一想法在同一个段落中出现两次重复。

张先生(中国)提出以下案文：

"教育的目的在于充分发展人的个性，加强对人权和基本自由的尊重，并促进国际友好。"

维尔凡先生(南斯拉夫)建议在中国代表提议的案文中增加以下短语：

"打击对民族、种族或宗教团体的不容忍和仇恨精神。"

南斯拉夫代表提议的修正案以 6 票对 4 票，5 票弃权获得通过。

中国代表提交的案文以 7 票对 5 票，2 票弃权获得通过。

整个第 27 条以 7 票对 4 票，3 票弃权获得通过。

21. 张彭春在联合国人权委员会
第三届第 70 次会议上的发言

1948 年 6 月 11 日下午 2 时 30 分,联合国人权委员会第三届第 70 次会议,在纽约成功湖召开,本次会议继续审议《国际人权宣言》草案。中国代表张彭春参加了本次会议,并在会议上发言,具体发言内容①会议纪要、纪要影像和纪要译文如下:

【会议纪要】

Consideration of Article 30

Mr. CASSIN (France) introduced his amendment suggesting the insertion of the words "in scientific research and" between the words "share" and "in the benefits". In answer to questions and suggestions by Mr. MALIK (Lebanon), Mr. LEBEAU (Belgium), the CHAIRMAN and Mr. CHANG (China), the French representative explained that cultural life included science but that he wished to lay particular stress on the participation of even uneducated persons in scientific progress.

Mr. CHANG (China) proposed the replacement of the last part of the sentence after "share" by "in scientific advancement" and recalled that the phrase was derived from Bacon.

After Mr. CHANG (China) had drawn the Commission's attention to the fact that the time originally set aside for the plenary meeting of the Commission had elapsed, Mr. CASSIN (France) moved that the discussion should be continued until a decision on the Article could be reached.

---

① UN Document: E/CN. 4/SR. 70, p. 4, p. 5.

Mr. CHANG（China）maintained that his amendment was furthest removed from the original text and consequently should be voted first.

Mr. CASSIN（France）withdrew his own amendment and supported the Chinese proposal.

After a short discussion the Chinese amendment was adopted by 8 votes to 3 with 5 abstentions.

【纪要影像】

CONSIDERATION OF ARTICLE 30

      Mr. CASSIN (France) introduced his amendment suggesting the insertion of the words "in scientific research and" between the words "share" and "in the benefits". In answer to questions and suggestions by Mr. MALIK (Lebanon), Mr. LEBEAU (Belgium), the CHAIRMAN and Mr. CHANG (China), the French representative explained that cultural life included science but that he wished to lay particular stress on the participation of even uneducated persons in scientific progress.

      Mr. CHANG (China) proposed the replacement of the last part of the sentence after "share" by "in scientific advancement" and recalled that the phrase was derived from Bacon.

图片 1.3.37:张彭春在联合国人权委员会第三届第 70 次会议发言纪要(1)

      After Mr. CHANG (China) had drawn the Commissions' attention to the fact that the time originally set aside for the plenary meeting of the Commission had elapsed, Mr. CASSIN (France) moved that the discussion should be continued until a decision on the Article could be reached.

      Mr. CHANG (China) maintained that his amendment was furthest removed from the original text and consequently should be voted first.

      Mr. CASSIN (France) withdrew his own amendment and supported the Chinese proposal.

After a short discussion the Chinese amendment was adopted by

8 votes to 3, with 5 abstentions.

图片 1.3.38：张彭春在联合国人权委员会第三届第 70 次会议发言纪要(2)

【纪要译文】

审议第 30 条

卡森先生(法国)介绍了他的修正案,建议在"分享"和"利益"之间插入"科学研究和"字样。在回答马利克先生(黎巴嫩)、勒博(Lebeau)先生(比利时)、主席和张先生(中国)提出的问题和建议时,法国代表解释说,文化生活包括科学,但他希望特别强调甚至未受过教育的人也参与科学进步。

张先生(中国)提议将"分享"之后的句子的最后一部分改为"科学进步",并回顾该短语源自培根。

在张先生(中国)提请委员会注意原先为委员会全体会议留出的时间已经过去之后,卡森先生(法国)提议继续讨论,直到就该条款达成决定。

张先生(中国)坚持认为,他的修正案与原文相去甚远,因此应首先表决。

卡森先生(法国)撤回他自己的修正案,支持中国的提议。

经过短暂的讨论,中国的修正案以 8 票对 3 票,5 票弃权获得通过。

22.张彭春在联合国人权委员会第三届第 71 次会议上的发言

1948 年 6 月 14 日上午 10 时 30 分,联合国人权委员会第三届第 71 次会议,在纽约成功湖召开,本次会议的主要议题是继续审议《国际人权宣言》草案。中国代表张彭春参加了本次会议,并在会议上先后多次发言,具体发言内容①会议纪要、纪要影像和纪要译文如下：

【会议纪要】

Articles 25 and 26

Mr. CHANG（China）wished to point out before a vote was taken on the first part of paragraph 1 that its provisions were fundamentally the same as those contained in the ILO text. To vote against the USSR text would, therefore, signify disagreement with its wording only, but not with the principles on which it was based.

The Commission then proceeded to consider the question of the vote, to be taken on the text submitted by the International Labour Organization as amended by the Chinese and United Kingdom representatives.

Mr. CHANG（China）did not see what possible objection there could be to that phrase when millions of people throughout the world were deprived of food and clothing.

Mr. CHANG（China）stated that the question raised in that paragraph would form the subject either of a separate "umbrella" clause or of a paragraph to be inserted in the Preamble. He added that his reasons for voting against the USSR text were connected with its wording.

Mr. CHANG（China）did not agree that the term "standard of living" was sufficiently precise. The question involved concerned not only the quantity but also the quality of food. The Chinese representative did not understand the wish to avoid reference to the two principal factors of an adequate standard of living.

The CHAIRMAN suggested that the words "including food and lodging, housing and medical care" should be inserted after the words "standard of living".

Mr. CHANG（China）agreed to that proposal.

---

① UN Document: E/CN. 4/SR. 71, p. 12, p. 13, p. 14.

The CHAIRMAN called for a vote on the question as to whether the words "food and clothing" should be included in the text.

It was decided to include these words by 11 votes to 3.

The CHAIRMAN put to the vote the Chinese amendment as a whole.

The Chinese amendment was adopted by 12 votes to none with 2 abstentions.

【纪要影像】

Articles 25 and 26

      Mr. CHANG (China) wished to point out before a vote was taken on the first part of paragraph 1 that its provisions were fundamentally the same as those contained in the ILO text. To vote against the USSR text would, therefore, signify disagreement with its wording only, but not with the principles on which it was based.

      The Commission then proceeded to consider the question of the vote. to be taken on the text submitted by the International Labour Organization as amended by the Chinese and United Kingdom representatives.

      Mr. CHANG (China) did not see what possible objection there could be to that phrase when millions of people throughout the world were deprived of food and clothing.

      Mr. CHANG (China) stated that the question raised in that paragraph would form the subject either of a separate "umbrella" clause or of a paragraph to be inserted in the Preamble. He added that his reasons for voting against the USSR text were connected with its wording.

图片 1.3.39:张彭春在联合国人权委员会第三届第 71 次会议发言纪要(1)

Mr. CHANG (China) did not agree that the term "standard of living" was sufficiently precise. The question involved concerned not only the quantity but also the quality of food. The Chinese representative did not understand the wish to avoid reference to the two principal factors of an adequate standard of living.

The CHAIRMAN suggested that the words "including food and lodging, housing and medical care" should be inserted after the words "standard of living".

Mr. CHANG (China) agreed to that proposal.

The CHAIRMAN called for a vote on the question as to whether the words "food and cloting" should be included in the text.

It was decided to include those words by 11 votes to 3.

The CHAIRMAN put to the vote the Chinese amendment as a whole.

The Chinese amendment was adopted by 12 votes to none with 2 abstentions.

图片 1.3.40:张彭春在联合国人权委员会第三届第 71 次会议发言纪要(2)

【纪要译文】

第 25 和 26 条

张先生(中国)希望在就第 1 段第一部分进行表决之前指出,该段的规定与劳工组织案文中的规定基本相同。因此,投票反对苏联的案文只意味着不同意其措辞,而不是不同意其所依据的原则。

委员会接着审议了对国际劳工组织提交的、经中国和英国代表修正的案文进行表决的问题。

张先生(中国)认为,在全世界数以百万计的人被剥夺食物和衣服的情况下,对这句话不会有什么异议。

张先生(中国)说,该段提出的问题将成为一个单独的"总括"条款或插入序言中的一个段落的主题。他补充说,他投票反对苏联案文的原因与其措辞有关。

张先生(中国)不认为"生活水平"一词足够准确。所涉及的问题不仅关系到食物的数量,也关系到食物的质量。中国代表不理解为什么希望避免提及适足生活水准的两个主要因素。

主席建议在"生活水平"一词之后插入"包括食宿、住房和医疗"一语。

张先生(中国)同意这一建议。

主席要求就"食物和衣服"一词是否应列入案文的问题进行表决。

以 11 票对 3 票决定列入这些文字。

主席将整个中国修正案付诸表决。

中国的修正案以 12 票对 0 票,2 票弃权获得通过。

23. 张彭春在联合国人权委员会第三届第 72 次会议上的发言

1948 年 6 月 14 日下午 2 时 30 分,联合国人权委员会第三届第 72 次会议,在纽约成功湖召开,本次会议的主要议题是继续审议《人权宣言》草案。中国代表张彭春参加了本次会议,并在会议上发言,具体发言内容①会议纪要、纪要影像和纪要译文如下:

【会议纪要】

Mr. CHANG (China), supported by Mr. MALIK (Lebanon), remarked that the original phrase, "economic, social and cultural rights enumerated below", appealed preferable. It contained a general statement, the meaning of which was wider than social security. If the Commission felt it necessary to use the term in the Declaration, it could do so when it revised the articles dealing with social rights.

Mr. CHANG (China) wondered whether it was the intention of the Com-

---

① UN Document: E/CN. 4/SR. 72, pp. 7-8, p. 10.

mission, by placing the covering article at the head of the articles dealing with economic and social rights, to create for them the name of "social security articles". He suggested that the clause referring to social security should be voted upon separately in both proposals.

The clause reading "particularly the right to social security" of the USSR proposal was adopted by 5 votes to 1, with 9 abstentions.

The first sentence of the USSR proposal was rejected by 11 votes to 4.

The second sentence of the USSR proposal was rejected by 10 votes to 4, with 1 abstention.

The phrase "Everyone... has the right to social security" of the amended French proposal was adopted by fifteen votes, with two abstentions.

The French proposal, as amended, was adopted by twelve votes, with five abstentions.

【纪要影像】

Mr. CHANG (China), supported by Mr. MALIK (Lebanon), remarked that the original phrase, "economic, social and cultural rights enumerated below", appeared preferable. It contained a general statement, the meaning of which was wider than social security. If the Commission felt it necessary to use the term in the Declaration, it could do so when it revised the articles dealing with social rights.

Mr. CHANG (China) wondered whether it was the intention of the Commission, by placing the covering article at the head of the articles dealing with economic and social rights, to create for them the name of "social security articles". He suggested that the clause referring to social security should be voted upon separately in both proposals.

联合国人权委员会和起草委员会

191

The clause reading "particularly the right to social security" of the USSR proposal was adopted by 5 votes to 1, with 9 abstentions.

The first sentence of the USSR proposal was rejected by 11 votes to 4.

The second sentence of the USSR proposal was rejected by 10 votes to 4, with 1 abstention.

The phrase "Everyone...has the right to social security" of the amended French proposal was adopted by fifteen votes, with two abstentions.

The French proposal,as amended, was adopted by twelve votes, with five abstentions.

图片 1.3.41：张彭春在联合国人权委员会第三届第 72 次会议发言纪要

【纪要译文】

张先生（中国）在马利克先生（黎巴嫩）的支持下说，原来的短语"下文列举的经济、社会和文化权利"更有吸引力。它包含一项一般性声明，其含义比社会保障更广泛。如果委员会认为有必要在《宣言》中使用这一术语，它可以在修订关于社会权利的条款时这样做。

张先生（中国）想知道，委员会将封面条款放在处理经济和社会权利的条款之首，是不是打算为这些条款起一个"社会保障条款"的名称。他建议对两项提案中提及社会保障的条款分别进行表决。

苏联提案中题为"特别是社会保障权"的条款以 5 票对 1 票，9 票弃权获得通过。

苏联提案的第一句以 11 票对 4 票被否决。

苏联提案的第二句以 10 票对 4 票，1 票弃权被否决。

经修正的法国提案中"人人……有权享受社会保障"一语以 15 票赞成、2 票弃权获得通过。

经修正的法国提案以 12 票赞成、5 票弃权获得通过。

24. 张彭春在联合国人权委员会
第三届第 74 次会议上的发言

　　1948 年 6 月 15 日下午 2 时 30 分,联合国人权委员会第三届第 74 次会议,在纽约成功湖召开,本次会议的主要议题是继续审议起草委员会提交给人权委员会的报告、继续审议各个代表团提交的宣言草案修正案。中国代表张彭春参加了本次会议,并在会议上先后多次发言,具体发言内容①会议纪要、纪要影像和纪要译文如下:

【会议纪要】

Article 30

The CHAIRMAN asked for observations on the additional text proposed by the Lebanese representative, which read as follows:"Cultural groups shall not be denied the right to free self-development."

Mr. CHANG (China) remarked that the ambiguity was caused by the fact that the word "cultural" could have two meanings; it could refer either to the practice of science and the arts, or to the ethnical origin of a community. There could be no doubt that in article 30 the word "cultural" was used in the former sense, and in the context the words:"cultural groups" could mean nothing but "cultural organizations". That article was perhaps not the best place to insert the text proposed by the Lebanese representative.

Article 31

The Chairman observed that, in her view, the amendment furthest removed from the original proposal appeared to be that of China, India and the U-

---

① UN Document:E/CN.4/SR.74, pp.3-4, p.5, p.9, p.11, p.13.

nited Kingdom, which proposed the deletion of the article.

Mr. CHANG (China) pointed out that the Commission should not give the impression that it had completely ignored the question of the protection of special religious or ethnical groups. In the article relating to the right to education there was a provision in favour of religious minorities.

Preamble

The CHAIRMAN read out the draft preamble prepared by the Committee on the Preamble, composed of the officers of the Commission (document E/CN. 4/138). She requested the members of the Commission to express their views regarding that text.

Mr. PAVLOV (Union of Soviet Socialist Republics) proposed a shorter text (document E/CN. 4/139).

The delegation of the Soviet Union thought that the text it proposed was more suitable than the one prepared by the Committee on the Preamble, because it was concise and contained all the elements that should appear in the Preamble to a Declaration on Human Rights.

Mr. CHANG (China) stressed the importance of the Preamble and the necessity of taking the utmost care in drafting it, and suggested that the consideration of the two texts submitted to the Commission should be deferred until the following day.

The Commission decided to defer the discussion of the Preamble to the Declaration until the following day.

Article 2, paragraph 2

Mr. LOUTFI (Egypt) agreed to revert to the wording adopted by the Style Committee for the beginning of the sentence, but he insisted on the addition of the words: "morality" and "public welfare".

In reply to a question by Mr. CHANG (China), he pointed out that, according to the French and Latin idea, the expression "general welfare" did not include morality and public order.

Mr. CHANG (China) supported that suggestion. He pointed out that, in the article which dealt with limitations to which human rights were to be subject, it would be well to avoid any enumeration which might give the impression that the Commission was inclining towards too much restriction.

【纪要影像】

Article 30

The CHAIRMAN asked for observations on the additional text proposed by the Lebanese representative, which read as follows: "Cultural groups shall not be denied the right to free self-development."

Mr. CHANG (China) remarked that the ambiguity was caused by the fact that the word "cultural" could have two meanings; it could refer either to the practice of science and the arts, or to the ethnical origin of a community. There could be no doubt that in article 30 the word "cultural" was used in the former sense, and in the context the words: "cultural groups" could mean nothing but "cultural organizations". That article was perhaps not the best place to insert the text proposed by the Lebanese representative.

Article 31

The CHAIRMAN observed that, in her view, the amendment furthest removed from the original proposal appeared to be that of China, India and the United Kingdom, which proposed the deletion of the article.

Mr. CHANG (China) pointed out that the Commission should not give the impression that it had completely ignored the question of the protection of special religious or ethnical groups. In the article relating to the right to education there was a provision in favour of religious minorities.

图片 1.3.42:张彭春在联合国人权委员会第三届第 74 次会议发言纪要(1)

联合国人权委员会和起草委员会

Preamble

The CHAIRMAN read out the draft preamble prepared by the Committee on the Preamble, composed of the officers of the Commission (document E/CN.4/138). She requested the members of the Commission to express their views regarding that text.

Mr. PAVLOV (Union of Soviet Socialist Republics) proposed a shorter text (document E/CN.4/139).

The delegation of the Soviet Union thought that the text it proposed was more suitable than the one prepared by the Committee on the Preamble, because it was concise and contained all the elements that should appear in the Preamble to a Declaration on Human Rights.

Mr. CHANG (China) stressed the importance of the Preamble and the necessity of taking the utmost care in drafting it, and suggested that the consideration of the two texts submitted to the Commission should be deferred until the following day.

The Commission decided to defer the discussion of the Preamble to the Declaration until the following day.

图片 1.3.43：张彭春在联合国人权委员会第三届第74次会议发言纪要(2)

Article 2, paragraph 2.

Mr. LOUTFI (Egypt) agreed to revert to the wording adopted by the Style Committee for the beginning of the sentence, but he insisted on the addition of the words: "morality" and "public welfare".

In reply to a question by Mr. CHANG (China), he pointed out that, according to the French and Latin idea, the expression "general welfare" did not include morality and public order.

Mr. CHANG (China) supported that suggestion. He pointed out that, in the article which dealt with limitations to which human rights were to be subject, it would be well to avoid any enumeration which might give the impression that the Commission was inclining towards too much restriction.

图片 1.3.44：张彭春在联合国人权委员会第三届第74次会议发言纪要(3)

第 30 条

主席要求就黎巴嫩代表提议的补充案文发表意见,该案文如下:"不得否认文化团体自由自我发展的权利。"

张先生(中国)说,这种含糊不清是因为"文化"一词可能有两种含义;它既可以指科学和艺术的实践,也可以指一个社区的民族起源。毫无疑问,在第 30 条中,"文化"一词是在前一种意义上使用的,在上下文中,"文化团体"可能只指"文化组织"。该条也许不是插入黎巴嫩代表提议的案文的最佳位置。

第 31 条

主席指出,在她看来,与原始提案距离最远的修正案似乎是中国、印度和英国的修正案,它们提议删除该条。

张先生(中国)指出,委员会不应给人以完全忽视保护特殊宗教或族裔群体问题的印象。在关于受教育权利的条款中,有一项有利于宗教少数群体的规定。

序言

主席宣读了由委员会主席团成员组成的序言委员会编写的序言草案(E/CN.4/138 号文件)。她请委员会成员就该案文发表意见。

帕夫洛夫先生(苏联)提出了一个较短的案文(E/CN.4/139 号文件)。

苏联代表团认为,它提出的案文比委员会就序言编写的案文更合适,因为它简明扼要,包含了人权宣言序言中应该出现的所有内容。

张先生(中国)强调序言的重要性和极其谨慎起草序言的必要性,并建议将提交给委员会的两个案文推迟到第二大审议。

委员会决定将对宣言序言的讨论推迟到第二天。

第 2 条第 2 款

卢特菲(Loutfi)先生(埃及)同意回到文体委员会通过的该句开头的措辞,但他坚持添加"道德"和"公共福利"等词。

在回答张先生(中国)的问题时,他指出,按照法国和拉丁哲学家的想法,"普遍福利"一词不包括道德和公共秩序。

张先生(中国)支持这一建议。他指出,在关于人权所受限制的条款中,最好避免列举,以免给人以委员会倾向于过多限制的印象。

25. 张彭春在联合国人权委员会第三届第 75 次会议上的发言

1948 年 6 月 16 日上午 10 时 45 分,联合国人权委员会第三届第 75 次会议,在纽约成功湖召开,本次会议的主要议题继续讨论《国际人权宣言》草案。中国代表张彭春参加了本次会议,并在会议上先后多次发言,具体发言内容①会议纪要、纪要影像和纪要译文如下:

【会议纪要】

Mr. CHANG (China) suggested that the order of the articles should be altered as follows: (a) the revised article 2 should be placed immediately before article 33 which had been adopted at the previous meeting; the article proposed by the representative of Lebanon should be placed before article 2; (b) the two paragraphs which made up article 3 might become two separate articles: the first paragraph would become article 2 and the second paragraph would become article 5 preceding the provisions concerning legal rights; (c) articles 4 and 5 would then become respectively articles 3 and 4; articles 6, 7 and 8 would remain unchanged.

Mr. CHANG (China) pointed out that his proposal should be taken as an amendment to the report of the Style Committee and should, therefore, be con-

---

① UN Document: E/CN.4/SR.75, p. 3, p. 5, p. 6, p. 8, p. 9, p. 12, p. 15.

sidered at the same time as that report.

Discussion of the Preamble to the Draft International Declaration of Human Rights

Mr. CHANG (China) hoped this paragraph would be adopted in view of its special importance and intrinsic value.

Paragraph 1 *was adopted by* 11 *votes to none, with* 5 *abstentions.*

Mr. CHANG (China) pointed out that the addition of the word "of" in the English text would narrow the meaning of the word "ignorance". Most of the members of the Style Committee had had in mind ignorance in general and not simply ignorance of human rights.

The CHAIRMAN agreed with the representative of China.

Mr. CHANG (China) explained that he had not approved the drafting of this paragraph. It was true that the Germans and the Japanese were to blame for their contempt of human rights, but it could not be said that they had been ignorant of those rights. The word "ignorance" in the English text was not the right word, and he would propose that it should be replaced in the English text by the words "indifference to".

Mr. CHANG (China) proposed that the substitution of the words "disregard of" for "ignorance" should be put to the vote.

The amendment was adopted by 10 *votes to* 1, *with* 5 *abstentions.*

Mr. HOOD (Australia) spoke again on the wording of the second paragraph. Although the Commission had decided to retain the much too dogmatic statement it contained, he wondered whether, in spite of that, it would not be wiser to define its scope more precisely by saying, in the English text, at the end of the sentence "and made it apparent to all that the fundamental freedoms were a (instead of "the") supreme issue of the conflict."

Mr. CHANG (China) pointed out that as the idea underlying the sentence was saved. It would be perfectly in order to submit amendments to that sentence.

The CHAIRMAN agreed.

Mr. CHANG (China) pointed out that the Preamble had not been drafted in accordance with a concept acceptable to all the members of the Committee. That was why the second paragraph had not been unanimously supported.

Paragraphs 4 and 5

Mr. CHANG (China) also wanted the need for an improvement in economic and social conditions mentioned. It could be done by borrowing the words of the Charter on that subject.

He suggested setting up a small committee to choose the appropriate quotations from the Charter.

The CHAIRMAN agreed with the Chinese representative's request and appointed a committee for that purpose, consisting of the representatives of China, the United Kingdom, Australia, the United States and Yugoslavia, which would meet in the early afternoon.

Mr. VILFAN (Yugoslavia) declined the offer as the Preamble as a whole, either wittingly or unwittingly, was based on a conception to which he could not subscribe; he could not make any concrete contributions to the preparation of a text based on a conception he did not share.

In reply to a question by Mr. Chang (China), he pointed out that the Preamble spoke only of the rights of the individual, whereas it could also have mentioned, as a compromise, and in deference to the ideas of all the members of the Commission, the rights of the Nation and of peoples.

The Preamble as submitted failed to recognized the duty of the individual to his Nation and to his State.

Mr. CHANG (China) suggested that the order of the articles should be altered as follows: (a) the revised article 2 should be placed immediately before article 33 which had been adopted at the previous meeting; the article proposed by the representative of Lebanon should be placed before article 2; (b) the two paragraphs which made up article 3 might become two separate articles: the first paragraph would become article 2 and the second paragraph would become article 5 preceding the provisions concerning legal rights; (c) articles 4 and 5 would then become respectively articles 3 and 4; articles 6, 7 and 8 would remain unchanged.

Mr. CHANG (China) pointed out that his proposal should be taken as an amendment to the report of the Style Committee and should, therefore, be considered at the same time as that report.

图片 1.3.45：张彭春在联合国人权委员会第三届第 75 次会议发言纪要(1)

DISCUSSION OF THE PREAMBLE TO THE DRAFT INTERNATIONAL DECLARATION OF HUMAN RIGHTS

Mr. CHANG (China) hoped this paragraph would be adopted in view of its special importance and intrinsic value.

Paragraph 1 was adopted by 11 votes to none, with 5 abstentions.

Mr. CHANG (China) pointed out that the addition of the word "of" in the English text would narrow the meaning of the word "ignorance". Most of the members of the Style Committee had had in mind ignorance in general and not simply ignorance of human rights.

The CHAIRMAN agreed with the representative of China.

Mr. CHANG (China) explained that he had not approved the drafting of this paragraph. It was true that the Germans and the Japanese were to blame for their contempt of human rights, but it could not be said that they had been ignorant of those rights. The word "ignorance" in the English text was not the right word, and he would propose that it should be replaced in the English text by the words "indifference to".

Mr. CHANG (China) proposed that the substitution of the words "disregard of" for "ignorance" should be put to the vote.

The amendment was adopted by 12 votes to 1 with 5 abstentions.

图片 1.3.46：张彭春在联合国人权委员会第三届第 75 次会议发言纪要(2)

Mr. HOOD (Australia) spoke again on the wording of the second paragraph. Although the Commission had decided to retain the much too dogmatic statement it contained, he wondered whether, in spite of that, it would not be wiser to define its scope more precisely by saying, in the English text, at the end of the sentence "and made it apparent to all that the fundamental freedoms were a (instead of "the") supreme issue of the conflict."

Mr. CHANG (China) pointed out that as the idea underlying the sentence was saved, it would be perfectly in order to submit amendments to that sentence.

The CHAIRMAN agreed.

Mr. CHANG (China) pointed out that the Preamble had not been drafted in accordance with a concept acceptable to all the members of the Committee. That was why the second paragraph had not been unanimously supported.

图片 1.3.47：张彭春在联合国人权委员会第三届第 75 次会议发言纪要(3)

Paragraphs 4 and 5

Mr. CHANG (China) also wanted the need for an improvement in economic and social conditions mentioned. It could be done by borrowing the words of the Charter on that subject.

He suggested setting up a small committee to choose the appropriate quotations from the Charter.

The CHAIRMAN agreed with the Chinese representative's request and appointed a committee for that purpose, consisting of the representatives of China, the United Kingdom, Australia, the United States and Yugoslavia, which would meet in the early afternoon.

Mr. VILFAN (Yugoslavia) declined the offer as the Preamble as a whole, either wittingly or unwittingly, was based on a conception to which he could not subscribe; he could not make any concrete contributions to the preparation of a text based on a conception he did not share.

In reply to a question by Mr. Chang (China), he pointed out that the Preamble spoke only of the rights of the individual, whereas it could also have mentioned, as a compromise, and in deference to the ideas of all the members of the Commission, the rights of the Nation and of peoples.

The Preamble as submitted failed to recognize the duty of the individual to his Nation and to his State.

图片 1.3.48：张彭春在联合国人权委员会第三届第 75 次会议发言纪要(4)

【纪要译文】

张先生(中国)建议将条款的顺序修改如下：(a)经修订的第 2 条应放在上次会议通过的第 33 条之前；黎巴嫩代表提议的条款应放在第 2 条之前；(b)构成第 3 条的两款可以成为两条独立的条款：第一款将成为第 2 条，第二款将成为第 5 条，放在有关法律权利的条款之前；(c)第 4 条和第 5 条将分别成为第 3 条和第 4 条；第 6、7 和 8 条保持不变。

张先生(中国)指出,他的提议应视为对文体委员会报告的修正,因此应与该报告同时审议。

讨论《国际人权宣言》草案的序言

张先生(中国)鉴于该段的特殊重要性和内在价值,希望该段获得通过。

第 1 段以 11 票对 0 票,5 票弃权获得通过。

联合国人权委员会和起草委员会

张先生(中国)指出,在英文文本中增加"of"一词会缩小"无知"一词的含义。风格委员会的大多数成员心目中一般的无知,并不仅仅是对人权的无知。

主席同意中国代表的意见。

张先生(中国)解释说,他不同意该段的措辞。的确,德国人和日本人应该为他们对人权的蔑视负责,但是不能说他们对这些权利一无所知。英文文本中的"ignorance"一词不恰当,他建议在英文文本中用"indifference to"一词代替。

张先生(中国)提议将"无视"一词改为"无知"一词付诸表决。

修正案以 10 票对 1 票,5 票弃权获得通过。

胡德先生(澳大利亚)再次就第二段的措辞发言。虽然委员会已决定保留其中过于教条的陈述,但他想知道,尽管如此,在英文文本中,在句尾说"并向所有人表明基本自由是冲突的一个十分重要的问题(而不是最为重要的问题)"是否更为明智。

张先生(中国)指出,该句的基本思想已经保留。对这句话提出修正案是完全合适的。

主席表示同意。

张先生(中国)指出,序言不是按照委员会所有成员都能接受的概念起草的。这就是第二段没有得到一致支持的原因。

第 4 段和第 5 段

张先生(中国)也希望提及改善经济和社会条件的必要性。可以借用《宪章》在这个问题上的措辞来做到这一点。

他建议成立一个小型委员会,从宪章中选择适当的引文。

主席同意中国代表的请求,并为此任命了一个委员会,由中国、英国、澳大利亚、美国和南斯拉夫的代表组成,将于下午早些时候开会。

维尔凡先生(南斯拉夫)拒绝了这一提议,因为整个序言有意或无意地基于一个他不能同意的概念;他不能对基于他不同意的概念的案文的编写作出任何具体贡献。

在回答张先生(中国)的问题时,他指出,序言只提到了个人的权利,而作为一种妥协,并尊重委员会所有成员的想法,序言也可以提到国家和人民的权利。

提交的序言没有承认个人对其民族和国家的责任。

26. 张彭春在联合国人权委员会第三届第 76 次会议上的发言

1948 年 6 月 16 日下午 2 时 30 分,联合国人权委员会第三届第 76 次会议,在纽约成功湖召开,本次会议的主要议题是审议小组委员会研究种族灭绝罪公约草案的报告(E/CN.4/136 号文件)、审议负责重新起草序言第四段的小组委员会提出的建议(E/CN.4/138 号文件)。中国代表张彭春参加了本次会议,并在会议上先后多次发言,具体发言内容①会议纪要、纪要影像和纪要译文如下:

【会议纪要】

Mr. CHANG (China) emphasized that the question of genocide was of cardinal importance for China, where the Japanese had committed that crime by various methods, in particular by means of narcotic drugs.

The question had been under consideration in the United Nations for over two years; world public opinion was expecting concrete action. Even though the Commission had not had sufficient time to study the Convention thoroughly, it could still express an opinion. He suggested that the word "study" should be replaced by "consider" and that the last sentence should be changed as follows: "The Commission is of the opinion that the draft Convention represents an

---

①   UN Document: E/CN.4/SR.76, pp. 8-9, p. 11, p. 14, p. 16.

appropriate basis for urgent consideration and decisive action by the Economic and Social Council and the General Assembly during their forthcoming sessions. "

Mr. CHANG (China) noted that the Commission was now faced with two proposals: the draft resolution drawn up by the Sub-Committee and amended in accordance with the suggestions of Chile and China, and the draft amendment submitted by the representative of the USSR.

It was apparent that all the members of the Commission agreed that genocide was a crime and that means should be found to combat that crime. Thus, the draft Convention was not perfect, but it would be deplorable if the Commission were to fail to state its views on the subject. The opinion of the Commission should therefore be indicated; in addition, it could be stated that certain members considered the draft Convention unsatisfactory.

The CHAIRMAN opened the discussion on the draft amendment submitted by the Chinese representative.

Mr. PAVLOV (Union of Soviet Socialist Republics) proposed to amend the Chinese amendment by saying that the draft constituted "an inappropriate basis".

Mr. CHANG (China) moved the closure of the debate.

Closure of debate was accepted by 11 *votes to* 4, *with* 2 *abstentions.*

Mr. CHANG (China) submitted the two proposals drawn up by the Sub-Committee and pointed out that the text of those proposals was taken from the preamble of the Charter.

Mr. CHANG (China) admitted that the work of the Drafting Committee had been unduly hurried and that it might be desirable to refer the matter to the next meeting.

【纪要影像】

Mr. CHANG (China) emphasized that the question of genocide was of cardinal importance for China, where the Japanese had committed that crime by various methods, in particular by means of narcotic drugs.

The question had been under consideration in the United Nations for over two years; world public opinion was expecting concrete action. Even though the Commission had not had sufficient time to study the Convention thoroughly, it could still express an opinion. He suggested that the word "study" should be replaced by "consider" and that the last sentence should be changed as follows: "The Commission is of the opinion that the draft Convention represents an appropriate basis for urgent consideration and decisive action by the Economic and Social Council and the General Assembly during their forthcoming sessions."

图片 1.3.49：张彭春在联合国人权委员会第三届第 76 次会议发言纪要(1)

Mr. CHANG (China) noted that the Commission was now faced with two proposals: the draft resolution drawn up by the Sub-Committee and amended in accordance with the suggestions of Chile and China, and the draft amendment submitted by the representative of the USSR.

It was apparent that all the members of the Commission agreed that genocide was a crime and that means should be found to combat that crime. True, the draft Convention was not perfect, but it would be deplorable if the Commission were to fail to state its views on the subject. The opinion of the Commission should therefore be indicated; in addition, it could be stated that certain members considered the draft Convention unsatisfactory.

图片 1.3.50：张彭春在联合国人权委员会第三届第 76 次会议发言纪要(2)

The CHAIRMAN opened the discussion on the draft amendment submitted by the Chinese representative.

Mr. PAVLOV (Union of Soviet Socialist Republics) proposed to amend the Chinese amendment by saying that the draft constituted "an inappropriate basis."

Mr. CHANG (China) moved the closure of the debate.

Closure of debate was accepted by 11 votes to 4, with 2 abstentions.

Mr. CHANG (China) submitted the two proposals drawn up by the Sub-Committee and pointed out that the text of those proposals was taken from the preamble of the Charter.

Mr. CHANG (China) admitted that the work of the Drafting Committee had been unduly hurried and that it might be desirable to refer the matter to the next meeting.

图片1.3.51：张彭春在联合国人权委员会第三届第76次会议发言纪要(3)

【纪要译文】

张先生(中国)强调,种族灭绝问题对中国来说是一个至关重要的问题,日本人曾以各种方式,特别是使用麻醉药品在中国犯下这一罪行。

这个问题在联合国已经审议了两年多;世界公众舆论期待着具体的行动。即使委员会没有足够的时间彻底研究《公约》,仍然可以发表意见。他建议将"研究"一词改为"审议",并将最后一句修改如下:"委员会认为,《公约》草案为经济及社会理事会和大会在即将举行的届会上进行紧急审议和采取果断行动奠定了适当的基础。"

张先生(中国)指出,委员会现在面临两项提案:小组委员会起草并根据智利和中国的建议修订的决议草案,以及苏联代表提交的修正案草案。

显然,委员会的所有成员都同意种族灭绝是一种罪行,应该找到打击这种罪行的手段。因此,公约草案并不完美,但如果委员会未能就这一主题发表意见,那将是令人遗憾的。因此,应表明委员会的意见;此外,可以说,某些成员认为公约草案不能令人满意。

主席宣布开始讨论中国代表提交的修正案草案。

帕夫洛夫(PAVLOV)先生(苏联)建议修改中国的修正案,他说该草案构成了"一个不适当的基础"。

张先生(中国)提出结束辩论的动议。

结束辩论的动议以11票对4票,2票弃权被接受。

张先生(中国)提交了小组委员会起草的两项提案,并指出这些提案的案文摘自《宪章》序言。

张先生(中国)承认起草委员会的工作过于仓促,最好将此事提交下次会议。

27. 张彭春在联合国人权委员会第三届第 77 次会议上的发言

1948 年 6 月 17 日上午 11 时,联合国人权委员会第三届第 77 次会议,在纽约成功湖召开,本次会议的主要议题是审议中国代表团提交的关于《宣言》条款顺序的提案、继续审议《人权宣言》序言。中国代表张彭春参加了本次会议,并在会议上先后多次发言,具体发言内容[①]会议纪要、纪要影像和纪要译文如下:

【会议纪要】

CONSIDERATION OF THE PROPOSAL SUBMITTED BY THE CHINESE DELEGATION REGARDING THE ORDER OF THE ARTICLES OF THE DECLARATION

Mr. CHANG (China) proposed making article 2 the penultimate article of the Declaration. An article which dealt with the limitations on the exercise of the rights, and freedoms proclaimed in the Declaration should not appear at the beginning of the Declaration before those rights and freedoms themselves had been set forth.

Mr. FONTAINA (Uruguay) supported the Chinese representative's proposal.

---

① UN Document: E/CN. 4/SR. 77, p. 2, p. 3, p. 4, p. 8, p. 9, p. 10.

He recalled his delegation's objections to the use of the terms "ordre public" (public order) in article 2, paragraph 2 (see document E/CN. 4/SR. 74). To place that article towards the end of the Declaration immediately before article 33 would reduce the possibility of misinterpreting that term.

Mr. LOPEZ (Philippines) supported the Chinese representative's proposal; since they were dealing with a Declaration on Human Rights, the rights of the individual should be stressed before his duties to society.

The Chinese representative's proposal was adopted by 8 votes to 7, with 1 abstention.

Mr. CHANG (China) proposed changing the order of the first five articles of the Declaration as follows: article 1 to remain where it was; article 3, paragraph 1 (principles of non-discrimination) to become article 2; article 3, paragraph 2 (principles of equality before the law) to become article 5; article 4 (right to life) to become article 3 and article 5 (respect for human dignity) to become article 4.

The Chinese representative's proposal was adopted by 9 votes to 1, with 6 abstentions.

Mr. CHANG (China) proposed placing article 13, which dealt with marriage, after article 9 which dealt with the family.

The Chinese representative's proposal was rejected by 5 votes to 4 with 7 abstentions.

Mr. CHANG (China) proposed placing article 15, on nationality, after article 12, which dealt with the right to recognition as a person before the law.

Mr. LOUTFI (Egypt) supported the proposal.

Mr. LOPEZ (Philippines) pointed out that article 12 itself had not been properly placed; it should follow article 3 which dealt with the rights to life and freedom.

Mr. CHANG (China) thought it would be better to place article 12 after article 5 which dealt with equality before the law.

Mr. PAVLOV (Union of Soviet Socialist Republics), supported by Mr. MALIK (Lebanon), suggested adopting both the proposals which had been made, namely, to place article 12 after article 3, which would be immediately followed by article 15.

His delegation would only vote for the Chinese representative's proposal to place article 15 after article 12 if the latter followed article 3 concerning the right to life and to liberty.

The CHAIRMAN called on the Commission to vote on the proposal to place article 12, which dealt with the right to recognition as a person before the law, after article 3 on the right to life and to liberty.

The proposal was rejected by 7 votes to 6, with 3 abstentions.

Mr. CHANG (China) said that there was something to be said for the USSR representative's interpretation: the paragraph, as drafted could mean that the obligation assumed by the Members of the United Nations would not be binding should agreement on a common conception not be reached.

The CHAIRMAN and Mr. CHANG (China) agreed that paragraph 6 was not essential and could, therefore, be deleted. Mr. Chang pointed out that any reservation regarding the pledge taken under the Charter would weaken that pledge.

Mr. CHANG (China) proposed appointing a small committee to draft a formula acceptable to all, bearing in mind the various comments made during the meeting.

Mr. JOCKEL (Australia) supported that proposal. His delegation considered paragraph 6 the most important of all the paragraphs of the Preamble, and it should be retained while an attempt was made to satisfy the USSR representative's justifiable objections.

The CHAIRMAN announced that the Drafting Sub-Committee to amend the form of paragraph 6 would be composed of the representatives of the following countries: China, France, Lebanon, the United Kingdom and the Union of Soviet Socialist Republics.

【纪要影像】

CONSIDERATION OF THE PROPOSAL SUBMITTED BY THE CHINESE DELEGATION REGARDING THE ORDER OF THE ARTICLES OF THE DECLARATION

Mr. CHANG (China) proposed making article 2 the penultimate article of the Declaration. An article which dealt with the limitations on the exercise of the rights and freedoms proclaimed in the Declaration should not appear at the beginning of the Declaration before those rights and freedoms themselves had been set forth.

Mr. FONTAINA (Uruguay) supported the Chinese representative's proposal.

He recalled his delegation's objections to the use of the term "ordre public" (public order) in article 2, paragraph 2 (see document E/CN.4/SR.74). To place that article towards the end of the Declaration immediately before article 33 would reduce the possibility of misinterpreting that term.

Mr. LOPEZ (Philippines) supported the Chinese representative's proposal; since they were dealing with a Declaration on Human Rights, the rights of the individual should be stressed before his duties to society.

The Chinese representative's proposal was adopted by 8 votes to 7, with 1 abstention.

图片 1.3.52：张彭春在联合国人权委员会第三届第 77 次会议发言纪要(1)

Mr. CHANG (China) proposed changing the order of the first five articles of the Declaration as follows: article 1 to remain where it was; article 3, paragraph 1 (principles of non-discrimination) to become article 2; article 3, paragraph 2 (principles of equality before the law) to become article 5; article 4 (right to life) to become article 3 and article 5 (respect for human dignity) to become article 4.

The Chinese representative's proposal was adopted by 9 votes to 1, with 6 abstentions.

Mr. CHANG (China) proposed placing article 13, which dealt with marriage, after article 9 which dealt with the family.

The Chinese representative's proposal was rejected by 5 votes to 4, with 7 abstentions.

Mr. CHANG (China) proposed placing article 15, on nationality, after article 12, which dealt with the right to recognition as a person before the law.

Mr. LOUTFI (Egypt) supported the proposal.

Mr. LOPEZ (Philippines) pointed out that article 12 itself had not been properly placed; it should follow article 3 which dealt with the right to life and freedom.

图片 1.3.53：张彭春在联合国人权委员会第三届第 77 次会议发言纪要(2)

Mr. CHANG (China) thought it would be better to place article 12 after article 5 which dealt with equality before the law.

Mr. PAVLOV (Union of Soviet Socialist Republics), supported by Mr. MALIK (Lebanon), suggested adopting both the proposals which had been made, namely, to place article 12 after article 3, which would be immediately followed by article 15.

His delegation would only vote for the Chinese representative's proposal to place article 15 after article 12 if the latter followed article 3 concerning the right to life and to liberty.

The CHAIRMAN called on the Commission to vote on the proposal to place article 12, which dealt with the right to recognition as a person before the law, after article 3 on the right to life and to liberty.

The proposal was rejected by 7 votes to 6, with 3 abstentions.

图片 1.3.54：张彭春在联合国人权委员会第三届第 77 次会议发言纪要(3)

Mr. CHANG (China) said that there was something to be said for the USSR representative's interpretation: the paragraph, as drafted could mean that the obligation assumed by the Members of the United Nations would not be binding should agreement on a common conception not be reached.

The CHAIRMAN and Mr. CHANG (China) agreed that paragraph 6 was not essential and could, therefore, be deleted. Mr. Chang pointed out that any reservation regarding the pledge taken under the Charter would weaken that pledge.

Mr. CHANG (China) proposed appointing a small committee to draft a formula acceptable to all, bearing in mind the various comments made during the meeting.

Mr. JOCKEL (Australia) supported that proposal. His delegation considered paragraph 6 the most important of all the paragraphs of the Preamble, and it should be retained while an attempt was made to satisfy the USSR representative's justifiable objections.

The CHAIRMAN announced that the Drafting Sub-Committee to amend the form of paragraph 6 would be composed of the representatives of the following countries: China, France, Lebanon, the United Kingdom and the Union of Soviet Socialist Republics.

图片 1.3.55:张彭春在联合国人权委员会第三届第 77 次会议发言纪要(4)

【纪要译文】

审议中国代表团提交的关于《宣言》条款顺序的提案

张先生(中国)提议将第 2 条列为宣言的倒数第二条。在阐述《宣言》所宣布的权利和自由之前,不应该在《宣言》的开头出现一个关于限制行使这些权利和自由的条款。

丰泰纳先生(乌拉圭)支持中国代表的提议。

他回顾说,美国代表团反对在第 2 条第 2 款中使用"公共秩序"(public order)一词(见 E/CN.4/SR.74 号文件)。将该条放在《宣言》末尾第 33 条之前,将减少误解该术语的可能性。

洛佩斯(Lopez)先生(菲律宾)支持中国代表的提议;由于他们正在处理一项人权宣言,个人的权利应该在他对社会的责任之前得到强调。

中国代表的提案以 8 票对 7 票,1 票弃权获得通过。

张先生(中国)建议将《宣言》前五条的顺序修改如下:第 1 条保持不

变;第 3 条第 1 款(不歧视原则)成为第 2 条;第 3 条第 2 款(法律面前平等的原则)成为第 5 条;第 4 条(生命权)成为第 3 条,第 5 条(尊重人的尊严)成为第 4 条。

中国代表的提案以 9 票对 1 票,6 票弃权获得通过。

张先生(中国)提议将涉及婚姻的第 13 条放在涉及家庭的第 9 条之后。

中国代表的提议以 5 票对 4 票,7 票弃权被否决。

张先生(中国)提议将关于国籍的第 15 条放在关于法律面前的人格得到承认的权利的第 12 条之后。

卢特菲先生(埃及)支持该提议。

洛佩斯先生(菲律宾)指出,第 12 条本身的位置不合适;它应遵循关于生命权和自由权的第 3 条。

张先生(中国)认为,最好将第 12 条放在关于法律面前平等的第 5 条之后。

帕夫洛夫先生(苏联)在马利克先生(黎巴嫩)的支持下建议采纳所提出的两项建议,即把第 12 条放在第 3 条之后,紧接着是第 15 条。

如果第 12 条放在关于生命权和自由权的第 3 条之后,他(苏联)的代表团只会投票赞成中国代表关于将第 15 条放在第 12 条之后的提议。

主席呼吁委员会就将第 12 条放在关于生命权和自由权的第 3 条之后的提议进行表决,该条涉及在法律面前人格得到承认的权利。

该提议以 7 票对 6 票,3 票弃权被否决。

张先生(中国)说,对苏联代表的解释有一些看法;该段的现有案文可能意味着,如果不能就共同概念达成协议,联合国会员国承担的义务将没有约束力。

主席和张先生(中国)同意,第 6 款不是必要的,因此可以删除。张先生指出,对根据《宪章》作出的承诺的任何保留都会削弱这一承诺。

张先生(中国)建议任命一个小型委员会,根据会议期间提出的各种意见,起草各方都能接受的方案。

乔基尔(Jockel)先生(澳大利亚)支持这一提议。他的代表团认为第6段是序言所有段落中最重要的,在试图满足苏联代表的合理化的反对意见时,应该保留该段。

主席宣布,修改第6段格式的起草小组委员会将由下列国家的代表组成:中国、法国、黎巴嫩、英国和苏联。

28. 张彭春在联合国人权委员会 第三届第 78 次会议上的发言

1948 年 6 月 17 日下午 2 时 30 分,联合国人权委员会第三届第 78 次会议,在纽约成功湖召开,本次会议的主要议题是继续审议《国际人权宣言》草案、讨论审议报告员报告的程序。中国代表张彭春参加了本次会议,并在会议上先后多次发言,具体发言内容①会议纪要、纪要影像和纪要译文如下:

【会议纪要】

Mr. MALIK (Lebanon), Rapporteur, submitted the following alternative text of paragraph 6 of the Preamble:

"WHEREAS a (definition) (common understanding) of these rights and freedoms is (necessary) (of the greatest importance) for the fulfillment of this pledge,"

Mr. CHANG (China) stated that he preferred "definition" to "common understanding" and "necessary" to "of the greatest importance".

He further suggested replacing "fulfillment" by "full realization".

The Commission decided, by 9 votes to 1 with 4 abstentions, in favour of the

---

① UN Document: E/CN. 4/SR. 78, p. 4, p. 5, p. 7, p. 10, p. 11, p. 14.

words "*common understanding*".

The Commission decided, by 6 votes to 4 with 4 abstentions, in favour of the words "of the greatest importance".

The Commission decided, by 8 votes to 2 with 4 abstentions, in favour of the words "full realization".

The Commission adopted the amended text by 13 votes to none, with 1 abstention.

Mr. CHANG (China) concurred in the idea behind the USSR proposal, i. e. there should be no doubt that peoples who did not at present enjoy self-government should be included in the Declaration. He thought, however, that the addition of the words "and peoples" after "all nations" would remove any possibility of misunderstanding.

Mr. CHANG (China) agreed with the USSR representative that the problem should be faced, but thought the Preamble was not the place to deal with it. If the USSR would propose the adoption of such a clause at the General Assembly, after the adoption of the Declaration, he would support it.

With regard to the USSR proposal, he pointed out that there were many more independent peoples than non-self-governing peoples in the world today. From a purely drafting point of view, therefore, the two phrases did not balance. Furthermore, the addition of the sentence proposed by the USSR made the paragraph unduly long.

The Chinese proposal was adopted by 8 votes to none with 5 abstentions.

The CHAIRMAN turned to consideration of an article originally suggested by the Lebanese representative and subsequently proposed by the Drafting Sub-Committee in the following form:

"Every one has the right to a good social and international order in which the rights and freedoms set out in this Declaration can be fully realized. "

Mr. CHANG (China) drew attention to two drafting points. Firstly, he questioned the juxtaposition of "social" and "international", which were not contrasting terms. "Social order, national and international" might be preferable. Secondly, he raised the point that "is entitled" might be substituted in the first line for "has the right" since the word "rights" was used further on in the article.

The CHAIRMAN, speaking as the United States representative, supported the proposed article, with the drafting changes mentioned by the Chinese representative.

After a short discussion of drafting in which the representatives of the Philippines, China and Lebanon took part, the CHAIRMAN put to the vote the first part of the article in the following form: "Every one is entitled to a good social and international order...".

The text was adopted by seven votes to none, with six abstentions.

Mr. CHANG (China) pointed out that the proposed article belonged more properly with measures for implementation.

Mr. CHANG (China) considered the first two paragraphs of the French-United States proposal unnecessary.

He further suggested an amendment to the third paragraph so that "after the eighth session of the Council in 1949" would be changed to "early in 1949". The date of the Council's eighth session was not as yet fixed.

The CHAIRMAN explained that the first two paragraphs of the proposal were designed to ensure that there should be no doubt of the fact that the Commission did not consider the Declaration a complete Bill of human rights.

Mr. CHANG (China) thought that idea might be included in the Rapporteur's report.

【纪要影像】

Mr. MALIK (Lebanon), Rapporteur, submitted the following alternative text of paragraph 6 of the Preamble:

"WHEREAS a (definition) (common understanding) of these rights and freedoms is (necessary) (of the greatest importance) for the fulfilment of this pledge,"

Mr. CHANG (China) stated that he preferred "definition" to "common understanding" and "necessary" to "of the greatest importance".

He further suggested replacing "fulfilment" by "full realization".

The Commission decided, by 9 votes to 1 with 4 abstentions, in favour of the words "common understanding".

The Commission decided, by 6 votes to 4 with 4 abstentions, in favour of the words "of the greatest importance".

The Commission decided, by 8 votes to 2 with 4 abstentions, in favour of the words "full realization".

The Commission adopted the amended text by 13 votes to none, with 1 abstention.

图片 1.3.56:张彭春在联合国人权委员会第三届第 78 次会议发言纪要(1)

Mr. CHANG (China) concurred in the idea behind the USSR proposal, i.e. there should be no doubt that peoples who did not at present enjoy self-government should be included in the Declaration. He thought, however, that the addition of the words "and peoples" after "all nations" would remove any possibility of misunderstanding.

Mr. CHANG (China) agreed with the USSR representative that the problem should be faced, but thought the Preamble was not the place to deal with it. If the USSR would propose the adoption of such a clause at the General Assembly, after the adoption of the Declaration, he would support it.

With regard to the USSR proposal, he pointed out that there were many more independent peoples than non-self-governing peoples in the world today. From a purely drafting point of view, therefore, the two phrases did not balance. Furthermore, the addition of the sentence proposed by the USSR made the paragraph unduly long.

The Chinese proposal was adopted by 8 votes to none with 5 abstentions.

图片 1.3.57:张彭春在联合国人权委员会第三届第 78 次会议发言纪要(2)

The CHAIRMAN turned to consideration of an article originally suggested by the Lebanese representative and subsequently proposed by the Drafting Sub-Committee in the following form:

"Every one has the right to a good social and international order in which the rights and freedoms set out in this Declaration can be fully realized."

Mr. CHANG (China) drew attention to two drafting points. Firstly, he questioned the juxtaposition of "social" and "international", which were not contrasting terms. "Social order, national and international" might be preferable. Secondly, he raised the point that "is entitled" might be substituted in the first line for "has the right" since the word "rights" was used further on in the article.

The CHAIRMAN, speaking as the United States representative, supported the proposed article, with the drafting changes mentioned by the Chinese representative.

After a short discussion of drafting in which the representatives of the Philippines, China and Lebanon took part, the CHAIRMAN put to the vote the first part of the article in the following form: "Every one is entitled to a good social and international order...".

The text was adopted by seven votes to none, with six abstentions.

图片 1.3.58：张彭春在联合国人权委员会第三届第 78 次会议发言纪要(3)

Mr. CHANG (China) pointed out that the proposed article belonged more properly with measures for implementation.

Mr. CHANG (China) considered the first two paragraphs of the French-United States proposal unnecessary.

He further suggested an amendment to the third paragraph so that "after the eighth session of the Council in 1949" would be changed to "early in 1949". The date of the Council's eighth session was not as yet fixed.

The CHAIRMAN explained that the first two paragraphs of the proposal were designed to ensure that there should be no doubt of the fact that the Commission did not consider the Declaration a complete Bill of human rights.

Mr. CHANG (China) thought that idea might be included in the Rapporteur's report.

图片 1.3.59:张彭春在联合国人权委员会第三届第78次会议发言纪要(4)

【纪要译文】

报告员马利克先生(黎巴嫩)提交了序言部分第 6 段的备选案文如下:

"鉴于对这些权利和自由的(定义)(普遍理解)是实现这一承诺的(必要的)(至关重要的),"

张先生(中国)说,他认为"定义"比"普遍理解"好,认为"必要的"比"至关重要的"好。

他进一步建议用"充分实现"取代"实现"。

委员会以 9 票对 1 票,4 票弃权,决定采用"普遍理解"一词。

委员会以 6 票对 4 票,4 票弃权决定,赞成"至关重要的"一词。

委员会以 8 票对 2 票,4 票弃权,决定采用"充分实现"一词。

委员会以 13 票对 0 票,1 票弃权通过了经修正的案文。

张先生(中国)同意苏联提案背后的想法,即毫无疑问,目前尚未享有自治的人民应包括在宣言中。然而,他认为,在"所有国家"之后加上"和人民"一词将消除任何误解的可能性。

张先生(中国)同意苏联代表的意见,认为应该正视这个问题,但认为序言不是处理这个问题的地方。如果苏联在宣言通过后提议在大会上通过这样一项条款,他将予以支持。

关于苏联的提案,他指出,当今世界上独立人民比非自治人民多得多。因此,从纯粹的起草角度来看,这两个短语并不均衡。此外,苏联提议增加的句子使该段过长。

中国的提案以 8 票对 0 票,5 票弃权获得通过。

主席开始审议最初由黎巴嫩代表提议、随后由起草小组委员会提议的条款,内容如下:

"人人有权要求一种良好的社会和国际秩序,在这种秩序中,本宣言所载的权利和自由能获得充分实现。"

张先生(中国)提请注意两个起草问题。首先,他质疑"社会"和"国际"的并列,这两个词并不对立。"国家和国际的社会秩序"可能更好。第二,他提出的观点是,第一行中的"赋予权利"可以替换为"有权",因为"权利"一词在该条中被进一步使用。

主席以美国代表的身份发言,支持拟议的条款,以及中国代表提到的起草方面的修改。

菲律宾、中国和黎巴嫩代表就起草问题进行了简短的讨论,随后,主席将该条第一部分付诸表决,内容如下:"人人有权享有良好的社会和国际秩序……"。

案文以 7 票对 0 票,6 票弃权获得通过。

张先生(中国)指出,拟议的条款更适合于实施措施。

张先生(中国)认为法国和美国联合提案的前两段没有必要。

他还建议修改第三段,将"1949 年理事会第八届会议之后"改为"1949 年初"。理事会第八届会议的日期尚未确定。

主席解释说,提案的前两段旨在确保委员会不认为《宣言》是一项完整的人权法案这一事实不容置疑。

张先生(中国)认为这一想法可纳入报告员的报告。

29. 张彭春在联合国人权委员会第三届第 80 次会议上的发言

1948 年 6 月 18 日上午 10 时 45 分,联合国人权委员会第三届第 80 次会议,在纽约成功湖召开,本次会议的主要议题是审议报告员提交的报告草稿(E/CN.4/148 号文件)、讨论工作计划中关于《国际人权宪章》(the

International Charter on Human Rights)的第 12 段。中国代表张彭春参加了本次会议,并在会议上先后多次发言,具体发言内容①会议纪要、纪要影像和纪要译文如下:

【会议纪要】

Mr. CHANG (China) recalled that he had been absent from the first meeting but that his alternate, Mr. Wu, had proposed the postponement of the second meeting until 26 May. The aim of that proposal had not been to await the arrival of the Byelorussian and Ukrainian representatives but to enable the members of the Commission to consider the various documents submitted to them.

Mr. CHANG (China) pointed out that it appeared from the speech made by Mr. WU as recorded in the summary record of the forty-sixth meeting that the Commission had postponed its work until 26 May following a proposal of the Chinese representative, not because the representatives of the Ukrainian and Byelorussian Soviet Socialist Republics had not yet arrive, but because members had not had sufficient time to examine the necessary documents.

Mr. CHANG (China) quoted a passage of the summary record concerned, according to which the Chairman had expressed her willingness that the Secretary-General should be informed of the sense of the meeting and of the substance of the discussion. Apart from that, only one formal decision — that relating to the Chinese proposal — had been recorded.

Mr. Chang proposed that the Rapporteur should proceed to re-draft paragraph 6 of the report.

There being no objection, that proposal was accepted.

Mr. CHANG (China) wondered whether it would not be better to include in that paragraph some explanation on the stage of the Commission's work on the

---

① UN Document: E/CN. 4/SR. 80, p. 7, p. 10, p. 11, p. 12, pp. 12−13.

Covenant and the measures to implement it.

Mr. CHANG (China) accepted the Rapporteur's proposal.

He went on to ask whether there was any special reason why certain members of the Commission did not wish a decision to be taken on the Declaration by the General Assembly at its next session, or whether the reason was that they preferred to present the drafts of the Covenant and the measures of implementation at the same time as the Declaration, so that they could be considered together. On the other hand, some members favored the idea of submitting the Declaration to the Assembly at once. He was of the opinion that the Declaration should be proclaimed without delay. The Commission should at least recommend that the Declaration should come before the General Assembly this year.

【纪要影像】

Mr. CHANG (China) recalled that he had been absent from the first meeting but that his alternate, Mr. Wu, had proposed the postponement of the second meeting until 26 May. The aim of that proposal had not been to await the arrival of the Byelorussian and Ukrainian representatives but to enable the members of the Commission to consider the various documents submitted to them.

Mr. CHANG (China) pointed out that it appeared from the speech made by Mr. WU as recorded in the summary record of the forty-sixth meeting that the Commission had postponed its work until 26 May following a proposal of the Chinese representative, not because the representatives of the Ukrainian and Byelorussian Soviet Socialist Republics had not yet arrived, but because members had not had sufficient time to examine the necessary documents.

图片 1.3.60:张彭春在联合国人权委员会第三届第 80 次会议发言纪要(1)

Mr. CHANG (China) quoted a passage of the summary record concerned, according to which the Chairman had expressed her willingness that the Secretary-General should be informed of the sense of the meeting and of the substance of the discussion. Apart from that, only one formal decision -- that relating to the Chinese proposal -- had been recorded.

Mr. Chang proposed that the Rapporteur should proceed to re-draft paragraph 6 of the report.

There being no objection, that proposal was accepted.

Mr. CHANG (China) wondered whether it would not be better to include in that paragraph some explanation on the stage of the Commission's work on the Covenant and the measures to implement it.

图片 1.3.61：张彭春在联合国人权委员会第三届第 80 次会议发言纪要(2)

Mr. CHANG (China) accepted the Rapporteur's proposal

He went on to ask whether there was any special reason why certain members of the Commission did not wish a decision to be taken on the Declaration by the General Assembly at its next session, or whether the reason was that they preferred to present the drafts of the Covenant and the measures of implementation at the same time as the Declaration, so that they could be considered together. On the other hand, some members favoured the idea of submitting the Declaration to the Assembly at once. He was of the opinion that the Declaration should be proclaimed without delay.

The Commission should at least recommend that the Declaration should come before the General Assembly this year.

图片 1.3.62：张彭春在联合国人权委员会第三届第 80 次会议发言纪要(3)

【纪要译文】

张先生(中国)回顾说,他没有出席第 1 次会议,但他的候补吴先生提议将第 2 次会议推迟到 5 月 26 日。该提议的目的不是等待白俄罗斯和乌克兰代表的到来,而是让委员会成员能够审议提交给他们的各种文件。

张先生(中国)指出,从第 46 次会议简要记录所载吴先生的发言来看,根据中国代表的提议,委员会已将其工作推迟到 5 月 26 日,这不是因为乌克兰和白俄罗斯苏维埃社会主义共和国的代表尚未到达,而是因为各成员没有足够的时间审查必要的文件。

张先生(中国)引用了有关简要记录中的一段话,根据这段话,主席表示她愿意将会议的意义和讨论的实质内容通知秘书长。除此之外,只记录了一项正式决定——与中国提案有关的决定。

张先生提议报告员着手重新起草报告第6段。

由于没有人反对,该建议被接受。

张先生(中国)想知道,在该段中列入一些关于委员会就《公约》开展工作的阶段和《公约》的实施措施的说明是否更好。

张先生(中国)接受报告员的建议。

他接着问,委员会的某些成员不希望大会在下一届会议上就《宣言》作出决定,是否有任何特殊的原因,或者是因为他们更愿意在提交《宣言》的同时提交《公约》草案和实施措施,以便能够一起审议。另一方面,一些成员赞成立即向大会提交《宣言》的想法。他认为应立即宣布该《宣言》。委员会至少应该建议,《宣言》应该在今年提交大会。

30. 张彭春在联合国人权委员会第三届第81次会议上的发言

1948年6月18日下午2时30分,联合国人权委员会第三届第81次会议,在纽约成功湖召开,本次会议的主要议题是继续讨论人权委员会提交经济及社会理事会的报告草稿(E/CN.4/148号文件)、讨论来文特设委员会的报告(E/CN.4/148/Add.2号文件)。中国代表张彭春参加了本次会议,并在会议上先后多次发言,具体发言内容①会议纪要、纪要影像和纪要译文如下:

---

① UN Document: E/CN.4/SR.81, p. 4, pp. 16–17.

Paragraph 6

Mr. MALIK (Lebanon) reminded the Commission that two amendments had been proposed to paragraph 6 of the report: (1) the Chinese representative had requested the insertion of the words: "because of the necessity for members to have ample time to examine the various documents" after the words: "of 26 May"; (2) the United States representative had requested that the words: "and in violation of the agreement" be replaced by the words: "and that certain members felt the delay was in violation of the agreement". It was for the Commission to decide on those two amendments.

The CHAIRMAN opened the discussion on the Chinese amendment first.

Mr. VILFAN (Yugoslavia) said that the Chinese amendment did not respect the chronological order of events. The Chinese representative's proposal to convene the second meeting of the Commission for the afternoon of 26 May "because of the necessity for members to have ample time to examine the various documents" had been moved only after the Commission had agreed in principle to inform the Secretary-General of the Byelorussian and Ukrainian representatives' delay in arriving.

Mr. CHANG (China) reminded the Commission that his proposal had been moved and adopted during the discussion on the USSR representative's proposal.

The Commission adopted the Chinese amendment by 11 votes to 4, with one abstention.

Paragraph 11

Mr. Chang (China) stated that, generally speaking, the Declaration on Human Rights could be said to represent the application of the Charter, while the Covenant was the application of the Declaration. The creation of committees

联合国人权委员会和起草委员会

of conciliation or of tribunals to deal with case of violation was a further degree of implementation. Though the Commission had agreed on the importance of the problem, it had not yet had time to study it in detail. The various proposals which had been submitted in that connection, and in particular the one submitted by Professor Cassin, deserved the Economic and Social Council's attention. In view of those facts, Mr. Chang supported the Rapporteur's proposal that the various proposals received should be transmitted to the Council with the explanation that the Commission had not had time to study them.

Mr. FONTAINA (Uruguay) supported the views of the representatives of China and the United States. The delegation of Uruguay agreed with the suggestion that the joint China-United States proposal should be transmitted to the Economic and Social Council at the same time as the other documents relationg to the question of implementation; but it wished it to be clearly understood, as the USSR representative had pointed out, that those documents did not in any way represent the views of the Commission as a whole.

Mr. LARRAIN (Chile) announced his delegation's support of the joint China-United States proposal. The fact that the Commission had not examined the Draft Covenant should not prevent it from transmitting to the Economic and Social Council any documents that were available on the question of implementation. The work which had already been accomplished could prove to be of great use in the Council's debates, and the objections which had been raised were, in the opinion of the Chilean delegation, only of a secondary character. The more comprehensive the documentation submitted to the Economic and Social Council was, the more useful it would be. The Chilean delegation was all the more willing to support the inclusion of document E/CN. 4/145 as it thought that the document containd some highly acceptable ideas corresponding to its own views.

REPORT OF THE *AD HOC* COMMITTEE ON COMMUNICATIONS (document E/CN. 4/148/Add. 2)

The CHAIRMAN stated that the Report of the *Ad Hoc* Committee on Communication would be inserted after paragraph 18.

Mr. CHANG (China) recalled that the names of members of other sub-committees dealing with other paragraphs had not been mentioned. He proposed therefore that the names of members of the *Ad Hoc* Committee on Communications should be omitted.

Mr. MALIK (Lebanon) pointed out that the *Ad Hoc* Committee on Communications had a different status. It was a permanent Committee of the Commission, and he thought that the names of its members should therefore be listed.

The CHAIRMAN recalled that the *Ad Hoc* Committee had been created for the third session and she asked the Commission to decide whether it should be maintained for the fourth session.

It was decided by 4 *votes to* 2, *with* 10 *abstentions, that the Ad Hoc Committee on communications should not be retained.*

The report of the Ad Hoc Committee on communication was adopted by 13 *votes to none, with* 3 *abstentions.*

Mr. CHANG (China) thought that the actual figures of the vote should be included in the Commission's report. The world should know that the Declaration produced after two years of serious work had obtained the support of twelve members, with four abstentions and no one opposed.

Mr. CHANG (China) expressed his appreciation for the great work of the Chairman.

【纪要影像】

Paragraph 6

Mr. MALIK (Lebanon) reminded the Commission that two amendments had been proposed to paragraph 6 of the report: (1) the Chinese representative had requested the insertion of the words: "because of the necessity for members to have ample time to examine the various documents" after the words: "of 26 May"; (2) the United States representative had requested that the words: "and in violation of the agreement" be replaced by the words: "and that certain members felt the delay was in violation of the agreement". It was for the Commission to decide on those two amendments.

The CHAIRMAN opened the discussion on the Chinese amendment first.

Mr. VILFAN (Yugoslavia) said that the Chinese amendment did not respect the chronological order of events. The Chinese representative's proposal to convene the second meeting of the Commission for the afternoon of 26 May "because of the necessity for members to have ample time to examine the various documents" had been moved only after the Commission had agreed in principle to inform the Secretary-General of the Byelorussian and Ukrainian representatives' delay in arriving.

Mr. CHANG (China) reminded the Commission that his proposal had been moved and adopted during the discussion on the USSR representative's proposal.

The Commission adopted the Chinese amendment by 11 votes to 4, with one abstention.

图片 1.3.63：张彭春在联合国人权委员会第三届第 81 次会议发言纪要(1)

Paragraph 11

Mr. CHANG (China) stated that, generally speaking, the
Declaration on Human Rights could be said to represent the application
of the Charter, while the Covenant was the application of the Declaration.
The creation of committees of conciliation or of tribunals to deal with

case of violation was a further degree of implementation. Though the
Commission had agreed on the importance of the problem, it had not yet had
time to study it in detail. The various proposals which had been submitted
in that connection, and in particular the one submitted by Professor Chang,
deserved the Economic and Social Council's attention. In view of those
facts, Mr. Chang supported the Rapporteur's proposal that the various
proposals received should be transmitted to the Council with the explanation
that the Commission had not had time to study them.

Mr. FONTAINA (Uruguay) supported the views of the representatives
of China and the United States. The delegation of Uruguay agreed with
the suggestion that the joint China-United States proposal should be transmitted to the Economic and Social Council at the same time as the other
documents relating to the question of implementation; but it wished it
to be clearly understood, as the USSR representative had pointed out, that
those documents did not in any way represent the views of the Commission
as a whole.

联合国人权委员会和起草委员会

Mr. LARRAIN (Chile) announced his delegation's support of the joint China-United States proposal. The fact that the Commission had not examined the Draft Covenant should not prevent it from transmitting to the Economic and Social Council any documents that were available on the question of implementation. The work which had already been accomplished could prove to be of great use in the Council's debates, and the objections which had been raised were, in the opinion of the Chilean delegation, only of a secondary character. The more comprehensive the documentation submitted to the Economic and Social Council was, the more useful it would be. The Chilean delegation was all the more willing to support the inclusion of document E/CN.4/145 as it thought that the document contained some highly acceptable ideas corresponding to its own views.

图片1.3.64：张彭春在联合国人权委员会第三届第81次会议发言纪要（2）

REPORT OF THE AD HOC COMMITTEE ON COMMUNICATIONS (document E/CN.4/148/Add.2)

The CHAIRMAN stated that the Report of the Ad Hoc Committee on Communications would be inserted after paragraph 18.

Mr. CHANG (China) recalled that the names of members of other sub-committees dealing with other paragraphs had not been mentioned. He proposed therefore that the names of members of the Ad Hoc Committee on Communications should be omitted.

Mr. MALIK (Lebanon) pointed out that the Ad Hoc Committee on Communications had a different status. It was a permanent committee of the Commission, and he thought that the names of its members should therefore be listed.

The CHAIRMAN recalled that the Ad Hoc Committee had been created for the third session and she asked the Commission to decide whether it should be maintained for the fourth session.

It was decided by 4 votes to 2, with 10 abstentions, that the Ad Hoc Committee on Communications should not be retained.

The report of the Ad Hoc Committee on Communications was adopted by 13 votes to none, with 3 abstentions.

Mr. CHANG (China) thought that the actual figures of the vote should be included in the Commission's report. The world should know that the Declaration produced after two years of serious work had obtained the support of twelve members, with four abstentions and no one opposed.

Mr. CHANG (China) expressed his appreciation for the great work of the Chairman.

图片 1.3.65:张彭春在联合国人权委员会第三届第 81 次会议发言纪要(3)

【纪要译文】

第 6 段

马利克先生(黎巴嫩)提醒委员会,对报告第 6 段提出了两项修正建议:(1)中国代表要求在"5 月 26 日"之后插入"由于委员们必须有充足的时间来审查各种文件";(2)美国代表要求将"并且违反协议"改为"一些委员认为拖延违反了协议"。应由委员会就这两项修正案做出决定。

主席首先开始讨论中国的修正案。

维尔凡先生(南斯拉夫)说,中国的修正案没有尊重事件发生的时间顺序。中国代表提议在 5 月 26 日下午召开委员会第 2 次会议,"由于委员们必须有充足的时间来审查各种文件",这一提议是在委员会原则上同意将白俄罗斯和乌克兰代表推迟抵达一事通知秘书长之后才提出的。

张先生(中国)提醒委员会说,他的提案是在讨论苏联代表的提案时提出并通过的。

委员会以 11 票对 4 票,1 票弃权通过了中国的修正案。

第 11 段

张先生(中国)说,一般来说,《人权宣言》可以说是《宪章》的应用,而《公约》则是《宣言》的应用。设立调解委员会或法庭来处理侵权案件是进一步落实。虽然委员会同意这个问题的重要性,但它还没有时间详细研究这个问题。在这方面提出的各种建议,特别是卡森教授提出的建议,值得经济及社会理事会注意。鉴于这些事实,张先生支持报告员的提议,即应将收到的各种提案转交理事会,并解释说委员会没有时间研究这些提案。

丰泰纳先生(乌拉圭)支持中国和美国代表的观点。乌拉圭代表团同意这样的建议,即中国和美国的联合提案应与有关实施问题的其他文件同时提交经济及社会理事会;但是,正如苏联代表所指出的,它希望人们清楚

联合国人权委员会和起草委员会

地理解,这些文件绝不代表整个委员会的观点。

拉腊因(Larrain)先生(智利)宣布智利代表团支持中国和美国的联合提案。委员会没有审查《公约》草案的事实不应妨碍它向经济及社会理事会转交关于实施问题的任何现有文件。已经完成的工作可以证明对理事会的辩论非常有用,智利代表团认为,提出的反对意见只是次要的。提交给经济及社会理事会的文件越全面,就越有用。智利代表团更愿意支持列入 E/CN.4/145 号文件,因为它认为该文件载有一些与其自己的观点相符的非常容易接受的想法。

来文特设委员会的报告(E/CN.4/148/Add.2 号文件)

主席说,特设通信委员会的报告将插在第 18 段之后。

张先生(中国)回顾说,没有提到处理其他段落的其他小组委员会成员的姓名。因此,他建议省略来文特设委员会成员的名字。

马利克先生(黎巴嫩)指出,来文特设委员会具有不同的地位。这是委员会的一个常设委员会,因此他认为应该列出其成员的姓名。

主席回顾说,特设委员会是为第三届会议设立的,她请委员会决定是否应在第四届会议上保留该委员会。

以 4 票对 2 票,10 票弃权决定,不应保留来文特设委员会。

特设通信委员会的报告以 13 票对 0 票,3 票弃权获得通过。

张先生(中国)认为,表决的实际数字应列入委员会的报告。全世界应该知道,经过两年认真工作后产生的宣言得到了 12 个成员的支持,4 票弃权,无人反对。

张先生(中国)对主席的出色工作表示赞赏。

第四章　联合国人权委员会第五届会议

继联合国人权委员会第四届会议[①]之后,联合国人权委员会第五届会议,于1949年5月9日至6月20日,在美国纽约成功湖举行。该届会议共召开了53次会议(即第83次会议至第135次会议),主要议题是讨论和审议《国际人权公约》草案、实施措施等。

中国代表张彭春参加了本届会议,在第83次会议上当选为第一副主席[②],并在本届共计9次会议上担任主席并主持全部或前半段会议,包括第84次会议、第85次会议、第99次会议、第100次会议、第122次会议、第123次会议、第126次会议和第127次会议。张彭春先生在该届会议中的30次会议上发言,包括第84次会议、第85次会议、第87次会议、第88次会议、第90次会议、第91次会议、第93次会议、第95次会议、第96次会议、第98次会议、第99次会议、第100次会议、第102次会议、第103次会议、第104次会议、第115次会议、第117次会议、第118次会议、第119次会议、第120次会议、第121次会议、第122次会议、第123次会议、第124次会议、第126次会议、第127次会议、第129次会议、第131次会议、第

---

① 联合人权委员会第四届会议是一届特别会议,既第82次会议,于1949年4月11日上午10时45分至11时50分,在美国纽约成功湖召开,本届会议的主要议题就是选举新闻和出版自由小组委员会的成员。张彭春参加了本次会议,并应会议主席邀请,与黎巴嫩查尔斯·马利克一起,对无记名投票结果进行唱票。据笔者推测本届会议上当选的该小组委员会成员名单中的一位张先生,应该不是张彭春先生(Mr. P. C. Chang),而是一位P. H. Chang。这一点从对该小组委员会会议记录也能得到证实。从联合国会议纪要来看,新闻和出版自由小组委员会从1947年5月19日至1952年3月21日,共召开了五届会议,共计112次会议(即第一届第1次会议至第五届第112次会议),这位张先生(Mr. P. H. Chang)一直担任该小组成员,并一度担任报告员。参考文献见: UN Document: E/CN. 4/Sub. 1/SR. 1, … E/CN. 4/Sub. 1/SR. 112。

② UN Document: E/CN. 4/SR. 83, p. 3. (法国代表卡森当选为第二副主席,黎巴嫩代表马利克当选为报告员。)

133 次会议和第 134 次会议。

　　本届会议中,张彭春先生缺席的会议仅有 7 次,即第 94 次会议、第 101 次会议、第 108 次会议、第 109 次会议、第 114 次会议、第 128 次会议和第 135 次会议。这几次会议都由查修先生参会。另外,张彭春先生还与查修先生共同参加了第 106 次会议和第 113 次会议。

1. 张彭春在人权委员会
第五届第 84 次会议上的发言

　　联合国人权委员会第五届第 84 次会议,于 1949 年 5 月 12 日上午 11 时至下午 1 时 30 分,在纽约成功湖举行,本次会议的主要议题是讨论和审议防止歧视和保护少数者委员会的报告。中国代表张彭春参加了本次会议,并担任会议主席,以会议主席身份先后多次发言,其具体发言内容①会议纪要、纪要影像和纪要译文如下:

【会议纪要】

The CHAIRMAN proposed that the Commission examine the report of the Committee on the prevention of discrimination and the protection of minorities (E/CN. 4/181).

The CHAIRMAN expressed the Secretariat's regret for the delay in distributing the document in question, which was due to the Secretariat's extremely heavy work load for the General Assembly. He assured the representative of the Union of Soviet Socialist Republics that his remarks would be acted on.

He also recognized that the remarks of the representative of France were fully justified.

---

① UN Document: E/CN. 4/SR. 84, p. 3, p. 5, p. 9.

The CHAIRMAN pointed out that the Sub-Commission's terms of reference were similar to those of man; other Committees or Commissions.

The CHAIRMAN, replying to the questions of the representative of the Union of Soviet Socialist Republics concerning procedure, stated that every delegation had the right to submit a motion for adjournment. It should be remembered however that the question of the Sub-Commission's terms of reference had been on the Commission's agenda for several meetings and a request for adjournment did not seem to be justified.

When the draft resolution was adopted any delegation could submit amendments subject to observance of the rules of procedure. He called the attention of the Commission to paragraph (b) of the draft resolution. According to that paragraph any delegation could submit proposals to the Commission on Human Rights or to the Economic and Social Council with a view to giving specific instructions to the Sub-Commission. The Sub-Commission could in this way be entrusted with the functions the delegation of the Union of Soviet Socialist Republics had in mind without alteration of the terms of reference defined in paragraph (a) of the draft resolution.

联合国人权委员会和起草委员会

【纪要影像】

The CHAIRMAN proposed that the Commission examine the report of the Committee on the prevention of discrimination and the protection of minorities (E/CN.4/181).

The CHAIRMAN expressed the Secretariat's regret for the delay in distributing the document in question, which was due to the Secretariat's extremely heavy work load for the General Assembly. He assured the representative of the Union of Soviet Socialist Republics that his remarks would be acted on.

He also recognized that the remarks of the represenative of France were fully justified.

The CHAIRMAN pointed out that the Sub-Commission's terms of reference were similar to those of many other Committees or Commissions.

图片1.4.1:张彭春在联合国人权委员会第五届第84次会议发言纪要(1)

The CHAIRMAN, replying to the questions of the representative of the Union of Soviet Socialist Republics concerning procedure, stated that every delegation had the right to submit a motion for adjournment. It should be remembered however that the question of the Sub-Commission's terms of reference had been on the Commission's agenda for several meetings and a request for adjournment did not seem to be justified.

When the draft resolution was adopted any delegation could submit amendments subject to observance of the rules of procedure. He called the attention of the Commission to paragraph (b) of the draft resolution. According to that paragraph any delegation could submit proposals to the Commission on Human Rights or to the Economic and Social Council with a view to giving specific instructions to the Sub-Commission. The Sub-Commission could in this way be entrusted with the functions the delegation of the Union of Soviet Socialist Republics had in mind without alteration of the terms of reference defined in paragraph (a) of the draft resolution.

图片1.4.2:张彭春在联合国人权委员会第五届第84次会议发言纪要(1)

【纪要译文】

主席提议委员会审查防止歧视和保护少数者委员会的报告(E/CN.4/181)。

主席对延迟分发有关文件表示遗憾,这是因为秘书处为大会承担了极其繁重的工作量。他向苏联代表保证,他的发言将得到执行。

他还承认法国代表的言论是完全有道理的。

主席指出,分设委员会的职权范围与其他事务委员会或委员会职权范围相似。

　　主席在回答苏联代表关于程序的问题时说,每个代表团都有权提出休会动议。然而,应当记住,分设委员会的职权范围问题已列入委员会几次会议的议程,休会请求被认为是没有道理的。

　　决议草案通过时,任何代表团都可以在遵守议事规则的前提下提交修正案。他提请委员会注意决议草案(b)段。根据该段,任何代表团都可以向人权委员会或经济及社会理事会提交提案,以便向分设委员会发出具体指示。可以这样委托分设委员会履行苏联代表团所设想的职能,而不改变决议草案(a)段所界定的职权范围。

2. 张彭春在人权委员会第五届第 85 次会议上的发言

　　联合国人权委员会第五届第 85 次会议,于 1947 年 5 月 12 日下午 3 时 15 分至 5 时 30 分,在纽约成功湖举行,本次会议的主要议题是继续讨论和审议防止歧视和保护少数者委员会的报告。中国代表张彭春参加了本次会议,并担任会议主席,以会议主席身份先后多次发言,其具体发言内容①会议纪要、纪要影像和纪要译文如下:

【会议纪要】

Chairman: Mr. P. C. CHANG (China)

The CHAIRMAN read the list of speakers, who were the representatives of Yugoslavia, Belgium, France and the Ukrainian SSR.

The CHAIRMAN stated that that procedure would be followed.

The CHAIRMAN pointed out that the USSR representative had not submit-

---

　　①　UN Document: E/CN.4/SR.85, p. 1, p. 2, p. 3, p. 5, pp. 5-6, p. 6.

ted a formal motion for postponement of the vote on draft resolution A. Although the list of speakers was closed, the USSR representative would be given an opportunity to clarify his position on the procedural matter before a vote was taken.

The CHAIRMAN asked the USSR representative whether he wished to submit a formal motion for postponement of the vote on the draft resolution or whether he would agree that a vote should be taken at that point and reserve his right subsequently to submit amendments.

The CHAIRMAN put the motion to adjourn the debate to the vote.

The motion was rejected by 7 votes to 4.

The CHAIRMAN interrupted the USSR representative on the ground that any reply to previous speakers was not in order as the speakers' list had been closed. He called for an interpretation of the speech only to the point where the USSR representative had begun to reply to the representative of France.

The CHAIRMAN ruled that the USSR representative could complete his speech after the vote was taken; he would then be able to explain the reasons for his vote.

The CHAIRMAN ruled that since only nine voting members were present, and ten were required to form a quorum, the meeting would adjourn.

```
Chairman:    Mr. P. C. CHANG              (China)
        The CHAIRMAN read the list of speakers, who were the repre-
sentatives of Yugoslavia, Belgium, France and the Ukrainian SSR.

        The CHAIRMAN stated that that procedure would be followed.

        The CHAIRMAN pointed out that the USSR representative had not
submitted a formal motion for postponement of the vote on draft reso-
lution A.    Although the list of speakers was closed, the USSR repre-
sentative would be given an opportunity to clarify his position on
the procedural matter before a vote was taken.

        The CHAIRMAN asked the USSR representative whether he wished
to submit a formal motion for postponement of the vote on the draft
resolution or whether he would agree that a vote should be taken at that
point and reserve his right subsequently to submit amendments.
```

图片 1.4.3:张彭春在联合国人权委员会第一届第 85 次会议发言纪要(1)

```
        The CHAIRMAN put the motion to adjourn the debate to the vote.
The motion was rejected by 7 votes to 4.

        The CHAIRMAN interrupted the USSR representative on the ground
that any reply to previous speakers was not in order as the speakers'
list had been closed.    He called for an interpretation of the speech only
to the point where the USSR representative had begun to reply to the
representative of France.

        The CHAIRMAN ruled that the USSR representative could complete
his speech after the vote was taken;  he would then be able to explain
the reasons for his vote.

        The CHAIRMAN ruled that since only nine voting members were
present, and ten were required to form a quorum, the meeting would adjourn.
```

图片 1.4.4:张彭春在联合国人权委员会第一届第 85 次会议发言纪要(2)

【纪要译文】

主席:张彭春先生(中国)

主席宣读了发言者名单,他们是南斯拉夫、比利时、法国和乌克兰苏维埃社会主义共和国的代表。

主席表示将遵循这一程序。

主席指出,苏联代表尚未提交推迟对决议草案 A 进行表决的正式动议。虽然发言名单已关闭,但苏联代表将有机会在表决前澄清其对程序问题的立场。

主席问苏联代表,他是否希望提交一份正式动议,要求推迟对该决议草案的表决,或者他是否同意此时进行表决,并保留随后提交修正案的权利。

主席将暂停辩论的动议付诸表决。

该动议以 7 票对 4 票被否决。

主席打断了苏联代表的发言,理由是,由于发言名单已关闭,对前几位发言者的任何答复都不妥当。他要求将发言解释到苏联代表开始答复法国代表的地方。

主席裁定苏联代表可以在投票后完成他的发言;然后,他将能够解释投票的原因。

主席裁定,由于只有九名有表决权的成员出席,并且需要十名成员构成法定人数,会议将休会。

3. 张彭春在人权委员会第五届第87次会议上的发言

联合国人权委员会第五届第87次会议,于1949年5月16日下午3时至晚上6时,在纽约成功湖举行,本次会议的主要议题是审议防止歧视和保护少数者委员会的首次报告等。中国代表张彭春参加了本次会议,并在会议上发言,其具体发言内容①会议纪要、纪要影像和纪要译文如下:

---

① UN Document：E/CN. 4/SR. 87, p. 8, p. 14, pp. 17−18.

Mr. CHANG (China) asked whether it was not true that the Commission so far set up by the Economic and Social Council were intended purely as study commissions without any executive functions.

The CHAIRMAN agreed that that was so.

Mr. SOERENSEN (Denmark) said the Committee had decided to increase the number of members of the Sub-Commission only after it had extended their term of office, and had done so owing to that extension. He asked that the vote be taken on the two paragraphs in that order, which was both chronological and logical and which was, moreover, the order in which they appeared in the draft text.

Mr. CHANG (China) shared that view.

Mr. P. C. CHANG (China), who had presided over the discussions of the eighty-fifth meeting of the Commission, wished to make an explanation.

At the time when Mr. Pavlov had been called upon to speak, the discussion of the substance of draft resolution A had been closed. He had had to answer only the question which the Chairman had put him, namely whether he wished to submit a formal motion for postponement of the vote on the draft resolution, or whether he would agree that a vote should be taken at that point and reserve his right subsequently to submit amendments. Mr. Pavlov had not explicitly asked for permission to reply to the representatives of France and Chile. Therefore, the Chairman had considered that the USSR representative should have confined himself to answering the question of procedure which had been addressed to him, any other remark being irrelevant. As the Chairman did not know Russian, he had been unable to follow the speech of the USSR representative and to interrupt him at the moment when he had digressed from the subject. It had been his duty to stop the interpretation of the speech as soon as he had become aware of that fact. Mr. Chang was convinced that Mr. Pavlov would have acted in the same way, had he been Chairman of the Commission.

【纪要影像】

Mr. CHANG (China) asked whether it was not true that the Commission so far set up by the Economic and Social Council were intended purely as study commissions without any executive functions.

The CHAIRMAN agreed that that was so.

Mr. SOERENSEN (Denmark) said the Committee had decided to increase the number of members of the Sub-Commission only after it had extended their term of office, and had done so owing to that extension. He asked that the vote be taken on the two paragraphs in that order, which was both chronological and logical and which was, moreover, the order in which they appeared in the draft text.

Mr. CHANG (China) shared that view.

图片1.4.5:张彭春在联合国人权委员会第一届第87次会议发言纪要(1)

Mr. P. C. CHANG (China), who had presided over the discussions of the eighty-fifth meeting of the Commission, wished to make an explanation.

At the time when Mr. Pavlov had been called upon to speak, the discussion of the substance of draft resolution A had been closed.

He had had to answer only the question which the Chairman had put him, namely whether he wished to submit a formal motion for postponement of the vote on the draft resolution, or whether he would agree that a vote should be taken at that point and reserve his right subsequently to submit amendments. Mr. Pavlov had not explicitly asked for permission to reply to the representatives of France and Chile. Therefore, the Chairman had considered that the USSR representative should have confined himself to answering the question of procedure which had been addressed to him, any other remark being irrelevant. As the Chairman did not know Russian, he had been unable to follow the speech of the USSR representative and to interrupt him at the moment when he had digressed from the subject. It had been his duty to stop the interpretation of the speech as soon as he had become aware of that fact. Mr. Chang was convinced that Mr. Pavlov would have acted in the same way, had he been Chairman of the Commission.

图片1.4.6:张彭春在联合国人权委员会第一届第87次会议发言纪要(2)

【纪要译文】

张先生(中国)问,经济及社会理事会迄今设立的委员会是否纯粹是作为研究委员会,没有任何行政职能。

主席赞同是这样。

瑟伦森(Soerensen)先生(丹麦)说,委员会只是在延长了分设委员会成员的任期之后才决定增加其成员的人数,而且是由于延长了任期才这样做的。他要求按时间顺序和逻辑顺序对这两段进行表决,而且这也是它们在案文草案中出现的顺序。

张先生(中国)同意这一观点。

主持委员会第85次会议讨论的张彭春先生(中国)希望作出解释。

在请帕夫洛夫先生发言时,关于决议草案A实质内容的讨论已经结束。他只需回答主席向他提出的问题,即他是否希望提交一项正式动议,要求推迟对该决议草案的表决,或者他是否同意此时进行表决,并保留随后提交修正案的权利。帕夫洛夫先生没有明确要求允许答复法国和智利代表。因此,主席认为,苏联代表本应只回答向他提出的程序问题,任何其他评论都无关紧要。由于主席不懂俄语,他无法听懂苏联代表的发言,也无法在他离题时打断他的话。一旦意识到这一事实,他就有责任停止对讲话的解释。张先生确信,如果帕夫洛夫是委员会主席,他也会以同样的方式行事。

4. 张彭春在人权委员会
第五届第 88 次会议发言纪要

联合国人权委员会第五届第88次会议,于1949年5月17日上午10时30分至下午1时,在纽约成功湖举行,本次会议的主要议题是讨论防止歧视和保护少数者小组委员会的职权范围、犹太组织协调委员会代表的发言和国际人权公约草案。中国代表张彭春参加了本次会议,并在会议上发言,其具体发言内容①会议纪要、纪要影像和纪要译文如下:

① UN Document:E/CN.4/SR.88, pp. 4–5.

【会议纪要】

Mr. CHANG (China) observed that on the basis of previous experience, there was no reason to think that the Economic and Social Council expected any of its subsidiary organs to do more than make studies; moreover, the words "the preparation of measures" in the Egyptian proposal confirmed that the purpose of the participation of members of the Sub-Commission in the visits to Trust Territories was to collect data and not to attempt to make changes of an administrative nature. If, then, the intention of the Egyptian proposal was that a study should be made, the field should be as wide as possible. Mr. Chang therefore suggested that the words "to the self-governing populations" should be added after the words "the full enjoyment of human rights and fundamental freedoms" in the original Egyptian proposal. Thus, the Sub-Commission might participate in visits to Trust Territories in order to obtain scientific data, on the basis of statistical sampling, for a study of the general question of how the full enjoyment of human rights and fundamental freedoms could be extended to non-self-governing peoples everywhere.

Speaking of the expression "periodical visits" used in the Egyptian proposal, Mr. Chang proposed the deletion of the word "periodical". The Sub-Commission should not be expected to take part in any visits other than those which it considered useful for the furtherance of the study it was making.

```
        Mr. CHANG (China) observed that on the basis of previous
experience, there was no reason to think that the Economic and Social
Council expected any of its subsidiary organs to do more than make

studies; moreover, the words "the preparation of measures" in the
Egyptian proposal confirmed that the purpose of the participation of
members of the Sub-Commission in the visits to Trust Territories was to
collect data and not to attempt to make changes of an administrative
nature.   If, then, the intention of the Egyptian proposal was that a
study should be made, the field should be as wide as possible.
Mr. Chang therefore suggested that the words "to the self-governing
populations" should be added after the words "the full enjoyment of
human rights and fundamental freedoms" in the original Egyptian
proposal.   Thus, the Sub-Commission might participate in visits to
Trust Territories in order to obtain scientific data, on the basis of
statistical sampling, for a study of the general question of how the
full enjoyment of human rights and fundamental freedoms could be
extended to non-self-governing peoples everywhere.
        Speaking of the expression "periodical visits" used in the
Egyptian proposal, Mr. Chang proposed the deletion of the word
"periodical".   The Sub-Commission should not be expected to take part
in any visits other than those which it considered useful for the
furtherance of the study it was making.
```

图片 1.4.7:张彭春在联合国人权委员会第五届第 88 次会议发言纪要

【纪要译文】

张先生(中国)说,根据以往的经验,没有理由认为经济及社会理事会期望其任何附属机构做的不仅仅是研究;此外,埃及提案中的"准备措施"一词证实,小组委员会成员参加对托管领土的访问的目的是收集数据,而不是试图进行行政性质的改变。那么,如果埃及提案的目的是进行研究,那么研究领域应该尽可能广泛。因此,张先生建议在埃及原提案中的"充分享受人权和基本自由"之前加上"自治人民"一词。因此,小组委员会可以参加对托管领土的访问,以便在统计抽样的基础上获得科学数据,研究如何将人权和基本自由的充分享受扩大到世界各地的非自治人民的一般问题。

谈到埃及提案中使用的"定期访问"一词,张先生建议删除"定期"一词。小组委员会不应参加除其认为有助于推动其正在进行的研究之外的任何访问。

联合国人权委员会和起草委员会

5. 张彭春在人权委员会
第五届第 90 次会议发言纪要

联合国人权委员会第五届第 90 次会议,于 1949 年 5 月 18 日上午 11 时至下午 1 时,在纽约成功湖举行,本次会议的主要议题是讨论黎巴嫩决议草案、讨论国际人权公约草案等。中国代表张彭春参加了本次会议,并在会议上发言,其具体发言内容①会议纪要、纪要影像和纪要译文如下:

【会议纪要】

Mr. CHANG (China) observed that, while he fully appreciated the desire of the Lebanese representative to expedite the work on the draft covenant, he felt obliged to remind the Commission of the larger objective which was its reason for being, and of which the covenant would be but a part. That objective was to assure to every individual the full exercise of human rights and fundamental freedoms; it could best be attained by bringing the full moral force of the United Nations to bear on Governments and public opinion. What the world needed most was education in the broadest sense of the word.

The draft covenant would, after all, be but another multilateral treaty, and a realistic view should be taken of the effectiveness of such treaties in the present state of civilization. It was always easier to ensure the observance of conventions on specific subjects, such as narcotic drugs. In a vast field like that of human rights, care should be taken to prepare the ground before a convention was launched, lest should become merely another international instrument for lawyers to play with.

---

① UN Document: E/CN. 4/SR. 90, pp. 4–5, pp. 12–13.

For that reason, while he did not oppose the Lebanese draft resolution, Mr. Chang did not think it wise to set definite dates for the completion of the draft covenant. The Commission would do better to devote cool intellectual attention to the production of a satisfactory document and a concentrated moral effort to the education of the world in the respect of human rights.

Mr. CHANG (China) reminded the Commission that its real objective was to supplement the aims outlined in article 3 of the Universal Declaration of Human Rights and in particular the principle that "everyone has the right to life ...". He pointed out that a covenant was really nothing more than an international treaty and that article 5 should be viewed in that light. It should be remembered that a treaty could be circumvented and that if the Commission wished to protect life it might do better to study the methods by which States protected the lives of their citizens at that time.

With regard to the United States text, he pointed out that if a State wished to deprive a person of life, it would have very little trouble in producing the requisite court records and sentence to justify its procedure. Consequently that draft of article 5 would not hamper the State and the covenant would really offer no protection to the individual.

With regard to the United Kingdom text, he considered that it might be difficult to enforce the fulfillment of contractual commitments assured under the covenant.

The Chinese delegation thought it might be wiser to prepare a compendium of States' laws concerning the protection of individuals. Such a document would effectively support and perhaps even enforce the Universal Declaration of Human Rights, which his delegation considered to be extremely valuable for the protection of individuals. The compilation of a compendium of international legislation in that field would certainly be within the purview of an international body and would seem to be the most practical way of attacking the problem.

The Chinese delegation was not convinced that the covenant, as then worded, would achieve any effective practical results.

【纪要影像】

Mr. CHANG (China) observed that, while he fully appreciated the desire of the Lebanese representative to expedite the work on the draft covenant, he felt obliged to remind the Commission of the larger objective which was its reason for being, and of which the covenant would be but a part. That objective was to assure to every individual the full exercise of human rights and fundamental freedoms; it could best be

attained by bringing the full moral force of the United Nations to bear on Governments and public opinion. What the world needed most was education in the broadest sense of the word.

The draft covenant would, after all, be but another multilateral treaty, and a realistic view should be taken of the effectiveness of such treaties in the present state of civilization. It was always easier to ensure the observance of conventions on specific subjects, such as narcotic drugs. In a vast field like that of human rights, care should be taken to prepare the ground before a convention was launched, lest it should become merely another international instrument for lawyers to play with.

For that reason, while he did not oppose the Lebanese draft resolution, Mr. Chang did not think it wise to set definite dates for the completion of the draft covenant. The Commission would do better to devote cool intellectual attention to the production of a satisfactory document and a concentrated moral effort to the education of the world in the respect of human rights.

图片 1.4.8：张彭春在联合国人权委员会第五届第 90 次会议发言纪要(1)

Mr. CHANG (China) reminded the Commission that its real objective was to supplement the aims outlined in article 3 of the Universal Declaration of Human Rights and in particular the principle that "everyone has the right to life...". He pointed out that a covenant was really nothing more than an international treaty and that article 5 should be viewed in that light. It should be remembered that a treaty could be circumvented and that if the Commission wished to protect life it might do better to study the methods by which States protected the lives of their citizens at that time.

With regard to the United States text, he pointed out that if a State wished to deprive a person of life, it would have very little trouble in producing the requisite court records and sentence to justify its procedure. Consequently that draft of article 5 would not hamper the State and the covenant would really offer no protection to the individual.

With regard to the United Kingdom text, he considered that it might be difficult to enforce the fulfillment of contractual commitments assumed under the covenant.

The Chinese delegation thought it might be wiser to prepare a compendium of States' laws concerning the protection of individuals. Such a document would effectively support and perhaps even enforce the Universal Declaration of Human Rights, which his delegation considered to be extremely valuable for the protection of individuals. The compilation of a compendium of international legislation in that field would certainly be within the purview of an international body and would seem to be the most practical way of attacking the problem. The Chinese delegation was not convinced that the covenant, as then worded, would achieve any effective practical results.

图片1.4.9:张彭春在联合国人权委员会第五届第90次会议发言纪要(2)

【纪要译文】

张先生(中国)说,虽然他完全理解黎巴嫩代表希望加快公约草案的工作,但他觉得有义务提醒委员会,更大的目标才是它存在的理由,公约只是其中的一部分。这一目标是确保每个人充分行使人权和基本自由;实现这一目标的最佳途径是让联合国的全部道德力量对各国政府和公众舆论施加影响。世界最需要的是广义上的教育。

毕竟,公约草案将只是另一项多边条约,应该以现实的眼光看待这些条约在当前文明状态下的效力。确保遵守关于麻醉药品等具体问题的公约总是比较容易的。在人权这样一个广阔的领域,应该注意在公约出台之前做好准备,以免成为律师们可以玩弄的另一个国际工具。

因此,尽管张先生不反对黎巴嫩的决议草案,但他认为确定完成公约草案的确切日期是不明智的。该委员会最好能将冷静的思想注意力放在编写一份令人满意的文件上,并集中精力于世界人权教育。

联合国人权委员会和起草委员会

张先生(中国)提醒委员会,它的真正目标是补充《世界人权宣言》第3条概述的目标,特别是"人人有生命权……"的原则。他指出,一项公约实际上只是一项国际条约,应该从这个角度看待第5条。应当记住,条约可以规避,而且如果委员会希望保护生命,最好研究各国当时保护其公民生命的方法。

关于美国的案文,他指出,如果一个国家希望剥夺一个人的生命,它在提供必要的法庭记录和判决以证明其程序正当性方面几乎没有困难。因此,第5条草案不会妨碍国家,《公约》实际上不会对个人提供保护。

关于英国的案文,他认为可能难以强制履行《公约》所保证的契约性承诺。

中国代表团认为,编写一份有关个人保护的国家法律概要可能更明智。这样一份文件将有效地支持甚至执行《世界人权宣言》,美国代表团认为该宣言对保护个人极为宝贵。编纂这一领域的国际立法简编当然属于一个国际机构的职权范围,而且似乎是解决这一问题的最实际的方式。中国代表团不相信《公约》当时的措辞会取得任何有效的实际结果。

6. 张彭春在人权委员会
第五届第 91 次会议发言纪要

联合国人权委员会第五届第91次会议,于1949年5月18日下午2时30分至5时40分,在纽约成功湖举行,本次会议的主要议题是讨论国际人权公约草案(第5条、第6条和第7条)。中国代表张彭春参加了本次会议,并在会议上发言,其具体发言内容①会议纪要、纪要影像和纪要译文如下:

---

① UN Document: E/CN. 4/SR. 91, p. 10, p. 14.

【会议纪要】

Mr. CHANG（China）suggested that the delegations of the United Kingdom, France and Lebanon, which had presented similar proposals for article 5, should meet informally in order to prepare and submit to the Commission a joint text containing the improvements suggested by Mr. Cassin.

Mr. CHANG（China）supported the Lebanese amendment to reproduce, in article 7 of the draft Covenant, the text of article 5 of the Declaration. He thought that, generally speaking, the articles of the draft Covenant should, whenever possible, repeat the provisions of the Declaration.

The Chinese delegation did not object to listing in article 6 the limitations of the right stated in that article. In drawing up such a list, account should be taken of various existing national laws. The Secretariat might be asked to compile the necessary material.

He therefore proposed that article 6 be deleted for the time being, and that article 7 might be retained in the form of article 5 of the Declaration.

【纪要影像】

> Mr. CHANG (China) suggested that the delegations of the United Kingdom, France and Lebanon, which had presented similar proposals for article 5, should meet informally in order to prepare and submit to the Commission a joint text containing the improvements suggested by Mr. Cassin.
>
> Mr. CHANG (China) supported the Lebanese amendment to reproduce, in article 7 of the draft Covenant, the text of article 5 of the Declaration. He thought that, generally speaking, the articles of the draft Covenant should, whenever possible, repeat the provisions of the Declaration.
>
> The Chinese delegation did not object to listing in article 6 the limitations of the right stated in that article. In drawing up such a list, account should be taken of various existing national laws. The Secretariat might be asked to compile the necessary material.
>
> He therefore proposed that article 6 be deleted for the time being, and that article 7 might be retained in the form of article 5 of the Declaration.

图片 1.4.10：张彭春在联合国人权委员会第五届第 91 次会议发言纪要

联合国人权委员会和起草委员会

【纪要译文】

张先生(中国)建议,就第 5 条提出类似提案的英国、法国和黎巴嫩代表团应举行非正式会议,以便编写一份联合案文,并向委员会提交一份包含卡森先生提出改进建议的案文。

张先生(中国)支持黎巴嫩的修正案,即在公约草案第 7 条中复制《宣言》第 5 条的案文。他认为,总的来说,公约草案的条款应尽可能重复《宣言》的规定。

中国代表团不反对在第 6 条中列出该条所述权利的限制。在拟定这样一份清单时,应考虑到各种现行的国家法律。可能会要求秘书处汇编必要的材料。

因此,他建议暂时删除第 6 条,并以《宣言》第 5 条的形式保留第 7 条。

7. 张彭春在人权委员会
第五届第 93 次会议发言纪要

联合国人权委员会第五届第 93 次会议,于 1947 年 5 月 19 日下午 2 时 30 分至 5 时 30 分,在纽约成功湖举行,本次会议的主要议题是讨论国际人权公约草案(第 8 条和第 5 条)。中国代表张彭春参加了本次会议,并在会议上发言,其具体发言内容①会议纪要、纪要影像和纪要译文如下:

【会议纪要】

Mr. CHANG (China) supported deferment of consideration of the second part of article 8. The very valid reasons advanced by the representative of Denmark called for more careful consideration of the numerous and complex prob-

---

① UN Document:E/CN. 4/SR. 93, p. 5, p. 13.

lems involved. The Commission, which was to complete its work before 22 June, should immediately take a decision on the first part of article 8; it could still return to the consideration of the second part if it felt it could do so before the end of the current session.

Mr. CHANG (China), like the representative of Guatemala, had intended to ask the representatives of the United Kingdom or Lebanon to delete sub-paragraph (b). Of course there had been wars, but by providing for the possibility of new wars, the covenant would make them almost inevitable. On the contrary, war must be definitely outlawed.

【纪要影像】

Mr. CHANG (China) supported deferment of consideration of the second part of article 8. The very valid reasons advanced by the representative of Denmark called for more careful consideration of the numerous and complex problems involved. The Commission, which was to complete its work before 22 June, should immediately take a decision on the first part of article 8; it could still return to the considera tion of the second part if it felt it could do so before the end of the current session.

Mr. CHANG (China), like the representative of Guatemala, had intended to ask the representatives of the United Kingdom or Lebanon to delete sub-paragraph (b). Of course there had been wars, but by providing for the possibility of new wars, the covenant would make them almost inevitable. On the contrary, war must be definitely outlawed.

图片 1.4.11:张彭春在联合国人权委员会第五届第 93 次会议发言纪要

【纪要译文】

张先生(中国)支持推迟审议第 8 条第二部分。丹麦代表提出的非常合理的理由要求更仔细地考虑所涉及的众多复杂问题。本应在 6 月 22 日之前完成工作的委员会应立即就第 8 条第一部分作出决定;如果它认为可以在本届会议结束前重新审议第二部分,它仍然可以这样做。

张先生(中国)与危地马拉代表一样,本打算请英国或黎巴嫩代表删除(b)分段。当然发生过战争,但通过提供新的战争的可能性,《公约》将使战争几乎不可避免。相反,战争肯定是非法的。

8. 张彭春在人权委员会第五届第95次会议发言纪要

联合国人权委员会第五届第 95 次会议,于 1949 年 5 月 20 日下午 2 时 30 分至 5 时 35 分,在纽约成功湖举行,本次会议的主要议题是讨论国际人权公约草案(第 9 条)。中国代表张彭春参加了本次会议,并在会议上发言,其具体发言内容①会议纪要、纪要影像和纪要译文如下:

【会议纪要】

Mr. CHANG (China) pointed out that the difficulty raised by restricting the exercise of a right occurred not only in the case under consideration. It also occurred in article 5 *inter alia*.

If contain exceptions were to be mentioned, they must be limited to the essential and general cases provided for in the legislation of all States.

It would be overambitious to try from the very beginning to draft a covenant anticipating all possible cases and giving all the consequent definitions. Even if the covenant which the Commission was drafting was not perfect, it would serve as a basis for a jurisprudence which would become increasingly important and significant. That jurisprudence would make it possible to complete the original covenant and to revise certain of its articles during the subsequent years.

Mr. Chang was therefore of the opinion that, for the time being, the Commission should limit its activities to the statement of general principles which ju-

---

① UN Document: E/CN. 4/SR. 95, pp. 10–11.

risprudence could clarify and make concrete by protocols which would complete the original covenant whenever such action seemed possible and desirable. By such progressive action, increasingly perfect definitions could be established and, for certain articles, increasingly complete lists of exceptions could be drawn up.

If a too perfect covenant was sought immediately, there would be the risk that the opposite result would be achieved and the moral prestige of the Declaration encroached upon.

He would therefore vote against the retention of a list of exceptions, namely, against paragraph 2 of the proposed article.

【纪要影像】

Mr. CHANG (China) pointed out that the difficulty raised by restricting the exercise of a right occurred not only in the case under consideration. It also occurred in article 5 inter alia.

If certain exceptions were to be mentioned, they must be limited to the essential and general cases provided for in the legislation of all States.

It would be overambitious to try from the very beginning to draft a covenant anticipating all possible cases and giving all the consequent definitions. Even if the covenant which the Commission was drafting was not perfect, it would serve as a basis for a jurisprudence which would become increasingly important and significant. That jurisprudence would make it possible to complete the original covenant and to revise certain of its articles during the subsequent years.

图片1.4.12:张彭春在联合国人权委员会第五届第95次会议发言纪要(1)

Mr. Chang was therefore of the opinion that, for the time being, the Commission should limit its activities to the statement of general principles which jurisprudence could clarify and make concrete by protocols which would complete the original covenant whenever such action seemed possible and desirable. By such progressive action, increasingly perfect definitions could be established and, for certain articles, increasingly complete lists of exceptions could be drawn up.

If a too perfect covenant was sought immediately, there would be the risk that the opposite result would be achieved and the moral prestige of the Declaration encroached upon.

He would therefore vote against the retention of a list of exceptions, namely, against paragraph 2 of the proposed article.

图片 1.4.13:张彭春在联合国人权委员会第五届第 95 次会议发言纪要(2)

【纪要译文】

张先生(中国)指出,限制行使一项权利所带来的困难不仅发生在所审议的案件中。尤其还出现在第 5 条中。

如果要提及例外情况,必须将其限于所有国家立法中规定的基本和一般情况。

如果从一开始就试图起草一份公约,预测所有可能的案例,并给出所有随后的定义,那就过于雄心勃勃了。即使委员会正在起草的公约并不完美,它也将成为判例的基础,判例将变得越来越重要和有意义。这一判例将使我们有可能完成最初的《公约》,并在随后的几年中修订其某些条款。

因此,张先生认为,委员会目前应将其活动限制在一般原则的陈述上,判例可以通过议定书加以澄清和具体化,只要这种行动似乎可行和可取,这些议定书将完成原始公约。通过这种循序渐进的行动,可以建立越来越完善的定义,对于某些条款,可以起草越来越完整的例外清单。

如果立即寻求一个过于完美的公约,就有可能取得相反的结果的风险,并损害《宣言》的道德声誉。

因此,他将投票反对保留"例外情况清单",即反对拟议条款的第 2 款。

9. 张彭春在人权委员会
第五届第96次会议发言纪要

联合国人权委员会第五届第96次会议,于1949年5月23日下午3时至5时30分,在纽约成功湖举行,本次会议的主要议题是讨论国际人权公约草案(第9条)。中国代表张彭春参加了本次会议,并在会议上发言,其具体发言内容①会议纪要、纪要影像和纪要译文如下:

【会议纪要】

Mr. CHANG (China) thought that the Commission should avoid putting into the covenant provisions which were peculiar to the laws of any one country, such as those dealing with arrest of minors and breaches of the peace. The legal system of the United Kingdom was peculiar to that country; no attempt should be made to impose it on other countries.

He reminded the Commission that there were only four weeks left before the close of the session; it would be better to agree on general principles rather than to try to reach agreement on questions of detail on which it would be more to the point to seek the advice of legal experts. The list of exceptions might provide a loophole and make it possible to disregard the covenant on the grounds that its provisions were difficult to put into effect.

---

① UN Document: E/CN. 4/SR. 96, p. 6.

【纪要影像】

> Mr. CHANG (China) thought that the Commission should avoid putting into the covenant provisions which were peculiar to the laws of any one country, such as those dealing with arrest of minors and breaches of the peace. The legal system of the United Kingdom was peculiar to that country; no attempt should be made to impose it on other countries.
>
> He reminded the Commission that there were only four weeks left before the close of the session; it would be better to agree on general principles rather than to try to reach agreement on questions of detail on which it would be more to the point to seek the advice of legal experts. The list of exceptions might provide a loophole and make it possible to disregard the covenant on the grounds that its provisions were difficult to put into effect.

图片1.4.14:张彭春在联合国人权委员会第五届第96次会议发言纪要

【纪要译文】

张先生(中国)认为,委员会应避免在《公约》中加入任何一个国家的法律所特有的条款,例如涉及逮捕未成年人和破坏和平的条款。英国的法律制度是该国特有的,不应试图将其强加给其他国家。

他提醒委员会,离会议结束只有四周了;最好是就一般原则达成一致,而不是试图就细节问题达成一致,在这些问题上,征求法律专家的意见更为恰当。例外情况清单可能会提供一个漏洞,使人们有可能以《公约》条款难以实施为由无视该《公约》。

10. 张彭春在人权委员会第五届第98次会议发言纪要

联合国人权委员会第五届第98次会议,于1949年5月24日下午2时30分至5时30分,在纽约成功湖举行,本次会议的主要议题是讨论国际人权公约草案(第 5 条和第 9 条)。中国代表张彭春参加了本次会议,并在会议上发言,其具体发言内容①会议纪要、纪要影像和纪要译文如下:

【会议纪要】

Mr. CHANG (China) requested that the first paragraph of the Chilean amendment should be voted in two parts, the word "arbitrarily" to be voted on separately.

The first paragraph of the Chilean amendment, with the exception of the word "arbitrarily" was adopted by 14 votes to none, with one abstention.

The word "arbitrarily" was not adopted, 7 votes being cast in favour and 7 against, with one abstention.

【纪要影像】

Mr. CHANG (China) requested that the first paragraph of the Chilean amendment should be voted in two parts, the word "arbitrarily" to be voted on separately.

The first paragraph of the Chilean amendment, with the exception of the word "arbitrarily" was adopted by 14 votes to none, with one abstention.

The word "arbitrarily" was not adopted, 7 votes being cast in favour and 7 against, with one abstention.

图片 1.6.15:张彭春在联合国人权委员会第五届第 98 次会议发言纪要

【纪要译文】

张先生(中国)要求将智利修正案的第一段分为两部分进行表决,"任

---

① UN Document: E/CN. 4/SR. 98, p. 12.

意"一词单独进行表决。

除"任意"一词外的智利修正案第一段,以 14 票对零票、1 票弃权获得通过。

"任意"一词未获通过,7 票赞成,7 票反对,1 票弃权。

11. 张彭春在人权委员会
第五届第 99 次会议发言纪要

联合国人权委员会第五届第 99 次会议,于 1947 年 5 月 25 日上午 11 时 30 分至下午 1 时,在纽约成功湖举行,本次会议的主要议题是讨论国际人权公约草案(第 9 条)。中国代表张彭春参加了本次会议,并担任会议主席,在会议上以主席身份先后多次发言,其具体发言内容①会议纪要、纪要影像和纪要译文如下:

【会议纪要】

Article 9

The CHAIRMAN recalled that the Commission had already adopted the first two paragraphs of article 9.

The United States delegation had presented an amendment (E/CN. 4/ 170) to paragraph 3, to which the French delegation, in turn, had presented an amendment. The United States text was intended to replace the Drafting Committee's text.

Finally, the USSR delegation had submitted an amendment (E/CN. 4/ 250) to paragraph 2 of the United Kingdom draft (E/CN. 4/188).

The CHAIRMAN explained that the USSR proposal was to replace the

---

① UN Document: E/CN. 4/SR. 99, p. 2, p. 3, p. 5, p. 6, p. 7.

words: "The accused in a criminal charge" by the words "Any person who is arrested on a charge of having committed a crime, or to prevent the commission of a crime for which he is making preparation, shall be"; then came the remainder of the text proposed by the United States of America. In his opinion, the words "he accused in a criminal charge" included the cases provided for by the USSR text.

The CHAIRMAN said that the expression "in a criminal charge" covered both the commission of the crime and the intent to commit the crime.

The CHAIRMAN answered that that question was the subject of the next paragraph of the draft.

The CHAIRMAN thought that, in order to speed up the work, it would be better not to delay the vote on paragraph 3. He assured the representative of Iran that the Commission was fully conscious of the connexion which existed between paragraphs 3 and 4. If paragraph 4 was rejected, the Commission could go back on its decision with regard to paragraph 3 so as to take into consideration the observations by the representative of Iran.

【纪要影像】

Article 9

The CHAIRMAN recalled that the Commission had already adopted the first two paragraphs of article 9.

The United States delegation had presented an amendment (E/CN.4/170) to paragraph 3, to which the French delegation, in turn, had presented an amendment. The United States text was intended to replace the Drafting Committee's text.

Finally, the USSR delegation had submitted an amendment (E/CN.4/250) to paragraph 2 of the United Kingdom draft (E/CN.4/188).

The CHAIRMAN explained that the USSR proposal was to replace the words: "The accused in a criminal charge" by the words "Any person who is arrested on a charge of having committed a crime, or to prevent the commission of a crime for which he is making preparation, shall be"; then came the remainder of the text proposed by the United States of America. In his opinion, the words "the accused in a criminal charge" included the cases provided for by the USSR text.

图片1.4.16:张彭春在联合国人权委员会第五届第99次会议发言纪要(1)

The CHAIRMAN said that the expression "in a criminal charge" covered both the commission of the crime and the intent to commit the crime.

The CHAIRMAN answered that that question was the subject of the next paragraph of the draft.

The CHAIRMAN thought that, in order to speed up the work, it would be better not to delay the vote on paragraph 3. He assured the representative of Iran that the Commission was fully conscious of the connexion which existed between paragraphs 3 and 4. If paragraph 4 was rejected, the Commission could go back on its decision with regard to paragraph 3 so as to take into consideration the observations by the representative of Iran.

图片1.4.17：张彭春在联合国人权委员会第五届第99次会议发言纪要(2)

【纪要译文】

第9条

主席回顾说,委员会已经通过了第9条的前两段。

美国代表团对第3段提出了一项修正案(E/CN.4/170),法国代表团也对其提出了一项修正案。美国的案文旨在取代起草委员会的案文。

最后,苏联代表团提交了对英国草案(E/CN.4/188)第2段的修正案(E/CN.4/250)。

主席解释说,苏联的提案是将"刑事指控中的被告"改为"任何因犯罪或出于预防犯罪而被逮捕的人,后者由于正在为犯罪作准备,应被逮捕";然后是美国提出的案文的剩余部分。他认为,"他在刑事指控中指控的"一语包括了苏联案文规定的情况。

主席说,"刑事指控"一词既包括犯罪,也包括犯罪意图。

主席回答说,这个问题是草案下一段的主题。

主席认为,为了加快工作,最好不要推迟对第3段的表决。他向伊朗代表保证,委员会充分意识到第3段和第4段之间的联系。如果第4段被否决,委员会可以撤回对第3段的决定,以便考虑到伊朗代表的意见。

12. 张彭春在人权委员会
第五届第 100 次会议发言纪要

联合国人权委员会第五届第 100 次会议,于 1947 年 5 月 25 日下午 2 时 30 分至 5 时 45 分,在纽约成功湖举行,本次会议的主要议题是讨论国际人权公约草案(第 9 条的第 3 段和第 4 段)。中国代表张彭春参加了本次会议,并担任会议主席主持了前半段会议,其具体发言内容①会议纪要、纪要影像和纪要译文如下:

【会议纪要】

Article 9, paragraph 3 (discussion continued)

The CHAIRMAN recalled that the Commission had before it the original text prepared by the Drafting Committee (E/800, E/CN. 4/212), the text proposed by the United States of America (E/CN. 4/170/Add. 4), the text proposed by the United Kingdom, and the amendments proposed by the USSR (E/CN. 4/250), France (E/CN. 4/259), and Lebanon (E/CN. 4/260).

The CHAIRMAN put to the vote the words "Any person arrested or detained ..."

Those words were adopted by 11 votes to 1, with 4 abstentions.

The CHAIRMAN put to the vote the rest of the amendment.

The rest of the amendment was adopted by 8 votes to 6, with 2 abstentions.

The USSR amendment as a whole was adopted by 10 votes to 5, with 1 abstention.

The CHAIRMAN put to the vote the first part of the United States proposal

---

① UN Document: E/CN. 4/SR. 100, p. 2, p. 5, p. 6.

as amended.

The United States text, as amended, was adopted by 13 votes to none, with 3 abstentions.

【纪要影像】

<pre>
Article 9, paragraph 3 (discussion continued)

        The CHAIRMAN recalled that the Commission had before it
the original text prepared by the Drafting Committee (E/800, E/CN.4/212),
the text proposed by the United States of America (E/CN.4/170/Add.4),
the text proposed by the United Kingdom, and the amendments proposed
by the USSR (E/CN.4/250), France (E/CN.4/259), and Lebanon (E/CN.4/260).

        The CHAIRMAN put to the vote the words "Any person
arrested or detained...".
        Those words were adopted by 11 votes to 1, with 4 abstentions.

        The CHAIRMAN put to the vote the rest of the amendment.
        The rest of the amendment was adopted by 8 votes to 6, with
2 abstentions.
        The USSR amendment as a whole was adopted by 10 votes to 5,
with 1 abstention.
        The CHAIRMAN put to the vote the first part of the
United States proposal as amended.
        The United States text, as amended, was adopted by 13 votes
to none, with 3 abstentions.
</pre>

图片 1.4.18：张彭春在联合国人权委员会第五届第 100 次会议发言纪要

【纪要译文】

第 9 条第 3 款(继续讨论)

主席回顾说,委员会收到了起草委员会编写的原始案文(E/800,E/CN.4/212)、美国提议的案文(E/CN.4/170/Add.4)、英国提议的案文以及苏联(E/CN.4/250)、法国(E/CN.4/259)和黎巴嫩(E/CN.4/260)提议的修正案。

主席将"任何被逮捕或拘留的人"等字付诸表决

这些文字以 11 票对 1 票,4 票弃权获得通过。

主席将修正案的其余部分付诸表决。

修正案的其余部分以 8 票对 6 票,2 票弃权获得通过。

整个苏联修正案以 10 票对 5 票,1 票弃权获得通过。

主席将经修正的美国提案的第一部分付诸表决。

经修正的美国案文以 13 票对 0 票,3 票弃权获得通过。

13. 张彭春在人权委员会
第五届第 102 次会议发言纪要

联合国人权委员会第五届第 102 次会议,于 1947 年 5 月 26 日下午 2 时 30 分至 5 时 30 分,在纽约成功湖举行,本次会议的主要议题是讨论国际人权公约草案(第 9 条)。中国代表张彭春参加了本次会议,并在会议上发言,其具体发言内容①会议纪要、纪要影像和纪要译文如下:

【会议纪要】

Mr. CHANG (China) believed that agreement might perhaps be reached on a text combining the original wording and that proposed by the French delegation. The English version of that text would read as follows:

"Every person who has been the victim of unlawful arrest or deprivation of liberty shall have an enforceable right to compensation."

Mr. CASSIN (France) accepted the new English translation of his text. He stressed the fact that no stronger term existed in French than "droit a reparation" (right to compensation) because to grant an individual a right was to give him the faculty to defend that right before the courts. If therefore the Commission accepted the French proposal, the present French text of the paragraph would not have to be modified and there would be no need to find an adequate translation for the English term "enforceable".

Mr. CHANG (China) was of the opinion that since the Commission had not yet taken a vote on the entire text of article 9, the only point on which a decision could be taken at that stage was the principle of combining articles 9 and 10.

---

① UN Document: E/CN. 4/SR. 102, p. 8, p. 12.

【纪要影像】

Mr. CHANG (China) believed that agreement might perhaps be reached on a text combining the original wording and that proposed by the French delegation. The English version of that text would read as follows:

"Every person who has been the victim of unlawful arrest or deprivation of liberty shall have an enforceable right to compensation."

Mr. CASSIN (France) accepted the new English translation of his text. He stressed the fact that no stronger term existed in French than "droit a reparation" (right to compensation) because to grant an individual a right was to give him the faculty to defend that right before the courts. If therefore the Commission accepted the French proposal, the present French text of the paragraph would not have to be modified and there would be no need to find an adequate translation for the English term "enforceable".

Mr. CHANG (China) was of the opinion that since the Commission had not yet taken a vote on the entire text of article 9, the only point on which a decision could be taken at that stage was the principle of combining articles 9 and 10.

图片 1.4.19:张彭春在联合国人权委员会第五届第 102 次会议发言纪要

【纪要译文】

张先生(中国)认为,也许可以就一个将原来的措辞和法国代表团提出的措辞结合起来的案文达成一致意见。该案文的英文版本如下:

"任何遭受非法逮捕或剥夺自由的人都有获得赔偿的强制性权利。"

卡森先生(法国)接受了他的案文的新的英文译文。他强调说,法语中没有比"获得赔偿的权利"更强有力的术语,因为赋予个人一项权利就是赋予他在法庭上捍卫这项权利的能力。因此,如果委员会接受法国的提议,该段目前的法文文本就不必修改,也没有必要为英文术语"enforceable"找到适当的翻译。

张先生(中国)认为,由于委员会尚未对第 9 条的整个案文进行表决,在此阶段唯一可以作出决定的是将第 9 条和第 10 条合并的原则。

14. 张彭春在人权委员会第五届第 103 次会议发言纪要

联合国人权委员会第五届第 103 次会议,于 1947 年 5 月 27 日上午 11 时 30 分至下午 1 时,在纽约成功湖举行,本次会议的主要议题是讨论人权委员会届会的会议地点问题、讨论国际人权公约草案等。中国代表张彭春参加了本次会议,并在会议上先后多次发言,其具体发言内容①会议纪要、纪要影像和纪要译文如下:

【会议纪要】

Mr. CHANG (China) was surprised that in paragraph 3 of the document submitted by the Secretariat, provision was made for simultaneous interpretation in all the official languages except Chinese.

The CHAIRMAN replied that the Secretariat had no doubt supposed, in view of the Chinese representative's perfect knowledge of English, that he would be so good as to use that language, and had made its arrangements accordingly.

Mr. CHANG (China) thought that personal considerations should not be introduced in a matter of principle. He added that his delegation had always been of the opinion that such an important session as that contemplated should be held only at the permanent Headquarters of the Organization.

Mr. CHANG (China) thought that the formula proposed by the French representative, whereby the first session of the Commission in 1950 should be held in Europe, to a certain extent prejudged the decision of the Economic and

---

① UN Document: E/CN.4/SR.103, p. 3, p. 4, p. 5, p. 7.

Social Council. In point of fact, the Council could decide that the Commission on Human Rights should hold only one session in 1950.

Mr. CASSIN (France) recognized the aptness of the Chinese representative's observation and proposed that the following wording should be used instead: "that the regular session of the Commission in 1950 be held in Geneva." He hoped that the Commission would accept the French proposal which had already been approved by a number of non-European delegations.

Mr. CHANG (China) pointed out that the public which generally attended the meetings of the Commission in Geneva was limited, composed only of Genevese. It could not be said therefore that that public represented European public opinion.

Moreover, telephonic and wireless communications between Geneva and other parts of the world, were not at all on the same scale as those connecting New York with the whole world. Therefore, if the publicity factor were considered from the angle of press communications and public attendance of meetings, it had to be recognized that the Commission on Human Rights had everything to gain by meeting in New York, where a considerable number of press correspondents followed the debates regularly.

Mr. Chang recognized that Europe was the cradle of modern civilization and that European public opinion was deeply interested in the question of human rights. But it could not be said that from the point of view of prestige and of close contact with public opinion, it was necessary for the Commission on Human Rights to meet in Geneva.

Mr. CHANG (China) pointed out that his delegation did not insist that the Commission on Human Rights and the organs of the United Nations in general should meet in the United States; what he had intended to convey was that his delegation felt the organs of the United Nations should meet at the Headquarters of the Organization, wherever those Headquarters were situated.

【纪要影像】

> Mr. CHANG (China) was surprised that in paragraph 3 of the document submitted by the Secretariat, provision was made for simultaneous interpretation in all the official languages except Chinese.
>
> The CHAIRMAN replied that the Secretariat had no doubt supposed, in view of the Chinese representative's perfect knowledge of English, that he would be so good as to use that language, and had made its arrangements accordingly.
>
> Mr. CHANG (China) thought that personal considerations should not be introduced in a matter of principle. He added that his delegation had always been of the opinion that such an important session as that contemplated should be held only at the permanent Headquarters of the Organization.

图片 1.4.20: 张彭春在联合国人权委员会第五届第 103 次会议发言纪要(1)

> Mr. CHANG (China) thought that the formula proposed by the French representative, whereby the first session of the Commission in 1950 should be held in Europe, to a certain extent prejudged the decision of the Economic and Social Council. In point of fact, the Council could decide that the Commission on Human Rights should hold only one session in 1950.
>
> Mr. CASSIN (France) recognized the aptness of the Chinese representative's observation and proposed that the following wording should be used instead: "that the regular session of the Commission in 1950 be held in Geneva." He hoped that the Commission would accept the French proposal which had already been approved by a number of non-European delegations.

图片 1.4.21: 张彭春在联合国人权委员会第五届第 103 次会议发言纪要(2)

联合国人权委员会和起草委员会

Mr. CHANG (China) pointed out that the public which generally attended the meetings of the Commission in Geneva was limited, composed only of Genevese. It could not be said therefore that that public represented European public opinion.

Moreover, telephonic and wireless communications between Geneva and other parts of the world, were not at all on the same scale as those connecting New York with the whole world. Therefore, if the publicity factor were considered from the angle of press communications and public attendance of meetings, it had to be recognized that the Commission on Human Rights had everything to gain by meeting in New York, where a considerable number of press correspondents followed the debates regularly.

图片 1.4.22:张彭春在联合国人权委员会第五届第 103 次会议发言纪要(3)

Mr. Chang recognized that Europe was the cradle of modern civilization and that European public opinion was deeply interested in the question of human rights. But it could not be said that from the point of view of prestige and of close contact with public opinion, it was necessary for the Commission on Human Rights to meet in Geneva.

Mr. CHANG (China) pointed out that his delegation did not insist that the Commission on Human Rights and the organs of the United Nations in general should meet in the United States; what he had intended to convey was that his delegation felt the organs of the United Nations should meet at the Headquarters of the Organization, wherever those Headquarters were situated.

图片 1.4.23:张彭春在联合国人权委员会第五届第 103 次会议发言纪要(4)

【纪要译文】

张先生(中国)感到惊讶的是,秘书处提交的文件第 3 段中规定,除中文外,所有官方语言都有同声传译。

主席回答说,鉴于中国代表对英语的精通,秘书处无疑认为他会很好地使用这种语言,并据此作出了安排。

张先生(中国)认为,原则上不应考虑个人因素。他补充说,他的代表团一贯认为,像这次设想的如此重要的会议只应在本组织的常设总部举行。

张先生(中国)认为,法国代表提出的 1950 年委员会第一届会议应在欧洲举行的方案在一定程度上预先判断了经济及社会理事会的决定。事实上,理事会可以决定人权委员会在 1950 年只举行一届会议。

卡森先生(法国)承认中国代表的意见是恰当的,并建议使用以下措辞:"委员会 1950 年常会在日内瓦举行。"他希望委员会接受法国的提案,该提案已经得到一些非欧洲代表团的批准。

张先生(中国)指出,一般参加委员会在日内瓦举行的会议的公众只有"日内瓦人"。因此,不能说该公众代表了欧洲的公众意见。

此外,日内瓦与世界其他地区之间的电话和无线通信,与纽约与全世界之间的通信规模完全不同。因此,如果从新闻传播和公众出席会议的角度来考虑宣传因素,就必须认识到,人权委员会在纽约开会可以获得一切好处,有相当多的新闻记者定期跟踪辩论。

张先生认识到欧洲是现代文明的摇篮,欧洲舆论对人权问题非常感兴趣。但是,从声望和与公众舆论密切接触的角度来看,不能说人权委员会有必要在日内瓦开会。

张先生(中国)指出,中国代表团并不坚持人权委员会和联合国各机构应在美国开会;他打算表达的意思是,他的代表团认为,联合国各机构应在联合国总部开会,无论这些总部位于何处。

15. 张彭春在人权委员会
第五届第 104 次会议发言纪要

联合国人权委员会第五届第 104 次会议,于 1947 年 5 月 27 日下午 2 时 45 分至 5 时 45 分,在纽约成功湖举行,本次会议的主要议题是讨论国际人权公约草案。中国代表张彭春参加了本次会议,并在会议上先后两次

发言,其具体发言内容①会议纪要、纪要影像和纪要译文如下:

【会议纪要】

Mr. CHANG (China) supported the proposal of the representative of Guatemala. He hoped the USSR representative would be satisfied with his second choice for the time being, on the understanding that when the final stage of rearrangement of the text was reached it could be decided whether slavery and servitude should be mentioned in the same paragraph.

Mr. SOERENSEN (Denmark) concurred in the proposals made by the representatives of the USSR, Guatemala and China.

The CHAIRMAN put to a vote the sentence: "No one shall be held in servitude".

The sentence was adopted by 15 votes to none.

Mr. CHANG (China) felt that the objection to killing on grounds of conscience was a very noble idea, but he wondered how many countries actually recognized it. If the number was found to be very small perhaps the Covenant should mention that fact, unless it wanted to encourage the recognition of the concept of the conscientious objector.

---

① UN Document: E/CN. 4/SR. 104, p. 4, p. 6.

Mr. CHANG (China) supported the proposal of the representative of Guatemala. He hoped the USSR representative would be satisfied with his second choice for the time being, on the understanding that when the final stage of rearrangement of the text was reached it could be decided whether slavery and servitude should be mentioned in the same paragraph.

Mr. SOERENSEN (Denmark) concurred in the proposals made by the representatives of the USSR, Guatemala and China.

The CHAIRMAN put to a vote the sentence: "No one shall be held in servitude".

The sentence was adopted by 15 votes to none.

Mr. CHANG (China) felt that the objection to killing on grounds of conscience was a very noble idea, but he wondered how many countries actually recognized it. If the number was found to be very small perhaps the Covenant should mention that fact, unless it wanted to encourage the recognition of the concept of the conscientious objector.

图片 1.4.24:张彭春在联合国人权委员会第五届第 104 次会议发言纪要

【纪要译文】

张先生(中国)支持危地马拉代表的提议。他希望苏联代表暂时对他的第二个选择感到满意,并理解在重新安排案文的最后阶段,可以决定是否应在同一段中提及奴隶制和奴役。

瑟伦森(Soerensen)先生(丹麦)同意苏联、危地马拉和中国代表提出的建议。

主席将以下句子付诸表决:"任何人不得被奴役"。

该句以 15 票对 0 票获得通过。

张先生(中国)认为,反对基于良心杀人是一个非常高尚的想法,但他想知道有多少国家真正承认这一点。如果发现人数非常少,也许《公约》应该提到这一事实,除非它想鼓励承认依良心拒服兵役者的概念。

联合国人权委员会和起草委员会

16. 张彭春在人权委员会
第五届第 115 次会议发言纪要

联合国人权委员会第五届第 115 次会议,于 1947 年 6 月 27 日上午 11 时,在纽约成功湖开幕,本次会议的主要议题是讨论国际人权公约:实施措施(E/800,E/CN.4/168,E/CN.4/274)。中国代表张彭春参加了本次会议,并在会议上发言,其具体发言内容①会议纪要、纪要影像和纪要译文如下:

【会议纪要】

Mr. CHANG (China) stated that he took a somewhat different view of the meaning of measures of implementation from that expressed by the majority of representatives. By implementation he meant positive measures for putting the Covenant into effect. It should not be dealt with merely from the negative angle; the emphasis should be less on complaints and petitions and more on international co-operation in the realization of human rights.

Mr. Chang pointed out that great advances had been made in the status of the individual during the past 150 years, particularly in the more highly industrialized countries, which had, incidentally, been influenced by Chinese philosophical thought. Although the ideals of human rights had been more fully put into effect in some countries than in others, they were recognized by all. Differences in the individual's position with regard to human rights naturally existed between highly industrialized countries, with opportunities for individual expansion, such as the United States of America, and others such as China which,

---

① UN Document:E/CN.4/SR.115, pp. 9-10.

although heirs to a great tradition of culture, were more backward industrially. It would therefore be easy for one country to complain of violations of human rights in the other but, on the political plane, such a complaint would merely lead to retaliation and would be of no constructive value.

On the question of the individual right of petition he agreed with the representatives of India and Lebanon. He felt, however, that the question of positive implementation was of much greater importance and proposed that, instead of provisions dealing with complaints, positive measures to stimulate international co-operation and encourage interest in the implementation of human rights should be taken.

【纪要影像】

Mr. CHANG (China) stated that he took a somewhat different view of the meaning of measures of implementation from that expressed by the majority of representatives. By implementation he meant positive measures for putting the Covenant into effect. It should not be dealt with merely from the negative angle; the emphasis should be less on complaints and petitions and more on international co-operation in the realization of human rights.

Mr. Chang pointed out that great advances had been made in the status of the individual during the past 150 years, particularly in the more highly industrialized countries, which had, incidentally, been influenced by Chinese philosophical thought. Although the ideals of human rights had been more fully put into effect in some countries than in others, they were recognized by all.

图片 1.4.25：张彭春在联合国人权委员会第五届第 115 次会议发言纪要(1)

Differences in the individual's position with regard to human rights naturally existed between highly industrialized countries, with opportunities for individual expansion, such as the United States of America, and others such as China which, although heirs to a great tradition of culture, were more backward industrially. It would therefore be easy for one country to complain of violations of human rights in the other but, on the political plane, such a complaint would merely lead to retaliation and would be of no constructive value.

On the question of the individual right of petition he agreed with the representatives of India and Lebanon. He felt, however, that the question of positive implementation was of much greater importance and proposed that, instead of provisions dealing with complaints, positive measures to stimulate international co-operation and encourage interest in the implementation of human rights should be taken.

图片1.4.26：张彭春在联合国人权委员会第五届第115次会议发言纪要(2)

【纪要译文】

张先生(中国)说,他对实施措施的含义的看法与大多数代表所表达的看法有些不同。他所说的实施是指为使《公约》生效而采取的积极措施。它不应该仅仅从消极的角度来处理;重点不应放在投诉和请愿上,而应放在实现人权的国际合作上。

张先生指出,在过去的150年里,个人的地位已经取得了巨大的进步,尤其是在工业化程度较高的国家,顺便说一句,这些国家受到了中国哲学思想的影响。虽然人权理想在一些国家比在其他国家得到了更充分的落实,但它们得到了所有国家的承认。在高度工业化的国家之间,个人在人权方面的立场自然存在差异,如美国等有个人扩张的机会,而中国等其他国家虽然继承了伟大的文化传统,但在工业上更加落后。因此,一个国家很容易抱怨另一个国家侵犯人权,但在政治层面上,这种抱怨只会导致报复,没有建设性价值。

关于个人请愿权问题,他同意印度和黎巴嫩代表的意见。然而,他认为,积极落实的问题更为重要,并提议,应当采取积极措施,刺激国际合作,鼓励对落实人权的兴趣,而不是制定处理投诉的条款。

17. 张彭春在人权委员会
第五届第117次会议发言纪要

联合国人权委员会第五届第117次会议,于1947年6月7日下午2时30分至5时55分,在纽约成功湖举行,本次会议的主要议题是讨论国际人权公约(第6条)。中国代表张彭春参加了本次会议,并在会议上发言,其具体发言内容①会议纪要、纪要影像和纪要译文如下:

【会议纪要】

Mr. CHANG (China) stated that a very interesting field had been opened up by the representative of the Ukrainian SSR but he would reserve his remarks on freedom of religion in China, where persons had complete liberty to change their beliefs.

He thought that it would be best to adopt article 18 of the Universal Declaration which had been discussed by fifty-eight nations at the first part of the third session of the Assembly. Such a text, if incorporated in the Covenant, would be more acceptable to the General Assembly than a more detailed and possibly more controversial draft.

Mr. CHANG (China) proposed that the Commission should vote first on paragraph 1 of the joint France-United States text of article 16.

---

① UN Document: E/CN.4/SR.117, p. 10, p. 11.

【纪要影像】

Mr. CHANG (China) stated that a very interesting field had been opened up by the representative of the Ukrainian SSR but he would reserve his remarks on freedom of religion in China, where persons had complete liberty to change their beliefs.

He thought that it would be best to adopt article 18 of the Universal Declaration which had been discussed by fifty-eight nations at the first part of the third session of the Assembly. Such a text, if incorporated in the Covenant, would be more acceptable to the General Assembly than a more detailed and possibly more controversial draft.

Mr. CHANG (China) proposed that the Commission should vote first on paragraph 1 of the joint France-United States text of article 16.

图片 1.4.27:张彭春在联合国人权委员会第五届第 117 次会议发言纪要

【纪要译文】

张先生(中国)说,乌克兰苏维埃社会主义共和国代表开辟了一个非常有趣的领域,但他将保留他关于中国宗教自由的言论,因为在中国,人们完全可以自由改变信仰。

他认为最好是采用《宣言》第 18 条,大会第三届第一期会议上有 58 个国家讨论了该条。如果将这样一个案文纳入《公约》,大会将比一个更详细、可能更具争议性的草案更能接受。

张先生(中国)提议,委员会应首先就第 16 条法美联合案文第 1 段进行表决。

18. 张彭春在人权委员会
第五届第118次会议发言纪要

联合国人权委员会第五届第118次会议,于1949年6月8日上午10时30分至下午1时,在纽约成功湖举行,本次会议的主要议题是讨论国际人权公约、讨论实施措施。中国代表张彭春参加了本次会议,并在会议上先后多次发言,其具体发言内容①会议纪要、纪要影像和纪要译文如下:

【会议纪要】

Mr. CHANG (China) thought the only question which arose was whether or not provisions relating to the right of individuals and organizations to petition should already be included in the Covenant. A vote on the draft resolution prepared by the Secretariat would make clear the position of the members of the Commission on that point.

Nevertheless, in view of the comments made by the representative of the Philippines, there was some excuse for wondering whether a vote on the draft resolution would be a vote for the adoption of the principle of petitions, while at the same time postponing the establishment of the means whereby that principle would be put into practice to a later date, or whether, on the contrary, as he himself understood it, it would be a vote for the immediate inclusion in the Covenant of provisions guaranteeing individuals and organizations the exercise of the right thus conferred upon them.

He asked the Chairman to give a ruling on the meaning to be attached to the draft resolution drawn up by the Secretariat.

---

① UN Document: E/CN. 4/SR. 118, p. 4, p. 8, p. 9, pp. 10-11, p. 11, p. 12.

Mr. CHANG (China) feared that the French proposal had serious disadvantages, in that it tended to separate the principle from its realization in practice. If the first part of the French text were accepted and the second rejected, the sole result of such a decision would be to awaken great hopes throughout the world, only to disappoint them immediately after. The members of the Commission must not forget that a Covenant on Human Rights was not to be compared with a Universal Declaration of Human Rights; a covenant was a treaty which the signatory States undertook to put into effect.

Mr. CHANG (China) suggested that the vote on that question should be postponed, so that a more thorough discussion of the proposals and suggestions which had just been submitted could take place.

Mr. CHANG (China) felt that the matter was important, and that the Commission should try to agree on an adequate text before voting on it.

He recalled that the representatives of Guatemala and of Iran had submitted suggestions which introduced new ideas. The representative of Iran had shown that a text might well be drafted in a negative form. Mr. Chang wondered whether the French representative could not accept the suggestion of the Iranian representative.

Mr. CHANG (China) withdrew his proposal to defer the vote and suggested that the French proposal should be amended to read as follows: "Resolves that provisions for individual and group petitions shall not be included in the measures of implementation at this time".

Mr. CHANG (China) pointed out that those who voted against the second part of the French proposal would likewise have to vote against the first part because, in a matter of such importance, the question of principle could not be separated from that of procedure. It was not possible to proclaim to the world that the right of petition by individuals and by groups of individuals was recognized, and at the same time declare that that right could not be exercised. The procedure making it possible to exercise that right had not yet been established. Consequently, the first part of the French proposal should be rejected for the same reason as the second part.

【纪要影像】

Mr. CHANG (China) thought the only question which arose was whether or not provisions relating to the right of individuals and organizations to petition should already be included in the Covenant. A vote on the draft resolution prepared by the Secretariat would make clear the position of the members of the Commission on that point.

Nevertheless, in view of the comments made by the representative of the Philippines, there was some excuse for wondering whether a vote on the draft resolution would be a vote for the adoption of the principle of petitions, while at the same time postponing the establishment of the means whereby that principle would be put into practice to a later date, or whether, on the contrary, as he himself understood it, it would be a vote for the immediate inclusion in the Covenant of provisions guaranteeing individuals and organizations the exercise of the right thus conferred upon them.

He asked the Chairman to give a ruling on the meaning to be attached to the draft resolution drawn up by the Secretariat.

图片 1.4.28:张彭春在联合国人权委员会第五届第 118 次会议发言纪要(1)

Mr. CHANG (China) feared that the French proposal had serious disadvantages, in that it tended to separate the principle from its realization in practice. If the first part of the French text were accepted and the second rejected, the sole result of such a decision would be to awaken great hopes throughout the world, only to disappoint them immediately after. The members of the Commission must not forget that a Covenant on Human Rights was not to be compared with a Universal Declaration of Human Rights; a covenant was a treaty which the signatory States undertook to put into effect.

Mr. CHANG (China) suggested that the vote on that question should be postponed, so that a more thorough discussion of the proposals and suggestions which had just been submitted could take place.

Mr. CHANG (China) felt that the matter was important, and that the Commission should try to agree on an adequate text before voting on it.

图片 1.4.29:张彭春在联合国人权委员会第五届第 118 次会议发言纪要(2)

He recalled that the representatives of Guatemala and of Iran had submitted suggestions which introduced new ideas. The representative of Iran had shown that a text might well be drafted in a negative form. Mr. Chang wondered whether the French representative could not accept the suggestion of the Iranian representative.

Mr. CHANG (China) withdrew his proposal to defer the vote and suggested that the French proposal should be amended to read as follows: "Resolves that provisions for individual and group petitions shall not be included in the measures of implementation at this time".

Mr. CHANG (China) pointed out that those who voted against the second part of the French proposal would likewise have to vote against the first part because, in a matter of such importance, the question of principle could not be separated from that of procedure. It was not possible to proclaim to the world that the right of petition by individuals and by groups of individuals was recognized, and at the same time declare that that right could not be exercised. The procedure making it possible to exercise that right had not yet been established. Consequently, the first part of the French proposal should be rejected for the same reason as the second part.

图片 1.4.30:张彭春在联合国人权委员会第五届第 118 次会议发言纪要(3)

【纪要译文】

张先生(中国)认为,出现的唯一问题是,是否应将有关个人和组织请愿权的条款纳入《公约》。对秘书处编写的决议草案进行表决将表明委员会成员在这一点上的立场。

然而,鉴于菲律宾代表所作的评论,有理由怀疑对该决议草案的表决是否会是对通过请愿原则的表决,同时,将确立实施这一原则的手段推迟到以后,或者是否如他本人所理解的那样,这将是投票赞成立即在《公约》中列入保障个人和组织行使由此赋予他们的权利的条款。

他请主席就秘书处起草的决议草案的含义作出裁决。

张先生(中国)担心法国的提案有严重的缺点,因为它倾向于将原则与其在实践中的实现分开。如果法文文本的第一部分被接受,而第二部分被拒绝,这样一个决定的唯一结果将是唤醒全世界的巨大希望,但之后却立即让他们失望。委员会成员决不能忘记,人权公约不能与《世界人权宣言》相比较;公约是签署国承诺实施的条约。

张先生(中国)建议推迟对该问题的表决,以便对刚刚提交的提案和建议进行更彻底的讨论。

张先生(中国)认为这一事项很重要,委员会应在就其进行表决之前就适当的案文达成一致。

他回顾说,危地马拉和伊朗的代表提交了一些建议,提出了新的想法。伊朗代表已经表明,案文很可能是以否定的形式起草的。张先生想知道法国代表是否能接受伊朗代表的建议。

张先生(中国)撤回了他推迟表决的提议,并建议将法国的提议修改如下:"决定此时不将有关个人和团体请愿的规定纳入实施措施。"

张先生(中国)指出,对法国提案第二部分投反对票的人也必须对第一部分投反对票,因为在如此重要的问题上,原则问题与程序问题是分不开的。不可能向全世界宣布个人和个人团体的请愿权得到承认,同时宣布这项权利不能行使。使行使这项权利成为可能的程序尚未确立。因此,法国提案的第一部分应被否决,理由与第二部分相同。

19. 张彭春在人权委员会第五届第119次会议发言纪要

联合国人权委员会第五届第119次会议,于1947年6月8日下午2时30分至晚上6时,在纽约成功湖举行,本次会议的主要议题是讨论国际人权公约、讨论实施措施(第2章:与个人权利相关的建议案)。中国代表张彭春参加了本次会议,并在会议上发言,其具体发言内容①会议纪要、纪要影像和纪要译文如下:

【会议纪要】

Mr. CHANG (China) felt that it had been agreed in the Economic and Social Council that votes on matters of substance could not be reconsidered at the same session, but that there was no such rule regarding votes on procedural

---

① UN Document：E/SR.344, p. 2.

285

联合国人权委员会和起草委员会

questions. He agreed that the Commission should finish its work by 20 June, but pointed out that in the short time at its disposal it could not hope to finish work on the draft covenant and the proposals regarding implementation.

Mr. CHANG (China) stated that he had not voted because he felt that the first vote was not clear. He asked whether the Lebanese proposal signified that the Commission would continue its discussion on the draft covenant up to and including 16 June.

Mr. CHANG (China) could not understand why, in connexion with such a serious question as freedom of religion or beliefs, the Commission should have imposed limitations which had not been considered necessary in other articles. He felt that those who really practised their religion would not feel complimented by the restrictions which had been imposed on them. Mr. Chang hoped that the Committee might eventually decide to delete the second paragraph of that article and replace it by a general limitation. It seemed to him inconsistent to promote, on the one hand, freedom of religious beliefs and, on the other, to limit such freedom not only by law but also by considerations of public safety, public order and health.

In that connexion, he mentioned the missionary effort in China. There had been a time when religion was not linked to "civilization", as in the seventeenth and eighteenth centuries when the Jesuits had gone to China not to civilize but simply to preach religion. A happy collaboration had existed and the Jesuits learned also a great deal from their Chinese friends. In the nineteenth century a different attitude had developed and trade and financial and other interests became linked to religious activities. Mr. Chang was glad to note that a change of attitude was developing and he hoped that religion and "civilization" would remain separate.

Mr. CHANG (China) felt that it had been agreed in the
Economic and Social Council that votes on matters of substance could
not be reconsidered at the same session, but that there was no such
rule regarding votes on procedural questions. He agreed that the
Commission should finish its work by 20 June, but pointed out that in
the short time at its disposal it could not hope to finish work on
the draft covenant and the proposals regarding implementation.

Mr. CHANG (China) stated that he had not voted because
he felt that the first vote was not clear. He asked whether the
Lebanese proposal signified that the Commission would continue its
discussion on the draft covenant up to and including 16 June.

Mr. CHANG (China) could not understand why, in connexion with
such a serious question as freedom of religion or beliefs, the Commission
should have imposed limitations which had not been considered necessary
in other articles. He felt that those who really practised their
religion would not feel complimented by the restrictions which had been

图片 1.4.31：张彭春在联合国人权委员会第五届第 119 次会议发言纪要(1)

imposed on them. Mr Chang hoped that the Committee might eventually
decide to delete the second paragraph of that article and replace it by
a general limitation. It seemed to him inconsistent to promote, on the
one hand, freedom of religious beliefs and, on the other, to limit such
freedom not only by law but also by considerations of public safety,
public order and health.

In that connexion, he mentioned the missionary effort in China.
There had been a time when religion was not linked to "civilization",
as in the seventeenth and eighteenth centuries when the Jesuits
had gone to China not to civilize but simply to preach religion.
A happy collaboration had existed and the Jesuits learned also a
great deal from their Chinese friends. In the nineteenth century
a different attitude had developed and trade and financial and other
interests became linked to religious activities. Mr. Chang was glad
to note that a change of attitude was developing and he hoped that
religion and "civilization" would remain separate.

图片 1.4.32：张彭春在联合国人权委员会第五届第 119 次会议发言纪要(2)

【纪要译文】

张先生(中国)认为,经济及社会理事会已经同意,不能在同一届会议上重新审议对实质性问题的表决,但对程序性问题的表决没有这样的规则。他同意委员会应在 6 月 20 日之前完成其工作,但指出,在可支配的短时间内,委员会不可能指望完成公约草案和关于实施的提案的工作。

张先生(中国)说,他没有投票,因为他觉得第一次投票不清楚。他问,黎巴嫩的提案是否意味着委员会将继续讨论公约草案,直至 6 月 16 日。

张先生(中国)无法理解,在涉及宗教或信仰自由这样一个严肃问题时,委员会为什么要施加在其他条款中被认为不必要的限制。他觉得那些真正信奉自己宗教的人不会因为受到的限制而感到受到赞扬。张先生希望委员会最终可能决定删除该条第二款,并以一般性限制取代。在他看来,一方面促进宗教信仰自由,另一方面不仅通过法律,而且考虑到公共安全、公共秩序和健康来限制这种自由,似乎是不一致的。

在这种联系中,他提到了传教士在中国的努力。曾经有一段时间,宗教与"文明"没有联系,就像在 17 和 18 世纪,耶稣会士来到中国不是为了文明,只是为了宣扬宗教。双方进行了愉快的合作,耶稣会士也从他们的中国朋友那里学到了很多东西。在 19 世纪,人们形成了一种不同的态度,贸易、金融和其他利益与宗教活动联系在一起。张先生高兴地注意到,态度正在发生变化,他希望宗教和"文明"保持分离。

20. 张彭春在人权委员会
第五届第 120 次会议发言纪要

联合国人权委员会第五届第 120 次会议,于 1947 年 6 月 9 日上午 10 时 30 分至下午 1 时,在纽约成功湖举行,本次会议的主要议题是讨论国际人权公约草案(第 17 条和第 18 条)。中国代表张彭春参加了本次会议,并在会议上发言,其具体发言内容[①]会议纪要、纪要影像和纪要译文如下:

---

① UN Document：E/CN.4/SR.120, p. 4, pp. 8-9.

Mr. CHANG (China) observed that paragraph 1 of article 17 as drafted by the United Nations Conference on Freedom of Information covered a very wide field and also dealt with freedom of thought and expression.

He suggested that, before taking a vote on the postponement of the consideration of article 17, the Commission should decide to request the views of Governments on the following two questions: (1) whether the Covenant should contain an article concerning freedom of information; (2) if so, what should the terms of that article be?

Mr. CHANG (China) considered the text of the United States amendment preferable to that of the Drafting Committee since it was clearer and more concise than the latter. All the same, he thought certain changes should be made in the United States text. In particular, he proposed to substitute for the first sentence, the negative form of which he did not approve, article 20, paragraph 1 of the Universal Declaration of Human Rights, which stated that "Everyone has the right to freedom of peaceful assembly and association."

Furthermore, it would seem to him preferable not to introduce restrictive provisions in article 18, but to provide for a general limiting clause applicable to the draft Covenant as a whole. If, however, the Commission did not share his opinion, he would suggest that the restrictive clauses proposed by the United States should be amended as follows: (1) the word "reasonable" which was too vague to be included in the draft International Covenant on Human Rights should be suppressed; (2) instead of sub-divisions (a), (b) and (c) commas should be used; (3) the words "the general interest" which were not specific enough, should be replaced by: "the prevention of public disorder."

【纪要影像】

Mr. CHANG (China) observed that paragraph 1 of article 17 as drafted by the United Nations Conference on Freedom of Information covered a very wide field and also dealt with freedom of thought and expression.

He suggested that, before taking a vote on the postponement of the consideration of article 17, the Commission should decide to request the views of Governments on the following two questions: (1) whether the Covenant should contain an article concerning freedom of information; (2) if so, what should the terms of that article be?

Mr. CHANG (China) considered the text of the United States amendment preferable to that of the Drafting Committee since it was

图片 1.4.33：张彭春在联合国人权委员会第五届第 120 次会议发言纪要(1)

clearer and more concise than the latter. All the same, he thought certain changes should be made in the United States text. In particular, he proposed to substitute for the first sentence, the negative form of which he did not approve, article 20, paragraph 1 of the Universal Declaration of Human Rights, which stated that "Everyone has the right to freedom of peaceful assembly and association."

Furthermore, it would seem to him preferable not to introduce restrictive provisions in article 18, but to provide for a general limiting clause applicable to the draft Covenant as a whole. If, however, the Commission did not share his opinion, he would suggest that the restrictive clauses proposed by the United States should be amended as follows: (1) the word "reasonable" which was too vague to be included in the draft International Covenant on Human Rights should be suppressed; (2) instead of sub-divisions (a), (b) and (c) commas should be used; (3) the words "the general interest" which were not specific enough, should be replaced by: "the prevention of public disorder."

图片 1.4.34：张彭春在联合国人权委员会第五届第 120 次会议发言纪要(2)

【纪要译文】

张先生(中国)说,联合国新闻和自由会议起草的第 17 条第 1 款涵盖了非常广泛的领域,也涉及思想和言论自由。

他建议,在就推迟审议第 17 条进行表决之前,委员会应决定就以下两个问题征求各国政府的意见:(1)公约是否应载有关于新闻自由的条款;(2)如果是,该条款的内容应该是什么?

张先生(中国)认为美国修正案的案文比起草委员会的案文更可取,因为它比后者更清楚、更简洁。尽管如此,他认为应该对美国文本进行某些修改。特别是,他提议用《世界人权宣言》第21条第1款——"人人有和平集会和结社自由的权利"来取代第一句。他不赞成第一句采用的否定形式。

此外,在他看来,最好不要在第18条中引入限制性条款,而是规定一项适用于整个公约草案的一般性限制条款。但是,如果委员会不同意他的意见,他将建议对美国提出的限制性条款进行如下修改:(1)禁止使用"合理"一词,因为该词过于模糊,无法纳入国际人权公约草案;(2)应使用逗号代替(a)、(b)和(c)子部分;(3)"总体利益"一词不够具体,应改为:"预防公共秩序混乱"。

21. 张彭春在人权委员会
第五届第121次会议发言纪要

联合国人权委员会第五届第121次会议,于1949年6月9日下午2时30分至5时35分,在纽约成功湖举行,本次会议的主要议题是讨论国际人权公约草案(第18条、第19条和第20条)。中国代表张彭春参加了本次会议,并在会议上发言,其具体发言内容①会议纪要、纪要影像和纪要译文如下:

【会议纪要】

Mr. CHANG (China) agreed to accept certain modifications proposed by

---

① UN Document:E/CN. 4/SR. 321, p. 2, p. 3, p. 15.

the French delegation (E/CN. 4/306) in the Chinese amendment to the Drafting Committee's text of article 18 (E/CN. 4/37). However, he wished to press for the retention of the word "national" before "security" in the second sentence of the Chinese amendment. He was anxious that there should be no confusion between national and social security.

Mr. CHANG (China) withdrew his amendment and proposed instead the insertion of the word "national" before "security" in whatever text was taken as a basis for voting.

Mr. CHANG (China) remarked that protection of the law under article 20 should not necessarily be restricted to the enjoyment of rights and freedoms set forth in the Covenant; other freedoms which, for some reason, might not be incorporated in the Covenant might deserve an equal measure of protection. He stressed that his remark was not intended as a formal proposal but only as a tentative suggestion for consideration by the Commission.

【纪要影像】

Mr. CHANG (China) agreed to accept certain modifications proposed by the French delegation (E/CN.4/306) in the Chinese amendment to the Drafting Committee's text of article 18 (E/CN.4/307). However, he wished to press for the retention of the word "national" before "security" in the second sentence of the Chinese amendment. He was anxious that there should be no confusion between national and social security.

Mr. CHANG (China) withdrew his amendment and proposed instead the insertion of the word "national" before "security" in whatever text was taken as a basis for voting.

Mr. CHANG (China) remarked that protection of the law under article 20 should not necessarily be restricted to the enjoyment of rights and freedoms set forth in the Covenant; other freedoms which, for some reason, might not be incorporated in the Covenant might deserve an equal measure of protection. He stressed that his remark was not intended as a formal proposal but only as a tentative suggestion for consideration by the Commission.

图片 1.4.35：张彭春在联合国人权委员会第五届第 121 次会议发言纪要

【纪要译文】

张先生(中国)同意接受法国代表团在中国对起草委员会第 18 条案文的修正案(E/CN. 4/307)中提出的某些修改(E/CN. 4/306)。然而,他希望敦促保留中国修正案第二句中"安全"之前的"国家"一词。他急切盼望国家安全和社会安全之间不应出现混淆。

张先生(中国)撤回了他的修正案,并提议在任何作为表决依据的文本中,在"安全"之前插入"国家"一词。

张先生(中国)说,根据第 21 条对法律的保护不一定限于享有《公约》规定的权利和自由;出于某种原因,可能没有被纳入《公约》的其他自由可能应该得到同等程度的保护。他强调说,他的话不是作为一项正式议案,而是作为一项供委员会审议的初步建议。

22. 张彭春在人权委员会第五届第 122 次会议发言纪要

联合国人权委员会第五届第 122 次会议,于 1949 年 6 月 10 日上午 10 时 30 分至下午 1 时 10 分,在纽约成功湖举行,本次会议的主要议题是继续讨论国际人权公约草案(第 20 条)。中国代表张彭春参加了本次会议,并担任会议主席,以主席身份在会议上先后多次发言,其具体发言内容[①]会议纪要、纪要影像和纪要译文如下:

【会议纪要】

Article 20

The CHAIRMAN stated that the French, Philippine and United States del-

---

① UN Document:E/CN. 4/SR. 122, p. 2, p. 3, p. 4, p. 6, p. 11, p. 12.

egations had submitted a joint text for article 20 (E/CN. 4/311).

However, the words "and to" in the first sentence of that proposal should be replaced by the words "in the enjoyment of" so that the text would read: "Everyone is entitled to equal protection of the law in the enjoyment of all the rights and freedoms, etc.".

The CHAIRMAN pointed out that the first sentence of article 7 of the Declaration of Human Rights, which stated: "All are equal before the law and are entitled without discrimination to equal protection of the law", went far beyond the idea contained in the first paragraph of the joint proposal, which spoke only of the "protection of the law in the enjoyment of all the rights and freedoms defined in this Covenant."

He consequently thought that the solution might be to repeat, in article 20, the first sentence of article 7 of the Declaration; the provisions of the joint proposal would then be included in article 20.

The CHAIRMAN thought that it was possible to reach a compromise solution between the views of the different delegations by drafting article 20 in the following manner: the first sentence of article 7 of the Declaration should be used; followed by the words "without discrimination of any kind, such as race ..." and without mentioning "the rights and freedoms defined in this Covenant".

Finally, a paragraph should be added concerning "protection against any discrimination in violation of this Covenant".

The CHAIRMAN pointed out that the Commission was therefore seized of two texts: one being the joint draft of the Philippines, France and the United States (E/CN. 4/311), and the other the Indian draft (E/CN. 4/312).

The CHAIRMAN explained that that idea was covered by the words "or other status"; it had not been stated in so many words in order to avoid re-opening a very old debate at that juncture.

The CHAIRMAN stressed that the proposed text read "the law" and not "the laws," and that it was evident that all those affected by the law were equal before that law.

【纪要影像】

Article 20

    The CHAIRMAN stated that the French, Philippine and United States delegations had submitted a joint text for article 20 (E/CN.4/311).

    However, the words "and to" in the first sentence of that proposal should be replaced by the words "in the enjoyment of" so that the text would read: "Everyone is entitled to equal protection of the law in the enjoyment of all the rights and freedoms, etc."

    The CHAIRMAN pointed out that the first sentence of article 7 of the Declaration of Human Rights, which stated: "All are equal before the law and are entitled without discrimination to equal protection of the law", went far beyond the idea contained in the first paragraph of the joint proposal, which spoke only of the "protection of the law in the enjoyment of all the rights and freedoms defined in this Covenant."

    He consequently thought that the solution might be to repeat, in article 20, the first sentence of article 7 of the Declaration; the provisions of the joint proposal would then be included in article 20.

图片 14.36：张彭春在联合国人权委员会第五届第 122 次会议发言纪要(1)

    The CHAIRMAN thought that it was possible to reach a compromise solution between the views of the different delegations by drafting article 20 in the following manner: the first sentence of article 7 of the Declaration should be used; followed by the words "without discrimination of any kind, such as race..." and without mentioning "the rights and freedoms defined in this Covenant".

    Finally, a paragraph should be added concerning "protection against any discrimination in violation of this Covenant".

    The CHAIRMAN pointed out that the Commission was therefore seized of two texts: one being the joint draft of the Philippines, France and the United States (E/CN.4/311), and the other the Indian draft (E/CN.4/312).

    The CHAIRMAN explained that that idea was covered by the words "or other status"; it had not been stated in so many words in order to avoid re-opening a very old debate at that juncture.

    The CHAIRMAN stressed that the proposed text read "the law" and not "the laws," and that it was evident that all those affected by the law were equal before that law.

图片 1.4.37：张彭春在联合国人权委员会第五届第 122 次会议发言纪要(2)

【纪要译文】

第 20 条

主席说,法国、菲律宾和美国代表团提交了第 20 条的联合案文(E/

CN. 4/311)。

然而,该提案第一句中的"和"应改为"享受",以便案文改为:"人人有权在享受所有权利和自由等方面受到法律的平等保护。"

主席指出,《人权宣言》第 7 条第一句规定:"法律面前人人平等,有权不受歧视地获得法律的平等保护。"这远远超出了联合提案第一段所载的想法,它只提到"在享受本公约规定的所有权利和自由方面的法律保护"。

因此,他认为解决办法可能是在第 20 条中重复《宣言》第 7 条的第一句话;然后,联合提案的条款将被纳入第 20 条。

主席认为,通过以下方式起草第 20 条,可以在不同代表团的意见之间达成折中解决办法:应使用《宣言》第 7 条第一句;然后是"没有任何歧视,比如种族……"而且没有提及"本公约所界定的权利和自由"。

最后,应增加一段关于"防止违反本公约的任何歧视"。

主席指出,委员会因此处理了两份案文:一份是菲律宾、法国和美国的联合草案(E/CN.4/311),另一份是印度草案(E/CN.4/312)。

主席解释说,"或其他地位"一词涵盖了这一想法;为了避免在那个时刻重新开始一场非常陈旧的辩论,没有用这么多的话来阐述这一点。

主席强调,拟议的案文是"法律"(the law)而不是"各种法律"(the laws),显然,所有受法律影响的人在该法律面前一律平等。

23. 张彭春在人权委员会
第五届第 123 次会议发言纪要

联合国人权委员会第五届第 123 次会议,于 1949 年 6 月 10 日下午 2 时 45 分至 5 时 35 分,在纽约成功湖举行,本次会议的主要议题是继续讨论国际人权公约草案(第 20 条、第 21 条和第 22 条)。中国代表张彭春参加了本次会议,并担任会议主席,在会议上以主席身份先后多次发言,其具体发言内容①会议纪要、纪要影像和纪要译文如下：

【会议纪要】

Draft International Covenant on Human Rights(E/800, E/N. 4/296, E/
CN. 4/312)

Article 20 (discussion continued)

The CHAIRMAN reopened the discussion on article 20 and suggested that
the Commission should treat the Indian amendment to that article (E/CN. 4/
312) as its basic working document.

Article 21

The CHAIRMAN opened the discussion on the above and referred members to document E/CN. 4/296, which contained the original text of article 21,
deleted by the Drafting Committee the previous year, and the text proposed by
the USSR.

The CHAIRMAN put to the vote the question whether consideration of article 21 should be postponed until article 17 was discussed.

The proposal was adopted by 5 votes to 3, with 4 abstentions.

The CHAIRMAN stated that when article 21 was eventually reconsidered,
the two texts proposed by the French and USSR representatives would be submitted to the Commission.

Article 22

The CHAIRMAN drew attention to the opinion expressed by the United
States representative in document E/CN. 4/296, to the effect that the article
was vague and unnecessary. After consultation with Mr. CASSIN (France) and
Mr. HOOD (Australia), he amended the draft proposed by the French delegation as follows：

"Nothing in this Covenant shall be interpreted as implying for any State,

---

① UN Document：E/CN. 4/SR. 123, p. 2, p. 4, p. 6, p. 7.

group or individual any right to engage in any activity or to perform any act aimed at the destruction or impairment of any of the rights and freedoms defined herein. "

That text combined the French and Australian proposals and brought the drafting into conformity with the terms of article 30 of the Universal Declaration of Human Rights.

【纪要影像】

DRAFT INTERNATIONAL COVENANT ON HUMAN RIGHTS (E/800, E/CN.4/296, E/CN.4/312)
Article 20 (discussion continued)

The CHAIRMAN reopened the discussion on article 20 and suggested that the Commission should treat the Indian amendment to that article (E/CN.4/312) as its basic working document.

Article 21

The CHAIRMAN opened the discussion on the above and referred members to document E/CN.4/296, which contained the original text of article 21, deleted by the Drafting Committee the previous year, and the text proposed by the USSR.

The CHAIRMAN put to the vote the question whether consideration of article 21 should be postponed until article 17 was discussed.

The proposal was adopted by 5 votes to 3, with 4 abstentions.

图片 1.4.38：张彭春在联合国人权委员第五届第 123 次会议发言纪要(1)

The CHAIRMAN stated that when article 21 was eventually reconsidered, the two texts proposed by the French and USSR representatives would be submitted to the Commission.

Article 22

The CHAIRMAN drew attention to the opinion expressed by the United States representative in document E/CN.4/296, to the effect that the article was vague and unnecessary. After consultation with Mr. CASSIN (France) and Mr. HOOD (Australia), he amended the draft proposed by the French delegation as follows:

"Nothing in this Covenant shall be interpreted as implying for any State, group or individual any right to engage in any activity or to perform any act aimed at the destruction or impairment of any of the rights and freedoms defined herein."

That text combined the French and Australian proposals and brought the drafting into conformity with the terms of article 30 of the Universal Declaration of Human Rights.

图片 1.4.39：张彭春在联合国人权委员会第五届第 123 次会议发言纪要(2)

【纪要译文】

国际人权公约草案(E/800、E/CN.4/296、E/CN.4/312)

第 20 条(讨论续)

主席重新开始讨论第 20 条,并建议委员会将印度对该条的修正案(E/CN.4/312)作为其基本工作文件。

第 21 条

主席开始讨论上述问题,并请成员们参阅文件:E/CN.4/296,其中载有起草委员会去年删除的第 21 条原文,以及苏联提出的案文。

主席将是否应将对第 21 条的审议推迟到讨论第 17 条的问题付诸表决。

该提案以 5 票对 3 票、4 票弃权获得通过。

主席说,最终重新审议第 21 条时,法国和苏联代表提出的两份案文将提交委员会。

第 22 条

主席提请注意美国代表在文件 E/CN.4/296 中表达的意见。大意是该条款含糊不清,没有必要。在与卡森先生(法国)和胡德先生(澳大利亚)协商后,他对法国代表团提出的草案修正如下:

"本公约的任何规定均不得解释为暗示任何国家、团体或个人有权从事任何旨在破坏或损害本公约所界定的任何权利和自由的活动或行为。"

该案文结合了法国和澳大利亚的提案,使草案符合《世界人权宣言》第 30 条的规定。

24. 张彭春在人权委员会
第五届第 124 次会议发言纪要

联合国人权委员会第五届第 124 次会议,于 1949 年 6 月 13 日上午 10 时 30 分至下午 1 时,在纽约成功湖举行,本次会议的主要议题是讨论国际人权公约草案(第 22 条)、审议公约草案第一部分。中国代表张彭春参加了本次会议,并在会议上发言,其具体发言内容①会议纪要、纪要影像和纪要译文如下:

【会议纪要】

Mr. CHANG (China), without expressing any opinion on the substance of the matter, thought that the French proposal was similar in meaning to the Australian alternative version—the formulation of which was, however, simpler.

Mr. CHANG (China) supported the United Kingdom suggestion. He pointed out that the paragraph had not been sufficiently discussed in the Drafting Committee, and that there had been no intention that both paragraphs should be included in one article. He suggested that the Commission might postpone consideration of both the paragraph and the United Kingdom amendment until a later date.

Mr. CHANG (China) pointed out that since the drafting of the text of the Covenant, the Commission had formulated the Declaration in which the term "civilized nations" had been deleted wherever it occurred, because of the difficulty of defining it. He therefore hoped that the Commission would see fit also to delete "civilized nations" from article 1 of the Covenant.

---

① UN Document: E/CN. 4/SR. 124, p. 2, p. 7, p. 15.

【纪要影像】

Mr. CHANG (China), without expressing any opinion on the substance of the matter, thought that the French proposal was similar in meaning to the Australian alternative version -- the formulation of which was, however, simpler.

Mr. CHANG (China) supported the United Kingdom suggestion. He pointed out that the paragraph had not been sufficiently discussed in the Drafting Committee, and that there had been no intention that both paragraphs should be included in one article. He suggested that the Commission might postpone consideration of both the paragraph and the United Kingdom amendment until a later date.

Mr. CHANG (China) pointed out that since the drafting of the text of the Covenant, the Commission had formulated the Declaration in which the term "civilized nations" had been deleted wherever it occurred, because of the difficulty of defining it. He therefore hoped that the Commission would see fit also to delete "civilized nations" from article 1 of the Covenant.

图片 1.4.40:张彭春在联合国人权委员会第五届第 124 次会议发言纪要

【纪要译文】

张先生(中国)没有就此事的实质内容发表任何意见,他认为法国的提案在意义上与澳大利亚的备选案文相似,但其提法更简单。

张先生(中国)支持英国的建议。他指出,起草委员会没有充分讨论该款,也没有打算将这两款纳入一条之中。他建议委员会将该款和英国修正案推迟到日后审议。

张先生(中国)指出,自起草《公约》案文以来,委员会制定了一项宣言,其中删除了"文明国家"一词,因为很难对其进行定义。因此,他希望委员会也认为应该从《公约》第 1 条中删除"文明国家"。

25. 张彭春在人权委员会
第五届第 126 次会议发言纪要

联合国人权委员会第五届第 126 次会议,于 1949 年 6 月 14 日上午 11 时 30 分至下午 1 时,在纽约成功湖举行,本次会议的主要议题是讨论国际人权公约草案(第 4 条)。中国代表张彭春参加了本次会议,并担任会议主席,在会议上以主席身份先后多次发言,其具体发言内容①会议纪要、纪要影像和纪要译文如下:

【会议纪要】

The CHAIRMAN opened the discussion on article 4 of the draft international covenant and the amendments submitted to it by the United States of America, the United Kingdom, France, and the Union of Soviet Socialist Republics (E/CN.4/319, E/CN.4/324, E/CN.4/325).

The CHAIRMAN noted three ideas in the proposal: (1) certain rights could be derogated from in certain circumstances; (2) while derogation from those rights was permissible in public emergencies, an exception should be made in respect of certain rights which must always remain unimpaired; (3) whenever there was a derogation from any rights, the Secretary-General must be informed thereof.

The first and third ideas seemed of a more general nature, whereas the second idea involved enumeration of the articles from which there should be no derogation. In view of the fact that the numerical order of the articles of the Covenant had not yet been determined and that more articles might later be in-

---

① UN Document: E/CN.4/SR.126, p. 2, p. 5, pp. 8-9, p. 10.

cluded in the light of comments which would be received from Governments, he suggested that the Commission should postpone any decision in respect of paragraph 2 of the United Kingdom proposal until it had become clear what provisions part II of the draft Covenant would contain.

The CHAIRMAN, speaking as the representative of China, expressed the view that if there were to be an article containing the ideas stated in the proposed article 4, it should not appear in part I. Those ideas were linked by their nature to the terms of article 22, as adopted. The essential character of the proposed article, dealing as it did with limitations, bore a marked resemblance to the subject matter of article 22; it should therefore be placed before or after that article.

The Commission would remember the discussions that had preceded the adoption of the Universal Declaration of Human Rights. The text of the Drafting Committee which was before the Commission was of an earlier date than the Universal Declaration of Human Rights. When, in drafting the latter, the Commission had dealt with the matter of limitations, it had agreed to place them after the enumeration of rights. If the limitation clause in the Covenant were placed in part I, he would be compelled to vote against the article.

He was opposed to mentioning war as a condition permitting derogation from the Covenant. It was not that he was unrealistic so far as the possibility of future wars was concerned, but to mention war as a condition permitting derogation of certain human rights would involve recognition of the concept of rules of war, which he deemed questionable, at the very least.

With regard to the enumeration of articles the limitation of which might be permitted under certain conditions, Mr. Chang believed that that should be considered later, since the articles subject to consideration in that respect might yet be added to or subtracted from.

CHAIRMAN put the proposal to postpone consideration of article 4 until part II of the Covenant was completed to vote.

【纪要影像】

The CHAIRMAN opened the discussion on article 4 of the draft
international covenant and the amendments submitted to it by the
United States of America, the United Kingdom, France, and the
Union of Soviet Socialist Republics (E/CN.4/319, E/CN.4/324, E/CN.4/325).

The CHAIRMAN noted three ideas in the proposal: (1) certain
rights could be derogated from in certain circumstances; (2) while
derogation from those rights was permissible in public emergencies, an
exception should be made in respect of certain rights which must always
remain unimpaired; (3) whenever there was a derogation from any rights,
the Secretary-General must be informed thereof.

The first and third ideas seemed of a more general nature, whereas
the second idea involved enumeration of the articles from which there
should be no derogation. In view of the fact that the numerical order
of the articles of the Covenant had not yet been determined and that
more articles might later be included in the light of comments which
would be received from Governments, he suggested that the Commission
should postpone any decision in respect of paragraph 2 of the
United Kingdom proposal until it had become clear what provisions
part II of the draft Covenant would contain.

图片 1.4.41：张彭春在联合国人权委员会第五届第 126 次会议发言纪要(1)

The CHAIRMAN, speaking as the representative of China, expressed
the view that if there were to be an article containing the ideas stated in
the proposed article 4, it should not appear in part I. Those ideas were
linked by their nature to the terms of article 22, as adopted. The essential character of the proposed article, dealing as it did with limitations, bore a marked resemblance to the subject matter of article 22; it
should therefore be placed before or after that article.

The Commission would remember the discussions that had preceded the
adoption of the Universal Declaration of Human Rights. The text of the
Drafting Committee which was before the Commission was of an earlier
date than the Universal Declaration of Human Rights. When, in drafting
the latter, the Commission had dealt with the matter of limitations,

图片 1.4.42：张彭春在联合国人权委员会第五届第 126 次会议发言纪要(2)

it had agreed to place them after the enumeration of rights. If the
limitation clause in the Covenant were placed in part I, he would be
compelled to vote against the article.

He was opposed to mentioning war as a condition permitting derogation
from the Covenant. It was not that he was unrealistic so far as the
possibility of future wars was concerned, but to mention war as a
condition permitting derogation of certain human rights would involve
recognition of the concept of rules of war, which he deemed questionable,
at the very least.

With regard to the enumeration of articles the limitation of which
might be permitted under certain conditions, Mr. Chang believed that
that should be considered later, since the articles subject to consideration in that respect might yet be added to or subtracted from.

The CHAIRMAN put the proposal to postpone consideration of
article 4 until part II of the Covenant was completed to the vote.

图片 1.4.43：张彭春在联合国人权委员会第五届第 126 次会议发言纪要(3)

【纪要译文】

主席开始讨论国际公约草案第 4 条以及美国、英国、法国和苏联提交
的修正案(E/CN.4/319、E/CN.4/324、E/CN.4/325)。

主席指出提案中有三个想法：(1)某些权利在某些情况下可能会受到
克减；(2)虽然在公共紧急情况下可以克减这些权利,但对于某些必须始
终不受损害的权利,应作出例外规定；(3)每当任何权利受到克减时,必须
通知秘书长。

第一个和第三个想法似乎更具一般性,而第二个想法涉及列举不应克
减的条款。鉴于《公约》条款的数字顺序尚未确定,而且根据各国政府提
出的意见,以后可能会列入更多条款,他建议委员会推迟到公约草案第二
部分将包含哪些条款明确时,再就英国提案第 2 段作出决定。

主席以中国代表的身份发言时表示,如果有一条包含拟议的第 4 条中
所述的观点,它则不应出现在第一部分中。这些观点的性质与通过的第
22 条的条款有关。拟议条款的本质特征与第 22 条的主题有明显的相似
之处,尽管它涉及限制；因此,应将其放在该条前后。

委员会将铭记《世界人权宣言》通过之前的讨论。委员会面前的起草
委员会的案文的日期早于《世界人权宣言》。在起草后者时,委员会处理
了限制问题,并同意将其置于权利列举之后。如果《公约》中的限制条款

被列入第一部分,他将被迫对该条款投反对票。

　　他反对把战争作为允许克减《公约》的条件。就未来战争的可能性而言,他并不是不切实际,而是说战争是允许克减某些人权的条件,这将涉及承认战争规则的概念,他认为这至少是有问题的。

　　关于列举在某些条件下可能允许限制的条款,张先生认为,这一点应在以后加以审议,因为在这方面需要审议的条款可能会增加或减少。

　　主席提议将对第 4 条的审议推迟到《公约》第二部分完成后进行表决。

26. 张彭春在人权委员会
第五届第 127 次会议发言纪要

　　联合国人权委员会第五届第 127 次会议,于 1949 年 6 月 14 日下午 2 时 50 分至 5 时 30 分,在纽约成功湖举行,本次会议的主要议题是讨论国际人权公约草案(第 4 条)。中国代表张彭春参加了本次会议,并担任会议主席,以会议主席身份在会议上先后多次发言(除最后一次发言外,本次会议的末尾罗斯福夫人继续担任会议主席),其具体发言内容①会议纪要、纪要影像和纪要译文如下:

【会议纪要】

The CHAIRMAN, replying to the remarks of the United Kingdom and Philippine representatives, agreed that principles could hardly be voted upon unless they were formulated in words. He pointed out that, if the Commission adopted a provisional text, it would remain free to improve it during its next succeeding session. The members of the Commission could, therefore, proceed

---

　　①　UN Document: E/CN. 4/SR. 127, p. 8, p. 9, p. 10, p. 11, p.14.

to vote immediately on (1) the principle of derogations from provisions of the Covenant "in time of war"; (2) the principle of derogations in the event of "other public emergency"; (3) the USSR amendment; and (4) paragraphs 2 and 3 of the United Kingdom amendment, should occasion arise.

The CHAIRMAN declared that the observations of the representative of Uruguay were worthy of the Commission's attention when it returned to the examination of the article in question.

The CHAIRMAN said he would take a vote on the second Indian proposal that the Commission should take a provisional decision on the United Kingdom text and reconsider the question when it had finished dealing with the second part of the Covenant.

The CHAIRMAN observed that the Commission had not taken a single final decision regarding the draft Covenant during the current session. It was, however, at liberty to decide that the vote on article 4 should be still more provisional in character.

The CHAIRMAN said that he would take a vote on the USSR amendment to the United Kingdom text (E/CN. 4/319) and then on the United Kingdom text itself.

Mr. CHANG (China) said that he had always opposed the inclusion of such an article in the draft Covenant, and expressed the hope that the Commission would ultimately decide, after careful consideration, to omit the article in its entirety. Should the Commission decide to maintain article 4, however, its position should be changed; it might perhaps be inserted after article 22, which concluded with a limitative provision.

联合国人权委员会和起草委员会

【纪要影像】

The CHAIRMAN, replying to the remarks of the United Kingdom and Philippine representatives, agreed that principles could hardly be voted upon unless they were formulated in words. He pointed out that, if the Commission adopted a provisional text, it would remain free to improve it during its next succeeding session. The members of the Commission could, therefore, proceed to vote immediately on (1) the principle of derogations from provisions of the Covenant "in time of war"; (2) the principle of derogations in the event of "other public emergency"; (3) the USSR amendment; and (4) paragraphs 2 and 3 of the United Kingdom amendment, should occasion arise.

The CHAIRMAN declared that the observations of the representative of Uruguay were worthy of the Commission's attention when it returned to the examination of the article in question.

The CHAIRMAN said he would take a vote on the second Indian proposal that the Commission should take a provisional decision on the United Kingdom text and reconsider the question when it had finished dealing with the second part of the Covenant.

图片1.4.44：张彭春在联合国人权委员会第五届第127次会议发言纪要(1)

The CHAIRMAN observed that the Commission had not taken a single final decision regarding the draft Covenant during the current session. It was, however, at liberty to decide that the vote on article 4 should be still more provisional in character.

The CHAIRMAN said that he would take a vote on the USSR amendment to the United Kingdom text (E/CN.4/319) and then on the United Kingdom text itself.

Mr. CHANG (China) said that he had always opposed the inclusion of such an article in the draft Covenant, and expressed the hope that the Commission would ultimately decide, after careful consideration, to omit the article in its entirety. Should the Commission decide to maintain article 4, however, its position should be changed; it might perhaps be inserted after article 22, which concluded with a limitative provision.

图片1.4.45：张彭春在联合国人权委员会第五届第127次会议发言纪要(2)

【纪要译文】

主席在答复英国和菲律宾代表的发言时同意,除非用文字表述,否则很难对原则进行表决。他指出,如果委员会通过一个临时案文,在下一届会议期间仍将保留改进该案文的自由。因此,委员会成员可以立即就(1)

在"战时"克减《公约》条款的原则进行表决;(2)在"其他公共紧急状态"情况下的克减原则;(3)苏联修正案;以及(4)英国修正案的第 2 段和第 3 段。

主席宣布,乌拉圭代表的意见值得委员会在重新审查有关条款时予以注意。

主席说,他将对印度的第二项提议进行表决,即委员会应对英国的案文作出临时决定,并在处理完《公约》第二部分后重新审议这一问题。

主席指出,委员会在本届会议期间没有就公约草案作出任何最后决定。然而,它可以自由决定对第 4 条的表决应该更加具有临时性质。

主席说,他将对英国案文(E/CN.4/319)的苏联修正案进行表决,然后对英国案文本身进行表决。

张先生(中国)说,他一直反对在公约草案中列入这样一个条款,并表示希望委员会经过认真审议后最终决定将该条款全部删除。然而,如果委员会决定保留第 4 条,其位置应该改变;它也许可以插在第 22 条之后,该条以一项限制性条款结束。

27. 张彭春在人权委员会
第五届第 129 次会议发言纪要

联合国人权委员会第五届第 129 次会议,于 1949 年 6 月 15 日下午 2 时 30 分至晚上 6 时 30 分,在纽约成功湖举行,本次会议的主要议题是讨论国际人权公约草案(第 23 条、第 24 条和第 25 条)。中国代表张彭春参加了本次会议,并在会议上发言,其具体发言内容①会议纪要、纪要影像和纪要译文如下:

---

① UN Document:E/CN.4/SR.129, p. 17.

【会议纪要】

Mr. CHANG (China) noted that the colonial clause had appeared in all the conventions prepared under the auspices of the United Nations, but that it had not effected much change in general appreciation of the necessity for recognizing the same rights and liberties for all peoples.

In the case of the Covenant on Human Rights, however, the Commission could not, it seemed, confine itself to reproducing one of the previously adopted clauses. The object of the Covenant was completely different from that of a convention such as had been adopted in connexion with the international transmission of news and the right of correction, which dealt primarily with the rights exercised by the Administering Authority and where the role played by the peoples of the Trust Territories or non-self-governing territories was passive. In respect of human rights, however, their role should be eminently an active one. For that reason the Covenant should apply in a more direct manner to such peoples, the more so as the Declaration had already expressly proclaimed the principle of the universality of human rights.

It would, therefore, be well to consider a new formula which would reproduce, in the first part, the second sub-paragraph of the United States amendment which would require the signatory State to take the necessary measures as soon as possible with a view to the implementation of the Covenant in territories for whose international relations it was responsible. The limitation clause regarding the consent of the territories could also be included in view of the fact that a number of them already enjoyed the right to decide such matters themselves. The rest of the article might make provision for certain exceptions which the signatory State would have to justify on the grounds that they met a real necessity arising out of a constitutional text.

The drafting of such an article raised a number of knotty questions of constitutional law which should first be studied by experts on the matter. The representative of China therefore suggested that the text of article 25 should be transmitted to Governments with all pertinent amendments and comments and that no decision should be taken on it until the various delegations were able to adopt a definite attitude towards it.

【纪要影像】

Mr. CHANG (China) noted that the colonial clause had appeared in all the conventions prepared under the auspices of the United Nations, but that it had not effected much change in general appreciation of the necessity for recognizing the same rights and liberties for all peoples.

In the case of the Covenant on Human Rights, however, the Commission could not, it seemed, confine itself to reproducing one of the previously adopted clauses. The object of the Covenant was completely different from that of a convention such as had been adopted in connexion with the international transmission of news and the right of correction, which dealt primarily with the rights exercised by the Administering Authority and where the role played by the peoples of the Trust Territories or non-self-governing territories was passive. In respect of human rights, however, their role should be eminently an active one. For that reason the Covenant should apply in a more direct manner to such peoples, the more so as the Declaration had already expressly proclaimed the principle of the universality of human rights.

图片 1.4.46：张彭春在联合国人权委员会第五届第 129 次会议发言纪要(1)

It would, therefore, be well to consider a new formula which would reproduce, in the first part, the second sub-paragraph of the United States amendment which would require the signatory State to take the necessary measures as soon as possible with a view to the implementation of the Covenant in territories for whose international relations it was responsible. The limitation clause regarding the consent of the territories could also be included in view of the fact that a number of them already enjoyed the right to decide such matters themselves. The rest of the article might make provision for certain exceptions which the signatory State would have to justify on the grounds that they met a real necessity arising out of a constitutional text.

The drafting of such an article raised a number of knotty questions of constitutional law which should first be studied by experts on the matter. The representative of China therefore suggested that the text of article 25 should be transmitted to Governments with all pertinent amendments and comments and that no decision should be taken on it until the various delegations were able to adopt a definite attitude towards it.

图片 1.4.47：张彭春在联合国人权委员会第五届第 129 次会议发言纪要(2)

【纪要译文】

张先生(中国)指出,在联合国主持下制定的所有公约中都出现了殖民地条款,但在普遍认识到必须承认所有人民的相同权利和自由方面,这一条款并没有带来太大变化。

然而,就《人权公约》而言,委员会似乎不能仅限于复制以前通过的一项条款。《公约》的目的与《国际新闻传播和矫正权公约》的目的完全不同,后者主要涉及管理当局行使的权利,托管领土或非自治领土人民所发挥的作用是消极的。然而,在人权方面,他们的作用应该是积极的。因此,《公约》应以更直接的方式适用于这些民族,因为《宣言》已经明确宣布了人权普遍性的原则。

因此,在第一部分中,我们将考虑一个新的方案。美国修正案的第二分段要求签署国尽快采取必要措施,以便在其负责国际关系的领土上执行《公约》。鉴于其中一些领土已经享有自行决定此类事项的权利,还可以列入关于领土同意的限制条款。该条的其余部分可能会对某些例外情况作出规定,签字国必须证明这些例外情况符合宪法文本所产生的实际必要性。

这一条款的起草提出了宪法中的一些棘手问题,这些问题应该首先由相关专家进行研究。因此,中国代表建议,第 25 条的案文应连同所有相关修正案和评论一并转交各国政府,在各代表团能够对其采取明确态度之前,不应就此作出决定。

28. 张彭春在人权委员会第五届第 131 次会议发言纪要

联合国人权委员会第五届第 131 次会议,于 1949 年 6 月 16 日下午 2 时 40 分至晚上 6 时,在纽约成功湖举行,本次会议的主要议题是讨论人权委员会第五届会议报告。中国代表张彭春参加了本次会议,并在会议上发言,其具体发言内容①会议纪要、纪要影像和纪要译文如下:

【会议纪要】

Mr. CHANG (China) was afraid the Danish draft resolution might be less satisfactory than it appeared at the first sight and might by-pass the real question, which was the inclusion of the economic and social rights in the Covenant. It seemed to him that the survey provided for in the proposal would be concerned exclusively with international action in connexion with the implementation of articles 22 to 27 of the Declaration; but, before taking any decision regarding the inclusion of economic and social rights in the Covenant, the Commission should try to obtain information on measures taken at the governmental level for the implementation of articles 22 to 27 of the Declaration. In order to improve the Danish draft resolution, therefore, he proposed that the words " of other bodies . . . within the scope" should be replaced by the words " in connexion with the realization of".

He also proposed that the word " their" before " specialized agencies" should be replaced by the word " the".

Mr. CHANG (China) proposed that the word " a" should be substituted

---

① UN Document: E/CN. 4/SR. 131, pp. 11-12, p. 15.

for the word "the" before the word "Covenant" in the Philippine amendment.

【纪要影像】

Mr. CHANG (China) was afraid the Danish draft resolution might be less satisfactory than it appeared at first sight and might by-pass the real question, which was the inclusion of the economic and social rights in the Covenant. It seemed to him that the survey provided for in the proposal would be concerned exclusively with international action in connexion with the implementation of articles 22 to 27 of the Declaration; but, before taking any decision regarding the inclusion of the economic and social rights in the Covenant, the Commission should try to obtain

information on measures taken at the governmental level for the implementation of articles 22 to 27 of the Declaration. In order to improve the Danish draft resolution, therefore, he proposed that the words "of other bodies... within the scope" should be replaced by the words "in connexion with the realization of".

He also proposed that the word "their" before "specialized agencies" should be replaced by the word "the".

Mr. CHANG (China) proposed that the word "a" should be substituted for the word "the" before the word "Covenant" in the Philippine amendment.

图片 1.4.48:张彭春在联合国人权委员会第五届第 131 次会议发言纪要

【纪要译文】

张先生(中国)担心丹麦的决议草案可能不如乍看之下令人满意,并可能绕过真正的问题,即将经济和社会权利纳入《公约》。在他看来,提案中规定的调查只涉及与执行《宣言》第 22 至 27 条有关的国际行动;但是,在就将经济和社会权利纳入《公约》作出任何决定之前,委员会应设法获得关于政府一级为执行《宣言》第 22 至 27 条而采取的措施的信息。因此,为了改进丹麦的决议草案,他提议将"范围内其他机构的"改为"与实现……有关的"。

他还建议将"专门机构"之前的词汇"their"改为"the"。

张先生(中国)提议,菲律宾修正案中"公约"一词之前的"a"应替换为"the"。

29. 张彭春在人权委员会
第五届第 133 次会议发言纪要

联合国人权委员会第五届第 133 次会议,于 1949 年 6 月 17 日下午 2 时 30 分至晚上 7 时 10 分,在纽约成功湖举行,本次会议的主要议题是讨论国际人权公约草案附加条款等。中国代表张彭春参加了本次会议,并在会议上发言,其具体发言内容①会议纪要、纪要影像和纪要译文如下:

【会议纪要】

Mr. CHANG (China) had abstained because, if the Declaration on Human Rights and later the Covenant were to be applied, every effort should first be made to find some practical measures to promote cooperation between nations. Any possibility of mutual recrimination and friction should therefore be reduced. The resolution gave too much weight to negative action.

【纪要影像】

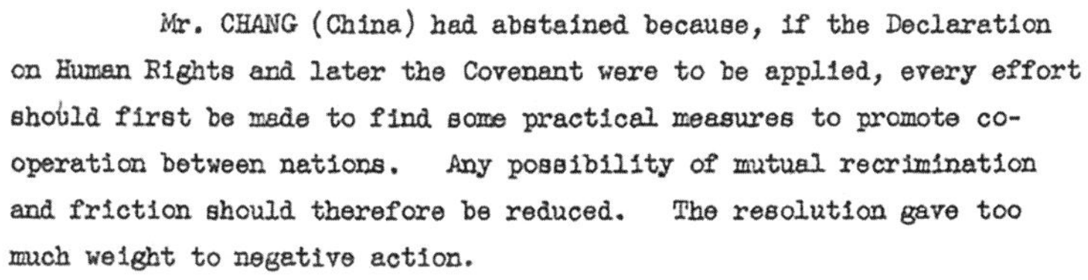

> Mr. CHANG (China) had abstained because, if the Declaration on Human Rights and later the Covenant were to be applied, every effort should first be made to find some practical measures to promote co-operation between nations. Any possibility of mutual recrimination and friction should therefore be reduced. The resolution gave too much weight to negative action.

图片 1.4.49:张彭春在联合国人权委员会第五届第 133 次会议发言纪要

---

① UN Document: E/CN. 4/SR. 131, pp. 11-12, p. 15.

【纪要译文】

张先生(中国)投了弃权票,因为如果要适用《人权宣言》和后来的《公约》,首先应尽一切努力找到一些促进国家间合作的实际措施。因此,应该减少任何相互指责和摩擦的可能性。该决议过于重视消极行动。

30. 张彭春在人权委员会第五届第 134 次会议发言纪要

联合国人权委员会第五届第 134 次会议,于 1949 年 6 月 20 日上午 10 时 30 分至下午 1 时 10 分,在纽约成功湖举行,本次会议的主要议题是继续讨论人权委员会第五届会议报告。中国代表张彭春参加了本次会议,并在会议上先后多次发言,其具体发言内容①会议纪要、纪要影像和纪要译文如下:

【会议纪要】

Mr. CHANG (China) hoped that the secretary should also see that the report was translated with as little delay into Chinese.

Mr. CHANG (China) said that the initial of his alternate, Mr. Cha, was "H".

Chapter XI: Yearbook on Human Rights

Mr. CHANG (China) would have preferred the language mentioned in paragraph 1 of part of the operative part of the resolution, to have been listed in the order in which they appeared in the Charter, namely: "Chinese, Russian, Spanish".

---

① UN Document: E/CN.4/SR.134, p. 3, p. 4, p. 7, p. 8, p. 10.

Mr. CHANG (China) said that the Committee had transmitted the proposals submitted by Ukraine (E/CN. 4/AC. 8/1) and by Guatemala (E/CN. 4/AC. 8/2) to the Commission together with its report. The first paragraph of Chapter XI could therefore mention all three documents.

It was so decided.

Chapter XI, as amended, was adopted.

Mr. CHANG (China) requested that no distinction should be made between the five official languages, and regards both interpretation and translation.

【纪要影像】

```
              Mr. CHANG (China) hoped that the Secretariat would also
see that the report was translated with as little delay into Chinese.
              Mr. CHANG (China) said that the initial of his alternate,
Mr. Cha, was "H".
     Chapter XI: Yearbook on Human Rights
              Mr. CHANG (China) would have preferred the languages mentioned
in paragraph 1 of the operative part of the resolution, to have been
listed in the order in which they appeared in the Charter, namely:
"Chinese, Russian, Spanish".
              Mr. CHANG (China) said that the Committee had transmitted the
proposals submitted by Ukraine (E/CN.4/AC.8/1) and by Guatemala
(E/CN.4/AC.8/2) to the Commission together with its report.  The first
paragraph of Chapter XI could therefore mention all three documents.
              It was so decided.
     Chapter XI, as amended, was adopted.
              Mr. CHANG (China) requested that no distinction should be made
between the five official languages, as regards both interpretation and
translation.
```

图片 1.4.50:张彭春在联合国人权委员会第五届第 134 次会议发言纪要

【纪要译文】

张先生(中国)希望秘书处也能尽快将报告翻译成中文。

张先生(中国)说,他的候补人查先生的首字母是"H"。

第十一章:人权年鉴

张先生(中国)希望决议执行部分第 1 段中提到的措辞能按照它们在

《宪章》中出现的顺序列出,即:"中文、俄文、西班牙文。"

张先生(中国)说,委员会已将乌克兰(E/CN.4/AC.8/1)和危地马拉(E/CN.4/AC.8/2)提交的提案连同其报告一并转交委员会。因此,第十一章的第一段可以提到所有三个文件。

就这样决定下来。

第十一章修正案通过。

张先生(中国)要求口译和笔译五种官方语言应该没有任何区别。

第五章 联合国人权委员会第六届会议

联合国人权委员会第六届会议,于 1950 年 3 月 27 日至 1950 年 5 月 19 日,在美国纽约成功湖举行,本届会议的中心议题是讨论和审议国际人权公约草案、实施措施及其各国提交的决议草案、修正案等。本届会议共召开了 66 次会议,即从第 136 次会议至第 201 次会议。张彭春出席了本届会议,实际共参加了本届 57 次会议,并在其中的 44 次会议上发言,包括第 136 次会议、第 137 次会议、第 138 次会议、第 139 次会议、第 140 次会议、第 142 次会议、第 143 次会议、第 145 次会议、第 146 次会议、第 147 次会议、第 148 次会议、第 149 次会议、第 150 次会议、第 151 次会议、第 152 次会议、第 153 次会议、第 155 次会议、第 156 次会议、第 157 次会议、第 158 次会议、第 159 次会议、第 161 次会议、第 163 次会议、第 164 次会议、第 165 次会议、第 166 次会议、第 167 次会议、第 170 次会议、第 171 次会议、第 173 次会议、第 174 次会议、第 175 次会议、第 182 次会议、第 183 次会议、第 184 次会议、第 186 次会议、第 189 次会议、第 192 次会议、第 193 次会议、第 195 次会议、第 197 次会议、第 198 次会议、第 199 次会议和第 201 次会议。张彭春在共计 7 次会议包括第 160 次会议、第 166 次会议、第 167 次会议、第 173 次会议、第 182 次会议、第 183 次会议和第 184 次会议中担任会议主席,以主席身份在会议上发言。他在本届因故缺席的会议共有 9 次,包括第 141 次会议、177 次会议、178 次会议、179 次会议、180 次会议、181 次会议、第 187 次会议、第 188 次会议和第 191 次会议。另外,张彭春与曹保颐先生共同参加的会议有三次,包括 190 次会议、197 次会议、199 次会议。张彭春与查修先生共同参加的会议有两次会议,包括第 196 次会议和第 198 次会议。

曹保颐先生参加的会议共有 12 次会议,并在其中的第 178 次会议①、第 179 次会议②、第 186 次会议③、第 188 次会议④、第 190 次会议⑤、第 197 次会议⑥和第 199 次会议⑦上发言;查修先生参加了三次会议(包括第 191 次会议、第 196 次会议和第 198 次会议),并在第 191 次会议⑧上发言。而曹保颐先生与查修先生共同参加的会议是第 191 次会议。

现将张彭春在本届会议发言的具体情况整理如下:

1. 张彭春在人权委员会第六届第 136 次会议发言纪要

1950 年 3 月 27 日上午 11 时至下午 12 时 45 分,联合国人权委员会第六届第 136 次会议,在纽约成功湖开幕,本次会议的主要议题是选举会议主席副主席、第二副主席和报告员。张彭春先生参加了本次会议,并在会议上发言,其具体发言内容⑨会议纪要、纪要影像和纪要译文如下:

【会议纪要】

12. Mr. CHANG（China）remarked that the proposal which had been laid before the Commission had not been unexpected. He considered it impossible to tolerate statements such as those which had been made, and which, mo-

---

① UN Document：E/CN. 4/SR. 178, p. 15.
② UN Document：E/CN. 4/SR. 179, p. 12.
③ UN Document：E/CN. 4/SR. 186, p. 14.
④ UN Document：E/CN. 4/SR. 188, p. 8.
⑤ UN Document：E/CN. 4/SR. 190, pp. 10-11.
⑥ UN Document：E/CN. 4/SR. 197, p. 17.
⑦ UN Document：E/CN. 4/SR. 199, p. 12, p. 13.
⑧ UN Document：E/CN. 4/SR. 191, p. 9.
⑨ UN Document：E/CN. 4/SR. 136, p. 5, pp. 8-9, p. 10, p. 11.

reover, had become hackneyed through stereotyped repetition.

14. The Chinese delegation had always defended the interests of the Chinese people and voiced their aspirations. A great human tragedy was taking place on Chinese territory; during that time the representative of the USSR was seeking to lead the Commission on Human Rights into an unworthy political manoeuvre. The tension which prevailed in the United Nations was caused by the withdrawal of the representatives of the USSR from its various organs rather than by the Chinese conflict. That refusal provided material for newspaper headlines; it did not contribute to the progress of the United Nations.

15. He appealed to the Commission not to allow itself to be diverted from its purposes but to continue its work.

34. Mr. CHANG (China) recalled that the Chinese people had made it clear that they would never renounce their independence and sovereign rights. They would never submit to foreign domination from any quarter. He wholeheartedly supported the Chairman's decision. The problem had been stated in perfectly clear terms: the representative of the USSR had not been concerned with the question of who was to represent China in the United Nations, but with imposing a specific policy on the Commission.

42. The CHAIRMAN asked the Commission to vote on the proposal that Mr. Chang, representative of China, should be elected first Vice-Chairman.

Mr. Chang (China) was elected first Vice-Chairman by 12 votes to none, with 2 abstentions.

52. Mr. CHANG (China) pointed out that the various delegations had had more than three years in which to state their positions. The Commission would no doubt desire to start drafting the final text of the draft covenant at its next meeting.

联合国人权委员会和起草委员会

【纪要影像】

12.　　Mr. CHANG (China) remarked that the proposal which had been laid before the Commission had not been unexpected. He considered it impossible to tolerate statements such as those which had been made, and which, moreover, had become hackneyed through stereotyped repetition.

14.　　The Chinese delegation had always defended the interests of the Chinese people and voiced their aspirations. A great human tragedy was taking place on chinese territory; during that time the representative of the USSR was seeking to lead the Commission on Human Rights into an unworthy political manoeuvre. The tension which prevailed in the United Nations was caused by the withdrawal of the representatives of the USSR from its various organs rather than by the Chinese conflict. That refusal provided material for newspaper headlines; it did not contribute to the progress of the United Nations.

15.　　He appealed to the Commission not to allow itself to be diverted from its purposes but to continue its work.

图片 1.5.1:张彭春在联合国人权委员会第六届第 136 次会议发言纪要(1)

34.　　Mr. CHANG (China) recalled that the Chinese people   i made it clear that they would never renounce their independence and sovere   rights.   They would never submit to foreign domination from any quarter.   wholeheartedly supported the Chairman's decision.   The problem had been stated in perfectly clear terms: the representative of the USSR had not been concerned with the question of who was to represent China in the United Nations, but with imposing a specific policy on the Commission.

42.　　The CHAIRMAN asked the Commission to vote on the proposal that Mr. Chang, representative of China, should be elected first Vice-Chairman.

　　Mr. Chang (China) was elected first Vice-Chairman by 12 votes to none, with 2 abstentions.

52.　　Mr. CHANG (China) pointed out that the various dele   ons had had more than three years in which to state their positions.   '   Commission would no doubt desire to start drafting the final text of the dr   covenant at its next meeting.

图片 1.5.2:张彭春在联合国人权委员会第六届第 136 次会议发言纪要(2)

【纪要译文】

12. 张先生(中国)说,向委员会提出的建议并非出乎意料。他认为不可能容忍像这样的言论,而且这些言论由于刻板的重复而变成陈词滥调。

14. 中国代表团①始终捍卫中国人民的利益,表达他们的愿望。一场

---

①　1949 年 10 月 1 日,中华人民共和国成立,国民政府在联合国的代表席位被认为是非法的,此处按字面意思翻译,特此说明。请读者明察。

巨大的人类悲剧正在中国领土上发生;在此期间,苏联代表试图领导人权委员会进行一次不值得的政治活动。联合国内普遍存在的紧张局势是由苏联代表退出其各机构而不是由中国冲突造成的。这种拒绝为报纸标题提供了素材;它没有对联合国的进展做出贡献。

15. 他呼吁委员会不要让自己偏离其宗旨,而是继续其工作。

34. 张先生(中国)回顾说,中国人民已经明确表示,他们永远不会放弃自己的独立和主权。他们绝不会屈服于任何一方的外国统治。他全心全意地支持主席的决定。这个问题已经用非常明确的措辞陈述了出来:苏联代表关心的不是谁将在联合国代表中国的问题,而是将一项具体政策强加给委员会的问题。

42. 主席请委员会就中国代表张彭春先生当选第一副主席的提议进行表决。

张先生(中国)以 12 票对零票、2 票弃权当选第一副主席。

52. 张先生(中国)指出,各代表团有三年多的时间表明立场。委员会无疑希望在下次会议上开始起草公约草案的最后文本。

2. 张彭春在人权委员会 第六届第 137 次会议发言纪要

1950 年 3 月 29 日上午 11 时至下午 1 时,联合国人权委员会第六届第 137 次会议,在纽约成功湖召开,本次会议的主要议题是讨论国际人权公约草案(序言)。张彭春先生参加了本次会议,并在会议上发言,其具体发言内容①会议纪要、纪要影像和纪要译文如下:

① UN Document:E/CN.4/SR. 137, p. 8, pp. 14-15.

【会议纪要】

27. Mr. CHANG (China) pointed out that an exchange of views on the general articles which would constitute part I of the draft covenant would undoubtedly be exceedingly useful at the current stage, provided that the Commission were given the possibility of changing its opinion at a later date, for it would be difficult, on account of the reasons given by the representatives of India and Lebanon, to take a final decision on those articles before the Commission had established the general purport of part II of the draft covenant.

28. In the circumstances, Mr. Chang suggested that a general debate should first take place on the preamble and the first four articles. The Commission would then study the provisions of part II of the draft covenant, basing its discussion on the principles which would have emerged in the course of the general debate. It would then return to the preamble and the general article and take its decision upon them on the basis of ripe consideration.

30. Mr. RAMADAN (Egypt) and Mrs. MEHTA (India) supported the Chinese representative's proposal.

The Chinese representative's proposal was adopted.

54. Mr. CHANG (China) thought that the Commission had done well to begin by discussing the preamble because that discussion would enable it to understand the scope and the true nature of the covenant which it was preparing. That was in fact the essential point which the Commission should try to settle. In the past, the covenant had been considered the most important part of the Charter of Human Rights and the Declaration was to constitute a kind of preamble to it. However, ever since its adoption, the Declaration had assumed more and more importance and meaning, exceeding the hopes of those who had drafted it. It had now become an historic document which would outlive political disturbances and nothing, not even the covenant, could diminish or weaken its

significance. In the circumstances, what was the specific purpose of the covenant which was being prepared? It was to ensure the implementation of the rights and fundamental freedoms proclaimed in the Declaration. It was clear that the covenant, unlike the Declaration which had rightly been described as "universal", could only have an international character inasmuch as it was supposed to bind the signatory States. But the question which immediately arose was how to ensure the effective implementation of the covenant, given the present stage of development of international law? In the absence of a universal constitution which would guarantee its implementation, it could be anticipated that States would seek to evade their responsibilities by invoking their sovereignty, and would reproach one another for failure to apply the provisions of the covenant.

55. That being so, the least that should be done was to draw the attention of Governments to their duties under the Charter in respect of human rights and fundamental freedoms. With that purpose in mind, Mr. Chang thought that the preamble of the covenant might reiterate the end of the introductory clause of the proclamation as it appeared in the Declaration.

56. Moreover, Mr. Chang thought that the representative of Australia had been right in deleting any reference in his draft to the general principles of the Charter. The Universal Declaration never mentioned principles; it spoke only of specific rights and freedoms. Every effort must be made to avoid statements concerning principles because States could always use the argument that practice could not in all cases be made to conform to principles. The Australian draft therefore quite rightly emphasized the fact that, by signing the Charter, States had undertaken to promote universal respect for human rights.

57. Mr. Chang thought that the operative part of the preamble proposed by the Australian delegation should be drafted so that it could not be construed to mean that the rights which were not specifically stated in the covenant were not

guaranteed by the contracting parties. Furthermore, Mr. Chang did not especially like the phrase "agree on the following articles" in the Australian text: he would prefer to replace it with "agree to give effect..." or a similar phrase such as that which appeared in the French text.

【纪要影像】

27.   Mr. CHANG (China) pointed out that an exchange of views on the general articles which would constitute part I of the draft covenant would undoubtedly be exceedingly useful at the current stage, provided that the Commission were given the possibility of changing its opinion at a later date, for it would be difficult, on account of the reasons given by the representatives of India and Lebanon, to take a final decision on those articles before the Commission had established the general purport of part II of the draft covenant.

28.   In the circumstances, Mr. Chang suggested that a general debate should first take place on the preamble and the first four articles. The Commission would then study the provisions of part II of the draft covenant, basing its discussion on the principles which would have emerged in the course of the general debate. It would then return to the preamble and the general articles and take its decision upon them on the basis of ripe consideration.

30.   Mr. RAMADAN (Egypt) and Mrs. MEHTA (India) supported the Chinese representative's proposal.

The Chinese representative's proposal was adopted.

图片 1.5.3：张彭春在联合国人权委员会第六届第 137 次会议发言纪要(1)

54.   Mr. CHANG (China) thought that the Commission had done well to begin by discussing the preamble because that discussion would enable it to understand the scope and the true nature of the covenant which it was preparing. That was in fact the essential point which the Commission should try to settle. In the past, the covenant had been considered the most important part of the Charter of Human Rights and the Declaration was to constitute a kind of preamble to it. However, ever since its adoption, the Declaration had assumed more and more importance and meaning, exceeding the hopes of those who had drafted it. It had now become an historic document which would outlive political disturbances and nothing, not even the covenant, could diminish or weaken its significance. In the circumstances, what was the specific purpose of the covenant which was being prepared? It was to ensure the implementation of the rights and fundamental freedoms proclaimed in the Declaration. It was clear that the covenant, unlike the Declaration which had rightly been described as "universal", could only have an international character inasmuch as it was supposed to bind the signatory States. But the question which immediately arose was how to ensure the effective implementation of the covenant, given the present stage of development of international law? In the absence of an universal constitution which would guarantee its implementation, it could be anticipated that States would seek to evade their responsibilities by invoking their sovereignty, and would reproach one another for failure to apply the provisions of the covenant.

图片 1.5.4：张彭春在联合国人权委员会第六届第 137 次会议发言纪要(2)

图片 1.5.5:张彭春在联合国人权委员会第六届第 137 次会议发言纪要(3)

【纪要译文】

27. 张先生(中国)指出,就构成公约草案第一部分的一般性条款交换意见,在现阶段无疑是非常有用的,倘若委员会有可能在以后改变其意见,因为这很难,鉴于印度和黎巴嫩代表提出的理由,我们决定在委员会确定公约草案第二部分的总主旨之前就这些条款作出最后决定。

28. 在这种情况下,张先生建议首先就序言和前四条进行一般性辩论。然后,委员会将研究公约草案第二部分的规定,并根据一般性辩论中可能出现的原则进行讨论。然后,它将回到序言和一般性条款,并在充分考虑的基础上作出决定。

30. 拉马丹(Ramadan)先生(埃及)和梅赫塔(Mehta)夫人(印度)支持中国代表的提议。

中国代表的提案获得通过。

54. 张先生(中国)认为,委员会从讨论序言开始做得很好,因为这种讨论将使它能够了解它正在拟订的《公约》的范围和真正性质。事实上,这是委员会应该努力解决的关键问题。过去,《公约》被认为是《人权宪章》最重要的组成部分,《宣言》将构成《公约》的序言。然而,自《宣言》通过以来,它的重要性和意义越来越大,超出了起草者的希望。它现在已成为一份历史性文件,将比政治争端更具生命力,任何东西,甚至《公约》都不能削弱其重要性。在这种情况下,正在制定的《公约》的具体目的是什么? 这是为了确保《宣言》中宣布的权利和基本自由得到落实。显然,《公约》与被正确地描述为"普遍性"的《宣言》不同,它只能具有国际性质,因为它本应约束签署国。但立即出现的问题是,鉴于目前国际法的发展阶段,如何确保《公约》的有效实施? 在没有一部保证其实施的普遍宪法的情况下,可以预见,各国将寻求通过援引其主权来逃避其责任,并因未能适用《公约》的规定而相互指责。

55. 既然如此,至少应该提请各国政府注意《宪章》规定的它们在人权和基本自由方面的义务。考虑到这一目的,张先生认为《公约》的序言可能会重申《宣言》中出现的序言条文的结尾部分。

56. 此外,张先生认为,澳大利亚代表在其草案中删除了对《宪章》一般原则的任何提及是正确的。《世界人权宣言》从未提及原则;它只提到具体的权利和自由。必须尽一切努力避免有关原则的陈述,因为各国总是可以使用这样的论点,即实践不能在所有情况下都符合原则。因此,澳大利亚草案非常正确地强调了一个事实,即各国通过签署《宪章》,已承诺促进对人权的普遍尊重。

57. 张先生认为,澳大利亚代表团提议的序言部分的实施部分应该起草,这样就不能解释为《公约》中没有具体规定的权利没有得到缔约方的保障。此外,张先生并不特别喜欢澳大利亚文本中的"同意以下条款"一词:他宁愿将其替换为"同意……生效"或类似的短语,如法语文本中出现的短语。

3. 张彭春在人权委员会
第六届第 138 次会议发言纪要

1950 年 3 月 29 日下午 2 时 30 分至下午 1 时,联合国人权委员会第六届第 138 次会议,在纽约成功湖召开,本次会议的主要议题是继续讨论国际人权公约草案(第 1 条和第 2 条)。张彭春先生参加了本次会议,并在会议上发言,其具体发言内容①会议纪要、纪要影像和纪要译文如下:

【会议纪要】

12. Mr. CHANG (China) supported the widely held view that article 1 should be deleted and that any valuable idea it might contain should, after further consideration, be placed in the preamble.

13. He felt that the draft covenant—like the Declaration—should contain no specific mention of the origin of human rights, in view of the controversial nature of the subject.

51. Mr. CHANG (China), reserving the right to enter into a fuller discussion of the many important and suggestive contributions made in the discussion so far, stated that he was prepared to accept the Australian suggestion that the word "recognized" should be substituted for the word "defined". He could also accept the addition of the words "respect and", as suggested by France.

52. The United Kingdom amendment to article 2, paragraph 1, raised a most important problem. Although the document under consideration was called a covenant, it was in effect a treaty or convention, differing from all other previous instruments of that kind in that it would cover a great variety of subjects.

---

① UN Document: E/CN. 4/SR. 138, p. 5, pp. 14–15.

A convention normally covered one subject only. The fact that the present draft Convention was intended to cover more subjects than any other should be borne in mind, if only to avoid future disappointments and disillusions.

53. The problem of how such a complex draft convention was to be ratified by the various national legislatures was admittedly most difficult but by no means hopeless.

54. The United Kingdom amendment was practical in that it introduced the possibility of specific reservations on particular provisions. He wondered, however, what nation would be frank enough to admit that its own legislation might not be up to the standards specified in the draft Covenant. He saw in that question a very real difficulty and suggested that serious study should be made of that point. He favoured some sort of provision for specific reservations on particular points, as a matter of principle, but would not at the moment commit himself concerning the methods to be used in the implementation of that principle.

55. Another fact to be borne in mind was that States differed in their legislative and constitutional practices. The second sentence of the first paragraph of article 2 might be acceptable. He sympathised with those who had doubts concerning the phrase "reasonable time" but considered that the fixing of a time-limit would also involve difficulties. He suggested that the matter should be left open for the time being and that the Commission should study each article in part II of the draft Convention, bearing in mind the points to which allusion had been made. The Commission could then return to part I and might well find that its consideration of part II had made it easier to agree upon a suitable text.

12.	Mr. CHANG (China) supported the widely held view that article 1 should be deleted and that any valuable idea it might contain should, after further consideration, be placed in the preamble.

13.	He felt that the draft covenant - like the Declaration - should contain no specific mention of the origin of human rights, in view of the controversial nature of the subject.

51.	Mr. CHANG (China), reserving the right to enter into a fuller discussion of the many important and suggestive contributions made in the discussion so far, stated that he was prepared to accept the Australian suggestion that the word "recognized" should be substituted for the word "defined". He could also accept the addition of the words "respect and", as suggested by France.

52.	The United Kingdom amendment to article 2, paragraph 1, raised a most important problem. Although the document under consideration was called a covenant, it was in effect a treaty or convention, differing from all other previous instruments of that kind in that it would cover a great variety of subjects. A convention normally covered one subject only. The fact that the present draft Convention was intended to cover more subjects than any other should be borne in mind, if only to avoid future disappointments and disillusions.

53.	The problem of how such a complex draft convention was to be ratified by the various national legislatures was admittedly most difficult but by no means hopeless.

图片 1.5.6:张彭春在联合国人权委员会第六届第 138 次会议发言纪要(1)

54.	The United Kingdom amendment was practical in that it introduced the possibility of specific reservations on particular provisions. He wondered, however, what nation would be frank enough to admit that its own legislation might not be up to the standards specified in the draft Covenant. He saw in that question a very real difficulty and suggested that serious study should be made of that point. He favoured some sort of provision for specific reservations on particular points, as a matter of principle, but would not at the moment commit himself concerning the methods to be used in the implementation of that principle.

55.	Another fact to be borne in mind was that States differed in their legislative and constitutional practices. The second sentence of the first paragraph of article 2 might be acceptable. He sympathised with those who had doubts concerning the phrase "reasonable time" but considered that the fixing of a time-limit would also involve difficulties. He suggested that the matter should be left open for the time being and that the Commission should study each article in part II of the draft Convention, bearing in mind the points to which allusion had been made. The Commission could then return to part I and might well find that its consideration of part II had made it easier to agree upon a suitable text.

图片 1.5.7:张彭春在联合国人权委员会第六届第 138 次会议发言纪要(2)

【纪要译文】

12. 张先生(中国)支持广泛持有的观点,即应删除第 1 条,并在进一步审议后将其可能包含的任何有价值的想法列入序言。

13. 他认为,鉴于人权问题的争议性,《公约》草案和《宣言》一样,不应具体提到人权的起源。

51. 张先生(中国)保留对迄今为止在讨论中所作的许多重要和具有启发性的贡献进行更充分讨论的权利。他说,他准备接受澳大利亚的建议,即"已确认"一词应取代"已定义"一词。他还可以接受法国建议添加"尊重和"等字。

52. 英国对第2条第1款的修正提出了一个最重要的问题。虽然审议中的文件被称为公约,但实际上它是一项条约《公约》,不同于以往所有其他此类文书,因为它将涵盖各种各样的主题。公约通常只涉及一个主题。应当铭记,本公约草案的目的是涵盖比任何其他公约都多的主题,即使只是为了避免未来的失望和幻灭。

53. 各国立法机构如何批准如此复杂的公约草案,这是公认的最困难的问题,但绝不是没有希望的。

54. 英国的修正案是切实可行的,因为它提出了对某些条款作出具体保留的可能性。然而,他想知道,哪个国家会坦率地承认自己的立法可能达不到公约草案规定的标准。他认为这个问题非常困难,并建议对这一点进行认真研究。作为一个原则问题,他赞成在某些特定问题上作出具体保留的某种规定,但目前不会就执行该原则所使用的方法作出承诺。

55. 另一个需要铭记的事实是,各国在立法和宪法实践方面存在差异。第2条第1款第二句或许可以接受。他同情那些对"合理时间"一词有疑问的人,但认为确定时限也会有困难。他建议暂时搁置这一问题,委员会应研究公约草案第二部分的每一条,同时铭记提及的要点。然后,委员会可以回到第一部分,很可能会发现,对第二部分的审议使商定适当案文变得更容易。

4. 张彭春在人权委员会
第六届第 139 次会议发言纪要

　　1950 年 3 月 30 日上午 11 时至下午 1 时,联合国人权委员会第六届第 139 次会议,在纽约成功湖召开,本次会议的主要议题是继续讨论国际人权公约草案(第 3-4 条)。张彭春先生参加了本次会议,并在会议上发言,其具体发言内容①会议纪要、纪要影像和纪要译文如下:

【会议纪要】

　　43. Mr. CHANG (China) thought that there was no conflict between national interests in the Commission, but rather an opposition between two or three legal systems. As the Commission was working on behalf of the United Nations, in which all the legal systems and philosophical ideas of the world were represented, it must try to reconcile those different systems. The best solution would therefore be to combine the various proposals relating to article 5 in such a way as to achieve as large a measure of agreement as possible and to reconcile the different viewpoints on the subject.

　　44. He therefore proposed that the first paragraph of the original draft article 5 should be retained in its absolute form, omitting any idea of intention or arbitrariness, which would considerably diminish its significance. In order, however, to satisfy States whose legislation provided for the death penalty, the text might be followed by a second paragraph drafted as follows:

　　"In countries where capital punishment exists, a sentence of death may be imposed only as a penalty for the most serious crimes pursuant to sentence by a

---

　　① UN Document: E/CN. 4/SR. 139, pp. 12-13.

competent court and in accordance with the law. Anyone sentenced to death may be granted amnesty or pardon or commutation of the sentence. "

45. Mr. Chang thought that only an article so drafted could obtain general support at the present stage in the evolution of international law. It would not be advisable at that time to include in article 5 too many detailed provisions, such as those which appeared in the third paragraph of the United Kingdom proposal, however important they might be. Any provisions of that sort would certainly create confusion and the Commission must at all costs avoid doing that when it was drafting the first covenant on human rights. In time a sort of jurisprudence on the subject would certainly be established, based on the comments of governments, and it would subsequently be possible to supplement the covenant in the light of that jurisprudence. So far as article 5 was concerned, the United Kingdom contribution, to which he paid tribute, was extremely important and would form one of the basic elements in any jurisprudence of that sort.

【纪要影像】

43.　　　Mr. CHANG (China) thought that there was no conflict between national interests in the Commission, but rather an opposition between two or three legal systems. As the Commission was working on behalf of the United Nations, in which all the legal systems and philosophical ideas of the world were represented, it must try to reconcile those different systems. The best solution would therefore be to combine the various proposals relating to article 5 in such a way as to achieve as large a measure of agreement as possible and to reconcile the different viewpoints on the subject.

44.　　　He therefore proposed that the first paragraph of the original draft article 5 should be retained in its absolute form, omitting any idea of intention or arbitrariness, which would considerably diminish its significance. In order, however, to satisfy States whose legislation provided for the death penalty, the text might be followed by a second paragraph drafted as follows:

"In countries where capital punishment exists, a sentence of death may be imposed only as a penalty for the most serious crimes pursuant to sentence by a competent court and in accordance with the law. Anyone sentenced to death may be granted amnesty or pardon or commutation of the sentence."

图片 1.5.8:张彭春在联合国人权委员会第六届第 139 次会议发言纪要(1)

图片1.5.9：张彭春在联合国人权委员会第六届第139次会议发言纪要(2)

【纪要译文】

43. 张先生(中国)认为,委员会中的国家之间没有利益冲突,而是两三个法律制度之间的对立。委员会代表联合国工作,代表了世界上所有的法律制度和哲学思想,因此它必须努力协调这些不同的制度。因此,最好的解决办法是将与第5条有关的各种提案结合起来,以便尽可能达成很大程度的一致,并调和关于这个问题的不同观点。

44. 因此,他提议,原第5条草案的第一款应以绝对形式保留,省略任何意图或任意性的概念,这将大大削弱其重要性。然而,为了满足其立法规定死刑的国家的要求,案文后面可能会有第二段,起草如下：

"在存在死刑的国家,死刑只能作为对最严重罪行的刑罚,由主管法院根据法律判处。任何被判处死刑的人都可以大赦、赦免或减刑。"

45. 张先生认为,在国际法发展的现阶段,只有这样起草的条款才能获得普遍支持。当时,在第5条中列入太多的详细规定,例如英国提案第三款中出现的规定,无论这些规定多么重要,都是不可取的。任何这类规定肯定会造成混乱,委员会在起草第一项人权公约时必须不惜一切代价避免这样做。随着时间的推移,根据各国政府的评论,肯定会建立一种关于这一主题的判例,随后将有可能根据这种判例补充《公约》。就第 5 条而言,他赞扬的英国的贡献极为重要,将构成任何此类判例的基本要素之一。

5. 张彭春在人权委员会
第六届第 140 次会议发言纪要

1950 年 3 月 30 日下午 2 时 30 分至 5 时 25 分,联合国人权委员会第六届第 140 次会议,在纽约成功湖召开,本次会议的主要议题是继续讨论国际人权公约草案(第 5 条)。张彭春先生参加了本次会议,并在会议上发言,其具体发言内容①会议纪要、纪要影像和纪要译文如下:

【会议纪要】

59. Mr. CHANG (China) observed that in the case of the draft covenant text and substance were so closely related that it was next to impossible to distinguish between them and to vote on them separately. At the same time, the covenant was a most important document, which required careful consideration and reflection. He therefore proposed that the Commission should agree to have two readings; votes would be taken at the first reading in the knowledge that any serious errors could still be corrected at the second and more rapid reading.

60. With respect to article 5, it would be unfortunate to omit paragraph 1 altogether, as the part of the covenant containing provisions on human rights would then begin by stating not a right but an exception to it. The Commission would find it much easier to reach a decision on that article if the Secretariat

---

① UN Document: E/CN. 4/SR. 140, p. 5.

were to prepare a paper listing all the amendments and proposing in what order they should be put to the vote.

【纪要影像】

59.　　Mr. CHANG (China) observed that in the case of the draft covenant text and substance were so closely related that it was next to impossible to distinguish between them and to vote on them separately.　At the same time, the covenant was a most important document, which required careful consideration and reflection.　He therefore proposed that the Commission should agree to have two readings; votes would be taken at the first reading in the knowledge that any serious errors could still be corrected at the second and more rapid reading.

60.　　With respect to article 5, it would be unfortunate to omit paragraph 1 altogether, as the part of the covenant containing provisions on human rights would then begin by stating not a right but an exception to it.　The Commission would find it much easier to reach a decision on that article if the Secretariat were to prepare a paper listing all the amendments and proposing in what order they should be put to the vote.

图片 1.5.10:张彭春在联合国人权委员会第六届第 140 次会议发言纪要

【纪要译文】

59. 张先生(中国)说,就公约草案而言,案文和实质内容是如此密切相关,几乎不可能区分它们,也不可能对它们分别进行表决。同时,《公约》是一份非常重要的文件,需要认真考虑和反思。因此,他提议委员会应同意进行二读;在获知任何严重错误仍可以在第二次以更快速度阅读中纠正的情况下,将在第一次阅读时进行投票。

60. 关于第 5 条,不幸的是第一段被完全省略,因为《公约》中载有人权条款的那一部分,一开始就不是一项权利,而是一项例外。如果秘书处编写一份文件,列出所有修正案,并提出将其付诸表决的顺序,委员会将发现就该条作出决定要容易得多。

联合国人权委员会和起草委员会

6. 张彭春在人权委员会
第六届第 142 次会议发言纪要

　　1950 年 3 月 31 日下午 2 时 30 分至 5 时 45 分,联合国人权委员会第六届第 142 次会议,在纽约成功湖召开,本次会议的主要议题是继续讨论国际人权公约草案(第 7 条)。张彭春先生参加了本次会议,并在会议上发言,其具体发言内容①会议纪要、纪要影像和纪要译文如下:

【会议纪要】

　　73. Mr. CHANG (China) supported the remarks of the Lebanese representative concerning paragraphs 2 and 3. He referred to article 4 of the Universal Declaration of Human Rights in connexion with the use of the word "servitude" and concluded that there was no need to qualify the word "servitude" at the present late stage.

【纪要影像】

　　73.　　Mr, CHANG (China) supported the remarks of the Lebanese representative concerning paragraphs 2 and 3.　He referred to article 4 of the Universal Declaration of Human Rights in connexion with the use of the word "servitude" and concluded that there was no need to qualify the word "servitude" at the present late stage.

图片 1.5.11:张彭春在联合国人权委员会第六届第 142 次会议发言纪要

【纪要译文】

　　73. 张先生(中国)支持黎巴嫩代表关于第 2 段和第 3 段的评论。他

---

① UN Document: E/CN. 4/SR. 142, p. 16.

提到《世界人权宣言》第 4 条与"劳役"一词的使用有关,并得出结论认为,在现阶段没有必要对"劳役"一词加以限定。

7. 张彭春在人权委员会
第六届第 143 次会议发言纪要

1950 年 4 月 3 日上午 11 时至下午 1 时,联合国人权委员会第六届第 143 次会议,在纽约成功湖召开,本次会议的主要议题是继续讨论国际人权公约草案(第 8 条)。张彭春先生参加了本次会议,并在会议上发言,其具体发言内容①会议纪要、纪要影像和纪要译文如下:

【会议纪要】

57. Mr. CHANG(China)felt that it was not so much a question of making regular provision for consultation among delegations as of ensuring that such consultations took place while the points at issue were clearly in members' minds. While it was open to the Commission to suspend discussion of paragraph 4 until the second reading, he felt that most members were in favour of reaching an immediate decision. He felt that a short period of consultation would be sufficient and he therefore suggested that the Commission should adjourn forthwith with a view to considering an agreed text at the following meeting.

58. The CHAIRMAN said that, while she agreed with Mr. Chang in principle on the usefulness of the procedure he suggested, she thought that, in the given instance, it would be difficult to reach an agreed solution in the limited time available before the following meeting.

72. Mr. CHANG(China)proposed that the Committee should suspend

---

① UN Document:E/CN. 4/SR. 143, p. 12, p. 14.

its discussion of article 8 until the drafting committee had completed its work. The drafting committee should work on the assumption that a second reading would take place.

【纪要影像】

57.　　Mr. CHANG (China) felt that it was not so much a question of making regular provision for consultation among delegations as of ensuring that such consultations took place while the points at issue were clearly in members' minds. While it was open to the Commission to suspend discussion of paragraph 4 until the second reading, he felt that most members were in favour of reaching an immediate decision. He felt that a short period of consultation would be sufficient and he therefore suggested that the Commission should adjourn forthwith with a view to considering an agreed text at the following meeting.

58.　　The CHAIRMAN said that, while she agreed with Mr. Chang in principle on the usefulness of the procedure he suggested, she thought that, in the given instance, it would be difficult to reach an agreed solution in the limited time available before the following meeting.

72.　　Mr. CHANG (China) proposed that the Committee should suspend its discussion of article 8 until the drafting committee had completed its work. The drafting committee should work on the assumption that a second reading would take place.

图片1.5.12:张彭春在联合国人权委员会第六届第143次会议发言纪要

【纪要译文】

57. 张先生(中国)认为,与其说是为各代表团之间的协商作出正常的规定,不如说是确保在成员们清楚地想到有关问题时进行这种协商。虽然委员会可以暂停对第4款的讨论,直到第二次阅读,但他认为大多数委员赞成立即作出决定。他认为,短时间的协商就足够了,因此他建议委员会立即休会,以便在下次会议上审议商定的案文。

58. 主席说,虽然她原则上同意张先生所建议的程序的有用性,但她认为,在具体情况下,很难在下次会议之前有限的时间内达成一致的解决办法。

72. 张先生(中国)提议委员会暂停对第8条的讨论,直到起草委员会完成其工作为止。起草委员会的工作应假定将进行二读。

8. 张彭春在人权委员会
第六届第 145 次会议发言纪要

1950 年 4 月 4 日下午 3 时至 5 时 30 分,联合国人权委员会第六届第 145 次会议,在纽约成功湖召开,本次会议的主要议题是继续讨论国际人权公约草案(第 8 条和第 9 条)。张彭春先生参加了本次会议,并在会议上发言,其具体发言内容①会议纪要、纪要影像和纪要译文如下:

【会议纪要】

47. Mr. CHANG (China) observed that the Commission had already discussed article 9 at length. The article had been submitted to Governments and those which had thought fit to do so had sent their comments and suggestions. It did not seem advisable at that stage to modify a text which had been so closely studied. It must not be forgotten that the Commission had reached the stage of giving final form to the draft covenant, It should devote its entire attention to and should only attempt to modify those articles which had been the subject of serious criticism—and article 9 was not among them. Otherwise it would not complete the work before it during the current session.

50. Mr. CHANG (China) thought that it was very difficult to make such subtle time distinctions in a single sentence. He preferred the original text.

---

① UN Document:E/CN. 4/SR. 145, p. 11, p. 12.

【纪要影像】

47.	Mr. CHANG (China) observed that the Commission had already discussed article 9 at length. The article had been submitted to Governments and those which had thought fit to do so had sent their comments and suggestions. It did not seem advisable at that stage to modify a text which had been so closely studied. It must not be forgotten that the Commission had reached the stage of giving final form to the draft covenant. It should devote its entire attention to and should only attempt to modify those articles which had been the subject of serious criticism -- and article 9 was not among them. Otherwise it would not complete the work before it during the current session.

50.	Mr. CHANG (China) thought that it was very difficult to make such subtle time distinctions in a single sentence. He preferred the original text.

图片 1.5.13：张彭春在联合国人权委员会第六届第 145 次会议发言纪要

【纪要译文】

47. 张先生(中国)说,委员会已经详细讨论了第 9 条。这一条已经提交给各国政府,那些认为适合这样做的国家已经发送了它们的评论和建议。在那个阶段,修改一份经过如此仔细研究的文本似乎是不可取的。不应忘记,委员会已经到了使公约草案具有最终形式的阶段,它应全神贯注于并只应努力修改那些受到严重批评的条款,而第 9 条不在其中。否则它将无法在本届会议期间完成面前的工作。

50. 张先生(中国)认为很难在一句话中作出如此微妙的时间区分。他更喜欢原文。

9. 张彭春在人权委员会
第六届第 146 次会议发言纪要

1950 年 4 月 5 日上午 11 时至下午 1 时,联合国人权委员会第六届第 146 次会议,在纽约成功湖召开,本次会议的主要议题是继续讨论国际人权公约草案(第 9 条)。张彭春先生参加了本次会议,并在会议上发言,其具体发言内容①会议纪要、纪要影像和纪要译文如下:

【会议纪要】

40. Mr. CHANG (China) was in favour of paragraphs 1 and 2 as they stood.

41. The corresponding paragraphs of the Lebanese amendment invoked law and legal procedure; but, when discussing the article at previous sessions, the Commission had been aware that laws alone were not sufficient to ensure justice and freedom. Dictators might well be able to accept the Lebanese text and twist it to suit their purposes; their will was law and could easily be made the law of the land. By excluding the concept or arbitrariness, contained in the original text, the Lebanese representative would open the door to abuses of human freedom carried out according to perfectly legal procedure. Sub-paragraph 2 (c) alone of the Lebanese amendment could be held to justify the most arbitrary methods. Freedom could be guaranteed only by a combination of proper laws and good faith on the part of every one concerned.

42. The word "arbitrary" as used in paragraph 1 of article 9 meant unjust, unfair, inconsiderate of others. It was quite right that that paragraph

---

① UN Document: E/CN. 4/SR. 146, pp. 11-12.

should contain a general exhortation of a moral character and should set a goal of justice and respect for the rights of others which the peoples of the world must strive to attain, and that the following paragraphs should deal with the more immediate and practical aspects of the matter.

43. He urged the Commission to have faith in the innate goodness of man, which would in the long run overcome all obstacles to liberty and justice.

【纪要影像】

40.　　Mr. CHANG (China) was in favour of paragraphs 1 and 2 as they stood.

41.　　The corresponding paragraphs of the Lebanese amendment invoked law and legal procedure; but, when discussing the article at previous sessions, the Commission had been aware that laws alone were not sufficient to ensure justice and freedom. Dictators might well be able to accept the Lebanese text and twist it to suit their purposes; their will was law and could easily be made the law of the land. By excluding the concept of arbitrariness, contained in the original text, the Lebanese representative would open the door to abuses of human freedom carried out according to perfectly legal procedure. Sub-paragraph 2 (c) alone of the Lebanese amendment could be held to justify the most arbitrary methods. Freedom could be guaranteed only by a combination of proper laws and good faith on the part of every one concerned.

42.　　The word "arbitrary" as used in paragraph 1 of article 9 meant unjust, unfair, inconsiderate of others. It was quite right that that paragraph should contain a general exhortation of a moral character and should set a goal of justice and respect for the rights of others which the peoples of the world must strive to attain, and that the following paragraphs should deal with the more immediate and practical aspects of the matter.

43.　　He urged the Commission to have faith in the innate goodness of man, which would in the long run overcome all obstacles to liberty and justice.

图片 1.5.14:张彭春在联合国人权委员会第六届第 146 次会议发言纪要

【纪要译文】

40. 张先生(中国)赞成目前的第 1 段和第 2 段。

41. 黎巴嫩修正案的相应段落援引了法律和法律程序;但是,在前几届会议上讨论该条款时,委员会意识到,仅靠法律不足以确保正义和自由。独裁者很可能会接受黎巴嫩文本,并根据自己的目的对其进行扭曲;他们的意志是法律,很容易成为国家的法律。通过排除原文中所载的概念或任意性,黎巴嫩代表将为根据完全合法的程序侵犯人的自由打开大门。仅黎巴嫩修正案第 2(c)分段就可以用来证明最武断的方法是正当的。自由只有通过适当的法律和有关各方的诚意才能得到保障。

42. 第 9 条第 1 段中使用的"任意"一词是指不公正、不公平、不顾他人的行为。这一段应该包含对道德品质的一般性劝诫,应该设定一个公正和尊重他人权利的目标,这是世界各国人民必须努力实现的目标,下面几段应该处理这个问题更直接和实际的方面,这是非常正确的。

43. 他敦促委员会相信人与生俱来的善良,从长远来看,这将克服自由和正义的一切障碍。

10. 张彭春在人权委员会
第六届第 147 次会议发言纪要

1950 年 4 月 5 日下午 2 时 45 分至 5 时 40 分,联合国人权委员会第六届第 147 次会议,在纽约成功湖召开,本次会议的主要议题是继续讨论国际人权公约草案(第 9 条)。张彭春先生参加了本次会议,并在会议上发言,其具体发言内容①会议纪要、纪要影像和纪要译文如下:

【会议纪要】

26. Mr. CHANG (China) said that there were two very interesting points in Mr. Malik's statement.

27. He was happy to note that Mr. Malik had acknowledged that the actions of the modern State were monstrous and was trying to protect individuals against State abuse of power. It would therefore seem logical for Mr. Malik to vote against his own amendment, in which the word "law" was mentioned in each sentence. Law emanated directly from the State and to vote for the Lebanese amendment would be to strengthen the already excessive power of the State, which itself enacted the laws which suited it. Mr. Malik had declared,

---

① UN Document: E/CN. 4/SR. 147, pp. 7-8, p. 11, p. 12.

moreover, that the covenant would not be immutable and might be revised. If that was so, all the exceptions that had been mentioned could be incorporated in the legislation which would develop as the provisions of the covenant were applied. He hoped that the Commission would have before it each year a report by the Secretariat on the progress of legislation in that field. Meanwhile, he considered that the members of the Commission should not lose sight of the fact that laws were essentially arbitrary and hung like a threat over human rights. For that reason he thought that the text adopted by the Commission at its fifth session was not as imperfect as some made out, and he would vote for it.

46. Mr. CHANG (China) thought that was not the proper time to try to give a final interpretation of the word "arbitrary". Delegations which wished to define the word clearly should present concrete proposals to that effect so that the Commission could examine them during the second reading of the draft.

53. Mr. CHANG (Chine) assured the Lebanese representative that his suggestion that the word "arbitrary" should not be defined until a study had been made of whether it was possible or desirable to define it had not been inspired by that representative's interpretation.

```
26.        Mr. CHANG (China) said that there were two very interesting points
in Mr. Malik's statement.
27.        He was happy to note that Mr. Malik had acknowledged that the actions
of the modern State were monstrous and was trying to protect individuals against
State abuse of power.  It would therefore seem logical for Mr. Malik to vote
against his own amendment, in which the word "law" was mentioned in each
sentence.  Law emanated directly from the State and to vote for the Lebanese
amendment would be to strengthen the already excessive power of the State, which
itself enacted the laws which suited it.  Mr. Malik had declared, moreover, that
the covenant would not be immutable and might be revised.  If that was so, all

the exceptions that had been mentioned could be incorporated in the legislation
which would develop as the provisions of the covenant were applied.  He hoped
that the Commission would have before it each year a report by the Secretariat
on the progress of legislation in that field.  Meanwhile, he considered that the
members of the Commission should not lose sight of the fact that laws were
essentially arbitrary and hung like a threat over human rights.  For that
reason he thought that the text adopted by the Commission at its fifth session
was not as imperfect as some made out, and he would vote for it.

46.        Mr. CHANG (China) thought that was not the proper time to try to give
a final interpretation of the word "arbitrary".  Delegations which wished to
define the word clearly should present concrete proposals to that effect so that
the Commission could examine them during the second reading of the draft.

53.        Mr. CHANG (China) assured the Lebanese representative that his
suggestion that the word "arbitrary" should not be defined until a study had been
made of whether it was possible or desirable to define it had not been inspired
by that representative's interpretation.
```

图片 1.5.15:张彭春在联合国人权委员会第六届第 147 次会议发言纪要

【纪要译文】

26. 张先生(中国)说,马利克先生的发言中有两点非常有趣。

27. 他高兴地注意到,马利克先生承认现代国家的行动是可怕的,并试图保护个人不受国家滥用权力之害。因此,马利克先生投票反对他自己的修正案似乎是合乎逻辑的,修正案中每句话都提到"法律"一词。法律直接来自国家,投票支持黎巴嫩修正案将加强国家已经过度的权力,国家本身制定了适合自己的法律。此外,马利克先生还宣布,《公约》不会一成不变,可能会被修订。如果是这样,所提到的所有例外都可以纳入随着《公约》条款的适用而发展的立法中。他希望委员会每年收到秘书处关于该领域立法进展情况的报告。同时,他认为,委员会成员不应忽视这样一个事实,即法律本质上是任意的,就像对人权的威胁一样悬而未决。因此,他认为委员会第五届会议通过的案文并不像一些人所说的那样不完善,他将投赞成票。

46. 张先生(中国)认为,现在不是对"任意的"一词作出最后解释的适当时机。希望明确定义该词的代表团应提出这方面的具体建议,以便委员会在草案二读期间加以审查。

53. 张先生(中国)向黎巴嫩代表保证,如果没有受到该代表解释的启发,在研究是否有可能或适宜对其进行定义之前,他建议不应给"任意的"一词下定义。

11. 张彭春在人权委员会
第六届第 148 次会议发言纪要

1950 年 4 月 6 日上午 11 时至下午 1 时,联合国人权委员会第六届第 148 次会议,在纽约成功湖召开,本次会议的主要议题是继续讨论国际人权公约草案(第 9 条和第 8 条)。张彭春先生参加了本次会议,并在会议上发言,其具体发言内容①会议纪要、纪要影像和纪要译文如下:

【会议纪要】

25. Mr. CHANG (China) suggested that the United States amendment (E/CN. 4/394) should be voted on in two parts, a first vote to be taken up to and including the word "compensation", and a second vote on the remainder. He was making that suggestion because he felt that the first part of the United States amendment was really all that was necessary, and that the second half dealt with matters that need not enter into the picture at all. He concluded from a comparison of the first part of the United States amendment with the text of paragraph 6, as worded in the draft covenant, that both versions were almost i-dentical, but that the United States draft had the merit of greater clarity.

26. He agreed with those who had held that the question was not one

---

① UN Document: E/CN. 4/SR. 148, pp. 6-7, p. 12, p. 14.

which could be resolved in a drafting committee.

60. Mr. CHANG (China) felt some misgivings about the wisdom of drafting the article in too great detail, because that method might logically have to be extended to other articles. The Drafting Group had successfully solved the problems which had arisen as a result of the original separation of paragraphs 3 and 4, but he was not convinced that stipulation in detail was a wholly desirable method.

69. Mr. CHANG (China) explained that he had abstained from voting because he doubted the wisdom of making the article so detailed. He hoped that a precedent would not be set for the inclusion of excessive detail in other articles.

【纪要影像】

25. Mr. CHANG (China) suggested that the United States amendment (E/CN.4/394) should be voted on in two parts, a first vote to be taken up to and including the word "compensation", and a second vote on the remainder. He was making that suggestion because he felt that the first part of the United States amendment was really all that was necessary, and that the second half dealt with matters that need not enter into the picture at all. He concluded from a comparison of the first part of the United States amendment with the text of paragraph 6, as worded in the draft covenant, that both versions were almost identical, but that the United States draft had the merit of greater clarity.

26. He agreed with those who had held that the question was not one which could be resolved in a drafting committee.

60. Mr. CHANG (China) felt some misgivings about the wisdom of drafting the article in too great detail, because that method might logically have to be extended to other articles. The Drafting Group had successfully solved the problems which had arisen as a result of the original separation of paragraphs 3 and 4, but he was not convinced that stipulation in detail was a wholly desirable method.

69. Mr. CHANG (China) explained that he had abstained from voting because he doubted the wisdom of making the article so detailed. He hoped that a precedent would not be set for the inclusion of excessive detail in other articles.

图片1.5.16:张彭春在联合国人权委员会第六届第148次会议发言纪要

【纪要译文】

25. 张先生(中国)建议,美国的修正案(E/CN. 4/394)应分两部分进行表决,第一部分是关于并包括"赔偿"一词的表决,第二部分是关于其余部分的表决。他之所以提出这一建议,是因为他觉得美国修正案的第一部分确实都是必要的,而第二部分涉及的是根本不需要出现。他通过比较美国修正案第一部分与公约草案第 6 款的案文得出结论,两个版本几乎相同,但美国草案的优点是更加明确。

26. 他同意那些认为这个问题不能在起草委员会中解决的人的意见。

60. 张先生(中国)对过于详细地起草该条是否明智感到有些疑虑,因为从逻辑上讲,这种方法可能必须推广到其他条款。起草小组成功地解决了由于最初将第 3 段和第 4 段分开而产生的问题,但他不相信详细规定是一种完全可取的方法。

69. 张先生(中国)解释说,他投了弃权票,因为他怀疑把这条写得如此详细是否明智。他希望不会为在其他条款中列入过多细节树立先例。

12. 张彭春在人权委员会 第六届第 149 次会议发言纪要

1950 年 4 月 6 日下午 2 时 30 分至 5 时 30 分,联合国人权委员会第六届第 148 次会议,在纽约成功湖召开,本次会议的主要议题是继续讨论国际人权公约草案(第 8 条和第 5 条)。张彭春先生参加了本次会议,并在会议上先后多次发言,其具体发言内容[①]会议纪要、纪要影像和纪要译文如下:

【会议纪要】

4. Mr. CHANG (China) observed that the Philippine proposal advocated the deletion of the original text of the first paragraph. There were, however, several other amendments affecting the text of that paragraph before the Com-

---

① UN Document:E/CN. 4/SR. 149, p. 3, p. 9, p. 10, p. 15.

mission, and it would hardly be possible to vote on its deletion before knowing just what was to be deleted.

44. Mr. CHANG (China) thought that the word "competent" would suffice for competent tribunal meant independent tribunal. Moreover, "intentional" was the key word of the paragraph. It was closely related to the interpretation of the exceptions listed in paragraph 4 of the Lebanese amendment. Therefore, Mr. Chang asked that a separate vote should be taken on that word.

48. Mr. CHANG (China) asked whether the United States amendment applied to paragraph 2 or paragraph 3 of article 5.

82. Mr. CHANG (China) reminded the Committee that it was working on a draft covenant capable of being accepted by all States and not on detailed conventions bearing on the various matters covered by each article.

83. He admitted that there was some foundation for the Egyptian representative's arguments and thought that he was quite right from the humane point of view. Nevertheless it would be somewhat inadvisable to overload the articles of the draft covenant with details which might make the document as a whole rather unbalanced.

84. The covenant should constitute a logical whole and only when it had been approved by Governments would the Commission be in a position to draw up a certain number of detailed conventions and to request the Secretariat to provide it with reports on the various legal systems.

85. Mr. Chang recalled that that was the reason why he had voted against the detailed provisions which it had been sought to introduce into article 8 and stated that he would do the same for article 5.

86. The CHAIRMAN agreed with the representative of China.

【纪要影像】

4.　　Mr. CHANG (China) observed that the Philippine proposal advocated the deletion of the original text of the first paragraph. There were, however, several other amendments affecting the text of that paragraph before the Commission, and it would hardly be possible to vote on its deletion before knowing just what was to be deleted.

44.　　Mr. CHANG (China) thought that the word "competent" would suffice for competent tribunal meant independent tribunal. Moreover, "intentional" was the key word of the paragraph. It was closely related to the interpretation of the exceptions listed in paragraph 4 of the Lebanese amendment. Therefore, Mr. Chang asked that a separate vote should be taken on that word.

48.　　Mr. CHANG (China) asked whether the United States amendment applied to paragraph 2 or paragraph 3 of article 5.

图片 1.5.17:张彭春在联合国人权委员会第六届第 149 次会议发言纪要(1)

82.　　Mr. CHANG (China) reminded the Committee that it was working on a draft covenant capable of being accepted by all States and not on detailed conventions bearing on the various matters covered by each article.

83.　　He admitted that there was some foundation for the Egyptian representative's arguments and thought that he was quite right from the humane point of view. Nevertheless it would be somewhat inadvisable to overload the articles of the draft covenant with details which might make the document as a whole rather unbalanced.

84.　　The covenant should constitute a logical whole and only when it had been approved by Governments would the Commission be in a position to draw up a certain number of detailed conventions and to request the Secretariat to provide it with reports on the various legal systems.

85.　　Mr. Chang recalled that that was the reason why he had voted against the detailed provisions which it had been sought to introduce into article 8 and stated that he would do the same for article 5.

86.　　The CHAIRMAN agreed with the representative of China.

图片 1.5.18:张彭春在联合国人权委员会第六届第 149 次会议发言纪要(2)

【纪要译文】

4. 张先生(中国)说,菲律宾的提案主张删除第一段的原文。然而,还有其他几项修正案影响到委员会面前该段的案文,在不知道要删除什么之前,很难就删除该段进行表决。

44. 张先生(中国)认为"合格"一词足以说明合格法庭是指独立法庭。此外,"故意"是该段的关键词。它与黎巴嫩修正案第 4 段所列例外情况的解释密切相关。因此,张先生要求对这个词进行单独表决。

48. 张先生(中国)问美国的修正案是否适用于第 5 条第 2 段或第 3 段。

82. 张先生(中国)提醒委员会,它正在拟订一项能够被所有国家接受的公约草案,而不是拟订涉及每一条所涉各种事项的详细公约。

83. 他承认埃及代表的论点有一定的根据,他认为从人道的观点来看,他是完全正确的。然而,在公约草案的条款中加入过多的细节可能会使整个文件相当不平衡,这在某种程度上是不可取的。

84.《公约》应构成一个合乎逻辑的整体,只有在得到各国政府批准后,委员会才能起草若干详细的公约,并请秘书处向其提供关于各种法律制度的报告。

85. 张先生回顾说,这就是他投票反对委员会试图将详细规定纳入第 8 条的原因,并表示他也将对第 5 条投反对票。

86. 主席同意中国代表的意见。

13. 张彭春在人权委员会 第六届第 150 次会议发言纪要

1950 年 4 月 6 日上午 11 时至下午 1 时,联合国人权委员会第六届第 150 次会议,在纽约成功湖召开,本次会议的主要议题是继续讨论国际人权公约草案(第 5 条)。张彭春先生参加了本次会议,并在会议上发言,其具体发言内容①会议纪要、纪要影像和纪要译文如下:

---

① UN Document:E/CN. 4/SR. 150, p. 3.

【会议纪要】

3. The CHAIRMAN thanked the Greek representative for his consideration and said that she would in fact have to be absent on Wednesday 12 April in order to attend the ceremonies to be held at Hyde Park. The Commission could, however, meet under the chairmanship of Mr. Chang.

4. Mr. CHANG (China), although quite prepared to act as chairman if the Commission so desired, was nevertheless in favour of holding no meeting on Wednesday 12 April, for the reasons given by the Greek representative.

【纪要影像】

3.　　The CHAIRMAN thanked the Greek representative for his consideration and said that she would in fact have to be absent on Wednesday 12 April in order to attend the ceremonies to be held at Hyde Park. The Commission could, however, meet under the chairmanship of Mr. Chang.

4.　　Mr. CHANG (China), although quite prepared to act as chairman if the Commission so desired, was nevertheless in favour of holding no meeting on Wednesday 12 April, for the reasons given by the Greek representative.

图片 1.5.19:张彭春在联合国人权委员会第六届第 150 次会议发言纪要

【纪要译文】

3. 主席感谢希腊代表的考虑,并说她实际上必须在 4 月 12 日星期三缺席,才能参加在海德公园举行的仪式。然而,该委员会可以在张先生的主持下举行会议。

4. 张先生(中国)虽然已准备好在委员会希望他担任主席时担任主席,但基于希腊代表所提出的理由,他还是赞成 4 月 12 日星期三不举行会议。

14. 张彭春在人权委员会
第六届第 151 次会议发言纪要

1950 年 4 月 10 日下午 2 时 30 分至 5 时 25 分,联合国人权委员会第六届第 151 次会议,在纽约成功湖召开,本次会议的主要议题是继续讨论国际人权公约草案(第 11 条)。张彭春先生参加了本次会议,并在会议上发言,其具体发言内容①会议纪要、纪要影像和纪要译文如下:

【会议纪要】

14. Mr. CHANG (China) thought that the substance of the article 11 ought to be embodied in the covenant and discussion, despite the difficulty of drafting it satisfactorily. The principle could be adopted at that stage, but it might be necessary to postpone the decision on the wording until the second reading. The right of liberty of movement was a very important one, particularly for peoples who had not previously enjoyed it.

15. He agreed with the Lebanese representative that the form of the article required further consideration. He felt that the wording of the limitations should be similar in all articles requiring them and that the general principle should be stated before the limitations. That would, however, have to be decided finally in the light of the decisions taken upon subsequent articles.

16. He could not accept the words "free from governmental interference in" which were in the United States amendment (E/CN. 4/365, page 34). All laws were a form of government interference, even though they were enacted in the interests of the majority of the people. If the interference occurred in the

① UN Document: E/CN. 4/SR. 151, p. 6, p. 14.

circumstances not governed by a law, it must be assumed to be arbitrary, while if it was under the law, the commission would be seeming to challenge the law, and that would be undesirable.

51. Mr. CHANG (China) thought that the Australian and the United States amendments were not mutually exclusive, and could therefore be combined, possibly by adding the phrase "and to return to his own country" to the United States amendment.

【纪要影像】

14.　　Mr. CHANG (China) thought that the substance of article 11 ought to be embodied in the covenant under discussion, despite the difficulty of drafting it satisfactorily. The principle could be adopted at that stage, but it might be necessary to postpone the decision on the wording until the second reading. The right of liberty of movement was a very important one, particularly for peoples who had not previously enjoyed it.

15.　　He agreed with the Lebanese representative that the form of the article required further consideration. he felt that the wording of the limitations should be similar in all articles requiring them and that the general principle should be stated before the limitations. That would, however, have to be decided finally in the light of the decisions taken upon subsequent articles.

16.　　He could not accept the words "free from governmental interference in", which were in the United States amendment (E/CN.4/365, page 54). All laws were a form of governmental interference, even though they were enacted in the interests of the majority of the people. If the interference occurred in circumstances not governed by a law, it must be assumed to be arbitrary, while if it was under the law, the Commission would be seeming to challenge the law, and that would be undesirable.

51.　　Mr. CHANG (China) thought that the Australian and the United States amendments were not mutually exclusive, and could therefore be combined, possibly by adding the phrase "and to return to his own country" to the United States amendment.

图片1.5.20:张彭春在联合国人权委员会第六届第151次会议发言纪要

【纪要译文】

14. 张先生(中国)认为,第11条的实质内容应当纳入讨论的《公约》之中,尽管很难令人满意地起草它。该原则可在该阶段通过,但可能有必要将有关措辞的决定推迟到二读。迁徙自由权是一项非常重要的权利,特别是对以前没有享受过这项权利的人民而言。

15. 他同意黎巴嫩代表的意见,即该条的形式需要进一步审议。他认为,在所有要求限制的条款中,限制的措辞都应该相似,并且应该在限制之前说明一般原则。然而,这最终必须根据对随后条款所作的决定而定。

16. 他不能接受美国修正案(E/CN. 4/365,第 34 页)中的"不受政府干预"字样。所有法律都是政府干预的一种形式,尽管它们是为了大多数人的利益而制定的。如果干预发生在不受法律管辖的情况下,则必须假定干预是任意的,而如果干预发生在法律之下,委员会似乎会对法律提出质疑,这是不可取的。

51. 张先生(中国)认为,澳大利亚和美国的修正案并不是相互排斥的,因此可以通过在美国的修正案中加上"并返回他自己的国家"一语来合并。

15. 张彭春在人权委员会
第六届第 152 次会议发言纪要

1950 年 4 月 11 日上午 11 时至下午 1 时 10 分,联合国人权委员会第六届第 152 次会议,在纽约成功湖召开,本次会议的主要议题是审议人权委员会第五届会议报告、继续讨论国际人权公约草案(第 5 条)。张彭春先生参加了本次会议,并在会议上发言,其具体发言内容①会议纪要、纪要影像和纪要译文如下:

【会议纪要】

42. Mr. CHANG (China) did not think it possible to combine the texts so rapidly without the danger of either repetition or unfortunate omissions.

43. He feared that some confusion might have arisen from the fact that in voting for the deletion of the world "international" from the revised Lebanese a-mendment to paragraph 2 (E/CN. 4/413), many representatives have consid-ered that that deletion also implied the deletion of paragraph 4 of the text pro-

---

① UN Document: E/CN. 4/SR. 152, p. 12, p. 13.

posed by Lebanon for article 5 (E/CN. 4/398).

44. The United Kingdom representative now expressed the opinion that there were ideas in paragraph 4 which should be kept. Mr. Chang agreed, but proposed that the vote on the question should be postponed until the Commission had a concrete proposal in writing before it.

50. Mr. CHANG (China) supported that point of view. There was nothing to prevent the Commission from voting first on the amendment proposed by the United States as a substitute for paragraphs 2 and 3 of the original text. If the amendments were rejected, the Commission could very well decide on those two paragraphs. The essential point was that no factor which might be of importance to the article as a whole should be omitted.

【纪要影像】

42.　　Mr. CHANG (China) did not think it possible to combine the texts so rapidly without the danger of either repetitions or unfortunate omissions.
43.　　He feared that some confusion might have arisen from the fact that in voting for the deletion of the word "intentional" from the revised Lebanese amendment to paragraph 2 (E/CN.4/413), many representatives had considered that that deletion also implied the deletion of paragraph 4 of the text proposed by Lebanon for article 5 (E/CN.4/398).
44.　　The United Kingdom representative now expressed the opinion that there were ideas in paragraph 4 which should be kept. Mr. Chang agreed, but proposed that the vote on the question should be postponed until the Commission had a concrete proposal in writing before it.
50.　　Mr. CHANG (China) supported that point of view. There was nothing to prevent the Commission from voting first on the amendment proposed by the United States as a substitute for paragraphs 2 and 3 of the original text. If the amendment was rejected, the Commission could very well decide on those two paragraphs. The essential point was that no factor which might be of importance to the article as a whole should be omitted.

图片 1.5.21：张彭春在联合国人权委员会第五届第 152 次会议发言纪要

【纪要译文】

42. 张先生(中国)认为,不可能如此迅速地合并案文而不出现重复或不幸遗漏的危险

43. 他担心,投票赞成从黎巴嫩对第 2 段的修订案(E/CN. 4/413)中

删除"国际的"一词可能会引起一些混乱,许多代表认为,删除也意味着删除黎巴嫩为第 5 条提议的案文(E/CN. 4/398)第 4 段。

44. 英国代表现在表示,第 4 段中有一些想法应予保留。张先生同意,但提议将对该问题的表决推迟到委员会收到一份具体的书面提案时进行。

50. 张先生(中国)支持这一观点。没有什么可以阻止委员会首先就美国提出的修正案进行表决,以取代原文第 2 段和第 3 段。如果修正案被否决,委员会完全可以就这两段作出决定。关键的一点是,不应忽略任何可能对整个条款具有重要意义的因素。

16. 张彭春在人权委员会 第六届第 153 次会议发言纪要

1950 年 4 月 11 日下午 2 时 45 分至 5 时 30 分,联合国人权委员会第六届第 153 次会议,在纽约成功湖召开,本次会议的主要议题是继续讨论国际人权公约草案。张彭春先生参加了本次会议,并在会议上发言,其具体发言内容①会议纪要、纪要影像和纪要译文如下:

【会议纪要】

12. At the request of Mr. CHANG (China), who wished to be able to vote separately on the words, "pursuant to the sentence of a competent court and", inasmuch as they were covered in the French text, the United States amendment to paragraphs 2 and 3 was put to the vote in four parts.

The words "In countries where capital punishment exists, sentence of death may be imposed only as a penalty for the most serious crimes" were adopted by 13

---

① UN Document: E/CN. 4/SR. 153, pp. 4-5.

votes to none, with one abstention.

The words "pursuant to the sentence of a competent court and" were adopted by 9 to none, with 5 abstentions.

The words "in accordance with law" were adopted by 12 votes to none, with 2 abstentions.

The words "not contrary to the Universal Declaration of Human Rights" were adopted by 9 votes to 2, with 3 abstentions.

The United States amendment as a whole was adopted by 12 votes to none, with 3 abstentions, becoming paragraph 3 of article 5.

【纪要影像】

12.　　At the request of Mr. CHANG (China), who wished to be able to vote separately on the words, "pursuant to the sentence of a competent court and", inasmuch as they were covered in the French text, the United States amendment to paragraphs 2 and 3 was put to the vote in four parts.

The words "In countries where capital punishment exists, sentence of death may be imposed only as a penalty for the most serious crimes" were adopted by 13 votes to none, with one abstention.

The words "pursuant to the sentence of a competent court and" were adopted by 9 votes to none, with 5 abstentions.

The words "in accordance with law" were adopted by 12 votes to none, with 2 abstentions.

The words "not contrary to the Universal Declaration of Human Rights" were adopted by 9 votes to 2, with 3 abstentions.

The United States amendment as a whole was adopted by 12 votes to none, with 3 abstentions, becoming paragraph 3 of article 5.

图片 1.5.22：张彭春在联合国人权委员会第六届第 153 次会议发言纪要

【纪要译文】

12. 应张先生（中国）的请求，他希望能够就"根据合格法院的判决和"等字分别进行表决，因为法文文本涵盖了这些内容，美国对第 2 段和第 3 段的修正案分四部分付诸表决。

"在存在死刑的国家，死刑只能作为对最严重罪行的惩罚"的措辞，以 13 票对 0 票、1 票弃权获得通过。

"根据合格法院的判决和"的措辞,以 9 票对 0 票、5 票弃权获得通过。

"根据法律"的措辞,以 12 票对 0 票、2 票弃权获得通过。

"不违反《世界人权宣言》"的措辞,以 9 票对 2 票、3 票弃权获得通过。

整个美国修正案,以 12 票对 0 票、3 票弃权获得通过,成为第 5 条第 3 段。

17. 张彭春在人权委员会第六届第 155 次会议发言纪要

1950 年 4 月 14 日下午 4 时至 5 时 25 分,联合国人权委员会第六届第 155 次会议,在纽约成功湖召开,本次会议的主要议题是继续讨论国际人权公约草案(第 12 条和第 13 条)。张彭春先生参加了本次会议,并在会议上发言,其具体发言内容①会议纪要、纪要影像和纪要译文如下:

【会议纪要】

51. Mr. Chang (China) explained that he had abstained from voting on the United States amendment because he thought that the word "entitled" could not be qualified by the words "shall be", since it referred to an inherent right, which could not be made mandatory. He did not object to the use of the words "shall be"——the orm usual in treaties——but hoped that a substitute for the word "entitled" would be found on second reading.

---

① UN Document:E/CN. 4/SR. 155, p. 11.

【纪要影像】

> 51.　Mr. CHANG (China) explained that he had abstained from voting on the
> United States amendment because he thought that the word "entitled" could not be
> qualified by the words "shall be", since it referred to an inherent right, which
> could not be made mandatory.　He did not object to the use of the words "shall
> be" -- the form usual in treaties -- but hoped that a substitute for the word
> "entitled" would be found on second reading.

图片 1.5.23：张彭春在联合国人权委员会第六届第 155 次会议发言纪要

【纪要译文】

51. 张先生(中国)解释说,他对美国的修正案投了弃权票,因为他认为"有权"一词不能用"应该"一词来限定,因为它指的是一种固有的权利,不能强制规定这种权利。他不反对使用"应为"一词,这是条约中常见的形式,但希望在二读时找到"有权"一词的替代词。

18. 张彭春在人权委员会
第六届第 156 次会议发言纪要

1950 年 4 月 17 日上午 11 时至下午 1 时 5 分,联合国人权委员会第六届第 156 次会议,在纽约成功湖召开,本次会议的主要议题是继续讨论国际人权公约草案(第 13 条)。张彭春先生参加了本次会议,并在会议上发言,其具体发言内容①会议纪要、纪要影像和纪要译文如下:

【会议纪要】

22. In order to eliminate redundancy in the use of the word "interest",

---

① 　UN Document：E/CN. 4/SR. 156, p. 6.

Mr. Chang (China) suggested that the phrase "for reasons of" should replace "in the interest of" before the word "morals".

It was so agreed.

【纪要影像】

22. ⋯⋯ In order to eliminate redundancy in the use of the word "interest" Mr. CHANG (China) suggested that the phrase "for reasons of" should replace "in the interest of" before the word "morals".
It was so agreed.

图片1.5.24:张彭春在联合国人权委员会第六届第156次会议发言纪要

【纪要译文】

22.为了消除"利益"一词的重复使用,张先生(中国)建议将"道德"一词前的"出于"一词改为"为了"。

就这样商定下来。

19.张彭春在人权委员会第六届第157次会议发言纪要

1950年4月17日下午3时至5时30分,联合国人权委员会第六届第157次会议,在纽约成功湖召开,本次会议的主要议题是继续讨论国际人权公约草案(第13条)。张彭春先生参加了本次会议,并在会议上发言,其具体发言内容①会议纪要、纪要影像和纪要译文如下:

【会议纪要】

41. Mr. CHANG (China) accepted the last text proposed by the United

---

① UN Document:E/CN.4/SR.157, p. 8.

Kingdom representative. He suggested the Commission should proceed to a vote and should request the Secretariat to give its opinion on the text before the second reading.

【纪要影像】

41. Mr. CHANG (China) accepted the last text proposed by the United Kingdom representative. He suggested the Commission should proceed to a vote and should request the Secretariat to give its opinion on the text before the second reading.

图片 1.5.25：张彭春在联合国人权委员会第六届第 157 次会议发言纪要

【纪要译文】

41. 张先生(中国)接受英国代表提出的最后案文。他建议委员会进行表决,并请秘书处在二读之前就案文发表意见。

20. 张彭春在人权委员会
第六届第 158 次会议发言纪要

1950 年 4 月 18 日上午 11 时至下午 1 时,联合国人权委员会第六届第 158 次会议,在纽约成功湖召开,本次会议的主要议题是继续讨论国际人权公约草案(第 13 条)。张彭春先生参加了本次会议,并在会议上发言,其具体发言内容①会议纪要、纪要影像和纪要译文如下:

【会议纪要】

30. Mr. CHANG (China) pointed out that the word "compensation" had

---

① UN Document：E/CN. 4/SR. 158, p. 8.

not been clearly defined. The article should provide for moral as well as material compensation in cases of erroneous conviction.

31. As to the text to be adopted, he preferred the French amendment to the original draft of paragraph 3.

32. He agreed with the representative of Lebanon with regard to the procedure to be followed. He would like to study a final text before deciding whether the paragraph should be deleted.

【纪要影像】

30. Mr. CHANG (China) pointed out that the word "compensation" had not been clearly defined. The article should provide for moral as well as material compensation in cases of erroneous convictions.
31. As to the text to be adopted, he preferred the French amendment to the original draft of paragraph 3.
32. He agreed with the representative of Lebanon with regard to the procedure to be followed. He would like to study a final text before deciding whether the paragraph should be deleted.

图片 1.5.26：张彭春在联合国人权委员会第六届第 158 次会议发言纪要

【纪要译文】

30. 张先生(中国)指出,"赔偿"一词没有明确的定义。该条应规定在错误定罪的情况下给予精神和物质赔偿。

31. 关于将要通过的案文,他倾向于法国的修正案,而不是第 3 段的原稿。

32. 他同意黎巴嫩代表关于应遵循的程序。在决定是否删除该段之前,他想研究一下最后文本。

21. 张彭春在人权委员会
第六届第 159 次会议发言纪要

1950 年 4 月 18 日下午 3 时至 5 时 20 分,联合国人权委员会第六届第 159 次会议,在纽约成功湖召开,本次会议的主要议题是继续讨论国际人权公约草案(第 13 条、第 14 条和第 15 条)。张彭春先生参加了本次会议,并在会议上发言,其具体发言内容①会议纪要、纪要影像和纪要译文如下:

【会议纪要】

51. Mr. CHANG (China) associated himself with the comments of the United States representative. He confirmed the fact that the Commission had decided against retaining the text proposed by the United Kingdom, not only because it thought that it was without value but also because it was afraid that it might lead to confusion and be exploited for purposes foreign to the intention of its authors. The Nurnberg trial was an exceptional case in international jurisprudence; it ought not therefore to be the subject of the special provision in a general convention on fundamental human rights and freedoms.

---

① UN Document: E/CN. 4/SR. 159, p. 11.

51.   Mr. CHANG (China) associated himself with the comments of the United
States representative. He confirmed the fact that the Commission had decided
against retaining the text proposed by the United Kingdom, not only because it
thought that it was without value but also because it was afraid that it might
lead to confusion and be exploited for purposes foreign to the intention of its
authors. The Nürnberg Trial was an exceptional case in international jurisprudence; it ought not therefore to be the subject of a special provision in a
general convention on fundamental human rights and freedoms.

图片 1.5.27:张彭春在联合国人权委员会第六届第 159 次会议发言纪要

【纪要译文】

51. 张先生(中国)赞同美国代表的意见。他证实,委员会决定不保留英国提出的案文,这不仅是因为它认为该案文没有价值,而且是因为它担心它可能导致混淆,并被用于与作者意图无关的目的。纽伦堡审判是国际法理学中的一个例外案例;因此,它不应成为关于基本人权和自由的一般性公约中特别条款的主题。

22. 张彭春在人权委员会 第六届第 161 次会议发言纪要

1950 年 4 月 19 日下午 3 时至 5 时 20 分,联合国人权委员会第六届第 161 次会议,在纽约成功湖召开,本次会议的主要议题是继续讨论国际人权公约草案(第 16 条和第 17 条)。张彭春先生参加了本次会议,并在会议上发言,其具体发言内容①会议纪要、纪要影像和纪要译文如下:

---

① UN Document:E/CN.4/SR.161, p. 9.

【会议纪要】

41. Mr. CHANG（China）pointed out that if a change of religion was made with fraudulent intent, it would obviously not be recognized by the civil authorities. In general, any act committed with fraudulous intent was not recognized; that was a general principle of civil codes. In any case fraud was covered by the paragraph which dealt with general limitations. The Egyptian amendment therefore seemed unnecessary.

【纪要影像】

41.　　Mr. CHANG (China) pointed out that if a change of religion was made with fraudulent intent, it would obviously not be recognized by the civil authorities.　In general, any act committed with fraudulent intent was not recognized; that was a general principle of civil codes.　In any case fraud was covered by the paragraph which dealt with general limitations.　The Egyptian amendment therefore seemed unnecessary.

图片1.5.28：张彭春在联合国人权委员会第六届第161次会议发言纪要

【纪要译文】

41. 张先生(中国)指出,如果宗教的改变是出于欺诈目的,民政当局显然不会承认。一般来说,任何带有欺诈意图的行为都不被承认;这是民法的一般原则。在任何情况下,欺诈都包含在涉及一般限制的段落中。因此,埃及的修正案似乎没有必要。

23. 张彭春在人权委员会
第六届第163次会议发言纪要

1950年4月20日下午3时至4时55分,联合国人权委员会第六届第163次会议,在纽约成功湖召开,本次会议的主要议题是继续讨论国际人

权公约草案(第13条)。张彭春先生参加了本次会议,并在会议上发言,其具体发言内容①会议纪要、纪要影像和纪要译文如下:

【会议纪要】

22. Mr. CHANG (China) suggested that, in view of the number of proposals and amendments before it, the Commission should adopt the procedure of making a separate study of a basic proposal, deciding whether it required amendments and then voting on the amendments.

23. Following his own suggestion, he would confine his comments to the text of the United States amendment (E/CN. 4/433/Rev. 1). The first paragraph of that text was satisfactory, but the words "of information and" should be inserted between the words "freedom" and "of expression" in the first line. Inasmuch as the Commission had been concerned for three years with the freedom of information, mention of it appeared indispensable. He also suggested that the words "without governmental interference" should be voted on separately, and that, for reasons of form, it would be better to replace the word "by" before "any other media" by the word "through".

24. He was opposed to the words "This right" at the beginning of paragraph 2. Reference to paragraph 1 showed that the right in question included "freedom to hold opinions, to seek, receive and impart information and ideas". The right to express opinions and the freedom to seek and receive information could not be subject to "such limitations as are provided by law", which could apply only to the right to impart information. He therefore suggested that the first line of paragraph 2 might be re-drafted to read:

"The right to impart information and ideas shall be subject only ...". He also suggested that the words "for the protection of" before "national security" should be replaced by "in the interest of", and that the words "for the protec-

---

① UN Document:E/CN. 4/SR. 163, p. 7, p. 13.

tion of" should be inserted before the phrase, "the rights, reputation or free-dom of other persons".

25. He explained that he had asked for a separate vote on the words "without governmental interference" because he considered them dangerous in that they might open the door to many abuses. There would, in any case, be governmental interference as only Governments could impose the limitations mentioned in paragraph 2. Arbitrary interference, however, should be prevented and if the Commission so decided, it could stipulate in paragraph 1 that the right to freedom of information and expression belonged to the individual and that there could be no arbitrary interference on the part of the Government.

26. The Commission was engaged in the study of an extremely broad subject; when future conventions and protocols were being drawn up it could return to the same questions and study them in a more detailed manner.

【纪要影像】

22.   Mr. CHANG (China) suggested that, in view of the number of proposals and amendments before it, the Commission should adopt the procedure of making a separate study of a basic proposal, deciding whether it required amendments and then voting on the amendments.

23.   Following his own suggestion, he would confine his comments to the text of the United States amendment (E/CN.4/433/Rev.1). The first paragraph of that text was satisfactory, but the words "of information and" should be inserted between the words "freedom" and "of expression" in the first line. Inasmuch as the Commission had been concerned for three years with the freedom of information, mention of it appeared indispensable. He also suggested that the words "without governmental interference" should be voted on separately, and that, for reasons of form, it would be better to replace the word "by" before "any other media" by the word "through".

24.   He was opposed to the words "This right" at the beginning of paragraph 2. Reference to paragraph 1 showed that the right in question included "freedom to hold opinions, to seek, receive and impart information and ideas". The right to express opinions and the freedom to seek and receive information could not be subject to "such limitations as are provided by law", which could apply only to the right to impart information. He therefore suggested that the first line of paragraph 2 might be re-drafted to read:

图片 1.5.29:张彭春在联合国人权委员会第六届第 163 次会议发言纪要(1)

```
"The right to impart information and ideas shall be subject only...".  He
also suggested that the words "for the protection of" before "national security"
should be replaced by "in the interest of", and that the words "for the
protection of" should be inserted before the phrase, "the rights, reputation
or freedom of other persons".
25.        He explained that he had asked for a separate vote on the words
"without governmental interference" because he considered them dangerous in
that they might open the door to many abuses.   There would, in any case, be
governmental interference as only Governments could impose the limitations
mentioned in paragraph 2.   Arbitrary interference, however, should be
prevented and if the Commission so decided, it could stipulate in paragraph 1
that the right to freedom of information and expression belonged to the
individual and that there could be no arbitrary interference on the part of
the Government.
26.        The Commission was engaged in the study of an extremely broad
subject;   when future conventions and protocols were being drawn up it could
return to the same questions and study them in a more detailed manner.
```

图片 1.5.30：张彭春在联合国人权委员会第六届第 163 次会议发言纪要(2)

【纪要译文】

22. 张先生(中国)建议,鉴于委员会收到的提案和修正案数目众多,委员会应采取对一项基本提案进行单独研究的程序,决定是否需要修正,然后就修正案进行表决。

23. 按照他自己的建议,他将把他的评论限于美国修正案(E/CN. 4/433/Rev. 1)的案文。该案文第一段令人满意,但应在第一行"表达自由"前增加"信息和"等字。鉴于委员会三年来一直关注新闻自由,提及它似乎是必不可少的。他还建议,应单独对"没有政府干预"一词进行表决,出于形式原因,最好将"任何其他媒介"之前的"借助"改为"通过"。

24. 他反对第 2 段开头的"这项权利"用词。提及第 1 段表明,所涉权利包括"持有意见、寻求、接受和传递信息和思想的自由"。表达意见的权利以及寻求和接受信息的自由不受"法律规定的限制",这种限制只能适用于传递信息的权利。因此,他建议将第 2 段第一行重新起草为:

"传播信息和思想的权利仅限于……"他还建议将"国家安全"之前的"为保护"改为"为了",并在"其他人的权利、名誉或自由"之前插入"为保护"。

25. 他解释说,他要求对"不受政府干预"一词进行单独表决,因为他认为这些词很危险,因为它们可能会为许多虐待行为敞开大门。无论如何,都会有政府干预,因为只有政府才能施加第 2 段所述的限制。但是,应当防止任意干涉,如果委员会作出决定,它可以在第 1 段中规定,信息和表达自由权属于个人,政府不得任意干涉。

26. 委员会正在研究一个非常广泛的问题;在起草未来的公约和议定书时,它可以回到同样的问题上来,并以更详细的方式研究它们。

24. 张彭春在人权委员会
第六届第 164 次会议发言纪要

1950 年 4 月 21 日上午 11 时至下午 1 时 5 分,联合国人权委员会第六届第 164 次会议,在纽约成功湖召开,本次会议的主要议题是继续讨论国际人权公约草案(第 17 条)。张彭春先生参加了本次会议,并在会议上先后多次发言,其具体发言内容①会议纪要、纪要影像和纪要译文如下:

【会议纪要】

4. Mr. CHANG (China) stressed the fact that the entire history of article 17 went to show that it had always been regarded as an article dealing with freedom of information rather than with freedom of expression. The repetition of the word "information" in the basic text was fully justified, because the general right was stated first and the specific definitions then followed.

8. Mr. CHANG (China) observed that article 19 of the Universal Declaration of Human Rights covered both the freedom of opinion and the freedom of information—the prerequisite for forming opinion and expressing it. The Indian delegation itself had originally wished to incorporate the text of that article in

---

① UN Document: E/CN. 4/SR. 164, p. 3, p. 4. p. 6, pp. 8–9, pp. 10–11, p. 11.

the draft covenant. The covenant should not be more restrictive than the Declaration. He would not object to a reproduction of the text of the Declaration, because he agreed with the representative of the United States that the paragraph would be inadequate if the concept of freedom of information was deleted from it.

12. Mr. CHANG (China) reserved the right to propose that the word "opinion" should be substituted for the word "information" in the third line, should the French amendment be adopted. The substance of article 19 of the Declaration could thus be incorporated in article 17 of the draft covenant, perhaps in a separate paragraph.

19. Mr. CHANG (China) urged the addition of the words "opinion and" to replace the words "information and" which the Commission had just voted to delete. He pointed out that article 19 of the Universal Declaration of Human Rights referred to "freedom of opinion and expression" and indicated that article 17 of the covenant was intended to supplement article 16 which did not fully cover freedom of opinion.

20. In reply to a question by Mr. WHITLAM (Australia) regarding the repetition which would occur in the rest of the text if the Chinese proposal were adopted, Mr. CHANG (China) noted that similar repetition occurred in article 19 of the Declaration and that therefore the Commission would merely be reinforcing the provisions of the Declaration. If the Commission saw fit, it could add the words "without interference" after the expression "to hold opinions" in lines 2 and 3 of paragraph 1.

37. Mr. CHANG (China) agreed with the views of the representatives of the United Kingdom, India and Lebanon and presented a proposal for article 17 which he hoped would also be acceptable to the French delegation. Instead of two separate articles, he suggested three paragraphs as follows: "1. Everyone has the right to freedom of opinion without interference." The second paragraph

would reproduce the text of E/CN. 4/433/Rev. 2 with the deletion which the Commission had agreed to as well as the deletion of the words "to hold opinions" in lines 2 and 3. Finally a third paragraph would state that the rights referred to in paragraph 2 would be subject to the limitations enumerated.

51. Mr. CHANG (China) feared that the Uruguayan amendment would only lead to renewed debate. He thought that both the representative of France, who wished to separate the concept of freedom of expression from that of freedom of opinion, and the representative of India, who did not think the two principles should be severed, would be satisfied if those ideas were presented in two separate paragraph within the same article.

52. He thought it could be left to the Style Committee to prepare a text which would meet the wishes of the Lebanese representative.

It was so decided.

57. Mr. CHANG (China) could accept the Australian text. He wondered, however, whether it would not be better to consider the matter more thoroughly before taking a decision.

【纪要影像】

4.   Mr. CHANG (China) stressed the fact that the entire history of article 17 went to show that it had always been regarded as an article dealing with freedom of information rather than with freedom of expression. The repetition of the word "information" in the basic text was fully justified, because the general right was stated first and the specific definitions then followed.

8.   Mr. CHANG (China) observed that article 19 of the Universal Declaration of Human Rights covered both the freedom of opinion and the freedom of information -- the prerequisite for forming opinion and expressing it. The Indian delegation itself had originally wished to incorporate the text of that article in the draft covenant. The covenant should not be more restrictive than the Declaration. He would not object to a reproduction of the text of the Declaration, because he agreed with the representative of the United States that the paragraph would be inadequate if the concept of freedom of information was deleted from it.

12.   Mr. CHANG (China) reserved the right to propose that the word "opinion" should be substituted for the word "information" in the third line, should the French amendment be adopted. The substance of article 19 of the Declaration could thus be incorporated in article 17 of the draft covenant, perhaps in a separate paragraph.

图片 1.5.31：张彭春在联合国人权委员会第六届第 164 次会议发言纪要(1)

19.   Mr. CHANG (China) urged the addition of the words "opinion and" to replace the words "information and" which the Commission had just voted to delete. He pointed out that article 19 of the Universal Declaration of Human Rights referred to "freedom of opinion and expression" and indicated that article 17 of the covenant was intended to supplement article 16 which did not fully cover freedom of opinion.

20.   In reply to a question by Mr. WHITLAM (Australia) regarding the repetition which would occur in the rest of the text if the Chinese proposal were adopted, Mr. CHANG (China) noted that similar repetition occurred in article 19 of the Declaration and that therefore the Commission would merely be reinforcing the provisions of the Declaration.   If the Commission saw fit, it could add the words "without interference" after the expression "to hold opinions" in lines 2 and 3 of paragraph 1.

37.   Mr. CHANG (China) agreed with the views of the representatives of the United Kingdom, India and Lebanon and presented a proposal for article 17 which he hoped would also be acceptable to the French delegation. Instead of

图片 1.5.32：张彭春在联合国人权委员会第六届第 164 次会议发言纪要(2)

two separate articles, he suggested three paragraphs as follows: "1. Everyone has the right to freedom of opinion without interference." The second paragraph would reproduce the text of E/CN.4/433/Rev.2 with the deletion which the Commission had agreed to as well as the deletion of the words "to hold opinions" in lines 2 and 3. Finally a third paragraph would state that the rights referred to in paragraph 2 would be subject to the limitations enumerated.

51.   Mr. CHANG (China) feared that the Uruguayan amendment would only lead to renewed debate. He thought that both the representative of France, who wished to separate the concept of freedom of expression from that of freedom of opinion, and

the representative of India, who did not think the two principles should be severed, would be satisfied if those ideas were presented in two separate paragraph within the same article.

52.   He thought it could be left to the Style Committee to prepare a text which would meet the wishes of the Lebanese representative.
    It was so decided.

57.   Mr. CHANG (China) could accept the Australian text. He wondered, however, whether it would not be better to consider the matter more thoroughly before taking a decision.

图片 1.5.33：张彭春在联合国人权委员会第六届第 164 次会议发言纪要(3)

【纪要译文】

4. 张先生(中国)强调,第 17 条的整个历史表明,该条一直被视为涉及信息自由而不是发表自由的条款。在基本案文中重复"信息"一词是完全合理的,因为首先陈述的是一般权利,然后才是具体定义。

8. 张先生(中国)注意到《世界人权宣言》第 19 条涵盖了主张自由和信息自由——这是形成主张和表达主张的先决条件。印度代表团本身原本希望将该条款的案文纳入公约草案。《公约》不应比《宣言》更具限制性。他不反对复制宣言的案文,因为他同意美国代表的意见,即如果从该段中删除信息自由的概念,该段将是不充分的。

12. 张先生(中国)保留提议将第三行中的"信息"一词改为"主张"的权利,如果法国的修正案获得通过的话。因此,《宣言》第 19 条的内容可以纳入《公约》草案第 17 条,或许放在一个单独的段落中。

19. 张先生(中国)敦促添加"主张和"一词,以取代委员会刚刚表决删除的"信息和"一词。他指出,《世界人权宣言》第 19 条提到"主张和发表意见的自由",并指出《公约》第 17 条旨在补充第 16 条,因为第 16 条没有充分涵盖主张自由。

20. 在回答惠特拉姆(Whitlam)先生(澳大利亚)提出的如果中国的提案获得通过,案文其余部分是否会出现重复的问题时,张先生(中国)指出,《宣言》第 19 条中也出现了类似的重复,因此委员会只是在加强《宣言》的规定。如果委员会认为合适,它可以在第 1 款第 2 行和第 3 行的"持有意见"一词之后加上"不受干涉"几个字。

37. 张先生(中国)同意英国、印度和黎巴嫩代表的意见,并提出了第 17 条的提案,他希望法国代表团也能接受该提案。他建议采用如下三段,而不是两条单独的条款:"1. 每个人都有不受干涉的主张自由的权利。"第 2 段将转载 E/CN.4/433/Rev.2 号文件的案文,删除委员会同意的内容,并删除第二行和第三行中的"持有主张"一词。最后,第 3 段将指出,第 2 段中提到的权利将受到所列举的限制。

51. 张先生(中国)担心乌拉圭的修正案只会导致新的辩论。他认为,希望将发表意见的自由的概念与主张自由的概念分开的法国代表和认为这两项原则不应分开的印度代表,如果在同一条内的两个单独段落中提出这些想法,都会感到满意。

52. 他认为可以让文体委员会编写一份符合黎巴嫩代表愿望的案文。

就这样决定下来。

57. 张先生(中国)可以接受澳大利亚的案文。然而,他想知道,在作出决定之前更彻底地考虑这个问题是否更好。

25. 张彭春在人权委员会
第六届第 165 次会议发言纪要

1950 年 4 月 21 日下午 3 时至 5 时 35 分,联合国人权委员会第六届第 165 次会议,在纽约成功湖召开,本次会议的主要议题是继续讨论国际人权公约草案(第 13 条)。张彭春先生参加了本次会议,并在会议上先后多次发言,其具体发言内容①会议纪要、纪要影像和纪要译文如下:

【会议纪要】

20. Mr. CHANG (China) said that the United States text should be more clearly defined. The text mentioned information and ideas, but those notions were not exclusive. He wished to know whether the French amendment, which made the text more specific, implied that critical comment should be deprecated. He thought it would be better to mention only facts and ideas.

31. Mr. CHANG (China) remarked that if the Commission embarked upon an etymological discussion, the debate might be prolonged unduly. He proposed that separate votes should be taken upon the several parts of the French amendment; first, upon the inclusion of the words "of all kinds" ("*de toute espèce*"); then, if the French representative insisted, upon the words "including facts ("*notamment des faits*"); and lastly, upon the words "critical comment" ("*des appréciations critiques*"). Further, if it was so desired, the Commission might vote upon the words "and ideas", appearing in the original text.

42. Mr. CHANG (China) wanted to know in what part of the sentence

---

① UN Document: E/CN. 4/SR. 165, p. 6, pp. 7-8, p. 9, p. 10, p. 13, p. 17, p. 18.

those words would be placed.

53. Mr. CHANG (China) thought that the wording of paragraph 1 as proposed by the United States was satisfactory and that it would be dangerous to adopt the restrictive formula suggested by the United Kingdom.

74. Mr. CHANG (China) considered that the United States text gave a narrower definition of the limitations provided by the law. The text of the French amendment was more concise but extended those limitations to freedom of information, which did not appear to be desirable.

103. Mr. CHANG (China) was gratified that the United Nations Conference on Freedom of Information had thought it wise to declare that the right in question carried with it duties and responsibilities. On the other hand, he did not think it necessary to remind the press of that fact once again in the draft international covenant on human rights. It would be well to retain the text of paragraph 2 submitted by the United States delegation.

104. The introduction of the word "special" would make the United Kingdom's amendment even less acceptable; it might well be wondered what were the special duties and responsibilities to which allusion was to be made.

110. Mr. CHANG (China) did not think the English word "protection" suitable. Abstractions such as national security, public order etc. could not be "protected".

20.　　Mr. CHANG (China) said that the United States text should be more clearly defined. The text mentioned information and ideas, but those notions were not exclusive. He wished to know whether the French amendment, which made the text more specific, implied that critical comment should be deprecated. He thought it would be better to mention only facts and ideas.

31.　　Mr. CHANG (China) remarked that if the Commission embarked upon an etymological discussion, the debate might be prolonged unduly. He proposed that separate votes should be taken upon the several parts of the French amendment; first, upon the inclusion of the words "of all kinds" ("de toute espèce"); then, if the French representative insisted, upon the words "including facts ("notamment des faits"); and lastly, upon the words "critical comment" ("des appréciations critiques"). Further, if it was so desired, the Commission might vote upon the words "and ideas", appearing in the original text.

42.　　Mr. CHANG (China) wanted to know in what part of the sentence those words would be placed.

图片 1.5.34：张彭春在联合国人权委员会第六届第 165 次会议发言纪要(1)

53.　　Mr. CHANG (China) thought that the wording of paragraph 1 as proposed by the United States was satisfactory and that it would be dangerous to adopt the restrictive formula suggested by the United Kingdom.

74.　　Mr. CHANG (China) considered that the United States text gave a narrower definition of the limitations provided by the law. The text of the French amendment was more concise but extended those limitations to freedom of information, which did not appear to be desirable.

103.　　Mr. CHANG (China) was gratified that the United Nations Conference on Freedom of Information had thought it wise to declare that the right in question carried with it duties and responsibilities. On the other hand, he did not think it necessary to remind the press of that fact once again in the draft international covenant on human rights. It would be well to retain the text of paragraph 2 submitted by the United States delegation.

104.　　The introduction of the word "special" would make the United Kingdom's amendment even less acceptable; it might well be wondered what were the special duties and responsibilities to which allusion was to be made.

110.　　Mr. CHANG (China) did not think the English word "protection" suitable. Abstractions such as national security, public order etc. could not be "protected".

图片 1.5.35：张彭春在联合国人权委员会第六届第 165 次会议发言纪要(2)

【纪要译文】

20. 张先生(中国)说,美国案文的定义应当更加明确。案文提到了信息和想法,但这些想法并不具有排他性。他想知道,使案文更加具体的法国修正案是否意味着批评意见应该被否决。他认为最好只提事实和想法。

31. 张先生(中国)说,如果委员会开始进行词源学讨论,辩论可能会拖得太久。他提议对法国修正案的几个部分进行单独表决:首先,列入了

"各种"("*de toute espèce*")一词;然后,如果法国代表坚持使用"包括事实"("*notamment des faits*")等词;最后,关于"批判性评论"("*des appréciations critiques*")这几个字。此外,如果愿意,委员会可以就原始案文中出现的"和想法"进行表决。

42. 张先生(中国)想知道这些词语将放在句子的什么部分。

53. 张先生(中国)认为,美国提议的第 1 段的措辞令人满意,采用英国提议的限制性措辞是危险的。

74. 张先生(中国)认为,美国案文对法律规定的限制下了较窄的定义。法国修正案的案文更加简洁,但将这些限制扩大到信息自由,这似乎并不可取。

103. 张先生(中国)感到欣慰的是,联合国新闻自由会议认为宣布这一权利带有义务和责任是明智的。另一方面,他认为没有必要在国际人权公约草案中再次提醒新闻界这一事实。最好保留美国代表团提交的第 2 款案文。

104. 引入"特别"一词将使英国的修正案更不可接受;人们很可能想知道,这暗示的特殊义务和责任是什么。

110. 张先生(中国)认为英文"protection"一词不合适。国家安全、公共秩序等抽象概念无法被"保护"。

26. 张彭春在人权委员会
第六届第 166 次会议发言纪要

1950 年 4 月 24 日上午 11 时 15 分至下午 1 时,联合国人权委员会第六届第 166 次会议,在纽约成功湖召开,本次会议的主要议题是继续讨论国际人权公约草案(第 13 条第 5 段和第 17 条第 3 段)。张彭春先生参加了本次会议,并担任会议主席,以会议主席的身份在会议上发言,其具体发言内容①会议纪要、纪要影像和纪要译文如下：

【会议纪要】

Article 13, paragraph 5 (E/CN. 4/365, E/CN. 4/441, E/CN. 4/445, E/CN. 4/448, E/CN. 4/L. 4) (continued)

1. The CHAIRMAN welcomed Mr. Cassin, French representative, who had so far not taken part in the Commission's work during the sixth session.

24. The CHAIRMAN, speaking as representative of China, pointed out that the word "*mineurs*" had been used in paragraph 1 of the French text and that it might be advisable to use it again. He proposed that the Commission should adopt the United States representative's suggestion and that its next meeting should accordingly be held at 3 p. m. and not at 2. 30 p. m.

It was so decided.

Article 17, paragraph 3 (E/CN. 4/365, E/CN. 4/424, E/CN. 4/433/ Rev. 2, E/CN. 4/434, E/CN. 4/438/Rev. 1)

25. The CHAIRMAN recalled that the Commission had not yet adopted a final text for paragraph 3 (originally paragraph 2) of article 17.

36. The CHAIRMAN said that, as all the members of the Commission appeared to be in agreement on the French amendment, it was unnecessary to put it to the vote.

It was so decided.

39. The CHAIRMAN then invited the members of the Commission to examine the United Kingdom amendment to replace the words "of public order" by the words "for prevention of disorder or crime" (E/CN. 4/365, page 50).

---

① UN Document: E/CN. 4/SR. 166, p. 3, p. 6, p. 7, p. 8.

【纪要影像】

```
Article 13, paragraph 5 (E/CN.4/365, E/CN.4/441, E/CN.4/445, E/CN.4/448,
E/CN.4/L.4) (continued)

1.      The CHAIRMAN welcomed Mr. Cassin, French representative, who had so
far not taken part in the Commission's work during the sixth session.

24.     The CHAIRMAN, speaking as representative of China, pointed out that
the word "mineurs" had been used in paragraph 1 of the French text and that it
might be advisable to use it again.  He proposed that the Commission should
adopt the United States representative's suggestion and that its next meeting
should accordingly be held at 3 p.m. and not at 2.30 p.m.
        It was so decided.

Article 17, paragraph 3 (E/CN.4/365, E/CN.4/424, E/CN.4/433/Rev.2, E/CN.4/434,
E/CN.4/438/Rev.1

25.     The CHAIRMAN recalled that the Commission had not yet adopted a final
text for paragraph 3 (originally paragraph 2) of article 17.

        The CHAIRMAN said that, as all the members of the Commission appeared
to be in agreement on the French amendment, it was unnecessary to put it to the
vote.
        It was so decided.

        The CHAIRMAN then invited the members of the Commission to examine
the United Kingdom amendment to replace the words "of public order" by the
words "for prevention of disorder or crime" (E/CN.4/365, page 50).
```

图片 1.5.36：张彭春在联合国人权委员会第六届第 166 次会议发言纪要

【纪要译文】

第 13 条第 5 款(E/CN. 4/365, E/CN. 4/441, E/CN. 4/445, E/CN. 4/448, E/CN. 4/L. 4)(续)

1. 主席对法国代表卡森先生表示欢迎,后者迄今尚未参加委员会第六届会议的工作。

24. 主席在作为中国代表发言时指出,法文文本第 1 款中使用了"mineurs"一词,最好再次使用该词。他提议委员会采纳美国代表的建议,因此下次会议应在下午 3 时而不是下午 2 时 30 分举行。

就这样决定了。

第 17 条第 3 款(E/CN. 4/365, E/CN. 4/424, E/CN. 4/433/Rev. 2, E/CN. 4/434, E/CN. 4/438/Rev. 1)

25. 主席回顾说,委员会尚未通过第 17 条第 3 款(原第 2 款)的最后案文。

36. 主席说,由于委员会所有成员似乎都同意法国的修正案,因此没有必要将其付诸表决。

就这样决定了。

39. 主席然后请委员会成员审查英国提出的将"公共秩序"改为"防止混乱或犯罪"的修正案(E/CN.4/365,第50页)。

27. 张彭春在人权委员会
第六届第167次会议发言纪要

1950年4月25日下午3时至5时35分,联合国人权委员会第六届第167次会议,在纽约成功湖召开,本次会议的主要议题是继续讨论国际人权公约草案(第17条和第13条)。张彭春先生参加了本次会议,并担任会议主席,以主席身份在会议上先后多次发言,其具体发言内容[①]会议纪要、纪要影像和纪要译文如下:

【会议纪要】

Welcome to the member of the commission on the status of women

1. The CHAIRMAN extended a cordial welcome to Mrs. Goldman, the member of the Commission on the Status of Women.

DRAFT INTERNATIONAL COVENANT ON HUMAN RIGHTS (continued)

Article 17 (E/1371, E/CN. 4/353/Add. 10, E/CN. 4/365, E/CN. 4/433/Rev. 2, E/CN. 4/434, E/CN. 4/438/Rev. 1, E/CN. 4/439, E/CN. 4/440, E/CN. 4/441, E/CN. 4/442, E/CN. 4/445, E/CN. 4/448, E/CN. 4/424) (continued)

---

① UN Document:E/CN.4/SR. 167, p. 3, p. 4, p. 6, p. 7, p. 8, p. 12, p. 14, p. 15, p. 17.

2. The CHAIRMAN invited the Commission to continue its discussion of the United States draft article 17 (E/CN. 4/433/Rev. 2) and the amendments to paragraph 2 of that proposal by the United Kingdom (E/CN. 4/440), France (E/CN. 4/438/Rev. 1), Egypt (E/CN. 4/434) and India (E/CN. 4/424).

10. The CHAIRMAN, speaking as representative of China, observed that the phrase "democratic society" had been used in article 29 of the Universal Declaration of Human Rights to quality the article as a whole, and not merely the phrase "public order". It might be better, however, to omit the reference from article 17 and draft an omnibus clause for the covenant as a whole.

19. The CHAIRMAN put the United Kingdom amendment to paragraph 2 of article 17 (E/CN. 4/440) to the vote. As a request had been made that the amendment should be voted upon in two parts, he first put to the vote the words "the prevention or disorder".

Those words were rejected by 7 votes to 6, with 2 abstentions.

20. The CHAIRMAN said that, as the first part of the United Kingdom amendment had been lost, he would not put the words "or crime" to the vote.

It was so agreed.

21. The CHAIRMAN put to the vote the French amendment to add the words "in a democratic society" after the words "public order" in paragraph 2 of article 17 (E/CN. 4/438/Rev. 1).

That amendment was rejected by 8 votes to 5, with 2 abstentions.

22. The CHAIRMAN then put to the vote the phrase "of national security, public order, safety, health or morals" in paragraph 2 of the United States draft article 17 (E/CN. 4/433/Rev. 2).

That phrase was adopted unanimously.

24. The CHAIRMAN put to the vote the last phrase of the second paragraph of the United States draft article 17 as amended (E/CN. 4/433/Rev. 2).

That phrase was adopted unanimously.

34. The CHAIRMAN, speaking as representative of China, agreed that the Indian amendment as it stood imposed an additional limitation on freedom of expression. He wondered whether it could be rephrased to meet that objection.

51. The CHAIRMAN put the Indian amendment (E/CN. 4/424) to the vote.

It was rejected by 6 votes to 5, with 4 abstentions.

54. In the absence of objection, the CHAIRMAN noted the general consensus that the United Kingdom amendments were covered by paragraph 2 and that a separate vote was therefore unnecessary.

55. He called for a vote on the text of article 17 as amended.

Article 17 as amended was adopted by 13 votes to none, with 2 abstentions.

67. The CHAIRMAN recalled that the Commission had agreed first to consider the United States text of article 17 and the various amendments thereto as its basic text and then to study the alternative texts submitted by the Philippines (E/CN. 4/365) and Yugoslavia (E/CN. 4/415).

71. The CHAIRMAN put the Yugoslav proposal for an alternative text of article 17 to the vote.

The Yugoslav proposal (E/CN. 4/415) was rejected by 5 votes to 1, with 8 abstentions.

Article 13 (E/CN. 4/449, E/CN. 4/L. 4) (continued)

73. The CHAIRMAN noted that the drafting group had submitted an agreed text for paragraph 2 (e) of article 13 (E/CN. 4/449).

85. The CHAIRMAN put the text submitted by the drafting group (E/CN. 4/440) to the vote.

The text submitted by the drafting group was unanimously accepted.

87. The CHAIRMAN put article 13 as amended to the vote.

Article 13 as amended was unanimously adopted.

【纪要影像】

WELCOME TO THE MEMBER OF THE COMMISSION ON THE STATUS OF WOMEN

1.   The CHAIRMAN extended a cordial welcome to Mrs. Goldman, the member of the Commission on the Status of Women.

DRAFT INTERNATIONAL COVENANT ON HUMAN RIGHTS (continued)

Article 17 (E/1371, E/CN.4/353/Add.10, E/CN.4/365, E/CN.4/433/Rev.2, E/CN.4/434, E/CN.4/438/Rev.1, E/CN.4/439, E/CN.4/440, E/CN.4/441, E/CN.4/442, E/CN.4/445, E/CN.4/448, E/CN.4/424) (continued)

2.   The CHAIRMAN invited the Commission to continue its discussion of the United States draft article 17 (E/CN.4/433/Rev.2) and the amendments to paragraph 2 of that proposal by the United Kingdom (E/CN.4/440), France (E/CN.4/438/Rev.1), Egypt (E/CN.4/434) and India (E/CN.4/424).

10.   The CHAIRMAN, speaking as representative of China, observed that the phrase "democratic society" had been used in article 29 of the Universal Declaration of Human Rights to qualify the article as a whole, and not merely the phrase "public order". It might be better, however, to omit the reference from article 17 and draft an omnibus clause for the covenant as a whole.

图片 1.5.37：张彭春在联合国人权委员会第六届第 167 次会议发言纪要(1)

19.   The CHAIRMAN put the United Kingdom amendment to paragraph 2 of article 17 (E/CN.4/440) to the vote. As a request had been made that the amendment should be voted upon in two parts, he first put to the vote the words "the prevention of disorder".
    Those words were rejected by 7 votes to 6, with 2 abstentions.

20.   The CHAIRMAN said that, as the first part of the United Kingdom amendment had been lost, he would not put the words "or crime" to the vote.
    It was so agreed.

21.   The CHAIRMAN put to the vote the French amendment to add the words "in a democratic society" after the words "public order" in paragraph 2 of article 17 (E/CN.4/438/Rev.1).
    That amendment was rejected by 8 votes to 5, with 2 abstentions.

22.   The CHAIRMAN then put to the vote the phrase "of national security, public order, safety, health or morals" in paragraph 2 of the United States draft article 17 (E/CN.4/433/Rev.2).
    That phrase was adopted unanimously.

图片 1.5.38：张彭春在联合国人权委员会第六届第 167 次会议发言纪要(2)

24.   The CHAIRMAN put to the vote the last phrase of the second paragraph of the United States draft article 17 as amended (E/CN.4/433/Rev.2).

That phrase was adopted unanimously.

34.   The CHAIRMAN, speaking as representative of China, agreed that the Indian amendment as it stood imposed an additional limitation on freedom of expression. He wondered whether it could be rephrased to meet that objection.

51.   The CHAIRMAN put the Indian amendment (E/CN.4/424) to the vote.

It was rejected by 6 votes to 5, with 4 abstentions.

54.   In the absence of objection, the CHAIRMAN noted the general consensus that the United Kingdom amendments were covered by paragraph 2 and that a separate vote was therefore unnecessary.

55.   He called for a vote on the text of article 17 as amended.

Article 17 as amended was adopted by 13 votes to none, with 2 abstentions.

图片 1.5.39：张彭春在联合国人权委员会第六届第 167 次会议发言纪要(3)

67.   The CHAIRMAN recalled that the Commission had agreed first to consider the United States text of article 17 and the various amendments thereto as its basic text and then to study the alternative texts submitted by the Philippines (E/CN.4/365) and Yugoslavia (E/CN.4/415).

71.   The CHAIRMAN put the Yugoslav proposal for an alternative text of article 17 to the vote.

The Yugoslav proposal (E/CN.4/415) was rejected by 5 votes to 1, with 8 abstentions.

Article 13 (E/CN.4/449, E/CN.4/L.4) (continued)

73.   The CHAIRMAN noted that the drafting group had submitted an agreed text for paragraph 2 (e) of article 13 (E/CN.4/449).

85.   The CHAIRMAN put the text submitted by the drafting group (E/CN.4/449) to the vote.

The text submitted by the drafting group was unanimously accepted.

87.   The CHAIRMAN put article 13 as amended to the vote.

Article 13 as amended was unanimously adopted.

图片 1.5.40：张彭春在联合国人权委员会第六届第 167 次会议发言纪要(4)

【纪要译文】

欢迎到来的妇女地位委员会成员

1.主席向妇女地位委员会成员戈尔德曼（Goldman）夫人表示热烈欢迎。

国际人权公约草案(续)

第 17 条(E/1371, E/CN.4/353/Add.10, E/CN.4/365, E/CN.4/433/

Rev. 2，E/CN. 4/434，E/CN. 4/438/Rev. 1，E/CN. 4/439，E/CN. 4/440，E/CN. 4/441，E/CN. 4/442，E/CN. 4/445，E/CN. 4/448，E/CN. 4/424）（续）

2. 主席请委员会继续讨论美国的第 17 条草案（E/CN. 4/433/Rev. 2）以及英国（E/CN. 4/440）、法国（E/CN. 4/438/Rev. 1）、埃及（E/CN. 4/434）和印度（E/CN. 4/424）对该提案第 2 款的修正。

10. 主席在作为中国代表发言时指出，《世界人权宣言》第 29 条中使用了"民主社会"一词来修饰整个条款，而不仅仅是"公共秩序"一词。然而，最好从第 17 条中删除这一提法，为整个《公约》起草一项总括条款。

19. 主席将英国对第 17 条第 2 款的修正案（E/CN. 4/440）付诸表决。由于有人要求对修正案分两部分进行表决，他首先将"预防或紊乱"几个字付诸表决。

这几个字以 7 票对 6 票，2 票弃权被否决。

20. 主席说，由于英国修正案的第一部分已经丢失，他不会将"或罪行"一词付诸表决。

就这样确定下来。

21. 主席将法国提出的在第 17 条第 2 款"公共秩序"一词之后增加"在民主社会"一词的提议付诸表决（E/CN. 4/438/Rev. 1）。

该修正案以 8 票对 5 票，2 票弃权被否决。

22. 主席随后将美国第 17 条草案（E/CN. 4/433/Rev. 2）第 2 款中的"国家安全、公共秩序、安全、健康或道德"一语付诸表决。

该短语获得一致通过。

24. 主席将经修正的美国第 17 条草案（E/CN. 4/433/Rev. 2）第二款最后一句付诸表决。

该句获得一致通过。

34. 主席作为中国代表发言，同意印度的修正案对表达自由施加了额外的限制。他想知道是否可以重新措辞以回应这一反对意见。

51. 主席将印度的修正案（E/CN. 4/424）付诸表决。

该提案以 6 票对 5 票,4 票弃权被否决。

54. 如果没有人反对,主席指出,普遍的共识是,英国的修正案已包括在第 2 款中,因此没有必要进行单独表决。

55. 他要求对修正后的第 17 条案文进行表决。

经修正的第 17 条以 13 票对 0 票,2 票弃权获得通过。

67. 主席回顾说,委员会同意首先审议美国第 17 条案文及其各种修正案作为其基本案文,然后研究菲律宾(E/CN.4/365)和南斯拉夫(E/CN.4/415)提交的备选案文。

71. 主席将南斯拉夫关于第 17 条备选案文的提案付诸表决。

南斯拉夫的提案(E/CN.4/415)以 5 票对 1 票,8 票弃权被否决。

第 13 条(E/CN.4/449,E/CN.4/L.4)(续)

73. 主席指出,起草小组提交了第 13 条第 2 款(E)项的商定案文(E/CN.4/449)。

85. 主席将起草小组提交的案文(E/CN.4/440)付诸表决。

起草小组提交的案文获得一致通过。

87. 主席将修正后的第 13 条付诸表决。

经修正的第 13 条获得一致通过。

28. 张彭春在人权委员会
第六届第 170 次会议发言纪要

1950 年 4 月 17 日上午 11 时至下午 1 时 20 分,联合国人权委员会第六届第 170 次会议,在纽约成功湖召开,本次会议的主要议题是继续讨论国际人权公约草案等。张彭春先生参加了本次会议,并在会议上发言,其具体发言内容①会议纪要、纪要影像和纪要译文如下:

---

① UN Document:E/CN.4/SR.170, pp. 11–12.

【会议纪要】

43. Mr. CHANG (China) traced the history of the draft convention on freedom of information and pointed out that the world situation had inevitably had its effect on the course of the United Nations' work. The Conference on Freedom of Information had been convened in Geneva in 1948 in accordance with a decision taken two years earlier. The Conference had drawn up three draft conventions, which had been examined in turn by the Economic and Social Council and by the General Assembly. It had not proved possible to adopt the third draft at the Council's ninth session on account of the large number or amendments submitted at a late stage by certain delegations; it should be borne in mind that at that time positions had hardened. It therefore seemed wiser to allow a certain period to elapse. The General Assembly had abstained from taking a final decision in the matter; it had preferred to refer it to the Commission on Human Rights and to ascertain the general lines of the article on freedom of information to be included in the covenant on human rights. Such was the actual situation; the Commission had drafted article 17 and would submit it to the General Assembly, which would of course take the final decision in the matter.

44. In all the circumstances, Mr. Chang felt that the time had come to take a vote. Outlining his views on the two texts before the Commission, he pointed out with reference to the joint draft resolution that the preparation of a convention was one means but not the only means of ensuring freedom of information and proposed that the text should be amended accordingly. Where the United States amendment was concerned, the desirability of preparing a convention on freedom of information had already been recognized by the General Assembly four years earlier. The only decision it was still required to take was related to the text of that convention. It would therefore be preferable to use the phrase "with respect to a special convention".

【纪要影像】

43.   Mr. CHANG (China) traced the history of the draft convention on freedom of information and pointed out that the world situation had inevitably had its effect on the course of the United Nations' work. The Conference on Freedom of Information had been convened in Geneva in 1948 in accordance with a decision taken two years earlier. The Conference had drawn up three draft conventions, which had been examined in turn by the Economic and Social Council and by the General Assembly. It had not proved possible to adopt the third draft at the Council's ninth session on account of the large number of amendments submitted at a late stage by certain delegations; it should be borne in mind that at that time positions had hardened. It therefore seemed wiser to allow a certain period to elapse. The General Assembly had abstained from taking a final decision in the matter; it had preferred to refer it to the Commission on Human Rights and to ascertain the general lines of the article on freedom of information to be included in the covenant on human rights. Such was the actual situation; the Commission had drafted article 17 and would submit it to the General Assembly, which would of course take the final decision in the matter.

44.   In all the circumstances, Mr. Chang felt that the time had come to take a vote. Outlining his views on the two texts before the Commission, he pointed out with reference to the joint draft resolution that the preparation of a convention was one means but not the only means of ensuring freedom of information and proposed that the text should be amended accordingly. Where the United States amendment was concerned, the desirability of preparing a convention on freedom of information had already been recognized by the General Assembly four years earlier. The only decision it was still required to take was related to the text of that convention. It would therefore be preferable to use the phrase "with respect to a special convention".

图片 1.5.41:张彭春在联合国人权委员会第六届第 170 次会议发言纪要

【纪要译文】

43. 张先生(中国)回顾了新闻自由公约草案的历史,指出世界形势不可避免地对联合国的工作进程产生了影响。根据两年前做出的决定,新闻自由会议于 1948 年在日内瓦召开。会议起草了三份公约草案,经济及社会理事会和大会依次审查了这些草案。由于某些代表团在较晚阶段提交了大量修正案,理事会第九届会议未能通过第三稿;应该记住,当时的立场已经变得强硬。因此,让一段时间过去似乎更明智。大会没有就此事做出最后决定;它倾向于将其提交人权委员会,并确定将列入《人权公约》的新闻自由条款的大致内容。这就是实际情况;委员会起草了第 17 条,并将提交给大会,大会当然会就此事作出最终决定。

44. 在所有这些情况下,张先生觉得投票表决的时候到了。他概述了他对委员会收到的两份案文的看法,并就联合决议草案指出,拟订一项公约是确保新闻自由的手段之一,但不是唯一的手段,并建议对案文进行相应的修正。就美国的修正案而言,大会早在四年前就已经认识到拟订一项新闻自由公约的可取性。它仍然需要作出的唯一决定与该公约的案文有关。因此,最好使用"关于一项特别公约"的短语。

29. 张彭春在人权委员会
第六届第 171 次会议发言纪要

　　1950 年 4 月 26 日下午 2 时 30 分至 5 时 30 分,联合国人权委员会第六届第 171 次会议,在纽约成功湖召开,本次会议的主要议题是继续讨论国际人权公约草案(第 17 条和第 19 条)。张彭春先生参加了本次会议,并在会议上发言,其具体发言内容①会议纪要、纪要影像和纪要译文如下:

【会议纪要】

　　4. Mr. CHANG (China) thought that in future it would be better to table all amendments before proceeding to the vote.

　　6. In reply to the CHAIRMAN, Mr. CHANG (China) said he was not proposing a procedure which should be strictly adhered to in future. He merely thought it commended itself as a more orderly method of work.

　　34. Mr. CHANG (China) supported the French amendment to paragraph 1, which was similar in form to article 18. If the original text were retained, however, paragraph 2 should be amended to read "This right shall be subject only to such limitations ..."

　　35. He also preferred the form of the limitations clause in article 18 to that in article 19. He proposed that the Style Committee should consider amending paragraph 2 to read: "to ensure national security, public order, the preservation of health or morals, or the protection of the fundamental rights and freedoms of others."

―――――――――――

　　① UN Document: E/CN. 4/SR. 171, p. 3, pp. 7-8, p. 17, p. 18.

36. In the interests of securing a more uniform style throughout the covenant he could accept the United Kingdom amendment if the specific limitations clause were deleted.

84. Mr. CHANG (China) saw no possibility of conflict between the two conventions. The covenant was intended to be a legal instrument to reinforce the rights proclaimed in the Declaration and to be further strengthened by existing conventions or future conventions dealing more specifically with the guarantees it provided. Only a new convention on freedom of association, adopted by the General Assembly, could prejudice the ILO Convention. There was no reason to retain paragraph 3 of article 19, especially since further safeguards against conflict with other conventions could be introduced in article 22.

88. Mr. CHANG (China) suggested that consideration of the Uruguayan amendment to paragraph 3 should be deferred until it had been distributed in writing and moved the adjournment of the meeting. He accepted the United Kingdom representative's suggestion, however, that a vote should be taken forthwith on paragraphs 1 and 2 of article 19.

89. Mr. ORIBE (Uruguay) accepted that compromise.

【纪要影像】

4.　　Mr. CHANG (China) thought that in future it would be better to table all amendments before proceeding to the vote.

6.　　In reply to the CHAIRMAN, Mr. CHANG (China) said he was not proposing a procedure which should be strictly adhered to in future. He merely thought it commended itself as a more orderly method of work.

34.　　Mr. CHANG (China) supported the French amendment to paragraph 1, which was similar in form to article 18. If the original text were retained, however, paragraph 2 should be amended to read "This right shall be subject only to such limitations..."

35.　　He also preferred the form of the limitations clause in article 18 to that in article 19. He proposed that the Style Committee should consider amending paragraph 2 to read: "to ensure national security, public order, the preservation of health or morals, or the protection of the fundamental rights and freedoms of others."

图片 1.5.42：张彭春在联合国人权委员会第六届第 171 次会议发言纪要(1)

36.　　In the interests of securing a more uniform style throughout the covenant he could accept the United Kingdom amendment if the specific limitations clause were deleted.

84.　　Mr. CHANG (China) saw no possibility of conflict between the two conventions. The covenant was intended to be a legal instrument to reinforce the rights proclaimed in the Declaration and to be further strengthened by existing conventions or future conventions dealing more specifically with the guarantees it provided. Only a new convention on freedom of association, adopted by the General Assembly, could prejudice the ILO Convention. There was no reason to retain paragraph 3 of article 19, especially since further safeguards against conflict with other conventions could be introduced in article 22.

88.　　Mr. CHANG (China) suggested that consideration of the Uruguayan amendment to paragraph 3 should be deferred until it had been distributed in writing and moved the adjournment of the meeting. He accepted the United Kingdom representative's suggestion, however, that a vote should be taken forthwith on paragraphs 1 and 2 of article 19.

89.　　Mr. ORIBE (Uruguay) accepted that compromise.

图片 1.5.43：张彭春在联合国人权委员会第六届第 171 次会议发言纪要(2)

【纪要译文】

4. 张先生(中国)认为,今后最好在进行表决前提出所有修正案。

6. 在回答主席的问题时,张先生(中国)说,他并不是建议今后应严格遵守的程序。他只是认为这是一种更有秩序的工作方法。

34. 张先生(中国)支持法国对第 1 款的修正,该修正在形式上类似于第 18 条。但是,如果保留原来的案文,第 2 款应修正为"这项权利只受……的限制"

35. 与第 19 条相比,他也更喜欢第 18 条中限制条款的形式。他建议文体委员会考虑将第 2 款修改为:"确保国家安全、公共秩序、维护健康或道德,或保护他人的基本权利和自由"。

36. 为了确保整个公约更加统一的风格,如果删除具体的限制条款,他可以接受英国的修正案。

84. 张先生(中国)认为这两项公约之间没有冲突的可能性。《公约》旨在成为一项法律文书,以加强《宣言》中宣布的权利,并通过现有公约或未来更具体地处理《公约》提供的保障的公约得到进一步加强。只有大会通过的关于结社自由的新公约才能损害国际劳工组织公约。没有理由保留第 19 条第 3 款,特别是因为防止与其他公约冲突的进一步保障措施可以在第 22 条中提出。

88. 张先生(中国)建议,乌拉圭对第 3 款的修正案应推迟到以书面形式分发后再审议,并提议休会。然而,他接受英国代表的建议,即应立即就第 19 条第 1 和第 2 款进行表决。

89. 奥里贝(Oribe)先生(乌拉圭)接受了这一妥协。

30. 张彭春在人权委员会第六届第 173 次会议发言纪要

1950 年 4 月 27 日下午 2 时 30 分至 5 时 50 分,联合国人权委员会第六届第 173 次会议,在纽约成功湖召开,本次会议的主要议题是继续讨论国际人权公约草案(第 20 条)。张彭春先生参加了本次会议,并担任会议主席,以主席身份在会议上发言,其具体发言内容①会议纪要、纪要影像和纪要译文如下:

---

① UN Document:E/CN.4/SR.173, p. 3, p. 6, p. 17, p. 18.

【会议纪要】

1. The CHAIRMAN invited the Commission to proceed with its consideration of article 20.

23. The CHAIRMAN, speaking as the representative of China, stressed the fact that article 20 was not an article on law but rather an article dealing essentially with equality. Human rights almost always involved comparison and questions of equal treatment. Although it was difficult to put article 1 of the Universal Declaration into legal terms, the covenant could at least provide for the essential of equality before the law.

24. The representative of China stated that the long discussion had not affected his support of the Commission's text of article 20.

88. The CHAIRMAN thought that the Commission could vote on the text of article 20 and consider the point raised by the Uruguayan representative at the second reading.

94. The CHAIRMAN put to the vote the motion to adjourn.

That motion was rejected by 7 votes to 6, with 2 abstentions.

95. In reply to Mr. ORIBE (Uruguay), the CHAIRMAN explained that the debate was not closed and that the Lebanese amendment could be admitted.

97. The CHAIRMAN too reminded the Commission that the word " discrimination" had been chosen as the best translation for the word " distinction" in the French text.

98. Mr. JEVERMOVIC (Yugoslavia) accepted the word " discrimination".

1.　　The CHAIRMAN invited the Commission to proceed with its consideration of article 20.

23.　　The CHAIRMAN, speaking as the representative of China, stressed the fact that article 20 was not an article on law but rather an article dealing essentially with equality. Human rights almost always involved comparison and questions of equal treatment. Although it was difficult to put article 1 of the Universal Declaration into legal terms, the covenant could at least provide for the essential of equality before the law.

24.　　The representative of China stated that the long discussion had not affected his support of the Commission's text of article 20.

88.　　The CHAIRMAN thought that the Commission could vote on the text of article 20 and consider the point raised by the Uruguayan representative at the second reading.

94.　　The CHAIRMAN put to the vote the motion to adjourn. That motion was rejected by 7 votes to 6, with 2 abstentions.

95.　　In reply to Mr. ORIBE (Uruguay), the CHAIRMAN explained that the debate was not closed and that the Lebanese amendment could be admitted.

97.　　The CHAIRMAN too reminded the Commission that the word "discrimination" had been chosen as the best translation for the word "distinction" in the French text.

98.　　Mr. JEVREMOVIC (Yugoslavia) accepted the word "discrimination".

图片 1.5.44：张彭春在联合国人权委员会第六届第 173 次会议发言纪要

【纪要译文】

1. 主席请委员会继续审议第 20 条。

23. 主席以中国代表的身份发言,强调第 20 条不是关于法律的条款,而是主要涉及平等的条款。人权几乎总是涉及比较和平等待遇的问题。虽然很难将《世界人权宣言》第一条变成法律条款,但《公约》至少可以规定法律面前人人平等的基本原则。

24. 中国代表说,长时间的讨论并不影响他对委员会第 20 条案文的支持。

88. 主席认为,委员会可以就第 20 条案文进行表决,并考虑乌拉圭代表在二读时提出的问题。

94. 主席将休会的动议付诸表决。

该动议以 7 票对 6 票,2 票弃权被否决。

95. 在答复奥里贝先生(乌拉圭)时,主席解释说,辩论没有结束,黎巴嫩的修正案可以被接受。

97. 主席也提醒委员会,"discrimination"(歧视)一词已被选为法文文本中"distinction"一词的最佳翻译。

98. 耶夫雷莫维奇(Jevremovic)先生(南斯拉夫)接受"discrimination"一词。

31. 张彭春在人权委员会第六届第 174 次会议发言纪要

1950 年 4 月 28 日上午 11 时至下午 1 时 5 分,联合国人权委员会第六届第 157 次会议,在纽约成功湖召开,本次会议的主要议题是继续讨论国际人权公约草案(第 20 条和第 21 条)。张彭春先生参加了本次会议,并在会议上发言,其具体发言内容①会议纪要、纪要影像和纪要译文如下:

【会议纪要】

11. Mr. CHANG (China), supported by Mr. KYROU (Greece), pointed out that it was most difficult to take a decision before the Lebanese delegation had submitted a formal proposal in writing.

17. Mr. CHANG (China) supported by Mr. CASSIN (France) asked that the discussion on article 20 should be postponed until the following meeting to enable representatives to study the written text of the Lebanese proposal and to give that very important article the thorough consideration it deserved.

18. The CHAIRMAN put the Chinese representative's proposal to the vote.

That proposal was adopted by 10 votes to none, with 4 abstentions.

49. Mr. CHANG (China) felt that the texts proposed for article 21 were

---

① UN Document:E/CN.4/SR.174, p. 4, p. 5, pp. 10–11, p. 14.

not entirely clear. The French draft was, of course, constructive. It resulted from the harrowing experiences of the Second World War and the memory of racial persecutions against the Jews. The words "fascist-Nazi" which appeared in the USSR text, could not, however, be accepted by some countries. Those words, in fact, designated ideologies which could be given other names, depending on the countries involved, and therefore had no place in a document such as the covenant.

50. The French draft expressed a principle which should not be overlooked. Application of that principle would no doubt meet with some difficulty and, as pointed out by the United States representative, might lead to abuse. Moreover, the use of such words as "national" and "religious" to qualify the word "hostility" was debatable. It would be difficult to give a definition of what constituted the national or religious domain. Caution should therefore be exercised to the use of such words.

51. He hoped that the French representative would review his text, making the necessary changes. The Commission should, in any event, take that text into account since it expressed a principle for which millions of men had given their lives in China as well as in France.

60. Mr. CHANG (China) considered that the Australian representative's proposal deserved careful consideration and he accordingly moved the adjournment of the debate.

It was decided to adjourn the debate.

【纪要影像】

11.　　Mr. CHANG (China), supported by Mr. KYROU (Greece), pointed out that it was most difficult to take a decision before the Lebanese delegation had submitted a formal proposal in writing.

17.　　Mr. CHANG (China) supported by Mr. CASSIN (France) asked that the discussion on article 20 should be postponed until the following meeting to enable representatives to study the written text of the Lebanese proposal and to give that very important article the thorough consideration it deserved.

18.　　The CHAIRMAN put the Chinese representative's proposal to the vote.
That proposal was adopted by 10 votes to none, with 4 abstentions.

19.　　Mr. CHANG (China) felt that the texts proposed for article 21 were not entirely clear. The French draft was, of course, constructive. It resulted from the harrowing experiences of the Second World War and the memory of racial persecutions against the Jews. The words "fascist-Nazi" which appeared in the USSR text, could not, however, be accepted by some countries. Those words, in fact, designated ideologies which could be given other names, depending on the countries involved, and therefore had no place in a document such as the covenant.

图片1.5.45：张彭春在联合国人权委员会第六届第174次会议发言纪要(1)

50.　　The French draft expressed a principle which should not be overlooked. Application of that principle would no doubt meet with some difficulty and, as pointed out by the United States representative, might lead to abuse. Moreover, the use of such words as "national" and "religious" to qualify the word "hostility" was debatable. It would be difficult to give a definition of what constituted the national or religious domain. Caution should therefore be exercised in the use of such words.

51.　　He hoped that the French representative would review his text, making the necessary changes. The Commission should, in any event, take that text into account since it expressed a principle for which millions of men had given their lives, in China as well as in France.

60.　　Mr. CHANG (China) considered that the Australian representative's proposal deserved careful consideration and he accordingly moved the adjournment of the debate.
It was decided to adjourn the debate.

图片1.5.46：张彭春在联合国人权委员会第六届第174次会议发言纪要(2)

【纪要译文】

11. 张先生(中国)在基鲁(Kyrou)先生(希腊)的支持下指出,在黎巴嫩代表团提交书面正式提案之前,很难作出决定。

17. 张先生(中国)在卡森先生(法国)的支持下要求将对第20条的讨

论推迟到下次会议,以便各位代表能够研究黎巴嫩提案的书面案文,并对这一非常重要的条款给予应有的充分考虑。

18. 主席将中国代表的提议付诸表决。

该提议以 10 票对 0 票,4 票弃权获得通过。

49. 张先生(中国)认为,为第 21 条提议的案文不完全清楚。法国的草案当然是建设性的。它源于第二次世界大战的悲惨经历和对犹太人种族迫害的记忆。然而,苏联文本中出现的"法西斯—纳粹"一词不能被一些国家接受。事实上,这些词语所指的意识形态可以有其他名称,这取决于所涉及的国家,因此不会出现在《公约》这样的文件中。

50. 法国的草案表达了一项不应被忽视的原则。该原则的适用无疑会遇到一些困难,而且正如美国代表所指出的,可能会导致滥用。此外,使用"民族的"和"宗教的"等词来修饰"敌意"一词是有争议的。很难给什么构成民族或宗教领域下定义。因此,应谨慎使用这些词语。

51. 他希望法国代表会审查他的案文,作出必要的修改。无论如何,委员会应考虑该案文,因为它表达了一项原则,数百万中国人和法国人为此献出了生命。

60. 张先生(中国)认为澳大利亚代表的建议值得认真考虑,因此他提出暂停辩论的动议。

决定暂停辩论。

32. 张彭春在人权委员会第六届第 175 次会议发言纪要

1950 年 4 月 28 日下午 2 时 30 分至 5 时 30 分,联合国人权委员会第六届第 175 次会议,在纽约成功湖召开,本次会议的主要议题是继续讨论国际人权公约草案(第 20 条和第 21 条)。张彭春先生参加了本次会议,并

在会议上发言,其具体发言内容①会议纪要、纪要影像和纪要译文如下:

【会议纪要】

32. Mr. CHANG (China) pointed out that while paragraph 1 was closely linked to the Declaration, it had to be interpreted in terms of the law; although the Commission might believe in the larger concept of equality, it could nevertheless accept the restrictive provisions of article 20 and thus take a significant step forward in the field of treaty protection. The Lebanese text stressed the notion of equality, whereas the covenant could only deal with equality before the law. He therefore wished to reserve his position on paragraph 1.

33. He also thought that paragraph 2 should be inserted in article 2, where it would apply to all rights.

34. He was opposed to the two drafting amendments which had been presented. He thought that if the Commission decided to retain the Lebanese amendment, it could leave such matters to the Style Committee.

43. Mr. CHANG (China) thought the Chilean amendment was academic because the term "ethnic origin" would convey but little to the common man.

44. The people who had suffered for many years, as European expansion fostered the concepts of discrimination based on race and colour, would not be satisfied with that term. To avoid misunderstanding, therefore, the Commission should adhere to the language of the Charter and the Univereal Declaration of Human Rights.

45. It was a matter of substance and not of drafting, and should be weighed carefully. In signing the Charter and in proclaiming the Declaration many nations had solemnly given sanction to the words "race" and "colour", which although not scientific terms, were clearly understood throughout the world. On the other hand, "ethnic origin", which included the notion of lan-

---

① UN Document: E/CN. 4/SR. 175, pp. 7-8, pp. 9-10, p. 11.

guage and religion, was too broad and confusing. Moreover, many nations still used the old terms in official documents. The Commission should therefore use those same words in preventing discrimination. If the Commission wished, it could use both "race" and "colour" in quotation marks in the covenant, but at all costs they should be retained.

46. He assured the Commission that the Chilean amendment could have misleading and far-reaching consequences and urged that it should be withdrawn until some future date, when public opinion was better prepared to understand its full implications.

47. He reserved the right to intervene again in the debate.

55. Mr. CHANG (China) stated that he had no doubt of the sincere desire of the representative of Chile to wipe out racial discrimination. In referring to the Chilean amendment as academic, he had voiced his opinion of the proposal, which he felt was inappropriate at that stage since it departed from the wording of the United Nations Charter and the Universal Declaration of Human Rights.

56. In reply to the representative of Uruguay, he made it clear that he had referred to Western expansion during the last two hundred years which had spread discrimination. It had not been his intention in speaking of that unfavourable aspect of Western development to minimize the valuable contributions of the West to the progress of mankind.

【纪要影像】

32. Mr. CHANG (China) pointed out that while paragraph 1 was closely linked to the Declaration, it had to be interpreted in terms of the law; although the Commission might believe in the larger concept of equality, it could nevertheless accept the restrictive provisions of article 20 and thus take a significant step forward in the field of treaty protection. The Lebanese text stressed the notion of equality, whereas the covenant could only deal with equality before the law. He therefore wished to reserve his position on paragraph 1.

33. He also thought that paragraph 2 should be inserted in article 2, where it would apply to all rights.

34. He was opposed to the two drafting amendments which had been presented. He thought that if the Commission decided to retain the Lebanese amendment, it could leave such matters to the Style Committee.

43. Mr. CHANG (China) thought the Chilean amendment was academic because the term "ethnic origin" would convey but little to the common man.

44. The people who had suffered for many years, as European expansion fostered the concepts of discrimination based on race and colour, would not be satisfied with that term. To avoid misunderstanding, therefore, the Commission should adhere to the language of the Charter and the Universal Declaration of Human Rights.

45. It was a matter of substance and not of drafting, and should be weighed carefully. In signing the Charter and in proclaiming the Declaration many nations had solemnly given sanction to the words "race" and "colour", which although not scientific terms, were clearly understood throughout the world. On the other hand, "ethnic origin", which included the notion of language and religion, was too broad and confusing. Moreover, many nations

图片 1.5.47:张彭春在联合国人权委员会第六届第 175 次会议发言纪要(1)

still used the old terms in official documents. The Commission should therefore use those same words in preventing discrimination. If the Commission wished, it could use both "race" and "colour" in quotation marks in the covenant, but at all costs they should be retained.

46. He assured the Commission that the Chilean amendment could have misleading and far-reaching consequences and urged that it should be withdrawn until some future date, when public opinion was better prepared to understand its full implications.

47. He reserved the right to intervene again in the debate.

55. Mr. CHANG (China) stated that he had no doubt of the sincere desire of the representative of Chile to wipe out racial discrimination. In referring to the Chilean amendment as academic, he had voiced his opinion of the proposal, which he felt was inappropriate at that stage since it departed from the wording of the United Nations Charter and the Universal Declaration of Human Rights.

56. In reply to the representative of Uruguay, he made it clear that he had referred to Western expansion during the last two hundred years which had spread discrimination. It had not been his intention in speaking of that unfavourable aspect of Western development to minimize the valuable contributions of the West to the progress of mankind.

图片 1.5.48:张彭春在联合国人权委员会第六届第 175 次会议发言纪要(2)

【纪要译文】

32.张先生(中国)指出,虽然第 1 段与《宣言》密切相关,但必须从法律的角度加以解释;虽然委员会可能相信更广泛的平等概念,但它仍然可以接受第 20 条的限制性规定,从而在条约保护领域向前迈出重要一步。

黎巴嫩文本强调平等的概念,而《公约》只能涉及法律面前的平等。因此,他希望保留他对第 1 段的立场。

33. 他还认为第 2 段应插入第 2 条,该条适用于所有权利。

34. 他反对已经提出的两项起草修正案。他认为,如果委员会决定保留黎巴嫩的修正案,它可以将这些事项留给文体委员会处理。

43. 张先生(中国)认为智利的修正案是学术性的,因为"民族起源"一词对普通人意义不大。

44. 由于欧洲的扩张助长了基于种族和肤色的歧视概念,多年来遭受苦难的人们不会对这个词感到满意。因此,为了避免误解,委员会应坚持《宪章》和《世界人权宣言》的语言。

45. 这是一个实质问题,而不是起草问题,应该仔细权衡。在签署《宪章》和宣布《宣言》时,许多国家庄严认可了"种族"和"肤色"这两个词,尽管它们不是科学术语,但全世界都清楚地理解。另一方面,包含语言和宗教概念的"民族起源"过于宽泛,令人困惑。此外,许多国家仍然在官方文件中使用旧词,因此委员会应该使用这些新词来防止歧视。如果委员会愿意,它可以在《公约》中使用加引号的"种族"和"肤色",但是无论如何都应予以保留。

46. 他向委员会保证,智利的修正案可能会产生误导和深远的后果,并敦促在公众舆论对其全部影响有了更好的理解之前撤回该修正案。

47. 他保留在辩论中再次发言的权利。

55. 张先生(中国)说,他毫不怀疑智利代表消除种族歧视的真诚愿望。在提到智利的提案是学术性的时,他表达了他对该提案的意见,他认为该提案在现阶段是不适当的,因为它背离了《联合国宪章》和《世界人权宣言》的措辞。

56. 在回答乌拉圭代表时,他明确表示,他指的是过去两百年间传播歧视的西方扩张。他在谈到西方发展负面方面时,无意贬低西方对人类进步的宝贵贡献。

33. 张彭春在人权委员会
第六届第 182 次会议发言纪要

1950 年 5 月 8 日下午 3 时至 5 时 30 分,联合国人权委员会第六届第 182 次会议,在纽约成功湖召开,本次会议的主要议题是继续讨论国际人权公约草案(第 7 条)。张彭春先生参加了本次会议,并担任会议主席,以主席身份在会议上发言,其具体发言内容①会议纪要、纪要影像和纪要译文如下:

【会议纪要】

1. The CHAIRMAN asked the Commission to continue its discussion of draft article 7. He drew attention in particular to statements concerning that article which had been submitted by the World Health Organization (E/CN. 4/ 359, E/CN. 4/389).

24. The CHAIRMAN asked the Commission whether it wished to state that it thought the atrocities contemplated under article 7 were definitely and categorically covered by article 6.

41. The CHAIRMAN wished to make it clear that in proposing a statement placing the Commission on record as believing that the substance of article 7 was covered by article 6, he had merely acted on the French representative's suggestion. He could therefore not claim credit for the suggestion itself.

42. The Lebanese representative had indicated that the Commission should formally and categorically declare that article 6 was intended to cover the substance of article 7, if it were decided to delete the latter. The Chairman as-

---

① UN Document: E/CN. 4/SR. 182, p. 3, p. 6, pp. 10–11, p. 15.

sumed that the Lebanese representative had in mind the adoption of a resolution in that sense by the Commission. If so, he would request the Lebanese representative to submit a suitable draft.

61. The CHAIRMAN answered the Lebanese representative that ample time would be given for consideration of the new texts.

【纪要影像】

1. The CHAIRMAN asked the Commission to continue its discussion of draft article 7. He drew attention in particular to statements concerning that article which had been submitted by the World Health Organization (E/CN.4/359,E/CN.4/389).

24. The CHAIRMAN asked the Commission whether it wished to state that it thought the atrocities contemplated under article 7 were definitely and categorically covered by article 6.

41. The CHAIRMAN wished to make it clear that in proposing a statement placing the Commission on record as believing that the substance of article 7 was covered by article 6, he had merely acted on the French representative's suggestion. He could therefore not claim credit for the suggestion itself.

42. The Lebanese representative had indicated that the Commission should formally and categorically declare that article 6 was intended to cover the substance of article 7, if it were decided to delete the latter. The Chairman assumed that the Lebanese representative had in mind the adoption of a resolution in that sense by the Commission. If so, he would request the Lebanese representative to submit a suitable draft.

61. The CHAIRMAN assured the Lebanese representative that ample time would be given for consideration of the new texts.

图片 1.5.49:张彭春在联合国人权委员会第六届第 182 次会议发言纪要

【纪要译文】

1. 主席请委员会继续讨论草案第 7 条。他特别提请注意世界卫生组织提交的关于该条的声明(E/CN.4/359,E/CN.4/389)。

24. 主席问委员会,它是否希望表明,它认为第 7 条所设想的暴行明确无误地包括在第 6 条中。

41. 主席希望说明,他提出一项声明,将委员会认为第 6 条涵盖了第 7 条的实质内容记录在案,只是按照法国代表的建议行事。因此,他不能声称建议本身是他的功劳。

42. 黎巴嫩代表表示,如果决定删除第 7 条,委员会应正式明确宣布第 6 条旨在涵盖第 7 条的实质内容。主席认为,黎巴嫩代表的意思是委员会通过一项这方面的决议。如果是这样,他将请黎巴嫩代表提交一份适当的草案。

61. 主席回答黎巴嫩代表说,将会有充足的时间来审议新的案文。

34. 张彭春在人权委员会
第六届第 183 次会议发言纪要

1950 年 5 月 9 日上午 11 时 20 分至下午 1 时 5 分,联合国人权委员会第六届第 183 次会议,在纽约成功湖召开,本次会议的主要议题是继续讨论国际人权公约草案(第 7 条和第 6 条)。张彭春先生参加了本次会议,并担任会议主席,以主席身份在会议上先后多次发言,其具体发言内容①会议纪要、纪要影像和纪要译文如下:

【会议纪要】

2. The CHAIRMAN noted the request of the United Kingdom representative.

3. The CHAIRMAN invited the Commission to continue the study of article 7. He recalled that several proposals had been submitted to the Commission—the French delegation's proposal that article 7 should be deleted and the substance of that article incorporated in article 6 (E/CN. 4/471), the Yugoslav delegation's proposal that article 7 should be amended (E/CN. 4/372), and the amendment to article 6 submitted by the Philippine delegation (E/CN. 4/472).

8. The CHAIRMAN said he would put the various proposals to the vote in

---

① UN Document: E/CN. 4/SR. 183, p. 3, p. 4, pp. 4–5, p. 10, p. 11, p. 12, p. 13.

the following order: he would first put to the vote the proposal that article 7 should be deleted, and if that were rejected, he would put the Yugoslav amendment to the vote. If the proposal for deletion were adopted, he would put the French amendment to article 6 (E/CN. 4/471) to the vote, and then the Philippine amendment to the same article (E/CN. 4/472).

11. The CHAIRMAN put to the vote the French proposal that article 7 should be deleted from the draft covenant.

The proposal was adopted by 11 votes to none, with 2 abstentions.

12. The CHAIRMAN said that in view of the Commission's decision it was unnecessary to put the Yugoslav amendment to article 7 to the vote. He then invited the members of the Commission to study the amendments submitted by France and the Philippines (E/CN. 4/471 and E/CN. 4/472), confining their remarks to the text of those amendments and not to the substance.

44. The CHAIRMAN invited the representatives of the Catholic International Union for Social Service and the International Union of Catholic Women's Leagues to state their views.

52. The CHAIRMAN closed the list of speakers which still included the representatives of the United Kingdom, the Philippines, Australia and Yugoslavia.

61. The CHAIRMAN read out and put to the vote paragraph 2 of the French proposal (E/CN. 4/471).

Paragraph 2 of the French proposal was adopted by 8 votes to 4, with 3 abstentions.

62. The CHAIRMAN called for a vote on the proposal of the Philippines (E/CN. 4/472).

The proposal of the Philippines was rejected by 5 votes to 4, with 5 abstentions.

63. The CHAIRMAN said that the Commission would have to vote on the

联合国人权委员会和起草委员会

whole of article 6 during the second reading.

66. The CHAIRMAN called upon the representative of the World Health Organization to make a statement.

【纪要影像】

2.   The CHAIRMAN noted the request of the United Kingdom representative.

3.   The CHAIRMAN invited the Commission to continue the study of article 7. He recalled that several proposals had been submitted to the Commission -- the French delegation's proposal that article 7 should be deleted and the substance of that article incorporated in article 6 (E/CN.4/471), the Yugoslav delegation's proposal that article 7 should be amended (E/CN.4/372), and the amendment to article 6 submitted by the Philippine delegation (E/CN.4/472).

8.   The CHAIRMAN said he would put the various proposals to the vote in the following order: he would first put to the vote the proposal that article 7 should be deleted, and if that were rejected, he would put the Yugoslav amendment to the vote. If the proposal for deletion were adopted, he would put the French amendment to article 6 (E/CN.4/471) to the vote, and then the Philippine amendment to the same article (E/CN.4/472).

11.   The CHAIRMAN put to the vote the French proposal that article 7 should be deleted from the draft covenant.
    The proposal was adopted by 11 votes to none, with 2 abstentions.

12.   The CHAIRMAN said that in view of the Commission's decision it was unnecessary to put the Yugoslav amendment to article 7 to the vote. He then invited the members of the Commission to study the amendments submitted by France and the Philippines (E/CN.4/471 and E/CN.4/472), confining their remarks to the text of these amendments and not to the substance.

图片 1.5.50：张彭春在联合国人权委员会第六届第 183 次会议发言纪要(1)

44.   The CHAIRMAN invited the representatives of the Catholic International Union for Social Service and the International Union of Catholic Women's Leagues to state their views.

52.   The CHAIRMAN closed the list of speakers which still included the representatives of the United Kingdom, the Philippines, Australia and Yugoslavia.

61.   The CHAIRMAN read out and put to the vote paragraph 2 of the French proposal (E/CN.4/471).
    Paragraph 2 of the French proposal was adopted by 8 votes to 4, with 3 abstentions.

62.   The CHAIRMAN called for a vote on the proposal of the Philippines (E/CN.4/472).
    The proposal of the Philippines was rejected by 5 votes to 4, with 3 abstentions.

63.   The CHAIRMAN said that the Commission would have to vote on the whole of article 6 during the second reading.

66.   The CHAIRMAN called upon the representative of the World Health Organization to make a statement.

图片 1.5.51：张彭春在联合国人权委员会第六届第 183 次会议发言纪要(2)

【纪要译文】

2. 主席注意到英国代表的请求。

3. 主席请委员会继续研究第 7 条。他回顾说，多项提案已经提交至委员会——法国代表团关于删除第 7 条并将该条的实质内容纳入第 6 条的提案（E/CN.4/471），南斯拉夫代表团关于修改第 7 条的提案（E/CN.4/372），以及菲律宾代表团提交的对第 6 条的修正案（E/CN.4/472）。

8. 主席说，他将按以下顺序将各项提案付诸表决：他首先将删除第 7 条的提案付诸表决，如果该提案被否决，他将把南斯拉夫的修正案付诸表决。如果删除的提议获得通过，他将把法国对第 6 条的修正案（E/CN.4/471）付诸表决，然后把菲律宾对同一条的修正案（E/CN.4/472）付诸表决。

11. 主席将法国关于从公约草案中删除第 7 条的提议付诸表决。

该提案以 11 票对 0 票，2 票弃权获得通过。

12. 主席说，鉴于委员会的决定，没有必要将南斯拉夫对第 7 条的修正案付诸表决。然后，他请委员会成员研究法国和菲律宾提交的修正案（E/CN.4/471 和 E/CN.4/472），将其评论限于这些修正案的案文，而不是实质内容。

44. 主席请天主教国际社会服务联合会和天主教妇女联合会的代表陈述他们的观点。

52. 主席宣布发言人名单截止，名单上仍有英国、菲律宾、澳大利亚和南斯拉夫的代表。

61. 主席宣读了法国提案（E/CN.4/471）的第 2 段，并将其付诸表决。

法国提案的第 2 段以 8 票对 4 票，3 票弃权获得通过。

62. 主席要求就菲律宾的提案（E/CN.4/472）进行表决。

菲律宾的提案以 5 票对 4 票，5 票弃权被否决。

63. 主席说，委员会必须在二读时对整个第 6 条进行表决。

66. 主席请世界卫生组织的代表发言。

35. 张彭春在人权委员会第六届第 184 次会议发言纪要

1950 年 5 月 9 日下午 2 时 30 分至 5 时 40 分,联合国人权委员会第六届第 184 次会议,在纽约成功湖召开,本次会议的主要议题是继续讨论国际人权公约草案第 II 部分插入附加条款的建议案。张彭春先生参加了本次会议,并担任会议主席,以主席的身份在会议上发言,其具体发言内容① 会议纪要、纪要影像和纪要译文如下:

【会议纪要】

1. The CHAIRMAN opened the discussion on proposals for additional articles to be inserted in part II of the draft covenant.

【纪要影像】

1.　　The CHAIRMAN opened the discussion on proposals for additional articles to be inserted in part II of the draft covenant.

图片 1.5.52:张彭春在联合国人权委员会第六届第 184 次会议发言纪要

【纪要译文】

1. 主席宣布开始讨论关于在公约草案第二部分增加条款的提案。

---

① UN Document:E/CN. 4/SR. 184, p. 3.

36. 张彭春在人权委员会第六届第 186 次会议发言纪要

1950 年 5 月 10 日下午 3 时至 6 时 30 分,联合国人权委员会第六届第 186 次会议,在纽约成功湖召开,本次会议的主要议题是继续讨论国际人权公约草案。张彭春先生参加了本次会议,并在会议上先后多次发言,其具体发言内容①会议纪要、纪要影像和纪要译文如下:

【会议纪要】

30. Mr. CHANG (China) supported the United States, Greek and Uruguayan representatives in their comments on the consolidated draft resolution (E/CN. 4/484). He in turn had several specific amendments to propose to that text. In paragraph 1 he suggested that the word "draft" should be inserted in the first line before the words "Covenant on human rights". Then the following phrase "on the drafting of which it has been engaged for several years" and the phrase "as it does" should be deleted. The words "some of" should be inserted in the second line before the words "the fundamental rights". In the third line the phrase "and to certain essential civil freedoms" should also be deleted because of the difficulty of defining that category of freedoms. In the fourth line the word "Standard" and in the fifth line the words "and secure the application of its primary principles as early as possible" should also be deleted. He objected to the word "Standard" for the reasons which had already been given; the last phrase should be deleted because the articles of the Universal Declaration were not, properly speaking, principles. The word "primary" was inadequate

---

① UN Document: E/CN. 4/SR. 186, p. 9, p. 17, p. 19.

and the phrase "secure the application" was vague.

31. He also suggested that paragraph 2 should be amended to read "consideration of additional Covenants and measures dealing with economic, social, cultural, political and other human rights, and to this end". He objected to the original formulation for the reasons given by the representative of Uruguay.

33. Mr. CASSIN (France) said that most of the Chinese amendments were acceptable. He would prefer, however, to retain the phrase "to certain essential civil freedoms" for that phrase had a specific meaning in French law. He would not insist on maintaining the last phrase of paragraph 1 if the Commission supported the Chinese amendment for deletion. He thought the Chinese amendment to paragraph 2 was helpful. It should be made perfectly clear, however, that categories of rights existed in fact and that the conditions of implementation of various rights required that some order should be imposed. He therefore would prefer to retain the phrase "by categories" although he would accept another suitable wording if that could be found.

70. Mr. CHANG (China), on a point of order, stated that inasmuch as the Chairman had called for the actuall vote on the amendment, further discussion thereon was out of order.

74. Mr. CHANG (China) stated that he would not press that part of his amendment, particularly in view of the fact that the phrase concerned contained the qualifying word "certain".

84. Mr. CHANG (China) agreed with the French representative. He would also invite attention to the words "additional covenants and measures" which formed the crux of the paragraph under consideration.

30.   Mr. CHANG (China) supported the United States, Greek and Uruguayan representatives in their comments on the consolidated draft resolution (E/CN.4/484). He in turn had several specific amendments to propose to that text. In paragraph 1 he suggested that the word "draft" should be inserted in the first line before the words "Covenant on human rights". Then the following phrase "on the drafting of which it has been engaged for several years" and the phrase "as it does" should be deleted. The words "some of" should be inserted in the second line before the words "the fundamental rights". In the third line the phrase "and to certain essential civil freedoms" should also be deleted because of the difficulty of defining that category of freedoms. In the fourth line the word "Standard" and in the fifth line the words "and secure the application of its primary principles as early as possible" should also be deleted. He objected to the word "Standard" for the reasons which had already been given; the last phrase should be deleted because the articles of the Universal Declaration were not, properly speaking, principles. The word "primary" was inadequate and the phrase "secure the application" was vague.
31.   He also suggested that paragraph 2 should be amended to read "consideration of additional Covenants and measures dealing with economic, social, cultural, political and other human rights, and to this end". He objected to the original formulation for the reasons given by the representative of Uruguay.

图片 1.5.53：张彭春在联合国人权委员会第六届第 186 次会议发言纪要（1）

33.   Mr. CASSIN (France) said that most of the Chinese amendments were acceptable. He would prefer, however, to retain the phrase "to certain essential civil freedoms" for that phrase had a specific meaning in French law. He would not insist on maintaining the last phrase of paragraph 1 if the Commission supported the Chinese amendment for deletion. He thought the Chinese amendment to paragraph 2 was helpful. It should be made perfectly clear, however, that categories of rights existed in fact and that the conditions of implementation of various rights required that some order should be imposed. He therefore would prefer to retain the phrase "by categories" although he would accept another suitable wording if that could be found.

70.   Mr. CHANG (China), on a point of order, stated that inasmuch as the Chairman had called for the actual vote on the amendment, further discussion thereon was out of order.

74.   Mr. CHANG (China) stated that he would not press that part of his amendment, particularly in view of the fact that the phrase concerned contained the qualifying word "certain".

84.   Mr. CHANG (China) agreed with the French representative. He would also invite attention to the words "additional covenants and measures" which formed the crux of the paragraph under consideration.

图片 1.5.54：张彭春在联合国人权委员会第六届第 186 次会议发言纪要（2）

【纪要译文】

30. 张先生（中国）支持美国、希腊和乌拉圭代表对综合决议草案的评论（E/CN.4/484）。他又对该案文提出了几项具体的修正案。在第 1 款中,他建议在第一行"人权公约"之后插入"草案"一词。^① 然后,应删除以下短语"委员会已就其起草工作进行了数年"和短语"正如其所做的那样"。应在第二行"基本权利"之前插入"一些"一词。第三行中的"和某些基本的公民自由"一语也应删除,因为很难界定这类自由。第四行中的"标准"一词和第五行中的"并确保尽早适用其主要原则"也应删除。他反对"标准"一词,理由已经说过了;最后一句应该删除,因为《世界人权宣言》的条款严格来说不是原则。"主要"一词是不够的,"保障适用程序"这个短语也很模糊。

31. 他还建议将第 2 段修改为"审议关于经济、社会、文化、政治和其他人权的其他公约和措施,并为此目的"。出于乌拉圭代表所述的原因,他反对最初的表述。

33. 卡森先生(法国)说,中国的大多数修正是可以接受的。然而,他倾向于保留"某些基本的公民自由"这一短语,因为该短语在法国法律中有特定的含义。如果委员会支持删除中国的修正案,他不会坚持保留第 1款的最后一句。他认为中国对第 2 款的修正是有帮助的。然而,应该十分明确的是,权利的类别实际上是存在的,而且各种权利的实施条件要求必须实行某种秩序。因此,他倾向于保留"按类别"这一短语,尽管如果可能的话,他会接受另一种合适的措辞。

70. 张先生(中国)就程序问题发言说,鉴于主席要求对修正案进行实际表决,进一步的讨论是不合适的。

74. 张先生(中国)说,他不会坚持他的修正案的这一部分,特别是考虑到有关的短语含有"某些"这个修饰词。

84. 张先生(中国)同意法国代表的意见。他还提请注意"附加公约和措施"一词,这是正在审议的这一段的核心。

---

① 编著者注:根据上下语境,中英文表达方式有所不同:这里英文习惯上是使用"before"(之前),而在中文语中则使用"之后",这是由于中英两种语言词语搭配习惯不同。

37. 张彭春在人权委员会
第六届第 189 次会议发言纪要

1950 年 5 月 12 日上午 11 时 15 分至下午 1 时,联合国人权委员会第六届第 189 次会议,在纽约成功湖召开,本次会议的主要议题是继续讨论国际人权公约草案(第 4 条、第 5 条和第 6 条)。张彭春先生参加了本次会议,并在会议上发言,其具体发言内容①会议纪要、纪要影像和纪要译文如下:

【会议纪要】

17. Mr. CHANG (China) wanted the Commission to vote on the words "and voting". The members of the committee ought to be highly respected and ought therefore to be elected by the majority of States parties to the covenant.

【纪要影像】

17.　　Mr. CHANG (China) wanted the Commission to vote on the words "and voting". The members of the committee ought to be highly respected and ought therefore to be elected by the majority of States parties to the covenant.

图片 1.5.55:张彭春在联合国人权委员会第六届第 189 次会议发言纪要

【纪要译文】

17. 张先生(中国)希望委员会就"和表决"一词进行表决。委员会成员应该受到高度尊重,因此应该由《公约》大多数缔约国选举产生。

---

① UN Document: E/CN. 4/SR. 189, p. 5.

38. 张彭春在人权委员会
第六届第 192 次会议发言纪要

1950 年 5 月 15 日上午 11 时至下午 1 时,联合国人权委员会第六届第 192 次会议,在纽约成功湖召开,本次会议的主要议题是继续讨论国际人权公约草案及实施措施。张彭春先生参加了本次会议,并在会议上发言,其具体发言内容①会议纪要、纪要影像和纪要译文如下:

【会议纪要】

46. Mr. CHANG (China) thought that insertion of the United Kingdom text would be superfluous at that stage. The International Court usually took from several months to a year to issue an advisory opinion: such a lengthy procedure was hardly appropriate for resolving the points of law likely to come up in the course of the committee's work. If fundamental differences of opinion requiring international arbitration should arise, the States concerned would in any event be free to put them before the Court.

57. Mr. CHANG (China) remarked that the second United Kingdom proposal was still less acceptable than the first, since it tended even more to confuse the character of the committee's functions. In creating the committee, the Commission had not intended to set up a juridical organ but a body of statesmen whose court of appeal would be the public opinion of the world. Both the United Kingdom proposals allowed that original intention to become obscured.

---

① UN Document: E/CN. 4/SR. 192, p. 13, p. 15.

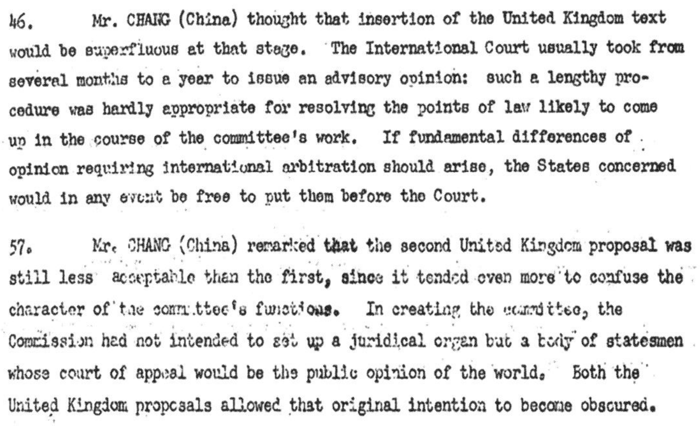

46.   Mr. CHANG (China) thought that insertion of the United Kingdom text would be superfluous at that stage.   The International Court usually took from several months to a year to issue an advisory opinion: such a lengthy procedure was hardly appropriate for resolving the points of law likely to come up in the course of the committee's work.   If fundamental differences of opinion requiring international arbitration should arise, the States concerned would in any event be free to put them before the Court.

57.   Mr. CHANG (China) remarked that the second United Kingdom proposal was still less acceptable than the first, since it tended even more to confuse the character of the committee's functions.   In creating the committee, the Commission had not intended to set up a juridical organ but a body of statesmen whose court of appeal would be the public opinion of the world.   Both the United Kingdom proposals allowed that original intention to become obscured.

图片 1.5.56：张彭春在联合国人权委员会第六届第 192 次会议发言纪要

【纪要译文】

46. 张先生(中国)认为,在现阶段插入英国的案文是多余的。国际法院通常需要几个月到一年的时间来发表咨询意见;如此漫长的程序对于解决委员会工作过程中可能出现的法律问题几乎是不合适的。如果出现需要国际仲裁的根本意见分歧,有关国家无论如何都可以向法院提出。

57. 张先生(中国)说,英国的第二项建议比第一项建议更不可接受,因为它更容易混淆委员会职能的性质。在设立委员会时,委员会并不打算设立一个司法机关,而是一个政治家团体,其上诉法院将是世界公众舆论。英国的两项提案都模糊了这一初衷。

39. 张彭春在人权委员会
第六届第 193 次会议发言纪要

1950 年 5 月 15 日下午 2 时 30 分至 6 时 40 分,联合国人权委员会第六届第 193 次会议,在纽约成功湖召开,本次会议的主要议题是继续讨论国际人权公约草案及实施措施、澳大利亚决议草案以及序言及第 1 条和第 2 条的内容。张彭春先生参加了本次会议,并在会议上发言,其具体发言内容①会议纪要、纪要影像和纪要译文如下:

【会议纪要】

17. Mr. CHANG (China) felt that the French amendment was couched in too general terms. In particular, it should not refer to proposals of an unoffical nature.

【纪要影像】

17.   Mr. CHANG (China) felt that the French amendment was couched in too general terms.   In particular, it should not refer to proposals of an unofficial nature.

图片 1.5.57:张彭春在联合国人权委员会第六届第 193 次会议发言纪要

【纪要译文】

17. 张先生(中国)认为法国的修正案措辞过于笼统。特别是,它不应提及非官方性质的提议。

---

① UN Document: E/CN. 4/SR. 193, p. 6.

40. 张彭春在人权委员会
第六届第 195 次会议发言纪要

1950 年 5 月 16 日下午 2 时 30 分至 7 时 10 分,联合国人权委员会第六届第 195 次会议,在纽约成功湖召开,本次会议的主要议题是继续讨论国际人权公约草案(第 2 条、第 3 条和第 4 条)。张彭春先生参加了本次会议,并在会议上发言,其具体发言内容①会议纪要、纪要影像和纪要译文如下:

【会议纪要】

16. Mr. CHANG(China)thought there was no point in inserting the word "domestic". He therefore suggested that the word should be deleted.

【纪要影像】

16.   Mr. CHANG (China) thought there was no point in inserting the word "domestic".   He therefore suggested that the word should be deleted.

图片 1.5.58:张彭春在联合国人权委员会第六届第 195 次会议发言纪要

【纪要译文】

16. 张先生(中国)认为插入"国内的"一词没有意义。因此,他建议删除该词。

---

① UN Document:E/CN.4/SR.195, p. 5.

41. 张彭春在人权委员会
第六届第 197 次会议发言纪要

1950 年 5 月 17 日下午 2 时 15 分至 6 时 50 分,联合国人权委员会第六届第 197 次会议,在纽约成功湖召开,本次会议的主要议题是继续讨论国际人权公约草案(第 24 条、第 25 条和第 26 条)。张彭春先生参加了本次会议,并在会议上发言,其具体发言内容①会议纪要、纪要影像和纪要译文如下:

【会议纪要】

13. Mr. CHANG (China) said that, having heard the explanation given by the representative of Belgium, he could not support the Belgian text. Indeed, it was essential not to give the covenant a bilateral character and, on the contrary, to lay stress on its wider scope.

109. Mr. CHANG (China) was prepared to support the United Kingdom amendment but thought that approval of an amendment to the covenant made by the General Assembly implied discussion of that amendment. If the United Kingdom representative would accept that interpretation, he was prepared to vote in favour of the United Kingdom proposal.

118. Mr. CHANG (China) asked whether the participation of non-member States would include the right to vote.

---

① UN Document: E/CN. 4/SR. 197, p. 5, p. 21, p. 23.

13. Mr. CHANG (China) said that, having heard the explanation given by the representative of Belgium, he could not support the Belgian text. Indeed, it was essential not to give the covenant a bilateral character and, on the contrary, to lay stress on its wider scope.

109. Mr. CHANG (China) was prepared to support the United Kingdom amendment but thought that approval of an amendment to the covenant made by the General Assembly implied discussion of that amendment. If the United Kingdom representative would accept that interpretation, he was prepared to vote in favour of the United Kingdom proposal.

118. Mr. CHANG (China) asked whether the participation of non-member States would include the right to vote.

图片 1.5.59：张彭春在联合国人权委员会第六届第 197 次会议发言纪要

【纪要译文】

13. 张先生(中国)说,听了比利时代表的解释后,他不能支持比利时的案文。事实上,至关重要的是不要赋予《公约》双边性质,相反,要强调其更广泛的范围。

109. 张先生(中国)准备支持英国的修正案,但认为大会批准《公约》的修正案意味着对该修正案的讨论。如果英国代表接受这种解释,他准备投票赞成英国的提议。

118. 张先生(中国)问,非会员国的参与是否包括表决权。

42. 张彭春在人权委员会第六届第 198 次会议发言纪要

1950 年 5 月 18 日上午 10 时 15 分至下午 1 时 10 分,联合国人权委员会第六届第 198 次会议,在纽约成功湖召开,本次会议的主要议题是继续讨论国际人权公约草案及法国、黎巴嫩、丹麦和英国分别提出的决议草案。张彭春先生参加了本次会议,并在会议上发言,其具体发言内容①会议纪要、纪要影像和纪要译文如下:

【会议纪要】

14. Mr. CHANG (China) thought the French draft resolution was a praiseworthy attempt to promote the implementation of the Universal Declaration on a wider scale than that envisaged in the covenant. He held no strong views on the proposed text, but would suggest that in the third paragraph the phrase "by their national law" should be deleted. The resolution could then be interpreted to include other, positive measures for promoting the observance of human rights, in addition to the purely negative approach of fostering respect for those rights through legislation. He had often expressed the view that in its work the Commission unduly emphasized the negative aspects of the implementation of human rights, and he had pointed out that such an approach might encourage states merely to engage in recriminations. In the interests of ensuring the effective observance of human rights, he would stress that educational measures in their widest sense, and other constructive programmes, should not be overlooked.

15. He had several drafting changes to suggest to the French proposal. It might be better to insert the sixth paragraph after either the second or the third paragraph, as it would be more logical to establish the regulations governing the contents of the annual report before laying down the mechanical procedure for transmitting them to the proper bodies. He also thought that the fourth and fifth paragraphs were superfluous and should be deleted.

16. He urged the Commission to consider the implications of the French draft resolution most carefully and to attempt to provide for constructive meas-

---

① UN Document: E/CN. 4/SR. 198, pp. 5-6.

ures to implement the principles proclaimed by the Declaration. If some positive results could be achieved, the entire cause of human rights would be advanced, but if it became necessary to rely entirely on legislative measures to a-
chieve those ends, he thought there was little hope that the Commission's efforts
would be highly successful.

17. The CHAIRMAN, speaking as representative of the United States of
America, said she agreed with the Chinese amendment to delete the phrase "by
their national law", in the third paragraph.

【纪要影像】

14.   Mr. CHANG (China) thought the French draft resolution was a
praiseworthy attempt to promote the implementation of the Universal Declaration
on a wider scale than that envisaged in the covenant. He held no strong views
on the proposed text, but would suggest that in the third paragraph the ·
phrase "by their national law" should be deleted. The resolution could then
be interpreted to include other, positive measures for promoting the observance
of human rights, in addition to the purely negative approach of fostering
respect for those rights through legislation. He had often expressed the
view that in its work the Commission unduly emphasized the negative aspects
of the implementation of human rights, and he had pointed out that such an
approach might encourage states merely to engage in recriminations.   In the
interests of ensuring the effective observance of human rights, he would stress
that educational measures in their widest sense, and other constructive
programmes, should not be overlooked.

图片 1.5.60：张彭春在联合国人权委员会第六届第 198 次会议发言纪要（1）

15.　　He had several drafting changes to suggest to the French proposal. It might be better to insert the sixth paragraph after either the second or the third paragraph, as it would be more logical to establish the regulations governing the contents of the annual report before laying down the mechanical procedure for transmitting them to the proper bodies. He also thought that the fourth and fifth paragrahs were superfluous and should be deleted.

16.　　He urged the Commission to consider the implications of the French draft resolution most carefully and to attempt to provide for constructive measures to implement the principles proclaimed by the Declaration. If some positive results could be achieved, the entire cause of human rights would be advanced, but if it became necessary to rely entirely on legislative measures to achieve those ends, he thought there was little hope that the Commission's efforts would be highly successful.

17.　　The CHAIRMAN, speaking as representative of the United States of America, said she agreed with the Chinese amendment to delete the phrase "by their national law", in the third paragraph.

图片 1.5.61：张彭春在联合国人权委员会第六届第 198 次会议发言纪要(2)

【纪要译文】

14. 张先生(中国)认为,法国的决议草案是在比《公约》设想的更大范围内促进落实《世界人权宣言》的一次值得称赞的尝试。他对拟议案文没有强烈的意见,但建议删除第三段中的"根据其国家法律"一语。除了通过立法促进尊重人权的纯粹消极的方法之外,该决议还可以被解释为包括促进尊重人权的其他积极措施。他经常表示,委员会在其工作中不适当地强调了落实人权的消极方面,他指出,这种做法可能只会鼓励各国相互指责。为了确保有效尊重人权,他强调不应忽视最广义的教育措施和其他建设性方案。

15. 他对法国的提案有几处文字上的改动。在第二段或第三段之后插入第六段可能更好,因为在规定将年度报告转交给适当机构的机械程序之前,先制定关于年度报告内容的条例更符合逻辑。他还认为第四段和第五段是多余的,应当删除。

16. 他敦促委员会非常仔细地考虑法国决议草案的影响,并试图提供建设性措施来落实《宣言》宣布的原则。如果能够取得一些积极成果,整个人权事业将会得到推进,但是如果必须完全依靠立法措施来实现这些目标,他认为委员会的努力取得高度成功的希望不大。

17. 主席作为美国代表发言说,她同意中国的修正案,删除第三段中的"根据其国家法律"一语。

43. 张彭春在人权委员会
第六届第 199 次会议发言纪要

1950 年 5 月 18 日下午 2 时 30 分至 7 时 25 分,联合国人权委员会第六届第 199 次会议,在纽约成功湖召开,本次会议的主要议题是继续讨论国际人权公约草案等。张彭春先生参加了本次会议,并在会议上发言,其具体发言内容①会议纪要、纪要影像和纪要译文如下:

【会议纪要】

8. Mr. CHANG (China) thought that the Lebanese proposal should be carried unanimously. In his opinion, there was no point in informing the Economic and Social Council that differences of opinion had arisen in the Commission on certain problems of major importance, because the Council would have before it the Commission's report and the summary records of its meetings. He also thought that the last paragraph of the United Kingdom draft resolution was pointless. It would be sufficient to transmit the Commission's report to the Council, which would decide for itself the steps to be taken.

9. He approved the first paragraph of the Lebanese draft resolution, and proposed that the following words would be added to that paragraph: "... and measures of implementation". He also suggested that the words "continued in annex A of this resolution" should be deleted.

22. Mr. CHANG (China) thought that the Commission should submit to

---

① UN Document: E/CN. 4/SR. 199, p. 5, p. 8.

the Economic and Social Council a draft resolution couched in the simplest terns; the Lebanese text would answer that purpose admirably. He also endorsed the Greek proposal for the inclusion of the third paragraph of the United Kingdom draft resolution as the last sentence of the report. Finally, in his opinion the Commission should draw the attention of the Council to the summary records of its meetings.

【纪要影像】

```
8.      Mr. CHANG (China)  thought that the Lebanese proposal should be  carried
unanimously.  In his opinion, there was no point in informing the Economic and
Social Council that differences of opinion had arisen in the Commission on certain
problems of major importance, because the Council would have before it the Com-
mission's report and the summary  records of its meetings.  He also  thought that
the last paragraph of the United Kingdom draft resolution was pointless.  It
would be sufficient to transmit the Commission's report to the Council, which
would decide for itself the steps to be taken.
9.      He approved the first paragraph of the  Lebanese draft resolution, and
proposed that the following words would be added to  that paragraph: "...and
measures of implementation".  He also suggested that the words "continued in
annex A of this resolution" should be deleted.

22.      Mr. CHANG (China) thought that the Commission should submit to the
Economic and Social Council a draft resolution couched in the simplest terms;
the Lebanese text would answer that purpose admirably. He also endorsed the
Greek proposal for the inclusion of the third paragraph of the United Kingdom
draft resolution as the last sentence of the report. Finally, in his opinion
the Commission should draw the attentionof the Council to the summary records
of its meetings.
```

图片1.5.62：张彭春在联合国人权委员会第六届第199次会议发言纪要

【纪要译文】

8.张先生(中国)认为黎巴嫩提案应获得一致通过。他认为,没有必要向经济及社会理事会通报委员会在某些重大问题上出现的意见分歧,因为理事会将收到委员会的报告及其会议的简要记录。他还认为英国决议草案的最后一段毫无意义。将委员会的报告转递给理事会就足够了,理事会将自己决定要采取的步骤。

9.他批准了黎巴嫩决议草案的第一段,并建议在该段中增加以下文字:"……和实施措施。"他还建议删除"本决议附件A中继续"等字。

22.张先生(中国)认为,委员会应向经济及社会理事会提交一份措辞最简洁的决议草案;黎巴嫩案文很好地满足了这一目的。他还赞同希腊关于将英国决议草案第三段作为报告最后一句的提议。最后,他认为委员会应提请理事会注意其会议纪要。

44. 张彭春在人权委员会
第六届第 201 次会议发言纪要

1950 年 5 月 19 日下午 2 时 30 分至 6 时 5 分,联合国人权委员会第六届第 201 次会议,在纽约成功湖召开,本次会议的主要议题是第二遍审议国际人权公约草案、审议法国决议草案及通过人权委员会第六届会议报告。张彭春先生参加了本次会议,并在会议上发言,其具体发言内容①会议纪要、纪要影像和纪要译文如下:

【会议纪要】

81. Mr. CHANG (China) said that it had been a pleasure for the members of the Commission to work under the inspiring leadership of the Chairman, whose widom and humanitarian spirit had greatly facilitated the accomplishment of their task.

【纪要影像】

81.　　Mr. CHANG (China) said that it had been a pleasure for the members of the Commission to work under the inspiring leadership of the Chairman, whose wisdom and humanitarian spirit had greatly facilitated the accomplishment of their task.

图片 1.5.63:张彭春在联合国人权委员会第六届第 201 次会议发言纪要

---

① UN Document:E/CN.4/SR.201, p. 15.

【纪要译文】

81. 张先生(中国)说,委员会成员很高兴在主席令人鼓舞的领导下工作,主席的智慧和人道主义精神大大促进了他们任务的完成。

联大第三委员会及联大全会

联大第三委员会(The UNGA Third Committee)Social,

Humanitarian and Cultural Questions

表2:张彭春在联大第三委员会及联大全会的发言情况

届会名称	会议时间	会议地点	会议总次数(会次)	档案资料情况	张彭春会议发言情况
联大第三委员会第一届会议	1946-1-11—1946-2-10;1946-10-24—1946-12-12	伦敦圣公会总部大楼;纽约成功湖	11(1—11)37(12—48)	会议纪要	在3次会议发言
联大第三委员会第二届会议	1947-4-28;1947-9-16—1947-11-11	纽约法拉盛草地公园;纽约成功湖	44(49—82)	会议纪要	在6次会议上发言
联大第三委员会第三届会议(第一部分)	1948-4-16—1948-12-8	纽约法拉盛草地公园+纽约成功湖+巴黎夏洛宫	98(83—180)	会议纪要	在45次会议上发言
联大第三委员会第三届会议(第二部分)	1949-4-6—1949-5-12	纽约成功湖	49(181—229)	会议纪要	在11次会议上发言
联大第三委员会第四届会议	1949-9-20—1949-11-28	纽约成功湖	40(230—269)	会议纪要	在1次会议上发言
联大第三委员会第五届会议	1950-9-20—1950-12-11	纽约成功湖	53(270—345)	会议纪要	在15次会议上发言
联大全体会议	1948-12-9—1948-12-10	巴黎夏洛宫	4(180—183)	会议纪要	在1次会议上发言
合计	大约6年	伦敦、纽约、巴黎等地	349	会议纪要	在82次会议上发言

第一章　联大第三委员会第一届会议

联大第三委员会(The United Nations General Assembly Third Committee,指的是社会、人道主义和文化委员会,英文名称为:the Social, Humanitarian and Cultural Committee)第一届会议,于 1946 年 1 月 11 日下午 3 时,在英国伦敦圣公会总部大楼开幕,本届会议包括两部分,共召开了 48 次会议。其中,第一部分包括 1946 年 1 月 11 日至 2 月 10 日,在英国伦敦圣公会总部大楼召开了 11 次会议(即第 1 次至第 11 次会议)。第二部分包括 1946 年 10 月 24 日至 12 月 12 日,在美国纽约成功湖召开了 37 次会议(即第 12 次至第 48 次会议)。这些会议重点讨论了难民问题及国际难民组织的建立、妇女的政治权利等问题。此外,于 1946 年 1 月 22 日晚上 5 时至 7 时和 1946 年 1 月 23 日上午 10 时 30 分至下午 12 时 55 分,与联大第二委员会联合召开了两次会议。

参加联大第三委员会第一部分的中国代表成员共有 5 位,其中张彭春先生(Mr. P. C. Chang)为首席代表,而参加第二部分会议的中国代表团成员有了调整和充实,共有 9 位成员,其中郭泰祺博士(Dr. Quo Tai-chi)为首席代表(见图 2.1.1)。

China:
H.E. Mr. P. C. Chang.
H.E. Mr. Victor Chi-tsai Hoo.
H.E. Mr. Lone Liang.
Mr. Kuo Yu-shou.
Mr. Szeming Sze.

China
H.E. Dr. Quo Tai-chi
H.E. Dr. P. C. Chang
H.E. Mr. C. J. Pao
Dr. Chang Chung-fu
Dr. Y. C. Yang
Mr. Hsuan-tsui Liu
Dr. Stephen Chao-yin Pan
Dr. Szeming Sze
Mrs. W. S. New

图片 2.1.1 联大第三委员会第一届会议中国代表团成员名单

　　张彭春先生参加了本届两部分全部会议,并在第 10 次会议[①]、第 14 次会议[②]和第 15 次会议[③]上发言。另有四位中国代表的发言出现在本届会议纪要中,包括郭泰祺先生在第 21 次会议[④]和第 46 次会议[⑤]上发言,杨先生(Mr. Yang)在第 21 次会议[⑥]、第 25 次会议[⑦]、第 35 次会议[⑧]、第 41 次会议[⑨]和第 48 次会议[⑩]上发言,牛夫人(Mrs. New)在第 24 次会议[⑪]上发言,而施思明先生(Mr. Szeming Sze)在第 33 次会议[⑫]上发言。现将张彭春先生的发言内容整理如下:

1. 张彭春在联大第三委员会
第一届第 10 次会议上的发言

　　联合国的第三委员会第一届第 10 次会议,于 1946 年 2 月 9 日上午 10 时 30 分,在英国伦敦圣公会总部大楼召开。本次会议讨论的是古巴代表所提出的关于建立文化委员会的决议草案,中国代表张彭春参加了本次会议,并在会议上发言,对古巴决议草案持反对态度,最后,该古巴建议案,以

---

① UN Document：A/C. 3/SR/10, p. 29.

② UN Document：A/C. 3/SR/14, p. 75.

③ UN Document：A/C. 3/SR/15, p. 84.

④ UN Document：A/C. 3/SR/21, p. 119.

⑤ UN Document：A/C. 3/SR/46, p. 298, p. 300.

⑥ UN Document：A/C. 3/SR/21, p. 121.

⑦ UN Document：A/C. 3/SR/25, p. 143.

⑧ UN Document：A/C. 3/SR/35, p. 201.

⑨ UN Document：A/C. 3/SR/41, p. 254.

⑩ UN Document：A/C. 3/SR/48, p. 315.

⑪ UN Document：A/C. 3/SR/24, p. 132.

⑫ UN Document：A/C. 3/SR/33, pp. 190-191, p. 193.

21 票对 13 票被否决。① 张彭春先生的具体发言内容②会议纪要、纪要影像和纪要译文如下：

【会议纪要】

Mr. CHANG (China) said that, while appreciating the Cuban delegate's suggestion, he was of the opinion that the newly formed Economic and Social Council already had sufficient tasks on hand; he urged that UNESCO should be given an opportunity to carry out the functions entrusted to it and suggested that the proposal to set up a cultural commission might be discussed at a future session of the Economic and Social Council.

【纪要影像】

Mr. CHANG (China) said that, while appreciating the Cuban delegate's suggestion, he was of the opinion that the newly formed Economic and Social Council already had sufficient tasks on hand; he urged that UNESCO should be given an opportunity to carry out the functions entrusted to it and suggested that the proposal to set up a cultural commission might be discussed at.a future session of the Economic and Social Council.

图片 2.1.2：张彭春在联大第三委员会第二届第 10 次会议发言纪要

【纪要译文】

张先生(中国)说,虽然他赞赏古巴代表的建议,但他认为新成立的经济及社会理事会手头已经有足够的任务;他敦促联合国教科文组织有机会履行赋予它的职能,并建议在经济及社会理事会下届会议上讨论设立文化委员会的建议。

① UN Document：A/C. 3/SR/10, p. 29.
② UN Document：A/C. 3/SR/10, p. 29.

2. 张彭春在联大第三委员会 第一届第 14 次会议上的发言

联大第三委员会第一届第 14 次会议，于 1946 年 11 月 2 日下午 3 时，在纽约成功湖召开，本次会议讨论联合国经社理事会关于将国联在行使关于麻醉药品国际协议、公约、议定书方面的权利移交联合国的报告。中国代表张彭春参加了本次会议，并在会议上第一个发言，其具体发言内容①会议纪要、纪要影像和纪要译文如下：

【会议纪要】

Mr. CHANG（China）pointed out that China had always been in the forefront as regards measures adopted for the international control of narcotic drugs. He therefore invited the Committee to adopt the draft resolution and approve the Protocol submitted to it. The signing of this Protocol during the present session of the Assembly would entail its immediate application and prevent any interruption in the international control of narcotic drugs.

---

① UN Document：A/C. 3/SR/14, p. 75.

【纪要影像】

> Mr. CHANG (China) pointed out that China had always been in the forefront as regards measures adopted for the international control of narcotic drugs. He therefore invited the Committee to adopt the draft resolution and approve the Protocol submitted to it. The signing of this Protocol during the present session of the Assembly would entail its immediate application and prevent any interruption in the international control of narcotic drugs.

图片 2.1.3:张彭春在联大第三委员会第一届第 14 次会议发言纪要

【纪要译文】

张先生(中国)指出,中国在采取国际麻醉药品管制措施方面一直走在前列。因此,他请委员会通过该决议草案并核准提交给它的议定书。在大会本届会议期间签署该议定书将需要立即实施该议定书,并防止麻醉药品国际管制的任何中断。

3. 张彭春在联大第三委员会第一届第 15 次会议上的发言

联大第三委员会第一届第 15 次会议,于 1946 年 11 月 4 日下午 4 时,在纽约成功湖召开,本次会议的主要议题是继续讨论经济及社会理事会关于国际红十字会的决议、讨论经济及社会理事会关于难民问题的报告和审议国际难民组织章程草案(A/127 号文件)。中国代表张彭春参加了本次

会议,并在会议上发言,其具体发言内容①会议纪要、纪要影像和纪要译文如下:

【会议纪要】

Mr. ARGYROPOULOS (Greece) and Mr. CHANG (China) emphasized the disadvantages of simultaneous interpretation.

【纪要影像】

Mr. ARGYROPOULOS (Greece) and Mr. CHANG (China) emphasized the disadvantages of simultaneous interpretation.

图片 2.1.4:张彭春在联大第三委员会第一届第 15 次会议发言纪要

【纪要译文】

阿伊罗普洛斯(Argyropoulos)先生(希腊)和张先生(中国)强调了同声传译的缺点。

---

① UN Document:A/C.3/SR/15, p. 84.

第二章 联大第三委员会第二届会议

联大第三委员会第二届会议,于 1947 年 9 月 16 日在法拉盛草地公园开幕(第 50 次会议),本届其后各次会议在成功湖举行,本届最后一次会议(第 82 次会议)于 1947 年 11 月 11 日在成功湖闭幕。值得说明的是,在本届会议召开之前,联大第三委员会于 1947 年 4 月 28 日在法拉盛草地公园召开了一次特别会议,即第 49 次会议。而这次特别会议通常也计入第二届会议,因此,本届共召开 44 次会议(即第 49 次至第 82 次会议)。

其中,中国代表张彭春参加了本届会议,并在本届第 55 次会议、第 57 次会议、第 58 次会议、第 59 次会议、第 60 次会议和第 67 次会议上发言。另有三位中国代表的发言出现在本届会议纪要中,包括杨先生(Mr. YANG)、牛夫人(Mrs. New)和施思明先生(Mr. Szeming Sze)。现将张彭春先生在本届各次会议上的发言内容整理如下:

1. 张彭春在联大第三委员会 第二届第 55 次会议上的发言

联大第三委员会第一届第 55 次会议,于 1947 年 9 月 29 日下午 3 时 30 分至晚上 6 时 10 分,在纽约成功湖召开,本次会议讨论联合国经社理事会报告的第 III 章内容,涉及到联合国文件:A/382,A/C. 3/152,A/C. 3/157。中国代表张彭春参加了本次会议,并在会议上发言,其具体发言内容①会议纪要、纪要影像和纪要译文如下:

---

① UN Document:A/C. 3/SR/55, p. 32.

【会议纪要】

Mr. CHANG (China) said that China reserved its right to speak on this question but he wished to draw attention to a point in the report of the Economic and Social Council which seemed important to him; namely, the question of narcotic drugs. The problem of synthetic drugs was urgent, and it was expedient strictly to limit and control their manufacture and use. He wished to thank and congratulate the Economic and Social Council, the Commission on Narcotic Drugs and the Secretariat for the striking results which they had achieved in such an important field. He concluded by remarking that not only drugs but sometimes big words were narcotic sand should perhaps be put under control.

【纪要影像】

> Mr. CHANG (China) said that China reserved its right to speak on this question but he wished to draw attention to a point in the report of the Economic and Social Council which seemed important to him; namely, the question of narcotic drugs. The problem of synthetic drugs was urgent, and it was expedient strictly to limit and control their manufacture and use. He wished to thank and congratulate the Economic and Social Council, the Commission on Narcotic Drugs and the Secretariat for the striking results which they had achieved in such an important field. He concluded by remarking that not only drugs but sometimes big words were narcotics and should perhaps be put under control.

图片 2.2.1:张彭春在联大第三委员会第二届第 55 次会议发言纪要

【纪要译文】

张先生(中国)说,中国保留就此问题发言的权利,但他希望提请注意经济及社会理事会报告中对他来说很重要的一点;即麻醉药品问题。合成药物的问题很紧迫,严格限制和控制它们的制造和使用是有利的。他要感谢并祝贺经济及社会理事会、麻醉药品委员会和秘书处在这一重要领域取得的显著成果。他最后指出，不仅毒品，有时大话也是麻醉品，或许应该加以控制。

2. 张彭春在联大第三委员会
第二届第 57 次会议上的发言

　　联大第三委员会第二届第 57 次会议，于 1946 年 10 月 3 日下午 3 时至晚上 6 时 15 分，在纽约成功湖召开，本次会议讨论英国关于社会福利咨询功能的决议草案、讨论有关世界卫生组织的决议草案等。中国代表张彭春参加了本次会议，并在会议上发言，其具体发言内容①会议纪要、纪要影像和纪要译文如下：

【会议纪要】

　　Mr. CHANG (China) said he wished to correct the misleading impression which might have been given by a statement by one member to the effect that if all the advisers recommended in the Secretary-General's programme[2] were sent to China that country's needs would still not be satisfied. China did not wish to absorb all those experts. Too much advice might lead to a certain amount of indigestion. So far China had had the benefit of the work of seven advisers for three months, and two were at present working in China. They had been assigned to a basic programme according to their qualifications. After describing the main points of the programme, Mr. Chang observed that the work of experts had stimulated local efforts, and he would like to point out in the first place that the duration of the service they had given was short; secondly, that the pro-

---

① UN Document：A/C. 3/SR/57, pp. 43-44; p. 48; p. 49.

联大第三委员会及联大全会

441

gramme had been scientifically planned; and thirdly that its implementation had cost the Chinese Government a sum much larger than salaries and expenses of the experts.

He appreciated the motives behind the United Kingdom resolution, but recalled that the Social Commission at its thirty-sixth meeting had disapproved of such a proposal and had decided by a vote of twelve to one in favour of continuing the services and approving the budget suggested by the Secretary-General. He considered the proper procedure was to endorse the Social Commission's conclusions. Finally, while the work of the Security Council might be more spectacular, the work of the Economic and Social Council in promoting such services was fundamental and lasting.

Mr. CHANG (China) opposed the proposal of the representative of New Zealand.

The CHAIRMAN said that it was his intention to provide the Fifth Committee with a summary of the discussions which had been held, irrespective of the decision regarding the New Zealand proposal.

The proposal of the representative of New Zealand was rejected by 36 votes to 5, with 9 abstentions.

Mr. CHANG (China) supported the United Kingdom resolution and recalled that his delegation had submitted the resolution calling for the convening of the International Health Conference. [1]

---

[2] See *Official Records of the Economic and Social Council*, *Second Year*, *Fifth Session*, *Annex 7*.

[1] See *Documents of the United Nations Conference on International Organization* (San Francisco, 1945, volume III, pages 631–632).

【纪要影像】

Mr. CHANG (China) said he wished to correct the misleading impression which might have been given by a statement by one member to the effect that if all the advisers recommended in the Secretary-General's programme[2] were sent to China that country's needs would

[1] See *Official Records of the Economic and Social Council*, Second Year, Fifth Session, Annex 7.

still not be satisfied. China did not wish to absorb all those experts. Too much advice might lead to a certain amount of indigestion. So far China had had the benefit of the work of seven advisers for three months, and two were at present working in China. They had been assigned to a basic programme according to their qualifications. After describing the main points of the programme, Mr. Chang observed that the work of experts had stimulated local efforts, and he would like to point out in the first place that the duration of the service they had given was short; secondly, that the programme had been scientifically planned; and thirdly that its implementation had cost the Chinese Government a sum much larger than salaries and expenses of the experts.

He appreciated the motives behind the United Kingdom resolution, but recalled that the Social Commission at its thirty-sixth meeting had disapproved of such a proposal and had decided by a vote of twelve to one in favour of continuing the services and approving the budget suggested by the Secretary-General. He considered the proper procedure was to endorse the Social Commission's conclusions. Finally, while the work of the Security Council might be more spectacular, the work of the Economic and Social Council in promoting such services was fundamental and lasting.

Mr. CHANG (China) opposed the proposal of the representative of New Zealand.

The CHAIRMAN said that it was his intention to provide the Fifth Committee with a summary of the discussions which had been held, irrespective of the decision regarding the New Zealand proposal.

The proposal of the representative of New Zealand was rejected by 36 votes to 5, with 9 abstentions.

Mr. CHANG (China) supported the United Kingdom resolution and recalled that his delegation had submitted the resolution calling for the convening of the International Health Conference.[1]

[1] See *Documents of the United Nations Conference on International Organization* (San Francisco, 1945, volume III, pages 631-632).

图片 3.2.2：张彭春在联大第三委员会第二届第 57 次会议发言纪要

【纪要译文】

张先生(中国)说,他希望纠正一位成员的发言可能造成的误导性印象,即如果秘书长方案中建议的所有顾问都被派往中国,该国的需要仍然无法得到满足。中国不希望吸收所有这些专家。太多的建议可能会导致一定程度的消化不良。迄今为止,中国已经受益于七位顾问三个月的工作,其中两位目前在中国工作。根据他们的资格,他们被分配到一个基本项目。在描述了该项目的要点之后,张先生指出,专家的工作刺激了当地的工作力度,他首先要指出,他们提供的服务期限很短;第二,该方案是经过科学规划的;第三,它的实施使中国政府付出的代价远远超过了专家的工资和开支。

他赞赏英国决议背后的动机,但回顾社会委员会第三十六次会议上不赞成这一提议,并以 12 票对 1 票决定继续提供服务并核准秘书长建议的预算。他认为适当的程序是认可社会委员会的结论。最后,虽然安全理事会的工作可能更引人注目,但经济及社会理事会在促进这类服务方面的工作是根本和持久的。

张先生(中国)反对新西兰代表的提案。

主席说,他打算向第五委员会提供已进行的讨论的摘要,而不论关于新西兰提案的决定如何。

新西兰代表的提案以 36 票对 5 票、9 票弃权被否决。

张先生(中国)支持英国的决议,并回顾其代表团提交了呼吁召开国际卫生会议的决议。

3. 张彭春在联大第三委员会 第二届第 58 次会议上的发言

联大第三委员会第二届第 58 次会议,于 1947 年 10 月 4 日下午 3 时 15 分至晚上 6 时,在纽约成功湖召开,本次会议讨论苏联关于新闻自由会议日程的决议草案。中国代表张彭春参加了本次会议,并在会议上发言,其具体发言内容①会议纪要、纪要影像和纪要译文如下:

【会议纪要】

Mr. CHANG (China) recalled that the opinion expressed by the USSR delegation had already been rejected by the majority on several occasions. He pointed out that Outer Mongolia, which for centuries had been an integral part of China, today had its own Government which had been recognized by the Chinese Government in very special circumstances during the war. The present attitude of the Government of the People's Republic of Outer Mongolia was forcing the Chinese Government to modify its general attitude towards it, as it did

---

① UN Document: A/C. 3/SR/58, pp. 59-60; p. 64.

not seem desirous of respecting China's frontiers. He described as dangerous the situation that would result from an invitation to the People's Republic of Outer Mongolia to attend the Conference on Freedom of Information.

In his view, the Committee's vote on this question would justify the opinion of his delegation, which held that the People's Republic of Outer Mongolia was not qualified to be invited to the Conference. China, he concluded, would vote against the USSR proposal, whether it was examined as a whole or point by point.

Mr. CHANG (China) wished to reply to the concordant statements of the representatives of the Ukrainian SSR and of the USSR. Those two speakers had, expressed the view that the People's Republic of Outer Mongolia should be invited to the Conference; their principal argument was the war effort of the Mongolian People's Republic in the struggle against Japan. He did not doubt that the small army formed in Mongolia had co-operated in the military effort of the USSR army. At present the air units and the divisions of that Mongolian army were directing their efforts against neighbouring territories. He refused to go further into that aspect of the question, but he also refused to believe that the recent activities of the Mongolian People's Republic rendered it particularly worthy of representation at the Conference.

【纪要影像】

Mr. CHANG (China) recalled that the opinion expressed by the USSR delegation had already been rejected by the majority on several occasions. He pointed out that Outer Mongolia, which for centuries had been an integral part of China, today had its own Government which had been recognized by the Chinese Government in very special circumstances during the war. The present attitude of the Government of the People's Republic of Outer Mongolia was forcing the Chinese Government to modify its general attitude towards it, as it did not seem desirous of respecting China's frontiers. He described as dangerous the situation that would result from an invitation to the People's Republic of Outer Mongolia to attend the Conference on Freedom of Information.

In his view, the Committee's vote on this question would justify the opinion of his delegation, which held that the People's Republic of Outer Mongolia was not qualified to be invited to the Conference. China, he concluded, would vote against the USSR proposal, whether it was examined as a whole or point by point.

Mr. CHANG (China) wished to reply to the concordant statements of the representatives of the Ukrainian SSR and of the USSR. Those two speakers had expressed the view that the People's Republic of Outer Mongolia should be invited to the Conference; their principal argument was the war effort of the Mongolian People's Republic in the struggle against Japan. He did not doubt that the small army formed in Mongolia had co-operated in the military effort of the USSR army. At present the air units and the divisions of that Mongolian army were directing their efforts against neighbouring territories. He refused to go further into that aspect of the question, but he also refused to believe that the recent activities of the Mongolian People's Republic rendered it particularly worthy of representation at the Conference.

图片 3.2.3:张彭春在联大第三委员会第二届第 58 次会议发言纪要

【纪要译文】

张先生(中国)回顾说,苏联代表团发表的意见已经在若干场合被多数人拒绝。他指出,几个世纪以来一直是中国不可分割的一部分的外蒙古,如今有了自己的政府,在战争期间非常特殊的情况下,得到了中国政府的承认。蒙古人民共和国政府目前的态度迫使中国政府改变对它的总体态度,因为它似乎不愿尊重中国的边界。他说,邀请蒙古人民共和国参加新闻自由会议将造成危险的局面。

他认为,委员会对这个问题的表决将证明他的代表团的意见是正确的,该代表团认为蒙古人民共和国没有资格被邀请参加会议。他总结说,中国将投票反对苏联的提案,无论是作为一个整体还是逐点审议。

张先生(中国)希望答复乌克兰苏维埃社会主义共和国和苏联代表一致的发言。这两位发言者表示,应邀请蒙古人民共和国参加会议;他们的主要论点是蒙古人民共和国在抗日斗争中的战争努力。他不怀疑,在蒙古国组建的小型军队与苏联军队的军事努力方面进行了合作。目前,蒙古国军的空军部队和各师正在努力针对相邻领土。他拒绝进一步探讨这个问

题的这一方面,但他也不认为蒙古人民共和国最近的活动使其特别值得派
代表出席会议。

4. 张彭春在联大第三委员会
第二届第 59 次会议上的发言

联大第三委员会第二届第 59 次会议,于 1947 年 10 月 6 日上午 11 时
至下午 1 时 5 分,在纽约成功湖召开,本次会议继续讨论苏联关于新闻自
由会议日程的决议草案。中国代表张彭春参加了本次会议,并在会议上发
言,其具体发言内容①会议纪要、纪要影像和纪要译文如下:

【会议纪要】

Mr. CHANG (China) said that the first question to be decided was
whether the Committee wished to recommend the Economic and Social Council
to reconsider the provisional agenda of the Conference on Freedom of Information. He did not think the vote on the USSR resolution could be taken paragraph by paragraph, without further careful discussion. He reminded the Chairman of the proposal by the representative of Panama and asked for his ruling on
that point.

---

① UN Document: A/C. 3/SR/59, pp. 70-71.

【纪要影像】

> Mr. CHANG (China) said that the first ques-
> tion to be decided was whether the Committee
> wished to recommend the Economic and Social
> Council to reconsider the provisional agenda of
> the Conference on Freedom of Information. He
> did not think the vote on the USSR resolution
> could be taken paragraph by paragraph, with-
> out further careful discussion. He reminded the
>
> Chairman of the proposal by the representative
> of Panama and asked for his ruling on that
> point.

图片 3.2.4：张彭春在联大第三委员会第二届第 59 次会议发言纪要

【纪要译文】

张先生(中国)说,有待决定的第一个问题是,委员会是否希望建议经济及社会理事会重新审议新闻自由会议的临时议程。他认为,在没有进一步仔细讨论的情况下,无法逐段对苏联决议进行表决。他提醒主席注意巴拿马代表的提案,并要求他就此作出裁决。

5. 张彭春在联大第三委员会第二届第 60 次会议上的发言

联大第三委员会第二届第 60 次会议,于 1947 年 10 月 7 日上午 11 时至下午 2 时,在纽约成功湖召开,本次会议讨论苏联关于新闻自由会议日程的决议草案。中国代表张彭春参加了本次会议,并在会议上先后多次发言,他在发言中所提出的建议被采纳,其具体发言内容①会议纪要、纪要影像和纪要译文如下：

---

① UN Document：A/C. 3/SR/60, p. 72; p. 73; p. 76; p. 78; p. 79.

【会议纪要】

Mr. CHANG (China) pointed out that the result of such a decision would be that the Indian proposal could be considered only after the other three resolutions which were already before the Committee. That was regrettable and it would be logical to proceed at once to a consideration of the Indian proposal.

Mr. CHANG (China) said that on the basis of rule 74 of the rules of procedure the first paragraph of section I ought to be considered separately and that the vote on that question ought to be taken separately from the vote on the nine points. The main question was whether or not the Committee agreed to make a recommendation.

Mr. CHANG (China) thought that the solution was simple: it was sufficient to start by voting only on the first paragraph of section I of the USSR proposal. Should the vote on the first paragraph be in the affirmative, the Committee would then be able to consider each point separately.

After some remarks by Mr. CHANG (China), the CHAIRMAN read the Panama delegation's amendment, adding that it had been decided not to accept any further amendments.

Mr. CHANG (China) supported the proposal of the United Kingdom and India and proposed that the Committee should vote on the first paragraph.

Mr. CHANG (China) asked that, as the debate was closed, the Committee should be called upon to vote.

The CHAIRMAN asked the Secretary of the Committee to read the preamble.

Mr. CHANG (China) interrupted the Secretary's reading of the preamble and asked that the Committee should vote not on the preamble but on sections I, II, III and IV.

Mr. CHANG (China) asked whether, in the event of the resolution being rejected in the ensuing vote, section IV would still stand.

【纪要影像】

Mr. CHANG (China) pointed out that the result of such a decision would be that the Indian proposal could be considered only after the other three resolutions which were already before the Committee. That was regrettable and it would be logical to proceed at once to a consideration of the Indian proposal.

Mr. CHANG (China) said that on the basis of rule 74 of the rules of procedure the first paragraph of section I ought to be considered separately and that the vote on that question ought to be taken separately from the vote on the nine points. The main question was whether or not the Committee agreed to make a recommendation.

Mr. CHANG (China) thought that the solution was simple: it was sufficient to start by voting only on the first paragraph of section I of the USSR proposal. Should the vote on the first paragraph be in the affirmative, the Committee would then be able to consider each point separately.

After some remarks by Mr. CHANG (China), the CHAIRMAN read the Panama delegation's amendment, adding that it had been decided not to accept any further amendments.

Mr. CHANG (China) supported the proposal of the United Kingdom and India and proposed that the Committee should vote on the first paragraph.

Mr. CHANG (China) asked that, as the debate was closed, the Committee should be called upon to vote.

The CHAIRMAN asked the Secretary of the Committee to read the preamble.

Mr. CHANG (China) interrupted the Secretary's reading of the preamble and asked that the Committee should vote not on the preamble but on sections I, II, III and IV.

Mr. CHANG (China) asked whether, in the event of the resolution being rejected in the ensuing vote, section IV would still stand.

图片 3.2.5：张彭春在联大第三委员会第二届第 60 次会议发言纪要

【纪要译文】

张先生(中国)指出,这一决定的结果是,印度的提案只能在委员会已经收到的其他三项决议之后审议。这是令人遗憾的,立即着手审议印度的提案是合乎逻辑的。

张先生(中国)说,根据议事规则第 74 条,第一部分第一段应单独审议,对该问题的表决应与对九个方面内容的表决分开进行。主要问题是委员会是否同意提出建议。

张先生(中国)认为解决办法很简单:首先只对苏联提案第一部分第一段进行表决就足够了。如果第一段的表决是肯定的,那么委员会就可以单独考虑每一方面。

在张先生(中国)发言后,主席宣读了巴拿马代表团的修正案,并补充说,已决定不接受任何进一步的修正案。

张先生(中国)支持英国和印度的提案,并提议委员会对第一段进行表决。

张先生(中国)要求在辩论结束时请委员会进行表决。

主席请委员会秘书宣读序言。

张先生(中国)打断了秘书对序言的阅读,要求委员会不就序言进行表决,而是就第一、二、三和四部分进行表决。

张先生(中国)问,如果该决议在随后的表决中被否决,第四部分是否仍然有效。

6. 张彭春在联大第三委员会第二届第 67 次会议上的发言

联大第三委员会第二届第 67 次会议,于 1947 年 10 月 22 日下午 3 时至 5 时 5 分,在纽约成功湖召开,本次会议讨论国际儿童应急基金问题。中国代表张彭春参加了本次会议,并在会议上发言,其具体发言内容①会议纪要、纪要影像和纪要译文如下:

【会议纪要】

Mr. Chang (China) said that his Government fully appreciated the value of the Fund to China and to the whole world. Through the Fund the United Nations would be able to do something really constructive. He supported the French resolution, and hoped that it would be adopted unanimously.

The draft resolution submitted by the delegation of France was adopted unanimously.

---

① UN Document: A/C. 3/SR. 67, p. 125.

451

【纪要影像】

> Mr. CHANG (China) said that his Government fully appreciated the value of the Fund to China and to the whole world. Through the Fund the United Nations would be able to do something really constructive. He supported the French resolution, and hoped that it would be adopted unanimously.
>
> *The draft resolution submitted by the delegation of France was adopted unanimously.*

图片 3.2.6：张彭春在联大第三委员会第二届第 67 次会议发言纪要

【纪要译文】

张先生(中国)说，中国政府充分认识到基金对中国和全世界的价值。通过该基金，联合国将能够做一些真正有建设性的事情。他支持法国的决议，并希望该决议获得一致通过。

法国代表团提交的决议草案获得一致通过。

第三章　联大第三委员会第三届会议
（第一部分）

　　联大第三委员会第三届会议第一部分会议,于 1948 年 4 月 16 日下午 12 时 50 分,在法拉盛草地公园开幕(即第 83 次会议),而 1948 年 12 月 8 日上午 11 时,在法国巴黎夏洛宫举行了第 180 次会议,这样,本届会议第一部分共计召开了 98 次会议,黎巴嫩的查尔斯·马利克(Charles Malik)担任会议主席,本届会议主要审议有关《国际人权宣言》草案的各种议案,并形成决议案。

图片 2.3.1:查尔斯·马利克先生任联大第三委员会主席

　　中国代表张彭春参加了本届会议,并在其中的 45 次会议上发言,包括第 88 次、第 91 次、第 95 次、第 96 次、第 97 次、第 98 次、第 99 次、第 100 次、第 101 次、第 103 次、第 105 次、第 107 次、第 108 次、第 109 次、第 110 次、第 113 次、第 114 次、第 119 次、第 125 次、第 126 次、第 127 次、第 131 次、第 133 次、第 134 次、第 141 次、第 142 次、第 143 次、第 144 次、第 145 次、第 146 次、第 149 次、第 150 次、第 151 次、第 152 次、第 153 次、第 154 次、第 156 次、第 157 次、第 158 次、第 166 次、第 167 次、第 175 次、第 176 次、第 177 次和第 178 次会议。这些会议发言内容,充分展现了中国代表张彭春为《世界人权宣言》的起草所做出的卓越贡献。

1. 张彭春在联大第三委员会
第三届第 88 次会议上的发言

联大第三委员会第三届第 88 次会议,于 1948 年 9 月 30 日上午 10 时 45 分至下午 1 时 15 分,在巴黎夏洛宫召开,本次会议主要讨论《国际人权宣言》草案。中国代表张彭春参加了本次会议,并在会议上发言,其具体发言内容①会议纪要、纪要影像和纪要译文如下:

【会议纪要】

Mr. CHANG (China) suggested, as a compromise, that the discussion on the preamble might begin immediately, a procedure which would permit every member to state his principles, since the preamble set out the principles on which the declaration was based. He proposed that the discussion should be divided into two parts, a discussion on principles and a discussion on drafting, so as to ascertain what wording would best express the principles accepted by the Commission.

There followed a brief discussion on the question whether the debate should deal with the draft declaration of human rights alone, or with all the drafts relating to human rights, including the covenant and the suggestions for implementation.

The CHAIRMAN asked the Committee to decide how the draft international declaration of human rights was to be examined.

The first proposal made was that a general discussion should take place in

---

① UN Document:A/C. 3/SR/88, pp. 28-29; pp. 30-31; p. 31.

which priority would be granted to representatives of the countries that had not taken part in the work of the Commission on Human Rights. The second proposal, put forward by the representative of China, was that the draft declaration of human rights be examined forthwith, beginning with the preamble, the substance and form of which would be considered in turn.

He asked the representatives to choose between those two proposals.

Mr. Contoumas (Greece) supported the proposal of the representative of China.

Mrs. Begtrup (Denmark) agreed with the representative of the United States that it would be advisable to limit discussion to the draft declaration of human rights which should, in accordance with the recommendation of the Economic and Social Council, be adopted by the General Assembly at its current session. The covenant had not yet been sufficiently elaborated for a useful study to be made.

She supported the Chinese proposal calling for general discussion on the preamble, to be followed by an examination of the other parts of the draft declaration.

Mr. CHANG (China) said that as his colleagues were in favour of a general discussion he would withdraw his proposal that the Committee should start immediately by studying the preamble. He would request the President, however, to ask the representatives whether they wished the discussion to deal solely with the draft declaration or with the whole report, including the covenant and the suggestions for implementation.

The Chairman referring to rule 107 of the rules of procedure said he would immediately put the motion for adjournment to the vote.

Mr. Chang (China) asked what exactly was the proposal before the Committee and upon what question would be vote be taken.

The Chairman stated the proposal in the following terms:

"*The Third Committee*

"*Decides to proceed immediately to a general discussion of item 2 of its agenda (Draft international declaration of human rights: items submitted by the Economic and Social Council), which includes the report of the Commission on Human Rights in its entirety.*"

The Chairman put his proposal to the vote.

The proposal was adopted.

【纪要影像】

Mr. CHANG (China) suggested, as a compromise, that the discussion on the preamble might begin immediately, a procedure which would permit every member to state his principles, since the preamble set out the principles on which the declaration was based. He proposed that the discussion should be divided into two parts, a discussion on principles and a discussion on drafting, so as to ascertain what wording would best express the principles accepted by the Commission.

There followed a brief discussion on the question whether the debate should deal with the draft declaration of human rights alone, or with all the drafts relating to human rights, including the covenant and the suggestions for implementation.

The CHAIRMAN asked the Committee to decide how the draft international declaration of human rights was to be examined.

The first proposal made was that a general discussion should take place in which priority would be granted to representatives of the countries that had not taken part in the work of the Commission on Human Rights. The second proposal, put forward by the representative of China, was that the draft declaration of human rights be examined forthwith, beginning with the preamble, the substance and form of which would be considered in turn.

He asked the representatives to choose between those two proposals.

Mr. CONTOUMAS (Greece) supported the proposal of the representative of China.

图片 3.3.1:张彭春在联大第三委员会第三届第 88 次会议发言纪要(1)

Mrs. BEGTRUP (Denmark) agreed with the representative of the United States that it would be advisable to limit discussion to the draft declaration of human rights which should, in accordance with the recommendation of the Economic and Social Council, be adopted by the General Assembly at its current session. The covenant had not yet been sufficiently elaborated for a useful study to be made.

She supported the Chinese proposal calling for a general discussion on the preamble, to be followed by an examination of the other parts of the draft declaration.

Mr. CHANG (China) said that as his colleagues were in favour of a general discussion, he would withdraw his proposal that the Committee should start immediately by studying the preamble. He would request the President, however, to ask the representatives whether they wished the discussion to deal solely with the draft declaration or with the whole report, including the covenant and the suggestions for implementation.

The CHAIRMAN referring to rule 107 of the rules of procedure said he would immediately put the motion for adjournment to the vote.

Mr. CHANG (China) asked what exactly was the proposal before the Committee and upon what question would the vote be taken.

The CHAIRMAN stated the proposal in the following terms:

"*The Third Committee*

"*Decides* to proceed immediately to a general discussion of item 2 of its agenda (Draft international declaration of human rights: item submitted by the Economic and Social Council), which includes the report of the Commission on Human Rights in its entirety."

The CHAIRMAN put his proposal to the vote.
The proposal was adopted.

图片 3.3.2:张彭春在联大第三委员会第三届第 88 次会议发言纪要(2)

【纪要译文】

张先生(中国)建议,作为一种折中办法,序言的讨论可以立即开始,程序是将允许每一个成员对其原则进行陈述,因为序言部分提出了《宣言》所依据的原则。他建议讨论应分为两部分,即对原则的讨论和对起草工作的讨论,以确定哪些措辞最能表达委员会所接受的原则。

随后,就辩论是应单独处理人权宣言草案,还是应处理与人权有关的所有草案——包括《公约》和执行建议的问题进行了简短的讨论。

主席请委员会决定如何审查国际人权宣言草案。

提出的第一项建议是,应进行一般性讨论,优先考虑尚未参加人权委员会工作的国家的代表。中国代表提出的第二项建议是,立即审查人权宣言草案,从序言开始,依次审议其实质和形式。

他请代表们在这两项提案中作出选择。

孔图玛斯(Contoumas)先生(希腊)支持中国代表的提案。

贝格特鲁普(Begtrup)夫人(丹麦)同意美国代表的意见,即最好将讨论范围限制在人权宣言草案上,根据经济及社会理事会的建议,人权宣言草案应在大会本届会议上通过。《公约》尚未得到充分的阐述,无法进行有益的研究。

她支持中国的建议,要求对序言进行大讨论,然后审查宣言草案的其他部分。

张先生(中国)说,由于他的同事们赞成进行大讨论,他将撤回他的建议,即委员会应立即开始讨论序言。但是,他请主席询问各位代表,他们是否希望讨论仅仅涉及宣言草案,还是涉及整个报告,包括《公约》和实施建议。

主席提到议事规则第107条说,他将立即将休会动议付诸表决。

张先生(中国)问在委员会面前的提案究竟是什么,将针对什么问题采取投票表决。

主席用以下措辞阐述了该提案:

"第三委员会

"决定立即对其议程项目 2(国际人权宣言草案:经济及社会理事会提交的项目)进行大讨论,其中包括人权委员会的报告全文。"

主席将他的提案付诸表决。

该提案获得通过。

2. 张彭春在联大第三委员会 第三届第 91 次会议上的发言

联大第三委员会第三届第 91 次会议,于 1948 年 10 月 2 日上午 10 时 30 分至下午 1 时 5 分,在巴黎夏洛宫召开,本次会议继续讨论《国际人权宣言》草案。中国代表张彭春参加了本次会议,并在会议上发言,其具体发言内容①会议纪要、纪要影像和纪要译文如下:

【会议纪要】

Mr. CHANG (China) stated that the draft international declaration of human rights which the General Assembly was about to adopt was a timely and noble document, for which there was urgent need. The Charter committed all Member States to the observance of human rights; the declaration stated those rights explicitly. It was only proper that their final formulation should take place in France, the birthplace of modern ideas of freedom.

In the eighteenth century, when progressive ideas with respect to human rights had been first put forward in Europe, translations of Chinese philosophers had been known to and had inspired such thinkers as Voltaire, Quesnay and Diderot in their humanistic revolt against feudalistic conceptions. Chinese ideas

---

① UN Document: A/C. 3/SR/91, pp. 47-48.

had been intermingled with European thought and sentiment on human rights at the time when that subject had been first speculated upon in modern Europe.

Stress should be laid upon the human aspect of human rights. A human being had to be constantly conscious of other men, in whose society he lived. A lengthy process of education was required before men and women realized the full value and obligations of the rights granted to them in the declaration; it was only when that stage had been achieved that those rights could be realized in practice. It was therefore necessary that the declaration should be approved as soon as possible, to serve as a basis and a programme for the humanization of man.

A declaration of human rights should be brief and readily understandable by all. It should be a document for all men everywhere, not merely for lawyers and scholars. It was with that object in mind that the Chinese delegation had introduced, at the third session of the Commission on Human Rights, a brief declaration containing ten articles and it was gratified by the fact that the document had aided in making the present draft declaration clear and relatively brief.

The Chinese delegation would give its general support to the draft declaration in its existing form, and reserved the right to present suggestions during the detailed examination of that document.

【纪要影像】

Mr. CHANG (China) stated that the draft international declaration of human rights which the General Assembly was about to adopt was a timely and noble document, for which there was urgent need. The Charter committed all Member States to the observance of human rights; the declaration stated those rights explicitly. It was only proper that their final formulation should take place in France, the birthplace of modern ideas of freedom.

In the eighteenth century, when progressive ideas with respect to human rights had been first put forward in Europe, translations of Chinese philosophers had been known to and had inspired such thinkers as Voltaire, Quesnay and Diderot in their humanistic revolt against feudalistic conceptions. Chinese ideas had been intermingled with European thought and sentiment on human rights at the time when that subject had been first speculated upon in modern Europe.

Stress should be laid upon the human aspect of human rights. A human being had to be constantly conscious of other men, in whose society he lived. A lengthy process of education was required before men and women realized the full value and obligations of the rights granted to them in the declaration; it was only when that stage had been achieved that those rights could be realized in practice. It was therefore necessary that the declaration should be approved as soon as possible, to serve as a basis and a programme for the humanization of man.

A declaration of human rights should be brief and readily understandable by all. It should be a document for all men everywhere, not merely for lawyers and scholars. It was with that object in mind that the Chinese delegation had introduced, at the third session of the Commission on Human Rights, a brief declaration containing ten articles[1] and it was gratified by the fact that the document had aided in making the present draft declaration clear and relatively brief.

The Chinese delegation would give its general support to the draft declaration in its existing form, and reserved the right to present suggestions during the detailed examination of that document.

图片3.3.3：张彭春在联大第三委员会第三届第91次会议发言纪要

【纪要译文】

张先生(中国)说,大会即将通过的《国际人权宣言》草案是一份及时和崇高的文件,这份文件是迫切需要的。《宪章》承诺所有会员国遵守人权;《宣言》明确规定了这些权利。它最终只有在现代自由理念的发源地法国制订,才是正确而适当的。

在18世纪,当欧洲首次提出关于人权的进步思想时,中国哲学家的译本为伏尔泰、魁奈和狄德罗等思想家所熟知,并激发了他们以人本主义反抗封建观念。在现代欧洲首次对人权问题进行思考时,中国的思想与欧洲的人权思想和情感交织在一起。

应强调人权的人的方面。一个人必须不断地意识到在他所生活的社会中的其他人。需要经历一个漫长的教育过程,男女才能够意识到在宣言中所赋予他们权利的全部价值和对应的义务;只有在那一阶段实现之后,那些权利才能在实践中得以实现。因此,有必要尽快批准《宣言》,作为人的人性化的基础和方案。

人权宣言应当简短,易于所有人理解。它应该是为各地所有人起草的一份文件,而不仅仅是为了律师和学者。正是考虑到这一目标,中国代表团在人权委员会第三届会议上提出了一项简短的宣言,其中载有十条内容,令人欣慰的一个现实是,该文件已经帮助使得这份宣言草案明确而相对简洁。

中国代表团将对现有形式的宣言草案给予普遍支持,并保留在详细审查该文件期间提出建议的权利。

3. 张彭春在联大第三委员会第三届第 95 次会议上的发言

联大第三委员会第三届第 95 次会议,于 1948 年 10 月 6 日下午 3 时 15 分至晚上 6 时 10 分,在巴黎夏洛宫召开,本次会议主要是继续讨论《国际人权宣言》草案(第 1 条)、讨论委员会的会议记录问题。中国代表张彭春参加了本次会议,并在会议上发言,其具体发言内容①会议纪要、纪要影像和纪要译文如下:

【会议纪要】

The CHAIRMAN read paragraphs 2 and 3 of the Egyptian delegation's proposal (A/C. 3/222), paragraph 1 having already been adopted at the 94th meeting:

"2. The Third Committee decides that the declaration of human rights shall be limited to the formulation of principles relating to human rights which presuppose the existence of corresponding duties on the part of States and defers the formulation of principles relating to the duties of States for incorporation in an appropriate instrument.

"3. The Third Committee decides that the declaration of human rights

---

① UN Document:A/C. 3/SR/95, p. 87; p. 93; p. 94.

shall deal both with human rights and with the duties corresponding thereto. "

Mr. CHANG (China) expressed his sympathy with the feelings which had motivated the proposal of the Egyptian representative.

It was not sufficient to resolve the question by invoking formal considerations such as that of the Committee's terms of reference. The Chinese representative felt that ethical considerations should play a greater part in the discussion. The question was not purely political. The aim of the United Nations was not to ensure the selfish gains of the individual but to try and increase man's moral stature. It was necessary to proclaim the duties of the individual for it was a consciousness of his duties which enabled man to reach a high moral standard.

Mr. SANTA CRUZ (Chile) formally proposed that the meetings of the Third Committee should be recorded verbatim in future or, if that were not possible, that a request should be made for fuller summary records.

Mr. Chang (China) observed that the representative of Chile had been wise in the wording of his request inasmuch as he had asked the Secretariat to provide verbatim records of meetings if possible, reserving the possibility of requesting summary records if it were impossible to have verbatim records.

Mr. Chang (China) had anticipated that the Committee would be more inclined to adopt the second part of the Chilean proposal than the first. Since a request had been made for separate votes, he would vote against the first part of the proposal and in favour of the second. If representatives wished to know the exact words spoken at a meeting, they could listen to the sound recordings.

The CHAIRMAN read paragraphs 2 and 3 of the Egyptian delegation's proposal (A/C.3/222), paragraph 1 having already been adopted at the 94th meeting:

"2. The Third Committee decides that the declaration of human rights shall be limited to the formulation of principles relating to human rights which presuppose the existence of corresponding duties on the part of States and defers the formulation of principles relating to the duties of States for incorporation in an appropriate instrument.

"3. The Third Committee decides that the declaration of human rights shall deal both with human rights and with the duties corresponding thereto."

Mr. CHANG (China) expressed his sympathy with the feelings which had motivated the proposal of the Egyptian representative.

It was not sufficient to resolve the question by invoking formal considerations such as that of the Committee's terms of reference. The Chinese representative felt that ethical considerations should play a greater part in the discussion. The question was not purely political. The aim of the United Nations was not to ensure the selfish gains of the individual but to try and increase man's moral stature. It was necessary to proclaim the duties of the individual for it was a consciousness of his duties which enabled man to reach a high moral standard.

Mr. SANTA CRUZ (Chile) formally proposed that the meetings of the Third Committee should be recorded verbatim in future or, if that were not possible, that a request should be made for fuller summary records.

Mr. CHANG (China) observed that the representative of Chile had been wise in the wording of his request inasmuch as he had asked the Secretariat to provide verbatim records of meetings *if possible*, reserving the possibility of requesting summary records if it were impossible to have verbatim records.

Mr. CHANG (China) had anticipated that the Committee would be more inclined to adopt the second part of the Chilean proposal than the first. Since a request had been made for separate votes, he would vote against the first part of the proposal and in favour of the second. If representatives wished to know the exact words spoken at a meeting, they could listen to the sound recordings.

图片 3.3.4：张彭春在联大第三委员会第三届第 95 次会议发言纪要

【纪要译文】

主席宣读了埃及代表团提案(A/C.3/222)第 2 段和第 3 段,第 94 次会议已通过第 1 段:

"2. 第三委员会决定,《人权宣言》应限于拟订与人权有关的原则,这些原则假定国家有相应的义务,并推迟拟订与国家义务有关的原则,以便纳入适当的文书。

"3. 第三委员会决定,《人权宣言》应涉及人权及其相应的义务。"

张先生(中国)对促使埃及代表提出建议的感情表示同情。

仅仅援引诸如委员会职权范围之类的正式考虑来解决这个问题是不够的。中国代表认为,伦理上的考虑应该在讨论中发挥更大的作用。这个问题并不是纯粹的政治问题。联合国的目标不是保证个人的私利,而是要努力提高人的道德境界。有必要宣布个人的义务职责,因为意识到其职责将使得他达到很高的道德标准。

桑塔·克鲁兹先生(智利)正式提议,今后应逐字记录第三委员会的会议,如果不可能,则应要求提供更完整的摘要记录。

张先生(中国)说,智利代表在其请求的措辞上是明智的,因为他要求秘书处尽可能提供会议的全文记录,如果无法提供全文记录,保留请求纪要的可能性。

张先生(中国)预计委员会更倾向于通过智利提案的第二部分而不是第一部分。由于有人要求进行单独表决,他将对提案的第一部分投反对票,对第二部分投赞成票。如果代表希望知道在会议上所说的确切言语,他们可以听录音。

4. 张彭春在联大第三委员会 第三届第 96 次会议上的发言

联大第三委员会第三届第 96 次会议,于 1948 年 10 月 7 日上午 10 时 30 分至下午 1 时 25 分,在巴黎夏洛宫召开,本次会议继续讨论《国际人权宣言》草案(第 1 条)。中国代表张彭春参加了本次会议,并在会议上发言,其具体发言内容①会议纪要、纪要影像和纪要译文如下:

【会议纪要】

Mr. CHANG (China) felt that article 1 of the declaration should remain where it was, and that the two sentences which made up that article should not be separated. A happy balance was struck by the broad statement of rights in the first sentence and the implication of duties in the second. Should article 1 be taken out of the body of the declaration, it would not claim as much of the reader's attention as it deserved to do; moreover, the various rights would appear more selfish if they were not preceded by the reference to "a spirit of

---

① UN Document: A/C. 3/SR/96, pp. 98-99; p. 102.

brotherhood". Similar reasoning applied to article 27, which contained a statement of duties. Statements of rights and duties should form an integral part of the declaration.

Mr. Chang supported the deletion in article 1 of the words "by nature", as suggested by the Belgian representative. That measure would obviate any theological question, which could not and should not be raised in a declaration designed to be universally applicable.

While the declaration would no doubt be accepted by a majority vote of Member States, in the field of human rights popular majority should not be forgotten. The Chinese representative recalled that the population of his country comprised a large segment of humanity. That population had ideals and traditions different from those of the Christian West. Those ideals included good manners, decorum, propriety and consideration for others. Yet although Chinese culture attached the greatest importance to manners as a part of ethics, the Chinese representative would refrain from proposing that mention of them should be made in the declaration. He hoped that his colleagues would show equal consideration and withdraw some of the amendments to article 1 which raised metaphysical problems. For Western civilization, too, the time for religious intolerance was over.

Mr. Chang agreed with the Lebanese representative that the word "born" in the first sentence of the English text of article 1 should be deleted; without that amendment the sentence was reminiscent of Rousseau and the theory that man was naturally good. For the purpose of the declaration it was better to start with a clean slate.

He also welcomed the fact that the delegation of the Union of South Africa had withdrawn its amendment to article 1 (A/C. 3/226).

The second sentence of article 1 called upon men to act towards one another in a spirit of brotherhood. That attitude was perfectly consistent with the Chinese attitude towards manners and the importance of kindly and considerate treatment of others. It was only when man's social behaviour rose to that level that he was truly human. Decorum was an ideal which should not be lost sight of—as unfortunately it often was—in the struggle to uphold noble principles.

In conclusion, Mr. Chang urged that articles 1, 2 and 3 should be left where they were.

Mr. CHANG (China) said that it would not be necessary to put that amendment to a vote because he could suggest another way of dealing with it. He wished to reserve the right to make that suggestion later.

【纪要影像】

Mr. CHANG (China) felt that article 1 of the declaration should remain where it was, and that the two sentences which made up that article should not be separated. A happy balance was struck by the broad statement of rights in the first sentence and the implication of duties in the second. Should article 1 be taken out of the body of the declaration, it would not claim as much of the reader's attention as it deserved to do; moreover, the various rights would appear more selfish if they were not preceded by the reference to "a spirit of brotherhood". Similar reasoning applied to article 27, which contained a statement of duties. Statements of rights and duties should form an integral part of the declaration.

Mr. Chang supported the deletion in article 1 of the words "by nature", as suggested by the Belgian representative. That measure would obviate any theological question, which could not and should not be raised in a declaration designed to be universally applicable.

While the declaration would no doubt be accepted by a majority vote of Member States, in the field of human rights popular majority should not be forgotten. The Chinese representative recalled that the population of his country comprised a large segment of humanity. That population had ideals and traditions different from those of the Christian West. Those ideals included good manners, decorum, propriety and consideration for others. Yet, although Chinese culture attached the greatest importance to manners as a part of ethics, the Chinese representative would refrain from proposing that mention of them should be made in the declaration. He hoped that his colleagues would show equal consideration and withdraw some of the amendments to article 1 which raised metaphysical problems. For Western civilization, too, the time for religious intolerance was over.

Mr. Chang agreed with the Lebanese representative that the word "born" in the first sentence of the English text of article 1 should be deleted; without that amendment, the sentence was reminiscent of Rousseau and the theory that man was naturally good. For the purposes of the declaration it was better to start with a clean slate.

图片 3.3.5:张彭春在联大第三委员会第三届第 96 次会议发言纪要(1)

He also welcomed the fact that the delegation of the Union of South Africa had withdrawn its amendment to article 1 (A/C.3/226).

The second sentence of article 1 called upon men to act towards one another in a spirit of brotherhood. That attitude was perfectly consistent with the Chinese attitude towards manners and the importance of kindly and considerate treatment of others. It was only when man's social behaviour rose to that level that he was truly human. Decorum was an ideal which should not be lost sight of—as unfortunately it often was—in the struggle to uphold noble principles.

In conclusion, Mr. Chang urged that articles 1, 2 and 3 should be left where they were.

Mr. CHANG (China) said that it would not be necessary to put that amendment to a vote because he could suggest another way of dealing with it. He wished to reserve the right to make that suggestion later.

图片 3.3.6：张彭春在联大第三委员会第三届第 96 次会议发言纪要(2)

【纪要译文】

张先生(中国)认为,《宣言》第 1 条应该保留在它现有的位置,由两个句子组成的这一条不应该被割裂。第一句有关权利的宽泛声明和第二句对于责任的暗示形成了一个很好的平衡。一旦第 1 条被从宣言的主体中剔除,就将不会让读者给予它本身应该得到的关注;而且,如果它们之前没有提及"以兄弟的精神相对待"的话,各种权利会显得更为自私。类似的推理适用于第 27 条,它包含一个职责的表述。权利和义务的声明应该是宣言的组成部分。

张先生支持按照比利时代表的建议,在第 1 条中删除"本性"一词。这一衡量标准将排除任何理论问题,它不能够也不应该在一个将为世界普遍适用的宣言中提出来。

宣言无疑将为(联合国)多数成员国接受时,在人权领域人口的多数性不应该被忘记。中国代表认为他的国家的人口占(世界)总人口的很大部分。这部分人口有着不同于基督教西方的理想和传统。那些思想中包括得体的举止、礼貌、礼仪和为他人着想。然而,尽管中国文化作为伦理道德的一个组成部分,对人们的行为方式有着极其重要的影响,但是,中国代表并没有提议在宣言中应该提及这些。他希望他的同事们表现出平等的态度,撤回在第 1 条修正案中提出的某些形而上学的东西。同样,对西方文明来说,宗教不容忍的时代结束了。

张先生同意黎巴嫩代表的意见,即应删除英文本第 1 条第一句中的"born"一词;没有这一修正案,这句话让人想起卢梭和人类天生善良的理论。就《宣言》而言,最好从头开始。

他还欢迎南非联盟代表团撤回对第 1 条的修正案。

第 1 条第二个句子呼吁人们以兄弟的精神相对待。这种态度是完全符合中国人对礼貌及亲切和体贴地对待他人的重要态度。只有当人的社会行为上升到那一水平,他才是一个真正的人。礼仪是一种不应被忽视的理想,但在奋力维护高尚原则方面,它又往往不幸地被忽视。

最后,张先生敦促将第 1 条、第 2 条和第 3 条应该保持在它们原来的位置。

张先生(中国)说,没有必要对该修正案进行表决,因为他可以提出另一种处理方法。他希望保留以后提出这一建议的权利。

5. 张彭春在联大第三委员会第三届第 97 次会议上的发言

联大第三委员会第三届第 97 次会议,于 1948 年 10 月 8 日下午 4 时 15 分至晚上 6 时 20 分,在巴黎夏洛宫召开,本次会议继续讨论《国际人权宣言》草案(第 1 条)。中国代表张彭春参加了本次会议,并在会议上发言,其具体发言内容①会议纪要、纪要影像和纪要译文如下:

---

① UN Document:A/C. 3/SR/97, p. 102; p. 103.

【会议纪要】

Mr. CHANG (China), speaking on a point of order, proposed a vote on the establishment of a co-ordinating committee before continuation of the discussion of article 1.

The CHAIRMAN interpreted the proposal of the representative of China as a motion for closure of the debate on article 1.

Mr. CHANG (China) withdrew his motion for closure of the debate.

【纪要影像】

Mr. CHANG (China), speaking on a point of order, proposed a vote on the establishment of a co-ordinating committee before continuation of the discussion of article 1.

The CHAIRMAN interpreted the proposal of the representative of China as a motion for closure of the debate on article 1.

Mr. CHANG (China) withdrew his motion for closure of the debate.

图片 3.3.7:张彭春在联大第三委员会第三届第 97 次会议发言纪要

【纪要译文】

张先生(中国)就程序问题发言,建议在继续讨论第 1 条之前就设立一个协调委员会进行表决。

主席将中国代表的提案解释为结束关于第 1 条的辩论的动议。

张先生(中国)撤回了结束辩论的动议。

联大第三委员会及联大全会

6. 张彭春在联大第三委员会
第三届第98次会议上的发言

联大第三委员会第三届第 98 次会议,于 1948 年 10 月 9 日上午 10 时 30 分至下午 1 时 20 分,在巴黎夏洛宫召开,本次会议继续讨论《国际人权宣言》草案(第 1 条)。中国代表张彭春参加了本次会议,并在会议上发言,其具体发言内容①会议纪要、纪要影像和纪要译文如下:

【会议纪要】

Mr. CHANG (China) thought that the basic text of article 1, with the amendments proposed by the Belgian (A/C. 3/234) and Lebanese (A/C. 3/235) representatives, would be acceptable to the Committee if it were understood on the basis of eighteenth century philosophy.

That philosophy was based on the innate goodness of man. Other schools of thought had said that man's nature was neutral and could be made good or bad, or again that his nature was all bad. The eighteenth century thinkers, whose work had led to the proclamation of the principles of liberty, equality and fraternity in France and, in the United States, to the Declaration of Independence, had realized that although man was largely animal, there was a part of him which distinguished him from animals. That part was the real man and was good, and that part should therefore be given greater importance. There was no contradiction between the eighteenth century idea of the goodness of man's essential nature and the idea of a soul given to man by God, for the concept of God laid particular stress on the human, as opposed to the animal, part of

---

① UN Document: A/C. 3/SR/98, pp. 113-114.

man's nature.

Mr. Chang urged that the Committee should not debate the question of the nature of man again but should build on the work of the eighteenth century philosophers. He thought the Committee should agree to a text beginning "All human beings are free. . ." —using "human beings" to refer to the non-animal part of man—as proposed by the Lebanese delegation, and should further agree to delete the words "by nature", as proposed by the Belgian delegation. If the words "by nature" were deleted, those who believed in God could still find in the strong opening assertion of the article the idea of God, and at the same time others with different concepts would be able to accept the text.

Mr. Chang hoped that in the light of his explanation the Brazilian delegation would be willing to withdraw its amendment (A/C. 3/215) and so spare the members of the Committee the task of deciding by vote on a principle which was in fact beyond the capacity of human judgment.

Mr. Chang paid a particular tribute to the contribution to the work of preparing the draft declaration made by Professor Cassin, the representative of France, who had so ably exposed French doctrines of the eighteenth century.

Concerning practical reality a point raised by the USSR representative, Mr. Chang said that all recognized the existence of wrongs, but the most efficacious way of correcting those wrongs was to set a common standard such as the draft declaration sought to establish. Recognition of the stark facts with which the world was faced should not, however, be termed realism but naturalism, for realism meant that which was truly real and which could be affirmed with the full force of the soul.

【纪要影像】

Mr. CHANG (China) thought that the basic text of article 1, with the amendments proposed by the Belgian (A/C.3/234) and Lebanese (A/C.3/235) representatives, would be acceptable to the Committee if it were understood on the basis of eighteenth century philosophy.

That philosophy was based on the innate goodness of man. Other schools of thought had said that man's nature was neutral and could be made good or bad, or again that his nature was all bad. The eighteenth century thinkers, whose work had led to the proclamation of the principles of liberty, equality and fraternity in France and, in the United States, to the Declaration of Independence, had realized that although man was largely animal, there was a part of him which distinguished him from animals. That part was the real man and was good, and that part should therefore be given greater importance. There was no contradiction between the eighteenth century idea of the goodness of man's essential nature and the idea of a soul given to man by God, for the concept of God laid particular stress on the human, as opposed to the animal, part of man's nature.

Mr. Chang urged that the Committee should not debate the question of the nature of man again but should build on the work of the eighteenth century philosophers. He thought the Committee should agree to a text beginning "All human beings *are* free . . ."—using "human beings" to refer to the non-animal part of man—as proposed by the Lebanese delegation, and should further agree to delete the words "by nature", as proposed by the Belgian delegation. If the words "by nature" were deleted, those who believed in God could still find in the strong opening assertion of the article the idea of God, and at the same time others with different concepts would be able to accept the text.

图片 3.3.8：张彭春在联大第三委员会第三届第 98 次会议发言纪要(1)

Mr. Chang hoped that in the light of his explanation the Brazilian delegation would be willing to withdraw its amendment (A/C.3/215) and so spare the members of the Committee the task of deciding by vote on a principle which was in fact beyond the capacity of human judgment.

Mr. Chang paid a particular tribute to the contribution to the work of preparing the draft declaration made by Professor Cassin, the representative of France, who had so ably exposed French doctrines of the eighteenth century.

Concerning practical reality a point raised by the USSR representative, Mr. Chang said that all recognized the existence of wrongs, but the most efficacious way of correcting those wrongs was to set a common standard such as the draft declaration sought to establish. Recognition of the stark facts with which the world was faced should not, however, be termed realism but naturalism, for realism meant that which was truly real and which could be affirmed with the full force of the soul.

图片 3.3.9：张彭春在联大第三委员会第三届第 98 次会议发言纪要(2)

【纪要译文】

张先生(中国)认为,第 1 条的基本案文以及比利时(A/C.3/234)和黎巴嫩(A/C.3/235)代表提出的修正案,如果根据 18 世纪的哲学加以理解,委员会将可以接受。

这一哲学是基于人类的本性是善良的。其他思想学派认为人的本性是中立的,可以变好或变坏,或者说,他的本性全是恶的。18 世纪思想家的作品,导致了法国的自由、平等和博爱原则和美国的独立宣言的发布,他们已经认识到,虽然人在很大程度上是动物,但人有一部分区别于动物。这部分是真实的人,是善良的,因此这部分应该给予更多的重视。在 18 世纪人的本性是善良的思想与上帝赋予人的灵魂的思想之间没有矛盾,因为上帝的概念特别强调的人性的一面,而不是部分人性中的动物性的一面。

张先生敦促委员会不要再辩论人的本性问题,而应该在 18 世纪哲学家的工作基础上再接再厉。他认为委员会应该同意文本开始的"所有人类都是自由的……"使用"人类"指的是由黎巴嫩代表团提出的非动物性的一部分,并应进一步同意删除比利时代表团提出的"本性"一词。如果说"本性"被删除,那些信仰上帝的人仍然能在该条开放性很强的断言中找到上帝的观念,同时其他持不同概念的人将可以接受文本内容。

张先生希望,根据他的解释,巴西代表团愿意撤回其修正案(A/C. 3/215),从而使委员会成员不必就一项事实上超出人类判断能力的原则进行表决。

张先生特别赞扬法国代表卡森教授对起草宣言草案的工作所作的贡献,他如此干练地揭示了 18 世纪法国的学说。

关于实际情况,苏联代表提出的一点,张先生说,大家都认识到错误的存在,但纠正这些错误最有效的方法就是要树立一个共同的标准,譬如起草宣言草案以寻求建立这一标准。意识到世界面临的刻板的事实,然而,却不应该称为现实主义,而是自然主义,因为现实主义意味着这是完全真实的,并且可能是由灵魂的全部力量来加以肯定的。

7. 张彭春在联大第三委员会
第三届第 99 次会议上的发言

联大第三委员会第三届第 99 次会议,于 1948 年 10 月 11 日下午 3 时至晚上 7 时 15 分,在巴黎夏洛宫召开,本次会议继续讨论《国际人权宣言》草案(第 1 条)。中国代表张彭春参加了本次会议,并在会议上发言,其具体发言内容①会议纪要、纪要影像和纪要译文如下:

【会议纪要】

Mr. CHANG (China) was in favour of the adoption of a strong affirmative statement without qualifications. If the word "born" were deleted, the question of whether human rights began at birth or at conception would not arise.

However, if the majority of the Committee wanted the word "born" to be retained, he suggested a further vote on the insertion of the words " and remain".

---

① UN Document:A/C. 3/SR/99, p. 124.

Mr. CHANG (China) was in favour of the adoption of a strong affirmative statement without qualifications. If the word "born" were deleted, the question of whether human rights began at birth or at conception would not arise.

However, if the majority of the Committee wanted the word "born" to be retained, he suggested a further vote on the insertion of the words "and remain".

图片 3.3.10:张彭春在联大第三委员会第三届第 99 次会议发言纪要

【纪要译文】

张先生(中国)赞成通过一项无保留的强有力的肯定声明。如果删除"出生"一词,就不会出现人权是从出生时开始还是从受孕时开始的问题。

然而,如果委员会多数成员希望保留"出生"一词,他建议就插入"和保留"一词进行进一步表决。

8. 张彭春在联大第三委员会 第三届第 100 次会议上的发言

联大第三委员会第三届第 100 次会议,于 1948 年 10 月 12 日上午 10 时 45 分至下午 1 时 20 分,在巴黎夏洛宫召开,本次会议继续讨论《国际人权宣言》草案(第 1 条)。中国代表张彭春参加了本次会议,并在会议上发言,其具体发言内容①会议纪要、纪要影像和纪要译文如下:

---

① UN Document：A/C. 3/SR/100, p. 128；p. 130.

【会议纪要】

Mr. CHANG (China) wished to stress that it was only after mature consideration that the Commission on Human Rights had decided to state the principles of equality and liberty in two separate articles of the draft declaration of human rights, which it was submitting to the General Assembly.

Article 2 did, in fact, aim at ensuring that everyone, without distinction of any kind, should enjoy all the rights and freedoms set forth in the declaration.

Article 6 aimed at translating that principle into a practical reality by granting everyone protection of the law against discrimination in violation of that declaration.

The Chinese delegation was in whole-hearted agreement with the Commission on Human Rights and hoped that the Third Committee would make a point of retaining article 2 in its existing form.

Speaking on the Cuban delegation's amendment Mr. Chang pointed out that, as the declaration did not make specific mention of duties as well as rights, it would be preferable to delete the words " and subject to the duties " from the proposed text. It had indeed been agreed that duties would be referred to only in article 27 which had to be further defined and amplified at a later date, and in the general declaration of article 1 on the spirit of brotherhood which should inspire the actions of all men.

In reply to the Chinese representative's remark with regard to duties, Mr. Pérez Cisneros said he appreciated the soundness of that criticism and accepted the deletion proposed by Mr. Chang.

Mr. CHANG (China) proposed, in order to simplify the procedure, that the new text submitted by the Cuban delegation for article 2 should be put to the vote. By voting for the adoption or rejection of that text, the Committee would show by implication whether it was for or against the principle of the fusion of texts.

The Chinese delegation could not, however, stress too much the importance which the fight against discrimination of any kind had for vast sections of the world's population. It was essential for those peoples that they should not only be protected within their national legislation against discrimination, but that the principle of equality in respect of all the fundamental freedoms and rights of mankind should be solemnly proclaimed.

Considered in that light, article 2 was of undeniable significance. For that reason, Mr. Chang requested the Cuban representative to withdraw his amendment, which tended to lessen the value of the article.

【纪要影像】

Mr. CHANG (China) wished to stress that it was only after mature consideration that the Commission on Human Rights had decided to state the principles of equality and liberty in two separate articles of the draft declaration of human rights, which it was submitting to the General Assembly.

Article 2 did, in fact, aim at ensuring that everyone, without distinction of any kind, should enjoy all the rights and freedoms set forth in the declaration.

Article 6 aimed at translating that principle into a practical reality by granting everyone protection of the law against discrimination in violation of that declaration.

The Chinese delegation was in whole-hearted agreement with the Commission on Human Rights and hoped that the Third Committee would make a point of retaining article 2 in its existing form.

Speaking on the Cuban delegation's amendment, Mr. Chang pointed out that, as the declaration did not make specific mention of duties as well as rights, it would be preferable to delete the words "and subject to the duties" from the proposed text. It had indeed been agreed that duties would be referred to only in article 27 which had to be further defined and amplified at a later date, and in the general declaration of article 1 on the spirit of brotherhood which should inspire the actions of all men.

In reply to the Chinese representative's remark with regard to duties, Mr. Pérez Cisneros said he appreciated the soundness of that criticism and accepted the deletion proposed by Mr. Chang.

Mr. CHANG (China) proposed, in order to simplify the procedure, that the new text submitted by the Cuban delegation for article 2 should be put to the vote. By voting for the adoption or rejection of that text, the Committee would show by implication whether it was for or against the principle of the fusion of texts.

The Chinese delegation could not, however, stress too much the importance which the fight against discrimination of any kind had for vast sections of the world's population. It was essential for those peoples that they should not only be protected within their national legislation against discrimination, but that the principle of equality in respect of all the fundamental freedoms and rights of mankind should be solemnly proclaimed.

Considered in that light, article 2 was of undeniable significance. For that reason, Mr. Chang requested the Cuban representative to withdraw his amendment, which tended to lessen the value of the article.

图片 3.3.11：张彭春在联大第三委员会第三届第 100 次会议发言纪要

【纪要译文】

张先生(中国)希望强调,人权委员会是在经过成熟的审议之后才决定在提交大会的人权宣言草案的两个单独条款中阐明平等和自由原则的。

第 2 条,事实上,其目的是确保人人应该没有任何区别地享有宣言中规定的所有权利和自由。

第 6 条的目的是把原则变成现实,通过给予每个人以法律保护来反对违反该宣言的歧视。

中国代表团完全同意人权委员会的意见,并希望第三委员会将重点保留现有形式的第 2 条。

在谈到古巴代表团的修正案时,张先生指出,由于《宣言》没有具体提到义务和权利,因此最好从拟议案文中删除"并受义务约束"等字。事实上,大家一致认为,只有在第 27 条中提及义务,该条必须在以后进一步界定和充实,并在关于兄弟情谊精神的第 1 条一般性宣言中提及义务,该精神应激励所有人的行动。

在回答中国代表关于关税的评论时,佩雷斯·西斯内罗斯(Pérez Cisneros)先生说,他赞赏这一批评的正确性,并接受张先生提出的删除建议。

张先生(中国)提议,为了简化程序,应将古巴代表团就第 2 条提交的新案文付诸表决。通过投票赞成或反对该案文,委员会将含蓄地表明它是赞成还是反对合并案文的原则。

然而,对于世界人口的广大地区来说,反对任何种类的歧视,中国代表团再强调其重要性都不过了。对那些民族来说,最基本的是他们不仅应在本国立法中得到免于歧视的保护,而且就人的所有基本自由和权利而言的平等原则应该被郑重宣布。

有鉴于此,第 2 条具有不可否认的重要意义。为此,张先生请古巴代表撤回他的修正案,因为这往往会降低该条的价值。

9. 张彭春在联大第三委员会第三届第 101 次会议上的发言

联大第三委员会第三届第 101 次会议,于 1948 年 10 月 13 日下午 3 时至 5 时 50 分,在巴黎夏洛宫召开,本次会议继续讨论《国际人权宣言》草案

(第2条)。中国代表张彭春参加了本次会议,并在会议上发言,其具体发言内容①会议纪要、纪要影像和纪要译文如下:

【会议纪要】

Mr. CHANG (China) pointed out that the question had been discussed fully in the Human Rights Commission. The concept of race, colour, social origin, and in most cases sex, involved the question of birth, while social origin also embraced the idea of class or caste.

The Commission's text seemed to him the clearest and least confused and he hoped that a large majority of the Committee would support it.

【纪要影像】

Mr. CHANG (China) pointed out that the question had been discussed fully in the Human Rights Commission. The concept of race, colour, social origin, and in most cases sex, involved the question of birth, while social origin also embraced the idea of class or caste.

The Commission's text seemed to him the clearest and least confused and he hoped that a large majority of the Committee would support it.

图片 3.3.12:张彭春在联大第三委员会第三届第 101 次会议发言纪要

【纪要译文】

张先生(中国)指出,人权委员会已经充分讨论了这个问题。种族、肤色、社会出身以及在大多数情况下性别的概念涉及出身问题,而社会出身

---

① UN Document: A/C. 3/SR/101, p. 139.

也包含阶级或种姓的概念。

在他看来,委员会的案文是最清楚和最不混乱的,他希望委员会的绝大多数成员会支持该案文。

10. 张彭春在联大第三委员会
第三届第 103 次会议上的发言

联大第三委员会第三届第 103 次会议,于 1948 年 10 月 15 日上午 10 时 45 分至下午 1 时 30 分,在巴黎夏洛宫召开,本次会议继续讨论《国际人权宣言》草案(第 3 条)。中国代表张彭春参加了本次会议,并在会议上发言,其具体发言内容①会议纪要、纪要影像和纪要译文如下:

【会议纪要】

Mr. CHANG（China）observed that all the amendments that had been submitted, even including those which had not been favourably received by the majority, had made a constructive contribution towards the preparation of a common declaration.

Members should not, however, lose sight of the draft declaration itself, which was the basic document before the Committee. That draft was the result of assiduous efforts and it had been reviewed with meticulous care. The original text prepared at Geneva had been submitted to the various Governments for their comments. It had then been examined by the Commission on Human Rights and had been altered in the light of the various comments and suggestions to which it had given rise. The draft declaration before the Committee was the final product of all that work, and it constituted only two-thirds of the original Geneva

---

① UN Document：A/C. 3/SR/103, pp. 153-154.

draft. It had, in fact, been realized that the clearer and the more concise the declaration was, the more effective and lasting it would be. The declaration was not intended for legal experts or scholars but for the general public; it should therefore be as striking as possible, and, accordingly as concise as possible. It would be best if the declaration were limited to ten articles, but, if that were not possible, it should at least be limited to the twenty-eight articles which composed the draft under consideration.

Mr. Chang then stated that the Third Committee had not studied the structure of the declaration as a whole. In his opinion, such a study was essential and therefore, in examining the declaration, he would refer specially to its logical structure.

Articles 1, 2 and 3 expressed the three main ideas of eighteenth century philosophy; article 1 expressed the idea of fraternity, article 2 that of equality, and article 3 that of liberty.

The idea of liberty was then analysed and applied to the human being in article 3. Article 3 set forth a basic principle, which was then defined and clarified in the nine following articles. Article 4 dealt with slavery, article 5 with the right to recognition as a person before the law, article 6 with equality before the law, article 7 with the need to establish the legality of arrest, article 8 with the right to a fair trial, article 9 with the right to be presumed innocent until proved guilty; article 10 forbade interference with a person's privacy and article 11 affirmed the right to freedom of movement.

In that series of articles the idea of liberty was gradually and progressively enlarged; it was applied first to the individual, then to the family, and finally to the country. That series of articles therefore served to develop and clarify the idea of liberty.

Articles 13 to 20 dealt individually with the various social institutions.

Article 20, like article 3, expressed a general idea which was explained and developed in the following articles. Article 20 set forth the idea of social security and that idea was defined and developed in articles 21 to 25.

The structure of the draft declaration was, therefore, perfectly clear and logical. The joint amendment submitted by the delegations of Lebanon, Uruguay and Cuba and especially its second part, which expressed the same idea as article 20, was not in harmony with that structure. It was for that reason that Mr. Chang thought that the draft declaration should be left as it was, since it possessed the qualities of logic, clarity and brevity, qualities which were indispensable if the declaration was to prove effective.

【纪要影像】

Mr. CHANG (China) observed that all the amendments that had been submitted, even including those which had not been favourably received by the majority, had made a constructive contribution towards the preparation of a common declaration.

Members should not, however, lose sight of the draft declaration itself, which was the basic document before the Committee. That draft was the result of assiduous efforts and it had been reviewed with meticulous care. The original text prepared at Geneva had been submitted to the various Governments for their comments. It had then been examined by the Commission on Human Rights and had been altered in the light of the various comments and suggestions to which it had given rise. The draft declaration before the Committee was the final product of all that work, and it constituted only two-thirds of the original Geneva draft. It had, in fact, been realized that the clearer and the more concise the declaration was, the more effective and lasting it would be. The declaration was not intended for legal experts or scholars but for the general public; it should therefore be as striking as possible, and, accordingly as concise as possible. It would be best if the declaration were limited to ten articles, but, if that were not possible, it should at least be limited to the twenty-eight articles which composed the draft under consideration.

Mr. Chang then stated that the Third Committee had not studied the structure of the declaration as a whole. In his opinion, such a study was essential and therefore, in examining the declaration, he would refer specially to its logical structure.

Articles 1, 2 and 3 expressed the three main ideas of eighteenth century philosophy; article 1 expressed the idea of fraternity, article 2 that of equality, and article 3 that of liberty.

The idea of liberty was then analysed and applied to the human being in article 3. Article 3 set forth a basic principle, which was then defined and clarified in the nine following articles. Article 4 dealt with slavery, article 5 with the right to recognition as a person before the law, article 6 with equality before the law, article 7 with the need to establish the legality of arrest, article 8 with the right to a fair trial, article 9 with the right to be presumed innocent until proved guilty; article 10 forbade interference with a person's privacy and article 11 affirmed the right to freedom of movement.

图片 3.3.13：张彭春在联大第三委员会第三届第 103 次会议发言纪要(1)

482

In that series of articles the idea of liberty was gradually and progressively enlarged; it was applied first to the individual, then to the family, and finally to the country. That series of articles therefore served to develop and clarify the idea of liberty.

Articles 13 to 20 dealt individually with the various social institutions.

Article 20, like article 3, expressed a general idea which was explained and developed in the following articles. Article 20 set forth the idea of social security and that idea was defined and developed in articles 21 to 25.

The structure of the draft declaration was, therefore, perfectly clear and logical. The joint amendment submitted by the delegations of Lebanon, Uruguay and Cuba and especially its second part, which expressed the same idea as article 20, was not in harmony with that structure. It was for that reason that Mr. Chang thought that the draft declaration should be left as it was, since it possessed the qualities of logic, clarity and brevity, qualities which were indispensable if the declaration was to prove effective.

图片 3.3.14：张彭春在联大第三委员会第三届第 103 次会议发言纪要(2)

【纪要译文】

张先生(中国)说,提交的所有修正案,甚至包括那些没有得到多数人赞同的修正案,都对编写共同宣言作出了建设性贡献。

尽管如此,委员们不应该忽视宣言草案本身,这是委员会面前的基本文件。该草案是不懈努力的结果,并且经过了细致的审查。在日内瓦准备的原始文本已提交给各国政府供其评论。然后,经人权委员会审查并根据提出的各种意见和建议对其进行了修改。委员会面前的宣言草案是所有这项工作的最后产物,它只包含了日内瓦原始草案的三分之二的内容。事实上,已经实现:宣言越是明确、越是更简洁、它将越是有效、越是持久。宣言不是为法律专家或学者而是为普通大众制订的;因此它应尽可能地引人注目,并尽可能简明扼要。宣言最好能限制在 10 条内容,但是如果不可能的话,它至少应该被限制在 28 条,以组成正在审议的草案。

张先生接着说,第三委员会没有研究整个《宣言》的结构。他认为,这种研究是必要的,因此,在审查《宣言》时,他将特别提到其逻辑结构。

第 1 条、第 2 条和第 3 条分别表达了 18 世纪哲学的三个主要思想。第 1 条表达的是博爱思想,第 2 条是平等思想,第 3 条是自由思想。

然后,第3条对自由的概念进行了分析,并将其适用于人。第3条设定了一项基本原则,这一原则由随后的9条所定义和澄清。第4条涉及的是奴隶制,第5条是法律面前人格权,第6条是法律面前人人平等,第7条是需要确立逮捕的合法性,第8条是公正审判权,第9条是在被证明有罪之前应有权被假定无罪;第10条是禁止干涉一个人的隐私,而第11条确认迁徙自由的权利。

在这一系列条款中,自由的思想被逐渐和依次放大;它首先应用于个人,然后应用于家庭,最后应用于国家。所以,这一系列条款起到发展和澄清自由思想的作用。

第13条到20条分别处理各项社会机制。

第20条像第3条一样表达了一个总的思想,它由后面的条款所解释和发展。第20条设定了社会安全的思想,并由其后的第21条到第25条所定义和发展。

所以,宣言草案的结构非常清楚、符合逻辑。黎巴嫩、乌拉圭和古巴代表团提交的联合修正案,特别是其第二部分,表达了与第20条相同的想法,与该结构不一致。正是出于这个原因,张先生认为宣言草案应该保持原样,因为它具有逻辑性、明确性和简洁性,如果宣言要被证明有效性的话,这些性质都是不可或缺的。

11. 张彭春在联大第三委员会 第三届第 105 次会议上的发言

联大第三委员会第三届第 105 次会议,于 1948 年 10 月 18 日上午 10 时 30 分至下午 1 时 25 分,在巴黎夏洛宫召开,本次会议继续讨论《国际人权宣言》草案(第 3 条)。中国代表张彭春参加了本次会议,并在会议上发

言,其具体发言内容①会议纪要、纪要影像和纪要译文如下:

【会议纪要】

Mr. CHANG (China) said he wished to give the correct version of the Chinese proverb mentioned by the representative of Belgium. It was: "Sweep the snow in front of one's own door. Overlook the frost on others' roof-tiles." That made for good neighbours.

He wished to lay great stress upon the need for careful consideration of the amendments before the Committee. Another Chinese proverb ran: "Matters allowed to mature slowly are free from sharp corners." That was the spirit in which the drafting of article 3 should be approached.

He had no objection to the drafting changes made in the revised version of the joint amendment submitted by Uruguay, Cuba and Lebanon (A/C. 3/274/Rev. 1). He agreed with the representative of Belgium, however, that the word "honour" in that amendment was not sufficiently concrete. The vote on that amendment should be taken only after mature consideration. If however, it were decided to take an immediate vote, he would vote against inclusion of the word "honour" and in favour of the retention of the wording used in the basic draft declaration.

He would also make a formal amendment combining article 3 with article 20, since the ideas contained in the joint amendment were already stated in that article. It might be desirable to express them in a general covering article. He would insist, however, that the new text should be placed in a separate paragraph in order to bring out its importance. His proposal would be to retain as a first paragraph the text of article 3 as worded in the draft declaration and to add the text of article 20 as a second paragraph, deleting, however, the words "has the right to social security and", and substituting for the words "set out below"

① UN Document: A/C. 3/SR/105, p. 177.

联大第三委员会及联大全会

the words "necessary to the full development of the personality", that phrase being taken, with the omission of the word "human", from the joint amendment.

He would vote against the joint amendment because he considered it incorrect to express two sets of ideas in a single paragraph.

While he would abstain from discussing the substance of the USSR amendment, he would vote against it because it dealt with implementation; that did not come within the scope of the declaration.

【纪要影像】

Mr. CHANG (China) said he wished to give the correct version of the Chinese proverb mentioned by the representative of Belgium. It was: "Sweep the snow in front of one's own door. Overlook the frost on others' roof-tiles." That made for good neighbours.

He wished to lay great stress upon the need for careful consideration of the amendments before the Committee. Another Chinese proverb ran: "Matters allowed to mature slowly are free from sharp corners." That was the spirit in which the drafting of article 3 should be approached.

He had no objection to the drafting changes made in the revised version of the joint amendment submitted by Uruguay, Cuba and Lebanon (A/C.3/274/Rev.1). He agreed with the representative of Belgium, however, that the word "honour" in that amendment was not sufficiently concrete. The vote on that amendment should be taken only after mature consideration. If however, it were decided to take an immediate vote, he would vote against inclusion of the word "honour" and in favour of the retention of the wording used in the basic draft declaration.

He would also make a formal amendment combining article 3 with article 20, since the ideas contained in the joint amendment were already stated in that article. It might be desirable to express them in a general covering article. He would insist, however, that the new text should be placed in a separate paragraph in order to bring out its importance. His proposal would be to retain as a first paragraph the text of article 3 as worded in the draft declaration and to add the text of article 20 as a second paragraph, deleting, however, the words "has the right to social security and", and substituting for the words "set out below" the words "necessary to the full development of the personality", that phrase being taken, with the omission of the word "human", from the joint amendment.

He would vote against the joint amendment because he considered it incorrect to express two sets of ideas in a single paragraph.

While he would abstain from discussing the substance of the USSR amendment, he would vote against it because it dealt with implementation; that did not come within the scope of the declaration.

图片 3.3.15：张彭春在联大第三委员会第三届第 105 次会议发言纪要

【纪要译文】

张先生(中国)说,他希望给出比利时代表提到的中国谚语的正确版本。它是:"各人自扫门前雪,莫管他人瓦上霜。"这就是好邻居。

他希望强调,有必要认真审议委员会面前的修正案。另一句中国谚语说:"事缓则圆,急难成效。"这就是起草第 3 条的精神。

他不反对乌拉圭、古巴和黎巴嫩提交的联合修正案修订本（A/C.3/274/Rev.1)中的措辞修改。然而,他同意比利时代表的意见,即该修正案中的"荣誉"一词不够具体。只有在经过充分考虑后,才能对该修正案进行表决。然而,如果决定立即进行表决,他将投票反对列入"荣誉"一词,并赞成保留基本宣言草案中使用的措辞。

他还将结合第 3 条和第 20 条提出一项正式修正案,因为联合修正案中所载的想法已在该条中阐明。最好用一条一般性的概括性条款来表达它们。然而,他坚持认为,新的文本应该放在一个单独的段落中,以突出其重要性。他的建议是保留以宣言草案文本措辞的第 3 条作为第一段,添加第 20 条的文本作为第二段,但删除"有权享受社会保障及",并在联合修正案中删除"人"一词,用"人格的全面发展十分必要"替代"以下阐明"一词。

他将投票反对联合修正案,因为他认为在一个段落中表达两组观点是不正确的。

虽然他会对苏联修正案的实质内容投弃权票,但他会投反对票,因为它涉及执行问题;这不在《宣言》的范围之内。

12. 张彭春在联大第三委员会第三届第 107 次会议上的发言

联大第三委员会第三届第 107 次会议,于 1948 年 10 月 19 日下午 3 时至晚上 6 时,在巴黎夏洛宫召开,本次会议继续讨论《国际人权宣言》草案(第 3 条)。中国代表张彭春参加了本次会议,并在会议上发言,其具体发言内容①会议纪要、纪要影像和纪要译文如下:

【会议纪要】

Mr. Pavlov（Union of Soviet Socialist Republics）protested against that

① UN Document：A/C. 3/SR/107, p. 184; p. 186; p. 191.

487

联大第三委员会及联大全会

procedure. As it stood, the basic text did not mention the rights and obligations of States. A proposal not to include in a draft ideas which were not there could not be considered and treated as an amendment to that draft. The Egyptian proposal could, on the other hand, be submitted in the form of an amendment to the USSR amendment, which actually took those rights and obligations into account.

Mr. Pavlov therefore considered that the Committee ought first to arrive at a decision regarding the draft amendment submitted by the delegation of the Soviet Union.

The Chinese representative had expressed the opinion that the USSR amendment would be tantamount to deleting from the articles the right of any individual to liberty and security of person, which right was included in the basic text; and he had been in favour of the inclusion of that right. Mr. Pavlov said that the amendment submitted by the Soviet Union did not intend to exclude that right; it was meant simply to ensure protection of the right to life. Should the corresponding clauses be adopted, and should the Chinese representative wish to add to the USSR amendment a paragraph affirming that every individual had a right to liberty and security of person, Mr. Pavlov would vote in favour of that amendment.

Replying to the USSR representative, Mr. CHANG (China) pointed out that the sole object of his remarks had been to propose a more convenient voting procedure. The first sentence of the Soviet Union amendment was identical with the basic text, but it omitted the words "liberty and security of person", Mr. Chang therefore proposed that the new draft should be considered as an amendment calling for the deletion of those words.

On a point of order, Mr. CHANG (China) questioned the desirability of voting on the Belgian delegation's amendment (A/C. 3/282), since the Committee had just voted against the addition of the words "physical integrity", which also appeared in that amendment.

Mr. Chang (China) endorsed the views expressed by the French and U-nited States representatives regarding the definition of the words "security of person". As those views would be recorded, he thought it useless to prolong the debate on that point.

【纪要影像】

Mr. PAVLOV (Union of Soviet Socialist Republics) protested against that procedure. As it stood, the basic text did not mention the rights and obligations of States. A proposal not to include in a draft ideas which were not there could not be considered and treated as an amendment to that draft. The Egyptian proposal could, on the other hand, be submitted in the form of an amendment to the USSR amendment, which actually took those rights and obligations into account.

Mr. Pavlov therefore considered that the Committee ought first to arrive at a decision regarding the draft amendment submitted by the delegation of the Soviet Union.

The Chinese representative had expressed the opinion that the USSR amendment would be tantamount to deleting from the articles the right of any individual to liberty and security of person, which right was included in the basic text; and he had been in favour of the inclusion of that right. Mr. Pavlov said that the amendment submitted by the Soviet Union did not intend to exclude that right; it was meant simply to ensure protection of the right to life. Should the corresponding clauses be adopted, and should the Chinese representative wish to add to the USSR amendment a paragraph affirming that every individual had a right to liberty and security of person, Mr. Pavlov would vote in favour of that amendment.

Replying to the USSR representative, Mr. CHANG (China) pointed out that the sole object of his remarks had been to propose a more convenient voting procedure. The first sentence of the Soviet Union amendment was identical with the basic text, but it omitted the words "liberty and security of person". Mr. Chang therefore proposed that the new draft should be considered as an amendment calling for the deletion of those words.

On a point of order, Mr. CHANG (China) questioned the desirability of voting on the Belgian delegation's amendment (A/C.3/282), since the Committee had just voted against the addition of the words "physical integrity", which also appeared in that amendment.

Mr. CHANG (China) endorsed the views expressed by the French and United States representatives regarding the definition of the words "security of person". As those views would be recorded, he thought it useless to prolong the debate on that point.

图片 3.3.16:张彭春在联大第三委员会第三届第 107 次会议发言纪要

【纪要译文】

帕夫洛夫先生(苏联)抗议这一程序。目前的基本案文没有提到国家的权利和义务。关于不在草案中列入不存在的想法的建议不能被视为对该草案的修正。另一方面,埃及的提案可以以对苏联修正案的修正案的形式提交,该修正案实际上考虑到了这些权利和义务。

因此,帕夫洛夫先生认为,委员会应首先就苏联代表团提交的修正案草案作出决定。

中国代表表示苏联修正案将等同于删除了包括在基本文本中的个人享有自由和人身安全的权利;他一直赞成将这项权利包括在内。帕夫洛夫先生说,苏联所提交的修正案不打算排除该权利,它只意味着确保对生命权的保护。如果相应条款获得通过,如果中国代表希望在苏联修正案中增加一段,确认每个人都有权享有人身自由和安全,帕夫洛夫先生将投票赞成该修正案。

张先生(中国)在答复苏联代表时指出,他发言的唯一目的是提出一种更为方便的表决程序。苏联修正案的第一句与基本案文相同,但它省略了"人身自由和安全"等字,因此,张先生建议,新草案应视为一项要求删除这些字的修正案。

关于顺序问题,张先生(中国)质疑是否有必要对比利时代表团的修正案(A/C. 3/282)进行表决,因为委员会刚刚投票反对在该修正案中添加"身体完整"一词。

张先生(中国)赞同法国和美国代表就"人身安全"一词的定义发表的意见。由于这些意见将被记录在案,他认为延长关于这一点的辩论是无用的。

13. 张彭春在联大第三委员会第三届第 108 次会议上的发言

联大第三委员会第三届第 108 次会议,于 1948 年 10 月 20 日下午 3 时 15 分至晚上 6 时 15 分,在巴黎夏洛宫召开,本次会议讨论了瑞典代表团关于加快委员会工作的提案(A/C. 3/281)。中国代表张彭春参加了本次会议,并发言支持该提案,其具体提案及张彭春的发言内容①会议纪要、纪要影像和纪要译文如下:

【会议纪要】

Proposal by the Swedish Delegation for Speeding up the Work of the Com-

---

① UN Document:A/C. 3/SR/108, p. 201.

mittee（A/C.3/281）

Mrs. LINDSTROM（Sweden）said that before the Committee went on to consider article of the draft declaration of human rights, she wished to make a proposal for speeding up its work.

In view of the limited number of meetings that remained for finishing their study of the declaration of rights, she deplored the length of the discussions. Many representatives had urgent work waiting to be done in their respective countries. She feared that they might not be able to stay in Paris until consideration of the draft declaration had been finished. For that reason, she proposed that the length of the speeches made in the Committee should be limited, in order to speed up the debates.

To that end, she submitted the following resolution to the Committee（A/C.3/281）:

"I. In accordance with rule 103 of the rules of procedure, the Committee fixes the following time-limit on speeches during the further consideration of the international declaration of human rights:

"1. Original speeches shall not exceed ten minutes;

"2. Second speeches shall not exceed five minutes.

"II. Acting under authority of rule 104 of the rules of procedure, the Chairman, with the consent of the Committee, shall declare the list of speakers closed at the end of one hour's debate on each article. This is subject to the Chairman's authority under this rule to accord the right to reply to any member if a speech delivered after he has declared the list closed makes this desirable. "

Mr. CHANG（China）supported the Swedish delegation's proposal.

【纪要影像】

图片 3.3.17：张彭春在联大第三委员会第三届第 108 次会议发言纪要

【纪要译文】

瑞典代表团关于加快委员会工作的提案（A/C. 3/281）

林斯特龙（Lindström）夫人（瑞典）说，在委员会审议人权宣言草案之前，她希望提出加速工作的建议。

鉴于完成《人权宣言》研究所需的会议数量有限，她对讨论时间过长表示遗憾。许多代表在各自国家都有迫切的工作要做。她担心，在完成对宣言草案的审议之前，他们可能无法留在巴黎。因此，她建议限制在委员会发言的长度，以加快辩论。

为此，她向委员会提交了以下决议案（A/C. 3/281）：

"一、根据议事规则第 103 条，委员会在进一步审议《国际人权宣言》期间对发言规定了以下时限：

"1. 初次发言不得超过十分钟；

"2. 第二次发言不得超过五分钟。

"二、主席根据议事规则第 104 条的授权行事，并征得委员会同意，应在就每一条进行一小时辩论后宣布发言名单截止。根据本条规则，主席有权在宣布名单结束后发表的讲话使任何成员有权作出答复时,给予该成员答辩权。"

张先生(中国)支持瑞典代表团的提案。

14. 张彭春在联大第三委员会
第三届第 109 次会议上的发言

联大第三委员会第三届第 109 次会议,于 1948 年 10 月 21 日下午 3 时至晚上 6 时 15 分,在巴黎夏洛宫召开,本次会议主要讨论议程项目 4(a) 的审议日期(难民和流离失所者:联合国调解人关于向难民提供巴勒斯坦援助的进度报告第三部分)、讨论《国际人权宣言》草案(第 4 条)。中国代表张彭春参加了本次会议,并在会议上发言,其具体发言内容①会议纪要、纪要影像和纪要译文如下:

【会议纪要】

Mr. CHANG (China) proposed that a small working group should be appointed to report back to the Committee as soon as possible, but that no time-limit should be set for its work. The Committee could discuss the report at its afternoon meetings, and could continue its examination of the draft declaration of human rights at the morning meetings.

While accepting the principle of appointing a working group, Mrs. ROOSEVELT (United States of America) stressed the need first to give the delegations an opportunity to consult their Governments on the assistance which the latter could make available. The proposal was quite new and many delegations had not yet considered the practical means by which their Governments might

---

① UN Document: A/C. 3/SR/109, p. 208.

give aid to the Palestine refugees. Certain questions, such as transport, were difficult to solve.

Mrs. Roosevelt therefore proposed that that item of the agenda should not be considered until the end of the following week. The working group could be set up at that time, and it could be guided by the information which the representatives had received from their Governments with regard to the assistance which the latter were in a position to give to the Palestine refugees.

The CHAIRMAN shared the view of the United States representative. He stressed that the immediate creation of a working group would also raise a procedural difficulty in view of the fact that such action presupposed that the Committee already had that item of its agenda before it, whereas it had not yet taken any decision on the matter.

He therefore proposed that the question should be included in the agenda of the meeting to be held on the afternoon of Friday, 29 October.

【纪要影像】

Mr. CHANG (China) proposed that a small working group should be appointed to report back to the Committee as soon as possible. but that no time-limit should be set for its work. The Committee could discuss the report at its afternoon meetings, and could continue its examination of the draft declaration of human rights at the morning meetings.

While accepting the principle of appointing a working group, Mrs. ROOSEVELT (United States of America) stressed the need first to give the delegations an opportunity to consult their Governments on the assistance which the latter could make available. The proposal was quite new and many delegations had not yet considered the practical means by which their Governments might give aid to the Palestine refugees. Certain questions, such as transport, were difficult to solve.

Mrs. Roosevelt therefore proposed that that item of the agenda should not be considered until the end of the following week. The working group could be set up at that time, and it could be guided by the information which the representatives had received from their Governments with regard to the assistance which the latter were in a position to give to the Palestine refugees.

The CHAIRMAN shared the view of the United States representative. He stressed that the immediate creation of a working group would also raise a procedural difficulty in view of the fact that such action presupposed that the Committee already had that item of its agenda before it, whereas it had not yet taken any decision on the matter.

He therefore proposed that the question should be included in the agenda of the meeting to be held on the afternoon of Friday, 29 October.

图片 3.3.18：张彭春在联大第三委员会第三届第 109 次会议发言纪要

【纪要译文】

张先生(中国)提议,应任命一个小型工作组尽快向委员会汇报工作,但不应为其工作设定时限。委员会可在下午的会议上讨论该报告,并可在上午的会议上继续审查人权宣言草案。

罗斯福夫人(美国)在接受任命一个工作组的原则的同时,强调必须首先让各国代表团有机会就后者可以提供的援助与本国政府协商。这是一项相当新的提案,许多代表团尚未考虑其政府可能向巴勒斯坦难民提供援助的实际手段。有些问题,例如运输,很难解决。

因此,罗斯福夫人提议在下一周结束之前不审议该议程项目。工作组可以在那时成立,工作组的指导方针可以是各国代表从其政府收到的关于后者能够向巴勒斯坦难民提供援助的资料。

主席同意美国代表的观点。他强调,立即设立一个工作组也会带来程序上的困难,因为这种行动的前提是委员会已经收到了该议程项目,而它尚未就此事项作出任何决定。

他因此提议将该问题列入定于 10 月 29 日星期五下午举行的会议议程。

15. 张彭春在联大第三委员会
第三届第 110 次会议上的发言

联大第三委员会第三届第 110 次会议,于 1948 年 10 月 22 日上午 10 时 45 分至下午 1 时 40 分,在巴黎夏洛宫召开,本次会议继续讨论《国际人权宣言》草案(第 4 条)。中国代表张彭春参加了本次会议,并在会议上先后多次发言,其具体发言内容①会议纪要、纪要影像和纪要译文如下:

---

① UN Document:A/C. 3/SR/110, p. 219; p. 220; p. 221; p. 222; p. 223.

【会议纪要】

Article 4 (*continued*)

Mr. CHANG (China) asked for clarification of the proposed sub-committee's terms of reference. The matters which it was to examine might not be complex enough to warrant setting up such a sub-committee.

Mr. CHANG (China) pointed out that in document E/800 (page 32) the USSR amendment was referred to as an addition; the USSR representative was describing it as a substitution. As an addition, it might be regarded rather as a method of implementing the original text than as a statement of principle. If taken in that sense, it was out of place in the declaration.

Mr. CHANG (China) said that if the USSR amendment were taken in substitution for the original text, he would vote against it. Prohibition of the slave trade need further study. Moreover, the phrase appeared to be merely a measure directing the implementation of the original text.

Mr. CHANG (China) suggested that a small sub-committee should be set up to make final drafting changes and that the vote on the whole article should be postponed until the following meeting.

Mr. CHANG (China) explained that he had not taken part in the vote because he considered that the text of the article was not satisfactory.

Mr. CHANG (China) asked for clarification of the proposed sub-committee's terms of reference. The matters which it was to examine might not be complex enough to warrant setting up such a sub-committee.

Mr. CHANG (China) pointed out that in document E/800 (page 32) the USSR amendment was referred to as an addition; the USSR representative was describing it as a substitution. As an addition, it might be regarded rather as a method of implementing the original text than as a statement of principle. If taken in that sense, it was out of place in the declaration.

Mr. CHANG (China) said that if the USSR amendment were taken in substitution for the original text, he would vote against it. Prohibition of the slave trade needed further study. Moreover, the phrase appeared to be merely a measure directing implementation of the original text.

Mr. CHANG (China) suggested that a small sub-committee should be set up to make final drafting changes and that the vote on the whole article should be postponed until the following meeting.

Mr. CHANG (China) explained that he had not taken part in the vote because he considered that the text of the article was not satisfactory.

图片 3.3.19：张彭春在联大第三委员会第三届第 110 次会议发言纪要

【纪要译文】

第 4 条(续)

张先生(中国)要求澄清拟议的小组委员会的职权范围。委员会要研究的事项可能没有复杂到有必要成立这样一个小组委员会。

张先生(中国)指出,在 E/800 号文件(第 32 页)中,苏联的修正案被称为增补;苏联代表将其描述为替代。此外,它可能被视为执行原文的一种方法,而不是一项原则声明。如果从这个意义上讲,它在宣言中是不合适的。

张先生(中国)说,如果以苏联修正案取代原文,他将投反对票。禁止贩卖奴隶需要进一步研究。此外,这一短语似乎只是指导实施原文的一项措施。

张先生(中国)建议,应设立一个小组委员会,以作最后的修改,并且对整条内容的表决应推迟到下一次会议。

张先生(中国)解释说,他没有参加表决,因为他认为该条的案文不令人满意。

联大第三委员会及联大全会

16. 张彭春在联大第三委员会
第三届第 113 次会议上的发言

联大第三委员会第三届第 113 次会议,于 1948 年 10 月 26 日下午 3 时至晚上 6 时 15 分,在巴黎夏洛宫召开,本次会议继续讨论《国际人权宣言》草案(第 6 条)。中国代表张彭春参加了本次会议,并在会议上发言,其具体发言内容①会议纪要、纪要影像和纪要译文如下:

【会议纪要】

Mr. CHANG (China), speaking on a point of order, suggested that the Mexican amendment might be put to the vote in parts and that the vote might be taken alternatively on the phrase "an effective judicial remedy" (A/C. 3/308) or the phrase "an effective remedy by the competent national tribunals" (A/C. 3/309).

He expressed a preference for the former; the word "national" might not be universally applicable, as a number of countries had state and provincial courts, which could not be considered national.

Mr. CHANG (China) stated that his suggestion had been made solely with a view to saving time and producing a more perfect text.

As it did not appear to have achieved its purpose, he withdrew it.

Mr. CHANG (China) declared that the draft in question was far from perfect. It should be rendered more definite, clearer and more clear cut. It should be realized that the text was intended to achieve improvement in the status of mankind. The adoption of certain substitutes proposed for the word "arbitrary"

---

① UN Document: A/C. 3/SR/113, p. 242; p. 251.

would disturb the balance of the article. He submitted that additions could doubtless be inserted in other articles.

The suggestion regarding exile might be included in article 13, and a sentence might be added to the effect that no person should be arbitrarily barred from entering his own country.

【纪要影像】

Mr. CHANG (China), speaking on a point of order, suggested that the Mexican amendment might be put to the vote in parts and that the vote might be taken alternatively on the phrase "an effective judicial remedy" (A/C.3/308) or the phrase "an effective remedy by the competent national tribunals" (A/C.3/309).

He expressed a preference for the former; the word "national" might not be universally applicable, as a number of countries had state and provincial courts, which could not be considered national.

Mr. CHANG (China) stated that his suggestion had been made solely with a view to saving time and producing a more perfect text.

As it did not appear to have achieved its purpose, he withdrew it.

Mr. CHANG (China) declared that the draft in question was far from perfect. It should be rendered more definite, clearer and more clear cut. It should be realized that the text was intended to achieve improvement in the status of mankind. The adoption of certain substitutes proposed for the word "arbitrary" would disturb the balance of the article. He submitted that additions could doubtless be inserted in other articles.

The suggestion regarding exile might be included in article 13, and a sentence might be added to the effect that no person should be arbitrarily barred from entering his own country.

图片 3.3.20：张彭春在联大第三委员会第三届第 113 次会议发言纪要

【纪要译文】

张先生(中国)就程序问题发言,建议墨西哥修正案可以进行部分投票,投票要么可以针对短语"一种有效的司法救济"(A/C.3/308)或者针对短语"一个由合格国家法庭的有效救济"(A/C.3/309)"进行表决。

他表示倾向于前者;"国家"一词可能并不普遍适用,因为一些国家有州和省法院,不能将其视为国家法院。

张先生(中国)说,他的建议完全是为了节省时间和编写更完善的案文。

由于它似乎没有达到目的,他撤回了它。

张先生(中国)宣布,讨论中的草案还远远没有完善。它应该变得更

联大第三委员会及联大全会

清楚、更清晰、更明确。应该意识到,文本是为了实现人类地位的提高。采用"任意的"一词的某些建议替代词会干扰条款的平衡。他认为,毫无疑问,可以在其他条款中加入补充条款。

关于流亡的建议可列入第 13 条,并可增加一句话,大意是不应任意禁止任何人进入其本国。

17. 张彭春在联大第三委员会 第三届第 114 次会议上的发言

联大第三委员会第三届第 114 次会议,于 1948 年 10 月 27 日下午 3 时至晚上 6 时 10 分,在巴黎夏洛宫召开,本次会议继续讨论《国际人权宣言》草案(第 7 条)。中国代表张彭春参加了本次会议,并在会议上发言,其具体发言内容①会议纪要、纪要影像和纪要译文如下:

【会议纪要】

Mr. Chang (China) said that he was certainly not opposed to including a prohibition of exile in the declaration.

He suggested the appointment of a sub-committee of three to draft an appropriate text after the Committee itself had decided the matter in principle.

He wondered, also, whether the idea might not be included in article 13.

---

① UN Document:A/C. 3/SR/114, p. 225.

【纪要影像】

Mr. CHANG (China) said that he was certainly not opposed to including a prohibition of exile in the declaration.

He suggested the appointment of a sub-committee of three to draft an appropriate text after the Committee itself had decided the matter in principle.

He wondered, also, whether the idea might not be included in article 13.

图片 3.3.21:张彭春在联大第三委员会第三届第 114 次会议发言纪要

【纪要译文】

张先生(中国)说,他肯定不反对在《宣言》中包括禁止被放逐的内容。

他建议任命一个由三人组成的小组委员会,在委员会原则上自行决定此事后起草一份适当的案文。

他还想知道这一想法是否可以不列入第 13 条。

18. 张彭春在联大第三委员会第三届第 119 次会议上的发言

联大第三委员会第三届第 119 次会议,于 1948 年 10 月 30 日下午 3 时至晚上 6 时 20 分,在巴黎夏洛宫召开,本次会议继续讨论《国际人权宣言》草案(第 10 条)。中国代表张彭春参加了本次会议,并在会议上发言,其具体发言内容①会议纪要、纪要影像和纪要译文如下:

① UN Document:A/C. 3/SR/119, p. 308;p. 314.

联大第三委员会及联大全会

【会议纪要】

Mr. CHANG (China) supported the United Kingdom amendment.

He agreed with the United States representative that the qualification "arbitrary" was far more comprehensive than "unreasonable" or the concept of "inviolability".

The Cuban amendment (A/C. 3/232) was interesting in that it extended the protection accorded to privacy, home, family and correspondence to honour and reputation, thus covering the subjective and social aspects of the human individual. Greater weight would attach to the Cuban provision to protect reputation and honour if it were placed in a separate paragraph.

Although the provision for legal protection might appear out of place in the declaration it might be inserted in the case under consideration since its omission might leave a loop-hole for such extralegal methods of protecting honour as dueling. He thought, however, that the United Kingdom amendment would be most satisfactory in the case in point.

Mr. CHANG (China), speaking on a point of order, stated that the Committee had before it an English text different from that which it had accepted. He and possibly other representatives had voted against the first version because it had not appeared to make sense. The Committee could not be asked to vote on the whole of an amendment the wording of which was different from the text on which the vote had been taken, in parts. Rather, it should take a second vote on the first paragraph, and be given an opportunity to reject it.

Mr. CHANG (China) supported the United Kingdom amendment.

He agreed with the United States representative that the qualification "arbitrary" was far more comprehensive than "unreasonable" or the concept of "inviolability".

The Cuban amendment (A/C.3/232) was interesting in that it extended the protection accorded to privacy, home, family and correspondence to honour and reputation, thus covering the subjective and social aspects of the human individual. Greater weight would attach to the Cuban provision to protect reputation and honour if it were placed in a separate paragraph.

Although the provision for legal protection might appear out of place in the declaration, it might be inserted in the case under consideration since its omission might leave a loop-hole for such extralegal methods of protecting honour as duelling. He thought, however, that the United Kingdom amendment would be most satisfactory in the case in point.

Mr. CHANG (China), speaking on a point of order, stated that the Committee had before it an English text different from that which it had accepted. He and possibly other representatives had voted against the first version because it had not appeared to make sense. The Committee could not be asked to vote on the whole of an amendment the wording of which was different from the text on which the vote had been taken, in parts. Rather, it should take a second vote on the first paragraph, and be given an opportunity to reject it.

图片 3.3.22：张彭春在联大第三委员会第三届第 119 次会议发言纪要

【纪要译文】

张先生(中国)支持英国的修正案。

他同意美国代表的意见,即"任意"的限制比"不合理"或"不可侵犯"的概念要全面得多。

古巴修正案(A/C.3/232)有趣的是,它扩展到给予隐私、家庭、住宅和通信、荣誉和声誉的保护,从而覆盖人类个体的主观方面和社会方面。如果要放在一个单独的段落,将给予古巴保护名誉和荣誉条款以更多重视。

虽然法律保护的规定可能在声明中显得不合适,但在审议的情况下它也可能被插入,因为如果不这样做,可能会给诸如决斗等保护名誉的法外方法留下一个漏洞。然而,他认为,英国的修正案最能令人满意。

张先生(中国)就程序问题发言说,委员会面前有一份不同于其所接受的英文文本。他和可能的其他代表投票反对第一个版本,因为它似乎没有意义。不能要求委员会就一项修正案的全部内容进行部分表决,该修正案的措辞与进行表决的案文不同。相反,它应该对第一段进行第二次投票,并有机会否决它。

19. 张彭春在联大第三委员会
第三届第 125 次会议上的发言

联大第三委员会第三届第 125 次会议,于 1948 年 11 月 8 日上午 10 时 45 分至下午 1 时 15 分,在巴黎夏洛宫召开,本次会议继续讨论《国际人权宣言》草案(第 14 条)。中国代表张彭春参加了本次会议,并在会议上发言,其具体发言内容①会议纪要、纪要影像和纪要译文如下:

【会议纪要】

Mr. CHANG(China)stated that his delegation had abstained from taking part in the final vote on article 14 because the gaps in that article were too serious to be overlooked.

That fact demonstrated once again the importance of avoiding undue haste in drafting; a document such as the one the Committee had to prepare must be the outcome of long reflection and thorough study.

The Chinese delegation thought that the General Assembly's attention should be drawn to the matter.

---

① UN Document:A/C. 3/SR/125, pp. 378-379.

Mr. CHANG (China) stated that his delegation had abstained from taking part in the final vote on

article 14 because the gaps in that article were too serious to be overlooked.

That fact demonstrated once again the importance of avoiding undue haste in drafting; a document such as the one the Committee had to prepare must be the outcome of long reflection and thorough study.

The Chinese delegation thought that the General Assembly's attention should be drawn to the matter.

图片 3.3.23:张彭春在联大第三委员会第三届第 125 次会议发言纪要

【纪要译文】

张先生(中国)说,他的代表团弃权不参加第 14 条的最终投票,因为那一条的分歧太严重不能被忽视。

这一事实再次证明了避免过于仓促起草的重要性;需要为委员会准备的这样一份文件必须是长期思考和深入研究的结果。

中国代表团认为,应提请联大注意这件事。

20. 张彭春在联大第三委员会 第三届第 126 次会议上的发言

联大第三委员会第三届第 126 次会议,于 1948 年 11 月 8 日下午 3 时至晚上 6 时 30 分,在巴黎夏洛宫召开,本次会议继续讨论《国际人权宣言》

草案(第15条)。中国代表张彭春参加了本次会议,并在会议上发言,其具体发言内容①会议纪要、纪要影像和纪要译文如下:

【会议纪要】

Mr. CHANG (China), while expressing appreciation of the amendments proposed, stated that his delegation preferred the original draft.

Mr. CHANG (China) realized that the right to private property was abused, but expressed the view that article 27 was the appropriate place for strengthening the limitations to the various rights. He recognized the good intentions of the authors of the two amendments, but still felt that the carefully prepared basic text was preferable.

【纪要影像】

Mr. CHANG (China), while expressing appreciation of the amendments proposed, stated that his delegation preferred the original draft.

Mr. CHANG (China) realized that the right to private property was abused, but expressed the view that article 27 was the appropriate place for strengthening the limitations to the various rights. He recognized the good intentions of the authors of the two amendments, but still felt that the carefully prepared basic text was preferable.

图片3.3.24:张彭春在联大第三委员会第三届第126次会议发言纪要

【纪要译文】

张先生(中国)在表示赞赏拟议修正案的同时表示,中国代表团倾向

---

① UN Document: A/C. 3/SR/126, p. 386; p. 388.

于原稿。

张先生(中国)认识到私有财产权被滥用,但认为第 27 条是加强对各种权利限制的适当位置。他承认两项修正案作者的良好意图,但仍然认为精心编写的基础案文更可取。

21. 张彭春在联大第三委员会第三届第 127 次会议上的发言

联大第三委员会第三届第 127 次会议,于 1948 年 11 月 9 日上午 10 时 50 分至下午 1 时 20 分,在巴黎夏洛宫召开,本次会议继续讨论《国际人权宣言》草案(第 16 条)。中国代表张彭春参加了本次会议,并在会议上发言,其具体发言内容①会议纪要、纪要影像和纪要译文如下:

【会议纪要】

Mr. CHANG(China)declared that in discussing article 16, the Committee was dealing with one of the most important principles in the declaration. From the eighteenth century, when the idea of human rights was born in Western Europe, freedom of thought had figured among the essential human freedoms and had covered the idea of religious freedom. He felt, moreover, that freedom of thought included freedom of conscience as well as religious freedom, but, as the declaration was destined for the vast mass of the world's population it should never be criticized for being too explicit.

He declared that 1869, the date of the publication of Darwin's treatises, really marked the beginning of the so-called conflict of religion and science. The effects, already eighty years old, of that manifestation of the human spirit

---

① UN Document:A/C. 3/SR/127, pp. 397-398.

could not be sufficiently deplored, and its influence could be felt in the Committee itself. For that reason he stressed the necessity of studying the problem of religious expression in its true perspective.

In order to throw more light on the question, he wished first of all to explain to the Committee how the Chinese approached the religious problem. Chinese philosophy was based essentially on a firm belief in a unitarian cause, expressed on the human plane by a pluralistic tolerance. That philosophy considered that man's actions were more important than metaphysics, that the art of living should be placed above knowledge of the causes of life, and that the best way for man to testify to the greatness of the Divinity was to give proof of an exemplary attitude in this world. In the eyes of Chinese philosophers, it was pluralistic tolerance, manifesting itself in every sphere of thought, conscience and religion, which should inspire men if they wished to base their relations on benevolence and justice.

Returning to article 16, Mr. Chang said he had heard with sympathy and respect the objections raised by the representative of Saudi Arabia. For the countries of the Far East, the nineteenth century, with its expansion of Western industrialism, had not always been very kind and he admitted that missionaries had not always limited themselves to their religious mission.

He expressed the opinion, however, that freedom of thought was well protected by the text proposed by the Commission on Human Rights. During the discussions in the latter, it had been agreed that freedom of belief was an integral part of freedom of thought and conscience, and if special emphasis was laid on the necessity of protecting it, that was to ensure the inviolability of that profound part of thought and conscience which, being largely emotional, was apt to lead mankind into unreasoned conflict.

Mr. CHANG (China) declared that in discussing article 16, the Committee was dealing with one of the most important principles in the declaration. From the eighteenth century, when the idea of human rights was born in Western Europe, freedom of thought had figured among the essential human freedoms and had covered the idea of religious freedom. He felt, moreover, that freedom of thought included freedom of conscience as well as religious freedom, but, as the declaration was destined for the vast mass of the world's population it should never be criticized for being too explicit.

He declared that 1869, the date of the publication of Darwin's treatises, really marked the beginning of the so-called conflict of religion and science. The effects, already eighty years old, of that manifestation of the human spirit could not be sufficiently deplored, and its influence could be felt in the Committee itself. For that reason he stressed the necessity of studying the problem of religious expression in its true perspective.

In order to throw more light on the question, he wished first of all to explain to the Committee how the Chinese approached the religious problem. Chinese philosophy was based essentially on a firm belief in a unitarian cause, expressed on the human plane by a pluralistic tolerance. That philosophy considered that man's actions were more important than metaphysics, that the art of living should be placed above knowledge of the causes of life, and that the best way for man to testify to the greatness of the Divinity was to give proof of an exemplary attitude in this world. In the eyes of Chinese philosophers, it was pluralistic tolerance, manifesting itself in every sphere of thought, conscience and religion, which should inspire men if they wished to base their relations on benevolence and justice.

Returning to article 16, Mr. Chang said he had heard with sympathy and respect the objections raised by the representative of Saudi Arabia. For the countries of the Far East, the nineteenth century, with its expansion of Western industrialism, had not always been very kind and he admitted that missionaries had not always limited themselves to their religious mission.

He expressed the opinion, however, that freedom of thought was well protected by the text proposed by the Commission on Human Rights. During the discussions in the latter, it had been agreed that freedom of belief was an integral part of freedom of thought and conscience, and if special emphasis was laid on the necessity of protecting it, that was to ensure the inviolability of that profound part of thought and conscience which, being largely emotional, was apt to lead mankind into unreasoned conflict.

图片 3.3.25：张彭春在联大第三委员会第三届第 127 次会议发言纪要

【纪要译文】

张先生(中国)宣布,在讨论第 16 条时,委员会正在处理《宣言》中最重要的原则之一。从 18 世纪,当人权思想在西欧产生,在人类基本自由之中自由的思想已经出现,它涵盖了宗教信仰自由的理念。此外,他认为,思想自由包括良心自由和宗教自由,但是,由于《宣言》的对象是世界上的大多数人,因此绝不能批评它过于明确。

他宣称,1869 年,达尔文论文的出版日期,真正标志着所谓的宗教和科学冲突的开始。已经存在了 80 年的这种人类精神的表现所产生的影响是不可低估的,它的影响在委员会本身就可以感觉到。因此,他强调有必要从真正的角度研究宗教表达问题。

为了进一步阐明这个问题,他希望首先向委员会解释中国人是如何处理宗教问题的。中国哲学基本上是建立在对一元论思想的坚定信念基础上的,这种信念在人的层面上表现为多元宽容,认为人的行为比形而上学更重要,认为生活艺术应该高于对人生事业的认识,人类证明神性伟大的最好方法就是证明在这个世界上有一种模范的态度。在中国哲学家看来,

联大第三委员会及联大全会

多元宽容体现在思想、良心和宗教的各个领域,如果人们希望将他们的关系建立在仁义的基础上,这种宽容应该会激励人们。

回到第 16 条,张先生说,他同情并尊重沙特阿拉伯代表提出的反对意见。对于远东国家来说,19 世纪,随着西方工业主义的扩张,并不总是很友好,他承认传教士并不总是局限于他们的宗教使命。

然而,他认为,人权委员会提出的案文很好地保护了思想自由。在后者的讨论中,人们一致认为信仰自由是思想和良心自由的一个组成部分,如果特别强调保护信仰自由的必要性,那就是确保思想和良心的深邃部分不可侵犯,而这一部分主要是情感的,很容易导致人类陷入毫无根据的冲突。

22. 张彭春在联大第三委员会
第三届第 131 次会议上的发言

联大第三委员会第三届第 131 次会议,于 1948 年 11 月 11 日下午 3 时至晚上 6 时 11 分,在巴黎夏洛宫召开,本次会议继续讨论《国际人权宣言》草案(第 18 条)。中国代表张彭春参加了本次会议,并在会议上发言,其发言内容①会议纪要、纪要影像和纪要译文如下:

【会议纪要】

Mr. CHANG (China) expressed his agreement with the representatives of Australia and Uruguay. It had so often been mentioned in the organs of the United Nations that the Charter could not be interpreted in any way which could justify interference in the internal affairs of Member States, that he feared that, if the Polish amendment were accepted, the right to freedom of assembly and

———————————

① UN Document: A/C. 3/SR/131, p. 441; p. 444; p. 446.

association might be interpreted as either restricting national legislation, or as being capable of exercise in defiance of the laws of the various States.

Mr. CHANG (China) pointed out that the amendment furthest removed from the Cuban amendment was the nearest to the basic text.

He asked whether the Belgian amendment, if adopted, should replace the basic text. He thought that the two texts should be compared.

Mr. CHANG (China) expressed his satisfaction at the adoption of the Uruguayan amendment, which established an important principle. But he was not too happy about the wording of article 18, because he considered the English text to be ambiguous on account of the fact that it was not certain whether the adjective "peaceful" was applicable only to the word "assembly", or to the two words "assembly" and "association".

【纪要影像】

Mr. CHANG (China) expressed his agreement with the representatives of Australia and Uruguay. It had so often been mentioned in the organs of the United Nations that the Charter could not be interpreted in any way which could justify interference in the internal affairs of Member States, that he feared that, if the Polish amendment were accepted, the right to freedom of assembly and association might be interpreted as either restricting national legislation, or as being capable of exercise in defiance of the laws of the various States.

Mr. CHANG (China) pointed out that the amendment furthest removed from the Cuban amendment was the nearest to the basic text.

He asked whether the Belgian amendment, if adopted, should replace the basic text. He thought that the two texts should be compared.

Mr. CHANG (China) expressed his satisfaction at the adoption of the Uruguayan amendment, which established an important principle. But he was not too happy about the wording of article 18, because he considered the English text to be ambiguous on account of the fact that it was not certain whether the adjective "peaceful" was applicable only to the word "assembly", or to the two words "assembly" and "association".

图片3.3.26：张彭春在联大第三委员会第三届第131次会议发言纪要

【纪要译文】

张先生(中国)表示同意澳大利亚和乌拉圭代表的意见。联合国各机构经常提到,对《宪章》的解释不能成为干涉会员国内政的理由,因此他担心,如果波兰的修正案被接受,集会和结社自由的权利可能被解释为限制国家立法,或解释为能够在违反各国法律的情况下实施。

张先生(中国)指出,离古巴修正案最远的修正案最接近基本案文。

他询问比利时修正案如果获得通过,是否应取代基本案文。他认为这两个文本应该进行比较。

张先生(中国)对乌拉圭修正案的通过表示满意,该修正案确立了一项重要原则。但他对第18条的措辞不太满意,因为他认为英文文本模棱两可,由于事实上不确定形容词"和平的"是只适用于"集会"一词,还是也适用于"集会"和"结社"两个词。

23. 张彭春在联大第三委员会 第三届第 133 次会议上的发言

联大第三委员会第三届第 133 次会议,于 1948 年 11 月 12 日上午 10 时 55 分至下午 1 时 20 分,在巴黎夏洛宫召开,本次会议继续讨论《国际人权宣言》草案(第 19 条)。中国代表张彭春参加了本次会议,并在会议上发言,其具体发言内容①会议纪要、纪要影像和纪要译文如下:

【会议纪要】

Mr. CHANG (China) said that he had listened very carefully to comments by the different delegations on article 19 of the declaration and proposed a new version of that article based on the suggestions of various delegations (A/C. 3/ 333).

Dealing first with paragraph 3, he said that the declaration should proclaim human rights and not stress the authority of Government, as the French

---

① UN Document:A/C. 3/SR/133, p. 462; p. 467.

delegation's amendment did. For that reason his delegation in paragraph 3 of its amendment proposed that "the will of the people" should become the subject of the first clause. The paragraph would read as follows:

"3. The will of the people is the source of the authority of government; this will shall be expressed in elections, universal, equal, periodic and by secret ballot, or manifested in equivalent free voting procedures."

In the first paragraph of article 19 his delegation proposed adding the words "as a citizen" immediately after the word "everyone". That addition took account of the amendments proposed by the delegations of Cuba and Uruguay. Moreover, the Human Rights Commission had adopted a similar wording in article 20, which began with the words "Everyone, as a member of society". The French text of this paragraph might be simplified by the omission of the words "qu'elle a".

In his country the civil service had been in existence for a long time and he emphasized the importance of the idea, not yet realized in the Western world, that civil servants should be recruited by the competitive method to make sure that only qualified persons took a direct part in the public service of their country. Hence he proposed paragraph 2 of article 19 should be amended to read as follows:

"2. Everyone has the right of free and equal access to public service in his country."

Mr. Abadi (Iraq), Mr. Contoumas (Greece) and Mr. Chang (China) also expressed themselves against the idea of appointing a drafting subcommittee to deal with article 19.

【纪要影像】

Mr. CHANG (China) said that he had listened very carefully to comments by the different delegations on article 19 of the declaration and proposed a new version of that article based on the suggestions of various delegations (A/C.3/333).

Dealing first with paragraph 3, he said that the declaration should proclaim human rights and not stress the authority of Government, as the French delegation's amendment did. For that reason his delegation in paragraph 3 of its amendment proposed that "the will of the people" should become the subject of the first clause. The paragraph would read as follows:

"3. The will of the people is the source of the authority of government; this will shall be expressed in elections, universal, equal, periodic and by secret ballot, or manifested in equivalent free voting procedures."

In the first paragraph of article 19 his delegation proposed adding the words "as a citizen" immediately after the word "everyone". That addition took account of the amendments proposed by the delegations of Cuba and Uruguay. Moreover, the Human Rights Commission had adopted a similar wording in article 20, which began with the words "Everyone, as a member of society". The French text of this paragraph might be simplified by the omission of the words "qu'elle a".

In his country the civil service had been in existence for a long time and he emphasized the importance of the idea, not yet realized in the Western world, that civil servants should be recruited by the competitive method to make sure that only qualified persons took a direct part in the public service of their country. Hence he proposed paragraph 2 of article 19 should be amended to read as follows:

"2. Everyone has the right of free and equal access to public service in his country."

Mr. ABADI (Iraq), Mr. CONTOUMAS (Greece) and Mr. CHANG (China) also expressed themselves against the idea of appointing a drafting sub-committee to deal with article 19.

图片 3.3.27：张彭春在联大第三委员会第三届第 133 次会议发言纪要

【纪要译文】

张先生(中国)说,他很认真地听取了就宣言第 19 条所发表的不同评论,并依据不同代表团的建议提出了该条的新版本(A/C. 3/333)。

首先谈到第 3 款,他说,不是像法国代表团的修正案那样,宣言应该宣扬人权而不应强调政府的权威。因此,美国代表团在其修正案第 3 款中提议,"人民的意愿"应成为第一条的主题。该款内容如下:

"3. 人民的意愿是政府权力的来源;这一意愿应在普遍、平等、定期和无记名选举中表达,或在同等的自由投票程序中体现。"

在第 19 条第 1 款中,他的代表团提议在"每个人"一词之后加上"作为公民"。这一补充考虑到古巴和乌拉圭代表团提出的修正案。此外,人权委员会在第 20 条中采用了类似的措辞,以"作为社会成员的每个人"开头。本款的法文案文可以通过省略"qu'elle a"来简化。

在他的国家,公职人员制度已经存在了很长一段时间,他强调了西方世界尚未认识到的这一思想的重要性,即公职人员应通过竞争的方式招聘,以确保只有合格的人才能够直接参与本国公务。因此,他提议将第 19

条第 2 款修改如下：

"2. 人人有自由权和以平等机会参加其本国公务之权。"

阿巴迪（Abadi）先生（伊拉克）、孔图玛斯（Contoumas）先生（希腊）和张先生（中国）也表示反对任命一个起草小组委员会处理第 19 条的想法。

24. 张彭春在联大第三委员会
第三届第 134 次会议上的发言

联大第三委员会第三届第 134 次会议，于 1948 年 11 月 12 日下午 4 时 30 分至晚上 6 时 30 分，在巴黎夏洛宫召开，本次会议继续讨论《国际人权宣言》草案（第 19 条）。中国代表张彭春参加了本次会议，并在会议上发言，具体发言内容会议纪要、纪要影像和纪要译文①如下：

【会议纪要】

Mr. CHANG（China）suggested a few changes in the compromise text which he had proposed for paragraph 3（A/C. 3/333）. The paragraph would read as follows：

"The will of the people is the basis of the authority of government；this will shall be expressed in periodic elections，which shall be universal，genuine，equal，and held by secret ballot，or manifested in equivalent free voting procedures. "

Mr. CHANG（China）thought the expression "the will of the people is the source of the authority . . . " was a positive statement of fact；"shall be the basis" on the contrary，would indicate that such was not always the case in certain countries. It was for that reason that he preferred "shall be the basis"，it

---

① UN Document：A/C. 3/SR/134, p. 468；pp. 470–471.

being generally understood that the will of the people should in all cases be the basis of the authority of the Government.

That wording should also satisfy the Argentine representative, since it was no longer a simple statement of fact, but the proclamation of a right.

He proposed the following wording for paragraph 3:

"The will of the people shall be the basis of the authority of government; this will shall be expressed in periodic and genuine elections, which shall be universal and equal, and shall be held by secret vote, or by equivalent free voting procedures".

【纪要影像】

Mr. CHANG (China) suggested a few changes in the compromise text which he had proposed for paragraph 3 (A/C.3/333). The paragraph would read as follows:

"The will of the people is the basis of the authority of government; this will shall be expressed in periodic elections, which shall be universal, genuine, equal, and held by secret ballot, or manifested in equivalent free voting procedures."

Mr. CHANG (China) thought the expression "the will of the people *is* the source of the authority . . ." was a positive statement of fact; "shall be the basis" on the contrary, would indicate that such was not always the case in certain countries. It was for that reason that he preferred "shall be the basis", it being generally understood that the will of the people should in all cases be the basis of the authority of the Government.

That wording should also satisfy the Argentine representative, since it was no longer a simple statement of fact, but the proclamation of a right.

He proposed the following wording for paragraph 3:

"The will of the people shall be the basis of the authority of government; this will shall be expressed in periodic and genuine elections, which shall be universal and equal, and shall be held by secret vote, or by equivalent free voting procedures".

图片 3.3.28：张彭春在联大第三委员会第三届第 134 次会议发言纪要

【纪要译文】

张先生(中国)建议对他提议的第 3 款折中案文(A/C.3/333)作一些修改。该款内容如下：

"人民意志应是政府权力的基础；这一意志应在定期选举中表达，选举应是普遍、真实、平等的，并以无记名投票方式进行，或以同等的自由投票程序体现。"

张先生(中国)认为"人民的意志是权威的源泉……"是对事实的肯定陈述;相反,"应为基础"将表明某些国家并非总是如此。正是出于这个原因,他更倾向于"应是基础",人们普遍认为,人民的意志在任何情况下都应是政府权力的基础。

这一措辞也应该使阿根廷代表满意,因为它不再是简单的事实陈述,而是宣布一项权利。

他提议第 3 款采用以下措辞:

"人民意志应是政府权力的基础;这一意志应以定期且真实的选举表达,选举应是普遍和平等的,并应通过无记名投票或同等的自由投票程序进行。"

25. 张彭春在联大第三委员会第三届第 141 次会议上的发言

联大第三委员会第三届第 141 次会议,于 1948 年 11 月 16 日晚上 8 时 30 分至 11 时 30 分,在巴黎夏洛宫召开,本次会议继续讨论国际人权宣言草案(第 21 条)。中国代表张彭春在本次会议上发言,并在会议上发言,其具体发言内容①会议纪要、纪要影像和纪要译文如下:

【会议纪要】

Mr. CHANG (China) thought that the adverse vote on the whole article did not indicate that the Committee had no intention of including an article guaranteeing the rights of labour, but might provide an opportunity for drafting some equivalent article to replace it. The unanimous vote in favour of paragraph 1 and the almost unanimous vote for paragraph 3 showed that it could

---

① UN Document:A/C.3/SR/141, pp. 453-454.

not be said that the Committee wished to exclude article 21 altogether from the declaration. The amended text, in any case, had certain drafting defects due as the representative of Cuba had suggested to lack of mature consideration. The words "and pay" appeared to be redundant in paragraph 1 in view of the text of paragraph 2; they might be deleted.

The narrow majority obtained in the vote on certain paragraphs suggested that the Committee had not been wholly satisfied with them. Article 22, which dealt with the right to a standard of living, was closely connected with the question of pay; it might be possible to merge the two. He supported the Peruvian motion, but believed it might be better to take up article 22 while the Committee meditated an improved draft for article 21.

【纪要影像】

Mr. CHANG (China) thought that the adverse vote on the whole article did not indicate that the Committee had no intention of including an article guaranteeing the rights of labour, but might provide an opportunity for drafting some equivalent article to replace it. The unanimous vote in favour of paragraph 1 and the almost unanimous vote for paragraph 3 showed that it could not be said that the Committee wished to exclude article 21 altogether from the declaration. The amended text, in any case, had certain drafting defects due, as the representative of Cuba had suggested, to lack of mature consideration. The words "and pay" appeared to be redundant in paragraph 1 in view of the text of paragraph 2; they might be deleted.

The narrow majority obtained in the vote on certain paragraphs suggested that the Committee had not been wholly satisfied with them. Article 22, which dealt with the right to a standard of living, was closely connected with the question of pay; it might be possible to merge the two. He supported the Peruvian motion, but believed it might be better to take up article 22 while the Committee meditated an improved draft for article 21.

图片 3.3.29:张彭春在联大第三委员会第三届第 141 次会议发言纪要

【纪要译文】

张先生(中国)认为,对整条的反对票并不表明委员会无意列入一条保障劳工权利的条款,而是可能提供一个机会,起草一些同等条款来取代该条款。一致投票赞成第 1 款和几乎一致投票赞成第 3 款表明,不能说委员会希望将第 21 条完全排除在宣言之外。无论如何,经修正的案文在措辞上存在某些缺陷,古巴代表认为,这是由于缺乏成熟的审议。鉴于第 2 款的案文,"及报酬"一词在第 1 款中似乎是多余的;它们可能会被删除。

在对某些条款的表决中获得的微弱多数表明,委员会对这些条款并不完全满意。关于生活水准权的第 22 条与工资问题密切相关;也许可以将两者合并。他支持秘鲁的动议,但认为在委员会考虑改进第 21 条草案时审议第 22 条可能更好。

26. 张彭春在联大第三委员会第三届第 142 次会议上的发言

联大第三委员会第三届第 142 次会议,于 1948 年 11 月 17 日上午 10 时 30 分至下午 1 时 30 分,在巴黎夏洛宫召开,本次会议继续讨论《国际人权宣言》草案(第 21 条)。中国代表张彭春参加了本次会议,并在会议上发言,其具体发言内容①会议纪要、纪要影像和纪要译文如下:

【会议纪要】

Mr. CHANG (China) urged that the Peruvian proposal should be put to the vote on the understanding that no particular text would be used as a basis for discussion but that any suggestion might be made which would lead to a satisfactory and generally acceptable text.

Mr. CHANG (China) said that the adoption of the Peruvian proposal would mean reconsideration of all the previous drafts of article 21. The amend-

---

① UN Document:A/C. 3/SR/142, p. 549.

ments set forth in document A/C. 3/298/Rev. 1, as well as those put forward at the previous meeting, could be reintroduced and new changes of a purely drafting character could be suggested. The USSR proposal, on the other hand, would limit the Committee to reconsidering the separate parts of the article which had been adopted at the previous meeting, to which only additions could be suggested.

The representatives of China, Peru and Cuba supported the Belgian proposal on the understanding that the group referred to by the Belgian representative would be an official drafting sub-committee.

【纪要影像】

Mr. CHANG (China) urged that the Peruvian proposal should be put to the vote on the understanding that no particular text would be used as a basis for discussion but that any suggestion might be made which would lead to a satisfactory and generally acceptable text.

Mr. CHANG (China) said that the adoption of the Peruvian proposal would mean reconsideration of all the previous drafts of article 21. The amendments set forth in document A/C.3/298/ Rev.1, as well as those put forward at the previous meeting, could be reintroduced and new changes of a purely drafting character could be suggested. The USSR proposal, on the other hand, would limit the Committee to reconsidering the separate parts of the article which had been adopted at the previous meeting, to which only additions could be suggested.

The representatives of CHINA, PERU and CUBA supported the Belgian proposal on the understanding that the group referred to by the Belgian representative would be an official drafting subcommittee.

图片 3.3.30:张彭春在联大第三委员会第三届第 142 次会议发言纪要

【纪要译文】

张先生(中国)敦促将秘鲁的提案付诸表决,但建立在不使用任何特定案文作为讨论的基础,但可以提出任何建议,从而产生令人满意和普遍接受的案文的理解上。

张先生(中国)说,采纳秘鲁的建议将意味着重新审议第 21 条以前的所有草案。A/C. 3/298/Rev. 1 号文件中提出的修正案以及上一次会议上提出的修正案可以重新提出,并可以提出纯粹起草性质的新的修改。另一方面,苏联的提案将限制委员会重新审议上一次会议通过的该条的单独部分,对这些部分只能提出补充意见。

中国、秘鲁和古巴代表支持比利时的提案,但有一项谅解,即比利时代表提到的小组将是一个正式起草小组委员会。

27. 张彭春在联大第三委员会 第三届第 143 次会议上的发言

联大第三委员会第三届第 143 次会议,于 1948 年 11 月 17 日下午 3 时 30 分至晚上 6 时 15 分,在巴黎夏洛宫召开,本次会议继续讨论《国际人权宣言》草案(第 21 条和第 22 条)。中国代表张彭春参加了本次会议,并在会议上发言,其具体发言内容①会议纪要、纪要影像和纪要译文如下:

【会议纪要】

Mr. CHANG (China) thought that the decision taken by the Committee at its previous meeting could not lend itself to more than one interpretation. The Belgian representative's suggestion had been accepted on the clear understanding that the Committee would immediately set up a drafting committee.

Mr. CHANG (China) asked that the discussion on the Uruguayan representative's proposal should be closed, and Mr. JIMÉNEZ DE ARÉCHAGA (Uruguay) asked for closure of the general debate.

The motion for closure was adopted by 26 votes to 7, with 3 abstentions.

---

① UN Document: A/C. 3/SR/143, p. 553; p. 554; p. 564.

The Chairman put to the vote the question of setting up a drafting committee.

It was decided to set up a drafting sub-committee by 27 votes to 2, with 6 abstentions.

Mr. CHANG (China) proposed the following wording for the first paragraph of article 22:

"Everyone has the right to a standard of living adequate for the needs of his family and himself, including food, clothing, housing, medical care and social services, and to security in the event of unemployment, sickness, disability, widowhood, old age or other loss of livelihood owing to circumstances beyond his control."

【纪要影像】

Mr. CHANG (China) thought that the decision taken by the Committee at its previous meeting could not lend itself to more than one interpretation. The Belgian representative's suggestion had been accepted on the clear understanding that the Committee would immediately set up a drafting committee.

Mr. CHANG (China) asked that the discussion on the Uruguayan representative's proposal should be closed, and Mr. JIMÉNEZ DE ARÉCHAGA (Uruguay) asked for closure of the general debate.

The motion for closure was adopted by 26 votes to 7, with 3 abstentions.

The CHAIRMAN put to the vote the question of setting up a drafting committee.

It was decided to set up a drafting sub-committee by 27 votes to 2, with 6 abstentions.

Mr. CHANG (China) proposed the following wording for the first paragraph of article 22:

"Everyone has the right to a standard of living adequate for the needs of his family and himself, including food, clothing, housing, medical care and social services, and to security in the event of unemployment, sickness, disability, widowhood, old age or other loss of livelihood owing to circumstances beyond his control."

图片 3.3.31:张彭春在联大第三委员会第三届第 143 次会议发言纪要

【纪要译文】

张先生(中国)认为,委员会在其上次会议上作出的决定只能有一种解释。比利时代表的建议已被接受,但有一项明确的谅解,即委员会将立即成立一个起草委员会。

张先生(中国)要求结束对乌拉圭代表提案的讨论,希门尼斯·德阿雷查加(Jiménez de Aréchaga)先生(乌拉圭)要求结束一般性辩论。

结束动议以 26 票对 7 票、3 票弃权获得通过。

主席将成立起草委员会的问题付诸表决。

会议以 27 票对 2 票、6 票弃权决定设立起草小组委员会。

张先生(中国)对第 22 条第一款提出以下措辞:

"人人有权享受足以满足其家庭和自身需要的生活水平,包括食物、衣着、住房、医疗和社会服务,并有权在失业、疾病、残疾、守寡、年老或因其无法控制的情况而丧失生计时获得保障。"

28. 张彭春在联大第三委员会
第三届第 144 次会议上的发言

联大第三委员会第三届第 144 次会议,于 1948 年 11 月 18 日上午 10 时 30 分至下午 1 时 20 分,在巴黎夏洛宫召开,本次会议继续讨论《国际人权宣言》草案(第 22 条)。中国代表张彭春参加了本次会议,并在会议上发言,其具体发言内容①会议纪要、纪要影像和纪要译文如下:

【会议纪要】

Mr. CHANG (China) said that he could accept certain drafting changes to his amendment. He agreed with the French and Chilean representatives that the words "health and well-being" should be restored; they should be substituted for the word "needs". He could not, however, wholly agree with the representative of France; social services certainly implied a support for an adequate standard of living, but they were not on the same level. It would, however, be possible to give emphasis to social services by inserting the word "necessary" before those words; it would refer to food, clothing, housing, etc. The word "and" would then be substituted for the comma after the word "housing".

---

① UN Document:A/C. 3/SR/144, pp. 571-572.//张彭春的建议与最后版本的比较表明,他的建议与最后版本几乎相同。在本次会议上,所有代表都谈到了中国的提案。在这种情况下,张彭春的提议成为第 144 次会议的讨论中心。在会上,讨论涉及许多修正案:美国修正案(A/C.3/343)、新西兰修正案(A/C.3/267)、多米尼加修正案(A/C.3/217/Corr. 2)、南斯拉夫修正案(A/C.3/233)、苏联修正案(GAOR C.3,P35)、阿根廷修正案(A/C.3/251)、黎巴嫩修正案(A/C.3/260)、挪威修正案(A/C.3/344)、古巴修正案(A/C.3/232/Corr. 1)、法国修正案(A/C.3/346)和澳大利亚修正案(A/C.3/348)。然而,中心议题围绕着中国的修正案(A/C.3/347)进行的。罗斯福夫人也撤回了美国的修改正案,继而支持中国的修正案。

He did not agree with the New Zealand proposal to insert the word "social" before the word "security". Social security had been mentioned in article 20, which had been intended to cover the subsequent articles. To repeat the words again in the present context would narrow their meaning. He agreed with the representative of Uruguay that the word *seguridad* was a more accurate translation of the word "security" than the word *seguros*, which implied insurance.

He did not object to the Norwegian proposal that the phrase "in circumstances beyond his control" should be voted separately. It might be well to include the words, however, because they would tend to encourage self-reliance.

The Australian alteration of paragraph 2 might be acceptable. His own abstract terms "motherhood" and "childhood" could not be used with the words "have the right"; the words "are entitled" should therefore be substituted in the English text.

Replying to the representative of the Dominican Republic, he pointed out that the word "childhood" covered all children born in or out of wedlock. He was glad to note that the USSR representative believed that the Yugoslav amendment needed drafting changes. That amendment would be voted on by roll-call, but he suggested that a vote should first be taken on its principle and, if that were accepted, the drafting changes could then be made. He agreed with the representatives of the Dominican Republic and France that the Yugoslav amendment in its present form was inappropriate to article 22 and belonged rather in some article dealing with the protection of social status.

【纪要影像】

Mr. CHANG (China) said that he could accept certain drafting changes to his amendment. He agreed with the French and Chilean representatives that the words "health and well-being" should be restored; they should be substituted for the word "needs". He could not, however, wholly agree with the representative of France; social services certainly implied a support for an adequate standard of living, but they were not on the same level. It would, however, be possible to give emphasis to social services by inserting the word "necessary" before those words; it would refer to food, clothing, housing, etc. The word "and" would then be substituted for the comma after the word "housing".

He did not agree with the New Zealand proposal to insert the word "social" before the word "security". Social security had been mentioned in article 20, which had been intended to cover the subsequent articles. To repeat the words again in the present context would narrow their meaning.

He agreed with the representative of Uruguay that the word *seguridad* was a more accurate translation of the word "security" than the word *seguros*, which implied insurance.

He did not object to the Norwegian proposal that the phrase "in circumstances beyond his control" should be voted separately. It might be well to include the words, however, because they would tend to encourage self-reliance.

The Australian alteration of paragraph 2 might be acceptable. His own abstract terms "motherhood" and "childhood" could not be used with the words "have the right"; the words "are entitled" should therefore be substituted in the English text.

Replying to the representative of the Dominican Republic, he pointed out that the word "childhood" covered all children born in or out of wedlock. He was glad to note that the USSR representative believed that the Yugoslav amendment needed drafting changes. That amendment would be voted on by roll-call, but he suggested that a vote should first be taken on its principle and, if that were accepted, the drafting changes could then be made. He agreed with the representatives of the Dominican Republic and France that the Yugoslav amendment in its present form was inappropriate to article 22 and belonged rather in some article dealing with the protection of social status.

图片 3.3.32：张彭春在联大第三委员会第三届第 144 次会议发言纪要

【纪要译文】

张先生(中国)说,他可以接受对其修正案的某些措辞修改。他同意法国和智利代表的意见,即应恢复"健康和福祉"一词;它们应取代"需要"一词。但是,他不能完全同意法国代表的意见;社会服务当然意味着对适当生活水平的支持,但它们并不在同一水平上。不过,在这些字眼前加上"必要"一词,可以强调社会服务;它指的是食物、衣服、住房等。然后用"和"一词取代"住房"一词后的逗号。

他不同意新西兰关于在"安全"一词之前插入"社会"一词的建议。第20条提到了社会保障,其目的是涵盖随后的条款。在当前上下文中重复这些词会缩小其含义。他同意乌拉圭代表的意见,即 seguridad 一词是对"安全"一词的更准确翻译,而 seguros 一词意味着保险。

他不反对挪威关于"在他无法控制的情况下"一语应单独表决的建议。不过,最好将这些词包括在内,因为它们往往会鼓励自力更生。

澳大利亚对第 2 款的修改可能是可以接受的。他自己的抽象术语"母性"和"童年"不能与"拥有权利"一起使用;因此,应在英文文本中替换"有权"一词。

他在答复多米尼加共和国代表时指出,"童年"一词涵盖了所有婚生或非婚生儿童。他高兴地注意到,苏联代表认为南斯拉夫的修正案需要修改措辞。该修正案将以唱名表决的方式进行表决,但他建议首先就其原则进行表决,如果这一点被接受,则可以对草案进行修改。他同意多米尼加共和国和法国代表的意见,即南斯拉夫目前形式的修正案不适用于第 22 条,而是属于关于保护社会地位的某些条款。

29. 张彭春在联大第三委员会第三届第 145 次会议上的发言

联大第三委员会第三届第 145 次会议,于 1948 年 11 月 18 日下午 3 时 15 分至晚上 6 时 5 分,在巴黎夏洛宫召开,本次会议继续讨论《国际人权宣言》草案(第 22 条)。中国代表张彭春参加了本次会议,并在会议上发言,其具体发言内容①会议纪要、纪要影像和纪要译文如下:

【会议纪要】

Mr. CHANG (China), with a view to avoiding procedural difficulties, withdrew the proposal he had made at the preceding meeting, in order to enable a vote to be taken on the principle of including the idea of the absolute equality of legitimate and illegitimate children.

Mr. CHANG (China) observed that the text presented by the French delegation differed in substance from the text submitted by his delegation. It contained three new ideas: individual resources, the need to supplement those re-

---

① UN Document: A/C. 3/SR/145, pp. 572-573; p. 574.

sources by social services, and the guarantee to the individual of well-being and health for himself and his family.

Mrs. Roosevelt (United States of America), Mrs. Corbet (United Kingdom) and Mr. Watt (Australia) agree with what had been said by the representative of China and drew attention to certain defects in the English translation of the French amendment.

The CHAIRMAN put to the vote the text proposed by the Chinese delegation for article 22, paragraph 1 (A/C. 3/347/Rev. 1).

The text proposed by the Chinese delegation was adopted as paragraph 1 of article 22, by 41 votes to none, with 3 abstentions.

The CHAIRMAN put to the vote the text proposed by the Chinese delegation for paragraph 2 (A/C. 3/347/Rev. 1).

The text was adopted by 25 votes to 7, with 12 abstentions.

【纪要影像】

Mr. CHANG (China), with a view to avoiding procedural difficulties, withdrew the proposal he had made at the preceding meeting, in order to

enable a vote to be taken on the principle of including the idea of the absolute equality of legitimate and illegitimate children.

Mr. CHANG (China) observed that the text presented by the French delegation differed in substance from the text submitted by his delegation. It contained three new ideas: individual resources, the need to supplement those resources by social services, and the guarantee to the individual of well-being and health for himself and his family.

Mrs. ROOSEVELT (United States of America), Mrs. CORBET (United Kingdom) and Mr. WATT (Australia) agreed with what had been said by the representative of China and drew attention to certain defects in the English translation of the French amendment.

The CHAIRMAN put to the vote the text proposed by the Chinese delegation for article 22, paragraph 1 (A/C.3/347/Rev.1).

The text proposed by the Chinese delegation was adopted as paragraph 1 of article 22, by 41 votes to none, with 3 abstentions.

The CHAIRMAN put to the vote the text proposed by the Chinese delegation for paragraph 2 (A/C.3/347/Rev.1).

The text was adopted by 25 votes to 7, with 12 abstentions.

图片 3.3.33:张彭春在联大第三委员会第三届第 145 次会议发言纪要

【纪要译文】

张先生(中国)为了避免程序上的困难,撤回了他在上一次会议上提出的建议,以便能够就包括合法子女和非婚生子女绝对平等这一概念的原则进行表决。

张先生(中国)说,法国代表团提交的案文与中国代表团提交的案文在实质内容上有所不同。它包含三个新的理念:个人资源,需要通过社会服务补充这些资源,以及保障个人及其家庭的福祉和健康。

罗斯福夫人(美国)、科比特(Corbet)夫人(英国)和瓦特(Watt)先生(澳大利亚)同意中国代表所说的话,并提请注意法国修正案英译本中的某些缺陷。

主席将中国代表团就第 22 条第 1 款提出的案文(A/C. 3/347/Rev. 1)

付诸表决。

中国代表团提出的案文以 41 票对零票、3 票弃权获得通过,成为第 22 条第 1 款。

主席将中国代表团提议的第 2 款案文(A/C. 3/347/Rev. 1)付诸表决。

案文以 25 票对 7 票,12 票弃权获得通过。

30. 张彭春在联大第三委员会
第三届第 146 次会议上的发言

联大第三委员会第三届第 146 次会议,于 1948 年 11 月 19 日上午 10 时 30 分至下午 1 时,在巴黎夏洛宫召开,本次会议继续讨论《国际人权宣言》草案(第 22 条)。中国代表张彭春参加了本次会议,并在会议上发言,其具体发言内容①会议纪要、纪要影像和纪要译文如下:

【会议纪要】

Mr. CHANG (China) said, in reply to the representative of the Dominican Republic, that he had not insisted and did not insist on the use, in the English text of paragraph 2, of the words "have the right".

He pointed out that paragraph 3——the former Norwegian amendment——was different in style from most articles in the declaration in that it began with a reference to a minority rather than to a broad general group. Moreover, it represented an enlargement of the statement in paragraph 2. He hoped that the Norwegian representative would agree to combine paragraphs 2 and 3 and to begin the latter with some such words as: "All children, including those born out of wedlock".

---

① UN Document: A/C. 3/SR/146, p. 579.

That suggestion might be dealt with at the same time as the suggestion of the representative of the Dominican Republic.

【纪要影像】

Mr. CHANG (China) said, in reply to the representative of the Dominican Republic, that he had not insisted and did not insist on the use, in the English text of paragraph 2, of the words "have the right".

He pointed out that paragraph 3—the former Norwegian amendment—was different in style from most articles in the declaration in that it began with a reference to a minority rather than to a broad general group. Moreover, it represented an enlargement of the statement in paragraph 2. He hoped that the Norwegian representative would agree to combine paragraphs 2 and 3 and to begin the latter with some such words as: "All children, including those born out of wedlock".

That suggestion might be dealt with at the same time as the suggestion of the representative of the Dominican Republic.

图片 3.3.34:张彭春在联大第三委员会第三届第 146 次会议发言纪要

【纪要译文】

张先生(中国)在答复多米尼加共和国代表时说,他没有坚称,也没有坚持在第 2 款的英文文本中使用"有权"一词。

他指出,挪威先前的修正案第 3 款在风格上与《宣言》中的大多数条款不同,因为它一开始提到的是少数群体,而不是广大的一般群体。此外,它扩大了第 2 款中的说明。他希望挪威代表同意将第 2 款和第 3 款合并在一起,并在第 3 款开头加上"所有儿童,包括非婚生儿童"等字。

这一建议可与多米尼加共和国代表的建议同时处理。

31. 张彭春在联大第三委员会
第三届第 149 次会议上的发言

联大第三委员会第三届第 149 次会议,于 1948 年 11 月 20 日上午 11 时至下午 1 时,在巴黎夏洛宫召开,本次会议继续讨论《国际人权宣言》草案(第 24 条)。中国代表张彭春参加了本次会议,并在会议上发言,其具体发言内容①会议纪要、纪要影像和纪要译文如下:

【会议纪要】

Mr. Chang (China) said he supported the basic text in preference to any of the amendments.

【纪要影像】

Mr. CHANG (China) said he supported the basic text in preference to any of the amendments.

图片 3.3.35:张彭春在联大第三委员会第三届第 149 次会议发言纪要

【纪要译文】

张先生(中国)说,他支持基本案文而不是任何修正案。

---

① UN Document:A/C. 3/SR/149, p. 613.

32. 张彭春在联大第三委员会第三届第 150 次会议上的发言

联大第三委员会第三届第 150 次会议,于 1948 年 11 月 20 日下午 3 时 15 分至下午 5 时 45 分,在巴黎夏洛宫召开,本次会议继续讨论《国际人权宣言》草案(第 24 条)。中国代表张彭春参加了本次会议,并在会议上发言,其具体发言内容①会议纪要、纪要影像和纪要译文如下:

【会议纪要】

Mr. CHANG (China) proposed a new version of the amendment, as follows:

"Everyone has the right to rest and leisure, including such provisions as reasonable limitation of working hours and periodical holidays with pay."

Mr. CHANG (China) had voted against the amendment on account of its wording, although his delegation had no objection to the principle on which it was based. The right to leisure was an abstract idea, the limitation of working hours was an abstract idea relating to a concrete reality, and holidays with pay were a concrete matter. For that reason, he considered that the wording of the New Zealand amendment, in giving equal importance to ideas of a very different nature and in expressing them without establishing any logical relation between them, was somewhat inadequate.

He appealed to the New Zealand delegation to consent to change the wording of its amendment.

---

① UN Document: A/C. 3/SR/150, p. 614.

【纪要影像】

Mr. CHANG (China) proposed a new version of the amendment, as follows:

"Everyone has the right to rest and leisure, *including such provisions as* reasonable limitation of working hours and periodical holidays with pay."

Mr. CHANG (China) had voted against the amendment on account of its wording, although his delegation had no objection to the principle on which it was based. The right to leisure was an abstract idea, the limitation of working hours was an abstract idea relating to a concrete reality, and holidays with pay were a concrete matter. For that reason, he considered that the wording of the New Zealand amendment, in giving equal importance to ideas of a very different nature and in expressing them without establishing any logical relation between them, was somewhat inadequate.

He appealed to the New Zealand delegation to consent to change the wording of its amendment.

图片 3.3.36：张彭春在联大第三委员会第三届第 150 次会议发言纪要

【纪要译文】

张先生(中国)提出修正案的新案文如下：

"人人有权休息和休闲,包括合理限制工作时间和定期带薪休假等规定。"

张先生(中国)对修正案的措辞投了反对票,尽管中国代表团不反对修正案所依据的原则。休闲权是一个抽象概念,工作时间限制是一个与具体现实相关的抽象概念,带薪假期是一个具体问题。因此,他认为,新西兰修正案的措辞,在同等重视性质迥异的想法和在表达这些想法时没有建立它们之间的任何逻辑关系,这在某种程度上是不够的。

他呼吁新西兰代表团同意修改其修正案的措辞。

33. 张彭春在联大第三委员会 第三届第 151 次会议上的发言

联大第三委员会第三届第 151 次会议,于 1948 年 11 月 22 日上午 10 时 50 分至下午 1 时 15 分,在巴黎夏洛宫召开,本次会议继续讨论《国际人权宣言》草案(第 25 条)。中国代表张彭春参加了本次会议,并在会议上发言,其具体发言内容①会议纪要、纪要影像和纪要译文如下:

【会议纪要】

Mr. CHANG (China), drew the attention of the members of the Committee to the last part of article 25, particularly the words "and to share in scientific advancement". As various delegations, in particular that of France, had already pointed out, not only must the right to share in the benefits of scientific advancement be guaranteed to everyone but also the right to participate in the work of scientific creation. In the arts, letters and sciences alike, aesthetic enjoyment had a dual aspect: a purely passive aspect when man appreciates beauty and an active aspect when he creates it. In this connexion Mr. Chang indicated that the expression "participate in" or "share in" did not express this dual aspect as precisely as it might. The text referred more clearly to creation than to passive enjoyment. He therefore proposed the addition, at the end of the first paragraph, of the words "and its benefits" (A/C. 3/361).

After stating that his delegation accepted the Peruvian amendment (150th meeting) proposing insertion of the word "freely" before the word "participate" in the first paragraph, he suggested a few drafting changes in the second

---

① UN Document: A/C. 3/SR/151, pp. 627-628.

paragraph of the joint amendment of Cuba, France and Mexico. The second paragraph would then read:

"Everyone has the right to the protection of the moral and material interests resulting from any scientific, literary or artistic production of which he is the author."

Mr. PÉREZ CISNEROS (Cuba) thanked the Chinese delegation for having clarified and improved the original text of the joint amendment. His delegation was glad to accept those changes, together with the amendment suggested by the Peruvian representative.

Mr. Cassin (France) approved the proposal of the representative of China to add the words "and its benefits" at the end of the first paragraph. Those words were preferable to the Cuban amendment since they avoided all ambiguity concerning the right to participate not only in scientific research but also in the benefits resulting from it.

【纪要影像】

Mr. CHANG (China), drew the attention of the members of the Committee to the last part of article 25, particularly the words "and to share in scientific advancement". As various delegations, in particular that of France, had already pointed out, not only must the right to share in the benefits of scientific advancement be guaranteed to everyone but also the right to participate in the work of scientific creation. In the arts, letters and sciences alike, aesthetic enjoyment had a dual aspect: a purely passive aspect when man appreciates beauty and an active aspect when he creates it. In this connexion Mr. Chang indicated that the expression "participate in" or "share in" did not express this dual aspect as precisely as it might. The text referred more clearly to creation than to passive enjoyment. He therefore proposed the addition, at the end of the first paragraph, of the words "and its benefits" (A/C.3/361).

After stating that his delegation accepted the Peruvian amendment (150th meeting) proposing insertion of the word "freely" before the word "participate" in the first paragraph, he suggested a few drafting changes in the second paragraph of the joint amendment of Cuba, France and Mexico. The second paragraph would then read:

"Everyone has the right to the protection of the moral and material interests resulting from any scientific, literary or artistic production of which he is the author."

Mr. PÉREZ CISNEROS (Cuba) thanked the Chinese delegation for having clarified and improved the original text of the joint amendment. His delegation was glad to accept those changes, together with the amendment suggested by the Peruvian representative.

Mr. CASSIN (France) approved the proposal of the representative of China to add the words "and its benefits" at the end of the first paragraph. Those words were preferable to the Cuban amendment since they avoided all ambiguity concerning the right to participate not only in scientific research but also in the benefits resulting from it.

图片 3.3.37：张彭春在联大第三委员会第三届第 151 次会议发言纪要

【纪要译文】

张先生(中国)提请委员会成员注意第 25 条最后一部分,特别是"和分享科学进步"等字。正如各代表团,特别是法国代表团已经指出的那样,不仅必须保障每个人分享科学进步利益的权利,而且还必须保障参与科学创造工作的权利。在艺术、文学和科学中,审美享受有两个方面:一个是欣赏美时纯粹的被动方面,另一个是创造美时的主动方面。在这种联系中,张先生表示,"参与"或"分享"一词并没有尽可能准确地表达这一双重方面。文本更明确地提到创造,而不是被动地享受。因此,他提议在第一段末尾加上"及其利益"(A/C. 3/361)。

他说,秘鲁代表团接受了秘鲁的修正案(第 150 次会议),建议在第一段"参与"一词之前插入"自由"一词,然后建议对古巴、法国和墨西哥联合修正案第二段的措辞作一些修改。第二段将改为:

"任何人都有权保护其作为作者的任何科学、文学或艺术作品所产生的精神和物质利益。"

佩雷斯·西斯内罗斯先生(古巴)感谢中国代表团澄清和改进了联合修正案的原文。秘鲁代表团很高兴接受这些修改以及秘鲁代表提出的修正案。

卡森先生(法国)赞成中国代表的建议,即在第一段末尾添加"及其利益"。这些话比古巴修正案更可取,因为它们避免了不仅参与科学研究的权利,而且也避免了参与科学研究所产生的利益的所有模糊性。

34. 张彭春在联大第三委员会
第三届第 152 次会议上的发言

　　联大第三委员会第三届第 152 次会议,于 1948 年 11 月 22 日下午 3 时至晚上 6 时 5 分,在巴黎夏洛宫召开,本次会议继续讨论《国际人权宣言》草案(第 25 条和第 26 条)。中国代表张彭春参加了本次会议,并在会议上发言,其具体发言内容①会议纪要、纪要影像和纪要译文如下:

【会议纪要】

Mr. CHANG (China) said that the text which appeared in document A/C. 3/361 had been attributed to the Chinese delegation. It was really a combined text: the insertion of the word "freely" was a Peruvian suggestion, the addition of the words "and its benefits" had been suggested by the Chinese delegation, and the second paragraph was really a joint Cuban, French and Mexican proposal. He asked that the second paragraph should be voted upon separately.

Mr. CHANG (China) was not at all sure that the word "social" did not include the idea of "international". Nor was he convinced that article 26 could be claimed to be a statement of a right. In his opinion, it would be wiser to postpone a decision on article 26 until the Committee had considered articles 27 and 28.

---

　　①　UN Document: A/C. 3/SR/152, p. 663.

Mr. CHANG (China) said that the text which appeared in document A/C.3/361 had been attributed to the Chinese delegation. It was really a combined text : the insertion of the word "freely" was a Peruvian suggestion, the addition of the words "and its benefits" had been suggested by the Chinese delegation, and the second paragraph was really a joint Cuban, French and Mexican proposal. He asked that the second paragraph should be voted upon separately.

Mr. CHANG (China) was not at all sure that the word "social" did not include the idea of "international". Nor was he convinced that article 26 could be claimed to be a statement of a right. In his opinion, it would be wiser to postpone a decision on article 26 until the Committee had considered articles 27 and 28.

图片 3.3.38：张彭春在联大第三委员会第三届第 152 次会议发言纪要

【纪要译文】

张先生(中国)说，A/C.3/361 号文件中的案文由中国代表团所作。它实际上是一个合并文本：插入"自由"一词是秘鲁的建议，添加"及其利益"一词是中国代表团建议的，第二段实际上是古巴、法国和墨西哥的联合提案。他要求对第二段进行单独表决。

张先生(中国)根本不确定"社会"一词是否包括"国际"的概念。他也不相信第 26 条可以被称为权利声明。他认为，在委员会审议第 27 条和第 28 条之前，推迟就第 26 条作出决定将更为明智。

联大第三委员会及联大全会

35. 张彭春在联大第三委员会
第三届第 153 次会议上的发言

联大第三委员会第三届第 153 次会议,于 1948 年 11 月 23 日下午 3 时 20 分至晚上 6 时,在巴黎夏洛宫召开,本次会议继续讨论《国际人权宣言》草案(第 27 条)。中国代表张彭春参加了本次会议,并在会议上发言,其具体发言内容①会议纪要、纪要影像和纪要译文如下:

【会议纪要】

Mr. CHANG (China) sympathized with the purpose of the French amendment to paragraph 1, but did not think that it had been achieved. It might perhaps be preferable, in the English text, to speak of the "free development of personality" rather than use the phrase "freely to develop his personality". It was not simple to improve the drafting of paragraph 1; unless an improvement could be effected the paragraph should be permitted to stand.

It was equally difficult to re-draft paragraph 2 in such a manner as to introduce the Uruguayan amendment in its proper place. As used by the Uruguayan representative, the words "prescribed by law" applied not only to public order and general welfare, which they might properly qualify, but also to such concepts as morality and recognition and respect for the rights of others, which surely could not and should not be prescribed by law.

Mr. Chang remarked that he found the original text of article 27 satisfactory in the main, but that he might at a later meeting present amendments of a drafting nature.

---

① UN Document: A/C. 3/SR/153, pp. 650-651.

Mr. CHANG (China) sympathized with the purpose of the French amendment to paragraph 1, but did not think that it had been achieved. It might perhaps be preferable, in the English text, to speak of the "free development of personality" rather than use the phrase "freely to develop his

personality". It was not simple to improve the drafting of paragraph 1; unless an improvement could be effected the paragraph should be permitted to stand.

It was equally difficult to re-draft paragraph 2 in such a manner as to introduce the Uruguayan amendment in its proper place. As used by the Uruguayan representative, the words "prescribed by law" applied not only to public order and general welfare, which they might properly qualify, but also to such concepts as morality and recognition and respect for the rights of others, which surely could not and should not be prescribed by law.

Mr. Chang remarked that he found the original text of article 27 satisfactory in the main, but that he might at a later meeting present amendments of a drafting nature.

图片 3.3.39:张彭春在联大第三委员会第三届第 153 次会议发言纪要

【纪要译文】

张先生(中国)赞同法国对第 1 款的修正案的目的,但不认为它已经实现。在英文文本中,也许更可取的说法是"个性的自由发展",而不是使用"自由地发展个性"一词。改进第 1 款的措辞并不简单;除非可以进行改进,否则应允许该款继续有效。

同样难以重新起草第 2 款,以便在适当的地方引入乌拉圭修正案。正如乌拉圭代表所使用的那样,"法律规定"一词不仅适用于公共秩序和一般福利,它们可以适当地加以限定,而且也适用于道德、承认和尊重他人权利等概念,这些概念当然不能也不应该由法律规定。

张先生说,他认为第 27 条的原文基本上令人满意,但他可能在以后的会议上提出草案性质的修正案。

36. 张彭春在联大第三委员会
第三届第 154 次会议上的发言

联大第三委员会第三届第 154 次会议,于 1948 年 11 月 24 日上午 11 时至下午 1 时 20 分,在巴黎夏洛宫召开,本次会议继续讨论《国际人权宣言》草案(第 27 条)。中国代表张彭春参加了本次会议,并在会议上发言,其具体发言内容①会议纪要、纪要影像和纪要译文如下:

【会议纪要】

Mr. CHANG (China) considered that the word "everyone" in the first sentence of article 27 already contained the meaning of the word "human", therefore need not be repeated.

The CHAIRMAN put to the vote the amendment formerly submitted by Australia, which had been taken up by the USSR delegation.

Mr. CHANG (China) asked that the amendment should be voted upon in parts so that the word "alone" might be voted on separately.

The CHAIRMAN put to the vote the proposal to include the word "alone" in the text of the USSR amendment.

That proposal was adopted by 23 votes to 5, with 14 abstentions.

The CHAIRMAN put to the vote the USSR amendment as a whole.

The amendment was adopted by 35 votes to none, with 6 abstentions.

---

① UN Document: A/C. 3/SR/154, p. 659; p. 660.

Mr. CHANG (China) considered that the word "everyone" in the first sentence of article 27 already contained the meaning of the word "human", therefore need not be repeated.

The CHAIRMAN put to the vote the amendment formerly submitted by Australia, which had been taken up by the USSR delegation.

Mr. CHANG (China) asked that the amendment should be voted upon in parts so that the word "alone" might be voted on separately.

The CHAIRMAN put to the vote the proposal to include the word "alone" in the text of the USSR amendment.

That proposal was adopted by 23 votes to 5, with 14 abstentions.

The CHAIRMAN put to the vote the USSR amendment as a whole.

The amendment was adopted by 35 votes to none, with 6 abstentions.

图片 3.3.40：张彭春在联大第三委员会第三届第 154 次会议发言纪要

【纪要译文】

张先生(中国)认为,第 27 条第一句中的"人人"一词已经包含了"人类"一词的含义,因此无需重复。

主席将澳大利亚以前提交的修正案付诸表决,该修正案已由苏联代表团处理。

张先生(中国)要求对修正案进行部分表决,以便对"单独"一词进行单独表决。

主席将在苏联修正案案文中加入"单独"一词的提案付诸表决。

该提案以 23 票对 5 票、14 票弃权获得通过。

主席将整个苏联修正案付诸表决。

修正案以 35 票对零票、6 票弃权获得通过。

联大第三委员会及联大全会

37. 张彭春在联大第三委员会
第三届第 156 次会议上的发言

联大第三委员会第三届第 156 次会议,于 1948 年 11 月 25 日上午 11 时至下午 1 时 10 分,在巴黎夏洛宫召开,本次会议继续讨论《国际人权宣言》草案(第 28 条和第 21 条:第三小组委员会的报告)。中国代表张彭春参加了本次会议,并在会议上发言,其具体发言内容①会议纪要、纪要影像和纪要译文如下:

【会议纪要】

Mr. CHANG (China) pointed out that he had agreed with the representative of Uruguay to replace the words "perform any acts" in the English text of the amendment submitted by the latter (A/C. 3/268) by the words "engage in any acts".

Mr. CHANG (China) said that, in view of the objections which his proposal had raised, he would not insist on it.

Mr. CHANG (China) thanked Sub-Committee 3 and its Rapporteur for having drawn up a decidedly better text than the previous one. He hoped that the Third Committee would work in the spirit of conciliation and impartiality, which had animated the members of the Sub-Committee.

Analysing the new text proposed for article 21, he expressed satisfaction at the skilful introduction of the idea of the free choice of employment in paragraph 1. The deletion of the words "and pay" in that paragraph, with a view to grouping everything connected with payment of the worker in paragraph 2, was

---

① UN Document:A/C. 3/SR/156, p. 672; p. 673; p. 675.

a debatable point, but the Chinese delegation would not oppose it. With regard to the non-discrimination clause, although he found the compromise formula adopted to be useless, he nevertheless approved the idea of not enumerating the possible causes of discrimination.

The representative of China said that his delegation would prefer not to keep the second sub-paragraph of paragraph 2 in its present form for, if the idea of payment came within the scope of article 21, that of the social protection required to meet the needs of the worker's family belonged on the contrary, to article 22, and it did not seem necessary to repeat it in article 21.

The Chinese delegation, whilst accepting paragraphs 1 and 3 without alteration, would have preferred paragraph 2 to be worded so as to retain merely the two following principles: the first sub-paragraph should include the principle that every working person had the right to just remuneration; the second su-- paragraph should include the principle of equal pay for equal work.

【纪要影像】

Mr. CHANG (China) pointed out that he had agreed with the representative of Uruguay to replace the words "perform any acts" in the English text of the amendment submitted by the latter (A/C.3/268) by the words "engage in any acts".

Mr. CHANG (China) said that, in view of the objections which his proposal had raised, he would not insist on it.

Mr. CHANG (China) thanked Sub-Committee 3 and its Rapporteur for having drawn up a decidedly better text than the previous one. He hoped that the Third Committee would work in the spirit of conciliation and impartiality, which had animated the members of the Sub-Committee.

Analysing the new text proposed for article 21, he expressed satisfaction at the skilful introduction of the idea of the free choice of employment in paragraph 1. The deletion of the words "and pay" in that paragraph, with a view to grouping everything connected with payment of the worker in paragraph 2, was a debatable point, but the Chinese delegation would not oppose it. With regard to the non-discrimination clause, although he found the compromise formula adopted to be useless, he nevertheless approved the idea of not enumerating the possible causes of discrimination.

The representative of China said that his delegation would prefer not to keep the second sub-paragraph of paragraph 2 in its present form for, if the idea of payment came within the scope of article 21, that of the social protection required to meet the needs of the worker's family belonged on the contrary, to article 22, and it did not seem necessary to repeat it in article 21.

The Chinese delegation, whilst accepting paragraphs 1 and 3 without alteration, would have preferred paragraph 2 to be worded so as to retain merely the two following principles: the first sub-paragraph should include the principle that every working person had the right to just

remuneration; the second sub-paragraph should include the principle of equal pay for equal work.

图片 3.3.41：张彭春在联大第三委员会第三届第 156 次会议发言纪要

【纪要译文】

张先生(中国)指出,他同意乌拉圭代表的意见,将后者提交的修正案(A/C.3/268)英文文本中的"从事任何行动"改为"采取任何行动"。

张先生(中国)说,鉴于他的提案提出的反对意见,他将不坚持提案。

张先生(中国)感谢第三小组委员会及其报告员起草了一份比前一份好得多的案文。他希望第三委员会将本着调解和公正的精神开展工作,这使小组委员会成员感到振奋。

在分析为第21条提出的新案文时,他对第1款巧妙地引入自由选择就业的概念表示满意。删除该款中的"和工资"一词,以便将与工人工资有关的所有事项都归入第2款,这是一个有争议的观点,但中国代表团不会反对。关于不歧视条款,尽管他认为所采用的折中方案毫无用处,但他还是赞成不列举歧视的可能原因的想法。

中国代表说,中国代表团不希望保留第2款第二分款目前的形式,因为如果支付的概念属于第21条的范围,则满足工人家庭需要所需的社会保护则属于第22条,而且似乎没有必要在第21条中重复这一点。

中国代表团在接受第1款和第3款不作改动的同时,更希望第2款的措辞仅保留以下两项原则:第一分款应包括每个工作人员都有权获得公正报酬的原则;第二分款应包括同工同酬原则。

38.张彭春在联大第三委员会
第三届第157次会议上的发言

联大第三委员会第三届第157次会议,于1948年11月25日下午3时至晚上6时30分,在巴黎夏洛宫召开,本次会议继续讨论《国际人权宣言》草案(第21条:第三小组委员会的报告)。中国代表张彭春参加了本次会

议,并在会议上发言,其具体发言内容①会议纪要、纪要影像和纪要译文
如下:

【会议纪要】

Mr. CHANG (China) indicated that article 21 might more accurately re-flect the real feelings of the Committee if it stated that everyone, without dis-crimination, was entitled to work. Of what use was it to forbid discrimination with respect to equal pay if people were not hired for discriminatory reasons?

He thought that the phrase beginning "supplemented by" in the second sub-paragraph of paragraph 2 should be in article 22 rather than article 21.

【纪要影像】

> Mr. CHANG (China) indicated that article 21 might more accurately reflect the real feelings of the Committee if it stated that everyone, without discrimination, was entitled to work. Of what use was it to forbid discrimination with respect to equal pay if people were not hired for discriminatory reasons?
>
> He thought that the phrase beginning "supplemented by" in the second sub-paragraph of paragraph 2 should be in article 22 rather than article 21.

图片 3.3.42:张彭春在联大第三委员会第三届第 157 次会议发言纪要

【纪要译文】

张先生(中国)指出,如果第 21 条规定人人都有权不受歧视地工作,

---

① UN Document:A/C. 3/SR/157, p. 684.

那么它可能更准确地反映委员会的真实想法。如果人们不是出于歧视性原因而被雇用,那么禁止同工同酬方面的歧视又有什么用呢?

他认为,第2款第二分款中以"补充"开头的短语应在第22条中,而不是在第21条中。

39. 张彭春在联大第三委员会
第三届第 158 次会议上的发言

联大第三委员会第三届第 158 次会议,于 1948 年 11 月 25 日晚上 8 时 30 分至 11 时,在巴黎夏洛宫召开,本次会议继续讨论《国际人权宣言》草案(第 21 条:第三小组委员会的报告)。中国代表张彭春参加了本次会议,并在会议上发言,其具体发言内容①会议纪要、纪要影像和纪要译文如下:

【会议纪要】

Mr. CHANG(China)stated that he had objected to the closure of the debate when the Byelorussian amendment had been under discussion as he had wanted more time in which to examine it. The introduction of that amendment had made article 21 more of a duplication of article 22 than before, and the Chinese delegation had abstained from voting on the second sentence of paragraph 2. Paragraph 3 of the new text was a definite improvement.

In the final vote on the article as a whole, the Chinese delegation had abstained, although it felt that the new text was certainly an improvement on the earlier text against which it had voted originally (141st meeting).

---

① UN Document:A/C. 3/SR/158, p. 692.

Mr. CHANG (China) stated that he had objected to the closure of the debate when the Byelorussian amendment had been under discussion as he had wanted more time in which to examine it. The introduction of that amendment had made article 21 more of a duplication of article 22 than before, and the Chinese delegation had abstained from voting on the second sentence of paragraph 2. Paragraph 3 of the new text was a definite improvement.

In the final vote on the article as a whole, the Chinese delegation had abstained, although it felt that the new text was certainly an improvement on the earlier text against which it had voted originally (141st meeting).

图片 3.3.43：张彭春在联大第三委员会第三届第 158 次会议发言纪要

【纪要译文】

张先生(中国)说，他反对在讨论白俄罗斯修正案时结束辩论,因为他希望有更多的时间来审议该修正案。该修正案的提出使第 21 条比以前产生了对第 22 条的更多重复,中国代表团对第 2 款第二句投了弃权票。新案文第 3 款是一个明显的改进。

在就整个条款进行的最后表决中,中国代表团投了弃权票,尽管它认为新案文肯定是对其最初投票反对的先前案文(第 141 次会议)的改进。

40. 张彭春在联大第三委员会
第三届第 166 次会议上的发言

联大第三委员会第三届第 166 次会议,于 1948 年 11 月 30 日下午 3 时至晚上 6 时 45 分,在巴黎夏洛宫召开,本次会议继续讨论《国际人权宣言》

草案(序言)。中国代表张彭春参加了本次会议,并在会议上发言,其具体发言内容①会议纪要、纪要影像和纪要译文如下:

【会议纪要】

Mr. CHANG (China) wished to make certain remarks concerning the a-mendments proposed to the first recital of the preamble. He recalled that he had had the honour of taking part in the work of the Commission on Human Rights and that the members of the Commission had then considered that first recital too long. The Netherlands amendment would make the text even more lengthy and more complex.

Moreover, if the idea of the divine origin of man were to be embodied in the declaration, it should be done in a separate paragraph so as to stress its im-portance; but, as certain delegations had pointed out, it was impossible to de-cide so important a problem by a vote which would only reflect political factors; for the consideration of such a question the number of votes for each country should be proportional to the size of its population.

For all those reasons, he hoped that the Netherlands delegation would withdraw its amendment.

Mr. CHANG (China) considered that the two first recitals in the text as submitted by the Commission on Human Rights should be retained. As for the third recital, it would be wise to accept the modification proposed by the United Kingdom delegation. On the other hand, he did not approve of the proposed ad-ditions to the fourth recital recapitulating ideas expressed in the Charter. Al-though the declaration dealt with all the rights of man, it was not necessary to refer to all of them in the preamble.

Mr. CHANG (China) shared the USSR representative's views on the ad-journment of the Committee's work during the meetings of the sub-committee.

----

① UN Document: A/C. 3/SR/166, pp. 771–772; p. 777; p. 780.

Mr. CHANG (China) wished to make certain remarks concerning the amendments proposed to the first recital of the preamble. He recalled that he had had the honour of taking part in the work of the Commission on Human Rights and that the members of the Commission had then considered that first recital too long. The Netherlands amendment would make the text even more lengthy and more complex.

Moreover, if the idea of the divine origin of man were to be embodied in the declaration, it should be done in a separate paragraph so as to stress its importance; but, as certain delegations had pointed out, it was impossible to decide so important a problem by a vote which would only reflect political factors; for the consideration of such a question the number of votes for each country should be proportional to the size of its population.

For all those reasons, he hoped that the Netherlands delegation would withdraw its amendment.

Mr. CHANG (China) considered that the two first recitals in the text as submitted by the Commission on Human Rights should be retained. As for the third recital, it would be wise to accept the modification proposed by the United Kingdom delegation. On the other hand, he did not approve of the proposed additions to the fourth recital recapitulating ideas expressed in the Charter. Although the declaration dealt with all the rights of man, it was not necessary to refer to all of them in the preamble.

Mr. CHANG (China) shared the USSR representative's views on the adjournment of the Committee's work during the meetings of the subcommittee.

图片 3.3.44：张彭春在联大第三委员会第三届第 166 次会议发言纪要

【纪要译文】

张先生(中国)希望就序言部分第一节的拟议修正案发表一些看法。他回顾说,他有幸参加了人权委员会的工作,委员会成员当时认为第一节陈述太长。荷兰的修正案将使案文更加冗长和复杂。

此外,如果《宣言》要体现人的神圣起源的思想,则应在单独的一段中进行,以强调其重要性;但是,正如某些代表团指出的那样,不可能通过只反映政治因素的表决来决定如此重要的问题;在审议这一问题时,每个国家的票数应与其人口数量成比例。

出于所有这些原因,他希望荷兰代表团撤回其修正案。

张先生(中国)认为,应保留人权委员会提交的案文中的前两节序言。至于第三节陈述,最好接受英国代表团提出的修改。另一方面,他不赞成在第四节序言中增加内容,概述《宪章》中表达的观点。虽然《宣言》涉及所有人的权利,但没有必要在序言中提及所有这些权利。

张先生(中国)同意苏联代表在小组委员会会议期间对委员会工作延期的看法。

联大第三委员会及联大全会

41. 张彭春在联大第三委员会
第三届第 167 次会议上的发言

联大第三委员会第三届第 167 次会议,于 1948 年 11 月 30 日晚上 9 时至 12 月 1 日凌晨 1 时 5 分,在巴黎夏洛宫召开,本次会议继续讨论《国际人权宣言》草案(序言)。中国代表张彭春参加了本次会议,并在会议上先后多次发言,其具体发言内容①会议纪要、纪要影像和纪要译文如下:

【会议纪要】

Mr. CHANG (China) said he was very surprised at the change of position which had occurred during the voting. The Chairman should take a vote on whether the two paragraphs which had been adopted should be substituted for the whole of the preamble or not, because a decision to add them to the preamble would create an entirely new situation.

Mr. CHANG (China) wondered where the text should be inserted, if the principle were accepted that the two paragraphs should be added to the preamble. Furthermore, should the two paragraphs be added to the actual preamble, or to the text proposed by the Ecuador delegation?

Mr. Chang proposed that, in order to save time, they should first take a vote, and then the USSR representative should explain in what form he wished the two paragraphs to be added.

The CHAIRMAN agreed with the Chinese representative's proposal.

In reply to a question by Mr. CHANG (China), the CHAIRMAN explained that the vote would be taken on whether the text proposed in the Ecua-

---

① UN Document: A/C. 3/SR/167, p. 782; p. 783; p. 787; p. 790.

dorean amendment should be substituted for the text of the Commission and not on the ideas expressed in the various parts of the amendment.

Mr. CHANG (China) proposed formally that the second paragraph of the amendment should be replaced by the last sentence of the first Australian amendment (A/C. 3/257): "... and have made apparent the supreme importance of the recognition and guarantee of fundamental freedoms".

He thought that everyone was acquainted with the fundamental freedoms proclaimed by President Roosevelt and set forth in the joint Australian-French amendment. To mention them would therefore be sufficient, but it was essential to provide for the recognition and guarantee of those fundamental freedoms.

The Chairman put to the vote the proposal just made by the Chinese representative in regard to the second paragraph of the joint Australian-French amendment.

The proposal was rejected by 17 votes to 9, with 10 abstentions.

Mr. CHANG (China) said the Cuban representative's proposal could not be accepted as the Committee had not yet finished voting on the preamble. Once the whole of the preamble had been voted upon, it would be possible for the Committee to take a decision on a proposal to reconsider its vote.

【纪要影像】

Mr. CHANG (China) said he was very surprised at the change of position which had occurred during the voting. The Chairman should take a vote on whether the two paragraphs which had been adopted should be substituted for the whole of the preamble or not, because a decision to add them to the preamble would create an entirely new situation.

Mr. CHANG (China) wondered where the text should be inserted, if the principle were accepted that the two paragraphs should be added to the preamble. Furthermore, should the two paragraphs be added to the actual preamble, or to the text proposed by the Ecuador delegation?

Mr. Chang proposed that, in order to save time, they should first take a vote, and then the USSR representative should explain in what form he wished the two paragraphs to be added.

The CHAIRMAN agreed with the Chinese representative's proposal.

In reply to a question by Mr. CHANG (China), the CHAIRMAN explained that the vote would be taken on whether the text proposed in the Ecuadorean amendment should be substituted for the text of the Commission and not on the ideas expressed in the various parts of the amendment.

Mr. CHANG (China) proposed formally that the second paragraph of the amendment should be replaced by the last sentence of the first Australian amendment (A/C.3/257): ". . . and have made apparent the supreme importance of the recognition and guarantee of fundamental freedoms".

He thought that everyone was acquainted with the fundamental freedoms proclaimed by President Roosevelt and set forth in the joint Australian-French amendment. To mention them would therefore be sufficient, but it was essential to provide for the recognition and guarantee of those fundamental freedoms.

The CHAIRMAN put to the vote the proposal just made by the Chinese representative in regard to the second paragraph of the joint Australian-French amendment.

The proposal was rejected by 17 votes to 9, with 10 abstentions.

Mr. CHANG (China) said the Cuban representative's proposal could not be accepted as the Committee had not yet finished voting on the preamble. Once the whole of the preamble had been voted upon, it would be possible for the Committee to take a decision on a proposal to reconsider its vote.

图片 3.3.45:张彭春在联大第三委员会第三届第 167 次会议发言纪要

【纪要译文】

张先生(中国)说,他对投票期间发生的立场变化感到非常惊讶。主席应就是否应以已通过的两段取代整个序言进行表决,因为将其添加到序言中的决定将造成一种全新的局面。

张先生(中国)想知道,如果接受在序言中增加这两段的原则,案文应该插入哪里。此外,这两段是应该添加到实际序言中,还是添加到厄瓜多尔代表团提议的案文中?

张先生建议,为了节省时间,他们应首先进行表决,然后苏联代表应解释他希望以何种形式添加这两段。

主席同意中国代表的建议。

在回答张先生(中国)的问题时,主席解释说,将对厄瓜多尔修正案中提议的案文是否应取代委员会的案文进行表决,而不是对修正案各部分表达的观点进行表决。

张先生(中国)正式提议将修正案第二段改为澳大利亚第一修正案(A/C. 3/257)的最后一句:"……并表明承认和保障基本自由的极端重

要性。"

他认为,每个人都熟悉罗斯福总统所宣布并在澳法联合修正案中阐述的基本自由。因此,提及它们就足够了,但必须规定承认和保障这些基本自由。

主席将中国代表刚才就澳法联合修正案第二段提出的提案付诸表决。

该提案以 17 票对 9 票、10 票弃权被否决。

张先生(中国)说,古巴代表的提案不能被接受,因为委员会尚未完成对序言部分的表决。一旦对整个序言部分进行表决,委员会就有可能就重新考虑其表决的提案作出决定。

42. 张彭春在联大第三委员会
第三届第 175 次会议上的发言

联大第三委员会第三届第 175 次会议,于 1948 年 12 月 4 日下午 4 时 15 分至晚上 6 时 55 分,在巴黎夏洛宫召开,本次会议继续讨论《国际人权宣言》草案(第 2 条)。中国代表张彭春参加了本次会议,并在会议上发言,其具体发言内容①会议纪要、纪要影像和纪要译文如下:

【会议纪要】

Mr. CHANG (China) favoured the text submitted by the Sub-Committee, for reasons of form.

Mr. CHANG (China) suggested the following wording: "... language, religion, national or social origin, political or other opinion, birth, property or other status".

Mr. AZKOUL (Lebanon) proposed the adoption of the following order of

---

① UN Document: A/C. 3/SR/175, p. 852.

enumeration in the first paragraph of article 2:

"... without distinction of any kind, such as race, colour, sex, language, religion, political or other opinion, national or social origin, property, birth or any other status".

The text was adopted unanimously.

【纪要影像】

Mr. CHANG (China) favoured the text submitted by the Sub-Committee, for reasons of form.

Mr. CHANG (China) suggested the following wording: "... language, religion, national or social origin, political or other opinion, birth, property or other status"

Mr. AZKOUL (Lebanon) proposed the adoption of the following order of enumeration in the first paragraph of article 2:

"... without distinction of any kind, such as race, colour, sex, language, religion, political or other opinion, national or social origin, property, birth or any other status".

The text was adopted unanimously.

图片 3.3.46：张彭春在联大第三委员会第三届第 175 次会议发言纪要

【纪要译文】

张先生（中国）出于形式原因赞成小组委员会提交的案文。

张先生（中国）建议使用以下措辞："……语言、宗教、民族或社会出身、政治或其他见解、出身、财产或其他身份。"

阿兹库勒（Azkoul）先生（黎巴嫩）提议在第 2 条第 1 款中采用以下列举顺序：

"……不分种族、肤色、性别、语言、宗教、政治或其他见解、国籍或社会出身、财产、出身或任何其他身份等任何区别"。

案文获得一致通过。

43. 张彭春在联大第三委员会
第三届第 176 次会议上的发言

联大第三委员会第三届第 177 次会议,于 1948 年 12 月 6 日上午 10 时 30 分至下午 1 时 10 分,在巴黎夏洛宫召开,本次会议继续讨论《国际人权宣言》草案(第 2 条)。中国代表张彭春参加了本次会议,并在会议上发言,其具体发言内容①会议纪要、纪要影像和纪要译文如下:

【会议纪要】

Mr. Cassin (France) stressed the fact that the question had already been discussed at length and that the Committee had taken a decision on the matter which there was no cause to reconsider. The term "arbitrary" was used on several occasions in the draft declaration and it was fully understood that it expressed two shades of meaning: that of illegality and that which the United Kingdom representative had sought to define by using the word "unreasonable".

Mr. BOGOMOLOV (Union of Soviet Socialist Republics), Mr. SAINT-LOT (Haiti), Mr. CHANG (China) and Mr. AIKMAN (New Zealand) shared the views expressed by the representative of France.

The CHAIRMAN asked the Committee to vote on the replacement of the term "arbitrary" by the word "unwarranted".

It was decided, by 34 votes to 2, with 5 abstentions, to retain the word "arbitrary".

Article 10 was adopted.

---

① UN Document: A/C. 3/SR/176, p. 864.

【纪要影像】

Mr. CASSIN (France) stressed the fact that the question had already been discussed at length and that the Committee had taken a decision on the matter which there was no cause to reconsider. The term "arbitrary" was used on several occasions in the draft declaration and it was fully understood that it expressed two shades of meaning: that of illegality and that which the United Kingdom representative had sought to define by using the word "unreasonable".

Mr. BOGOMOLOV (Union of Soviet Socialist Republics), Mr. SAINT-LOT (Haiti), Mr. CHANG (China) and Mr. AIKMAN (New Zealand) shared the views expressed by the representative of France.

The CHAIRMAN asked the Committee to vote on the replacement of the term "arbitrary" by the word "unwarranted".

It was decided, by 34 votes to 2, with 5 abstentions, to retain the word "arbitrary".

Article 10 was adopted.

图片 3.3.47：张彭春在联大第三委员会第三届第 176 次会议发言纪要

【纪要译文】

卡森先生(法国)强调,这个问题已经进行了详细讨论,委员会已经就这个问题作出了决定,没有理由重新考虑。宣言草案中多次使用"任意"一词,人们完全理解它表达了两种含义:非法性和英国代表试图用"不合理"一词来界定的含义。

博戈莫洛夫(Bogomolov)先生(苏联)、桑特·劳特(Saint Lot)先生(海地)、张先生(中国)和艾克曼(Aikman)先生(新西兰)赞同法国代表表达的观点。

主席请委员会就"任意"一词改为"无根据"一词进行表决。

会议以 34 票对 2 票、5 票弃权决定保留"任意"一词。

第 10 条获得通过。

44. 张彭春在联大第三委员会第三届第 177 次会议上的发言

联大第三委员会第三届第 177 次会议,于 1948 年 12 月 6 日下午 3 时 30 分至晚上 6 时 40 分,在巴黎夏洛宫召开,本次会议继续讨论《国际人权宣言》草案(第 16 条和第 23 条)。中国代表张彭春参加了本次会议,并在会议上发言,其具体发言内容①会议纪要、纪要影像和纪要译文如下:

【会议纪要】

In reply to a question by Mr. CHANG (China), the CHAIRMAN stated that the replacement of *ou* by *et* in French must involve a corresponding change in the English text. He pointed out, however, that the word "either" in the English text made it clear that freedom to manifest religion or belief in public by no means excluded the freedom to do so in private.

Mr. CHANG (China) recalled that the current form of the first phrase of paragraph 3 had been established, as a compromise solution, as the result of a concession by the French delegation, which had always expressed preference for the use of the present indicative. After some debate, the Committee had decided in favour of the current wording.

While expressing no personal preference, he suggested that, in order to avoid loss of time and a possible disparity between the French and English texts, the sentence should be retained as it stood.

Mr. CHANG (China) observed that he had submitted a slight amendment (A/C. 3/397) to paragraph 1 of article 23, chiefly for the sake of uniformity of

---

① UN Document: A/C. 3/SR/177, p. 865, p. 867; p. 868; p. 869.

style.

The first two sentences of the paragraph would remain unchanged; the third would read as follows: "Elementary education shall be compulsory; technical and professional education shall be made generally available; and higher education shall be equally accessible to all on the basis of merit."

The CHAIRMAN put to the vote the first two sentences of paragraph 1.

The first two sentences were adopted by 27 votes to 8.

The CHAIRMAN put to the vote the Chinese amendment to the remainder of paragraph 1.

The amendment was adopted by 13 votes to 1, with 7 abstentions.

Paragraph 2 of article 23 was adopted.

Mr. CHANG (China) suggested replacing the words "to their children" by the words "to their offspring in their early childhood".

【纪要影像】

In reply to a question by Mr. CHANG (China), the CHAIRMAN stated that the replacement of *ou* by *et* in French must involve a corresponding change in the English text. He pointed out, however, that the word "either" in the English text made it clear that freedom to manifest religion or belief in public by no means excluded the freedom to do so in private.

Mr. CHANG (China) recalled that the current form of the first phrase of paragraph 3 had been established as a compromise solution, as the result of a concession by the French delegation, which had always expressed preference for the use of the present indicative. After some debate, the Committee had decided in favour of the current wording.

While expressing no personal preference, he suggested that, in order to avoid loss of time and a possible disparity between the French and English texts, the sentence should be retained as it stood.

Mr. CHANG (China) observed that he had submitted a slight amendment (A/C.3/397) to paragraph 1 of article 23, chiefly for the sake of uniformity of style.

The first two sentences of the paragraph would remain unchanged; the third would read as follows: "Elementary education shall be compulsory; technical and professional education shall be made generally available; and higher education shall be equally accessible to all on the basis of merit."

The CHAIRMAN put to the vote the first two sentences of paragraph 1.

The first two sentences were adopted by 27 votes to 8.

The CHAIRMAN put to the vote the Chinese amendment to the remainder of paragraph 1.

The amendment was adopted by 13 votes to 1, with 7 abstentions.

Paragraph 2 of article 23 was adopted.

Mr. CHANG (China) suggested replacing the words "to their children" by the words "to their offspring in their early childhood".

图片 3.3.48：张彭春在联大第三委员会第三届第 177 次会议发言纪要

【纪要译文】

在回答张先生（中国）的问题时，主席说，要在法语文本中用 et 替换 ou 必须涉及英文文本的相应更改。然而，他指出，英文文本中的"或"一词明确表明，公开表明宗教或信仰的自由绝不排除私下表明宗教或信仰的自由。

张先生（中国）回顾说，第 3 款第一句的现行形式是作为折中解决办法确定的，这是法国代表团作出让步的结果，法国代表团一直表示倾向于使用本指示性案文。经过一些辩论，委员会决定赞成目前的措辞。

虽然他没有表示个人偏好，但他建议，为了避免浪费时间和法文和英文文本之间可能存在的差异；这句话应该保留原样。

张先生（中国）说，他对第 23 条第 1 款提出了稍微的修正（A/C. 3/397），主要是为了风格的统一。

该款前两句将保持不变；第三句内容如下："基础教育应为义务教育；应普遍提供技术和专业教育；所有人应根据成绩平等接受高等教育。"

主席将第 1 款前两句付诸表决。

前两句以 27 票对 8 票获得通过。

主席将中国对第 1 款其余部分的修正案付诸表决。

修正案以 13 票对 1 票、7 票弃权获得通过。

第 23 条第 2 款获得通过。

张先生（中国）建议将"对其子女"改为"对其幼年子女"。

45. 张彭春在联大第三委员会
第三届第 178 次会议上的发言

联大第三委员会第三届第 178 次会议,于 1948 年 12 月 6 日晚上 8 时 30 分至 7 日凌晨 3 时 10 分,在巴黎夏洛宫召开,本次会议继续讨论《国际人权宣言》草案(第 28 条、附加条款、条款的安排)。中国代表张彭春参加了本次会议,并在会议上先后多次发言,其具体发言内容①会议纪要、纪要影像和纪要译文如下:

【会议纪要】

ADDITIONAL ARTICLE

Mr. CAMPOS ORTIZ (Mexico), Mr. CHANG (China) and Mr. AZ-KOUL (Lebanon) suggested drafting changes whereby the word également, in the French text, would be replaced by the words en pleine égalité, and the English text would read as follows:

"The rights set forth in this Declaration apply equally to all inhabitants of Trust and Non-Self-Governing Territories. "

The CHAIRMAN put the additional article, as amended, to the vote.

The additional article, as amended, was adopted.

REARRANGEMENT OF ARTICLES

Mr. CHANG (China) called attention to the fact that various bodies had worked on the declaration for two years, and that all the Governments had had an opportunity of considering it and making comments. The order in which the articles appeared in the declaration had stood the test of time; the document

---

① UN Document: A/C. 3/SR/178, p. 874; pp. 876-877; p. 878; p. 880; p. 882.

possessed an organic unity which should not be tampered with lightly, at the very end of the Committee's work.

With regard to the Cuban proposal, if article 14 were inserted between articles 7, 8 and 9, which granted purely legal rights, and article 10, which dealt only incidentally with the family and called for legal protection with respect to a number of other matters, a logical sequence would be destroyed.

The Lebanese suggestion was equally unacceptable since articles 11, 12 and 13, dealing with freedom; of movement, asylum, and nationality, were much more closely associated in meaning with article 10 than was article 14.

He pleaded with the Committee not to alter the order of any of the articles save for good and sufficient reasons.

Mr. CHANG (China) suggested a rearrangement of certain articles with a view to ensuring that there was no break in the organic progression from articles on the right to life and the right to liberty to articles on the protection and enjoyment of those rights.

He agreed with the Brazilian representative that priority should be given to article 16, which should follow article 3; he felt, however, that articles 17, 18 and 19, which all dealt with the rights of the individual in relation to society, should continue to follow immediately upon article 16.

He would not object to the USSR proposal concerning the additional article if it met with the Committee's approval.

The Chairman put to the vote the Chinese proposal for the insertion of articles 18 and 19 after articles 16 and 17 in their new position.

The proposal was adopted by 21 votes to 3, with 12 abstentions.

Mr. CHANG (China) withdrew his earlier suggestions. He pointed out that the new position of articles 16 and 17 had caused the confusion.

He supported the Haitian proposal for the reconsideration of the Committee 's decisions.

Mr. CHANG (China) suggested that paragraph (c) of the Cuban amendment should be changed to read as follows:

"... not only in the official languages, but also, using every means at his disposal, in all possible languages".

It was so agreed.

Mr. CHANG (China) supported the views of the representatives of Haiti and Mexico and proposed that the third paragraph of the New Zealand draft resolution should be deleted.

【纪要影像】

ADDITIONAL ARTICLE

Mr. CAMPOS ORTIZ (Mexico), Mr. CHANG (China) and Mr. AZKOUL (Lebanon) suggested drafting changes whereby the word *également*, in the French text, would be replaced by the words *en pleine égalité*, and the English text would read as follows:

"The rights set forth in this Declaration apply equally to all inhabitants of Trust and Non-Self-Governing Territories."

The CHAIRMAN put the additional article, as amended, to the vote.

The additional article, as amended, was adopted.

ARRANGEMENT OF ARTICLES

Mr. CHANG (China) called attention to the fact that various bodies had worked on the declaration for two years, and that all the Governments had had an opportunity of considering it and making comments. The order in which the articles appeared in the declaration had stood the test of time; the document possessed an organic unity which should not be tampered with lightly, at the very end of the Committee's work.

With regard to the Cuban proposal, if article 14 were inserted between articles 7, 8 and 9, which granted purely legal rights, and article 10, which dealt only incidentally with the family and called for legal protection with respect to a number of other matters, a logical sequence would be destroyed.

The Lebanese suggestion was equally unacceptable, since articles 11, 12 and 13, dealing with freedom of movement, asylum, and nationality, were much more closely associated in meaning with article 10 than was article 14.

He pleaded with the Committee not to alter the order of any of the articles save for good and sufficient reasons.

图片 3.3.46:张彭春在联大第三委员会第三届第 178 次会议发言纪要(1)

Mr. CHANG (China) suggested a rearrangement of certain articles with a view to ensuring that there was no break in the organic progression from articles on the right to life and the right to liberty to articles on the protection and enjoyment of those rights.

He agreed with the Brazilian representative that priority should be given to article 16, which should follow article 3; he felt, however, that articles 17, 18 and 19, which all dealt with the rights of the individual in relation to society, should continue to follow immediately upon article 16.

He would not object to the USSR proposal concerning the additional article if it met with the Committee's approval.

The CHAIRMAN put to the vote the Chinese proposal for the insertion of articles 18 and 19 after articles 16 and 17 in their new position.

The proposal was adopted by 21 votes to 3, with 12 abstentions.

Mr. CHANG (China) withdrew his earlier suggestions. He pointed out that the new position of articles 16 and 17 had caused the confusion.

He supported the Haitian proposal for the reconsideration of the Committee's decisions.

Mr. CHANG (China) suggested that paragraph (c) of the Cuban amendment should be changed to read as follows:

" . . . not only in the official languages, but also, using every means at his disposal, in all possible languages".

It was so agreed.

Mr. CHANG (China) supported the views of the representatives of Haiti and Mexico and proposed that the third paragraph of the New Zealand draft resolution should be deleted.

图片 3.3.46:张彭春在联大第三委员会第三届第 178 次会议发言纪要(2)

【纪要译文】

附加条款

坎波斯·奥尔蒂斯先生先生(墨西哥)、张先生(中国)和阿兹库尔先生(黎巴嫩)建议对措词进行修改,将法文文本中的 également 一词改为 en pleine égalité,英文文本如下:

"本《宣言》所载权利同样适用于托管和非自治领土的所有居民。"

主席将修正后的附加条款付诸表决。

经修正的该附加条款获得通过。

条款的安排

张先生(中国)提请注意这样一个事实,即各机构为《宣言》工作了两年,所有政府都有机会审议该宣言并发表意见。这些条款在宣言中出现的顺序经受了时间的考验;该文件具有有机的统一性,在委员会工作结束时不应轻易篡改。

关于古巴的建议,如果在第 7 条、第 8 条和第 9 条之间插入第 14 条,该条授予纯粹的法律权利,而第 10 条只附带涉及家庭,并要求在一些其他事项上提供法律保护,那么逻辑顺序就会被破坏。

黎巴嫩的建议同样不能接受,因为第 11 条、第 12 条和第 13 条涉及自由;与第 14 条相比,迁徙、庇护和国籍的定义在意义上与第 10 条有更密切的联系。

他恳求委员会不要改变任何条款的顺序,除非有充分的理由。

张先生(中国)建议对某些条款进行重新安排,以确保从关于生命权和自由权的条款到关于保护和享受这些权利的条款的有机发展不会中断。

他同意巴西代表的意见,即应优先考虑第 16 条,该条应在第 3 条之后;然而,他认为,第 17 条、第 18 条和第 19 条都涉及个人与社会的权利,应继续紧随第 16 条之后。

如果得到委员会的批准,他不会反对苏联关于附加条款的提案。

主席将中国关于在第 16 条和第 17 条之后插入第 18 条和第 19 条的提案付诸表决。

该提案以 21 票对 3 票、12 票弃权获得通过。

张先生(中国)撤回了他先前的建议。他指出,第 16 条和第 17 条的新位置造成了混乱。

他支持海地关于重新审议委员会决定的建议。

张先生(中国)建议将古巴修正案(c)款改为:

"……不仅用官方语言,而且用他所掌握的一切手段,用所有可能的语言。"

此项达成了一致。

张先生(中国)支持海地和墨西哥代表的意见,并建议删除新西兰决议草案的第三款。

第四章 联大第三委员会第三届会议 （第二部分）

    联大第三委员会于 1949 年 4 月 6 日至 5 月 12 日，在纽约成功湖召开了第三届（第二部分）会议，包括 181 次至 229 次会议，该届大会共举行了 49 次会议。张彭春作为中国驻联大代表，参加了本届会议，并在其中的 11 次会议上发言，包括第 182 次、第 183 次、第 184 次、第 185 次、第 188 次、第 189 次、第 190 次、第 193 次、第 194 次、第 218 次和第 219 次会议，根据对会议纪要的统计显示，张彭春在本部分共有 25 次发言，但鉴于会议纪要一般不可能把所有发言都记录在案，因此，张彭春的实际发言次数应该远远大于 25 次。另有参加本届会议的中方顾问查修先生（Mr. Cha）参加了第 209 次会议①、第 222 次会议②和第 224 次会议③，并在会上分别发言。而本届会议的议程主要是讨论联合国经社理事会有关"新闻自由"的报告，起草新闻收集和国际传播公约。

    根据联合国官方档案会议纪要（档案文献来源：UN Document：A/C. 3/SR. 181–229 等）。联大第三委员会第三届（第二部分）第 181 次会议于 1949 年 4 月 6 日下午 3 时，在纽约成功湖举办，参加本届会议的中方人员共有 7 人，其中，张彭春作为中国代表，另有候补 1 人，顾问 5 人，具体参加会议人员名单（名字采用威妥玛拼音）如下：

---

    ① UN Document.：A_C-3_SR-181-229-EN, p. 277. / UN Doc.：A_C-3_SR-209-EN, p. 277.

    ② UN Document.：A_C-3_SR-181-229-EN, p. 383. /UN Doc.：A_C-3_SR-222-EN, p. 383.

    ③ UN Document.：A_C-3_SR-181-229-EN, p. 403. /UN Doc.：A_C-3_SR-224-EN, p. 403.

CHINA

Representative
H.E. Dr. P. C. Chang
Alternate
H.E. Dr. Pao Chin-jien
Advisers
Dr. H. Cha
Dr. K. P. Fengsen
Dr. Ho Hao-ju
Dr. Simon Cheng
Mr. P. Y. Tsao

图片 2.4.1:联大第三委员会第三届会议(第二部分)中国代表团名单

现将张彭春的发言内容依据其所参加的各次会议先后整理如下:

1. 张彭春在联大第三委员会
第三届第 182 次会议上的发言

联大第三委员会第三届第 182 次会议,于 1949 年 4 月 7 日下午 3 时至晚上 6 时 20 分,在纽约成功湖召开,本次会议主要议题是继续讨论新闻自由:经济及社会理事会的报告、继续讨论《新闻收集和国际传播公约》草案和第 1 条。中国代表张彭春参加了本次会议,并在会议上发言,其具体发言内容①会议纪要、纪要影像和纪要译文如下:

【会议纪要】

Mr. Chang (China) recalled the history of the draft convention under discussion. The texts of three draft conventions, carefully prepared by the United

---

① UN Doc.: A_C-3_SR-181-229-EN, P. 7-8; P. 10. / UN Doc.: A_C-3_SR-182 -EN, P. 7-8; P. 10.

Nations Conference on Freedom of Information held at Geneva—a conference at which approximately fifty States had been represented—had been submitted together with a number of resolutions to the Economic and Social Council's seventh session. The Council had referred the texts to its Committee on Human Rights, which had produced the amended text of the first draft convention, as it appeared in document E/1065, but which, for lack of time, had been unable to examine the remaining two draft conventions or the resolutions. The Council, moreover, had not considered the amended draft convention in plenary session, although statements of views had been made by separate members, but had referred the three draft conventions to the General Assembly. [1] Consequently, it could not be said that the first draft convention, even though it had been amended by a Council committee of the whole, bore the official stamp of the Council's approval.

In view of those considerations, the Chinese representative urged the Committee to keep in mind the text prepared by the Geneva Conference. Article 1, paragraph B of that text referred to a foreign correspondent as "the holder of a valid passport"; as in the majority of cases holders of passports were foreigners residing abroad, the strong presumption was that the definition contained in paragraph B applied only to such persons and not to nationals of a State employed by a foreign information agency. The Chinese representative had certainly gained that impression at the Geneva Conference.

The omission of the word "foreign" from the text before the Committee showed that the Human Rights Committee of the Economic and Social Council had inclined to the broader interpretation; it would consequently be useful for the Third Committee, when making its decision, to keep in mind the original Conference text, to which the United States representatives, incidentally, had

---

① See Official Records of the Economic and Social Council, third year, seventh session, 202nd meeting.

no objection.

If the Committee wished, it could of course extend the protection provided by the convention to both categories of persons; before making such a decision it should, however, see clearly the principle involved.

Mr. CHANG (China) in turn was surprised by the United Kingdom representative's interpretation of paragraph 2. The reason given when the Council Committee on Human Rights had revised that text had been that it was open to the interpretation of applying to foreigners only. The phrase introduced in the Council text, "when outside his State", made it clear that the foreign correspondent might be residing in his State; in other words, he might be the national of that State employed by a foreign news agency in the capacity of correspondent. The Conference text, on the other hand, specified that a foreign correspondent had to be the holder of a valid passport, the inference being that he was a foreigner residing abroad. There was consequently strong doubt whether that text applied to nationals of a State as well as to foreigners.

Mr. Chang thought the Conference text should be considered by the Committee as an alternative. That text too was open to amendments. The important thing for the Committee to decide was the question of principle: whether or not the protection afforded by the draft convention should extend to the nationals of a State acting in the capacity of correspondents for a foreign agency as well as to foreign correspondents residing abroad.

Mr. CHANG (China) recalled the history of the draft convention under discussion. The texts of three draft conventions, carefully prepared by the United Nations Conference on Freedom of Information held at Geneva — a conference at which approximately fifty States had been represented — had been submitted together with a number of resolutions to the Economic and Social Council's seventh session. The Council had referred the texts to its Committee on Human Rights, which had produced the amended text of the first draft convention, as it appeared in document E/1065, but which, for lack of time, had been unable to examine the remaining two draft conventions or the resolutions. The Council, moreover, had not considered the amended draft convention in plenary session, although statements of views had been made by separate members, but had referred the three draft conventions to the General Assembly.[1] Consequently, it could not be said that the first draft convention, even though it had been amended by a Council committee of the whole, bore the official stamp of the Council's approval.

[1] See *Official Records of the Economic and Social Council*, third year, seventh session, 202nd meeting.

In view of those considerations, the Chinese representative urged the Committee to keep in mind the text prepared by the Geneva Conference. Article 1, paragraph B of that text referred to a foreign correspondent as "the holder of a valid passport"; as in the majority of cases holders of passports were foreigners residing abroad, the strong presumption was that the definition contained in paragraph B applied only to such persons and not to nationals of a State employed by a foreign information agency. The Chinese representative had certainly gained that impression at the Geneva Conference.

The omission of the word "foreign" from the text before the Committee showed that the Human Rights Committee of the Economic and Social Council had inclined to the broader interpretation; it would consequently be useful for the Third Committee, when making its decision, to keep in mind the original Conference text, to which the United States representatives, incidentally, had no objection.

If the Committee wished, it could of course extend the protection provided by the convention to both categories of persons; before making such a decision it should, however, see clearly the principle involved.

图片 2.4.2：张彭春在联大第三委员会第三届第 182 次会议发言纪要(1)

Mr. CHANG (China) in turn was surprised by the United Kingdom representative's interpretation of paragraph 2. The reason given when the Council Committee on Human Rights had revised that text had been that it was open to the interpretation of applying to foreigners only. The phrase introduced in the Council text, "when outside his State", made it clear that the foreign correspondent might be residing in his State; in other words, he might be the national of that State employed by a foreign news agency in the capacity of correspondent. The Conference text, on the other hand, specified that a foreign correspondent had to be the holder of a valid passport, the inference being that he was a foreigner residing abroad. There was consequently strong doubt whether that text applied to nationals of a State as well as to foreigners.

Mr. Chang thought the Conference text should be considered by the Committee as an alternative. That text too was open to amendments. The important thing for the Committee to decide was the question of principle: whether or not the protection afforded by the draft convention should extend to the nationals of a State acting in the capacity of correspondents for a foreign agency as well as to foreign correspondents residing abroad.

图片 3.4.3：张彭春在联大第三委员会第三届第 182 次会议发言纪要(2)

【纪要译文】

张先生(中国)回顾了正在讨论的公约草案的历史。在日内瓦举行的联合国信息自由会议——约有 50 个国家派代表出席了该会议——仔细编写的三项公约草案案文已连同若干决议提交经济及社会理事会第七届会议。理事会已将案文提交其人权委员会,该委员会提出了 E/1065 号文件所载的公约草案第一稿的修正案文,但由于时间不够,该委员会未能审查其余两项公约草案或决议。此外,理事会在全体会议上没有审议经修正的公约草案,尽管有个别成员发表了意见声明,但已将这三项公约草案提交大会。① 因此,不能说第一项公约草案已获得理事会的正式批准,尽管它已由理事会全体委员会修订。

鉴于这些考虑,中国代表敦促委员会牢记日内瓦会议编写的案文。该案文第 1 条 B 款将外国记者称为"有效护照持有人";由于在大多数情况下,护照持有人都是居住在国外的外国人,因此强烈的推定是,B 款所载的定义只适用于这些人,而不适用于外国新闻机构雇用的国家国民。中国代表在日内瓦会议上当然获得了这种印象。

委员会面前的案文中省略了"外国"一词,表明经济及社会理事会人权事务委员会倾向于更广泛的解释;因此,第三委员会在作出决定时,最好记住会议的原始案文,顺便说一句,美国代表并不反对该案文。

如果委员会愿意,它当然可以将《公约》提供的保护扩大到这两类人;然而,在作出这样的决定之前,它应该清楚地看到所涉及的原则。

张先生(中国)对英国代表对第 2 款的解释感到惊讶。理事会人权委员会重新修订该案文时给出的理由是,该案文只适用于外国人。理事会案文中引入的"在其国家境外"一语明确表示,外国记者可能居住在其国家;换句话说,他可能是一家外国通讯社以通讯员身份雇用的该国国民。另一方面,会议文本规定,外国记者必须持有有效通行证,由此推断他是居住在国外的外国人。因此,人们强烈怀疑该案文是否适用于一国国民以及外

---

① 见《经济及社会理事会正式记录》,第三年,第七届会议,第 202 次会议》。

国人。

张先生认为,委员会应将会议案文作为备选案文加以审议。该案文也可以修改。委员会要决定的重要事项是原则问题:公约草案提供的保护是否应扩大到以外国机构通讯员身份行事的国家国民以及居住在国外的外国通讯员。

2. 张彭春在联大第三委员会
第三届第 183 次会议上的发言

联大第三委员会第三届第 183 次会议,于 1949 年 4 月 8 日下午 3 时至晚上 6 时 25 分,在纽约成功湖召开,本次会议主要议题是继续讨论新闻自由:经济及社会理事会的报告、继续讨论《新闻收集和国际传播公约》草案和第 1 条。中国代表张彭春参加了本次会议,并在会议上发言,其具体发言内容①会议纪要、纪要影像和纪要译文如下:

【会议纪要】

Mr. Chang (China) remarked that it was for the Committee to decide what meaning it wished to give to the term "foreign correspondent" and then to redraft the definition contained in paragraph 2 accordingly. The intentions of those who had prepared the earlier drafts of that paragraph were consequently not relevant to the task in hand.

Nevertheless, it was clear from the documents used at the United Nations Conference on Freedom of Information that the earliest conception of a foreign correspondent had been that of a person residing abroad and engaged in trans-

---

① UN Doc.: A_C-3_SR-181-229-EN, P. 14-15; P. 21-22; P. 24. / UN Doc.: A_C-3_SR-183-EN, P. 14-15; P. 21-22; P. 24.

mitting information beyond the frontiers of the State in which he resided. In support of that statement, Mr. Chang quoted from the earliest draft of the convention under discussion,[①] article 2 of which stated that no restrictions should be imposed by any of the Contracting States upon the entry and egress of foreign correspondents, while article 3 said that foreign correspondents sent from one State to another should be permitted to travel freely across the territory of intervening States. It was clear that those provisions could apply only to foreign nationals.

Moreover, a proposal concerning the entry, residence and egress of foreign correspondents, submitted at the Conference, was based on the principle that Governments should encourage the interchange of foreign correspondents, while a similar proposal was to be found in an amendment presented by none other than the United Kingdom.

There could consequently be no doubt concerning the intention behind the earliest drafts of the convention. The Human Rights Committee of the Economic and Social Council had altered that intention, as it had had every right to do. In the same manner, the Third Committee was entitled to make any change it wished.

The Chinese representative pointed out that he had not intended to move the amendment ascribed to him in document A/C. 3/419, to replace "correspondent" by "foreign correspondent" in the first sentence of paragraph 2. If the Committee agreed in principle that the term "correspondent" should apply only to correspondents residing abroad and not to the nationals of a State residing in that State but employed by a foreign news agency, a number of consequential amendments would have to be made. That would not be as difficult, however, as had been represented: whenever the term "correspondent" occurred in the Council text, the corresponding Conference text could be used as

---

① See document E/Conf. 6/41

the basis for discussion.

Mr. CHANG (China) appreciated the spirit of compromise shown by the United States representative and fully agreed with the aspirations he had expressed. The gathering and international transmission of news was an extremely important factor in international relations and the question should therefore be handled with care. It would indeed be ideal if the international flow of information could be supervised by the United Nations, but in that case there would be no need for any convention on the subject.

The draft convention was not directly concerned with questions of employment and finance, although those considerations should be borne in mind. What was important was that the realities of the situation should be recognized. As the representative of India had stated earlier in the meeting, some countries were less highly developed than others in the field of news transmission and were therefore not in a position to send correspondents abroad. Such countries were in the majority and those which employed foreign correspondents were comparatively few. The United Kingdom representative had stated that there would not be any discrimination as among the nationals of a State, if the draft convention were to apply to all correspondents employed by foreign information agencies, regardless of their nationality. Mr. Chang felt, however, that there would be a certain amount of discrimination, as the correspondent working in his own country would feel himself to be in a privileged position if he received pay from abroad and was entitled to protection under an international convention. If the whole exchange of information could be carried on internationally, the question would naturally not arise, but in the existing circumstances it had to be taken into account.

He maintained his opinion that the words foreign correspondent used in the original Conference text had not been intended to cover correspondents who were nationals of the State in which they worked. If that had been the case, there would have been no need to amend the text, as had been done during the Economic and Social Council's seventh session.

He appreciated the good intentions of the countries which were in a position to send correspondents abroad, but felt that the position of under-developed countries should be borne in mind. If the opinion expressed by the representatives of the United States and the United Kingdom were adopted, it would be very difficult for the under-developed countries to sign the convention.

Mr. Chang (China) did not consider that the majority obtained in the recent vote had been overwhelming and wondered whether the representatives who had made up that majority might not be willing to reconsider their decision. If the Mexican proposal were adopted as a compromise, it would enable many more countries to sign the convention.

【纪要影像】

Mr. Chang (China) remarked that it was for the Committee to decide what meaning it wished to give to the term "foreign correspondent" and then to re-draft the definition contained in paragraph 2 accordingly. The intentions of those who had prepared the earlier drafts of that paragraph were consequently not relevant to the task in hand.

Nevertheless, it was clear from the documents used at the United Nations Conference on Freedom of Information that the earliest conception of a foreign correspondent had been that of a person residing abroad and engaged in transmitting information beyond the frontiers of the State in which he resided. In support of that statement, Mr. Chang quoted from the earliest draft of the convention under discussion,[1] article 2 of which stated that no restrictions should be imposed by any of the Contracting States upon the entry and egress of foreign correspondents, while article 3 said that foreign correspondents sent from one State to another should be permitted to travel freely across the territory of intervening States. It was clear that those provisions could apply only to foreign nationals.

[1] See document E/Conf.6/41.

Moreover, a proposal concerning the entry, residence and egress of foreign correspondents, submitted at the Conference, was based on the principle that Governments should encourage the interchange of foreign correspondents, while a similar proposal was to be found in an amendment presented by none other than the United Kingdom.

There could consequently be no doubt concerning the intention behind the earliest drafts of the convention. The Human Rights Committee of the Economic and Social Council had altered that intention, as it had had every right to do. In the same manner, the Third Committee was entitled to make any change it wished.

The Chinese representative pointed out that he had not intended to move the amendment ascribed to him in document A/C.3/419, to replace "correspondent" by "foreign correspondent" in the first sentence of paragraph 2. If the Committee agreed in principle that the term "correspondent" should apply only to correspondents residing abroad and not to the nationals of a State residing in that State but employed by a foreign news agency, a number of consequential amendments would have to be made. That would not be as difficult, however, as had been represented: whenever the term "correspondent" occurred in the Council text, the corresponding Conference text could be used as the basis for discussion.

图片 3.4.4:张彭春在联大第三委员会第三届第 183 次会议发言纪要(1)

Mr. CHANG (China) appreciated the spirit of compromise shown by the United States representative and fully agreed with the aspirations he had expressed. The gathering and international transmission of news was an extremely important factor in international relations and the question should therefore be handled with care. It would indeed be ideal if the international flow of information could be supervised by the United Nations, but in that case there would be no need for any convention on the subject.

The draft convention was not directly concerned with questions of employment and finance, although those considerations should be borne in mind. What was important was that the realities of the situation should be recognized. As the representative of India had stated earlier in the meeting, some countries were less highly developed than others in the field of news transmission and were therefore not in a position to send correspondents abroad. Such countries were in the majority and those which employed foreign correspondents were comparatively few. The United Kingdom representative had stated that there would not be any discrimination as among the nationals of a State, if the draft convention were to apply to all correspondents employed by foreign information agencies, regardless of their nationality. Mr. Chang felt, however, that there would be a certain amount of discrimination, as the correspondent working in his own country would feel himself to be in a privileged position if he received pay from abroad and was entitled to protection under an international convention. If the whole exchange of information could be carried on internationally, the question would naturally not arise, but in the existing circumstances it had to be taken into account.

He maintained his opinion that the words "foreign correspondent" used in the original Conference text had not been intended to cover correspondents who were nationals of the State in which they worked. If that had been the case, there would have been no need to amend the text, as had been done during the Economic and Social Council's seventh session.

He appreciated the good intentions of the countries which were in a position to send correspondents abroad, but felt that the position of under-developed countries should be borne in mind. If the opinion expressed by the representatives of the United States and the United Kingdom were adopted, it would be very difficult for the under-developed countries to sign the convention.

Mr. CHANG (China) did not consider that the majority obtained in the recent vote had been overwhelming and wondered whether the representatives who had made up that majority might not be willing to reconsider their decision. If the Mexican proposal were adopted as a compromise, it would enable many more countries to sign the convention.

图片 3.4.5：张彭春在联大第三委员会第三届第 183 次会议发言纪要(2)

【纪要译文】

张先生(中国)说,应由委员会决定它希望赋予"外国通讯员"一词什么含义,然后据此重新起草第 2 款所载的定义。因此,编写该款早期草案的人的意图与手头的任务无关。

然而,从联合国新闻自由会议使用的文件中可以清楚地看出,外国通讯员的最早概念是居住在国外并从事在其居住国境外传播信息的人。为支持这一说法,张先生引述了正在讨论的公约最早的草案①,其中第 2 条规定,任何缔约国不应对外国通讯员的出入施加任何限制,而第 3 条规定,从一个国家派往另一个国家的外国通讯员应被允许自由穿越介入国的领土。显然,这些规定只能适用于外国国民。

此外,在会议上提交的关于外国记者入境、居留和出境的提案所依据的原则是,各国政府应鼓励外国通讯员交流,而只有英国提出的修正案中也有类似提案。

因此,公约最早草案背后的意图是毫无疑问的。经济及社会理事会人权委员会改变了这一意图,因为它完全有权这样做。同样,第三委员会有

---

① 见文件:E/Conf. 6/41.

权作出它所希望的任何改变。

中国代表指出,他无意动议 A/C. 3/419 号文件中所述的修正案,将第 2 款第一句中的"通讯员"改为"外国通讯员"。如果委员会原则上同意"通讯员"一词只适用于居住在国外的通讯员,而不适用于居住在该国但受雇于外国通讯社的一国国民,则必须作出若干相应的修正。然而,这并不像人们所说的那样困难:只要理事会案文中出现"通讯员"一词,相应的会议案文就可以作为讨论的基础。

张先生(中国)赞赏美国代表表现出的妥协精神,并完全同意他表达的愿望。新闻的收集和国际传播是国际关系中一个极其重要的因素,因此应谨慎处理这个问题。如果联合国能够监督信息的国际流动,这确实是理想的,但在这种情况下,就没有必要就此问题订立任何公约。

公约草案并不直接涉及就业和金融问题,但应铭记这些考虑。重要的是应该认识到局势的现实。正如印度代表早些时候在会议上指出的那样,一些国家在新闻传播领域不如其他国家发达,因此无法向国外派遣记者。这些国家占大多数,雇用外国记者的国家相对较少。英国代表说,如果公约草案适用于外国新闻机构雇用的所有通讯员,而不论其国籍如何,一国国民之间就不会有任何歧视。然而,张先生认为会有一定程度的歧视,因为在自己国家工作的通讯员如果从国外获得报酬并有权根据国际公约得到保护,就会觉得自己处于特权地位。如果整个信息交流能够在国际上进行。这个问题自然不会出现,但在目前的情况下,必须加以考虑。

他坚持认为,会议原文中使用的"外国通讯员"一词并不是为了涵盖作为其工作国国民的通讯员。如果是这样,就没有必要像经济及社会理事会第七届会议期间那样修改案文。

赞赏有能力向国外派遣通讯员的国家的良好意愿,但认为——应铭记不发达国家的立场。如果美国和英国代表的意见获得通过,欠发达国家将很难签署该公约。

张先生(中国)没有考虑到在最近的投票中获得的多数是压倒性的,并且怀疑那些组成了多数的代表可能不愿意重新考虑他们的决定。如果墨西哥的提案作为折中方案获得通过,将使更多的国家能够签署该公约。

3. 张彭春在联大第三委员会
第三届第 184 次会议上的发言

联大第三委员会第三届第 184 次会议,于 1949 年 4 月 11 日上午 11 时 30 分至下午 1 时 20 分,在纽约成功湖召开,本次会议主要议题是继续讨论新闻自由:经济及社会理事会的报告、继续讨论《新闻收集和国际传播公约》草案和第 1 条。中国代表张彭春参加了本次会议,并在会议上发言,其具体发言内容①会议纪要、纪要影像和纪要译文如下:

【会议纪要】

Mr. Chang (China) was glad that the question of the vote taken at the 183rd meeting had been raised, because he felt there really was some need for clarification. The whole question should be approached from the educational rather than from the political point of view, because of the nature of the draft convention itself. The definition of "correspondent" in paragraph 2 of article 1 was of fundamental importance to the draft convention as a whole, and the question should therefore be settled unequivocally before the other articles could be discussed. In order to be free, information should be fair, full and frank, and the discussion in the Third Committee should also have those attributes if the convention were to be successful and to receive the maximum number of signatures.

He pointed out that an absolute majority had not been obtained in the vote

---

① UN Doc.: A_C-3_SR-181-229-EN, P. 26-27. / A_C-3_SR-184-EN, P. 26-27.

taken at the 183rd meeting. The same could also be said of the vote taken on the subject in the Human Rights Committee of the Economic and Social Council,[2] when 8 representatives had voted in favour of including the nationals of the country in which the news was collected and from which it was transmitted, 7 had voted against that concept and 3 had abstained. Thus the voting had been very close each time and such a narrow majority could not be considered satisfactory where a question of such vital importance was concerned. Mr. Chang thought it would be better to place the discussion on a less legalistic footing — to attempt to reach a compromise rather than to hurry to a vote. Such had been the procedure followed during the discussion of resolution 19 adopted by the Conference on Freedom of Information, with the result that the resolution had eventually been adopted unanimously.

In his opinion, the Conference text of the draft convention was infinitely preferable to the re-draft adopted by the Human Rights Committee of the Economic and Social Council and he very much regretted that the Conference text, which had been prepared by fifty-four countries, had not been taken as a basis for discussion rather than the re-draft, which had been considered by only eighteen countries. The United States representative had said he would be willing to return to the wording of the Conference text and Mr. Chang hoped the Committee would eventually decide to follow that course. In his opinion, the Conference text had been perfectly clear and straightforward and there had been no intention of including correspondents who were nationals of the country in which they worked.

The question was one of great importance under-developed countries, which were in the vast majority. The Netherlands representative had stated, at the 183rd meeting, that a large proportion of correspondents working for foreign agencies in his country were of Dutch nationality and he had argued that such

---

② See document E/AC. 27/SR. 15.

correspondents should be covered by the draft convention. Mr. Chang felt, however, that the position was different where under-developed countries were concerned. As he had already stated at the 183rd meeting, the difficulty would not arise if all information agencies could be internationalized. If, however, nationals of the country in which the news was collected and from which it was transmitted were included in the draft convention, it would amount to internationalizing the employees without internationalizing the agencies which employed them. Moreover, the third draft convention,[①]which dealt with freedom of information as a whole, gave general protection to all correspondents. The first draft convention should therefore keep to its real purpose, which was, in his opinion, to protect the rights of foreign correspondents working outside the country of which they were nationals.

He did not wish to make a formal proposal for reconsideration of the vote taken at the 183rd meeting, but he hoped that some of those who had formed the majority of 22 might agree to reconsider their decision. He suggested that a small informal group might be set up to give the matter more careful consideration and to reach a more general understanding, since the question was one of such paramount importance.

联大第三委员会及联大全会

---

① See Resolutions adopted by the Economic and Social Council at its seventh session, resolution 152 B (VII) , page 24.

【纪要影像】

Mr. CHANG (China) was glad that the question of the vote taken at the 183rd meeting had been raised, because he felt there really was some need for clarification. The whole question should be approached from the educational rather than from the political point of view, because of the nature of the draft convention itself. The definition of "correspondent" in paragraph 2 of article 1 was of fundamental importance to the draft convention as a whole, and the question should therefore be settled unequivocally before the other articles could be discussed. In order to be free, information should be fair, full and frank, and the discussion in the Third Committee should also have those attributes if the convention were to be successful and to receive the maximum number of signatures.

He pointed out that an absolute majority had not been obtained in the vote taken at the 183rd meeting. The same could also be said of the vote taken on the subject in the Human Rights Committee of the Economic and Social Council,[2] when 8 representatives had voted in favour of including the nationals of the country in which the news was collected and from which it was transmitted,

*See document E/AC.27/SR.15.

7 had voted against that concept and 3 had abstained. Thus the voting had been very close each time and such a narrow majority could not be considered satisfactory where a question of such vital importance was concerned. Mr. Chang thought it would be better to place the discussion on a less legalistic footing — to attempt to reach a compromise rather than to hurry to a vote. Such had been the procedure followed during the discussion of resolution 19 adopted by the Conference on Freedom of Information, with the result that the resolution had eventually been adopted unanimously.

In his opinion, the Conference text of the draft convention was infinitely preferable to the re-draft adopted by the Human Rights Committee of the Economic and Social Council and he very much regretted that the Conference text, which had been prepared by fifty-four countries, had not been taken as a basis for discussion rather than the re-draft, which had been considered by only eighteen countries. The United States representative had said he would be willing to return to the wording of the Conference text and Mr. Chang hoped the Committee would eventually decide to follow that course. In his opinion, the Conference text had been perfectly clear and straightforward and there had been no intention of including correspondents who were nationals of the country in which they worked.

图片 3.4.6:张彭春在联大第三委员会第三届第 184 次会议发言纪要(1)

The question was one of great importance to under-developed countries, which were in the vast majority. The Netherlands representative had stated, at the 183rd meeting, that a large proportion of correspondents working for foreign agencies in his country were of Dutch nationality and he had argued that such correspondents should be covered by the draft convention. Mr. Chang felt, however, that the position was different where under-developed countries were concerned. As he had already stated at the 183rd meeting, the difficulty would not arise if all information agencies could be internationalized. If, however, nationals of the country in which the news was collected and from which it was transmitted were included in the draft convention, it would amount to internationalizing the employees without internationalizing the agencies which employed them. Moreover, the third draft convention,[1] which dealt with freedom of information as a whole, gave general protection to all correspondents. The first draft convention should therefore keep to its real purpose, which was, in his opinion, to protect the rights of foreign correspondents working outside the country of which they were nationals.

He did not wish to make a formal proposal for reconsideration of the vote taken at the 183rd meeting, but he hoped that some of those who had formed the majority of 22 might agree to reconsider their decision. He suggested that a small informal group might be set up to give the matter more careful consideration and to reach a more general understanding, since the question was one of such paramount importance.

[1] See *Resolutions adopted by the Economic and Social Council at its seventh session*, resolution 152 B (VII), page 24.

图片 3.4.7:张彭春在联大第三委员会第三届第 184 次会议发言纪要(2)

【纪要译文】

张先生(中国)感到高兴的是,第 183 次会议上的表决问题已经提出,因为他认为确实需要澄清。由于公约草案本身的性质,应该从教育的角度而不是从政治的角度来处理整个问题。第 1 条第 2 款中"通讯员"的定义对整个公约草案具有根本重要性,因此,在讨论其他条款之前,应明确解决这一问题。为了自由,信息应该是公平、充分和坦率的,如果《公约》要取得成功并获得最大程度的签署,第三委员会的讨论也应该具有这些特点。

他指出,第 183 次会议的表决没有获得绝对多数。经济及社会理事会人权委员会就这一问题进行的表决也是如此[2],有 8 名代表投票赞成将收集和传播新闻的国家的国民包括在内,7 人投票反对这一概念,3 人投票弃权。因此,每次投票都非常接近,在如此重要的问题上,如此微弱的多数不能被认为是令人满意的。张先生认为,最好将讨论放在一个不那么法律化的基础上——试图达成妥协,而不是匆忙投票。这就是讨论信息自由会议通过的第 19 号决议时遵循的程序,结果该决议最终获得一致通过。

他认为,公约草案的会议案文比经济及社会理事会人权委员会通过的重新的草案要好得多,他非常遗憾的是,由 54 个国家编写的会议案文没有被作为讨论的基础,而作为讨论基础的草案,只有 18 个国家审议过。美国代表曾表示,他愿意回到会议案文的措辞上来,张先生希望委员会最终决定遵循这一方针。他认为,会议案文十分明确和直截了当,没有打算将通讯员包括在其工作所在国的国民中。

在欠发达国家占绝大多数的情况下,这是一个非常重要的问题。荷兰代表在第 183 次会议上指出,在荷兰为外国机构工作的记者中有很大一部分是荷兰国籍的,他认为公约草案应涵盖这些记者。然而,张先生认为,就欠发达国家而言,情况有所不同。正如他在第 183 次会议上所说,如果所有新闻机构都能国际化,就不会出现困难。但是,如果在公约草案中列入收集和传播新闻的国家的国民,这将等于使雇员国际化,而不是使雇用他们的机构国际化。此外,涉及整个信息自由的第三项公约草案[1]对所有通讯员提供了一般性保护。因此,公约草案初稿应符合其真正目的,他认为,

---

② 见文件 E/AC. 27/SR. 15。
① 见经济及社会理事会第七届会议通过的决议,第 152 B(VII)号决议,第 24 页。

这是为了保护在其国籍国以外工作的外国记者的权利。

他不想正式提议重新审议第 183 次会议上的表决,但他希望占 22 票多数的一些人可能同意重新审议他们的决定。他建议设立一个小型非正式小组,对这一问题进行更仔细的审议,并达成更广泛的理解,因为这一问题非常重要。

4. 张彭春在联大第三委员会
第三届第 185 次会议上的发言

联大第三委员会第三届第 185 次会议,于 1949 年 4 月 11 日下午 2 时 30 分至晚上 6 时 25 分,在纽约成功湖召开,本次会议主要议题是继续讨论新闻自由:经济及社会理事会的报告、继续讨论《新闻收集和国际传播公约》草案和第 1 条第 1 款和第 2 款。中国代表张彭春参加了本次会议,并在会议上先后多次发言,其具体发言内容①会议纪要、纪要影像和纪要译文如下:

【会议纪要】

Mr. CHANG (China) recalled that the Committee had adopted a decision on principle during the 183rd meeting, in accordance with which the word "correspondent" would apply to both national and non-national correspondents. It had not taken a formal decision on the Chinese amendment.

The term "foreign correspondent" had appeared in all previous drafts. The draft convention, in his opinion, concerned foreign correspondents, even if some representatives believed that the application of that term should be extend-

---

① UN Document:A/C. 3/SR. 181-229, P. 32-33; P. 35; P. 37; P. 37; P. 38. / UN Document:A/C. 3/SR. 185, P. 32-33; P. 35; P. 37; P. 37; P. 38.

ed to cover correspondents who were nationals of the country in which they carried on their professional activities. The Committee could, therefore, while respecting the decision it had taken at its 183rd meeting, insert the word "foreign" before the word "correspondent" as proposed in the Chinese amendment.

Mr. Chang suggested that the words "gathering and international transmission of news" might be substituted for the words "the collection and reporting of news material", so that the aims of the convention should be explicitly recalled. If there were any objection to that suggestion, however, he would not insist that it should be put to the vote.

Mr. CHANG (China) noted that his suggestions had given rise to objections on the part of some delegations, but had received the approval of others. He wished to point out that it would be illogical not to adopt the expression "foreign correspondent", if the Committee agreed to replace the words "the collection and reporting of news material" by the words "the gathering and international transmission of news".

Mr. Chang proposed that his two amendments should be put to the vote separately. He further requested that a vote should be taken on the question of retaining the words "when outside his State". He would either vote against the retention of those words or he would abstain, according to whether his two preceding amendments had been rejected or adopted. Such an attitude was consistent with his opinion that a correspondent must not be able to invoke the provisions of an international convention, should he have to defend himself before the laws of his own country.

Mr. CHANG (China) stated that, if the Committee accepted his two proposals to the effect that the term "foreign correspondent" and the wording "is regularly engaged in the gathering and international transmission of news" should be used, he would agree to withdraw his suggestion that the words "when outside his State" should be voted on separately.

Mr. CHANG (China) said he would withdraw his suggestion that a separate vote should be taken on the retention of the words "when outside his State". He pointed out moreover that he had not made any formal proposal to that effect.

He recalled the comments he had made at the time when he had put forward his suggestion and stated that he was maintaining his position: a "correspondent" should be the national of a State other than the one in which he worked; otherwise it might be possible for nationals of a given State to invoke the provisions of an international convention in an action against the laws of their own country.

Mr. CHANG (China) stated that he was withdrawing all the proposals which he had presented in connexion with the text of paragraph 2.

【纪要影像】

Mr. CHANG (China) recalled that the Committee had adopted a decision on principle during the 183rd meeting, in accordance with which the word "correspondent" would apply to both national and non-national correspondents. It had not taken a formal decision on the Chinese amendment.

The term "foreign correspondent" had appeared in all previous drafts. The draft convention, in his opinion, concerned foreign correspondents, even if some representatives believed that the application of that term should be extended to cover correspondents who were nationals of the country in which they carried on their professional activities. The Committee could, therefore, while respecting the decision it had taken at its 183rd meeting, insert the word "foreign" before the word "correspondent" as proposed in the Chinese amendment.

Mr. Chang suggested that the words "gathering and international transmission of news" might be substituted for the words "the collection and reporting of news material", so that the aims of the convention should be explicitly recalled. If there were any objection to that suggestion, however, he would not insist that it should be put to the vote.

Mr. CHANG (China) noted that his suggestions had given rise to objections on the part of some delegations, but had received the approval of others. He wished to point out that it would be illogical not to adopt the expression "foreign correspondent", if the Committee agreed to replace the words "the collection and reporting of news material" by the words "the gathering and international transmission of news".

Mr. Chang proposed that his two amendments should be put to the vote separately. He further requested that a vote should be taken on the question of retaining the words "when outside his State". He would either vote against the retention of those words or he would abstain, according to whether his two preceding amendments had been rejected or adopted. Such an attitude was consistent with his opinion that a correspondent must not be able to invoke the provisions of an international convention, should he have to defend himself before the laws of his own country.

图片 3.4.8：张彭春在联大第三委员会第三届第 185 次会议发言纪要(1)

Mr. CHANG (China) stated that, if the Committee accepted his two proposals to the effect that the term "foreign correspondent" and the wording "is regularly engaged in the gathering and international transmission of news" should be used, he would agree to withdraw his suggestion that the words "when outside his State" should be voted on separately.

Mr. CHANG (China) said he would withdraw his suggestion that a separate vote should be taken on the retention of the words "when outside his State". He pointed out moreover that he had not made any formal proposal to that effect.

He recalled the comments he had made at the time when he had put forward his suggestion and stated that he was maintaining his position: a "correspondent" should be the national of a State other than the one in which he worked; otherwise it might be possible for nationals of a given State to invoke the provisions of an international convention in an action against the laws of their own country.

Mr. CHANG (China) stated that he was withdrawing all the proposals which he had presented in connexion with the text of paragraph 2.

图片 3.4.9:张彭春在联大第三委员会第三届第185次会议发言纪要(2)

【纪要译文】

张先生(中国)回顾说,委员会在第183次会议上通过了一项原则性决定,根据该决定,"通讯员"一词将适用于本国和非本国通讯员。它尚未就中国的修正案作出正式决定。

"外国通讯员"一词出现在所有以前的草案中。他认为,公约草案涉及外国通讯员,即使一些代表认为,该术语的适用范围应扩大到包括从事专业活动的国家的国民。因此,委员会在尊重其在第183次会议上作出的决定的同时,可以按照中国修正案的建议,在"通讯员"一词之前插入"外国"一词。

张先生建议,可以用"新闻的收集和国际传播"取代"新闻材料的收集和报道",以便明确回顾《公约》的宗旨。但是,如果有人反对这一建议,他不会坚持将其付诸表决。

张先生(中国)指出,他的建议引起了一些代表团的反对,但得到了其他代表团的批准。他希望指出,如果委员会同意将"收集和报道新闻材料"改为"收集和国际传播新闻",则不采用"外国通讯员"一词是不合逻辑的。

张先生提议将他的两项修正案分别付诸表决。他还要求就保留"在其国家境外"字样的问题进行表决。他要么投票反对保留这些文字,要么弃权,这取决于他之前的两项修正案是否被否决或通过。这种态度与他的观点是一致的,即如果通讯员必须在自己国家的法律面前为自己辩护,他就不能援引国际公约的规定。

张先生(中国)说,如果委员会接受了他的两项建议,即应使用"外国通讯员"一词和"经常从事新闻的收集和国际传播"一词,他将同意撤回其关于"在其国家之外"一词的建议应该单独进行表决。

张先生(中国)说,他将撤回他的建议,即对保留"不在其国家"一词进行单独表决。他还指出,他没有就此提出任何正式建议。

他回顾了他在提出建议时所作的评论,并表示他坚持自己的立场:"通讯员"应当是他工作所在国以外的国家的国民;否则,某一国家的国民可能会在违反本国法律的诉讼中援引国际公约的规定。

张先生(中国)说,他撤回了自己就第2款案文提出的所有提案。

5. 张彭春在联大第三委员会
第三届第188次会议上的发言

联大第三委员会第三届第188次会议,于1949年4月14日上午10时30分至下午1时10分,在纽约成功湖召开,本次会议主要议题是选举一位新的副主席、继续讨论新闻自由:经济及社会理事会的报告、继续讨论《新闻收集和国际传播公约》草案和第2条。中国代表张彭春参加了本次

会议,并在会议上发言,其具体发言内容①会议纪要、纪要影像和纪要译文如下:

【会议纪要】

Mr. CHANG (China) appreciated the contributions to the discussion made by the representatives of Belgium and the Philippines. Reading from the draft for article 2 submitted by the United States delegation①to the Conference on Freedom of Information, he noted that the word "facilitate" was used in that draft and that the words "encourage", "expedite" and "discriminate" did not appear. In his opinion, those words might give rise to difficulties of interpretation and he preferred the original United States draft to the text before the Committee.

He noted that article 2 was the first place in which the word "correspondent" was used following its definition in article 1. If that definition were borne in mind, it would be seen that article 2 first mentioned "correspondents" (that is, both the nationals and non-nationals of the country in which the news was collected and from which it was transmitted) and then went on to speak of "correspondents of other Contracting States". The sentence was thus obviously unbalanced. In order to obviate that difficulty, the expression "foreign correspondents" could be used at the beginning of the article, in its restricted and, in his opinion, true sense.

He did not wish to make any concrete suggestion, but he emphasized the fact that his remarks were always made in the interests of clarity. He felt sure that, in time, the true, straightforward meaning of the article would emerge. In the meantime, he would be obliged to abstain from voting because of the confu-

---

① UN Doc.: A_C-3_SR-181-229-EN, P. 63-64 / UN Doc.: A_C-3_SR-188-EN, P. 63-64.

① See E/Conf. 6/41.

sion in the text.

【纪要影像】

Mr. CHANG (China) appreciated the contributions to the discussion made by the representatives of Belgium and the Philippines. Reading from the draft for article 2 submitted by the United States delegation[1] to the Conference on Freedom of Information, he noted that the word "facilitate" was used in that draft and that the words "encourage", "expedite" and "discriminate" did not appear. In his opinion, those words might give rise to difficulties of interpretation and he preferred the original United States draft to the text before the Committee.

He noted that article 2 was the first place in which the word "correspondent" was used following its definition in article 1. If that definition were borne in mind, it would be seen that article 2 first mentioned "correspondents" (that is, both the nationals and non-nationals of the country in which the news was collected and from which it was transmitted) and then went on to speak of "correspondents of other Contracting States". The sentence was thus obviously unbalanced. In order to obviate that difficulty, the expression "foreign correspondents" could be used at the beginning of the article, in its restricted and, in his opinion, true sense.

He did not wish to make any concrete suggestion, but he emphasized the fact that his remarks were always made in the interests of clarity. He felt sure that, in time, the true, straightforward meaning of the article would emerge. In the meantime, he would be obliged to abstain from voting because of the confusion in the text.

[1] See E/Conf.6/41.

图片 3.4.10：张彭春在联大第三委员会第三届第 188 次会议发言纪要

【纪要译文】

张先生(中国)赞赏比利时和菲律宾代表对讨论所作的贡献。在阅读美国代表团①提交给新闻自由会议的第 2 条草案时,他指出,该草案使用了"便利"一词,"鼓励""加快"和"歧视"都没有出现。他认为,这些词语可能会造成解释上的困难,他更喜欢美国的原稿而不是委员会面前的案文。

他指出,第 2 条是在第 1 条的定义之后首先使用"通讯员"一词的地方。如果铭记这一定义,可以看出,第 2 条首先提到了"通讯员"(即新闻收集国和传播国的国民和非国民),然后又提到了"其他缔约国的通讯员"。因此,这个句子显然是不平衡的。为了避免这一困难,可以在条款开头使用"外国通讯员"一词,他认为这是一个有限制的、真正意义上的词语。

---

① 见文件：E/Conf. 6/41

他不想提出任何具体建议,但他强调,他的发言始终是为了澄清。他确信,该条款的真正、直截了当的意义迟早会显现出来。同时,由于案文混乱,他将不得不投弃权票。

6. 张彭春在联大第三委员会
第三届第 189 次会议上的发言

联大第三委员会第三届第 189 次会议,于 1949 年 4 月 14 日下午 2 时 30 分至晚上 6 时 20 分,在纽约成功湖召开,本次会议主要议题是继续讨论新闻自由:经济及社会理事会的报告、继续讨论《新闻收集和国际传播公约》草案和第 2 条和第 3 条。中国代表张彭春参加了本次会,并在会议上发言,其具体发言内容①如下:

【会议纪要】

Mr. Chang（China）suggested the deletion of the words "official and non-official" in article 3. That would allay the anxiety of the Indian delegation and at the same time answer the objections that had been made to the Indian amendment.

He pointed out that the wording of article 3 was not good. Its obscurity was the result of the Committee's decision to use the word "correspondent" to designate both foreign correspondents and those who were nationals of the State in whose territory they carried on their activities. Consequently, the text under consideration spoke of the State's "own correspondents", which was neither accurate nor acceptable.

---

① UN Doc.: A_C-3_SR-181-229-EN, P. 74-75. / UN Doc.: A_C-3_SR-189-EN, P. 74-75.

The Committee would continue to encounter difficulties of that kind so long as it had not formulated a clear definition of the term "correspondent".

【纪要影像】

Mr. CHANG (China) suggested the deletion of the words "official and non-official" in article 3. That would allay the anxiety of the Indian delegation and at the same time answer the objections that had been made to the Indian amendment.

He pointed out that the wording of article 3 was not good. Its obscurity was the result of the Committee's decision to use the word "correspondent" to designate both foreign correspondents and those who were nationals of the State in whose territory they carried on their activities. Consequently, the text under consideration spoke of the State's "own correspondents", which was neither accurate nor acceptable.

The Committee would continue to encounter difficulties of that kind so long as it had not formulated a clear definition of the term "correspondent".

图片 3.4.11：张彭春在联大第三委员会第三届第 189 次会议发言纪要

【纪要译文】

张先生(中国)建议删除第 3 条中的"官方和非官方"一词。这将减轻印度代表团的焦虑,同时回答对印度修正案提出的反对意见。

他指出,第 3 条的措辞不好。其费解的是因为委员会决定使用"通讯员"一词来指定外国通讯员和那些在其境内进行活动的国家的国民。因此,审议中的案文谈到该国的"自己的通讯员",这既不准确也不可接受。

只要委员会没有对"通讯员"一词作出明确定义,它就会继续遇到这种困难。

7. 张彭春在联大第三委员会
第三届第 190 次会议上的发言

联大第三委员会第三届第 190 次会议,于 1949 年 4 月 18 日上午 11 时至下午 1 时 20 分,在纽约成功湖召开,本次会议主要议题是继续讨论新闻自由:经济及社会理事会的报告、继续讨论《新闻收集和国际传播公约》草案和第 3 条。中国代表张彭春参加了本次会议,并在会议上先后多次发言,其具体发言内容①会议纪要、纪要影像和纪要译文如下:

【会议纪要】

Mr. Chang (China) recalled that he had endeavoured, on several occasions, to call attention to the difficulties which were bound to arise throughout the study of the draft convention as a result of the Committee's decision not to use the term "foreign correspondent".

Mr. Chang felt compelled to protest again, on the occasion of the verbal proposal made by the United Kingdom representative at the 189th meeting to replace the words "its own correspondents" by the words "the correspondents employing by its national Press". Such a formula was not satisfactory for numerous reasons. In the first place, the word "Press" was not appropriate in view of the fact that there were other means of communicating information, such as radio broadcasting and motion pictures. Moreover, the use of the word "national" as opposed to the word "foreign" also led to confusion. The aim was to ensure to a foreign correspondent working for a foreign information agency the same protec-

① UN Doc.: A_C-3_SR-181-229-EN, P. 78-79; P. 83; P. 85; P. 86. / UN doc.: A_C-3_SR-190-EN, P. 78-79; P. 83; P. 85; P. 86.

tion as was enjoyed by a correspondent who was a national of the country in which he carried on his professional activities—whether or not he worked for a foreign agency. Such a distinction between correspondents of foreign nationality and non-foreign correspondents was not evident in the formula proposed by the United Kingdom representative which, furthermore, did not do away with the ambiguity of the text. Lastly, Mr. Chang remarked that the word "employed", which he liked on account of its honesty, did not provide the necessary clarity either, since domestic news agencies also employed foreign personnel.

The representative of China requested the Committee to take no decision, for the time being, on that delicate question of drafting, which had already caused so much difficulty and would continue to do so if it were not judiciously settled. He warned the Committee that it would be confronted with the same problem until it found an entirely satisfactory formula to define what it meant by the term "correspondent".

Mr. CHANG (China) pointed out that the United Kingdom proposal did not altogether meet the concern he had expressed. The difficulty which had arisen in connexion with article 3 would appear in the case of other articles; it was not enough, therefore, to propose a formula for article 3. Furthermore, the United Kingdom proposal was likely to increase the ambiguity of the article; he could not vote for it. He again suggested that no hasty decision should be taken on the matter, and that the Committee should wait until all the articles of the convention had been considered.

Mr. CHANG (China) emphasized once more the necessity of avoiding any confusion in article 3. He repeated that there was no need for the Committee to decide so hastily on such an important question. If the United Kingdom amendment were put to the vote, he would be obliged to abstain.

Mr. CHANG (China) stated that the Peruvian amendment completely changed the meaning of article 3, and was contrary to the decision of principle taken by the Committee.

【纪要影像】

Mr. CHANG (China) recalled that he had endeavoured, on several occasions, to call attention to the difficulties which were bound to arise throughout the study of the draft convention as a result of the Committee's decision not to use the term "foreign correspondent".

Mr. Chang felt compelled to protest again, on the occasion of the verbal proposal made by the United Kingdom representative at the 189th meeting to replace the words "its own correspondents" by the words "the correspondents employed by its national Press". Such a formula was not satisfactory for numerous reasons. In the first place, the word "Press" was not appropriate in view of the fact that there were other means of communicating information, such as radio broadcasting and motion pictures. Moreover, the use of the word "national" as opposed to the word "foreign" also led to confusion. The aim was to ensure to a foreign correspondent working for a foreign information agency the same protection as was enjoyed by a correspondent who was a national of the country in which he carried on his professional activities — whether or not he worked for a foreign agency. Such a distinction between correspondents of foreign nationality and non-foreign correspondents was not evident in the formula proposed by the United Kingdom representative which, furthermore, did not do away with the ambiguity of the text. Lastly, Mr. Chang remarked that the word "employed", which he liked on account of its honesty, did not provide the necessary clarity either, since domestic news agencies also employed foreign personnel.

The representative of China requested the Committee to take no decision, for the time being, on that delicate question of drafting, which had already caused so much difficulty and would continue to do so if it were not judiciously settled. He warned the Committee that it would be confronted with the same problem until it found an entirely satisfactory formula to define what it meant by the term "correspondent".

图片 3.4.12：张彭春在联大第三委员会第三届第 190 次会议发言纪要（1）

Mr. CHANG (China) pointed out that the United Kingdom proposal did not altogether meet the concern he had expressed. The difficulty which had arisen in connexion with article 3 would appear in the case of other articles; it was not enough, therefore, to propose a formula for article 3. Furthermore, the United Kingdom proposal was likely to increase the ambiguity of the article; he could not vote for it. He again suggested that no hasty decision should be taken on the matter, and that the Committee should wait until all the articles of the convention had been considered.

Mr. CHANG (China) emphasized once more the necessity of avoiding any confusion in article 3. He repeated that there was no need for the Committee to decide so hastily on such an important question. If the United Kingdom amendment were put to the vote, he would be obliged to abstain.

Mr. CHANG (China) stated that the Peruvian amendment completely changed the meaning of article 3, and was contrary to the decision of principle taken by the Committee.

图片 3.4.13：张彭春在联大第三委员会第三届第 190 次会议发言纪要（2）

【纪要译文】

张先生(中国)回顾说,由于委员会决定不使用"外国通讯员"一词,他曾多次努力提请注意在整个公约草案研究过程中必然会出现的困难。

英国代表在第189次会议上口头提议将"本国通讯员"改为"本国新闻界雇用的通讯员"之际,张先生感到不得不再次提出抗议。由于许多原因,这样一个公式并不令人满意。首先,"新闻"一词不合适,因为还有其他传播信息的手段,如无线电广播和电影。此外,使用"国家"一词而不是"外国"一词也导致混淆。目的是确保为外国新闻机构工作的外国记者享有与其从事专业活动所在国国民相同的保护,无论他是否为外国机构工作。在英国代表提出的方案中,外国籍通讯员和非外国通讯员之间的这种区别并不明显,而且,这并没有消除案文的模糊性。最后,张先生说,他因诚实而喜欢的"雇用"一词也没有提供必要的明确性,因为国内新闻机构也雇用外国人员。

中国代表要求委员会暂时不对这一微妙的起草问题作出决定,因为这一问题已经造成了很大的困难,如果不明智地加以解决,它将继续造成极大困难。他警告委员会,在找到一个完全令人满意的方案来定义"通讯员"一词的含义之前,它将面临同样的问题。

张先生(中国)指出,英国的提案没有完全满足他所表示的关切。与第3条有关的困难将出现在其他条款中;因此,为第3条提出一个方案是不够的。此外,英国的提议可能会增加该条的模糊性;他不能投赞成票。他再次建议,不应就此事仓促作出决定,委员会应等到《公约》所有条款都审议完毕后再作出决定。

张先生(中国)再次强调有必要避免第3条中的任何混淆。他重申,委员会没有必要就如此重要的问题作出如此仓促的决定。如果将英国的修正案付诸表决,他将不得不弃权。

张先生(中国)说,秘鲁的修正案完全改变了第3条的含义,违反了委员会作出的原则决定。

8. 张彭春在联大第三委员会
第三届第 193 次会议上的发言

联大第三委员会第三届第 193 次会议,于 1949 年 4 月 19 日下午 3 时至晚上 6 时 45 分,在纽约成功湖召开,本次会议主要议题是继续讨论新闻自由:经济及社会理事会的报告、继续讨论《新闻收集和国际传播公约》草案和第 5 条、第 6 条、第 7 条和第 1 条。中国代表张彭春参加了本次会议,并在会议上发言,其具体发言内容①会议纪要、纪要影像和纪要译文如下:

【会议纪要】

Mr. CHANG (China) , speaking in explanation of his vote, referred to the comments he had made during the discussion on article 2 at the 188th meeting. At that time he had pointed out that the wording adopted for article 2 was illogical and unbalanced: after the word "correspondents" had been used near the beginning of the article, meaning both the nationals and non-nationals of the country concerned according to the definition adopted in article 1, there was a reference further on in the same sentence to "correspondents of other Contracting States". In his opinion the wording just adopted for article 5 had the same defects since it first mentioned "correspondents" and later "correspondents of other Contracting States". If representatives were to refer back to the original Conference text (E/Conf. 6/79) of article 5, they would find the wording perfectly logical, since the term "foreign correspondents" was used throughout. Avoidance of the expression "foreign correspondents" had thus made the article

① UN Doc.: A_C-3_SR-181-229-EN, P. 109-110; P. 115; P. 120. / UN Doc.: A _C-3_SR-193-EN, P. 109-110; P. 115; P. 120.

unbalanced. Moreover, the use of the word "correspondents", which included the nationals of the country concerned, destroyed the original meaning of the first part of the article. It was perfectly obvious that nationals of a country would have to conform to the laws inforce and to state that fact might imply that it was possible for them not to conform to those laws. If the word "foreign" was inserted the whole meaning would immediately Become quite clear.

Those remarks would apply equally to the wording adopted for article 4 and, in his opinion, the clarity of the whole draft convention was being jeopardized by a mistaken aversion for the expression "foreign correspondents". He trusted, however, that the illogical dislike of that expression would eventually be overcome and that a really clear text would at last emerge.

Mr. CHANG (China) remarked that the replacement of the term "foreign correspondent" by "correspondent" throughout the draft convention frequently resulted in ambiguity. Rectification of terms was called for in several instances, including article 7, where it was not clear whether or not the words "of other Contracting States" qualified the word "correspondents".

Mr. PAYSSÉ REYES (Uruguay), supported by Mrs. FIGUEROA (Chile) and Mr. CHANG (China), strongly objected to the permissive meaning. States had the obvious right to take what measures they thought fit; no international convention could properly confer such a right upon them.

【纪要影像】

Mr. CHANG (China), speaking in explanation of his vote, referred to the comments he had made during the discussion on article 2 at the 188th meeting. At that time he had pointed out that the wording adopted for article 2 was illogical and unbalanced: after the word "correspondents" had been used near the beginning of the article, meaning both the nationals and non-nationals of the country concerned according to the definition adopted in article 1, there was a reference further on in the same sentence to "correspondents of other Contracting States". In his opinion the wording just adopted for article 5 had the same defects since it first mentioned "correspondents" and later "correspondents of other Contracting States". If representatives were to refer back to the original Conference text (E/Conf.6/79) of article 5, they would find the wording perfectly logical, since the term "foreign correspondents" was used throughout. Avoidance of the expression "foreign correspondents" had thus made the article unbalanced. Moreover, the use of the word "correspondents", which included the nationals of the country concerned, destroyed the original meaning of the first part of the article. It was perfectly obvious that nationals of a country would have to conform to the laws in force and to state that fact might imply that it was possible for them not to conform to those laws. If the word "foreign" was inserted the whole meaning would immediately become quite clear.

Those remarks would apply equally to the wording adopted for article 4 and, in his opinion, the clarity of the whole draft convention was being jeopardized by a mistaken aversion for the expression "foreign correspondents". He trusted, however, that the illogical dislike of that expression would eventually be overcome and that a really clear text would at last emerge.

Mr. CHANG (China) remarked that the replacement of the term "foreign correspondent" by "correspondent" throughout the draft convention frequently resulted in ambiguity. Rectification of terms was called for in several instances, including article 7, where it was not clear whether or not the words "of other Contracting States" qualified the word "correspondents".

Mr. PAYSSÉ REYES (Uruguay), supported by Mrs. FIGUEROA (Chile) and Mr. CHANG (China), strongly objected to the permissive meaning. States had the obvious right to take what measures they thought fit; no international convention could properly confer such a right upon them.

图片 3.4.14:张彭春在联大第三委员会第三届第 193 次会议发言纪要

【纪要译文】

张先生(中国)在解释投票立场时提到了他在第 188 次会议上讨论第 2 条时所作的评论。当时他指出,为第 2 条采用的措辞是不合逻辑和不平衡的:在该条开头附近使用了"通讯员"一词之后,根据第 1 条通过的定义,这意味着有关国家的国民和非国民,同一句中还提到"其他缔约国的通讯员"。他认为,刚刚为第 5 条采用的措辞也有同样的缺陷,因为它首先提到"通讯员",后来又提到"其他缔约国的通讯员"。如果各位代表回顾会议第 5 条的原始案文(E/Conf.6/79),他们会发现该措辞完全合乎逻辑,因为"外国通讯员"一词贯穿始终。因此,避免使用"外国通讯员"一词使该条不平衡。此外,使用包括有关国家国民在内的"通讯员"一词破坏了该条第一部分的原有含义。很明显,一个国家的国民必须遵守有效的法律,并说明这一事实可能意味着他们可能不遵守这些法律。如果加上"外国"一词,整个意思将立即变得十分清楚。

这些评论同样适用于为第 4 条通过的措辞,他认为,对"外国通讯员"

联大第三委员会及联大全会

一词的错误厌恶正在损害整个公约草案的清晰度。然而,他相信,对这一表达不合逻辑的厌恶最终会被克服,最终会出现一个真正明确的文本。

张先生(中国)说,在整个公约草案中将"外国通讯员"一词改为"通讯员",常常造成歧义。在一些情况下,包括在第 7 条中,要求更正术语,因为不清楚"其他缔约国"一词是否限定了"通讯员"一词。

派赛·雷耶斯(Payssé Reyes)先生(乌拉圭)在菲格罗亚(Figueroa)女士(智利)和张先生(中国)的支持下,强烈反对这种放任的含义。各国显然有权采取它们认为合适的措施;任何国际公约都不能适当地赋予他们这种权利。

9. 张彭春在联大第三委员会第三届第 194 次会议上的发言

联大第三委员会第三届第 194 次会议,于 1949 年 4 月 20 日上午 10 时 30 分至下午 1 时,在纽约成功湖召开,本次会议主要议题是继续讨论新闻自由:经济及社会理事会的报告、继续讨论《新闻收集和国际传播公约》草案和第 1 条、第 8 条。中国代表张彭春参加了本次会议,并在会议上发言,其具体发言内容①会议纪要、纪要影像和纪要译文如下:

【会议纪要】

Mr. CHANG (China) thought that since article 1 as a whole had already been voted upon by the Committee, a new paragraph could not be added to it. Any proposal for an additional paragraph would be equivalent to a request for a fresh discussion of the article.

---

① UN Doc.: A_C-3_SR-181-229-EN, P. 121-122. / UN Doc.: A_C-3_SR-193-EN, P. 121-122.

Article 1 contained definitions of three expressions which were used several times in the convention. The expression "news dispatches" was used only once, in the article under discussion. There was therefore no need to insert a definition of it in article 1: it was in fact more logical to have it appear immediately following article 7, as a second paragraph to that article or as a footnote.

【纪要影像】

Mr. CHANG (China) thought that since article 1 as a whole had already been voted upon by the Committee, a new paragraph could not be added to it. Any proposal for an additional paragraph would be equivalent to a request for a fresh discussion of the article.

Article 1 contained definitions of three expressions which were used several times in the convention. The expression "news dispatches" was used only once, in the article under discussion. There was therefore no need to insert a definition of it in article 1; it was in fact more logical to have it appear immediately following article 7, as a second paragraph to that article or as a footnote.

图片 3.4.15:张彭春在联大第三委员会第三届第 194 次会议发言纪要

【纪要译文】

张先生(中国)认为,由于委员会已经对整个第 1 条进行了表决,因此不能在其中增加新的一款。任何增加一款的建议都相当于要求重新讨论该条。

第 1 条载有《公约》多次使用的三个用语的定义。"新闻快讯"一词在讨论的该条中只使用过一次。因此,没有必要在第 1 条中插入该条的定义:事实上,将其作为该条的第二款或脚注出现在第 7 条之后更符合逻辑。

10. 张彭春在联大第三委员会
第三届第 218 次会议上的发言

联大第三委员会第三届第 218 次会议,于 1949 年 5 月 6 日上午 11 时至下午 1 时 30 分,在纽约成功湖召开,本次会议主要议题是继续讨论新闻自由:经济及社会理事会的报告、继续讨论《新闻收集和国际传播公约》草案和荷兰代表提交的程序议案。中国代表张彭春参加了本次会议,并在会议上发言,其具体发言内容①会议纪要、纪要影像和纪要译文如下:

【会议纪要】

Mr. CHANG（China）asked the Committee to consider certain points with regard to international agreements and their importance. He emphasized that of all the protocols which States had signed, the protocol placing certain synthetic drugs under international control①and the protocols relating to the suppression of the traffic in women and children and traffic in obscene publications②had proved to be the most effective. Those protocols owed their effectiveness to the fact that they had been supported by the great majority, if not all, of the General Assembly and that they had received the moral sanction of all the peoples of the world.

If the Committee wished to ensure that the convention on the freedom of in-

---

① UN Doc.: A_C-3_SR-181-229-EN, P. 350-351; P. 355. / UN Doc.: A_C-3_SR-218-EN, P. 350-351; P. 355.

① See Official Records of the third session of the General Assembly, Part I, Resolutions, No. 211 A（III）.

② See Official Records of the third session of the General Assembly, Part I, Resolutions, No. 126 A（II）.

formation had the same universal character, it should be guided by the moral principles which had governed the drafting of the protocols he had mentioned. If the Committee allowed itself to be guided by legal or practical considerations only, it would establish an instrument the scope of which could not fail to be limited and provisional.

It was not a question of concluding a merely technical agreement to regulate freedom of information, but an agreement which would create the moral atmosphere necessary to enable the spirit of man to shake off all bonds. If that were the case—and Mr. Chang was convinced that it could not fail to be so—the Committee had far too important a work to accomplish to be held back by considerations of time and procedure. It was better to do the work well than to do it quickly.

For those reasons the Chinese delegation would vote for the Netherlands proposal, which it considered the most sensible in the circumstances.

Mr. CHANG (China) recalled that the Third Committee had been set up to deal with social, humanitarian and cultural questions. Those questions required careful consideration and mutual understanding on the part of members of the Committee. If the Committee wished to accomplish lasting work it should, therefore, take decisions only by a very large majority, if not unanimously. Bearing that aspect in mind, he thought that the Committee should not refer the consideration of the draft convention to an *ad hoc* committee, because that procedure would create an atmosphere of haste which would be harmful to the work.

The question of freedom of information could be considered from various points of view. The Committee should do its utmost to prepare a document which would be acceptable to all Member States. Only if it worked in a spirit of mutual understanding would the Committee be able to draft a convention of lasting value.

【纪要影像】

Mr. CHANG (China) asked the Committee to consider certain points with regard to international agreements and their importance. He emphasized that of all the protocols which States had signed, the protocol placing certain synthetic drugs under international control[1] and the protocols relating to the suppression of the traffic in

[1] See *Official Records of the third session of the General Assembly, Part I, Resolutions*, No. 211 A (III).

women and children and traffic in obscene publications[1] had proved to be the most effective. Those protocols owed their effectiveness to the fact that they had been supported by the great majority, if not all, of the General Assembly and that they had received the moral sanction of all the peoples of the world.

[1] See *Official Records of the second session of the General Assembly, Resolutions*, No. 126 (II).

If the Committee wished to ensure that the convention on the freedom of information had the same universal character, it should be guided by the moral principles which had governed the drafting of the protocols he had mentioned. If the Committee allowed itself to be guided by legal or practical considerations only, it would establish an instrument the scope of which could not fail to be limited and provisional.

It was not a question of concluding a merely technical agreement to regulate freedom of information, but an agreement which would create the moral atmosphere necessary to enable the spirit of man to shake off all bonds. If that were the case — and Mr. Chang was convinced that it could not fail to be so — the Committee had far too important a work to accomplish to be held back by considerations of time and procedure. It was better to do the work well than to do it quickly.

For those reasons the Chinese delegation would vote for the Netherlands proposal, which it considered the most sensible in the circumstances.

图片 3.4.16：张彭春在联大第三委员会第三届第 218 次会议发言纪要(1)

Mr. CHANG (China) recalled that the Third Committee had been set up to deal with social, humanitarian and cultural questions. Those questions required careful consideration and mutual understanding on the part of members of the Committee. If the Committee wished to accomplish lasting work it should, therefore, take decisions only by a very large majority, if not unanimously. Bearing that aspect in mind, he thought that the Committee should not refer the consideration of the draft convention to an *ad hoc* committee, because that procedure would create an atmosphere of haste which would be harmful to the work.

The question of freedom of information could be considered from various points of view. The Committee should do its utmost to prepare a document which would be acceptable to all Member States. Only if it worked in a spirit of mutual understanding would the Committee be able to draft a convention of lasting value.

图片 3.4.17：张彭春在联大第三委员会第三届第 218 次会议发言纪要(2)

【纪要译文】

张先生(中国)要求委员会考虑关于国际协定的某些要点及其重要性。他强调,在各国签署的所有议定书中,将某些合成药物置于国际管制之下的议定书①和关于禁止贩卖妇女和儿童以及贩卖淫秽物品的议定书②已证明是最有效的。这些议定书之所以有效,是因为它们得到了大会绝大多数(如果不是全部的话)的支持,并得到了世界各国人民的道义制裁。

如果委员会希望确保《新闻自由公约》具有同样的普遍性,它就应当以他所提到的起草议定书的道德原则为指导。如果委员会允许自己仅以法律或实际考虑为指导,它将制定一项文书,其范围必须是有限的和临时的。

这不仅仅是缔结一项规范新闻自由的技术协议的问题,而是一项能够创造必要的道德氛围,使人类精神摆脱一切束缚的协议,如果是这样的话,张先生相信这是不可能的,因此委员会有一项太重要的工作要完成,不能因为时间和程序的考虑而拖延。把这项工作做好比把它快点做完更好。

出于这些原因,中国代表团将对荷兰的提案投赞成票,它认为在目前情况下这是最明智的。

张先生(中国)回顾说,设立第三委员会是为了处理社会、人道主义和文化问题。这些问题需要委员会成员认真审议和相互理解。因此,如果委员会希望完成持久的工作,它应该以绝大多数作出决定,如果不是一致的话。考虑到这一方面,他认为委员会不应将公约草案的审议交给特设委员会,因为这一程序将造成一种匆忙的气氛,这将对工作有害。

新闻自由问题可以从不同的角度加以考虑。委员会应尽最大努力编写一份所有会员国都能接受的文件。只有本着相互理解的精神,委员会才能起草一项具有持久价值的公约。

---

① 见:《联大第三届会议正式记录,第一部分,决议》,第 211 A(III)号。
② 见:《联大第三届会议正式记录,第一部分,决议》,第 126 (II)号。

11. 张彭春在联大第三委员会
第三届第 219 次会议上的发言

联大第三委员会第三届第219次会议,于1949年5月6日下午3时至5时40分,在纽约成功湖召开,本次会议主要议题是继续讨论新闻自由:经济及社会理事会的报告、讨论印度代表提交的程序议案和巴西代表提交的程序议案、继续讨论《新闻收集和国际传播公约》草案。中国代表张彭春参加了本次会议,并在会议上发言,其具体发言内容①会议纪要、纪要影像和纪要译文如下:

【会议纪要】

Dr. CHANG (China) did not think the Committee should feel that if it did not produce a convention at that session, it had failed in its task. If the Colombian and Brazilian representatives would agree not to press for an immediate vote on their proposals, the Committee might continue its work, take up consideration of the convention later and come to a decision.

With regard to the Brazilian proposal, he wished to substitute for the words "be not open for signature before the second convention" the words "be open for signature at the same time as the convention on freedom of information".

Dr. CHANG (China) wished to withdraw his proposal on the ground that it had not been a formal amendment and was no longer necessary in view of the subsequent amendments to the text proposed by India.

---

① UN Doc.: A_C-3_SR-181-229-EN, P. 359. / UN Doc.: A_C-3_SR-219-EN, P. 359.

Dr. CHANG (China) did not think the Committee should feel that if it did not produce a convention at that session, it had failed in its task. If the Colombian and Brazilian representatives would agree not to press for an immediate vote on their proposals, the Committee might continue its work, take up consideration of the convention later and come to a decision.

With regard to the Brazilian proposal, he wished to substitute for the words "be not open for signature before the second convention" the words "be open for signature at the same time as the convention on freedom of information".

Dr. CHANG (China) wished to withdraw his proposal on the ground that it had not been a formal amendment and was no longer necessary in view of the subsequent amendments to the text proposed by India.

图片 3.4.18：张彭春在联大第三委员会第三届第 219 次会议发言纪要

【纪要译文】

张博士(中国)不认为，如果没有在该届会议上产生一项公约，委员会应感到自己的任务失败了。如果哥伦比亚和巴西代表同意不要求立即就其提案进行表决，委员会可以继续工作，稍后审议《公约》，并作出决定。

关于巴西的提案，他希望用"与《新闻自由公约》同时开放供签署"取代"在第二项公约之前不开放供签署"。

张博士(中国)希望撤回其提案，理由是该提案不是一项正式修正案，鉴于印度随后对案文提出的修正案，该提案不再必要。

联大第三委员会及联大全会

第五章 联大第三委员会第四届会议

1949 年 9 月 20 日至 11 月 28 日,联大第三委员会第四届会议,在纽约成功湖召开,本届会议从第 230 次至 269 次会议共召开了 40 次会议,中国代表团有两位正式代表参加,分别为程天放博士(*Tien-fong Cheng*)和张彭春先生。参加本届会议的中国代表发言次数最多的是查修先生(Mr. Cha),他在 1949 年 10 月 5 日下午 3 时举行的第 242 次会议①、1949 年 10 月 6 日上午 10 时 45 分举行的第 243 次会议②、1949 年 10 月 11 日上午 10 时 45 分举行的第 245 次会议③、1949 年 10 月 18 日上午 10 时 45 分举行的第 252 次会议④和 1949 年 10 月 19 日上午 10 时 45 分举行的第 254 次会议⑤上,共有 6 次发言内容。另外,本届会议程博士和曹保颐先生(Mr. Tsao)各有一次发言,其中程博士的发言⑥是在 1949 年 9 月 27 日下午 3 时举行的第 234 次会议上,而曹先生的发言⑦是在 1949 年 11 月 21 日下午 3 时举行的第 267 次会议上。

张彭春先生在本届会议上只有一次发言,是在 1949 年 10 月 26 日下午 3 时举行的第 255 次会议上。

---

① UN Document:A/C.3/SR/242,p. 44.(参与讨论禁止贩卖人口及取缔意图营利使人卖淫的公约草案。)

② UN Document:A/C.3/SR/243,p. 45;pp. 46-47.(参与讨论禁止贩卖人口及取缔意图营利使人卖淫的公约草案。)

③ UN Document:A/C.3/SR/245,p. 59.(参与讨论禁止贩卖人口及取缔意图营利使人卖淫的公约草案。)

④ UN Document:A/C.3/SR/252,p. 92.(参与讨论社会福利咨询服务。)

⑤ UN Document:A/C.3/SR/254,p. 96.(参与讨论社会福利咨询服务。)

⑥ UN Document:A/C.3/SR/234,pp. 10-11.(参与讨论新闻自由公约草案。)

⑦ UN Document:A/C.3/SR/267,pp. 164-165.(参与讨论联合国国际儿童紧急基金:(a)联合国国际儿童紧急基金的报告-(b)联合国为儿童呼吁。)

图片 2.5.1:联大第三委员会第四届会议中国代表团名单

1. 张彭春在联大第三委员会第四届第 255 次会议上的发言

联大第三委员会第四届第 255 次会议,于 1949 年 10 月 26 日下午 3 时至 5 时 40 分,在纽约成功湖举行,本次会议主要议题是讨论经社理事会的报告的第三章内容。张彭春先生参加了本次会议,并在会议上发言,其具体发言内容①会议纪要、纪要影像和纪要译文如下:

【会议纪要】

1. The CHAIRMAN opened the discussion on chapter III of the report of the Economic and Social Council.

2. Mr. CHANG (China) called attention to the fact that a document prepared by the Third Committee—the Universal Declaration of Human Rights—

———————————

① UN Document:A/C. 3/SR/255, p. 103.(参与讨论经济及社会理事会报告的第三章。)

had been placed, together with the Charter of the United Nations, within the cornerstone of the United Nations Permanent Headquarters. The preparation of that Declaration had been a historic achievement which would live long in the memory of mankind. The work in that field had not yet been completed, for the covenant remained to be drafted, but a very important initial step had been taken in the adoption of the Declaration.

3. He congratulated the Third Committee on all the work it had accomplished during the preceding year. Besides its work on the Universal Declaration of Human Rights, the Committee had also considered the draft convention for the suppression of the traffic in persons and of the exploitation of the prostitution of others. Much had also been done to strengthen the control over narcotic drugs during the three years since the United Nations had taken over that task. Two protocols had been adopted on the subject: one on 11 December 1946 and the other on 19 November 1948. Moreover, the Commission on Narcotic Drugs was doing valuable work in the preparation of a new single convention to replace the existing international treaties on the subject.

4. Concluding his remarks of appreciation, he submitted the following draft resolution (A/C. 3/L. 24) for adoption by the Committee:

"*The General Assembly*,

"*Takes note of chapter III of the report of the Economic and Social Council.*"

1. The CHAIRMAN opened the discussion on chapter III of the report of the Economic and Social Council.

2. Mr. CHANG (China) called attention to the fact that a document prepared by the Third Committee—the Universal Declaration of Human Rights—had been placed, together with the Charter of the United Nations, within the cornerstone of the United Nations Permanent Headquarters. The preparation of that Declaration had been a historic achievement which would live long in the memory of mankind. The work in that field had not yet been completed, for the covenant remained to be drafted, but a very important initial step had been taken in the adoption of the Declaration.

3. He congratulated the Third Committee on all the work it had accomplished during the preceding year. Besides its work on the Universal Declaration of Human Rights, the Committee had also considered the draft convention for the suppres-sion of the traffic in persons and of the exploitation of the prostitution of others. Much had also been done to strengthen the control over narcotic drugs during the three years since the United Nations had taken over that task. Two protocols had been adopted on the subject: one on 11 December 1946 and the other on 19 November 1948. Moreover, the Commission on Narcotic Drugs was doing valuable work in the preparation of a new single convention to replace the existing international treaties on the subject.

4. Concluding his remarks of appreciation, he submitted the following draft resolution (A/C.3/L.24) for adoption by the Committee:

"The General Assembly,

"Takes note of chapter III of the report of the Economic and Social Council."

图片 3.5.2：张彭春在联大第三委员会第四届第 255 次会议发言纪要

【纪要译文】

1. 主席开始讨论经济及社会理事会报告第三章。

2. 张先生(中国)提请注意,第三委员会编写的一份文件《世界人权宣言》与《联合国宪章》一起被置于联合国常设总部的基石之内。该宣言的编写是一项历史性的成就,将在人类的记忆中长期存在。该领域的工作尚未完成,因为《公约》仍有待起草,但在通过《宣言》方面已采取了非常重要的初步步骤。

3. 他祝贺第三委员会在前一年所完成的所有工作。除了关于《世界人权宣言》的工作外,委员会还审议了禁止贩卖人口和取缔逼迫他人卖淫的公约草案。自联合国接管这项任务以来的三年中,在加强对麻醉药品的管制方面也做了大量工作。就这个问题通过了两项议定书:一项于 1946 年 12 月 11 日通过,另一项于 1948 年 11 月 19 日通过。此外,麻醉药品委员会正在开展宝贵的工作,拟订一项新的单一公约,以取代关于这一问题的现有国际条约。

联大第三委员会及联大全会

4. 在结束他的赞赏发言时,他提交了下列决议草案(A/C. 3/L. 24)供委员会通过:

"联大,

"注意到经济及社会理事会报告第三章。"

第六章　联大第三委员会第五届会议

　　1950 年 9 月 20 日上午 11 时 30 分,联合国第三委员会第五届第 270 次会议(即本届首次会议),在纽约成功湖召开,本届会议共召开了 53 次会议。在已有的联合国官方会议纪要中,发现中国人曹保颐(Mr. TSAO)先生的身影出现在 1950 年 10 月 19 日之前和 11 月 29 日之后的会议上,并在本届第 282 次会议①、第 283 次会议②、第 286 次会议③、第 287 次会议④、第 329 次会议⑤、第 330 次会议⑥、第 332 次会议⑦、第 333 次会议⑧和第 337 次会议⑨上做了发言。

　　而在本届会议上张彭春先生的发言内容在官方会议纪要中首次出现

---

　　① 本次会议于 1950 年 10 月 11 日上午 11 时 45 分,在纽约成功湖举行,见:UN Doc. : A/C.3/SR/282, p. 74.

　　② 本次会议于 1950 年 10 月 13 日上午 11 时 45 分,在纽约成功湖举行,见:UN Doc. : A/C.3/SR/282, p. 81.

　　③ 本次会议于 1950 年 10 月 16 日下午 3 时,在纽约成功湖举行,见:UN Doc. : A/C.3/SR/286, p. 94.

　　④ 本次会议于 1950 年 10 月 18 日上午 11 时,在纽约成功湖举行,见:UN Doc. : A/C.3/SR/287, p. 101.

　　⑤ 本次会议于 1950 年 11 月 29 日上午 10 时 45 分,在纽约成功湖举行,见:UN Doc. : A/C.3/SR/329, p. 362.

　　⑥ 本次会议于 1950 年 11 月 30 日下午 3 时,在纽约成功湖举行,见:UN Doc. : A/C.3/SR/330, p. 368; p. 370.

　　⑦ 本次会议于 1950 年 12 月 1 日下午 3 时,在纽约成功湖举行,见:UN Doc. : A/C.3/SR/332, p. 376; p. 379.

　　⑧ 本次会议于 1950 年 12 月 2 日上午 10 时 45 分,在纽约成功湖举行,见:UN Doc. : A/C.3/SR/333, p. 387.

　　⑨ 本次会议于 1950 年 12 月 6 日上午 10 时 45 分,在纽约成功湖举行,见:UN Doc. : A/C.3/SR/337, p. 414.

图片 2.6.1:2017 年 6 月 8 日,张彭春的雕像揭幕仪式在南开大学周恩来管理学院
中央花园举行(雕像图片由孙平华拍摄于揭幕仪式现场)

在 1950 年 10 月 20 日下午 3 时召开的第 291 次会议①上,其后,张彭春先
生在第 292 次会议②、第 295 次会议③、第 299 次会议④、第 301 次会议、第
302 次会议⑤、第 304 次会议⑥、第 308 次会议⑦、第 309 次会议⑧、第 312 次

---

① 本次会议于 1950 年 10 月 20 日下午 3 时,在纽约成功湖举行,见:UN Doc.:A/C.
3/SR/291, p. 127.

② 本次会议于 1950 年 10 月 25 日下午 3 时,在纽约成功湖举行,见:UN Doc.:A/C.
3/SR/292, p. 138.

③ 本次会议于 1950 年 10 月 27 日上午 11 时 45 分,在纽约成功湖举行,见:UN
Doc.:A/C. 3/SR/295, pp. 158−159.

④ 本次会议于 1950 年 10 月 31 日下午 3 时,在纽约成功湖举行,见:UN Doc.:A/C.
3/SR/292, pp. 185−186.

⑤ 本次会议于 1950 年 11 月 2 日下午 3 时,在纽约成功湖举行,见:UN Doc.:A/C.
3/SR/302, p. 204; p. 205.

⑥ 本次会议于 1950 年 11 月 6 日上午 11 时 45 分,在纽约成功湖举行,见:UN Doc.:
A/C. 3/SR/302, p. 214.

⑦ 本次会议于 1950 年 11 月 8 日下午 3 时,在纽约成功湖举行,见:UN Doc.:A/C.
3/SR/308, pp. 235−236.

⑧ 本次会议于 1950 年 11 月 9 日 10 时 45 分,在纽约成功湖举行,见:UN Doc.:A/
C. 3/SR/309, p. 238; p. 239.

会议①、第 313 次会议②、第 315 次会议③、第 316 次会议④、第 318 次会议⑤、第 322 次会议⑥上分别进行了大会发言,这样在本届会议上张彭春共在其中的 15 次会议上进行了大会发言。下面按照先后顺序,分别列出张彭春先生会议发言的内容:

1. 张彭春在联大第三委员会
第五届第 291 次会议上的发言

联大第三委员会第五届第 291 次会议,于 1950 年 10 月 20 日下午 3 时至 5 时 50 分,在纽约成功湖举行,本次会议的主要议题是起草第一国际人权公约和实施措施。张彭春先生参加了本次会议,并在会议上发言,其具体发言内容⑦会议纪要、纪要影像和纪要译文如下:

【会议纪要】

26. Mr. CHANG（China）stated that before the Committee could com-

---

① 本次会议于 1950 年 11 月 13 日上午 10 时 45 分,在纽约成功湖举行,见:UN Doc.：A/C. 3/SR/312, pp. 251-252.

② 本次会议于 1950 年 11 月 14 日下午 3 时,在纽约成功湖举行,见:UN Doc.：A/C. 3/SR/313, pp. 257.

③ 本次会议于 1950 年 11 月 16 日上午 10 时 45 分,在纽约成功湖举行,见:UN Doc.：A/C. 3/SR/315, p. 272; p. 273.

④ 本次会议于 1950 年 11 月 16 日下午 3 时,在纽约成功湖举行,见:UN Doc.：A/C. 3/SR/316, pp. 275.

⑤ 本次会议于 1950 年 11 月 17 日下午 3 时,在纽约成功湖举行,见:UN Doc.：A/C. 3/SR/318, p. 286.

⑥ 本次会议于 1950 年 11 月 21 日下午 3 时,在纽约成功湖举行,见:UN Doc.：A/C. 3/SR/322, pp. 315-316.

⑦ 本次会议于 1950 年 10 月 20 日下午 3 时,在纽约成功湖举行,见:UN Doc.：A/C. 3/SR/291, p. 127.

ment upon the adequacy of the first eighteen articles, it must consider what was meant by "adequate". That word implied certain criteria, as to both commission and omission, in relation to the subject matter and style of the draft covenant. The selection of proper criteria also necessitated thorough consideration of the purpose and applicability of the draft covenant. The instrument under discussion was described as a "covenant", and it was hoped that many States would ratify it. It was therefore a treaty and thus raised the question of the effectiveness of treaties.

27. Much might be learned from a comparison with the Universal Declaration of Human Rights. The purpose of the Declaration had been clearly stated and that was a guarantee that its significance would increase with the passage of time. In its resolution 217 (III), the General Assembly had proclaimed it as "a common standard of achievement for all peoples and all nations, to the end that every individual and every organ of society, keeping this Declaration constantly in mind, shall strive by teaching and education to promote respect for these rights and freedoms and by progressive measures, national and international, to secure their universal and effective recognition and observance, both among the peoples of Member States themselves and among the peoples of territories under their jurisdiction".

28. The purpose of the draft covenant should be made equally clear. Some members had urged the Committee to avoid turning the draft covenant into a second edition of the Universal Declaration of Human Rights. He agreed with that counsel. He also agreed most emphatically that nothing must be done to undermine the Declaration.

29. The question was how to forge a connecting link between the drafting, signing and ratifying of the draft covenant, on the one hand, and, on the other, the promotion and protection of the rights of individual human beings in various parts of the world. Mere ratification would obviously not automatically grant en-

joyment of the rights in question to every individual. The Secretariat might be able to elucidate that important question.

30. Judging from the debate, there appeared to be no need of a draft covenant at all, for every speaker claimed that the constitution of his own country already provided rights far in excess of those contemplated in the draft covenant. If that were indeed true, the only result of the adoption of the draft covenant would be to lower, rather than to raise, standards of human rights. He suspected, however, that the actual situation was less encouraging than appeared from the debate; that there was a very real need to protect the enjoyment of human rights; and that such a task could be accomplished by the adoption of a suitable covenant.

【纪要影像】

26. Mr. CHANG (China) stated that before the Committee could comment upon the adequacy of the first eighteen articles, it must consider what was meant by "adequate". That word implied certain criteria, as to both commission and omission, in relation to the subject matter and style of the draft covenant. The selection of proper criteria also necessitated thorough consideration of the purpose and applicability of the draft covenant. The instrument under discussion was described as a "covenant", and it was hoped that many States would ratify it. It was therefore a treaty and thus raised the question of the effectiveness of treaties.

27. Much might be learned from a comparison with the Universal Declaration of Human Rights. The purpose of the Declaration had been clearly stated and that was a guarantee that its significance would increase with the passage of time. In its resolution 217 (III), the General Assembly had proclaimed it as "a common standard of achievement for all peoples and all nations, to the end that every individual and every organ of society, keeping this Declaration constantly in mind, shall strive by teaching and education to promote respect for these rights and freedoms and by progressive measures, national and international, to secure their universal and effective recognition and observance, both among the peoples of Member States themselves and among the peoples of territories under their jurisdiction".

28. The purpose of the draft covenant should be made equally clear. Some members had urged the Committee to avoid turning the draft covenant into a second edition of the Universal Declaration of Human Rights. He agreed with that counsel. He also agreed most emphatically that nothing must be done to undermine the Declaration.

29. The question was how to forge a connecting link between the drafting, signing and ratifying of the draft covenant, on the one hand, and, on the other, the promotion and protection of the rights of individual human beings in various parts of the world. Mere ratification would obviously not automatically grant enjoyment of the rights in question to every individual. The Secretariat might be able to elucidate that important question.

30. Judging from the debate, there appeared to be no need of a draft covenant at all, for every speaker claimed that the constitution of his own country already provided rights far in excess of those contemplated in the draft covenant. If that were indeed true, the only result of the adoption of the draft covenant would be to lower, rather than to raise, standards of human rights. He suspected, however, that the actual situation was less encouraging than appeared from the debate; that there was a very real need to protect the enjoyment of human rights; and that such a task could be accomplished by the adoption of a suitable covenant.

图片 3.6.2:张彭春在联大第三委员会第五届第 291 次会议发言纪要

【纪要译文】

26. 张先生(中国)说,在委员会就前 18 条是否充分发表意见之前,它必须考虑"充分"是什么意思。该词暗示了与公约草案的主题和文体有关的关于作为和不作为的某些标准。选择适当的标准还需要彻底审议公约草案的宗旨和适用性。讨论中的文书被称为"公约",希望许多国家批准该文书。所以它是一项条约,因此提出了条约效力的问题。

27. 从与《世界人权宣言》的比较中可以学到很多东西。《宣言》的目的已经明确说明,这保证了其重要性将随着时间的推移而增加。大会在其第217(Ⅲ)号决议中宣布该决议为:"所有人民和所有国家的努力实现的共同标准,以期每一个人和每一社会机构时刻铭记本宣言,努力通过教诲和教育促进对这些权利和自由的尊重,并通过国家和国际的渐进措施,确保这些权利和自由在会员国人民之间和在其管辖下的领土人民中得到普遍和有效的承认和遵行。"

28. 公约草案的目的应该同样明确。一些成员敦促委员会避免将公约草案变成《世界人权宣言》的第二版。他同意这一意见。他还同意极为强调不得采取任何行动破坏《宣言》。

29. 问题是如何在起草、签署和批准《公约》草案与在世界各地促进和保护个人权利之间建立联系。仅仅批准显然不会自动赋予每个人享有这些权利,秘书处或许能够澄清这一重要问题。

30. 从辩论的情况来看,似乎根本不需要一项公约草案,因为每一位发言者都声称,他自己国家的宪法已经提供了远远超过公约草案所设想的权利。如果情况确实如此,通过公约草案的唯一结果将是降低而不是提高人权标准。然而,他怀疑实际情况并不像辩论中表现的那样令人鼓舞;确实需要保护享有人权;这项任务可以通过一项适当的公约来完成。

2. 张彭春在联大第三委员会
第五届第 292 次会议上的发言

联大第三委员会第五届第 292 次会议,于 1950 年 10 月 25 日下午 3 时至晚上 6 时,在纽约成功湖举行,本次会议的主要议题是起草第一国际人权公约和实施措施。张彭春先生参加了本次会议,并在会议上发言,其具体发言内容①会议纪要、纪要影像和纪要译文如下:

【会议纪要】

69. Mr. CHANG (China) said that the Committee should try to view the question of the federal clause in its proper perspective. Economic and social considerations had only acquired international importance comparatively recently; federal States had originally been formed for purely military and defensive purposes and the decisions taken by their governments had related only to questions of war or peace. If a federal government did not consider itself competent to settle questions which were not strictly military or diplomatic, it was difficult to see where the responsibility for solving them lay. Furthermore, if that government maintained that such questions were the responsibility of its constituent parts, whether they were described as states, provinces or cantons, it might be asked why in those circumstances the responsible parts were not represented on the same footing as the federal government itself.

70. That was a question which called for study, and he would be glad to have the views of the Secretariat and of members of the Committee on the point.

---

① 本次会议于 1950 年 10 月 25 日下午 3 时,在纽约成功湖举行,见: UN Doc.: A/C. 3/SR/292, p. 138.

【纪要影像】

69. Mr. CHANG (China) said that the Committee should try to view the question of the federal clause in its proper perspective. Economic and social considerations had only acquired international importance comparatively recently; federal States had originally been formed for purely military and defensive purposes and the decisions taken by their governments had related only to questions of war or peace. If a federal government did not consider itself competent to settle questions which were not strictly military or diplomatic, it was difficult to see where the responsibility for solving them lay. Furthermore, if that government maintained that such questions were the responsibility of its constituent parts, whether they were described as states, provinces or cantons, it might be asked why in those circumstances the responsible parts were not represented on the same footing as the federal government itself.

70. That was a question which called for study, and he would be glad to have the views of the Secretariat and of members of the Committee on the point.

图片 3.6.3：张彭春在联大第三委员会第五届第 292 次会议发言纪要

【纪要译文】

69. 张先生(中国)说,委员会应设法从适当的角度看待联邦条款问题。经济和社会考虑只是在最近才获得国际重要性;联邦国家最初纯粹是为了军事和防御目的而成立的,其政府所作的决定只涉及战争或和平问题。如果联邦政府不认为自己有能力解决不严格的军事或外交问题,那么很难看出解决这些问题的责任在哪里。此外,如果该国政府坚持认为这些问题是其组成部分的责任,无论它们被称为州、省或州,可能会有人问,为什么在这些情况下,负责的部分没有得到与联邦政府本身同等的体现出来。

70. 这是一个需要研究的问题,他很高兴听取秘书处和委员会成员关于这一问题的看法。

3. 张彭春在联大第三委员会
第五届第 295 次会议上的发言

联大第三委员会第五届第 295 次会议,于 1950 年 10 月 27 日上午 10 时 45 分至下午 1 时 10 分,在纽约成功湖举行,本次会议的主要议题是起草第一国际人权公约和实施措施。张彭春先生参加了本次会议,并在会议上发言,其具体发言内容①会议纪要、纪要影像和纪要译文如下:

【会议纪要】

21. Mr. CHANG (China) congratulated the Committee on the current debate, which had not only clarified the problem of the inclusion of a colonial clause but had practically solved it.

22. The representative of the United States had said (294th meeting) that her country, while supporting the inclusion of such a clause, did not itself require it. At the same meeting the French representative had made it clear that his country did not require the colonial clause in respect of the first eighteen articles of the draft covenant.

23. He would emphasize that the draft covenant did not deal with such matters as road traffic, customs duties or narcotic drugs: it dealt with human rights, and no one could assert that such rights should be qualified.

24. Some had argued that a colonial clause was necessary in order to permit consultation with local authorities in Non-Self-Governing Territories. The argument appeared to be sound and in keeping with the Charter. The point

---

① 本次会议于 1950 年 10 月 27 日上午 10 时 45 分,在纽约成功湖举行,张彭春在本次会议上的发言见: UN Doc. : A/C. 3/SR/295, pp. 158-159.

was, however, that there could surely be no reason to suppose that the people of the territories involved did not desire human rights. Furthermore, if the colonial Powers truly desired to develop the system of consultation with local authorities—and such a desire was highly commendable—they could easily consult the local authorities in question during the minimum interval of one year which would have to elapse before the draft covenant would be ready for signature.

25. A second argument centred around something that had been dignified by the name of "levels of civilization". During the rapid growth of empires in the nineteenth century there had been a tendency to equate the terms "imperial growth" and "civilization". It was then that the word "native" had acquired a new meaning as a designation of non-Europeans, a definition which, he feared, might still linger in the minds of some people. Civilization had largely meant European rule. A reaction to that attitude had begun to develop by the early twentieth century and, after two world wars, the world ought to have a different idea of the meaning of civilization. It was true that there were different degrees of technological and other forms of advancement but, as the Charter clearly showed, that did not mean that less-developed areas were to be exploited by outsiders.

26. Some argued that the administration of Non-Self-Governing Territories was beneficial to the Administering Authority, while others argued that it was a heavy responsibility unselfishly assumed. The responsibility could not be so very heavy, however, for all the nations concerned had been most anxious to assume it. Yet, in a sense, colonial administration was both a burden and a blessing. Apart from the sufferings of the peoples of the Non-Self-Governing Territories and from the benefits accruing to the colonial Powers, the latter also suffered because power corrupted them. The United Nations should help them by ensuring that they were no longer corrupted by such power. The non-inclusion of a colonial clause in the draft convention would be a step in the direc-

tion.

27. He noted from paragraph 34 of the Secretary-General's report on the question (E/1721 and Corr. 1) that the General Assembly had eliminated the colonial clause from the 1921 Convention for the Suppression of the Traffic in Women and Children, and the 1933 Convention for the Suppression of Traffic in Women of Full Age and the 1923 Convention for the Suppression of the Circulation of, and Traffic in, Obscene Publications. If it had been possible to eliminate the colonial clause from those conventions it would surely be inadvisable to reintroduce it by including it in the draft covenant. After all, the draft covenant dealt with the field of human rights and it would be difficult for the United Nations to explain why those rights should not be applied in the Non-Self-Governing Territories.

【纪要影像】

21. Mr. CHANG (China) congratulated the Committee on the current debate, which had not only

clarified the problem of the inclusion of a colonial clause but had practically solved it.

22. The representative of the United States had said (294th meeting) that her country, while supporting the inclusion of such a clause, did not itself require it. At the same meeting the French representative had made it clear that his country did not require the colonial clause in respect of the first eighteen articles of the draft covenant.

23. He would emphasize that the draft covenant did not deal with such matters as road traffic, customs duties or narcotic drugs: it dealt with human rights, and no one could assert that such rights should be qualified.

24. Some had argued that a colonial clause was necessary in order to permit consultation with local authorities in Non-Self-Governing Territories. The argument appeared to be sound and in keeping with the Charter. The point was, however, that there could surely be no reason to suppose that the people of the territories involved did not desire human rights. Furthermore, if the colonial Powers truly desired to develop the system of consultation with local authorities—and such a desire was highly commendable—they could easily consult the local authorities in question during the minimum interval of one year which would have to elapse before the draft covenant would be ready for signature.

25. A second argument centred around something that had been dignified by the name of "levels of civilization". During the rapid growth of empires in the nineteenth century there had been a tendency to equate the terms "imperial growth" and "civilization". It was then that the word "native" had acquired a new meaning as a designation of non-Europeans, a definition which, he feared, might still linger in the minds of some people. Civilization had largely meant European rule. A reaction to that attitude had begun to develop by the early twentieth century and, after two world wars, the world ought to have a different idea of the meaning of civilization. It was true that there were different degrees of technological and other forms of advancement but, as the Charter clearly showed, that did not mean that less-developed areas were to be exploited by outsiders.

图片 3.6.4:张彭春在联大第三委员会第五届第 295 次会议发言纪要(1)

26. Some argued that the administration of Non-Self-Governing Territories was beneficial to the Administering Authority, while others argued that it was a heavy responsibility unselfishly assumed. The responsibility could not be so very heavy, however, for all the nations concerned had been most anxious to assume it. Yet, in a sense, colonial administration was both a burden and a blessing. Apart from the sufferings of the peoples of the Non-Self-Governing Territories and from the benefits accruing to the colonial Powers, the latter also suffered because power corrupted them. The United Nations should help them by ensuring that they were no longer corrupted by such power. The non-inclusion of a colonial clause in the draft convention would be a step in that direction.

27. He noted from paragraph 34 of the Secretary-General's report on the question (E/1721 and Corr.1) that the General Assembly had eliminated the colonial clause from the 1921 Convention for the Suppression

of the Traffic in Women and Children, the 1933 Convention for the Suppression of Traffic in Women of Full Age and the 1923 Convention for the Suppression of the Circulation of, and Traffic in, Obscene Publications. If it had been possible to eliminate the colonial clause from those conventions it would surely be inadvisable to reintroduce it by including it in the draft covenant. After all, the draft covenant dealt with the field of human rights and it would be difficult for the United Nations to explain why those rights should not be applied in the Non-Self-Governing Territories.

图片 3.6.5：张彭春在联大第三委员会第五届第 295 次会议发言纪要(2)

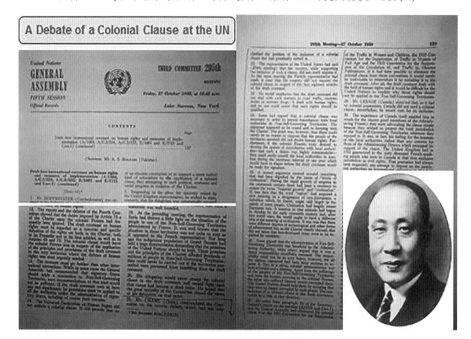

图片 3.6.6：张彭春在联大第三委员会第五届第 295 次会议发言纪要(3)

【纪要译文】

21. 张先生(中国)祝贺委员会目前的辩论,这次辩论不仅澄清了列入殖民地条款的问题,而且实际上解决了这个问题。

22. 美国代表说(第 294 次会议),美国虽然支持列入这一条款,但它本身并不要求这样做。在同一次会议上,法国代表明确表示,法国对公约草案的前十八条不要求有殖民地条款。

23. 他要强调的是,公约草案没有涉及道路交通、关税或麻醉药品等事项;它涉及人权,没有人可以断言这些权利应该是有条件的。

24. 有些人争辩说,为了允许与非自治领土的地方当局协商,有必要订立殖民地条款。这一论点似乎是合理的,符合《宪章》。然而,问题是,肯定没有理由认为有关领土的人民不渴望人权。此外,如果殖民地国家确实希望发展与地方当局协商的制度,而且这种愿望是值得高度赞扬的,那么它们可以很容易地在公约草案准备签署之前至少一年的时间内与有关地方当局协商。

25. 第二个论点围绕着被称为"文明水平"的东西展开。在十九世纪帝国迅速发展的时期,有一种将"帝国发展"和"文明"等同起来的趋势。正是在那时,"原住民"一词作为非欧洲人的称谓获得了新的含义,他担心这一定义可能仍然萦绕在一些人的脑海中。文明在很大程度上意味着欧洲的统治。对这种态度的反应在二十世纪初开始形成,在两次世界大战之后,世界应该对文明的意义有不同的看法。诚然,有不同程度的技术和其他形式的进步,但正如《宪章》明确表明的那样,这并不意味着欠发达地区将被外来者剥削。

26. 一些人认为,非自治领土的管理有利于管理当局,而另一些人则认为,这是无私地承担的重大责任。然而,责任不可能如此沉重,因为所有有关国家都急于承担责任。然而,从某种意义上说,殖民地管理既是一种负担,也是一种福祉。除了非自治领土人民的苦难和殖民列强所获得的利益外,殖民列强也因为权力腐败而遭受苦难。联合国应该帮助他们,确保他们不再被这种权力所腐蚀。不在公约草案中列入殖民地条款将是朝着这一方向迈出的一步。

27. 他从秘书长关于这个问题的报告(E/1721 和 Corr. 1)第 34 段中注意到,大会已从 1921 年《禁止贩卖妇女和儿童公约》、1933 年《禁止贩卖成年妇女公约》和 1923 年《禁止淫秽出版物流通和贩卖公约》中删除了殖民地条款。如果有可能从这些公约中删除殖民地条款,那么将其列入公约草案肯定是不可取的。毕竟,公约草案涉及人权领域,联合国很难解释为什么这些权利不应适用于非自治领土。

4. 张彭春在联大第三委员会
第五届第 299 次会议上的发言

联大第三委员会第五届第 299 次会议,于 1950 年 10 月 31 日下午 3 时至 5 时 55 分,在纽约成功湖举行,本次会议的主要议题是起草第一国际人权公约和实施措施。张彭春先生参加了本次会议,并在会议上发言,其具体发言内容①会议纪要、纪要影像和纪要译文如下:

【会议纪要】

1. Mr. CHANG (China) noted that four main controversial issues had developed in the debate on the desirability of including special articles on economic, social and cultural rights in the draft first international covenant on human rights: the relative importance of individual rights and economic and social rights, the relative priority to be given to the latter, the relative complexity of defining them and the relative urgency of including them in the first draft cove-

---

① 本次会议于 1950 年 10 月 31 日下午 3 时,在纽约成功湖举行,见: UN Doc. : A/C. 3/SR/292, pp. 185-186.

nant.

2. The French representative had produced a solution of the question of relative urgency by proposing (298th meeting) that two separate covenants should be prepared simultaneously before the sixth session of the General Assembly. The principal difficulty inherent in such a solution, admirable as it was in intention, was that it would be extremely difficult to obtain general agreement on the choice of the economic, social and cultural rights to be included in a separate covenant.

3. He wondered, however, whether there were really cogent arguments for speed in drafting and adopting the covenant before the Committee. Urgency had been more or less assumed on the ground that, the Universal Declaration of Human Rights having only a moral force, it must be supplemented as soon as possible by a covenant with mandatory force, if human rights were to be effectively protected. The Commission on Human Rights had wisely decided to begin by preparing the Declaration rather than the draft covenant, as had originally been proposed; but every effort must be made to see that the covenant did not detract from the value of the Declaration, which had already acquired greater force and prestige than had been expected.

4. Before it accepted the assumption that the completion of the draft covenant was really urgently required, the Committee should ask itself how large a majority of its members would be able to approve the draft at the following session, how many would be able to sign and how many to ratify. Unless a new approach was found, it seemed that members would be fairly equally divided on the first question.

5. It had been argued that the number of initial signatures was unimportant; that others would gradually accede by force of example. A covenant on human rights was not, however, on the same level as a technical convention; it was something much more lofty and concerned the cause of international peace

much more closely.

6. There was a real danger that the covenant on human rights might actually augment the causes of international dispute. Although the word "covenant" gave the impression that something sacrosanct was intended, a covenant in fact was merely a convention and had only the status of a treaty. If relatively unimportant technical conventions gave rise to disputes, such as weeping document would be likely to cause even greater contention. Breaches of the covenant would take place within the domestic jurisdiction of States; complaints would, therefore, be regarded as infringements of national sovereignty and there would probably be no means of obtaining redress without causing international disputes. That was no imaginary danger; the Commission on Human Rights had already received hundreds of petitions and complaints from individuals invoking the Universal Declaration of Human Rights. A covenant signed at the existing stage of developments in international relations might, therefore, not only fail to protect human rights but might become the direct cause of an increase in international tension. Until there was some method of controlling a State's domestic behaviour without infringing its sovereignty, the provision of disciplinary measures appeared to be premature.

7. The Committee seemed to have failed to envisage that aspect of the problem clearly; both the Commission on Human Rights and the Economic and Social Council should be asked to take that view into account before they proceeded further with the preparation of the draft covenant on human rights.

Draft first international covenant on human rights and measures of implementation (A/1384, A/C.3/534, A/C.3/535 and E/1681) (*continued*)

[Item 63]*

1. Mr. CHANG (China) noted that four main controversial issues had developed in the debate on the desirability of including special articles on economic, social and cultural rights in the draft first international covenant on human rights: the relative importance of individual rights and economic and social rights, the relative priority to be given to the latter, the relative complexity of defining them and the relative urgency of including them in the first draft covenant.

2. The French representative had produced a solution of the question of relative urgency by proposing (298th meeting) that two separate covenants should be prepared simultaneously before the sixth session of the General Assembly. The principal difficulty inherent in such a solution, admirable as it was in intention, was that it would be extremely difficult to obtain general agreement on the choice of the economic, social and cultural rights to be included in a separate covenant.

3. He wondered, however, whether there were really cogent arguments for speed in drafting and adopting the covenant before the Committee. Urgency had been more or less assumed on the ground that, the Universal Declaration of Human Rights having only a moral force, it must be supplemented as soon as possible by a covenant with mandatory force, if human rights were to be effectively protected. The Commission on Human Rights had wisely decided to begin by preparing the Declaration rather than the draft covenant, as had originally been proposed; but every effort must be made to see that the covenant did not detract from the value of the Declaration, which had already acquired greater force and prestige than had been expected.

4. Before it accepted the assumption that the completion of the draft covenant was really urgently re-

* Indicates the item number on the General Assembly agenda.

图片 3.6.7：张彭春在联大第三委员会第五届第 299 次会议发言纪要（1）

quired, the Committee should ask itself how large a majority of its members would be able to approve the draft at the following session, how many would be able to sign and how many to ratify. Unless a new approach was found, it seemed that members would be fairly equally divided on the first question.

5. It had been argued that the number of initial signatures was unimportant; that others would gradually accede by force of example. A covenant on human rights was not, however, on the same level as a technical convention; it was something much more lofty and concerned the cause of international peace much more closely.

6. There was a real danger that the covenant on human rights might actually augment the causes of international dispute. Although the word "covenant" gave the impression that something sacrosanct was intended, a covenant in fact was merely a convention and had only the status of a treaty. If relatively unimportant technical conventions gave rise to disputes, such a sweeping document would be likely to cause even greater contention. Breaches of the covenant would take place within the domestic jurisdiction of States;

complaints would, therefore, be regarded as infringements of national sovereignty and there would probably be no means of obtaining redress without causing international disputes. That was no imaginary danger; the Commission on Human Rights had already received hundreds of petitions and complaints from individuals invoking the Universal Declaration of Human Rights. A covenant signed at the existing stage of developments in international relations might, therefore, not only fail to protect human rights but might become the direct cause of an increase in international tension. Until there was some method of controlling a State's domestic behaviour without infringing its sovereignty, the provision of disciplinary measures appeared to be premature.

7. The Committee seemed to have failed to envisage that aspect of the problem clearly; both the Commission on Human Rights and the Economic and Social Council should be asked to take that view into account before they proceeded further with the preparation of the draft covenant on human rights.

图片 3.6.8：张彭春在联大第三委员会第五届第 299 次会议发言纪要（2）

【纪要译文】

1. 张先生(中国)指出,在第一项国际人权公约草案中列入关于经济、社会和文化权利的特别条款是否可取的辩论中,出现了四个主要有争议的问题:个人权利和经济及社会权利的相对重要性,对后者给予的相对优先权,对其进行界定的相对复杂性,以及将其纳入第一份公约草案的相对紧迫性。

2. 法国代表提议(第 298 次会议)在大会第六届会议之前同时拟订两项单独的公约,从而解决了相对紧迫的问题。这种解决办法所固有的主要困难,尽管其用意令人钦佩,但却是极难就选择列入单独公约的经济、社会和文化权利达成普遍协议。

3. 然而,他想知道,是否确实有令人信服的理由要求委员会加快起草和通过《公约》。人们或多或少地假定了紧迫性,因为《世界人权宣言》只有一种道德力量,如果要有效地保护人权,就必须尽快通过一项具有强制性的公约加以补充。人权委员会明智地决定首先编写宣言,而不是原先提议的公约草案;但是,必须尽一切努力确保《公约》不减损《宣言》的价值,该宣言已经获得了比预期更大的力量和威望。

4. 在接受确实迫切需要完成公约草案这一假设之前,委员会应当问问自己,在下届会议上有多少成员能够批准该草案,有多少成员能够签署,有多少成员能够批准。除非找到一种新的办法,否则在第一个问题上,各成员的意见似乎会相当分歧。

5. 有人认为初始签署性质的数量并不重要;其他人会逐渐以身作则。然而,人权公约与技术公约不在同一水平上;这是一件更崇高的事情,与国际和平事业密切相关。

6.《人权公约》实际上可能增加国际争端的起因,这是一种真正的危险。虽然"盟约"(covenant)一词给人的印象是神圣不可侵犯的,但盟约实际上只是一项公约(convention),具有条约(treaty)的地位。如果相对不重要的技术公约引起争议,比如概括性的文件可能会引起更大的争议。违反

《公约》的行为将在各国国内管辖范围内发生;因此,申诉将被视为侵犯国家主权,可能无法在不引起国家间争端的情况下获得补救。这不是想象中的危险;人权委员会已经收到数百份援引《世界人权宣言》的个人请愿书和投诉。因此,在国际关系发展的现有阶段签署的公约不仅不能保护人权,而且可能成为国际紧张局势加剧的直接原因。在有某种方法控制一国的国内行为而不侵犯其主权之前,提供纪律措施似乎为时过早。

7. 委员会似乎没有清楚地设想问题的这一方面;应要求人权委员会和经济及社会理事会在进一步编写人权公约草案之前考虑到这一观点。

5. 张彭春在联大第三委员会第五届第 301 次会议上的发言

联大第三委员会第五届第 301 次会议,于 1950 年 11 月 1 日下午 3 时至 5 时 25 分,在纽约成功湖举行,本次会议的主要议题是起草第一国际人权公约和实施措施。张彭春先生参加了本次会议,并在会议上发言,其具体发言内容①会议纪要、纪要影像和纪要译文如下:

【会议纪要】

18. Mr. CHANG (China) considered that the designation "human rights committee" was not altogether fortunate and that the use of the word "Committee" might give rise to confusion. The Economic and Social Council was considering the question of changing the nomenclature of its subsidiary organs; there was even a possibility that the Commission on Human Rights might be renamed "Committee on Human Rights". He felt sure that an appropriate designation of

---

① 本次会议于 1950 年 11 月 1 日下午 3 时,在纽约成功湖举行,见: UN Doc.: A/C. 3/SR/301, p. 198; p. 201.

the proposed body could be found; it might perhaps be called the "human rights board".

19. He also felt that more attention should be paid to the important question of functions and that the relevant provisions of the draft covenant should be stated in greater detail. While articles 19 to 37, which dealt with organization, went into considerable detail, articles 38 to 41, dealing with functions, were more general.

20. Three functions were foreseen: article 38, paragraph 1, provided for direct negotiation between States; article 41, paragraph 1, assigned the function of good offices to the human rights committee, and article 41, paragraph 3, provided, in effect, for an appeal to world public opinion. Three successive stages were thus envisaged: first, direct negotiation; secondly, if that failed, an appeal to the good offices of the human rights committee; and, thirdly, if that also failed, an appeal to world public opinion. The general picture that emerged was that considerably more attention had been paid to the question of organization than to providing details about functions.

21. With regard to implementation, he had constantly urged that it should not be visualized as an essentially negative concept referring almost exclusively to complaints concerning violations of human rights, but that due attention should also be paid to its positive aspect, that is, education and promotion and protection of human rights. Much of the current debate did not actually centre on implementation so much as on complaints; he feared the development of a tendency to look for complaints. Experience in other fields showed that complaints and stern discipline were neither the only nor the best methods of promoting the achievement of positive goals.

22. There were differences between advanced and under-developed countries in that respect. Countries which had accumulated great wealth as a result of the industrial revolution had been able to use that wealth in part to secure

better primary education for their citizens. The growth of education had facilitated the attainment of human rights in the advanced countries so that the under-developed countries were placed at a relative disadvantage. That inequality due to economic factors might cause under-developed countries to hesitate before joining the more fully developed countries in a covenant on human rights. He did not believe that the situation could be remedied merely by the exertion of pressure in the form of a multitude of complaints.

23. Perhaps the best way to progress was to use the Universal Declaration of Human Rights as a positive instrument for the promotion of ideals, and he hoped that the Committee would do nothing that might decrease its efficacy and influence.

62. Mr. CHANG (China) replied that he had not intended to convey the idea that economically under-developed countries would be less willing or able to ensure observance of human rights than the advanced countries; he had meant merely that it would be more difficult for them to provide such material equipment required for the protection of human rights as schools and courts.

【纪要影像】

18. Mr. CHANG (China) considered that the designation "human rights committee" was not altogether fortunate and that the use of the word "committee" might give rise to confusion. The Economic and Social Council was considering the question of changing the nomenclature of its subsidiary organs; there was even a possibility that the Commission on Human Rights might be renamed "Committee on Human Rights". He felt sure that an appropriate designation of the proposed body could be found; it might perhaps be called the "human rights board".

19. He also felt that more attention should be paid to the important question of functions and that the relevant provisions of the draft covenant should be stated in greater detail. While articles 19 to 37, which dealt with organization, went into considerable detail, articles 38 to 41, dealing with functions, were more general.

20. Three functions were foreseen: article 38, paragraph 1, provided for direct negotiation between States; article 41, paragraph 1, assigned the function of good offices to the human rights committee; and article 41, paragraph 3, provided, in effect, for an appeal to world public opinion. Three successive stages were thus envisaged: first, direct negotiation; secondly, if that failed, an appeal to the good offices of the human rights committee; and, thirdly, if that also failed, an appeal to world public opinion. The general picture that emerged was that considerably more attention had been paid to the question of organization than to providing details about functions.

21. With regard to implementation, he had constantly urged that it should not be visualized as an essentially negative concept referring almost exclusively to complaints concerning violations of human rights, but that due attention should also be paid to its positive aspect, that is, education and promotion and protection of human rights. Much of the current debate did not actually centre on implementation so much as on complaints; he feared the development of a tendency to look for complaints. Experience in other fields showed that complaints and stern discipline were neither the only nor the best methods of promoting the achievement of positive goals.

22. There were differences between advanced and under-developed countries in that respect. Countries which had accumulated great wealth as a result of the industrial revolution had been able to use that wealth in part to secure better primary education for their citizens. The growth of education had facilitated the attainment of human rights in the advanced countries so that the under-developed countries were placed at a relative disadvantage. That inequality due to economic factors might cause under-developed countries to hesitate before joining the more fully developed countries in a covenant on human rights. He did not believe that the situation could be remedied merely by the exertion of pressure in the form of a multitude of complaints.

23. Perhaps the best way to progress was to use the Universal Declaration of Human Rights as a positive instrument for the promotion of ideals, and he hoped that the Committee would do nothing that might decrease its efficacy and influence.

62. Mr. CHANG (China) replied that he had not intended to convey the idea that economically under-developed countries would be less willing or able to ensure observance of human rights than the advanced countries; he had meant merely that it would be more difficult for them to provide such material equipment required for the protection of human rights as schools and courts.

图片 3.6.9:张彭春在联大第三委员会第五届第 301 次会议发言纪要

【纪要译文】

18. 张先生(中国)认为,"人权事务委员会"的名称并不十分幸运,使用"委员会"一词可能会引起混淆。经济及社会理事会正在审议改变其附属机构名称的问题;甚至有可能将人权委员会(the Commission on Human Rights)改名为"人权事务委员会"(Committee on Human Rights)。他确信可以找到对拟议机构的适当名称;它可能被称为"人权理事会"(human rights board)。

19. 他还认为,应更加注意重要的职能问题,并应更详细地说明公约草案的有关规定。关于组织的第 19 条至第 37 条相当详细,而关于职能的第 38 条至第 41 条则更一般。

20. 预见了三项职能:第 38 条第 1 款规定了国家之间的直接谈判;第 41 条第 1 款将斡旋职能分配给人权事务委员会,第 41 条第 3 款实际上规定了向世界舆论发出呼吁。因此设想了三个连续的阶段:第一,直接谈判;第二,如果失败,则呼吁人权事务委员会进行斡旋;第三,如果这也失败了,那就是呼吁世界舆论。出现的总体情况是,对组织问题的关注远远超过了对职能细节的关注。

21. 关于执行问题,他一直敦促不应将其视为一个基本上是消极的概念,几乎只提到侵犯人权的申诉,而是也应适当注意其积极方面,即教育、促进和保护人权。目前的辩论实际上并不是以执行为中心,而是以申诉为中心;他担心会出现寻求投诉的趋势。其他领域的经验表明,抱怨和严厉的纪律既不是促进实现积极目标的唯一方法,也不是最好的方法。

22. 发达国家和欠发达国家在这方面存在差异。由于工业革命而积累了大量财富的国家能够部分地利用这些财富为其公民提供更好的初等教育。教育的增长促进了发达国家实现人权,使欠发达国家处于相对劣势。由于经济因素造成的这种不平等可能导致欠发达国家在加入较发达国家的人权公约之前犹豫不决。他不相信仅仅通过以大量诉状的形式施加压力就可以补救这种情况。

23. 也许取得进展的最佳办法是利用《世界人权宣言》作为促进理想的积极工具,他希望委员会不要做任何可能削弱其效力和影响的事情。

62. 张先生(中国)答复说,他无意传达这样一种想法,即经济上不发达的国家比发达国家更不愿意或更不能够确保遵守人权;他只是说,他们将更难提供学校和法院等保护人权所需的物质设备。

6. 张彭春在联大第三委员会
第五届第 302 次会议上的发言

联大第三委员会第五届第 302 次会议,于 1950 年 11 月 2 日下午 3 时至晚上 6 时 5 分,在纽约成功湖举行,本次会议的主要议题是起草第一国际人权公约和实施措施。张彭春先生参加了本次会议,并在会议上发言,其具体发言内容①会议纪要、纪要影像和纪要译文如下:

【会议纪要】

12. Mr. CHANG (China), supported by Mr. KOHN (Israel), suggested that all the draft resolutions should be classified according to the four questions asked by the Economic and Social Council and should be considered in that order.

44. Mr. CHANG (China) and Mr. LEQUESNE (United Kingdom) proposed minor drafting changes.

---

① 本次会议于 1950 年 11 月 2 日下午 3 时,在纽约成功湖举行,见: UN Doc.: A/C. 3/SR/302, p. 204; p. 205.

【纪要影像】

12.　Mr. CHANG (China), supported by Mr. KOHN (Israel), suggested that all the draft resolutions should be classified according to the four questions asked by the Economic and Social Council and should be considered in that order.

44.　Mr. CHANG (China) and Mr. LEQUESNE (United Kingdom) proposed minor drafting changes.

图片 3.6.10：张彭春在联大第三委员会第五届第 302 次会议发言纪要

【纪要译文】

12. 张先生（中国）在科恩（Kohn）先生（以色列）的支持下，建议所有决议草案应按照经济及社会理事会提出的四个问题分类，并应按顺序审议。

44. 张先生（中国）和勒凯纳（Lequesne）先生（英国）提议对措辞作一些小改动。

7. 张彭春在联大第三委员会
第五届第 304 次会议上的发言

联大第三委员会第五届第 304 次会议，于 1950 年 11 月 6 日上午 10 时 45 分时至下午 1 时，在纽约成功湖举行，本次会议的主要议题是起草第一国际人权公约和实施措施。张彭春先生参加了本次会议，并在会议上发

言,其具体发言内容①会议纪要、纪要影像和纪要译文如下:

【会议纪要】

54. Mr. CHANG (China) thought that it might be helpful if the sponsors of amendments to the joint draft resolution could present a joint and simplified text.

【纪要影像】

54. Mr. CHANG (China) thought that it might be helpful if the sponsors of amendments to the joint draft resolution could present a joint and simplified text.

图片 3.6.11:张彭春在联大第三委员会第五届第 304 次会议发言纪要

【纪要译文】

54. 张先生(中国)认为,如果联合决议草案修正案的提案国能够提出一份联合和简化的案文,可能会有所帮助。

8. 张彭春在联大第三委员会
第五届第 308 次会议上的发言

联大第三委员会第五届第 308 次会议,于 1950 年 11 月 8 日下午 3 时至晚上 6 时 10 分,在纽约成功湖举行,本次会议的主要议题是起草第一国际人权公约和实施措施。张彭春先生参加了本次会议,并在会议上发言,

---

① 本次会议于 1950 年 11 月 6 日上午 11 时 45 分,在纽约成功湖举行,见:UN Doc.: A/C. 3/SR/304, p. 214.

其具体发言内容①会议纪要、纪要影像和纪要译文如下：

【会议纪要】

74. Mr. CHANG（China）thought that with goodwill it should be possible to draft a text which would gain the approval of all delegations.

75. The problems raised by the federal clause could not be compared with those raised by the colonial clause. If the problems of the federal clause were to be seen in their true perspective, they should be examined in the light of history. At the time of the establishment of federal States international relations pertained primarily to military or political problems while economic and social questions came essentially within the domestic jurisdiction of States. Since that time the situation had developed and those questions were becoming more and more the subject of international conventions. Hence the constitutional difficulties which had been indicated in connexion with the covenant on human rights.

76. Consequently the problem was to bear those difficulties in mind and at the same time to seek to remedy that state of affairs. The proposal in sub-paragraph（c）of the basic text（A/C. 3/L. 76）, requesting the Commission on Human Rights to study the federal State article—that is, to work on texts—was not enough; the Commission should be requested to grapple with the deep-rooted causes of the problem.

77. After an analysis of the text of sub-paragraph（c）and the various amendments proposed to it, he suggested the following text:

"（c）To study the problems envisaged in draft article 43 with a view to extending the application of the covenant in all the constituent states or provinces forming a federation."

78. That was simply a suggestion which he was inviting the members of the

① 本次会议于 1950 年 11 月 8 日下午 3 时,在纽约成功湖举行,见:UN Doc.：A/C. 3/SR/308, pp. 235–236.

Committee to consider, in the hope that the authors of the various drafts could use it as a basis in the preparation of a single text acceptable to all.

【纪要影像】

74. Mr. CHANG (China) thought that with goodwill it should be possible to draft a text which would gain the approval of all delegations.

75. The problems raised by the federal clause could not be compared with those raised by the colonial clause. If the problems of the federal clause were to be seen in their true perspective, they should be examined in the light of history. At the time of the establishment of federal States international relations pertained primarily to military or political problems while economic and social questions came essentially within the domestic jurisdiction of States. Since that time the situation had developed and those questions were becoming more and more the subject of international conventions. Hence the constitutional difficulties which had been indicated in connexion with the covenant on human rights.

76. Consequently the problem was to bear those difficulties in mind and at the same time to seek to remedy that state of affairs. The proposal in sub-paragraph (c) of the basic text (A/C.3/L.76), requesting the Commission on Human Rights to study the federal State article—that is, to work on texts—was not enough; the Commission should be requested to grapple with the deep-rooted causes of the problem.

77. After an analysis of the text of sub-paragraph (c) and the various amendments proposed to it, he suggested the following text:

"(c) To study the problems envisaged in draft article 43 with a view to extending the application of the covenant in all the constituent states or provinces forming a federation."

78. That was simply a suggestion which he was inviting the members of the Committee to consider, in the hope that the authors of the various drafts could use it as a basis in the preparation of a single text acceptable to all.

图片 3.6.12:张彭春在联大第三委员会第五届第 308 次会议发言纪要

【纪要译文】

74. 张先生(中国)认为,只要有诚意,就可以起草一份将获得所有代表团批准的案文。

75. 联邦条款提出的问题不能与殖民地条款提出的问题相比。如果要从真实的角度看待联邦条款的问题,就应该从历史的角度来审视这些问题。在建立联邦国家时,国际关系主要涉及军事或政治问题,而经济和社会问题基本上属于国家的国内管辖范围。自那时以来,情况有所发展,这些问题越来越成为国际公约的主题。因此,在与《人权公约》有关的问题上指出了宪法上的困难。

76. 因此,问题是要牢记这些困难,同时设法纠正这种状况。基本案文(A/C. 3/L. 76)分段(c)中要求人权委员会研究联邦国家条款,即就案文开展工作的建议是不够的;应要求委员会努力解决这一问题的深层次原因。

77.在分析了(c)分段的案文和对其提出的各种修正之后,他提出了以下案文:

"(c)研究第43条草案设想的问题,以期将《公约》的适用范围扩大到组成联邦的所有组成州或省。"

78.这仅仅是他邀请委员会成员考虑的一个建议,希望各种草案的作者能把它作为准备一个可接受的单一文本的基础。

9.张彭春在联大第三委员会第五届第309次会议上的发言

联大第三委员会第五届第309次会议,于1950年11月9日上午10时45分至下午1时5分,在纽约成功湖举行,本次会议的主要议题是起草第一国际人权公约和实施措施。张彭春先生参加了本次会议,并在会议上先后多次发言,其具体发言内容①会议纪要、纪要影像和纪要译文如下:

【会议纪要】

23. The CHAIRMAN drew the Committee's attention to an amendment submitted orally by the Chinese delegation at the 308th meeting, concerning the words "the federal State article" in paragraph 2 (c) of the joint draft resolution (A/C. 3/L. 76).

24. Mr. CHANG (China) observed that no federal state article currently existed for study, as appeared from the note under the heading "Article 43" in annex I of the report of the Commission on Human Rights (sixth session) (E/

---

① 本次会议于1950年11月9日上午10时45分,在纽约成功湖举行,见: UN Doc.: A/C. 3/SR/309, p. 238; p. 239.

1681）．

25. Mr. PRATT DE MARIA（Uruguay）suggested that that difficulty could be removed by substituting "a federal State article" for "the federal State article".

26. Mr. CHANG accepted that suggestion.

31. The CHAIRMAN drew the Committee's attention to a second amendment submitted orally by the Chinese delegation, calling for the deletion of the words "for the consideration of the General Assembly at its sixth session".

32. Mr. CHANG（China）explained that, in his opinion, the words were redundant, as that phrase already appeared in paragraph 2（a）.

33. Mrs. ROOSEVELT（United States of America）said that such repetition was usual in United Nations resolutions and that its retention would make the joint draft resolution more precise.

34. Mr. CHANG（China）withdrew his amendment.

【纪要影像】

23. The CHAIRMAN drew the Committee's attention to an amendment submitted orally by the Chinese delegation at the 308th meeting, concerning the words "the federal State article" in paragraph 2 (c) of the joint draft resolution (A/C.3/L.76).

24. Mr. CHANG (China) observed that no federal state article currently existed for study, as appeared from the note under the heading "Article 43" in annex I of the report of the Commission on Human Rights (sixth session) (E/1681).

25. Mr. PRATT DE MARIA (Uruguay) suggested that that difficulty could be removed by substituting "a federal State article" for "the federal State article".

26. Mr. CHANG accepted that suggestion.

31. The CHAIRMAN drew the Committee's attention to a second amendment submitted orally by the Chinese delegation, calling for the deletion of the words "for the consideration of the General Assembly at its sixth session".

32. Mr. CHANG (China) explained that, in his opinion, the words were redundant, as that phrase already appeared in paragraph 2 (a).

33. Mrs. ROOSEVELT (United States of America) said that such repetition was usual in United Nations resolutions and that its retention would make the joint draft resolution more precise.

34. Mr. CHANG (China) withdrew his amendment.

图片 3.6.13：张彭春在联大第三委员会第五届第 309 次会议发言纪要

【纪要译文】

23. 主席提请委员会注意中国代表团在第 308 次会议上口头提出的关于联合决议草案（A/C. 3/L. 76）第 2（c）款中"联邦国家条款"一词的修正案。

24. 张先生（中国）说，正如人权委员会（第六届会议）报告（E/1681）附件一"第 43 条"标题下的说明所示，目前没有联邦国家条款可供研究。

25. 普拉特·德玛利亚（Pratt de Maria）先生（乌拉圭）建议用"一个联邦国家条款"代替"该联邦国家条款"，以消除这一困难。

26. 张先生接受了这一建议。

31. 主席提请委员会注意中国代表团口头提交的第二项修正案，要求删除"供大会第六届会议审议"等字。

32. 张先生（中国）解释说，他认为这些词语是多余的，因为这些词在第 2（a）款中已经出现了。

33. 罗斯福夫人（美国）说，这种重复在联合国决议中很常见，保留这种重复将使联合决议草案更加准确。

34. 张先生（中国）撤回其修正案。

10. 张彭春在联大第三委员会第五届第 312 次会议上的发言

联大第三委员会第五届第 312 次会议，于 1950 年 11 月 13 日上午 10时 45 分至下午 1 时，在纽约成功湖举行，本次会议的主要议题是起草第一国际人权公约和实施措施。张彭春先生参加了本次会议，并在会议上发

言,其具体发言内容①会议纪要、纪要影像和纪要译文如下:

【会议纪要】

9. Mr. CHANG (China) said that he had not spoken on the item under discussion because it must be obvious to everyone that his delegation was in favour of the amendment of Afghanistan and Saudi Arabia.

10. However, he felt that the Commission on Human Rights and the Secretariat would be glad to have some explanation of the terms of the amendment and he would therefore try to bring out the principal ideas, of which there were three. First, the effect of the amendment was to reaffirm a principle—the right of peoples to self-determination. Secondly, the text requested the Commission on Human Rights to draw up an article and he felt that it would be advisable for delegations to submit drafts to the Commission. Lastly, to use the phraseology of the amendment, a study should be made of ways and means which would ensure the right of peoples and nations to self-determination. Such a study should not be the exclusive responsibility of the Commission on Human Rights; the delegations also would have to take part in it. Some aspects of the matter might be outside the competence of the Commission on Human Rights but that need not prevent it from working for more extensive and tangible enjoyment of the right in question.

---

① 本次会议于 1950 年 11 月 13 日上午 10 时 45 分,在纽约成功湖举行,见: UN Doc.: A/C. 3/SR/312, pp. 251−252.

【纪要影像】

> 9. Mr. CHANG (China) said that he had not spoken on the item under discussion because it must be obvious to everyone that his delegation was in favour of the amendment of Afghanistan and Saudi Arabia.
>
> 10. However, he felt that the Commission on Human Rights and the Secretariat would be glad to have some explanation of the terms of the amendment and he would therefore try to bring out the principal ideas, of which there were three. First, the effect of the amendment was to reaffirm a principle—the right of peoples to self-determination. Secondly, the text requested the Commission on Human Rights to draw up an article
>
> and he felt that it would be advisable for delegations to submit drafts to the Commission. Lastly, to use the phraseology of the amendment, a study should be made of ways and means which would ensure the right of peoples and nations to self-determination. Such a study should not be the exclusive responsibility of the Commission on Human Rights; the delegations also would have to take part in it. Some aspects of the matter might be outside the competence of the Commission on Human Rights but that need not prevent it from working for more extensive and tangible enjoyment of the right in question.

图片 3.6.14：张彭春在联大第三委员会第五届第 312 次会议发言纪要

【纪要译文】

9. 张先生（中国）说，他没有就讨论中的项目发言，因为每个人都必须清楚地看到，中国代表团赞成阿富汗和沙特阿拉伯的修正案。

10. 然而，他认为人权委员会和秘书处将乐于对修正案的条款作一些解释，因此他将设法提出主要的意见，其中有三个意见。首先，修正案的作用是重申人民自决权的原则。第二，案文请人权委员会起草一条条款并且他认为各代表团最好向委员会提交草案。最后，使用修正案的措辞，应当研究确保人民和国家自决权的方式方法。这种研究不应完全由人权委员会负责；各代表团也必须参加。这一事项的某些方面可能不属于人权委员会的职权范围，但这不一定妨碍它为更广泛和切实地享受这一权利而努力。

11. 张彭春在联大第三委员会
第五届第313次会议上的发言

联大第三委员会第五届第313次会议,于1950年11月14日下午3时至晚上6时25分,在纽约成功湖举行,本次会议的主要议题是起草第一国际人权公约和实施措施。张彭春先生参加了本次会议,并在会议上发言,提出加快委员会工作进度的方法,其具体发言内容①会议纪要、纪要影像和纪要译文如下:

【会议纪要】

9. Mr. CHANG (China) suggested that the reduction of the interval between morning and afternoon meetings might be achieved by prolonging the morning meeting by twenty or thirty minutes.

【纪要影像】

9. Mr. CHANG (China) suggested that the reduction of the interval between morning and afternoon meetings might be achieved by prolonging the morning meeting by twenty or thirty minutes.

图片3.6.15:张彭春在联大第三委员会第五届第313次会议发言纪要

【纪要译文】

9. 张先生(中国)建议,可以通过将上午会议延长二十或三十分钟来缩短上午和下午会议的间隔时间。

---

① 本次会议于1950年11月14日下午3时,在纽约成功湖举行,见: UN Doc.: A/C.3/SR/313, pp. 257.

12. 张彭春在联大第三委员会
第五届第 315 次会议上的发言

联大第三委员会第五届第 315 次会议，于 1950 年 11 月 16 日上午 10 时 45 分至下午 1 时 30 分，在纽约成功湖举行，本次会议的主要议题是起草第一国际人权公约和实施措施。张彭春先生参加了本次会议，并在会议上发言，其具体发言内容①会议纪要、纪要影像和纪要译文如下：

【会议纪要】

59. Mr. CHANG (China) also approved the proposal of the delegation of the United States. However, the Chinese delegation would not be entirely satisfied if 10 December were to mark simply a commemoration: it was important not only to recall the anniversary of the adoption of the Universal Declaration of Human Rights, but also to encourage governments and peoples to pursue their efforts to make it a living reality.

60. To that end, he proposed that the Secretary-General should also be asked to report each year to the General Assembly on the steps taken in the various countries to publish the Declaration as widely as possible.

73. Mr. CHANG (China) said that in paying a tribute to the Members of the United Nations, the General Assembly would be addressing compliments to itself. The Assembly could obviously express its appreciation to the other countries which were not represented in the Organization, but he wondered whether it was really necessary.

---

① 本次会议于 1950 年 11 月 16 日上午 10 时 45 分，在纽约成功湖举行，见：UN Doc.：A/C.3/SR/315, p. 272；p. 273.

80. Mr. CHANG (China) said that in view of the many amendments which had been made in the draft resolution in the course of the discussion, it would be preferable if the Committee could have a written text of the whole resolution before taking a final vote.

【纪要影像】

59. Mr. CHANG (China) also approved the proposal of the delegation of the United States. However, the Chinese delegation would not be entirely satisfied if 10 December were to mark simply a commemoration: it was important not only to recall the anniversary of the adoption of the Universal Declaration of Human Rights, but also to encourage governments and peoples to pursue their efforts to make it a living reality.

60. To that end, he proposed that the Secretary-General should also be asked to report each year to the General Assembly on the steps taken in the various countries to publish the Declaration as widely as possible.

73. Mr. CHANG (China) said that in paying a tribute to the Members of the United Nations, the General Assembly would be addressing compliments to itself. The Assembly could obviously express its appreciation to the other countries which were not represented in the Organization, but he wondered whether it was really necessary.

80. Mr. CHANG (China) said that in view of the many amendments which had been made in the draft resolution in the course of the discussion, it would be preferable if the Committee could have a written text of the whole resolution before taking a final vote.

图片 3.6.16:张彭春在联大第三委员会第五届第 315 次会议发言纪要

【纪要译文】

59. 张先生(中国)也同意了美国代表团的提案。然而,如果 12 月 10 日仅仅是一个纪念活动,中国代表团将不会完全满意:重要的是不仅要回顾《世界人权宣言》通过一周年,而且要鼓励各国政府和人民努力使其成为现实。

60. 为此,他提议还应请秘书长每年向大会报告各国为尽可能广泛地发表《宣言》所采取的步骤。

73. 张先生(中国)说,大会在向联合国会员国致敬时,是在向自己致意。大会显然可以向本组织没有代表的其他国家表示感谢,但他想知道这是否真的必要。

80. 张先生(中国)说,鉴于在讨论过程中对决议草案作了许多修正,委员会最好在进行最后表决之前有一份整个决议的书面文本。

13. 张彭春在联大第三委员会第五届第 316 次会议上的发言

联大第三委员会第五届第 316 次会议,于 1950 年 11 月 16 日下午 3 时至 4 时 35 分,在纽约成功湖举行,本次会议的主要议题是讨论人权日:美国代表提交的决议草案、讨论议程项目的优先次序(A/C. 3/531)。张彭春先生参加了本次会议,并在会议上发言,其具体发言内容①会议纪要、纪要影像和纪要译文如下:

【会议纪要】

4. Lord MACDONALD (United Kingdom) thought that, as a rule, sad events were "commemorated", while joyful occasions were "celebrated" ...

5. He therefore suggested the substitution of the word "celebrate" for the word "commemorate" in the first paragraph of the operative part.

6. Mr. CHANG (China) proposed that the end of that paragraph should read: "... and to exert increasing effort in this field of human progress".

7. Mrs. ROOSEVELT (United States of America) accepted the suggestions of the United Kingdom and Chinese representatives.

---

① 本次会议于 1950 年 11 月 16 日下午 3 时,在纽约成功湖举行,见: UN Doc.: A/C. 3/SR/316, pp. 275.

4. Lord MACDONALD (United Kingdom) thought that, as a rule, sad events were "commemorated", while joyful occasions were "celebrated".

5. He therefore suggested the substitution of the word "celebrate" for the word "commemorate" in the first paragraph of the operative part.

6. Mr. CHANG (China) proposed that the end of that paragraph should read: "... and to exert increasing effort in this field of human progress".

7. Mrs. ROOSEVELT (United States of America) accepted the suggestions of the United Kingdom and Chinese representatives.

图片 3.6.17:张彭春在联大第三委员会第五届第 316 次会议发言纪要

【纪要译文】

4.麦克唐纳(MacDonold)勋爵(英国)认为,通常悲伤的事件用"纪念"一词,而欢乐的事件用"庆祝"一词。

5.因此,他建议将执行部分第一段中的"纪念"一词改为"庆祝"。

6.张先生(中国)提议该段末尾改为:"……并在人类进步的这一领域作出更大的努力"。

7.罗斯福夫人(美国)接受英国和中国代表的建议。

14.张彭春在联大第三委员会第五届第 318 次会议上的发言

联大第三委员会第五届第 318 次会议,于 1950 年 11 月 17 日下午 3 时至晚上 6 时 25 分,在纽约成功湖举行,本次会议的主要议题是起草第一国际人权公约和实施措施、讨论新闻自由。张彭春先生参加了本次会议,并

在会议上发言,其具体发言内容①会议纪要、纪要影像和纪要译文如下:

【会议纪要】

12. Mr. CHANG (China) supported that view. The draft resolution was irregular in structure, but it served its purpose; partial improvement would do more harm than good.

【纪要影像】

12. Mr. CHANG (China) supported that view. The draft resolution was irregular in structure, but it served its purpose; partial improvement would do more harm than good.

图片 3.6.18:张彭春在联大第三委员会第五届第 318 次会议发言纪要

【纪要译文】

12. 张先生(中国)支持这一观点。该决议草案结构不规则,但达到了目的;局部改善弊大于利。

15. 张彭春在联大第三委员会 第五届第 322 次会议上的发言

联大第三委员会第五届第 322 次会议,于 1950 年 11 月 21 日下午 3 时至晚上 6 时 15 分,在纽约成功湖举行,本次会议的主要议题是讨论新闻自由公约草案。张彭春先生参加了本次会议,并在会议上发言,其具体发言

---

① 本次会议于 1950 年 11 月 17 日下午 3 时,在纽约成功湖举行,见:UN Doc.:A/C. 3/SR/318, p. 286.

内容①会议纪要、纪要影像和纪要译文如下:

【会议纪要】

4. Mr. CHANG (China) recalled that the United Nations Conference on Freedom of Information, held at Geneva in 1948, had felt that it ought to transmit the result of its work to the Economic and Social Council instead of opening for signature the three draft conventions it had prepared. Subsequently, when the drafts had come before the Economic and Social Council, some delegations, in their anxiety to achieve perfection, had proposed a few dozen amendments to them, with the result that the General Assembly, at its third session, was presented with incomplete and imperfect instruments. The first two conventions had already been dealt with. Everyone recognized the importance of the third, but the subject of dispute was the date by which it would be completed.

5. In the opinion of the authors of the joint draft resolution (A/C. 3/L. 110/Rev. 1), the matter was clearly urgent and should be settled before the next session of the General Assembly by setting up a committee of fifteen members and convening a conference of plenipotentiaries. The United States held that the question could only be settled after the completion of the draft covenant on human rights.

6. He considered that it was premature to fix a definite date at the moment. The Economic and Social Council was to meet in July 1951, and it would have to invite the conference in question to meet before August, which left too short a time. Moreover, the Council was to meet at Geneva, but it appeared that the expenses involved by the conference would be less if it were held at the United Nations headquarters: it would therefore be difficult for the Secretariat members concerned to attend both the conference and the Council session.

----

① 本次会议于 1950 年 11 月 21 日下午 3 时,在纽约成功湖举行,见: UN Doc. : A/C. 3/SR/322, pp. 315–316.

7. At the end of the Geneva conference the participants, relatively satisfied with the results achieved, had thought that it would be possible three or five years later to convene an international conference to study the evolution of the situation. But it was no simple matter to convene an international conference, and the preparations for the last conference had lasted almost a year. While the United Nations was impatient to have the convention prepared and perfected, it was improbable that the work could be done before 1 August 1951 if it were to be done by a conference. The question should therefore be considered in a practical spirit, lest too much haste should lead to mistakes.

8. Certain persons believed in the need for an international conference, while others thought it advisable to follow the ordinary process offered by the regular organs of the United Nations, in order to save money. Since opinions were not unanimous, the question should be considered calmly.

9. In conclusion, he expressed the hope that, if the General Assembly decided to refer the question to a conference, it would endeavour to make that conference really international by providing for the largest possible number of participants.

【纪要影像】

4. Mr. CHANG (China) recalled that the United Nations Conference on Freedom of Information, held at Geneva in 1948, had felt that it ought to transmit the result of its work to the Economic and Social Council instead of opening for signature the three draft conventions it had prepared. Subsequently, when the drafts had come before the Economic and Social Council, some delegations, in their anxiety to achieve perfection, had proposed a few dozen amendments to them, with the result that the General Assembly, at its third session, was presented with incomplete and imperfect instruments. The first two conventions had already been dealt with. Everyone recognized the importance of the third, but the subject of dispute was the date by which it would be completed.

5. In the opinion of the authors of the joint draft resolution (A/C.3/L.110/Rev.1), the matter was clearly urgent and should be settled before the next session

of the General Assembly by setting up a committee of fifteen members and convening a conference of plenipotentiaries. The United States held that the question could only be settled after the completion of the draft covenant on human rights.

6. He considered that it was premature to fix a definite date at the moment. The Economic and Social Council was to meet in July 1951, and it would have to invite the conference in question to meet before August, which left too short a time. Moreover, the Council was to meet at Geneva, but it appeared that the expenses involved by the conference would be less if it were held at the United Nations headquarters: it would therefore be difficult for the Secretariat members concerned to attend both the conference and the Council session.

7. At the end of the Geneva conference the participants, relatively satisfied with the results achieved, had thought that it would be possible three or five years later to convene an international conference to study the evolution of the situation. But it was no simple matter to convene an international conference, and the preparations for the last conference had lasted almost a year. While the United Nations was impatient to have the convention prepared and perfected, it was improbable that the work could be done before 1 August 1951 if it were to be done by a conference. The question should therefore be considered in a practical spirit, lest too much haste should lead to mistakes.

8. Certain persons believed in the need for an international conference, while others thought it advisable to follow the ordinary process offered by the regular organs of the United Nations, in order to save money. Since opinions were not unanimous, the question should be considered calmly.

9. In conclusion, he expressed the hope that, if the General Assembly decided to refer the question to a conference, it would endeavour to make that conference really international by providing for the largest possible number of participants.

图片 3.6.19：张彭春在联大第三委员会第五届第 322 次会议发言纪要

【纪要译文】

4. 张先生(中国)回顾说,1948 年在日内瓦举行的联合国新闻自由会议认为,它应当将其工作成果转交经济及社会理事会,而不是将它拟订的三项公约草案开放供签署。后来,当这些草案提交经济及社会理事会时,一些代表团急于达到完美,对其提出了几十项修正案,结果导致大会第三届会议收到了不完整和不完美的文书。前两项公约已经讨论过。每个人都认识到第三个问题的重要性,但争议的主题是它的完成日期。

5. 联合决议草案(A/C.3/L.110/Rev.1)的作者们认为,这个问题显然是紧急的,应该在大会下届会议之前通过设立一个由 15 名成员组成的委员会和召开一次全权代表会议来解决。美国认为,这个问题只有在人权公约草案完成之后才能得到解决。

6. 他认为目前确定一个确切的日期为时过早。经济及社会理事会将于 1951 年 7 月举行会议,它必须邀请有关会议在 8 月之前举行会议,因为时间太短。此外,理事会将在日内瓦举行会议,但如果会议在联合国总部举行,会议所涉费用似乎会减少;因此,有关秘书处成员难以同时出席会议和理事会届会。

7. 在日内瓦会议结束时,与会者对所取得的成果比较满意,认为可以在三年或五年后召开一次国际会议,研究局势的演变。但召开一次国际会议绝非易事,上一次会议的筹备工作持续了近一年。虽然联合国迫不及待地要起草和完善《公约》,但如果想通过一次会议来完成,这项工作不可能在 1951 年 8 月 1 日之前完成。因此,应本着务实的精神考虑这个问题,以免操之过急会导致错误。

8. 有些人认为有必要举行一次国际会议,而另一些人则认为,为了节省经费,宜遵循联合国各常设机构提供的一般程序。由于意见不一致,这个问题应该冷静考虑。

9. 最后,他表示希望,如果大会决定将这个问题提交会议,它将通过提供尽可能多的与会者,努力使该会议真正具有国际性。

第七章　联合国大会全体会议

1948 年 12 月 9 日至 10 日,联合国大会全会在法国巴黎夏洛宫,举行了第 180 次至 183 次会议,各国代表分别在这些会议做最后陈述。中国代表张彭春参加了这几次全会,并在第 182 次全会上发言。

在这次联大全会之前,联大第三委员会举行了 81 次会议,讨论整个宣言草案和个别条款。在辩论过程中提交了 168 份正式决议草案,其中载有对各条款的修正案。讨论的详细摘要见《1948—1949 年联合国年鉴》,第 526–529 页。第三委员会在第 178 次会议上对整个案文进行了表决。该宣言草案以 29 票赞成、0 票反对和 7 票弃权的唱名表决方式获得通过。(A/PV. 178)

人权委员会主席在第三委员会发言时指出,《宣言》只是制定《宪章》所要求的人权方案的第一步。宣言草案是不可剥夺的人权基本原则的声明,为所有人民和所有国家设立了努力实现的共同标准。(A/C. 3/SR. 89)

中国代表张彭春在联大第 182 次会议上的发言如下:

1. 张彭春在联大第 182 次全会上的发言

就在《世界人权宣言》即将发布的当天下午,即 1948 年 12 月 10 日下午 3 时 20 分至晚上 6 时 20 分,联大第 182 次全会在法国巴黎夏洛宫召开,澳大利亚伊瓦特(Evatt)担任大会主席,中国代表张彭春参加了本次会

议,并对他所参加起草的宣言进行了最后总体陈述,其发言内容①会议纪要、纪要影像和纪要译文如下:

【会议纪要】

Mr. CHANG（China）pointed out that, in the course of the long debate on the universal declaration of human rights, representatives had reached agreement whenever they were concerned first and foremost with the defence of human rights. The disagreements had been due to preoccupation of a purely political nature.

Mr. Chang, who had worked for two years on drafting the declaration, hoped that it might prosper, nourished by the hope of mankind.

In the eighteenth century, when solemn declarations of the rights of man had been made in the west, the emphasis had been laid on human rights as contrasted with the divine right claimed by kings. The speaker stressed that Chinese thought had not been without influence on the evolution of those ideas in the western world. The first condition for defence of the rights of man was tolerance towards the various opinions and beliefs held throughout the world. Uncompromising dogmatism had caused much harm, by accentuating disputes, and lending them an ideological basis. In the present times, and more particularly during the years following the First World War, there had been a tendency to impose a standardized way of thinking and a single way of life. With that approach, equilibrium could be reached only at the cost of moving away from the truth, or employing force. But, however violent the methods employed, equilibrium achieved in that way could never last. If harmony was to be maintained in the human community and humanity itself was to be saved, everyone had to accept, in a spirit of sincere tolerance, the different view and beliefs of his fellow men.

---

① UN Document：A/C. 3/SR/182, pp. 895−896.

On the other hand, it was important that conceptions should be very accurately defined; that was no purely academic question. In the modern world, it was considered clever statesmanship to confuse one's adversary; but a real statesman could not tolerate confusion. Social order and peaceful co-operation could be achieved only if people learned to express clear ideas in precise terms. The disagreements all around were only too often the result of confusion spread by the use—whether willful or not—of inaccurate and ambiguous terms.

By pleading for tolerance of all opinions and beliefs and by insisting on precision of terminology, the Chinese delegation had striven to introduce certain improvements into the universal declaration of human rights.

【纪要影像】

Mr. CHANG (China) pointed out that, in the course of the long debate on the universal declaration of human rights, representatives had reached agreement whenever they were concerned first and foremost with the defence of human rights. The disagreements had been due to preoccupation of a purely political nature.

Mr. Chang, who had worked for two years on drafting the declaration, hoped that it might prosper, nourished by the hope of mankind.

In the eighteenth century, when solemn declarations of the rights of man had been made in the west, the emphasis had been laid on human rights as contrasted with the divine right claimed by kings. The speaker stressed that Chinese thought had not been without influence on the evolution of those ideas in the western world. The first condition for defence of the rights of man was tolerance towards the various opinions and beliefs held throughout the world. Uncompromising dogmatism had caused much harm, by accentuating disputes, and lending them an ideological basis. In the present times, and more particularly during the years following the First World War, there had been a tendency to impose a standardized way of thinking and a single way of life. With that approach, equilibrium could be reached only at the cost of moving away from the truth, or employing force. But, however violent the methods employed, equilibrium achieved in that way could never last. If harmony was to be maintained in the human community and humanity itself was to be saved, everyone had to accept, in a spirit of sincere tolerance, the different views and beliefs of his fellow men.

On the other hand, it was important that conceptions should be very accurately defined; that was no purely academic question. In the modern world, it was considered clever statesmanship to confuse one's adversary; but a real statesman could not tolerate confusion. Social order and peaceful co-operation could be achieved only if people learned to express clear ideas in precise terms. The disagreements all around were only too often the result of confusion spread by the use — whether wilful or not — of inaccurate and ambiguous terms.

By pleading for tolerance of all opinions and beliefs and by insisting on precision of terminology, the Chinese delegation had striven to introduce certain improvements into the universal declaration of human rights.

图片 3.7.1:张彭春在联大全体会议第 182 次会议发言纪要(英文版)

【纪要译文】

在《世界人权宣言》的长期争论过程中,无论何时首先关注人权保护,各国代表达成了共识。未达成一致的原因是一种对纯粹政治性的关注。

张彭春先生,花了两年时间参加起草宣言工作,他希望《宣言》因由全

联大第三委员会及联大全会

人类的希望滋养而将会获得成功。

在 18 世纪,当庄严的人权宣言在西方产生,强调人权可与国王宣称的王权相比拟。演讲者张彭春强调指出,中国思想对西方这些主张的发展不是没有影响。捍卫人权的首要条件就是要宽容全世界各种不同观点和不同信仰。不妥协的教条主义,造成很多危害,它借助于强调争端,并为其提供了一个思想基础。在当代,尤其是在第一次世界大战之后的岁月,越是有一种趋势将一种标准的思维方式和单一的生活方式强加于人。那种方法也能达到安宁,但只有以背离真理或使用暴力为代价。但是,无论使用怎样暴虐的方法,所获得的安宁也绝不会持久。如果要保持人类社会和谐、要拯救人类自己,每个人都必须以真诚的宽容精神去接受他人的不同观点和不同信仰。

另一方面,很重要的一点是概念应该非常准确的界定,那不是纯粹的学术问题。在现代世界,被认为是聪明的政治家搞乱了自己的敌人;但是,一个真正的政治家将不能容忍混乱。只有当人们学会以精确的词语表达清楚的观点时,社会秩序及和平合作才能实现。所有的争议,常常只是通过有意无意地使用不准确和模糊的词语而导致混乱造成的。

通过恳求对所有观点和信仰的宽容,并坚持使用精确的措辞,中国代表已经努力使《世界人权宣言》有了一定的改进。

張彭春先生(中國)稱,在關於世界人權宣言之長期討論中,各國代表對維護人權極關重要之事項,類能達成協議,今日紛歧意見之存在,純因未能捐棄政治上之成見。

張先生參加宣言之起草工作,已達兩年,深望以人類期望之切,可使宣言力量發揚光大。

當十八世紀西方國家鄭重宣示人權之際,其所著重者為與君權神授說相對之人權。西方此種觀念之演進,殆與中國思想不無關係。維護人權之首要條件為對於全世界所有不同之意見與信仰,抱容恕之態度。不妥協之獨斷思想,為害已多,爭端因之而益劇,爭持者又利用之以為理論上之根據。時至近代,尤以第一次世界大戰後之數年間,思想與生活,均有被強納於一軌之趨勢。依此進行,必須舍棄真理或使用武力,始可望達成平衡。

然無論用力如何強暴,如何獲得之平衡,決無持久之理。欲保人類社會之和融或使人類本身不遭坎難,則人人必須以真誠容恕之精神,接受他人不同之意見與信仰。

此外,有若干觀念,必須予以正確之界說。此事並非純屬學術上之問題。今人極關混淆對方思想乃政治上之高明手腕,但真正之政治家,則決不容惝恍之辭,而必須明白辨正。欲救社會安定,和平合作,則人人均應以精確之文詞,表達明白之思想。今日各方意見之所以紛歧,大都係有意無意之間,詞句含混,用字失常之結果。

中國代表團籲請各方對各種意見與信仰,力行容恕之道,並堅持宣言之用字措詞,必須精確適當。中國代表團已本此二種宗旨,提出意見,力求世界人權宣言之改進。

图片 3.7.2:张彭春在联大全体会议第 182 次会议发言纪要(中文版)

【中文纪要·简体字版】

张彭春先生(中国)称,在关于《世界人权宣言》之长期讨论中,各国代表对维护人权极关重要之事项。类能达成协议,今日分歧意见之存在,纯因未能捐弃政治上之成见。

张先生参加宣言之起草工作,已达两年,深望以人类期望之切,可使宣言力量发扬光大。

当 18 世纪西方国家郑重宣示人权之际,其所着重者为与君权神授说相对之人权。西方此种观念之演进,殆与中国思想不无关系。维护人权之首要条件为对于全世界所有不同之意见与信仰,抱容恕之态度。不妥协之独断思想,为害已多,争端因之而益剧,争持者又利用之以为理论上之根据。时至近代,尤以第一次世界大战后之数年间,思想与生活,均有被强纳于一轨之趋势。依此进行,必须舍弃真理或使用武力,始可望达成平衡。然无论用力如何强暴,如何获得之平衡,绝无持久之理。欲保人类社会之

---

① UN Document:A/PV.182, p. 304.

联大第三委员会及联大全会

和融或使人类本身不遭劫难,则人人必须以真诚容恕之精神,接受他人不同之意见与信仰。

此外,有若干信念,必须予以正确之界说。此事并非纯属学术上之问题,今人恒谓混淆对方思想乃政治上之高明手腕,但真正之政治家,则决不容恫恍之辞,而必须明白辩正。欲救社会安定,和平合作,则人人均应以精确之文词,表达明白之思想。今日各方意见之所以分歧,大都系有意无意之间,词句含混,用字失当之结果。

中国代表团吁请各方对各种意见与信仰,力行容恕之道,并坚持宣言之用字措辞,必须精确适当。中国代表团已本此二种宗旨,提出意见,力求《世界人权宣言》之改进。

附　录

《世界合作共赢的中国贡献：张彭春在联合国经济及社会理事会的发言》内容补正说明

　　本部分内容作为笔者所编著的《世界合作共赢的中国贡献：张彭春在联合国经济及社会理事会的发言》(简称《世界合作共赢的中国贡献》)一书中"第三章　联合国经社理事会第三届会议(纪要)"部分(见原书第85-124页)的全文记录内容。

　　虽然联合国经济及社会理事会(简称联合国经社理事会)第三届会议的全文记录在《世界合作共赢的中国贡献》一书正式出版①之前就已经找到,但由于联合国图书馆并未及时扫描上传联合国正式文件系统,而该部分内容上传之后(联合国正式文件系统标注的发布时间是 2022 年 6 月 21日),笔者又因忙于《全球人权治理的中国智慧》一书的撰写,因此,该部分内容未能及时收集、整理、研究并收入《世界合作共赢的中国贡献》一书,留下遗憾。现借助《全球人权治理的中国智慧》出版之际,将联合国经社理事会第三届会议的全文会议记录中涉及到中国代表张彭春的发言内容作为附录收入本书,以作为对《世界合作共赢的中国贡献》一书的补充和完善。

　　值得说明的是:由于全面获得第三届会议的全文记录,数据更新的结果发现张彭春在第三届第 16 次会议上也有发言,而在会议纪要文件中并没涉及这次会议。这样对《世界合作共赢的中国贡献》张彭春所参与发言

---

① 　2022 年 4 月 22 日,张彭春先生诞辰 130 周年纪念活动在天津举行,为了交流的需要,该书印制了数十册样书,当时样书上的出版时间是 2022 年 5 月,该样书由于赶时间,里面仍然存在一些问题。纪念活动之后,经笔者进一步修改完善,最终第一版正式出版时间推迟到 2023 年 1 月,但令人遗憾的是,联合国经社理事会第三届会议的全文记录部分却未能及时收入。

的联合国经社理事会的会议次数从原来所说的不少于 164 次提高到不少于 165 次。还有一点值得说明的是,在《世界合作共赢的中国贡献》一书中,联合国经社理事会第三届第 5 次会议的全文记录当时只有法语本,这次也更新为英语本。另外,通过全文记录,发现除了中国代表助理施思明参加了会议并在第 4 次①和第 9 次②会议上发言外,杨博士(Dr. Y. C. Yang)分别在第 8 次会议、第 16 次会议、第 17 次会议、第 20 次会议和第 21 次会议上发言,这都反映了中国对全球治理的贡献。

---

① UN Document:E/PV. 19, p. 32.
② UN Document:E/PV. 24, pp. 61–62.

第三章　联合国经社理事会
第三届会议

联合国经社理事会第三届会议第 1 次会议,于 1946 年 9 月 11 日上午 10 时 30 分至下午 12 时 40 分,在纽约成功湖举行。至 1946 年 10 月 3 日晚,本届会议共召开 21 次会议。另外,理事会还于 1946 年 12 月 10 日下午 3 时至晚上 6 时,在纽约法拉盛草地公园(Flushing Meadow,当时联合国临时总部)召开了一次特别会议。① 本届会议的主要议题有:通过会议日程、讨论经济和就业委员会各小组委员会的职权范围、任命一个审议难民问题的委员会、秘书长关于世界卫生会议的报告、委员会成员的费用支付、审议理事会关于世界卫生组织的决议草案、讨论各委员会的费用问题、审议和讨论国际难民组织决议草案及修正案、讨论国际儿童基金、审议建立人口委员会议案、审议哥伦比亚代表关于建立财政委员会的修正案、国际难民组织特别委员会财政报告、讨论法国代表提交的关于设立联合国研究实验室的决议草案、理事会非政府组织主席报告、讨论理事会第四届会议日期等。

附
录

---

① 　UN Document：E/SR. 21.

China

Delegate:
Dr. P. C. CHANG

Assistants:
Dr. Y. C. YANG
Dr. Szeming Sze
Dr. Y. L. Wu
Mr. P. N. CHENG

Secretary:
Mr. P. Y. TSAO

图片 3.1:联合国经济及社会理事会第三届会议中国代表团名单

中国代表张彭春参加了本届会议,并在其中的 16 次会议上发言,包括本届第 1 次会议、第 2 次会议、第 3 次会议、第 5 次会议、第 6 次会议、第 7 次会议、第 12 次会议、第 14 次会议、第 15 次会议、第 16 次会议、第 17 次会议、第 18 次会议、第 19 次会议、第 20 次会议、第 21 次会议和特别会议上分别发言。根据联合国正式文件系统新上传的全文记录,以"会议发言全文记录及译文"体例,以"全文记录"和"全文译文"呈现本届会议上张彭春先生的发言内容,从而弥补《世界合作共赢的中国贡献》相关部分(即第三章"联合国经社理事会第三届会议",见原书第 85–124 页)所缺少的全文记录部分。考虑到将来《世界合作共赢的中国贡献》一书的修订版,这部分内容有可能会替换掉原书中的第三章内容,尽管有部分重复内容,但考虑到体例的统一,该补正内容既包括会议发言全文记录也包括内容纪要两部分。

1. 张彭春在经社理事会 第三届第1次会议上的发言

联合国经社理事会第三届第1次会议,于1946年9月11日上午10时30分至下午12时40分,在纽约成功湖开幕,本次会议的主要议题是通过会议日程。中国代表张彭春率团参加了本次会议,并在会议上发言,其发言内容如下:

(1) 会议发言全文记录①及译文

【全文记录】

Dr. Chang (China): Mr. President, it seems as though we have already spoken enough on this matter of agenda. The general trend is to agree with the suggestion made by the Belgian Representative and later on supported by the Indian Representative. I would also support this suggestion, and especially, to be concrete, to adopt this as our target time-table, with the exception of Friday, September 13—Item 2. In considering the organization of the Demographic Commission, I think the suggestion of the United States Representative as well as the Representative of the Soviet Union to have the organization of the six commissions, which already started working, first, and then to put the organization of the other commissions—not necessarily to postpone them until the next session, but to put them toward the end of this session is good. In case time allows, we shall proceed with the discussion of the organization; if not, we shall postpone them until the next session.

---

① UN Document: E/PV. 16, p. 61, p. 72.

Therefore, Mr. President, I should like to save time and propose the adoption of this provisional target time-table for the rest of this meeting, with the deletion of Item 2 from the Friday-proposed agenda. Furthermore, Mr. President, just in order to clarify this in our mind, I really think there are two categories of problems before us at this session, one proper organization, which is not yet finished. Therefore, we should proceed with the discussion of the Economic and Employment Commission, and later on, with the organization and the election of the commission and the expenses of the commissions. That is on the organizational side, category one. And then, in category 2 we might call them "the current problems", the problems that must be tackled, namely, the Refugees and later on the devastated areas and health, and so forth. They are the current problems and, therefore, these two categories should be carried on side by side.

Therefore, I agree. I rather see the advisability of following such a schedule.

Dr. Chang (China): I still think we need some sort of target program to go by; otherwise, we won't know what we are going to discuss at the next session or the next two or three days. Shouldn't we, Mr. President, just to have an understanding, that except for the two items already commented on, namely, Friday, Item 2, Demographic Commission which should be naturally postponed for one day in view of the fact that the documents are not yet thoroughly digested. Aside from these two exceptions, we should follow this target program as far as we can. If that is the case, we should like to know after Mr. La Guardia's—I am sure most energetic statement—what are we going to do this afternoon; because we may have to prepare ourselves in case Items 18 and 19 should be brought up, and we should do something in preparation. Or shall we keep on discussing that problem tomorrow morning?

Dr. Chang (China): Item 18 and Item 19.

【全文译文】

张博士(中国):主席先生,关于议程问题,我们似乎已经说得够多了。总的趋势是同意比利时代表提出的、后来得到印度代表支持的建议。我也支持这一建议,特别是具体地说,通过这一建议作为我们的目标时间表,但9月13日星期五除外——项目2。在考虑人口委员会的组织问题时,我认为美国代表和苏联代表的建议是,首先组织已经开始工作的六个委员会,然后组织其他委员会——不一定要推迟到下届会议,而是在本届会议快结束时进行,这是好的。如果时间允许,我们将着手讨论组织问题;如果没有,我们将把它们推迟到下届会议。

因此,主席先生,我想节省时间,提议通过本次会议剩余时间的暂定目标时间表,从星期五提议的议程中删除项目2。此外,主席先生,为了在我们的头脑中澄清这一点,我确实认为本届会议有两类问题摆在我们面前,一类是适当的组织问题,这一问题尚未完成。因此,我们应该着手讨论经济和就业委员会,然后讨论委员会的组织和选举以及委员会的费用。这是在组织方面,第一类。然后,在第二类中,我们可以称之为"当前的问题",即必须解决的问题,即难民问题以及随后的灾区和卫生问题,等等。它们是当前的问题,因此,这两个类别应该同时进行。

所以,我同意。我认为遵循这样的时间表是明智的。

张博士(中国):我仍然认为我们需要某种目标方案作为依据;否则,我们将不知道我们将在下一次会议或今后两三天讨论什么。主席先生,我们难道不应该有这样一种理解,即除了已经评论过的两个项目,即星期五的项目2,人口委员会自然应该推迟一天,因为文件还没有完全消化。除了这两个例外,我们应该尽可能地遵循这个目标计划。如果是这样的话,我们想知道在拉·瓜迪亚先生——我确信是最有力的发言——之后,我们今天下午要做什么;因为我们可能要做好准备,以防第18项和第19项被提出来,我们应该做些准备。还是我们明天早上继续讨论那个问题?

张博士(中国):项目18和项目19。

（2）会议发言内容纪要①

本次会议【会议纪要】【纪要影像】和【纪要译文】又见《世界合作共赢的中国贡献》一书第 89–91 页。②

【会议纪要】

Mr. CHANG（China）agreed with the delegates for Belgium and India. The provisional time table might, however, be modified to comply with the suggestions of the United States and Soviet delegates that item 13 concerning the Demographic Commission be discussed at a later date.

The Council was faced with two categories of problems：organizational problems, such as the setting up of commissions, the election of their members and the payment of their expenses；and current problems such as refugee and health questions and the reconstruction of devastated areas. He agreed that the two types of problems must be dealt with side by side as envisaged in the Secretariat time table.

Mr. CHANG（China）asked that before the meeting rose an understanding should be reached on the programme for the next two or three days. The time table proposed by the Secretariat might be adopted with the exception of the postponement of the item referring to the Demographic Commission and possibly of one meeting of the Committee on Refugees. Would items 18 and 19 of the agenda be taken up at the afternoon meeting, after the statement by Mr. La Guardia?

---

① UN Document：E/SR. 1, pp. 14–15, pp. 15–16.

② 孙平华编著:《世界合作共赢的中国贡献:张彭春在联合国经济及社会理事会的发言》,天津社会科学院出版社 2023 年 1 月版,第 89–91 页。

Mr. CHANG (China) agreed with the delegates for Belgium and India. The provisional time table might, however, be modified to comply with the suggestions of the United States and Soviet delegates that item 13 concerning the Demographic Commission be discussed at a later date.

The Council was faced with two categories of problems: organizational problems, such as the setting up of commissions, the election of their members and the payment of their expenses; and current problems such as refugee and health questions and the reconstruction of devastated areas. He agreed that the two types of problems must be dealt with side by side as envisaged in the Secretariat time table.

Mr. CHANG (China) asked that before the meeting rose an understanding should be reached on the programme for the next two or three days. The time table proposed by the Secretariat might be adopted with the exception of the postponement of the item referring to the Demographic Commission and possibly of one meeting of the Committee on Refugees. Would items 18 and 19 of the agenda be taken up at the afternoon meeting, after the statement by Mr. La Guardia?

图片 3.2:张彭春在经社理事会第三届第 1 次会议发言纪要

【纪要译文】

张先生(中国)同意比利时和印度的代表的意见。但是,临时时间表可以修改,以符合美国和苏联代表的建议,即关于人口委员会的项目 13 将在以后讨论。

理事会面临两类问题:组织问题,如设立委员会、选举其成员和支付其费用;以及当前问题如难民和健康问题以及灾区重建等。他同意,这两类问题必须按照秘书处时间表的设想同时处理。

张先生(中国)要求在会议开始之前,就今后两三天的方案达成谅解。秘书处提议的时间表可以采纳,除了人口委员会的项目可能推迟,以及难民委员会可能推迟一次会议之外。在拉·瓜迪亚先生发言之后,下午会议是否会讨论议程项目 18 和 19?

附

录

2. 张彭春在经社理事会 第三届第 2 次会议上的发言

联合国经社理事会第三届第 2 次会议,于 1946 年 9 月 11 日下午 2 时至 5 时,在纽约成功湖举行,本次会议的主要议程是审议经济和就业委员会各小组委员会的职权范围等。中国代表张彭春率团参加了本次会议,并在会议上发言,其发言内容如下:

(1)会议发言全文记录①及译文

【全文记录】

Dr. Chang (China): Mr. President, my comments will be very few and very short. There has been a paper circulated called a Memorandum on the Terms of the Reference of the Sub-Commission on Economic Developments. I am sure Members of the Council have either read or will read this short statement. I must, on this occasion, make one point clear, namely, that we hope that the organization of the Economic and Employment Commission will follow the functional basis, especially on the level of policy-making, while, in the carrying out of the policies and decisions passed by the Council, regional agencies or offices maybe either permanently or temporarily set up. In other words, we should all have within our range a clear distinction as to the functional and regional divisions of work. On the policy-making level, it should be functional; on the operation side, it may be regional.

The reason why this point is brought out here, especially for reference

---

① UN Document: E/PV. 17, p. 111, p. 112, pp. 132-133,

when the Sub-Committee will come to discuss this matter, is that I understand this temporary Sub-Commission on the Economic Reconstruction for Devastated Areas is likely to present to this Council a suggestion for the creation of a so called Economic Commission for Europe. If so, I think we should make proper reservations at the present time that this principle should be followed, namely, in regard to policy making it should be functional, in regard to operation it may be regional. That is the point I want to make at this juncture.

Secondly, in circulating this proposal on the terms of reference of the Sub-Commission on Economic Development, the Chinese Delegation still wishes to make the same reservation as it did during the second session. During the Second Session—may I just quote this sentence from the statement of the Chinese Delegation made during the second Session—"The Chinese Delegation is inclined to think that the Council might find a Sub-Commission inadequate to cope with such a vast program. . . "—especially as we have outlined here in this short paper. "We therefore may, in due course, wish to propose the enlarging of the Sub-Commission into a full Commission devoting its concentrated attention to the problem of economic development of. . . "—what I have called in the last Session—"below pressure areas, not only for the welfare of the peoples in these areas, but for the betterment of man's estate in all parts of the world—".

The Chinese Delegation, at this Third Session, while agreeing for the time being to the creation of a Sub-Commission of Economic Development under the Economic and Employment Commission, if there should be no new suggestions concerning new Commissions to be created—while we agree to that—we reserve the bringing up of the matter, in due course of the time, as the work to be promoted under this a present Sub-Commission on Economic Developments develops.

Thank you.

Mr. Chang (China): Mr. President, I think those of us who were here at the Second Session remember clearly that was toward the end of the Session, the program was so extremely crowded that we did not have much time to discuss the terms of reference for the sub-commissions of the Economic and Social Council. The procedure followed during the last session, if I'm not mistaken, was to put this matter under our Committee, you might say, on Economic Affairs, composed of the Representatives as enumerated by our Belgian colleague. Therefore, I would endorse the suggestion already put forth by our Norwegian colleague, if the President will be gracious enough to change his mind as he has the right to, of turning the matter over to that Committee on Economic Affairs to follow our general procedure—as a matter of fact to continue the discussion that was interrupted at the last session.

It is not setting a new precedent at all; it is simply continuation of the discussion during the last session. Furthermore, in regard to the little paper that the Chinese Delegation has circulated, it is nothing new at all; there is no new principle suggested. If you look at the Resolution and compare it to the terms of reference which we rushed over without proper discussion, it is a mere amendment. If you will kindly turn over to paper E/107, page 3, you will find under the Resolutions "The Sub-commission Economic Development shall study the methods of increasing production, productivity and levels of consumption with special attention to the less-developed regions of the world". That is exactly the same wording as we had during the last session, and where the amendment really comes in is, "it shall (a)..., (b)..., (c)...". The (a), (b), and (c), are the new suggestions of carrying out that big tremendous function; that is all—it is nothing new.

The second, "2. Examine the effects of industrialization and technological change on world economic conditions and the adjustments required," is the exact wording of what we had during the last session, so there is nothing new, no big principle involved.

In the circumstances, Mr. President—we have ten minutes to go before five o'clock—may I suggest that these two terms should be given to the Committee on Economic Affairs to bring back to the Council a statement on the terms of reference. I am sure the Secretariat would like to present terms of reference for all the three sub-commissions, not only the Sub-commission on Economic Development alone, so we will then give the Secretariat a chance of working out that statement within the next day or two.

【全文译文】

张博士(中国):主席先生,我的评论很少、很短。已经分发了一份,称为关于经济发展小组委员会职权范围备忘录的文件。我相信理事会成员已经或将要阅读这个简短声明。我必须在这一场合澄清一点,即我们希望经济和就业委员会的组织将遵循职能基础,特别是在决策一级,同时,在执行理事会通过的政策和决定时,可以永久或临时设立区域机构或办事处。换句话说,我们都应该在我们的工作范围内明确区分职能和区域分工。在决策层面,应该是功能性的;运营方面,可能是区域性的。

之所以在这里提出这一点,特别是在小组委员会将要讨论这一问题时作为参考,是因为我知道这个关于灾区经济重建的临时小组委员会可能会向理事会提出一项建议,成立一个所谓的欧洲经济委员会。如果是这样的话,我认为我们目前应该做出适当的保留,即应该遵循这一原则,即就决策而言,它应该是功能性的,就运作而言,它可以是区域性的。这是我在这个关头想说的一点。

第二,在分发关于经济发展小组委员会职权范围的提案时,中国代表团仍希望像在第二届会议上一样持保留意见。在第二届会议期间,我想引用中国代表团在第二届会议上的发言中的这句话,"中国代表团倾向于认为,理事会可能会认为一个小组委员会不足以处理如此庞大的方案……"特别是正如我们在该短文中所概述的那样。"因此,我们可能希望在适当的时候建议将小组委员会扩大为一个正式的委员会,集中关注……"——

我在上一届会议中称之为——"低压地区之下的经济发展问题,这不仅是为了这些地区人民的福利,也是为了改善世界各地人民的生活……"。

中国代表团在第三次会议上,虽然暂时同意在经济和就业委员会下设立一个经济发展小组委员会,但如果没有关于设立新的委员会的新建议,我们同意,但我们保留在适当的时候提出这一问题,因为目前的经济发展小组委员会将推动工作的发展。

谢谢大家。

张先生(中国):主席先生,我想我们参加第二届会议的人都清楚地记得,在届末,会议安排得非常拥挤,我们没有太多时间讨论经社理事会小组委员会的职权范围。如果我没有弄错的话,上届会议遵循的程序是将此事提交给我们的经济事务委员会,该委员会由比利时同事列举的代表组成。因此,我赞同我们的挪威同事已经提出的建议,如果主席能够改变他的想法——他有权这样做——把这个问题交给那个经济事务委员会,按照我们的一般程序处理——事实上是继续上届会议中断的讨论。

这根本不是开创一个新的先例;这只是上届会议讨论的延续。此外,关于中国代表团分发的小文件,这根本不是什么新东西;没有提出新的原则。如果你看一下这项决议,并把它与我们未经适当讨论就匆忙制定的职权范围相比较,它仅仅是一项修正案。请翻到 E/107 号文件第 3 页,你会发现在这些决议下"经济发展小组委员会应研究增加生产、生产力和消费水平的方法,特别注意世界上较不发达的地区"。这与我们在上届会议中的措辞完全相同,真正需要修正的是,"它应当(a)……、(b)……、(c)……"。(a)、(b)和(c)是执行那个巨大功能的新建议;仅此而已——这并不新鲜。

第二个,"2. 审查工业化和技术变革对世界经济状况的影响以及所需的调整",这是我们在上届会议的确切措辞,因此没有什么新内容,也没有什么大原则。

主席先生,在这种情况下——我们离五点还有十分钟——我是否可以建议将这两个任期交给经济事务委员会,以便向理事会带回一份关于职权范围的声明。我确信,秘书处希望提出所有三个小组委员会的职权范围,而不仅仅是经济发展小组委员会的职权范围,因此我们将让秘书处有机会在一两天内拟定这一声明。

(2) 会议发言内容纪要①

本次会议【会议纪要】【纪要影像】和【纪要译文】又见《世界合作共赢的中国贡献》一书第 92-95 页。②

【会议纪要】

Mr. CHANG（China）drew attention to a memorandum on the terms of reference of the Sub-Commission on Economic Development（document E/107）, which had been distributed. In studying this document, the members of the Council should, he thought, keep before them the following distinction: whereas the organization of the Economic and Employment Commission must, at the higher level, be functional it might, at the executive level, be regional.

He had stressed this distinction because he felt sure the temporary Sub-Commission on the Economic Reconstruction of Devastated Areas would ask the Council to establish an Economic Commission for Europe and, in that case, the principle on which he had just laid stress ought to be applied.

With regard to this proposal concerning the terms of reference of the Sub-Commission on Economic Development, the Chinese delegation felt bound to make the same reservation as it had made during the second session, namely, that in its view a sub-commission was inadequate to cover such a vast field; it should be enlarged so as to constitute a full commission.

The Chinese delegation would agree to the establishment of a Sub-Commis-

---

① UN Document: E/SR. 2, pp. 24-25, p. 26.

② 孙平华编著:《世界合作共赢的中国贡献:张彭春在联合国经济及社会理事会的发言》,天津社会科学院出版社 2023 年 1 月版,第 92-95 页。

sion on Economic Development under the authority of the Economic and Employment Commission, if no other suggestions for the establishment of new commissions were submitted, but it reserved the right to raise the question again at the proper time.

Mr. CHANG (China) said the procedure followed at the second session had been to refer the terms of reference of a sub-commission to a committee, which might be called the Committee on Economic Questions, for the composition of which the representative of Belgium had made a suggestion. He accordingly supported the Norwegian proposal and pointed out that action on these lines would simply imply the continuation of a discussion suspended in June.

On the other hand, as regards the resolution submitted to the Council by the Chinese delegation, members would soon see, if they studied document E/107, page 3, that it proposed only one amendment to the terms of reference which had been drawn up by the Council after a hurried discussion. No new factor had been introduced and the amendment did not affect any principle.

He therefore suggested that this task should be entrusted to the Committee on Economic Questions, which would submit a proposal on the terms of reference to the Council.

He felt sure the Secretariat would be prepared to draw up the terms of reference of the three sub-commissions and not merely that of the Sub-Commission on Economic Development.

【纪要影像】

Mr. CHANG (China) drew attention to a memorandum on the terms of reference of the Sub-Commission on Economic Development (document E/107), which had been distributed. In studying this document, the members of the Council should, he thought, keep before them the following distinction: whereas the organization of the Economic and Employment Commission must, at the higher level, be functional it might, at the executive level, be regional.

He had stressed this distinction because he felt sure the temporary Sub-Commission on the Economic Reconstruction of Devastated Areas would ask the Council to establish an Economic Commission for Europe and, in that case, the principle on which he had just laid stress ought to be applied.

With regard to this proposal concerning the terms of reference of the Sub-Commission on Economic Development, the Chinese delegation felt bound to make the same reservation as it had made during the second session, namely, that in its view a sub-commission was inadequate to cover such a vast field; it should be enlarged so as to constitute a full commission.

The Chinese delegation would agree to the establishment of a Sub-Commission on Economic Development under the authority of the Economic and Employment Commission, if no other suggestions for the establishment of new commissions were submitted, but it reserved the right to raise the question again at the proper time.

Mr. CHANG (China) said the procedure followed at the second session had been to refer the terms of reference of a sub-commission to a committee, which might be called the Committee on Economic Questions, for the composition of which the representative of Belgium had made a suggestion. He accordingly supported the Norwegian proposal and pointed out that action on these lines would simply imply the continuation of a discussion suspended in June.

On the other hand, as regards the resolution submitted to the Council by the Chinese delegation, members would soon see, if they studied document E/107, page 3, that it proposed only one amendment to the terms of reference which had been drawn up by the Council after a hurried discussion. No new factor had been introduced and the amendment did not affect any principle.

He therefore suggested that this task should be entrusted to the Committee on Economic Questions, which would submit a proposal on the terms of reference to the Council.

He felt sure the Secretariat would be prepared to draw up the terms of reference of the three sub-commissions and not merely that of the Sub-Commission on Economic Development.

图片 3.3:张彭春在经社理事会第三届第 2 次会议发言纪要

【纪要译文】

张先生(中国)提请注意已分发的关于经济发展小组委员会职权范围的备忘录(E/107 号文件)。他认为,在研究这份文件时,理事会成员应注意以下区别:经济和就业委员会的组织必须在较高一级必须是职能性的,但在执行一级可能是区域性的。

他强调了这一区别,因为他确信灾区经济重建临时小组委员会将要求理事会设立一个欧洲经济委员会,在这种情况下,他刚才强调的原则应该适用。

关于这一涉及经济发展小组委员会职权范围的建议,中国代表团认为有必要作出与第二届会议相同的保留,即认为一个小组委员会不足以涵盖如此广泛的领域;它应该扩大,以便成为一个正式的委员会。

如果没有其他关于设立新委员会的建议提交,中国代表团将同意在经济和就业委员会管辖之下设立经济发展小组委员会,但保留在适当时候再次提出这一问题的权利。

附
录

张先生(中国)说,第二届会议遵循的程序是将分设委员会的职权范围提交一个委员会,该委员会可称为经济问题委员会,比利时代表对其组成提出了建议。因此,他支持挪威的建议,并指出按照这些思路采取行动只会意味着继续进行6月份暂停的讨论。

另一方面,关于中国代表团向理事会提交的决议,如果各位成员研究了E/107号文件第3页,他们很快就会看到,该决议只对理事会在匆忙讨论后起草的职权范围提出了一项修正。没有引入新的因素,修正案不影响任何原则。

因此,他建议将这项任务委托给经济问题委员会,该委员会将向理事会提交一份关于职权范围的提案。

他确信秘书处将准备起草三个分设委员会的职权范围,而不仅仅是经济发展分设委员会的职权范围。

3. 张彭春在经社理事会
第三届第3次会议上的发言

联合国经社理事会第三届第3次会议1946年9月12日上午10时30分至下午1时30分,在纽约成功湖举行,本次会议的主要议题是向联合国转让国际联盟在麻醉药品方面行使的权力、听取秘书长关于国际卫生会议的报告(作为世界卫生组织创立过程的一个环节,为了更好地了解中国代表的在该组织缔造过程的贡献,这里将整个呈现秘书长的这个报告)、讨论委员会成员费用的支付等。中国代表张彭春率团参加了本次会议,并先后两次在会议上发言,其发言内容如下:

(1) 会议发言全文记录①及译文

【全文记录】

Mr. Chang (China): Mr. President, in the establishment of the Commission on Narcotic Drugs, the Chinese Delegation from the days of the Preparatory Commission of the United Nations has had the honor of supporting the measure, not only on the organization of the Commission, but also in maintaining a deep interest in the international efforts to control the traffic in narcotic drugs.

We are, therefore, particularly happy to note the good progress which has been made in preparing for the first meeting of the Commission and for the continuation by the Commission of the important international work in the field of drug control, which was conducted by the League of Nations.

We have given careful study to the documents which have been prepared for the Secretariat, and wish to take this opportunity to commend the Secretariat on the excellence of the documents so far prepared. The two draft resolutions and the draft protocol embodied in these documents are in general acceptable to the Chinese Delegation. We are glad to state our approval of the procedure recommended in these documents. There are only one or two minor changes of a drafting nature which we should like to have considered, and since other Delegation we understand, may also have some similar changes to suggest, we should like to see a small drafting committee appointed which may study and incorporate changes which the Representatives wish to make.

Report of the Secretary-General on the International Health Conference

The President: Now, we have to proceed, and take up point 3 of our Agenda today. This is the Report of the Secretary-General on the International Health Conference.

---

① UN Document: E/PV. 18, p. 12, pp. 32-40, pp. 91-110.

I am very happy to see here Dr. Chisholm, who was appointed Executive Secretary of the Interim Commission of the newly-created World Health Organization. May I ask Dr. Chisholm to give his statement?

(Dr. Chisholm assumed a seat at the table.)

Dr. G. B. Chisholm (Canada): Mr. President, may I make a brief statement about the present stage of development of the World Health Organization? You will not need to be reminded of its origin in proposals made by Brazil and China; the invitation by the Economic and Social Council to eighteen experts to meet in Paris as a Technical Preparatory Committee in April; the report of that Committee to the Economic and Social Council here; the gathering together of the International Health Conference attended by 61 nations, some of whom had the status of observers; and a meeting, lasting some four weeks, of that Conference here in New York.

There was agreement reached, an astonishing degree of agreement, so that eventually sixty-one nations signed documents, forty-seven of the nations signed without reservations, agreement on the setting up of the Interim Commission. The Interim Commission as elected by the Conference has the following Members:

Australia

Brazil

Canada

China

Egypt

France

India

Liberia

Mexico

Netherlands

Norway

Peru

United Kingdom

United States of America

Union of Soviet Social Republics

Venezuela

Yugoslavia

Dr. Stampar, your President, was elected the Chairman of the Interim Commission of the World Health Organization.

Further committees were set up, the Committee on Administration and Finance; a Negotiating Committee to undertake to develop the reletionships of the World Health Organization with other bodies including bodies of the United Nations, and an Epidemiological Intelligence and Quarantine Comnission.

According to its Constitution, the World Health Orgenization will be set up whenever twenty-six nations have ratified their signatures to the appropriate documents. At that time the Interim Commission will go out of existence. The United Nations Secretariat and other bodies have been extraordinarily helpful in assisting in every way the beginning of the World Health Organization. Its Interim Commission has been able to secure temporery quarters in the New York Academy of Medicine for which we are very grateful to the New York Doctors.

The administrative policies of the Interim Commission of the World Health Organization and its financial policies will by constitutional direction conform to those of the United Nations bodies; its personnel policy also. Liaison and joint committees are now in process of exploration with other bodies of the United Nations.

附录

The future relationships and areas of responsibility are gradually being worked out. The Interim Commission has called its next meeting for some time in November, tentatively that meeting was called for Geneva. It will in any case meet somewhere in Europe because it is expecting to explore posibilities as to where it may locate its headquarters in the future.

I think there is nothing further, Mr. President.

The President: Does any Member of the Council wish more explanation from Dr. Chisholm? He is free to put any question he likes.

Dr. Chang (China): The Delegation of China naturally notes with deep satisfaction the report of progress that is made by the World Health Organization. I feel that our Council can congratulate ourselves on having sponsored the birth of such a very healthy offspring which has arrived on schedule according to the timetable we set at our first Session in London. We accept, I think, the report of this Organization and as to what further action is needed to regularize the relationship of this newborn Organization to the United Nations—the matter can be left to our Negotiations Committee until such time when the organization will be further completed.

We are very happy indeed to see how the war against microbes, suggested by China, is now actually in the real healthy way of being carried out.

Thank you.

Dr. Chang (China): Mr. President, it seems to me the major factor to be considered as to whether the United Nations or the respective governments should shoulder the expenses of the members of the commissions in carrying out these duties is the status of these members as seen in the light of the nature of their functions. I agree with the distinction made by the Belgian Representative that there are commissions that are gatherings of representatives of governments for special subjects to be considered. From that point of view the present temporary sub-commission on the Economic Reconstruction for the Devastated Areas, now meeting in London, probably by nature belongs to that type. That is, the different participating governments have direct interests. Now, the commissions which we are considering of composing, mainly the six so far constituted—they are really of the nature of advisers to the Council. These commissions have no executive function in particular, unless they are given such by the Council. Their chief function, as we all agree, is to advise the Council. They submit their reports to the Council. There are no differences of opinion at all on the part of all members of the Council, as well as on the part, I think, of all people who have taken part in these various commissions. It is that their function is to advise the Council.

Now we did have a difference of opinion concerning how these advisers to the Council should be selected. That was the difference of opinion. One opinion was that this should be individuals. The other opinion was that these advisers were to be representatives of governments. That is a clear thing. When the vote was taken, unfortunately the issue was not clearly drawn. There was no time for it. I voted for the thing and some of my colleagues here also voted, not exactly "of" representatives of governments. We voted for representatives "from" governments. There is a great distinction there. Some of us felt that inasmuch as these experts are not still well-known, especially experts who happen to speak and write in languages that are not so widely read or heard. It is not quite appropriate or fitting, or if you like to use a stronger word, fair to consider only the people who write in languages that are well-known as experts and consider others who happen to write in language not well-known as not experts.

Therefore, under these circumstances at least the Chinese Delegation made the suggestion that for a trial period of say two, three, or four years, the governments should nominate these expert advisers to serve on the commissions to advise the Council. I hope that point is clear. At least so far as the standing made by the Chinese Delegation as well as it is in the minds of the Representatives at the Second Session.

There was no time allowed for this discussion. The vote was taken and then it was considered to be representatives "of" governments. Let's go back to

附
录

this. In accordance with the resolution of the Economic and Social Council a-dopted on the 21 of June 1946, Documents E/84, Revision 1, "All commissions are to consist of one representative from each of ..." Please remember that appeared in this document. A representative "from ... a certain numbers of the United Nations selected by the Council ..." that is, "... the commissions are to consist of representatives from members of the United Nations selected by the Council to serve on the respective commissions."

Further, "...With a view to securing a balanced representation in the various fields covered by the commission, the Secretary General shall consult with the governments so selected before the representatives are finally nominated by these governments and confirmed by the Council." That was definitely stated in the reporting of the Resolution. Whereas the Council Resolution definitely speaks of members from governments selected by the Council the possibility of misunderstanding regarding the real status of the commission members cannot be ruled out. Thus, for instance, according to the report of the Secretary General on the work of the Organization, the pamphlet, document, very ably prepared by the Secretariat, that is, Document A/65, page 14, the commissions are to consist of representatives "of" governments. I thought that was very unfortunate to make that mistake. The persons writing it did not know how much time we spent discussing this matter. It is therefore necessary to clarify the status of the members of the commissions without leaving any more doubt. The decision that members of the commissions should be representatives "from" governments or member states selected by the Council representatives from member states selected by the Council, was first reached in connection with the discussion on the composition of the commissions in general and that of the Economic and Employment Commission in particular. That is Document E/J. C/1, and E/J. C/2. By "representative" the Council meant persons designated by governments. That is how it was interpreted. In the discussions which followed the

President made it quite clear that "... the governments selected by the Council or the Member States selected by the Council had the option to send either a governmental representative or an expert outside the government."

... (At this point Mr. Noel-Baker arrived and assumed the Chair of the United Kingdom Delegation) ...

I think many of us still remember that interpretation because I forced the President to make that statement. Otherwise I should consider the decision not clear. That appears in E/J. C/2, page 4. It was further agreed that whether a member nominated by a government should be a representative of that govern-ment—again quotation—"the representative of that government should speak for the government concerned" or not would be "a matter for individual govern-ments to decide." That again appeared in E/J. C/2, page 4. Now that is all very clear—at least very clear to most of us who voted for that resolution—that we were not voting for representatives of governments, though some Members who voted for the resolution voted for members of governments. Many of us, or several, voted for representatives from Member States selected by the Council to serve on the different Commissions. If that is clear it seems that the matter of payment of expenses should follow, namely, for Members of Commissions of an advisory function to the Council, while the process of selection is for the time being so fixed as to have the Member States selected by the Council as a first instance, and then the Member States would designate the representatives, and these representatives may be representatives of governments, or they may be not directly employed by the governments; they may speak for the governments or may speak for themselves. From the point of view of the Council, however, they all speak as individual experts. I think that is the understanding of many of the people who voted for that measure, and of course I am sure there are rea-sons why people should say that these representatives must be representatives of governments. These reasons were also very clearly stated, and I am just stating

附
录

it, for some of the Members who voted for that voted for representatives from Member States selected by the Council to serve as Members of the Commissions. I do not believe it is necessary to go back again, to reverse the vote. That is not a good procedure, so let us keep the instructions we have, as the President made it clear that while some Members voted for representatives of governments and some other Members I am sure would have, but because of the presence of those Members in that vote, that vote was able to be a majority and they voted for the governments from Member States selected by the Council. If that is the case, let us leave the vote as it is, but at the same time keep the functions of the Members of these Commissions clear, namely advisory to the Council. If that is the case, it seems as though the payment of expenses should be borne by the United Nations.

(Mr. Davila returned and assumed the seat of the Chilean Delegation.)

【全文译文】

张先生(中国):主席先生,在麻醉药品委员会的成立过程中,中国代表团从联合国筹备委员会时期起就有幸支持这一措施,不仅是在委员会的组织方面,而且也是在对控制麻醉药品贩运的国际努力方面保持高度兴趣。

因此,我们特别高兴地注意到在筹备委员会第一次会议和委员会继续推进国际联盟在药物管制领域开展的重要国际工作方面取得的良好进展。

我们仔细研究了为秘书处准备的文件,并希望借此机会赞扬秘书处迄今为止准备的出色文件。中国代表团总体上可以接受这两项决议草案和议定书草案。我们很高兴地声明我们同意这些文件中推荐的程序。只有一两个草案性质的小改动,我们本想考虑,而且因为我们知道其他代表团也可能有一些类似的改动建议,我们希望任命一个小型起草委员会,研究并采纳代表们希望做出的改动。

秘书长关于国际卫生会议的报告

主席：现在，我们必须着手处理今天议程的第三点。这是秘书长关于国际卫生大会的报告。

我很高兴在这里见到齐索姆（Chisholm）博士，他被任命为新成立的世界卫生组织临时委员会的执行秘书。我可以请齐索姆博士发表他的声明吗？

（齐索姆博士在桌旁就座。）

齐索姆博士（加拿大）：主席先生，请允许我就世界卫生组织目前的发展阶段作一简短发言。不需要提醒你们其起源是巴西和中国的提案；经济及社会理事会邀请18名专家于4月在巴黎举行会议，作为技术筹备委员会；委员会这里提交经济及社会理事会的报告；61个国家一起参加的国际卫生会议，其中一些国家拥有观察员地位；以及在纽约这里举行的一次为期约四周的会议。

达成了协议，惊人程度的协议，最终61个国家签署了文件，其中47个国家毫无保留地签署了关于成立临时委员会的协议。会议选出的临时委员会成员如下：

澳大利亚、巴西、加拿大、中国、埃及、法国、印度、利比里亚、墨西哥、荷兰、挪威、秘鲁、英国、美国、苏维埃社会共和国联盟、委内瑞拉、南斯拉夫。

你们的主席斯坦帕（Stampar）博士当选为世界卫生组织临时委员会主席。

成立了更多的委员会，即行政和财务委员会；一个谈判委员会，负责发展世界卫生组织与包括联合国机构在内的其他机构的关系，以及一个流行病情报和检疫委员会。

根据其章程，世界卫生组织将在26个国家批准签署相应文件后成立。届时，临时委员会将不复存在。联合国秘书处和其他机构在以各种方式协助世界卫生组织的成立方面提供了极大的帮助。它的临时委员会能够在纽约医学院获得临时办公场所，为此我们非常感谢纽约的医生们。

世界卫生组织临时委员会的行政政策及其财政政策将根据宪法指示

符合联合国各机构的政策;其人事政策也是如此。联络和联合委员会目前正在与联合国其他机构进行探讨。

未来的关系和责任范围正在逐步确定。临时委员会将于 11 月召开下一次会议,暂定在日内瓦召开。无论如何,它将在欧洲的某个地方举行会议,因为它希望探索将来把总部设在哪儿的可能性。

我想没有其他问题了,主席先生。

主席:是否有理事会成员希望齐索姆博士作更多解释? 他可以自由地提出任何他喜欢的问题。

张博士(中国):中国代表团当然十分满意地注意到世界卫生组织所作的进展报告。我觉得我们的理事会可以祝贺我们自己赞助了这样一个非常健康的后代的出生,它按照我们在伦敦第一次会议上制定的时间表如期到来。我认为,我们接受该组织的报告,至于需要采取什么进一步行动来使这个新生组织与联合国的关系正常化,这个问题可以留给我们的谈判委员会,直到该组织进一步完善。

我们确实非常高兴地看到,由中国提议的反对微生物的战争现在正以真正健康的方式进行。

谢谢大家。

张博士(中国):主席先生,在我看来,应由联合国还是各国政府承担委员会成员履行这些职责的费用的主要考虑因素是这些成员根据其职能的性质所具有的地位。我同意比利时代表所作的区分,即有些委员会是政府代表为要审议的特殊议题而聚集在一起的。从这个角度来看,目前正在伦敦开会的灾区经济重建临时分设委员会可能本质上属于这种类型。也就是说,不同的参与政府有直接的利益。现在,我们正在考虑组成的委员会,主要是迄今组成的六个委员会——它们实际上具有理事会顾问的性质。这些委员会没有具体的行政职能,除非理事会赋予它们这种职能。我们都同意,他们的主要职能是向理事会提出建议。他们向理事会提交报告。理事会所有成员没有任何意见分歧,我想参加这些委员会的所有人也是如此。他们的职能是向理事会提供建议。

现在,我们确实对如何挑选这些理事会顾问有不同意见。那是意见的分歧。一种意见认为,这应该是个人。另一种意见是,这些顾问应该是政府的代表。这是很清楚的事情。进行投票时,不幸的是,这个问题没有明确提出。在这个问题上没时间了。我投了赞成票,我的一些同事也投了票,不完全是政府"的"代表。我们投票选举"来自"政府的代表。这里有很大的区别。我们中的一些人认为,由于这些专家仍然不太出名,特别是那些碰巧使用不太被广泛阅读或听到的语言说话和写作的专家。仅仅将那些用众所周知的语言写作的人视为专家,而将那些碰巧用不广为人知的语言写作的人视为非专家是不太恰当的。其实说得更直白一点,就是不公平。

因此,在这种情况下,至少中国代表团建议,在两年、三年或四年的试验期内,各国政府应提名这些专家顾问参加向理事会提供咨询意见的委员会。我希望这一点是清楚的。至少就中国代表团的立场以及在第二届会议上代表们的想法而言是如此。

没有时间进行这种讨论。进行了投票,然后被认为是政府"的"代表。让我们回到这个话题。根据经济及社会理事会 1946 年 6 月 21 日通过的决议,E/84 号文件,第一次修订版,"所有委员会将由来自……的一名代表组成",请记住文件中的这一点。一名代表"由理事会从……若干联合国成员中选出……"即"……各委员会将由理事会选出在各委员会任职的联合国会员国代表组成。"

此外,"……为了确保委员会所涉各个领域的均衡代表性,秘书长应在这些政府最后提名代表并经理事会确认之前,与如此选出的政府进行协商"。这一点在决议的报告中得到了明确阐述。

尽管理事会决议明确提到由理事会选出的来自政府的成员,但不能排除对委员会成员的真实身份产生误解的可能性。因此,例如,根据秘书长关于本组织工作的报告,即秘书处非常干练地编写的小册子、文件,即 A/65 号文件第 14 页,委员会将由政府"的"代表组成。我认为犯这样的错误是非常不幸的。这样写的人不知道我们花了多少时间讨论这个问题。因此,有必要澄清委员会成员的地位,不要再留下任何疑问。关于各委员会成员应该是理事会挑选的"来自"政府或会员国的代表的决定,是在讨论各委员会的一般组成,特别是经济和就业委员会的组成时首次达成的。这是 E/J. C/1 号和 E/J. C/2 号文件。理事会的"代表"是指政府指定的人。这就是对它的解释。在随后的讨论中,主席明确表示"……理事会选定的政府或理事会选定的成员国可以选择派遣政府代表或政府以外的专家。"

我想我们许多人仍然记得那个解释,因为我迫使主席发表了那个声明。否则我会认为这个决定不明确。这出现在 E/J. C/2 号文件第 4 页。与会者还同意,一国政府提名的成员是否应作为该国政府的代表——再次引用——"该国政府的代表应代表有关政府发言",将"由各国政府决定"这再次出现在 E/J. C/2 号文件第 4 页。现在一切都很清楚——至少对我们大多数投票赞成该决议的人来说非常清楚——我们不是投票支持政府代表,尽管一些投票赞成该决议的成员投票支持政府成员。我们中的许多人,或者几个人,投票支持由理事会选出的会员国代表在不同的委员会中任职。如果这一点很清楚,那么接下来似乎应该是支付费用的问题,即理事会咨询职能委员会成员的费用,而挑选过程目前是固定的,首先由理事会挑选成员国,然后由成员国指定代表,这些代表可以是政府代表,也可以不直接受雇于政府;他们可能代表政府说话,也可能代表自己说话。然而,从理事会的角度来看,他们都是以个人专家的身份发言。我想这是许多投票赞成这项措施的人的理解,当然,我相信人们有理由说这些代表必须是政府的代表。这些原因也已经非常清楚地阐述过,我现在只是在阐述,因为一些投赞成票的成员投票支持理事会选出的会员国代表担任委员会成员。我不认为有必要再次回去改变投票。这不是一个好的程序,所以让我们保持现有的指示,因为主席明确表示,虽然一些成员投票支持政府代表,而我确信其他一些成员也会这样做,但由于那些成员在投票中在场,那一票能够成为多数票,他们投票支持理事会选定的会员国政府。如果是这样,我们就让表决保持原样,但同时明确这些委员会成员的职能,即向理事会提供咨询。如果是这样的话,似乎费用应该由联合国支付。

[戴维拉（Davila）先生返回并在智利代表团的席位上就座。]……（此时，诺埃尔·贝克先生抵达并就任英国代表团团长）……

(2)会议发言内容纪要[①]

本次会议【会议纪要】【纪要影像】和【纪要译文】又见《世界合作共赢的中国贡献》一书第96-98页。[②]

【会议纪要】

Mr. CHANG（China）congratulated the Secretariat on the work it had done, approved the contents of the report presented and recommended the setting up of a small committee to settle certain details of drafting. The representatives of the UNITED STATES OF AMERICA and BELGIUM associated themselves with the views expressed by the Chinese representative.

The representative of INDIA supported what Mr. Chang（China）had said, and stated that his country, being particularly interested in the fight against diseases carried by microbes, considered it necessary that the nations should ratify the Convention and Protocol of the new Organization as a matter of the greatest urgency.

Mr. MARTIN（Canada）pointed out that his country was the first to have formally agreed to the decisions taken at New York.

Replying to a question by the Canadian representative, the CHAIRMAN stated that, up to date, only three nations had ratified the legal instruments of the World Health Organization（Canada, China and the United Kingdom）but he hoped that within a year, the other nations would have signified their approval.

---

① UN Document：E/SR. 3, p. 28, p. 29, p. 31.
② 孙平华编著：《世界合作共赢的中国贡献：张彭春在联合国经济及社会理事会的发言》，天津社会科学院出版社 2023 年 1 月版，第 96-98 页。

Mr. CHANG (China) pointed out that those commissions had no executive functions; they acted mainly as advisers to the Council. It was a pity that the Council, in altering the composition of the commissions, had not expressed itself sufficiently clearly on this point in its resolution. The Council's attitude was that members of commissions acted in an advisory capacity for the Council; their expenses should therefore be borne by the United Nations.

【纪要影像】

Mr. CHANG (China) congratulated the Secretariat on the work it had done, approved the contents of the report presented and recommended the setting up of a small committee to settle certain details of drafting. The representatives of the UNITED STATES OF AMERICA and BELGIUM associated themselves with the views expressed by the Chinese representative.

The representative of INDIA supported what Mr. Chang (China) had said, and stated that his country, being particularly interested in the fight against diseases carried by microbes, considered it necessary that the nations should ratify the Convention and Protocol of the new Organization as a matter of the greatest urgency.

Mr. MARTIN (Canada) pointed out that his country was the first to have formally agreed to the decisions taken at New York.

Replying to a question by the Canadian representative, the CHAIRMAN stated that, up to date, only three nations had ratified the legal instruments of the World Health Organization (Canada, China and the United Kingdom) but he hoped that within a year, the other nations would have signified their approval.

Mr. CHANG (China) pointed out that those commissions had no executive functions; they acted mainly as advisers to the Council. It was a pity that the Council, in altering the composition of the commissions, had not expressed itself sufficiently clearly on this point in its resolution. The Council's attitude was that members of commissions acted in an advisory capacity for the Council; their expenses should therefore be borne by the United Nations.

图片 3.4：张彭春在经社理事会第三届第 3 次会议发言纪要

【纪要译文】

张先生(中国)对秘书处所做的工作表示祝贺,同意所提交报告的内容,并建议成立一个小型委员会来解决起草工作的某些细节问题。美国代表和比利时代表赞同中国代表所表达的意见。

印度代表支持张先生(中国)的发言,并指出,印度对防治微生物携带的疾病特别感兴趣,认为各国有必要将批准新组织的公约和议定书作为最紧迫的事项。

马丁(Martin)先生(加拿大)指出,加拿大是第一个正式同意在纽约作出的决定的国家。

主席在答复加拿大代表的问题时说,迄今为止,只有三个国家(加拿大、中国和英国)批准了世界卫生组织的法律文书,但他希望在一年内,其他国家会表示签署同意。

张先生(中国)指出,这些委员会没有行政职能;他们主要担任委员会的顾问。遗憾的是,理事会在改变各委员会的组成时,没有在其决议中就这一点充分明确地表达自己的看法。理事会的态度是,委员会成员以理事会的咨询身份行事;因此,他们的费用应由联合国承担。

4. 张彭春在经社理事会 第三届第 5 次会议上的发言

联合国经社理事会第三届第 5 次会议,于 1946 年 9 月 21 日上午 10 时 30 分至下午 1 时 35 分,在纽约成功湖举行。本次会议的主要议题是建议大会授权理事会请求国际法院发表咨询意见、讨论附加议程项目、讨论各个委员会的费用问题等。中国代表张彭春率团参加了本次会议,并在会议上发言,其发言内容如下:

(1)会议发言全文记录①及译文

【全文记录】

Mr. Chang (China): The Chinese Delegation is very much interested indeed in the urgent and important matters covered by this resolution. Therefore, we should like to see that it be placed on the Agenda of the Council at this ses-

---

① UN Document:E/PV. 20, p. 41. (说明:该部分英文全文记录替代了孙平华编著的《世界合作共赢的中国贡献:张彭春在联合国经济及社会理事会的发言》,天津社会科学院出版社 2023 年 1 月版中第 99–100 页对应的法语全文记录。)

sion.

【全文译文】

张先生(中国):中国代表团确实非常关心这项决议所涉及的紧迫和重要的问题。因此,我们希望看到它被列入理事会本届会议的议程。

(2)会议发言内容纪要(无)

5. 张彭春在经社理事会第三届第6次会议上的发言

联合国经社理事会第三届第6次会议,于1946年9月21日下午2时30分至4时35分,在纽约成功湖举行。本次会议的主要议题是继续讨论委员会成员的费用问题等。中国代表张彭春率团参加了本次会议,并在会议上发言,提出三条建议案,其发言内容如下:

(1)会议发言全文记录①及译文

【全文记录】

Dr. Chang (China): Mr. President, you surprised me by calling me, but nevertheless I would like to say just two things. One is, let us emphasize the advisory nature of the commissions and sub-commissions. The discussion of how these Members are to be selected came much later. Originally we made the decision of having these commissions organized to assist and advise the Council on various important matters in which the Council is seriously interested. For the

---

① UN Document:E/PV.21, pp. 11-15, p. 21, p. 51, p. 61.

time being, let us not go back to that problem as to how these Members are to be selected. There is an agreed *modus operandi*. As to whether they are "of" or "from" I will not go into, but we do know from all the discussions that different people seem to understand it differently. However, we do agree that these people come to visit the Council. I think that is the most important thing. If that is the case, as a Council, as an important organ of the United Nations, we should remunerate the people who come here to advise us. That is the most important point. Whether these people speak as "of" the Government, namely speaking of the word "of" Government, or these people happen simply to be recommended by the Government there would be a difference. Our understanding was that this difference would be allowed. When they come however, they are here to advise the Council. If so, the Council at the part of the United Nations should pay for their travel expenses as well as the *per diem* subsistence. That is the first point.

I would like to stress that because we're beginning in our organization. It seems that it is very important for us to see clearly these things instead of getting so confused. These commissions and sub-commissions are here to advise the Council.

The second point I'd like to draw your attention to is the fact that expenses really are not limited to the traveling expenses and the *per diem* expenses. We must not forget that these people, especially when they come from a long distance, have to be paid their salaries. Take for instance, a person coming from my humble country. Even by air, it will take him about a week to two weeks to get here and then going back it will take about the same time. Now it takes about a month, roughly speaking to attend the meeting, more than a month. And then, at twice a year, it would be two or three months. That part of the salary must be taken care of. So we consider that that should be the contribution from the different Governments.

The governments may nominate them from private origin or from public offices. That part of it the different Governments will take care of. So that part of it must not be forgotten. There is that part of the expenses (to be paid) in some ways, you see. They're not at all free. We are not paying them salaries. We simply pay them *per diem* expenses while they're meeting.

Then as to another point, namely whether we should pay more than one Member to a commission or a sub-commission. I am inclined to think that in as much as these people who come to advise us are taken to be experts, they really come here at individuals. Naturally they have no assistance of a private secretary, they would enjoy it, but on the other hand we want them as individual experts. Therefore, I would like to see it simply stated like this because the Members of commissions and sub-commissions come to the United Nations to assist in this respect, the Council. Therefore, their travel expenses and their *per diem* expenses during the meeting should be taken care of by the United Nations. That is one. Secondly, in as much as they are invited to come to serve as experts we pay only the experts and if the expert should need another assistant or another expert or somebody to help him, that is up to him.

Some of them for instance, if they have positions in their own Governments or in their own research institutes, perhaps they can get an assistant to come, but that is another matter. So I should think in general, we would make it a rule that the United Nations will only pay one Member from each of the Member States selected by the Council to serve on the commission or sub-commissions.

Mr. Chang (China) seconded by M. Bousquet (France), suggested that the proposal be composed only of delegates or persons designated by governments.

The President clarified the question by saying that the proposal amounted to the Council nominating countries only, and he asked for a vote on the Soviet proposal.

Decision: *The proposal was adopted by eleven votes for and five against.* [1]

Dr. Chang (China): Mr. President, I may be saying something that is already in the wise mind of the President. I have a feeling perhaps that you may be leading that way. After hearing the hesitation and difficulty on the part of the Representative of the United States Delegation in the voting, if the position is put in a complex way, I think the President may have already thought of it, and probably was on the point of suggesting voting according to a simple manner. In other words, split the thing into three parts. Therefore I would like to reinstitute—I think probably the President would do so—the procedure as suggested by the Representative from the United Kingdom. That is very logical. First, how many agree to have traveling expenses paid by the United Nations, that is the first. Secondly, how many agree to have the *per diem* paid by the United Nations, of one Representative, and then how many would agree to have an assistant to both paid by the United Nations.

I think that is the logical thing. Probably that is already in the wise mind of the President.

The President: Now if the Chinese Representative will pardon my rather poor mind, I think I can put the matter to a vote.

Dr. Chang (China): Mr. President, I think it may be altogether advisable to begin our discussion in a meeting as the whole. If necessary, we may have a Drafting Committee over the details.

【全文译文】

张博士(中国):主席先生,你呼唤我让我很吃惊,但我还是想说两点。一是,让我们强调委员会和分设委员会的咨询性质。关于如何选择这些成员的讨论是在很久以后才开始的。最初,我们决定组织这些委员会,就理

附

录

---

① 编著说:该部分斜体为苏联代表费奥诺夫(Feonov)宣读的之前会议决定中的部分内容,其中涉及到张彭春先生。

事会非常关心的各种重要问题向理事会提供协助和咨询。目前,让我们不要回到如何选择这些成员的问题上来。有一个商定的工作方式。至于它们是"of"还是"from",我就不多说了,但我们从所有的讨论中确实知道,不同的人似乎对此有不同的理解。然而,我们确实同意这些人来访问理事会。我认为这是最重要的事情。如果是这样的话,作为理事会,作为联合国的一个重要机构,我们应该给来这里向我们提供建议的人报酬。这是最重要的一点。无论这些人是以"政府"的身份说话,即以政府"的"一员说话,还是这些人只是由政府推荐,都会有所不同。我们的理解是,这种差异是允许的。然而,当他们来的时候,他们是来这里向理事会提出建议的。如果是这样,联合国方面的理事会应该支付他们的旅费和每日生活津贴。这是第一点。

我想强调这一点,因为我们的组织刚刚起步。看清楚这些事情,而不是变得这么迷茫,似乎对我们来说很重要。这些委员会和分设委员会在此向理事会提供咨询意见。

我想提请您注意的第二点是,费用并不仅限于差旅费和每日津贴。我们不能忘记,这些人,尤其是来自远方的人,必须得到他们的工资。举个例子,一个人来自我卑微的国家。即使乘飞机,他也要花一周到两周的时间才能到达这里,然后回来也要花同样的时间。现在大概需要一个月,粗略来说参加会议,一个多月。然后,一年两次,这将是两三个月。那部分工资一定要管。因此,我们认为这应该是不同政府的贡献。

政府可以从私人或公职部门提名他们。这一部分将由不同的政府负责。所以这一部分不能被遗忘。你知道,在某些方面有那部分(要支付的)费用。他们一点也不自由。我们没有给他们发工资。我们只是在他们开会时支付他们每日的费用。

然后是另一个问题,即我们是否应该向委员会或分设委员会支付超过一名成员的费用。我倾向于认为,这些来给我们提建议的人被认为是专家,他们实际上是以个人身份来这里的。自然,他们没有私人秘书的帮助,他们会喜欢有人帮助,但另一方面,我们希望他们作为个人专家。因此,我希望简单地这样说,因为委员会和小组委员会的成员到联合国来是为了在这方面协助理事会。因此,他们在会议期间的旅费和每日津贴应由联合国负责。这是其一。第二,只要他们被邀请来担任专家,我们就只付给专家报酬,如果专家需要另一名助手或另一名专家或其他人来帮助他,那就由他决定。

例如,他们中的一些人,如果他们在自己的政府或自己的研究机构中有职位,也许他们可以请一名助手来,但那是另一回事。因此,我认为,总的来说,我们将制定一项规则,即联合国将只向理事会选出的每个成员国支付一名成员在委员会或小组委员会任职的费用。

张先生(中国)在布斯凯(Bousquet)先生(法国)的附议下建议,该提案只应由各国政府指定的代表或人员组成。

主席澄清了这个问题,他说这个提案只涉及理事会提名国家,他要求对苏联的提案进行表决。

决定:该提案以 11 票赞成、5 票反对获得通过。

张博士(中国):主席先生,我可能说了主席明智的想法。我有一种感觉,也许你正朝那个方向走。在听到美国代表团代表在表决中的犹豫和困难之后,如果以复杂的方式表明立场,我想主席可能已经想到了,并且可能正要建议以简单的方式进行表决。换句话说,把事情分成三部分。因此,我想恢复英国代表建议的程序——我想主席可能会这样做。这非常符合逻辑。首先,有多少人同意由联合国支付旅费,这是第一个问题。第二,有多少人同意由联合国支付一名代表的每日津贴,又有多少人同意由联合国支付代表和其助理的费用。

我认为这是合乎逻辑的事情。或许这已经是主席明智的想法了。

主席:如果中国代表原谅我的愚笨,我想我可以将这个问题付诸表决。

张博士(中国):主席先生,我认为以全体会议的形式开始我们的讨论是完全可取的。如果有必要,我们可能会有一个起草委员会来处理细节问题。

（2）会议发言内容纪要①

本次会议【会议纪要】【纪要影像】和【纪要译文】又见《世界合作共赢的中国贡献》一书第 101-102 页。②

【会议纪要】

Mr. CHANG（China）considered it advisable to stress the fact that these commissions should be regarded as advisory organs of the Council. It would then be logical for the United Nations to pay the travelling expenses and subsistence allowances of commission members. He suggested, however, that the expenses of the experts accompanying the advisers should not be paid by the United Nations.

Mr. CHANG（China）formulated the three proposals to be put to the vote：

（1）The proposal that the travelling expenses of members of commissions and sub-commissions should be paid by the United Nations.

Decision：*This proposal was adopted by seventeen votes to one.*

（2）The proposal that subsistence allowances of members of commissions and sub-commissions should be borne by the United Nations.

Decision：*This proposal was adopted by ten votes to eight.*

（3）The proposal that the United Nations should pay the travelling expenses and subsistence allowances of experts attached to a commission or sub-commission.

Decision：*This proposal was rejected by twelve votes to five, with one abstention.*

---

① UN Document：E/SR. 6, p. 42, p. 43.

② 孙平华编著：《世界合作共赢的中国贡献：张彭春在联合国经济及社会理事会的发言》，天津社会科学院出版社 2023 年 1 月版，第 101-102 页。

【纪要影像】

Mr. CHANG (China) considered it advisable to stress the fact that these commissions should be regarded as advisory organs of the Council. It would then be logical for the United Nations to pay the travelling expenses and subsistence allowances of commission members. He suggested, however, that the expenses of the experts accompanying the advisers should not be paid by the United Nations.

Mr. CHANG (China) formulated the three proposals to be put to the vote:

(1) The proposal that the travelling expenses of members of commissions and sub-commissions should be paid by the United Nations.

Decision: *This proposal was adopted by seventeen votes to one.*

(2) The proposal that subsistence allowances of members of commissions and sub-commissions should be borne by the United Nations.

Decision: *This proposal was adopted by ten votes to eight.*

(3) The proposal that the United Nations should pay the travelling expenses and subsistence allowances of experts attached to a commission or sub-commission.

Decision: *This proposal was rejected by twelve votes to five, with one abstention.*

图片 3.5:张彭春在经社理事会第三届第 6 次会议发言纪要

【纪要译文】

张先生(中国)认为应该强调,这些委员会应被视为理事会的咨询机构。因此,联合国支付委员会成员的旅费和生活津贴是合乎逻辑的。但是,他建议,陪同顾问的专家的费用不应由联合国支付。

张先生(中国)提出了三项付诸表决的提案:

(1)委员会和小组委员会成员的旅费应由联合国支付的建议。

决定:该提案以 17 票对 1 票获得通过。

(2)委员会和小组委员会成员的生活津贴应由联合国负担的建议。

决定:该提案以 10 票对 8 票获得通过。

(3)由联合国支付附属于委员会或小组委员会的专家的旅费和生活津贴的建议。

决定:该提案以 12 票对 5 票、1 票弃权被否决。

附
录

703

6.张彭春在经社理事会
第三届第7次会议上的发言

联合国经社理事会第三届第7次会议,于1946年9月23日上午10时30分至下午1时30分,在纽约成功湖举行。本次会议的主要议题是讨论和审议国际难民组织决议草案等。中国代表张彭春率团参加了本次会议,并在会议上发言,其发言内容如下:

(1)会议发言全文记录①及译文

【全文记录】

Dr. Chang (China): Mr. President, my remarks will be very brief, indeed. I only suggest a verbal alteration, a verbal amendment. Article II, paragraph (a) instead of the second line having "country of origin", to amend it to "countries of nationality of former habitual residents." That is just to bring it to uniformity with the Preamble. The third paragraph of the Preamble says "countries of nationality of former habitual residents". That is all.

【全文译文】

张博士(中国):主席先生,我的发言确实很简短。我只建议口头替换、口头修正。第二条第(a)款,将第二行的"原籍国"改为"前惯常居民的国籍国"。这只是为了与序言保持一致。序言第三段说"前惯常居民的国籍国"。仅此而已。

---

① UN Document: E/PV. 22, pp. 36–40.

(2)会议发言内容纪要①

本次会议【会议纪要】【纪要影像】和【纪要译文】又见《世界合作共赢的中国贡献》一书第 103-104 页。②

【会议纪要】

Mr. Chang (China), supported by Mr. Martin (Canada), suggested that the words "country of origin" in article II, paragraph 1(a) should be replaced by the words "countries of nationality or former habitual residence."

【纪要影像】

Mr. CHANG (China), supported by Mr. MARTIN (Canada), suggested that the words "country of origin" in article II, paragraph 1 (a) should be replaced by the words "countries of nationality or former habitual residence."

图片 3.6:张彭春在经社理事会第三届第 7 次会议发言纪要

【纪要译文】

张先生(中国)在马丁先生(加拿大)的支持下建议将第二条第 1 款(a)项中的"原籍国"改为"国籍国或前惯常居住地国"。

附
录

---

① UN Document:E/SR. 7, p. 46.
② 孙平华编著:《世界合作共赢的中国贡献:张彭春在联合国经济及社会理事会的发言》,天津社会科学院出版社 2023 年 1 月版,第 103-104 页。

7. 张彭春在经社理事会第三届第 12 次会议上的发言

　　联合国经社理事会第三届第 12 次会议,于 1946 年 9 月 28 日下午 2 时 45 分至晚上 7 时 15 分,在纽约成功湖举行。本次会议主要议题是讨论苏联代表关于与临时国际航空组织的关系的请求、讨论任命与非政府组织协商安排常设委员会等。中国代表张彭春率团参加了本次会议,并在会议上发言,其发言内容如下:

(1) 会议发言全文记录①及译文

【全文记录】

　　Dr. Chang (China): Quiet all day. Now, few words.

　　PICAO is analogous to a Postal Union. It is technical. Therefore, advisable to consider technical necessity.

　　Sir Girja Shankar Bajpai (India): I don't wish to interrupt my colleague from China, Mr. President, but on a point of order, if we agree upon a closure, we agree upon a closure for all.

　　Dr. Chang (China): Second point. Soviet Resolution suggests the suspending of all negotiations with PICAO. It did not say, or does not say, suspending all relationships with PICAO. I understand the negotiations are practically over. I am wondering whether the Soviet Delegation would like to amend their Resolution, otherwise the effect would not be so very clear.

　　Would it only stop negotiations and not stop further relationships?

---

　　①　UN Document: E/PV. 27, p. 106, pp. 121–122, p. 122, pp. 123–125

Dr. Chang (China): I have been waited the whole day to[①] make this beautiful speech of mine.

It is my very pleasant duty as well as real enjoyment to make this suggestion:

As you can see, Mr. President, on Page 483 there is s Standing Committee that has already been constituted. Page 483, Number I: "The Economic and Social Council shall establish a Standing Committee, composed of the President of the Council and five Members of the Council, who will be assisted by the Assistant Secretary-General, ... This Committee will review applications for consultative status submitted by non-governmental organizations, and make recommendations to the Council. It shall be known as the Committee on Arrangements for Consultation with Non-Governmental Organizations."

When that Committee was constituted, its duty was to review applications. Being a Member of that Committee, I must say that the reviewing of the applications is rather a burdensome job, if not exactly a tedious one. Naturally there are Members on this Committee who have done more work than others—especially the Representative of the United Kingdom Delegation and the Representative from the United States Delegation. They have been doing a great deal of work—especially the gentleman who has gone over the long list of women's organizations. Inasmuch as he has done so much of the burdensome duty, we must not deprive him of the pleasure of seeing the ladies after they are admitted.

Consequently, I propose that the Standing Committee that we already have—and this is the sort of a job that really has no political implication to be

附录

---

① 由于本句残缺，对照了法语版全文记录（见 E/P. V. 27, p. 86.）: "M. Chang (Chine)(Interprétation): J'ai attend toute la jourée pour faire ce magnique discours et c'est pour moi un plaisir et un devoir que de présenter cette suggestion. 汉语大意是: 张先生（中国）: 我等了一整天才发表这个神奇的演讲，提出这个建议对我来说是一种荣幸和责任。

read into it—should deal not only with the reviewing of applications but also with consultations. In other words, we shall combine reception and hospitality and allow the people who do the application-reviewing to also do the pleasant duty of shaking hands with the organizations that are admitted.

Sir, I recommend that the same Committee shall take on the two duties. ①

Mr. Chernykov (Soviet Union) (Second interpretation; original in Russian): The Delegation of the Soviet Union supports the proposal made by the Chinese Representative.

Dr. Chang (China): Mr. President, may I make a suggestion—that on Monday, if the President should see fit, he may require all Members speaking to speak in code.

Mr. Chernykov (Soviet Union) (Second interpretation; original in Russian): I think it would be in the interest of the work we perform here to adjourn now until Monday.

Dr. Chang (China): I support the proposal of the Representative of the Soviet Union.

【全文译文】

张博士(中国):安静一整天。现在,简单说几句。

临时国际航空组织(PICAO)类似于邮政联盟。这是技术性的。因此,考虑技术必要性是明智的。

吉尔贾·尚卡尔·巴杰帕伊(Girja Shankar Bajpai)爵士(印度):主席

---

① 2023 年 5 月 23 日,笔者就该文件中所存在的问题,通过邮件与联合国图书馆联系(https://www.un.org/en/library/contact-us),随后收到回复(ask@un.libanswers.com)说图书馆正在翻新,可能 7 月份才能返回图书馆帮助核查相关内容。(Janine Pickardt:Dear Pinghua Sun, Thank you very much for bringing this to our attention. We will have to check the original print copy to see if information got lost in the scanning process or if the original text is already missing this text. Due to ongoing renovation work in the Library building, we currently do not have access to our print collection. We are planning to return to the Library in July 2023.) 2023 年 7 月 12 日再次收到回复说没有问题,原文就是这样。

先生,我不想打断我的中国同事,但就程序问题而言,如果我们同意结束,我们就同意对所有人结束。

张博士(中国):第二点。苏联决议建议中止与临时国际航空组织的所有谈判。它过去或现在没有说,中止与临时国际航空组织的一切关系。我知道谈判实际上已经结束了。我不知道苏联代表团是否想修改他们的决议,否则效果不会如此明显。

它只会停止谈判而不会停止进一步的关系吗?

张博士(中国):主席先生,我等了整整一天来做我的这个漂亮的演讲。

提出这个建议是我非常愉快的职责,也是我真正的享受:

正如你所看到的,主席先生,在第483页,有一个已经组成的常设委员会。第483页,第一号:"经济及社会理事会应设立一个常设委员会,由理事会主席和五名理事会成员组成,并由助理秘书长协助,……该委员会将审查非政府组织提出的咨商地位申请,并向理事会提出建议。它将被称为与非政府组织协商安排委员会。"

该委员会成立时,其职责是审查申请。作为该委员会的成员,我必须说,审查申请是一项相当繁重的工作,如果不是一项十分乏味的工作的话。自然,本委员会中有些成员比其他人做了更多的工作,特别是英国代表团的代表和美国代表团的代表。他们做了大量的工作——特别是那位检查了一长串妇女组织名单的先生。因为他做了这么多的繁重的职责,我们不能剥夺他看到女士们被接纳后的快乐。

因此,我提议,我们已经设立的常设委员会——这是一项真正没有任何政治含义的工作——不仅应该审查申请,而且应该进行协商。换句话说,我们将把接待和款待结合起来,让审查申请的人也能愉快地与被接纳的组织握手。

主席先生,我建议由同一委员会负责这两项职责。

切尔尼科夫先生(苏联)(第二次口译,原文俄语):苏联代表团支持中国代表提出的建议。

张博士(中国):主席先生,我可以提一个建议吗——星期一,如果主席认为合适,他可以要求所有发言的成员用暗语发言。

切尔尼科夫先生(苏联)(第二次口译,原文俄语):我认为现在休会到星期一将有利于我们在这里进行的工作。

张博士(中国):我支持苏联代表的建议。

(2)会议发言内容纪要①

本次会议【会议纪要】【纪要影像】和【纪要译文】又见《世界合作共赢的中国贡献》一书第105-106页。②

【会议纪要】

Mr. CHANG (China) remarked that the proposal of the Union of Soviet Socialist Republics suggested that negotiations should be suspended, but did not mean that the relationship should be terminated.

Mr. CHANG (China) pointed out that there was already in existence a committee to consider applications for admission from non-governmental organizations, known as the NGO Committee, and he thought that the same committee might well take over both functions.

---

① UN Document: E/SR. 12, p. 81, p. 82.
② 孙平华编著:《世界合作共赢的中国贡献:张彭春在联合国经济及社会理事会的发言》,天津社会科学院出版社2023年1月版,第105-106页。

Mr. CHANG (China) remarked that the proposal of the Union of Soviet Socialist Republics suggested that negotiations should be suspended, but did not mean that the relationship should be terminated.

Mr. CHANG (China) pointed out that there was already in existence a committee to consider applications for admission from non-governmental organizations, known as the NGO Committee, and he thought that the same committee might well take over both functions.

图片 3.7:张彭春在经社理事会第三届第 12 次会议发言纪要

【纪要译文】

张先生(中国)评论,苏维埃社会主义共和国联盟的提案建议暂停谈判,但并不意味着终止关系。

张先生(中国)指出,已经存在一个委员会负责审议非政府组织的申请,称为非政府组织委员会,他认为同一个委员会可以很好地同时承担这两项职能。

8. 张彭春在经社理事会第三届第 14 次会议上的发言

联合国经社理事会第三届第 14 次会议,于 1946 年 9 月 30 日下午 2 时 45 分至晚上 7 时 45 分,在纽约成功湖举行。本次会议主要议题是讨论联合国善后救济总署议案开展的与国际儿童应急基金有关的福利工作等。中国代表张彭春率团参加了本次会议,并在会议上发言,其发言内容如下:

（1）会议发言全文记录①及译文

【全文记录】

Dr. Chang（China）：I think that inasmuch as we are going to have maybe two days, if not three days, more we should conserve some of our energy. Furthermore, the teams are not all of the same size. If that had been the case, we could have longer sessions. Then, people could take turns, substitutes could be put in. It happens that my Delegation is not the smallest and there are many that are smaller than mine. Consequently, considering the smaller Delegations, we should not work them too hard. So, I am personally of the opinion that at least for Monday and Tuesday we should stop at 7:00, and if there is a necessity for meetings on Wednesday and Thursday we can continue.

Dr. Chang（China）：Mr. President, the Chinese Delegation heartily supports the resolution. While we help the children, the children can help us. Confucius said, "A great man is he who has not lost the heart of the child." Therefore, we hope that in doing this, we may all be benefited.

【全文译文】

张博士（中国）：我认为，由于我们可能只有两天——如果不是三天的话，我们应该节省一些精力。此外，这些团队的规模也不尽相同。如果是这样的话，我们可以有更长的会议。然后，人们可以轮流，可以纳入替补人员。碰巧我国代表团规模不是最小的，还有许多比我国代表团小的代表团。因此，考虑到较小的代表团，我们不应该让他们太辛苦。因此，我个人认为，至少在星期一和星期二，我们应该在7点停止，如果有必要在星期三和星期四开会，我们可以继续。

张博士（中国）：主席先生，中国代表团衷心支持这项决议。当我们帮

---

① UN Document：E/PV. 29, p. 11, pp. 136–140.

助孩子们时,孩子们也能帮助我们。孔子说:"大人者,不失其赤子之心。"①因此,我们希望在这样做的时候,我们都能受益。

(2)会议发言内容纪要②

本次会议【会议纪要】【纪要影像】和【纪要译文】又见《世界合作共赢的中国贡献》一书第 107 页。③

【会议纪要】

Mr. Chang (China) warmly supported the proposals submitted to the Council.

【纪要影像】

Mr. CHANG (China) warmly supported the proposals submitted to the Council.

图片 3.8:张彭春在经社理事会第三届第 14 次会议发言纪要

【纪要译文】

张先生(中国)热烈支持提交理事会的提案。

---

① 其实,这里可能是张彭春误将孟子的话说成孔子的话了,该句话见:《孟子·离娄章句下》,通过对联合国经济及社会理事会会议记录的研究,发现张彭春先生在该理事会第五届第 88 次会议上,也援引了孟子的这句名言(见 UN Document:E/PV.88,p. 61.)。又见孙平华编著:《世界合作共赢的中国贡献:张彭春在联合国经济及社会理事会的发言》,天津:天津社会科学院出版社 2023 年 1 月版,第 241 页和第 244 页。
② UN Document:E/SR. 14,p. 98.
③ 孙平华编著:《世界合作共赢的中国贡献:张彭春在联合国经济及社会理事会的发言》,天津社会科学院出版社 2023 年 1 月版,第 107 页。

9.张彭春在经社理事会
第三届第 15 次会议上的发言

联合国经社理事会第三届第 15 次会议,于 1946 年 10 月 1 日上午 10 时 30 分至下午 1 时 33 分,在纽约成功湖举行。本次会议主要议题是审议哥伦比亚代表关于建立财政委员会的修正案、审议建立人口委员会的议案等。中国代表张彭春率团参加了本次会议,并在会议上发言,其发言内容如下:

(1)会议发言全文记录①及译文

【全文记录】

Mr. Chang (China): Mr. President, the Chinese Delegation has already expressed its support of this resolution for the establishment of a Fiscal Commission and the Chinese Delegation would like to see its early realization. We also appreciate the contribution made by the distinguished Representative of Colombia.

【全文译文】

张先生(中国):主席先生,中国代表团已表示支持设立财政委员会的决议,并希望这一决议早日实现。我们还赞赏尊敬的哥伦比亚代表所做的贡献。

---

① UN Document: E/PV.30, p. 21

(2)会议发言内容纪要①

本次会议【会议纪要】、【纪要影像】和【纪要译文】又见《世界合作共赢的中国贡献》一书第 108-109 页。②

【会议纪要】

Mr. Dávila (Chile) supported the Colombian proposal. It had been on the agenda since the first session of the Council, and prompt action was desirable. Mr. Noel-Baker (United Kingdom) and Mr. Chang (China) also supported this proposal.

【纪要影像】

Mr. DÁVILA (Chile) supported the Colombian proposal. It had been on the agenda since the first session of the Council, and prompt action was desirable. Mr. NOEL-BAKER (United Kingdom) and Mr. CHANG (China) also supported the proposal.

图片 3.9:张彭春在经社理事会第三届第 15 次会议发言纪要

【纪要译文】

达维拉(Dávila)先生(智利)支持哥伦比亚的提议。自理事会第一届会议以来,它就一直列在议程上,需要立即采取行动。内欧·贝克(Noel Baker)先生(英国)和张先生(中国)也支持这项提议。

---

① UN Document:E/SR. 15, p. 100.
② 孙平华编著:《世界合作共赢的中国贡献:张彭春在联合国经济及社会理事会的发言》,天津社会科学院出版社 2023 年 1 月版,第 108-109 页。

10. 张彭春在经社理事会
第三届第 16 次会议上的发言

联合国经社理事会第三届第 16 次会议,于 1946 年 10 月 1 日下午 2 时 45 分至晚上 7 时 15 分,在纽约成功湖举行。本次会议主要议题是审议特别委员会国际难民组织财政报告等。中国代表张彭春率团参加了本次会议,并在会议上发言①,其发言内容如下:

(1)会议发言全文记录及译文

【全文记录】

The President：This paper was circulated only today and is rather voluminous and very important. Therefore I propose that we should take it into consideration tomorrow morning. Do you agree?

Now the report of the Council Non-Governmental Organizations Committee.

Dr. Chang (China)：A point of order Mr. President. I did not understand how we disposed of this report.

The President：We will take it tomorrow morning.

Dr. Chang (China)：We will have a chance of suggesting amendments?

The President：Yes certainly. It is document E/189.

【全文译文】

主席:这份文件今天才分发,篇幅很大,非常重要。因此,我建议我们

---

① UN Document：E/PV. 31, p. 102.

明天上午考虑这个问题。你同意吗?

现在是理事会非政府组织委员会的报告。

张博士(中国):程序问题,主席先生。我不明白我们是如何处理这份报告的。

主席:我们将在明天上午进行表决。

张博士(中国):我们将有机会提出修正案吗?

主席:是的,当然。这是 E/189 号文件。

(2)会议发言内容纪要(无)

11. 张彭春在经社理事会第三届第 17 次会议上的发言

联合国经社理事会第三届第 17 次会议,于 1946 年 10 月 2 日上午 10 时 30 分至下午 1 时 30 分,在纽约成功湖举行。本次会议主要议题是审议特别委员会国际难民组织财政报告等。中国代表张彭春率团参加了本次会议,并在会议上发言,其发言内容如下:

(1)会议发言全文记录①及译文

【全文记录】

Dr. Chang (China): First of all, may I add my humble words of appreciation for the work done by the *ad hoc* committee, under the leadership of our distinguished Indian colleague. I do not have much to say. A few lines have been passed around. May I just call your attention to page 8? As a matter of

① UN Document: E/PV. 32, pp. 11-20, pp. 22-25.

fact, this is not a request so much for additional appropriations; it is really a matter of making this report look a little better worded. By that I mean, if you look at Page 8, you will find on the second line "... for the repatriation of 62,911 overseas Chinese." Then it is followed all the way through with this detail figure, 62,911. For instance, about the middle, that is, the fourteenth line, again you will see that figure. The question has been raised as to how we know the exact figure down to one person, not one more nor one less. I understand this matter was given some attention at the Committee meeting, but later on, due to other things, it was not finally rounded out. So, I suggest something like this: That the figure of 62,911 overseas Chinese, who are desiring to return to their places of habitual residence, be reduced to around figure, to 60,000. After all, it is a mere rough estimate. The number of registered people in China, wanting to return, seems to be increasing almost from day to day, because a latest figure I got about a week or ten days ago were thirty or forty more than the report received some few weeks before that. So, we cannot estimate the detail numbers. It does not look well on the report to make the number so detailed, so I suggest that we decrease that estimate to a round figure of 60,000, and add, however, a little on to the other item, namely, the Chinese stranded abroad on account of the war, who desire repatriation to China. The later figure I have received, in round numbers, is about 10,000 already estimated. They come from different parts, mostly from around China, but also some in Italy, some in Germany. The numbers are now being investigated, the detailed numbers. So, they are really displaced persons also coming within our definition. I am suggesting this little change in the language. I think it will make the report look better. I have consulted with some of the Members of the Committee, and they seem to agree that this minor change would not really alter the report very much.

The changes then will be as follows. Will you kindly turn to Page 8, line

2? Change the first figure, 3,140,000—that is calculated on the basis of 62,911—to 3,250,000. You can see that that is changing that figure of 62,911 to 60,000, a round figure, and allowing 5,000, a round figure, for the stranded Chinese who desire repatriation to China. That is all. So the whole thing should read like this: You see, the second figure, 62,911 is changed to 60,000, and then after the words "overseas Chinese", at the end of the second line, you add these words "... and 5,000 Chinese stranded abroad on account of the war, who desire repatriation to China."

If you like, we can add to these few words, "... who desire repatriation to China." Then, at the beginning of line 14, change the figure 62,911 to 60,000, so that it is just round figures. Then, at the end of the paragraph, at the end of 5(a), add the following: "With reference to 10,000 Chinese stranded abroad, the *ad hoc* Committee is of the opinion that roughly half of the number may be transported back to China during the first financial year. Figuring on the lowest average cost of transportation at $50.00 per person, an item of $250,000 is included in the provisional budget." In other words, it is counting on the same average.

The whole suggestion is to round the figures out, instead of having just to say "nine hundred eleven". Nobody knows, and I think at this moment the registered people, perhaps, is already 27 more—I do not know. Also, to take into account that there are such people who are being registered and being prepared to return from abroad. The rough figure I have received is around 10,000, so we say about 5,000 may be taken care of during the next year.

That is all. Mr. President.

Dr. Chang (China): Mr. President, I appreciate the remarks of my distinguished colleagues; especially do I appreciate and accept the correction suggested by the United States Representative. I think it does make it clearer, although, as you may see, as amended, it would read, you see, like this: The

附
录

first two lines: "$3,250,000 for the repatriation of 60,000 overseas Chinese, and 5,000 Chinese stranded abroad on account of the war, who desire repatriation to China."

So, it is also very clearly stated, it is not in addition to the budget at all. But the United States Representative did make this clear. So I accept his alteration. The last line of my amendment, instead of "is included in the Provisional Budget," is to read: "is included in the amount $3,250,000, as mentioned above." That is quite acceptable, and that does make it clearer.

【全文译文】

张博士(中国):首先,请允许我对特设委员会在我们尊敬的印度同事的领导下所做的工作表示赞赏。我没什么好说的。传阅了几行内容。我可以请你注意第 8 页吗?事实上,这并不是要求额外拨款;这确实是一个让这份报告看起来措辞更好一点的问题。我的意思是,如果你看第 8 页,你会发现在第 2 行"……遣返 62,911 名华侨。"然后是这个详细数字——62,911。例如,在中间,也就是第 14 行,你会再次看到那个数字。有人提出这样一个问题,即我们如何知道精确到一个人的确切数字,而不是多一个或少一个。据我所知,这件事在委员会会议上得到了一些关注,但后来,由于其他事情,它没有得到最终解决。因此,我的建议是这样的:希望返回故里的 62,911 名海外华人应减少到 60,000 人左右。毕竟,这只是一个粗略的估计。希望回国的中国登记人数似乎每天都在增加,因为我大约一周或十天前得到的最新数字比几周前收到的报告多三四十人。因此,我们无法估计具体的数字。在报告中把这个数字写得如此详细是不合适的,所以我建议我们把这个估计数减少到 6 万的整数,但在另一个项目上增加一点,即由于战争而滞留国外并希望返回中国的中国人。我收到的后来的数字,大概是 10,000。他们来自不同的地方,大部分来自中国各地,但也有一些在意大利,一些在德国。现在正在调查这些数字,详细的数字。因此,他们是真正的流离失所者,也符合我们的定义。我建议在语言上做一点小小的改变。我认为这会使报告看起来更好。我同委员会的一些成员进行了磋商,他们似乎同意这一微小的改动不会真正对报告产生很大的影响。

接下来的变化如下。请翻到第 8 页第 2 行好吗? 将第一个数字 3,140,000(根据 62,911 计算)更改为 3,250,000。你可以看到,这将把 62,911 人的数字改为 60,000 人,一个整数,并允许 5,000 人,一个整数,给那些希望返回中国的滞留中国人。仅此而已。所以整个事情应该是这样的:你看,第二个数字,62,911 改为 60,000,然后在"海外华人"一词之后,在第 2 行的末尾,你加上这些话"⋯⋯和 5,000 名因战争而滞留国外的中国人,他们希望返回中国"。

如果你愿意,我们可以在这几句话后面加上"⋯⋯希望被遣返中国的人"。然后,在第 14 行的开头,将数字 62,911 更改为 60,000,这样它只是一个整数。然后,在该段末尾,在第 5(a)段末尾,增加以下内容:"关于滞留在国外的 10,000 名中国人,特设委员会认为,在第一个财政年度,大约有一半的人数可能被送回中国。按每人 50 美元的最低平均运输费用计算,临时预算中包括一个 250,000 美元的项目。"换句话说,它指的是同一个平均值。

整个建议是把数字四舍五入,而不是只说"911"。没有人知道,我想目前登记的人数可能已经超过 27 人——我不知道。此外,要考虑到有些人正在登记并准备从国外返回。我收到的粗略数字是大约 10,000 人,所以我们说在下一年中可能会照顾到大约 5,000 人。

仅此而已。主席先生。

张博士(中国):主席先生,我感谢尊敬的同事们的发言;我尤其赞赏并接受美国代表建议的更正。我认为它确实说得更清楚了,尽管,正如你可能看到的,经修正后,它将读作这样:头两行:"3,250,000 美元用于遣返 60,000 名海外中国人和 5000 名因战争而滞留国外、希望返回中国的中国人。"

所以,它也说得很清楚,它根本不是在预算之外。但是美国代表确实清楚地表明了这一点。所以我接受他的改变。我的修正案的最后一行不是"包括在临时预算中",而是"包括在上述 3,250,000 美元的数额中"。这是完全可以接受的,这确实使事情变得更加清楚。

(2)会议发言内容纪要①

本次会议【会议纪要】【纪要影像】和【纪要译文】又见《世界合作共赢的中国贡献》一书第 110-112 页。②

【会议纪要】

Mr. CHANG(China)suggested that in paragraph 5(a),page 8, the number of Overseas Chinese,who desired to return to their place of habitual residence,could be reduced to a round figure since that number was based on a rough estimate and changed constantly;on the other hand, the second item, covering Chinese stranded abroad on account of the war and desiring repatriation to China, could be slightly increased. Mr. Chang accordingly proposed that paragraph 5(a)should be amended as follows:

Second line:Change the figure 62,911 to 60,000; change $3,140,550——calculated on the basis of 62,911——to $3,250,000. At the end of the line, add the words:"and 5,000 Chinese stranded abroad on account of the war."

Fourteenth line:change the figure 62,911 to 60,000. At the end of the paragraph, add the following sentence:"With reference to 10,000 Chinese stranded abroad, the ad hoc Committee is of the opinion that roughly half of them may be transported back to China during the first financial year. Figuring on the lowest average cost of transportation at $50 per person, an item of $250,000 is included in the provisional budget".

---

① UN Document:E/SR.17, pp. 116-117, p. 117.
② 孙平华编著:《世界合作共赢的中国贡献:张彭春在联合国经济及社会理事会的发言》,天津社会科学院出版社 2023 年 1 月版,第 110-112 页。

Mr. CHANG (China) accepted the correction proposed by the representative of the United States, and suggested that the last line of para-graph 5 (a) should then read: "... is included in the amount of $3.250,000 mentioned above."

【纪要影像】

Mr. CHANG (China) suggested that in paragraph 5 (a), page 8, the number of Overseas Chinese, who desired to return to their place of habitual residence, could be reduced to a round figure since that number was based on a rough estimate and changed constantly; on the other hand, the second item, covering Chinese stranded abroad on account of the war and desiring repatriation to China, could be slightly increased. Mr. Chang accordingly proposed that paragraph 5 (a) should be amended as follows:

Second line: Change the figure 62,911 to 60,000; change $3,140,550—calculated on the basis of 62,911—to $3,250,000. At the end of the line, add the words: "and 5,000 Chinese stranded abroad on account of the war."

Fourteenth line: change the figure 62,911 to 60,000. At the end of the paragraph, add the following sentence: "With reference to 10,000 Chinese stranded abroad, the *ad hoc* Committee is of the opinion that roughly half of them may be transported back to China during the first financial year. Figuring on the lowest average cost of transportation at $50 per person, an item of $250,000 is included in the provisional budget".

Mr. CHANG (China) accepted the correction proposed by the representative of the United States, and suggested that the last line of para-graph 5 (a) should then read: "... is included in the amount of $3,250,000 mentioned above."

图片 3.10:张彭春在经社理事会第三届第 17 次会议发言纪要

【纪要译文】

张先生(中国)建议,在第 8 页第 5(a)段中,希望返回惯常居住地的海外华侨人数可以减少到一个整数,因为这个数字是根据粗略估计得出的,并且不断变化;另一方面,第二项涉及因战争而滞留国外并希望返回中国的中国人,可能会略微增加。

因此,张先生提议将第 5(a)段修正如下:

第二行:将数字 62,911 改为 60,000;将 3,140,550 美元(62,911 基础上计算)改为 3,250,000 美元。在这一行的末尾,加上一句"还有 5,000 名中国人因战争而滞留国外。"

第十四行:将数字 62,911 改为 60,000。在本段末尾,增加如下一句话:"关于滞留海外的 10,000 中国人,特设委员会认为,其中大约一半可能在第一个财政年度被运回中国。根据每人 50 美元的最低平均运输成本计算,临时预算中包括 250,000 美元的项目。"

张先生(中国)接受美国代表提出的更正,并建议将第 5(a)段最后一行改为:"……包括在上述 3,250,000 美元的数额中。"

12. 张彭春在经社理事会 第三届第 18 次会议上的发言

联合国经社理事会第三届第 18 次会议,1946 年 10 月 2 日下午 2 时 45 分至晚上 7 时 30 分,在纽约成功湖举行。本次会议主要议题是关于粮农组织的法国建议案、法国代表提交的关于设立联合国研究实验室的决议草案、选举委员会成员等。中国代表张彭春率团参加了本次会议,并在会议上发言,其发言内容如下:

(1)会议发言全文记录①及译文

【全文记录】

Dr. Chang (China): Mr. President, the Chinese Delegation has the honor and pleasure of supporting this French proposal most heartily.

There is no need for me to add anything to the already lucid and generous statement made by the distinguished Representative of France. Therefore, I would like to see an explorative effort made by the Secretariat along this line of promoting cooperative research efforts in the world under the auspices of the United Nations.

Dr. Chang (China): Mr. President, several Representatives around me

---

① UN Document: E/PV. 33, pp. 33-35, p. 72, pp. 76-80.

have suggested that we might use this sheet and check on it instead of writing fifteen separate names. Some of us may have handwriting which may not be extremely legible.

Dr. Chang (China): Mr. President, may I just make it clear. It is really a suggestion by the distinguished colleague to my right who said that he wanted me to speak. Instead of using the white ballot, we can use this one—that is the first thing. The second thing is that instead of checking States which may be very indistinct, we simply cancel out the ones that we do not want. Then the rest of it will be simple cancel out the ones that we do not want. Then the rest of it will be simpler. Cross lines through the names we do not want. It is not at all signed. This is secret balloting.

Dr. Chang (China): Are we voting for the Transport Commission?

The President: No—only prepare yourself.

【全文译文】

张博士(中国):主席先生,中国代表团非常荣幸和高兴地衷心支持法国的这一提案。

我没有必要对尊敬的法国代表已经清晰而慷慨的发言做任何补充。因此,我希望看到秘书处沿着这一方向做出探索性努力,在联合国的主持下促进全世界的合作研究努力。

张博士(中国):主席先生,我周围的几位代表建议,我们可以用这张表核对一下,而不是分别写 15 个单独的名字。我们有些人的笔迹可能不是很清晰。

张博士(中国):主席先生,请允许我澄清一下。这实际上是我右边那位尊敬的同事提出的建议,他说他想让我发言。我们可以不用白色选票,而用这张——这是第一件事。第二件事是,我们不是检查可能非常模糊的状态,而是简单地取消我们不想要的状态。那么剩下的就简单了,取消掉我们不想要的。那么剩下的就简单多了。在我们不想要的名字上划线。

它根本无需签名。这是秘密投票。

张博士(中国):我们是要投票给运输委员会吗?

主席:不是——只是做好准备。

(2)会议发言内容纪要①

本次会议【会议纪要】【纪要影像】和【纪要译文】又见《世界合作共赢的中国贡献》一书第113-114页。②

【会议纪要】

Mr. CHANG（China）, Mr. Agyropoulos（Grecce）, Mr. Noel-Baker（United Kingdom）and Mr. Dávila（Chile）supported the French proposal. Mr. MALIK（Lebanon）also expressed approval, suggesting, however, that the United Nations research laboratories should be situated in the countries least favourably equipped in that respect.

【纪要影像】

Mr. CHANG (China), Mr. ARGYROPOULOS (Greece), Mr. NOEL-BAKER (United Kingdom) and Mr. DÁVILA (Chile) supported the French proposal. Mr. MALIK (Lebanon) also expressed approval, suggesting, however, that the United Nations research laboratories should be situated in the countries least favourably equipped in that respect.

图片3.11:张彭春在经社理事会第三届第18次会议发言纪要

---

① UN Document：E/SR.18, p. 126.

② 孙平华编著:《世界合作共赢的中国贡献:张彭春在联合国经济及社会理事会的发言》,天津社会科学院出版社2023年1月版,第113-114页。

【纪要译文】

张先生(中国)、阿伊罗普洛斯先生(希腊)、内欧·贝克先生(英国)和达维拉先生(智利)支持法国的提案。马利克先生(黎巴嫩)也表示赞同,但他建议联合国研究实验室应设在这方面设施最不完善的国家。

13. 张彭春在经社理事会
第三届第 19 次会议上的发言

联合国经社理事会第三届第 19 次会议,于 1946 年 10 月 3 日上午 10 时 30 分至下午 1 时 22 分,在纽约成功湖举行。本次会议主要议题是讨论人口委员会决议修正案等。中国代表张彭春率团参加了本次会议,并在会议上发言,其发言内容如下:

(1)会议发言全文记录①及译文

【全文记录】

Dr. Chang (China):Mr. President, that shows China is very sound fiscally.

Dr. Chang (China):Mr. President, just in line with the correction or amendment already made, please to turn to page 2, first line. I think the words "... be entitled to" should be deleted. "Such representatives shall take part in the proceedings of the Commission and shall not vote." That is enough.

Dr. Chang (China):I deeply appreciate the Indian Representative's calling my attention to this wording. It really should not be "shall"; just to make it

---

① UN Document:E/PV. 34, pp. 16-20, p. 66, pp. 67-70, p. 72, p. 81,

very simple "Such representatives may take part in the proceedings of the Commission but may not vote."

Secretary-General：The last proposal is quite clear. The last three sentences are deleted, but it does not mean anything because it is the duty of the Secretariat to invite all the specialized agencies to all meetings of the Committees.

Dr. Chang（China）：You are right.

Secretary-General：Therefore, the World Health Organization will be invited.

Dr. Chang（China）：You are right.

Dr. Chang（China）：I seem to have the same understanding as the Representative of the United States that the function of the corresponding Members is to correspond.

【全文译文】

张博士(中国)：主席先生,这表明中国的财政状况非常稳健。

张博士(中国)：主席先生,根据已经做出的更正或修正,请翻到第2页,第一行。我认为"……有权"这几个字应该删除。"这些代表应参加委员会的会议,但无表决权。"这就够了。

张博士(中国)：我非常感谢印度代表提醒我注意这一措辞。实在不应该是"应当";简单地说,"这些代表可以参加委员会的会议,但不能投票。"

秘书长：最后一项建议相当明确。最后三句被删除,但这没有任何意义,因为秘书处有责任邀请所有专门机构参加委员会的所有会议。

张博士(中国)：你说得对。

秘书长：因此,将邀请世界卫生组织。

张博士(中国)：你说得对。

张博士(中国)：我似乎与美国代表有着相同的理解,即准成员的职能是通信。

（2）会议发言内容纪要^①

本次会议【会议纪要】【纪要影像】和【纪要译文】又见《世界合作共赢的中国贡献》一书第 115-116 页。^②

【会议纪要】

Mr. Feonov（Union of Soviet Socialist Republics）proposed that in view of the fact that representatives of the three other commissions were not to be members of the Population Commission, the words "shall also include" should be changed to "shall invite." He also agreed to the suggestion of Mr. CHANG（China）that the words "be entitled to" should be deleted.

Following a suggestion by Sir Girja Shankar Bajpai（India）, Mr. CHANG（China）proposed the substitution of the word "shall" by the word "may." The proposal met with no objection.

Mr. Stinebower（United States of America）pointed out that the footnote on page 1 of the resolution（document E/226）was inaccurate, since the Council had made no decision regarding corresponding members.

He proposed the deletion in the text of the words：corresponding members" and of the footnote itself. Corresponding members were to correspond and not to appear in person. Mr. CHANG（China）agreed.

附

录

---

① UN Document：E/SR. 19, p. 137, p. 138.

② 孙平华编著：《世界合作共赢的中国贡献：张彭春在联合国经济及社会理事会的发言》，天津社会科学院出版社 2023 年 1 月版，第 115-116 页。

【纪要影像】

Mr. FEONOV (Union of Soviet Socialist Republics) proposed that in view of the fact that representatives of the three other commissions were not to be members of the Population Commission, the words "shall also include" should be changed to "shall invite." He also agreed to the suggestion of Mr. CHANG (China) that the words "be entitled to" should be deleted.

Following a suggestion by Sir Girja Shankar BAJPAI (India), Mr. CHANG (China) proposed the substitution of the word "shall" by the word "may." The proposal met with no objection.

Mr. STINEBOWER (United States of America) pointed out that the footnote on page 1 of the resolution (document E/226) was inaccurate, since the Council had made no decision regarding corresponding members.

He proposed the deletion in the text of the words: "corresponding members" and of the footnote itself. Corresponding members were to correspond and not to appear in person. Mr. CHANG (China) agreed.

图片 3.12：张彭春在经社理事会第三届第 19 次会议发言纪要

【纪要译文】

费奥诺夫(Feonov)先生(苏联)提议,鉴于其他三个委员会的代表不是人口委员会的成员,应将"还应包括"改为"应邀请"。他还同意张先生(中国)的建议,即删除"有权"一词。

根据吉尔拉·山卡尔·巴杰帕伊爵士(印度)的建议,张先生(中国)提议将"应"(shall)一词改为"可"(may)。这项提议没有遭到反对。

斯坦鲍尔(Stinebower)先生(美国)指出,决议(E/226 号文件)第 1 页的脚注不准确,因为理事会没有就准成员作出决定。

他建议删除案文中的"准成员"和脚注本身。准成员是采用通信方式,而不是亲自到场。张先生(中国)同意。

14. 张彭春在经社理事会
第三届第 20 次会议上的发言

联合国经社理事会第三届第 19 次会议 1946 年 10 月 3 日下午 2 时 45 分,在纽约成功湖举行,本次会议主要议题是审议关于受灾地区经济重建临时小组委员会报告的决议草案等。中国代表张彭春率团参加了本次会议,并在会议上发言,其发言内容如下:

(1)会议发言全文记录①及译文

【全文记录】

Dr. Chang (China): This concerns the rectification of a term, the correction of an anomaly.

We have considered the report of the Temporary Sub-Commission for Economic Reconstruction of Devastated Areas. As a matter of fact, the Sub-Commission is "sub" to nothing. It is, as a matter of fact, a Commission, directly advising the Council. It is not a sub-commission advising the Commission on Economic and Employment, as it was first contemplated. So, I have been informed by certain Members of Delegations, as well as of the Secretariat, that this anomaly has created some inconvenience. It is always right to make a rectification of a term as soon as that anomaly is detected. So, the Chinese Delegation has the honor in proposing this: the change of status to recognize the anomaly and to alter it as soon as possible.

In regard to the terms of reference, I think it does no harm to let the

① UN Document: E/PV. 35, pp. 47–50, p. 51, pp. 51–52, pp. 107–110, p. 111.

changed status, namely, the Temporary Commission for Economic Reconstruction of Devastated Areas, to keep the same set of references until our next session. For, after all, this Sub-Commission is a temporary one. The change of the name is, after all, only a matter of correcting an anomaly. However, when this suggestion was brought out, I was informed that this might cause some prejudice to the proposal for the establishment of an Economic Commission for Europe. In the spirit that the Chinese Delegation would like to promote, namely, conciliation, I agreed to leave this proposal to be dealt with together with the proposal for the creation of an Economic Commission for Europe. If that proposal should be discussed in the General Assembly—of course, this may be referred to the General Assembly altogether—but there is this consideration, namely, this is strictly a Council matter. It is not a matter that can be dealt with properly by the General Assembly.

So, Mr. President, I should like to find out the opinion of the Members here as to whether we might not take an action on this immediately. But if there should be any serious objection to its influence on the consideration of the proposal for the creation of an Economic Commission for Europe, if there should be, I should like to hear the reason. I am still ready to follow the spirit of conciliation.

Dr. Chang (China): Yes, Mr. President. I would have said nothing at all had not Resolution V been changed. If Resolution V had not been changed then Resolution VI would follow the same procedure. Now, inasmuch as Resolution V has been changed, to referring the matter to the General Assembly, I see some difficulty—or is my understanding correct that Resolution V has been changed?

The President: Resolution V is taken as it stands; no changes. Only two Representatives have said that they reserve the right to raise this question at the Assembly, but every Representative has the right to do so.

Dr. Chang (China): If that is the case, I also will follow the text as it stands.

The President: Resolution VI is approved.

Dr. Chang (China): Mr. President, before we got to the next item, may I just say one word in appreciation of what the Council has decided under Resolution III. The Chinese Delegation appreciates deeply the special significance of the decision of the Council to convene a meeting of the Far Eastern Working Group of the Sub-commission on Economic Reconstruction of Devastated Areas, in Nanking. This will be the first time for any agency of the United Nations to visit China, and to hold its meetings in China, and it is my hope, Mr. President, that we may be honored by the presence of the Secretary-General.

Dr. Chang (China): I think the suggestion of bringing this matter to the attention of the General Assembly, concerning the relationship with PICAO, is altogether wise and acceptable, because I think not only the Chinese Delegation, but others, may feel the same. However, I will speak for the Chinese Delegation, that the last vote taken was, as I expressed in my cold language,— we considered the matter technical, from both points of view; technical in the sense that having started negotiations, it was not necessary to stop it half way. However, the negotiations were finished, and I think it may be remembered that at that time I suggested the resolution proposed by the Soviet Delegation should be amended to include not only the negotiations, but also the relationship with the PICAO, and today that has been brought out.

It seems as though I would not, at this stage, vote again on that question, because if I should vote on the technical issue, it may be understood that I am politically sympathizing with some Government which we expressed, the Chinese Delegation expressed, very definitely, in the vote on the Narcotic Protocol, our attitude.

So, I think it is altogether wise for us not to take a vote on this issue, but to bring the matter to the General Assembly, because even though there should be an expression here, I think the matter would be brought up before the Assembly anyway.

Dr. Chang (China): Mr. President, in view of the fact that this is an Economic and Social Council, naturally the greatest emphasis should be on economic and social problems. There is that item in the Charter, but the Council, it seems to me, has the prerogative to decide which terms are exactly within our competence and which terms are not.

May I then, if there has been a resolution already, suggest an amendment saying that the question suggested should be referred to the General Assembly. In other words the so-called terms really could be so interpreted as not to include things which the Council feels itself requiring some higher mandate for us to get a directive.

【全文译文】

张博士(中国):这涉及一个术语的纠正,一个异常现象的纠正。

我们审议了灾区经济重建临时分设委员会的报告。事实上,分设委员会是微不足道的。事实上,它是一个委员会,直接向理事会提供咨询意见。它不是最初设想的向经济和就业委员会提供咨询意见的分设委员会。因此,一些代表团成员以及秘书处通知我,这种不正常现象造成了一些不便。一旦发现异常,立即对术语进行纠正总是正确的。因此,中国代表团荣幸地提出这一建议:改变现状,以认识到这种不正常现象,并尽快加以改变。

关于职权范围,我认为让已经改变的状态,即灾区经济重建临时委员会,在我们的下届会议之前保持同样的职权范围并无坏处。因为这个分设委员会毕竟是临时的。毕竟,名称的改变只是纠正一个异常现象。然而,当这项建议提出时,我被告知,这可能对设立欧洲经济委员会的提议造成一些损害。本着中国代表团希望推动的和解精神,我同意将这一提议与设立欧洲经济委员会的提议一并处理。如果应提议在大会讨论——当然,这可以完全提交给大会——但有这样一种考虑，即这完全是理事会的事情。这不是一个可以由大会适当处理的问题。

因此，主席先生，我想了解一下各位成员对我们是否可以不立即就此采取行动的看法。但是，如果有人强烈反对它对审议建立欧洲经济委员会的建议的影响，如果有人反对，我想听听理由。我仍然愿意遵循和解的精神。

张博士（中国）：是的，主席先生。如果第五号决议没有改变，我什么也不会说。如果决议五没有改变，那么决议六将遵循同样的程序。现在，由于决议五已被修改，我认为将该问题提交大会有一些困难——或者我的理解是决议五已被修改是正确的吗？

主席：决议五照原样通过；没有变化。只有两位代表说，他们保留在大会上提出这个问题的权利，但每位代表都有权这样做。

张博士（中国）：如果是这样，我也将依照原样文本。

主席：决议六获得批准。

张博士（中国）：主席先生，在我们讨论下一个项目之前，我想说一句话，对理事会根据第三号决议做出的决定表示赞赏。中国代表团高度赞赏经社理事会决定在南京召开灾区经济重建分设委员会远东工作组会议的特殊意义。这将是联合国任何一个机构第一次访问中国，并在中国举行会议，主席先生，我希望我们能因秘书长的光临而感到荣幸。

张博士（中国）：我认为，将这一涉及与临时国际航空组织关系的问题提请大会注意的建议是完全明智和可以接受的，因为我认为不仅中国代表团，而且其他代表团也可能有同感。然而，我将代表中国代表团说，正如我用冷漠的语言所表达的那样，我们从两个角度都认为这是一个技术性问题；技术性，因为谈判已经开始，没有必要中途停止。然而，谈判已经结束，我想人们可能记得，当时我建议对苏联代表团提出的决议进行修正，以便不仅包括谈判，而且包括与临时国际航空组织的关系，今天这一点已经提出。

看来我在现阶段不会再次就这个问题投票，因为如果我要就技术问题投票,可能会被理解为我在政治上同情我们所表达的某些政府,中国代表团在关于麻醉品议定书的表决中非常明确地表达了我们的态度。

因此,我认为,我们完全明智的做法是不就这个问题进行表决,而是将这个问题提交大会,因为即使在这里应该有所表示,我认为这个问题无论如何都会提交大会。

张博士(中国):主席先生,鉴于这是一个经济及社会理事会,最大的重点自然应该是经济和社会问题。《宪章》中有这一项内容,但在我看来,理事会有权决定哪些项目完全属于我们的职权范围,哪些项目不属于。

如果已经有了一项决议,我是否可以建议一项修正案,说所建议的问题应该提交大会。换句话说,所谓的项目实际上可以被解释为不包括理事会认为自己需要更高授权才能得到指示的事情。

(2)会议发言内容纪要①

本次会议【会议纪要】【纪要影像】和【纪要译文】又见《世界合作共赢的中国贡献》一书第 117-118 页。②

【会议纪要】

Mr. CHANG (China) thought, with regard to resolution VI, that the Temporary Sub-Commission for Economic Reconstruction of Devastated Areas should be raised to the status of a temporary commission, provided such action did not prejudice the establishment of an economic commission for Europe. With regard to resolution II, he expressed gratification that an agency of the United Nations would visit China, and expressed the hope that the Secretary-General would accompany it.

Mr. CHANG (China) supported the suggestion that the matter of PICAO

---

① UN Document:E/SR. 20, p. 143, p. 146, p. 147.

② 孙平华编著:《世界合作共赢的中国贡献:张彭春在联合国经济及社会理事会的发言》,天津社会科学院出版社 2023 年 1 月版,第 117-118 页。

should be submitted to the General Assembly. He would not vote on the USSR proposal, because it raised not a technical, but a political issue.

Mr. CHANG (China) proposed that the question of PICAO should be referred to the General Assembly.

Mr. CHANG (China) replied that one was a matter of signing a protocol, and the other was a matter of considering PICAO as a technical institution. He pointed out that in the Universal Postal Union there were members who did not agree completely in their political structures.

【纪要影像】

Mr. CHANG (China) thought, with regard to resolution VI, that the Temporary Sub-Commission for Economic Reconstruction of Devastated Areas should be raised to the status of a temporary commission, provided such action did not prejudice the establishment of an economic commission for Europe. With regard to resolution III, he expressed gratification that an agency of the United Nations would visit China, and expressed the hope that the Secretary-General would accompany it.

Mr. CHANG (China) supported the suggestion that the matter of PICAO should be submitted to the General Assembly. He would not vote on the USSR proposal, because it raised not a technical, but a political issue.

Mr. CHANG (China) proposed that the question of PICAO should be referred to the General Assembly.

Mr. CHANG (China) replied that one was a matter of signing a protocol, and the other was a matter of considering PICAO as a technical institution. He pointed out that in the Universal Postal Union there were members who did not agree completely in their political structures.

图片 3.13:张彭春在经社理事会第三届第 20 次会议发言纪要

【纪要译文】

张先生(中国)认为,关于第六号决议,应将灾区经济重建临时小组委员会提升为一个临时委员会,但这种行动不得妨碍欧洲经济委员会的成立。关于第三号决议,他对联合国一个机构将访问中国表示满意,并希望秘书长陪同访问。

张先生(中国)支持将临时国际民用航空组织(PICAO:Provisional International Civil Aviation Organization)问题提交大会的建议。他不会对苏联的提案进行投票,因为它提出的不是技术问题,而是政治问题。

张先生(中国)提议临时国际民用航空组织问题提交大会。

附录

张先生(中国)回答说,一个是签署议定书的问题,另一个是将临时国际民用航空组织视为一个技术机构的问题。他指出,在万国邮政联盟中,有些成员在其政治结构方面,并未达成一致意见。

15. 张彭春在经社理事会第三届第 21 次会议上的发言

联合国经社理事会第三届第 21 次会议,于 1946 年 10 月 3 日上午 8 时至 11 时 35 分,在纽约成功湖召开。本次会议主要议题是理事会非政府组织主席报告、讨论理事会会议安排以确认委员会成员、讨论理事会第四届会议日期等。中国代表张彭春率团参加本次会议,并在会议上发言,发言内容如下:

(1) 会议发言全文记录①及译文

【全文记录】

Dr. Chang (China): Including translation.

Dr. Chang (China): Mr. President, may I suggest that the present Representative of Colombia should be requested to take the chair for that special meeting.

Dr. Chang (China): There is another document—E/224.

Before commenting on it, may I particularly impressed sincere appreciation for the great and courteous consideration on the part of our Soviet colleague in using English in our deliberations this evening. Aside from my sincere respect for his high personal qualities—even though he is a Government Repre-

① UN Document: /PV. 36, p. 6, p. 76, pp. 81–85, pp. 87–90, p. 96, pp. 96–99.

sentative, he also has personal qualities—and, especially in appreciation of the great courtesy of his not using his great, beautiful language, *otchinkrassivaia*, I shall not speak in Chinese.

So very quickly, I am proposing something which I think my Soviet colleague would like to have an instituted—namely, a plan, if not a five-year plan, for our meetings, instead of having this haphazard way of meeting at all times of the year. As we all realize, we have just completed the election of the Members of the Commissions, so we shall be having at least and eleven-ring circus going.

By the eleven rings, I mean the eight Commissions just elected, the Narcotic Commission, the Refugee problem and the Devastated areas. We shall have at least eleven, if not more.

Now, if these various Commissions are going to meet on the average of two times every year, I really can envisage the terrible mess we shall be in during this coming year. So, I am suggesting these two things—although, as a matter of fact, I claim no originality in this; it came out of a discussion with our most patient and objective President.

The first point is:

"In order to assist members of the Council and the Secretariat in making plans for the work of the Council and its Commissions during 1947," somebody suggests "that the Secretary-General should be asked to prepare a calendar of sessions for the year, indicating approximately when meetings of the Council and of the Commissions and Sub-Commissions will take place. It would, of course, be understood that this calendar would not be binding on the Council or the Commissions but would serve as a useful guide in making forward plans."

That is one part of it.

This is the second part:

"Rule 2 of the Rules of Procedure prescribes that the Economic and Social

附

录

Council should meet 'not less than three times a year'. " Somebody "considers that if the Council is to carry out its heavy programme of work it will be necessary to hold four sessions . . . " and instead of "a year", we say "to hold four sessions in 1947".

We do not know how this will work; we can go on in an experimental spirit. I think in 1947 we shall have our busiest year, because all these various new Commissions will be meeting, and they will be submitting requests, reports, for us to make decisions on. So, I think, instead of "a year", I change it to "1947". That means that for next year we will try out this idea of having four sessions next year. At the end of next year, if we want to try something else, we may then change.

(*Continuing reading document E/224*) ". . . at approximately three monthly intervals. If it is generally agreed among members of the Council that four regular meetings should be held. . . "—then just delete "each year"—somebody "suggests that the Secretary-General should make appropriate provision in the calendar suggested above. "

As the matter fact, the plan is like this: to have four sessions next year—approximately, one in February, one in May, one in August and one in November. Then, with our eleven circuses going, it would be divided approximately into two groups—one group sandwiched in between, let us say, before February and before August; another group sandwiched in before May and before November. Thereby, the Council will be discussing, say, only five or six reports at one time, instead of maybe eight, nine or eleven all mixed together.

Also, we must remember that the specialized agencies are to take part in our discussions. It would be extremely useful for them to know ahead of time as to when we are going to meet. Then, they will be able to arrange their meeting accordingly.

So, from all these various points of view, I think it is altogether appropriate and necessary that we should have a plan for this coming year, the meeting, I should rather think, around the middle of each of these months. I have a reason for that "middle", because the middle of August will be just about two to three weeks before the General Assembly, so I should suggest, roughly speaking, about the middle of February, the middle of May, the middle of August, the middle of November, and having the other Commission sandwiched in between. I think with that sort of a plan we can get somewhere.

Thank you.

Dr. Chang (China): Mr. President, I am very much tempted to support the resolution introduced by my Soviet colleague that not only Representatives and Members of the Commissions should be considered in regard to their families, but also their consorts. However, that is not on the agenda. I do, however, to save time, accept all so far said. Let us pass the first one, namely, that we suggest to the Secretary-General that he do such a thing. Then, in regard to the second, I accept my French colleague's suggestion that they may serve as a basis for consideration. That is my second point.

My third point concerns a date for the next session. Instead of saying February 15th to February 28th, which will probably mean March 1st, let us just say, about February 15th. By that, I mean that it will not be without prejudice if you adopt my four-session plan, especially the 15th of August, because that will give two or three weeks before the General Assembly.

I still believe my Soviet colleagues, after thinking it over—I am not going to argue the case at the time—will come to see the wisdom of it, although it may cause him to do such much traveling, namely, with this sort of regularity we can get something simplified, and then all your specialized agencies will fix their dates according to our schedule. If we keep ourselves floating the specialized agencies don't know what to do. UNESCO will fix November, and then somebody else, and we have to fix our schedule according to their plans. We

附
录

are the Economic and Social Council of the United Nations; we are supposed to coordinate. Consequently, it is very important that we have a master plan and let them fix their program according to ours. I am not going to speak any more but I think the suggestion is very strong although there is no vote.

Dr. Chang (China): Mr. President, I think it is nothing but appropriate that one of the five official languages, namely, Chinese, should be heard, and I am sure the translators will be able to translate.

(*Dr. Chang then continued speaking, in Chinese*)

I think I will ask my colleague, Dr. Yang, to interpret.

Dr. Yang (China) (Interpretation of Dr. Chang's remarks): I am happy to be in the same crowd with our distinguished interpreter.

Mr. President, I feel particularly happy in congratulating the Council for its success because I can claim a good part of the success myself since I was the person who nominated the Honorable President, Dr. Stampar. So I can claim to have a share in what he has succeeded in doing. I am therefore particularly happy in congratulating this Council for having such a splendid Chairman to preside over our deliberations.

Dr. Chang (China): I have another sentence yet, please. I think considering the late hour, I will continue in English, but we must not, Mr. President, forget our Secretariat. The Secretary-General and all the Secretarial Staff have worked most devotedly and therefore they deserve a vote of sincere thanks from all of us. Furthermore, some of us have enjoyed the special hospitality of the Navy Cars. Therefore, may we ask the Secretary-General to send a note of appreciation on our part saying what courteous drivers they have been, these boys. I think a letter from us would be the proper thing to do.

Then, last of all, Mr. President, may I congratulate the Council for one thing very particularly. A while ago, about an hour ago, I went out and talked to one of the Members of the Secretariat. I said, "Have meetings here ever been held so late?" He said, "Once the Security Council."

I said, "How late?" He said, "Eleven o'clock."

So, Mr. President, I congratulate the Council for having broken that record.

【全文译文】

张博士(中国):包括翻译。

张博士(中国):主席先生,我可否建议请哥伦比亚现任代表担任这次特别会议的主席。

张博士(中国):还有一份 E/224 号文件。

在就此发表评论之前,请允许我对我们的苏联同事在今晚的讨论中使用英语所表现出的极大的礼貌表示由衷的赞赏。除了我对他崇高的个人品质——尽管他是政府代表,但他也有个人品质——的真诚敬意之外,特别是为了感谢他没有使用他伟大而优美的语言(otchin krassivaia[①])的极为礼貌,我将不使用中文发言。

因此,我很快提出一个我认为我的苏联同事希望制定的东西——即为我们的会议制定一个计划——如果不是一个五年计划的话,而不是在一年中的任何时候举行这种随意的会议。众所周知,我们刚刚完成了委员会成员的选举,因此我们将至少有 11 环表演。

我说的 11 个环指的是刚刚选出的 8 个委员会,即麻醉药品委员会、难民问题和灾区。我们至少会有 11 个,如果不是更多的话。

现在,如果这些不同的委员会平均每年举行两次会议,我真的可以想象在未来的一年里我们将会陷入一片混乱。所以,我建议这两件事——尽管,事实上,我并不认为这有什么独创性;这是与我们最有耐心、最客观的主席讨论后得出的结论。

---

① 编著者注:这里张彭春先生借用了两个俄语单词,意为"非常漂亮",被会议全文记录成英文字母组合,但由于档案文件中前一个字母组合的最后字母不是很清楚,只好按照俄语发音来大致确认。

附录

第一点是：

"为了协助理事会成员和秘书处为理事会及其各委员会在1947年期间的工作制定计划"，有人建议，"应请秘书长编制一份该年的会议日历，表明理事会和各委员会及小组委员会会议的大致时间。当然，可以理解的是，这一日历对理事会或各委员会没有约束力，但可以作为制定未来计划的有益指南。"

这是其中的一部分。

这是第二部分：

"议事规则第2条规定，经济及社会理事会应'每年至少开三届会议'。"有人"认为，如果理事会要执行其繁重的工作方案，就必须举行四届会议……"，我们说"在1947年举行四届会议"，而不是"一年"。

我们不知道这将如何运作；我们可以本着实验的精神继续下去。我认为1947年将是我们最忙的一年，因为所有这些新的委员会都将开会，他们将提交请求和报告，供我们做出决定。所以，我想，不是"一年"，而是改成了"1947年"。这意味着明年我们将尝试举行四次会议的想法。明年年底，如果我们想尝试别的东西，我们可能会改变。

（继续阅读E/224号文件）"……大约每三个月一届。如果理事会成员普遍同意应举行四届定期会议……"——那么就删除"每年"——有人"建议秘书长在上述日历中做出适当安排。"

事实上，计划是这样的：明年大约举行四次会议，一届在2月，一届在5月，一届在8月，一届在11月。然后，我们的11个巡回会议，它会被分成大约两组——一组夹在中间，让我们说，在2月之前和8月之前；另一组夹在5月和11月之前。因此，理事会一次只能讨论5或6份报告，而不是8、9或11份报告混在一起讨论。

此外，我们必须记住，专门机构将参加我们的讨论。让他们提前知道我们什么时候开会是非常有用的。然后，他们将能相应地安排他们的会议。

因此，从所有这些不同的角度来看，我认为我们应该为明年的会议制定一个计划,这是完全适当和必要的,我想应该是在每个月的中旬左右。我有一个选择"中旬"的理由,因为 8 月中旬将在大会之前大约两到三个星期,所以我应该建议,粗略地说,大约在 2 月中旬、5 月中旬、8 月中旬、11 月中旬,并让另一个委员会夹在中间。我认为有了那种计划,我们就能取得进展。

谢谢你。

张博士(中国):主席先生,我很想支持我的苏联同事提出的决议,即不仅应该考虑委员会代表和成员的家属,还应该考虑他们的配偶。然而,这不在议程上。不过,为了节省时间,我确实接受了迄今为止所说的一切。让我们通过第一条,即我们建议秘书长这样做。然后,关于第二点,我接受我的法国同事的建议,即它们可以作为审议的基础。这是我的第二点。

我的第三点涉及下届会议的日期。不要说 2 月 15 日到 2 月 28 日,这可能意味着 3 月 1 日,让我们只说,大约 2 月 15 日。我的意思是,如果你们通过我的四届会议计划,特别是 8 月 15 日的计划,这将不会没有影响,因为这将在大会召开之前有两三个星期的时间。

我仍然相信,我的苏联同事在仔细考虑之后——我当时不打算争辩——会明白这样做的明智之处,尽管这可能会使他进行如此多的旅行,也就是说,有了这种规律性,我们可以简化一些事情,然后你们所有的专门机构将根据我们的时间表确定它们的日期。如果我们继续放任自流,专门机构就不知道该怎么办了。联合国教科文组织将确定 11 月,然后其他人,我们必须根据他们的计划确定我们的日程。我们是联合国经济及社会理事会;我们应该协调。因此,我们有一个总体计划,让他们根据我们的计划来调整他们的计划,这是非常重要的。我不打算再发言了,但我认为尽管没有表决,这个建议是非常有力的。

张博士(中国):主席先生,我认为听取五种官方语言之一,即中文的发言是非常恰当的,我相信翻译人员能够翻译。

(张博士继续用中文发言)

我想我会请我的同事杨博士来翻译一下。

杨博士(中国)(张博士发言的口译):我很高兴与我们尊敬的口译员站在一起。

主席先生,我特别高兴地祝贺理事会取得的成功,因为我可以说我自己也取得了很大的成功,因为我是提名尊敬的主席斯坦帕博士的人。因此,我可以声称在他的成功中分享一份。因此,我特别高兴地祝贺理事会有这样一位出色的主席主持我们的审议。

张博士(中国):我还有一句话要说。考虑到时间已晚,我将继续用英语发言,但主席先生,我们不能忘记我们的秘书处。秘书长和所有秘书处工作人员都非常尽心尽力地工作,因此他们应该得到我们所有人的真诚感谢。此外,我们中的一些人享受了海军汽车的特殊款待。因此,我们可否请秘书长发出一封我们的感谢信,说这些男孩是多么有礼貌的司机。我认为我们写封信是合适的。

主席先生,最后,我谨就一件非常特别的事情向理事会表示祝贺。不久前,大约一个小时前,我出去与秘书处的一名成员交谈。我说:"这里的会议开过这么晚吗?"他说:"理安会有过一次。"

我说:"多晚?"他说:"十一点。"

因此,主席先生,我祝贺理事会打破了这一纪录。

(2)会议发言内容纪要①

本次会议【会议纪要】【纪要影像】和【纪要译文】又见《世界合作共赢的中国贡献》一书第119—121页。②

【会议纪要】

Mr. CHANG (China) nominated Dr. Zuleta Angel, representative of Colombia, as Acting Chairman; the nomination was seconded by the representa-

---

① UN Document:E/SR.21, p. 156, pp. 156—157, p. 157.

② 孙平华编著《世界合作共赢的中国贡献:张彭春在联合国经济及社会理事会的发言》,天津社会科学院出版社2023年1月版,第119—121页。

tives of Yugoslavia and Peru, and Dr. Zuleta Angel was unanimously elected.

Mr. CHANG (China), with reference to the suggestion of the Chinese delegation (document E/224), believed these suggestions would facilitate the work of the Council and the eleven commissions. The first proposal was that the Secretary-General should be asked to prepare a calendar of sessions for the coming year, indicating approximately when the meetings of the Council and of the commissions and sub-commissions would take place. Secondly, he proposed that the Council should hold four sessions in 1947, in view of the heavy schedule of work with which it had to deal. The sessions, according to his plan, would take place in February, May, August and November, with half of the commissions meeting before the February and August sessions, and the other half meeting before the May and November sessions. He further suggested that the Council should meet about the middle of February, May, August and November, in order to have one session two to three weeks before the General Assembly.

Mr. CHANG (China) agreed to the acceptance of the first point, and accepted the suggestion of the representative of France that the second point should serve as a basis for consideration.

附
录

【纪要影像】

Mr. CHANG (China) nominated Dr. Zuleta Angel, representative of Colombia, as Acting Chairman; the nomination was seconded by the representatives of Yugoslavia and Peru, and Dr. Zuleta Angel was unanimously elected.

Mr. CHANG (China), with reference to the suggestion of the Chinese delegation (document E/224), believed these suggestions would facilitate the work of the Council and the eleven commissions. The first proposal was that the Secretary-General should be asked to prepare a calendar of sessions for the coming year, indicating approximately when the meetings of the Council and of the commissions and sub-com-missions would take place. Secondly, he proposed that the Council should hold four sessions in 1947, in view of the heavy schedule of work with which it had to deal. The sessions, according to his plan, would take place in February, May, August and November, with half of the commissions meeting before the February and August sessions, and the other half meeting before the May and November sessions. He further suggested that the Council should meet about the middle of February, May, August and November, in order to have one session two to three weeks before the General Assembly.

Mr. CHANG (China) agreed to the acceptance of the first point, and accepted the suggestion of the representative of France that the second point should serve as a basis for consideration.

图片 3.14：张彭春在联合国经济及社会理事会第三届第 21 次会议发言纪要

【纪要译文】

张先生(中国)提名哥伦比亚代表祖莱塔·安吉尔(Zuleta Angel)博士为代理主席；南斯拉夫和秘鲁的代表附议了这一提名。祖莱塔·安吉尔博士全票当选。

张先生(中国)提到中国代表团的建议(E/224 号文件)，认为这些建议将有助于理事会和十一个委员会的工作。第一项建议是，应请秘书长为下一年编制一份会议日历，说明理事会、各委员会和小组委员会会议的大致举行时间。第二，鉴于理事会必须处理繁重的工作日程，他建议理事会在 1947 年举行四届会议。根据他的计划，这些会议将在 2 月、5 月、8 月和 11 月举行，其中一半的委员会会议在 2 月和 8 月的会议之前举行，另一半在 5 月和 11 月的会议之前举行。他还建议理事会大约在 2 月中旬、5 月中旬、8 月中旬和 11 月中旬召开会议，以便在大会召开前两至三周举行一届会议。

张先生(中国)同意接受第一点，并接受法国代表的建议，即第二点应作为审议的基础。

16. 张彭春在经社理事会第三届特别会议上的发言

联合国经社理事会第三届特别会议,于 1946 年 12 月 10 日下午 3 时至晚上 6 时,在法拉盛草地公园举行。本次会议的主要议题是确定经社理事会委员会成员任命。中国代表张彭春参加了这次特别会议,并在会议上发言,其发言内容如下:

(1) 会议发言全文记录①及译文

【全文记录】

Mr. Chang（China）：Mr. Chairman, this Document E/250—before we approve or confirm the names here listed, I suppose we would like to know who they are, and surely the information given here, concerning the Chinese nominees mostly show who they are not.

Page 2, China, Dr. Franklin Ho, a Member of the Central Planning Board. He is not. He was the Vice-Minister of Economics, Ministry of Economics, and Deputy-Secretary-General of the Central Planning Board. That is one mistake.

Then page 4, China, Mr. Frank Kefung, Railway and Highway Director

---

① UN Document：E/PV. 37, pp. 21-25；E/PV. 37/Add. 1, p. 2, p. 7, p. 11, p. 12. (值得指出的是:本次会议全文记录不完整,只记录下张彭春的一次发言内容,因为全文记录者为了参加联大全会的一个会议而中途离开,造成了全文记录缺少下午 3 时 50 分之后的内容。后一个文件作为对全文记录的补正,包含了会议纪要的内容,目的是弥补全文记录不全的缺陷。而根据会议纪要,张彭春先生在本次会议上发言内容被记录了四次,见: UN Document：E/SR. 21, p. 159, p. 162, p. 164, p. 165.)

in China. He is not.

Well, sir, it is extremely confusing. Statistical Member Mr. Lieu, formerly Director of Statistics, Central Bank of China. Not exactly this wording.

Fiscal Commission, Mr. S. K. Fong, Member Tariff Commission of China. No, no he is not.

Human Rights—There is a humble gentleman by the name of Dr. P. C. Chang. He was some years ago Minister to Chile. I do not know why they should pick that up. Of course it was a great honour, I realize. I will always feel with a great deal of satisfaction that I was once in the honoured country of the neighbor to my left, but why should they pick that alone. It is really odd.

And again, gentlemen, page 8, the Chinese nominee, Dr. Yang, President of Soochow University, Adviser to the Chinese Government. Where? Never.

It is really uniformly incorrect.

So, Mr. Chairman, you look at this and on page 10 the same gentleman, Dr. Franklin L. Ho, given another title, Adviser, Kin Chenk Banking Corporation. It is really most, most wonderfully uniform in being not what they are.

Well, however, I am not criticizing anyone in particular, but please, when you consider these names, just delete all the qualifications as attached in this Document—that is, especially for the Press and for the information. Please do not announce them as these high offices given to them in this Document.

【全文译文】

张先生(中国):主席先生,第 E/250 号文件——在我们批准或确认这里所列的名字之前,我想我们想知道他们是谁——当然这里提供了信息,关于中国被提名者的资料大多展示他们不是何人。

第 2 页,中国,富兰克林·何博士①,中央计划委员会成员。他不是。他曾任经济部经济副部长和中央计划委员会副秘书长。这是一个错误。

然后第 4 页,中国,弗兰克·凯丰(Frank Kefung)先生,中国铁路和公路总监。他不是。

嗯,先生,这是非常令人困惑的。前中国中央银行统计处处长刘先生。这样的措辞不确切。

中国关税税则委员会成员,财政委员会。不,不,他不是。

人权——有一位谦逊的绅士,名叫张彭春博士。几年前他是驻智利公使。我不知道他们为什么要提到那个。当然,我意识到这是一个巨大的荣誉。我将永远感到极大的满足,我曾经在我左边邻居的荣耀的国家,但为什么他们要单独提那个。这真的很奇怪。

再次,先生们,第 8 页,中国提名人,东吴大学校长、中国政府顾问杨博士。在哪里?从来没有。

这确实是完全不正确的。

所以,主席先生,你看这份报告,在第 10 页上,这位先生,富兰克林·何廉博士,换了另一个头衔,建兴银行顾问。这真的是在是与不是之间最、最奇妙的统一。

然而,我并没有特别批评任何人,但是,当你考虑这些名字时,请删除本文件中所附的所有限制条件——也就是说,特别是对媒体和新闻而言。请不要在这份文件中宣布他们担任这些高级职务。

---

① 笔者注:根据《何廉回忆录》(中国文史出版社 1988 年版)作者介绍:"何廉(Franklin Ho,1895-1975 年),湖南邵阳人,是中国著名的经济学家及教育家。何廉于 1919 年赴美国耶鲁大学留学,并曾在欧文·费雪(Irving Fisher)身边工作了三年,研究指数。1926 年回到中国,任南开大学商科教授,基于'建立适应中国特点经济学',成立了南开经济研究所。1931 年任南开大学经济学院院长。在这期间,他一方面编制了南开经济指数,成为日后研究中国当时经济状况的绝佳数据;另一方面,他亦翻译了大量经济学著作,使西方经济学引入中国。后来在国民政府中任顾问职务,专责经济发展政策。但在 1941 年成为了政治的替罪羊而被迫退出政府。1947 年赴美国,在普林斯顿大学任访问学者,后来成为哥伦比亚大学教授。1975 年逝世于纽约。"(见网址:https://baike.baidu.com/item/何廉回忆录/8246233? fr=aladdin)

（2）会议发言内容会议纪要①

本次会议【会议纪要】【纪要影像】和【纪要译文】又见《世界合作共赢的中国贡献》一书第 122-124 页。②

【会议纪要】

Mr. CHANG（China）pointed out that the titles attributed to the candidates proposed by the Chinese Government, in document E/250, were not always correct and asked that the mistakes should be rectified.

Mr. CHANG（China）stated that his Government had submitted precise and detailed lists to the Secretariat, but that the latter had made an arbitrary choice among the qualifications mentioned. He, therefore, proposed that it should be definitely laid down that the Secretariat should consult delegations.

Mr. CHANG（China）proposed the following text:

"Members of Commissions nominated subsequent to the present special meeting and prior to the next session of the Economic and Social Council, after consultation between the Governments concerned and the Secretary-General, in accordance with the Economic and Social Council's decisions of 21 June and 1, 2 and 3 October 1946, may serve provisionally on Commissions pending confirmation by the Economic and Social Council at its next regular session."

Mr. CHANG（China）, on behalf of the Economic and Social Council, expressed the gratitude of its members for the successful efforts of the Chairman, who had been kind enough to preside at this meeting, despite his present poor state of health.

---

① UN Document: E/SR. 21, p. 159, p. 162, p. 164, p. 165.

② 孙平华编著:《世界合作共赢的中国贡献:张彭春在联合国经济及社会理事会的发言》,天津社会科学院出版社 2023 年 1 月版,第 122-124 页。

【纪要影像】

Mr. CHANG (China) pointed out that the titles attributed to the candidates proposed by the Chinese Government, in document E/250, were not always correct and asked that the mistakes should be rectified.

Mr. CHANG (China) stated that his Government had submitted precise and detailed lists to the Secretariat, but that the latter had made an arbitrary choice among the qualifications mentioned. He, therefore, proposed that it should be definitely laid down that the Secretariat should consult delegations.

Mr. CHANG (China) proposed the following text:

"Members of Commissions nominated subsequent to the present special meeting and prior to the next session of the Economic and Social Council, after consultation between the Governments concerned and the Secretary-General, in accordance with the Economic and Social Council's decisions of 21 June and 1, 2 and 3 October 1946, may serve provisionally on Commissions pending confirmation by the Economic and Social Council at its next regular session."

Mr. CHANG (China), on behalf of the Economic and Social Council, expressed the gratitude of its members for the successful efforts of the Chairman, who had been kind enough to preside at this meeting, despite his present poor state of health.

图片 3.15：张彭春在联合国经济及社会理事会第三届特别会议发言纪要

【纪要译文】

张先生(中国)指出，第 E/250 号文件中中国政府提出的候选人的头衔并不总是正确的，他要求纠正错误。

张先生(中国)说，中国政府已向秘书处提交了准确和详细的清单，但秘书处对所提到的资格条件作出了任意选择。因此，他建议明确规定秘书处应与各代表团协商。

张先生(中国)提出以下案文：

"在本次特别会议之后、经济及社会理事会下届会议之前，根据经济及社会理事会 1946 年 6 月 21 日和 10 月 1 日、2 日和 3 日的决定，经有关政府与秘书长协商后提名的委员会成员，可暂时在委员会任职，直至经济及社会理事会下届常会确认。

张先生(中国)代表经济及社会理事会表示，理事会成员感谢主席的成功努力，感谢他在目前的健康状况不佳的情况下主持了这次会议。